ACES AT KURSK
The Battle for Aerial Supremacy on the Eastern Front, 1943

This book is dedicated to my father

Colonel William A. Lawrence
(United States Army) 1931–2000

He was the combat aviator that I grew up with.

ACES AT KURSK
The Battle for Aerial Supremacy on the Eastern Front, 1943

Christopher A. Lawrence
The Dupuy Institute

ACES AT KURSK
The Battle for Aerial Supremacy on the Eastern Front, 1943

First published in Great Britain in 2024 by
Air World
An imprint of
Pen & Sword Books Ltd
Yorkshire – Philadelphia

Copyright © Christopher A. Lawrence, 2024

ISBN 978 1 39908 143 6

The right of Christopher A. Lawrence to be identified as Author of this work has been asserted by him in accordance with the Copyright, Designs and Patents Act 1988.

A CIP catalogue record for this book is available from the British Library.

All rights reserved. No part of this book may be reproduced or transmitted in any form or by any means, electronic or mechanical including photocopying, recording or by any information storage and retrieval system, without permission from the Publisher in writing.

Typeset by SJmagic DESIGN SERVICES, India.

Printed and bound in the UK by CPI Group (UK) Ltd.

Pen & Sword Books Limited incorporates the imprints of Atlas, Archaeology, Aviation, Discovery, Family History, Fiction, History, Maritime, Military, Military Classics, Politics, Select, Transport, True Crime, Air World, Frontline Publishing, Leo Cooper, Remember When, Seaforth Publishing, The Praetorian Press, Wharncliffe Local History, Wharncliffe Transport, Wharncliffe True Crime and White Owl.

For a complete list of Pen & Sword titles please contact

PEN & SWORD BOOKS LIMITED
George House, Units 12 & 13, Beevor Street, Off Pontefract Road,
Barnsley, South Yorkshire, S71 1HN, England
E-mail: enquiries@pen-and-sword.co.uk
Website: www.pen-and-sword.co.uk

or
PEN AND SWORD BOOKS
1950 Lawrence Rd, Havertown, PA 19083, USA
E-mail: uspen-and-sword@casematepublishers.com
Website: www.penandswordbooks.com

CONTENTS

Illustrations and Maps		vi
Acknowledgements		vii
Prologue		ix
Chapter One	The Strategic Air Campaign	1
Chapter Two	Both Sides Prepare	22
Chapter Three	The Strike at Dawn	51
Chapter Four	The Fight for Air Superiority	76
Chapter Five	The Air War Continues	120
Chapter Six	A Less Intense Air War Continues	147
Chapter Seven	The Air Battle to Support the Offensive North of Kursk	160
Chapter Eight	The Soviet Counteroffensives	223
Chapter Nine	Winding Down	255
Chapter Ten	The Last Air Offensive	270
Appendix I	German and Soviet Terminology	286
Appendix II	Air Campaign Statistics	296
Appendix III	The Structure of the German Ground Offensive	371
Appendix IV	Commander Biographies	376
Bibliography		385
Biographical Information		399

ILLUSTRATIONS AND MAPS

Situation Map, 18 March 1943	xi
Voronezh Front, 31 March 1943	xiii
Eastern Front, 4 July 1943	xvii
German and Soviet Dispositions, 28 June 1943	xviii
Soviet Defense Lines, 4 July 1943	xix
Soviet Strength and Casualties by Quarter	xx
Comparative Losses by Quarter	xxi
Kharkov, Belgorod and Kursk Map	2
A German chart showing the times of sunrise, sunset, and the phases of the moon for Konotop	39
II Guard Tank Corps Map for 1800, 6 July 1943	83
German vs Soviet Daytime Sorties	149
German vs Soviet Daytime Losses	150
German vs Soviet Percent Losses per Daytime Sorties	150
Tank Losses at Prokhorovka, 12 July 1943	231
XVIII Tank Corps Deployment, 11 – 17 July 1943	234
XXIX Tank Corps, 12 July 1943	236
German Offensive, 5 – 17 July 1943	250
Soviet Air Claims vs German Air Losses	274
German Air Claims vs Soviet Air Losses	275
Soviet Air Claims vs Soviet Air Losses	275
Soviet Offensive, 12 July – 23 August 1943	277
Daily Situation Map, 04 July 1943	372
Tank Situation at Kursk, Southern Front 4 July 1943 evening	373
Tank Situation at Kursk, Southern Front 11 July 1943 evening	373
Tank Losses at Kursk, Southern Front 12 and 13 July 1943	374
Tank Situation at Kursk, Southern Front 18 July 1943 evening	374
Daily Situation Map, 18 July 1943	375

ACKNOWLEDGEMENTS

This book has been created based upon my 1,662-page mega-book: *Kursk: The Battle of Prokhorovka*. That book covered the entire German Belgorod offensive in the south, from 4 July to 24 July 1943. It incorporated the actions of two German infantry corps and three German panzer corps against most of the Soviet Voronezh Front and reinforcing forces. It was a massive battle that was detailed down to division-level for each day of the operation

This book examines the air actions over the battlefield from 4 to 18 July 1943 that were part of German Army Group South's offensive around Belgorod. South of Kursk, the air campaign involved in supporting the large German ground offensive was larger than the Battle of Britain. It included many of the top German and Russian aces and some of their most famous aviators. It was the first significant air battle on the Eastern Front since the Soviet Air Force had been gutted in the initial German onslaught of June of 1941. It was the first time the Soviet Air Force had attempted to contend with the German Air Force for control of the skies.

The Battle of Kursk was the subject of a large data base that we assembled at *The Dupuy Institute* from 1993 to 1996 for the US Army Concepts Analysis Agency (CAA), now called the Center for Army Analysis. I was the program manager for this large research and database effort. We assembled unit records from the German side and, uniquely, obtained access to the Soviet Army files from the Russian Military Archives just outside of Moscow, at Podolsk. This effort included over a dozen people and resulted in a database being delivered to CAA for use in model validation. CAA never used it for such.

As we were sitting on a collection of unique material, I felt an obligation to prepare a book using this large collection of unique research. The original Kursk book was written from late 1999 to around the middle of 2003 and was almost completed then but, because of the large amount of material we had assembled, the draft of the book came out much larger than I originally planned. Because of the work load at *The Dupuy Institute*, I was unable to complete it at that time. Therefore, I was only able to start back to work on it in late 2009 and the behemoth was published in 2015.

A detailed description of this effort is provided in my original book and in articles written since then.[1] Many people were important in this effort and are all acknowledged in that book. The key personnel that are acknowledged are: Colonel Trevor N. Dupuy (USA); E.G. Vandiver (Director of the Center for Army Analysis); Dr. Fyodor Davidovich Sverdlov (Colonel, USSR); Dr. Anatolii Vainer (Colonel, USSR); Major General G.G. Nessonov (USSR); Colonel Valerii Akimov (Russia); Vyacheslav Viktorovich Stepashkin; Dr Richard

Harrison; Colonel John Sloan (USA, Ret.); Richard C. Anderson; Major General Dieter Brand (Bundeswehr, Ret.); L. Jay Karamales; Major General Nicholas Krawciw (USA, Ret.) and Dr. Arthur Volz. They all played a major role in assisting with the Kursk Data Base or in preparing the book. Also among other people who provided help and are acknowledged in the original book are: Walter Baumen, Dr. Ronald Bellamy (Col. USA, Ret.), Christer Bergstrom, Wulf-Dietrich Brand, Frederick L. Clemens, Jeff Chrisman, Dr. George Daoust (Col. USA), Alexander Dinsmoor, Gary Dickson, Anders Frankson, Dr. Karl-Heinz Frieser (Col. Bundeswehr), David M. Glantz (Col. USA, Ret.), Harvey Gough, Alex Hellmund, Jukka Juutinen, Grigori A. Kultonov (Col. USSR), Paul Krawciw, Thomas Peters, Tom Petteys (Aberdeen Books), Dr. Yan Mann, Edward Milligan (Lt. Col. USA), Dmitri Myslivschenko, Rainer Prill (Lt. Col. Bundeswehr, Ret.), Dr. Dmitri Ryabushkin, Jonna Schwarz, Susan Sims, Mikhail Serykh, Ariane C. Smith, Howard Whitley, Niklas Zetterling, Yun Zhang, and, of course, Tatiana Samsonova Lawrence. All of these people played a role in completing the Kursk Data Base or helping with the original Kursk book.

This is my third book about the Battle of Kursk. My original 1,662 page mega-book covered the entire offensive by Army Group South from 4 to 24 July 1943. My next book focused only on the Battle of Prokhorovka. This book is focused entirely on the air campaign. As the Battle of Kursk was the largest battle of the Second World War, there are many other books that could be written about it. An air campaign during the German offensive north of Kursk is also discussed here, although not in the same depth, along with an air campaign that was generated in support of the Soviet counteroffensive in the north, around Orel, that started on 12 July 1943. There was also an air campaign generated in support of the Soviet counteroffensive south of Kursk that started on 3 August 1943. Being a huge battle, I can only do justice in this book to the air campaign conducted in response to the German offensive to the south of Kursk. We do briefly cover the air campaign in response to the German attack north of Kursk from 5 to 11 July 1943. It is in a separate chapter in this book.

Central to this new effort has been John Barry Grehan (Pen & Sword Books). Also assisting me in preparing, research and reviewing of this book was Dr. Andrew Arthy, Christer Bergstrom, L. Jay Karamales, Patrick R. Plummer and Ariane C. Smith (Capital A).

Note

1. See Christopher A. Lawrence, *Kursk: The Battle of Prokhorovka* (Aberdeen Books, Sheridan, Colorado, 2015), 19–24 (Preface: The Kursk Data Base) and 25–26 (Acknowledgements). Also see Christopher A. Lawrence, "Did I Just Write the Largest History Book Ever?" at http://www.aberdeenbookstore.com/the-largest-history-book-ever, and a shorter version of the same article at the *History News Network* at https://historynews network.org/article/161443, dated January 2016.

PROLOGUE

I feel as if I am pushing open the door to a dark room never seen before, without knowing what lies behind the door.

Adolf Hitler
21 June 1941[1]

The German Air Force (the Luftwaffe) had not been seriously challenged in the first two years of this war in the East. On 22 June 1941 Germany attacked the Soviet Union. At the start of the German offensive, *Operation Barbarossa*, the German Air Force struck the Soviet Air Force on the ground at their airfields. Many Soviet aircraft were caught and destroyed there. Many others were shot down in the following days through subsequent strikes and aerial combat. By the end of July, the Soviet Air Force had been seriously attritted. They had lost over 5,000 planes![2] Their strength was now around 3,500 planes, putting them closer to the Germans in quantity, but they were well behind them in quality and training.[3] On 22 July 1941, the first German air raids against Moscow were conducted, although the damage was slight.[4]

As the ground war waxed and waned over the next two years, the Soviet Union continued to build new planes, develop their aircraft, and train new pilots. With multiple competing aircraft design bureaus, they had already developed their next generation of fighters, the Mig-3, the LaGG-3 and the Yak-1 to replace their obsolete Polikarpov I-16 and bi-plane I-15 and I-153 fighters that populated most of their fighter regiments. These new planes were good competition to the ubiquitous German fighter, the Messerschmitt Bf-109, also known as the Me-109. But it would take time for the Soviet Union to produce the new aircraft and replace the obsolete aircraft in their air force. Their air force, still of considerable size, was always present during these early stages of the war, but it was a force in transition, training and rebuilding, and it was having to do so in the middle of the largest and bloodiest ground campaign in history. They maintained over 2,000 aircraft throughout and every day sent up hundreds of sorties.[5] But the Soviet air force failed to establish itself as a force to be reckoned with during the first two years of this war. In the subsequent major ground battles, the Battle of Moscow, the Siege of Leningrad, and the Battle of Stalingrad, the Soviet Air Force was present, but did not decisively influence the ground battle. Rarely were they able to successfully contend for the skies with the German Air Force. For the first two years of the war, the Germans could establish air superiority over any area of the battlefield that they choose to. Major German ground operations usually had the benefit of air support while major Soviet ground operations rarely did. It was a lopsided scenario.

This was demonstrated at the Battle of Kharkov in May 1942, which was initiated with a Soviet offensive. The Soviet air support consisted of over 900 aircraft.[6] They had control of the sky on the first day. And then as General Semyon K. Timoshenko, the Soviet commander of the attacking Southwestern Front, is quoted as reporting "From the second day of our offensive the enemy achieved air superiority, and by means of continuous strikes by a large quantity of aircraft our forces were deprived of freedom of manoeuvre on the battlefield."[7]

Even during the infamous Battle of Stalingrad from August 1942-February 1943, the Germans often maintained control of the air. On 19 November, the Red Army launched *Operation Uranus,* their offensive to encircle the German and Romanian troops fighting for Stalingrad. This offensive was supported by three newly-formed Soviet air armies, including the Seventeenth Air Army under the restored Major General Stepan Krasovskii.[8] They outnumbered the Germans in aircraft.[9] The Third and Fourth Romanian Armies, portions of the German Fourth Panzer Army and the German Sixth Army were encircled around Stalingrad on 23 November 1942, leaving 284,000 men surrounded.[10] The Soviet encircling attacks were done with limited air support by either side because of the weather.

The Germans then tried to resupply the surrounded troops by air, as promised by the head of the Luftwaffe, Reich Marshal Hermann Goering.[11] This was well beyond the Luftwaffe's capability. This resupply effort fell short, not because of the Soviet Air Force, although they did intercept some transport aircraft; but because of the limitations of the German transport fleet, the ever increasing distances they had to fly as the Soviet Army pushed the German Army back, and the degrading effects of the harsh winter weather. As the new year rolled around the Germans were driven back and forced to do their resupply flights to Stalingrad from bases over 200 miles away. The German losses for these failed resupply operations were high, although most of their losses were not caused by the Soviet air force.[12]

The ground fighting after the encirclement of Stalingrad was dramatic. This included stopping a German attempt in late November to reconnect with the German Sixth Army surrounded in Stalingrad. This vain effort was commanded by Field Marshal Erich von Manstein, who had just come down from Leningrad to take command in the south. It was followed by a desperate retreat of 650 kilometers by the German forces that had pushed all the way down to the Caucasus Mountains. This was then followed up by multiple devastating Soviet offenses. This was initiated with *Operation Little Saturn* which was a massive offensive that included the entire southern half of the Eastern Front.[13] It started 12 December 1942 and continued until 18 February 1943. This offensive destroyed the Italian Eighth Army, effectively removing the Italians from the Eastern Front. The Soviet Army then encircled and annihilated the Hungarian Second Army. The German Army was reeling and they had been stripped of four allied armies. The German Sixth Army had started their summer offensive in June 1942 from just east of Kharkov. From there they had driven all the way to Stalingrad while other German forces pushed down into the Caucasus Mountains. Now, on 15 February 1943, Kharkov fell to the Red Army.

On 12 February Field Marshal Manstein was placed in command of the re-formed Army Group South. The following day Hitler entrusted Manstein with command of the entire

PROLOGUE

southern front. In late February he launched a counterattack against the overextended and exhausted Soviet forces. This attack retook Kharkov on 14 March 1943 and continued rolling north, taking the small city of Belgorod on 18 March, over 60 kilometers to the north. North of Belgorod they encountered the Twenty-first Army, later called the Sixth Guards Army, which was furiously preparing a defense. Army Group South's offensive ended around 25 March 1943. The spring rains were arriving and the troops were exhausted. This halted military operations for a while.

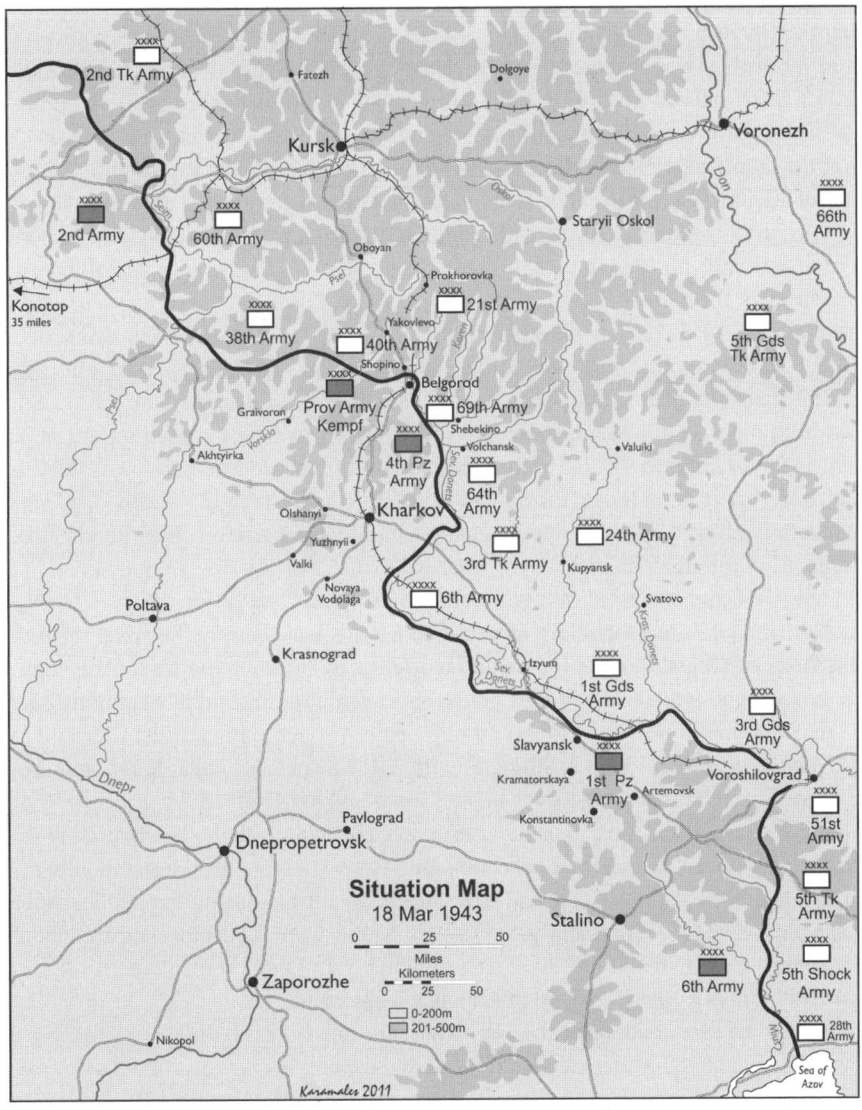

Army Group South Situation, 18 March 1943.

xi

With poor weather, and much of the fighting done in winter weather, the air forces of both sides played a lesser role. The rapid movement of the front often left them without proper airbases to operate from. Between the weather, the continued activity, the constant movement and extended combat and operations, their serviceability levels often dropped below 50% (meaning less than half the aircraft were operational on any given day). It was only after the front lines had stabilized, the weather improved and the forces regrouped, that the two air forces could again re-engage.

As this fighting ended, it left a 2,000 kilometer front line running from just outside Leningrad (now St. Petersburg) down to the Black Sea. There was a large bulge at Kursk and another large bulge just north of it at Orel. The Germans also had a foothold in the south at the Kuban bridgehead, the area where Crimea connects to Russia across the Sea of Azov. Hitler insisted on holding this bridgehead for further offensive operations. The Kuban bridgehead would become the scene of an extended air battle in April and May 1943.

After the dramatic winter battles of late 1942 and early 1943, the lines stabilized towards the end of March 1943. With both sides exhausted, and the spring "mud season" arriving, all the offensives had halted. At the end of March, the front went into a two-month period of relative peace, while rain and mud dominated the battlefield. The two sides rebuilt their forces and prepared for the coming summer. This was to be the third summer of the war in the East.

The German Air Force on the Eastern Front on 30 January 1943 consisted of 2,165 aircraft of all types, with only 989 of them ready-for-action. Among those aircraft were 479 Ju-52 transport planes that were part of the attempt to resupply the German forces trapped in Stalingrad. These transports were to shortly leave for the Mediterranean theater to help in the buildup at Tunis.[14] The German Air Force had been seriously bled in the attempt to resupply Stalingrad, losing 224 bombers and 266 Ju-52s in this desperate and futile resupply effort.[15] This air force was now significantly weaker than the air force that had originally supported the invasion of Russia. The German Air Force on the Eastern Front on 21 June 1941 had consisted of 3,664 aircraft, with 2,815 ready-for-action.[16]

The German Air Force, especially in southern Russia, was then shuffled over the next two months from emergency to emergency in an attempt to shore up the front. This kept their forces stressed and stretched. With the pause in hostilities at the end of March, the German Air Force was finally able to rest and rebuild. This was a significant recovery and by the end of May, they were back up to strength, with 3,415 airplanes available for operations on the Eastern Front. This was just over half of the deployed German Air Force strength, as facing the Western allies were considerable assets, particularly fighters, attempting to attrit and halt the UK and U.S. strategic air campaign.[17] In particular, the German bomber forces in the east had been rebuilt. These had been seriously attrited during the winter, especially as they were used to help resupply Stalingrad. There were 1,728 airplanes in the Army Group South area with the Fourth Air Fleet, of which 1,134 were combat aircraft (excluding harassment bombers, transports and miscellaneous aircraft).[18]

The Soviet air force had spent the last two years slowly and painfully rebuilding itself. It now became engaged in an extended fight with the Germans for control of the air over the Kuban bridgehead. The Kuban bridgehead was just east of Crimea, across the Kerch Strait in the Taman Peninsula. It was only 90 by 80 kilometers, creating a very small space for what

PROLOGUE

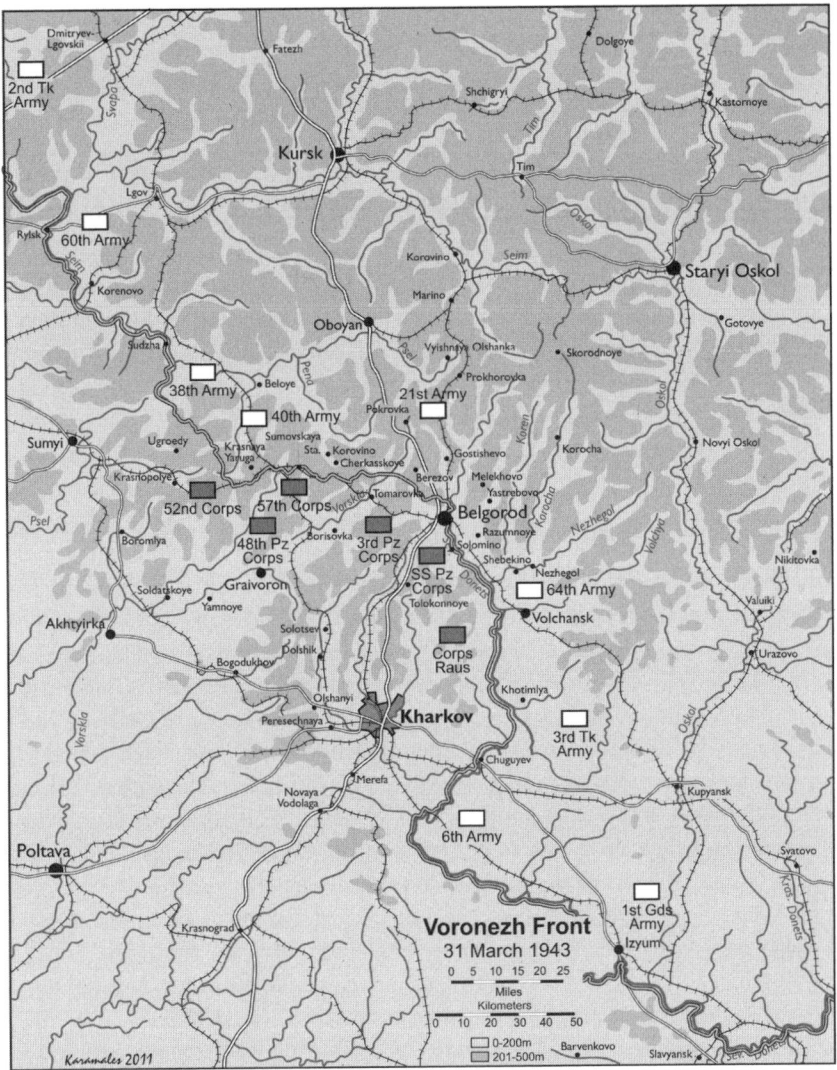

Voronezh Front, German and Soviet Dispositions, 31 March 1943.

became a rather extended battle. This bridgehead was created in late December when the German forces from the Caucasus withdrew through Rostov and formed a bridgehead there. It was now held by the German Seventeenth Army and consisted of around 15 divisions and some Romanian troops. The German Fourth Air Fleet had originally deployed the VIII Air Corps there, but replaced it with the I Air Corps. The Soviets had committed the Fourth and Fifth Air Armies along with air forces of the Black Sea Fleet.

On 28 March, STAVKA, headed by Stalin, ordered an attack on the Kuban bridgehead. The two months of fighting there was initiated with a rather unsuccessful Soviet offensive starting on 4 April. On 17 April, the Germans started their own offensive in the area, *Operation Neptune*, to destroy a Soviet bridgehead at Myiskhako that had been created by a small amphibious landing along the Black Sea coast in February. This Soviet bridgehead was only ten kilometers deep and eight kilometers wide. This attack also stalled out after several days of hard fighting. On 29 April, the Soviets then launched a flanking maneuver to take the coastal town of Anapa. This also stalled out by 10 May with heavy air losses. After a period of quiet, the Soviets shifted their offensive efforts north to a major assault on the German fortified "blue line" on 26 May. This attack also stalled out with heavy ground and air losses. On the ground, this was a campaign that did not accomplish much for either side and for two months, the lines hardly moved. Being the only major operation on the Eastern Front during that time, there was an extended air campaign tied to it. The supporting air campaign was significant to the Soviet air force as they were able to test, modify and improve their doctrine, tactics, and training.

The Soviets forces, Major General Nikolai F. Naumenko's Fourth Air Army, Major General Sergei K. Goryunov's Fifth Air Army and Major General Vasilii Ermachenkov's Black Sea air forces, were augmented by 60 bombers from their Long Range Aviation force (abbreviated as the ADD, Aviatsiya Dalnego Deistiviya) for a total of 570 aircraft.[19] Coordinating these three air groups was Major General Konstantin A. Vershinin.

The Germans, on the defensive, had replaced the VIII Air Corps with General Guenther Korten's I Air Corps, still part of the Fourth Air Army. Defending this area was also the 15th Flak Division. Overall command was exercised by the Luftwaffe Command Kuban under General Otto Dessloch. The I Air Corps initially had at least 250 German, Romanian, Croatian and Slovak aircraft.[20] On 5 April, after the start of the Soviet attacks, the bridgehead was reinforced to nearly 600 combat aircraft.[21] By 20 April, the air battle had turned into a significant effort with 541 Soviet sorties that day, countered by 859 German sorties,[22] and on the 21st the Soviet air force flew more sorties over the Kuban then the German Air Force although at a cost.[23] The Soviets continued to reinforce until by early May they had added 490 aircraft there.[24] Meanwhile the Germans handed back control of the air in late April when the III/3rd Fighter Wing, I/52nd Fighter Wing and III/55th Bomber Wing were transferred to Ukraine in anticipation of the Kursk offensive. This was two of their five fighter groups, or 40% of their fighter force.[25] The air battle had grown lopsided in favor of the Soviet Union, with them putting up 1,054 sorties on 29 April while the Germans were only able to put up 414.[26] On 3 May, having air superiority, the Soviets forced elements of the German Seventeenth Army to retreat. The German fighter units were soon called back to Crimea, but their return was delayed because of a massive Soviet air strike against the German airfields in Ukraine on 6 May. This air strike is discussed in more depth in Chapter One of this book.

The Soviets also escalated their efforts with another 234 aircraft in mid-April, then added another 256 aircraft to the Fourth Air Army and then in May added another 300 aircraft while the Black Sea air forces also added more aircraft. They now had 848 aircraft, with 719 of them in the Fourth Air Army. The Long Range Aviation force (the ADD) also provided another 140 bombers and on 1 May organized the VI Bomber Corps for operations there under command of General Major Georgii Tupikov. By 7 May, significant elements of the Luftwaffe had returned from Ukraine and the battle again swung back in favor of the

PROLOGUE

German Air Force. On 8 May the Germans flew 736 sorties, opposed by only 455 sorties by the Soviet Fourth Air Army.[27] The situation on the ground had stabilized.

The next Soviet offensive in the Kuban was on 26 May. By the end of May the Soviet strength had grown to 924 aircraft.[28] There were also command changes with Goryunov and the Fifth Air Army being transferred north to the Voronezh Front on 24 April and Naumenko transferred to the north to command the Fifteenth Air Army on 1 May while Vershinin took over command of the Fourth Air Army. This extended two-month campaign was close to being an even air battle, with the Soviet Union having a definite quantitative advantage. The attack penetrated about 10 kilometers into German lines before stalling out. This created the most intense day of the campaign, with Soviet aviation doing 1,426 sorties on this day.[29] The activity remained high for the next three days.[30] The Soviet ground offensive was halted on 30 May, but air activity continued for several days after that.[31] The fighting then died down by 7 June, ending the two month rather intensive air campaign in the Kuban.

It was the fighting at the Kuban bridgehead that many of the recently arriving lend-lease aircraft first came into extensive use. This included the United States supplied Bell P-39 Airacobras and Douglas A-20 Havoc bombers (often called Bostons), and in smaller numbers the Curtiss P-40 Kittyhawks and the British Supermarine Spitfire Vs. The aerial operations around the Kuban bridgehead in April and May created an extended air campaign on the Eastern Front. Both sides were employing planes relatively similar in capability. It is where many of the Soviet units and pilots got their initial combat experience. It is where the famous Soviet ace, Alexander I. Pokryishkin, first established his reputation. Also deployed there in late May was the first Soviet all-female air regiment, the 588th Night Bomber Regiment. It was also called the "Kuban Meat Grinder" by some.

The Russians finally halted their offensive in early June. By that time the Fourth Air Army had flown 10,250 sorties, the Fifth Air Army had flown 2,299 sorties, and the Long Range Aviation had flown at least 2,419 sorties.[32] The two air armies had lost 240 aircraft to enemy action in the fighting, with another 851 seriously damaged of which 308 were cannibalized and 73 scrapped. The I Corps reported 192 aircraft lost to enemy action and 132 to accidents.[33] If these figures are complete (which they probably are not), this would indicate at least a one-to-three exchange ratio in favor of the Germans.[34]

The German fighter forces included the II and III Groups of the 3rd Fighter Wing and all three groups of the 52nd Fighter Wing. It included many of their top aces on the Eastern Front, including Guenther Rall. The Germans then pulled many of their aircraft out of the Kuban in preparation for Kursk. By June 7, major air operations over the Kuban ended as the Germans withdrew their aircraft. The next big air battle would be the Battle of Kursk.

The VIII Air Corps was pulled from Crimea in late March and sent to Kharkov in preparation of the Kursk offensive. But many of the air units assigned to it remained in and around Crimea, including the 3rd and 52nd Fighter Wings. The Germans would re-assign the II and III Groups of the 3rd Fighter Wing and the I and IIII Groups of the 52nd Fighter Wing back to the VIII Air Corps in preparation for the Battle of Kursk. Only the II/52nd Fighter Wing would remain back in the Taman Peninsula along with some Romanian air units. The rest of the fighter units south of Kursk were assigned to the upcoming offensive. General Dessloch would take over temporary command of the Fourth Air Fleet around 11 June 1943.

The Soviet Fifth Air Army was also later transferred north to serve as the air army for the Steppe Military District (later called the Steppe Front), which was held in reserve during the defensive phase of the Battle of Kursk.

In June 1943, the Germans had 5,003 "front-line aircraft." In July, only 2,500 of them were on the Eastern Front.[35] The Western allies were occupying the attention of half the Luftwaffe. The Axis had 960 front-line German aircraft and around 300 Italian aircraft in the central Mediterranean, and around 800 aircraft on home defense in Germany, along with some 600 night-fighters. Of the 2,500 aircraft in the East, over 1,800 were committed to the Kursk offensive.

The forces deployed in the south, ready to conduct the offensive, were under Army Group South commanded by the famous German strategist, Field Marshal Erich von Manstein. Committed to the offensive were three panzer corps, from left to right (west to east), the XLVIII (48th) Panzer Corps, the SS Panzer Corps and the III Panzer Corps. On each flank was a supporting infantry corps, in the west it was the LII (52nd) Corps and on the right flank was Corps Raus. A total of 17 German divisions were prepared for this offensive in the south. It included four large panzer grenadier divisions, five panzer divisions, and eight infantry divisions. The four large panzer grenadier divisions included the elite Gross Deutschland Division and three recently expanded SS Divisions. They were supported by the VIII Air Corps under command of Major General Hans Seidemann. This unit had over 1,100 aircraft.[36] This was most of the planes of its parent organization, the Fourth Air Fleet under command of General Otto Dessloch.

The Soviet Union defended this area with the Voronezh Front commanded by the always aggressive General Nikolai F. Vatutin and supported by his earthy political commissar, Lt. General Nikita Khrushchev. The Voronezh Front consisted of five infantry armies, a tank army of three armored corps, two other tank corps and a reserve infantry corps. It was supported by the Second Air Army commanded by Lt. General Stepan A. Krasovskii. On 1 July 1943 the Second Air Army had 881 airplanes.[37] Attached to the neighboring Southwest Front was the Seventeenth Air Army commanded by Lt. General Vladimir A. Sudets. On 1 July 1943 it had 735 airplanes.[38] It also provided considerable air support to the Soviet defense, especially in the first few days.

North of Kursk was the German Ninth Army, under command of Colonel General Walter Model. It conducted a smaller offensive simultaneous with Manstein's southern offensive. They were supported by the Sixth Air Fleet under Colonel General Robert Ritter von Greim. Its First Air Division had around 730 aircraft.[39] They were facing the Central Front commanded by Lt. General Konstantin K. Rokossovskii. It was supported by Sixteenth Air Army under command of Lt. General Sergei I. Rudenko. On 1 July 1943 it had 1,034 airplanes.[40]

In reserve, behind these two Soviet Fronts, mostly deployed along the base of the Kursk bulge was a large reserve force. This was the Steppe Military District, later renamed the Steppe Front. At the beginning of July it had six infantry armies, one tank army (the famous Fifth Guard Tank Army) of two armored corps, three tank corps and three cavalry corps.[41] It was commanded by General Ivan S. Konev. It was supported by the Fifth Air Army, commanded by Lt. General Sergei K. Goryunov.

Between all the forces in and around the Kursk bulge, the Soviets had at least 2,650 planes.[42] According to Vasilevskii the Soviet Army in the summer of 1943 had 8,300

PROLOGUE

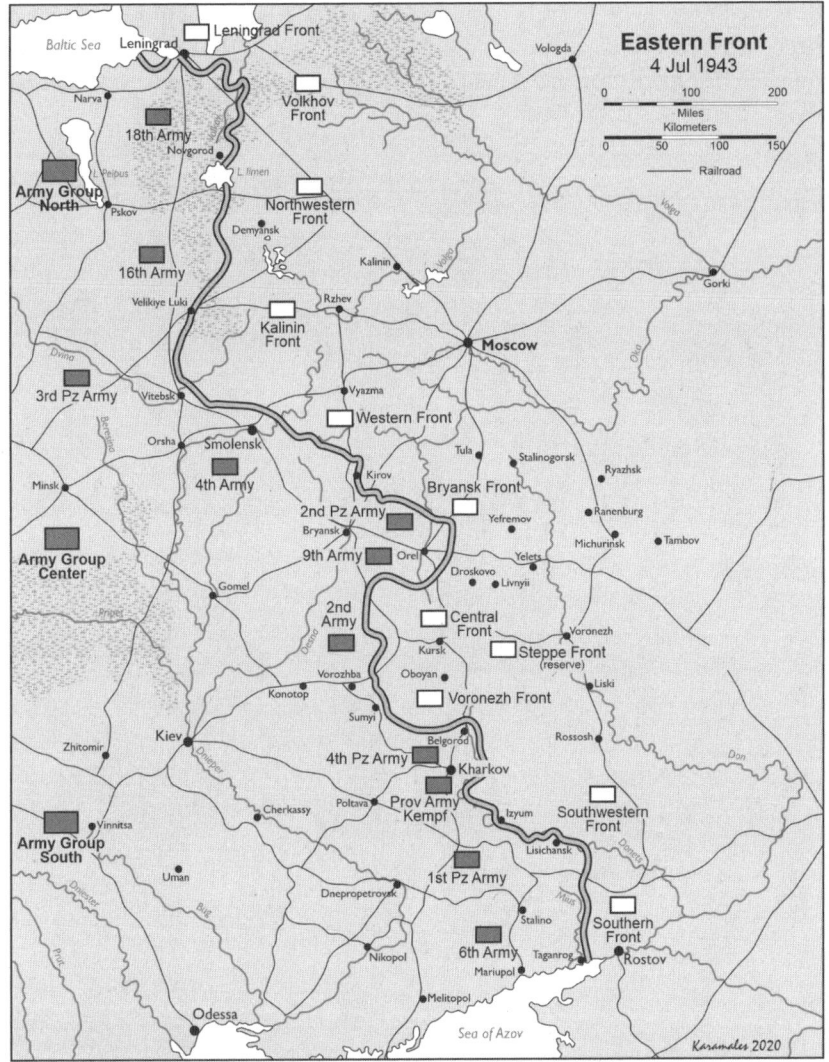

Eastern Front, 04 Jul 1943.

warplanes.[43] Counting the Steppe Front's planes, this would mean that the Soviet Army had committed 32% of their aircraft to the defense of the Kursk bulge.

But a significant part of the story of the first half of 1943 was the increase in the number of Soviet planes. Up until now, production rate had been so low that the Soviet industry was only producing enough planes to replace their losses. In 1941 many of the Soviet aircraft factories had been relocated to the east, some to the Ural Mountains and beyond. With the factories now producing and the flow of lend lease planes also well underway, the Soviet plane strength grew notably. In the first half of 1943, the Soviet operational plane strength started to grow without bounds. In November 1942 one estimate places Soviet plane strength at 3,100, but has them with 8,300 planes in July 1943.[44] The Germans would be outnumbered at the Kuban and would also be outnumbered at Kursk. It would become the norm for the air war in the East.

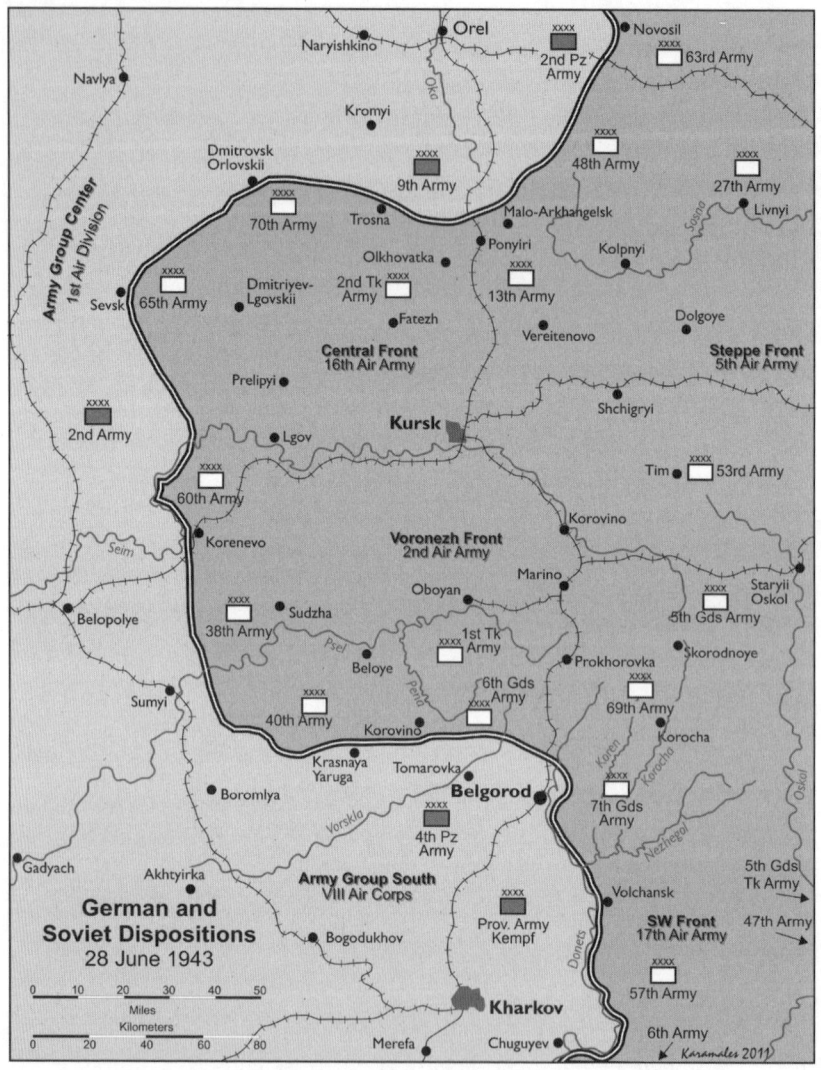

German and Soviet Dispositions, 28 Jun 1943.

After a series of delays that lasted for the better part of two months, the German offensive was scheduled to start 5 July 1943.

But from the end of March until the offensive started, the Eastern Front lay silent for a full three months. It was certainly the quietest period of this bloody war. This quiet period encouraged the German Air Force to conduct its first strategic air campaign on the Eastern Front.

PROLOGUE

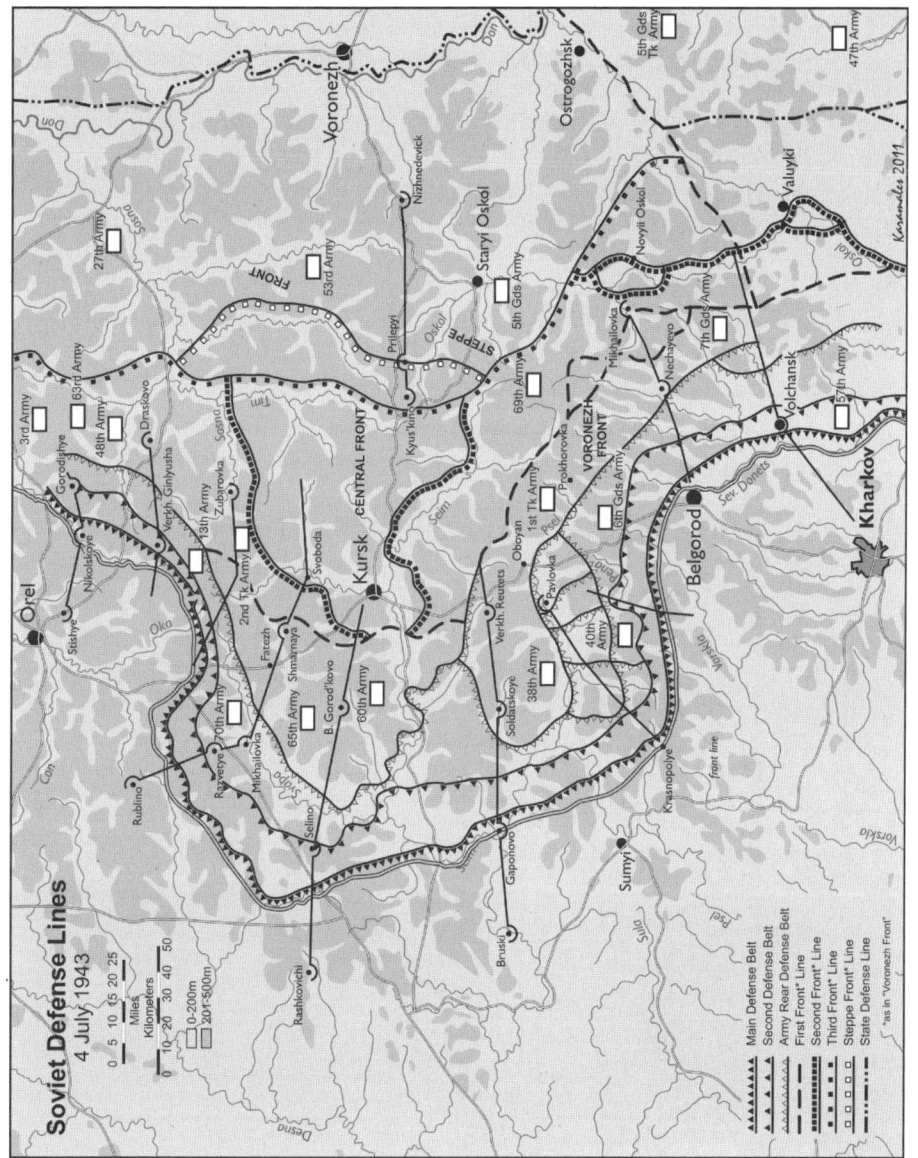

Soviet Defense Lines.

THE CYCLE OF THE WAR

The following chart lists the Soviet casualties by calendar quarter (killed and missing) and total casualties. It also includes total strength.

This chart is drawn from figures in Krivosheyev's book.[45] They are a summation of losses for the Fronts, and as such are less than total Soviet losses. Still, they show a clear pattern. The two bloodiest periods of the war are the two German summer offensives in the 3rd quarter of 1941 and 1942. The third and fourth periods with the highest casualties (although not the highest killed and missing) are the two Soviet winter offensives in the first quarter of 1942 and 1943. Then there is the very quiet period of the 2nd quarter of 1943, which was indeed the quietest period of the war, suffering even fewer losses than the Soviet Army suffered in the 3rd quarter of 1945, when Germany surrendered with the fighting ended less than half way through the quarter.

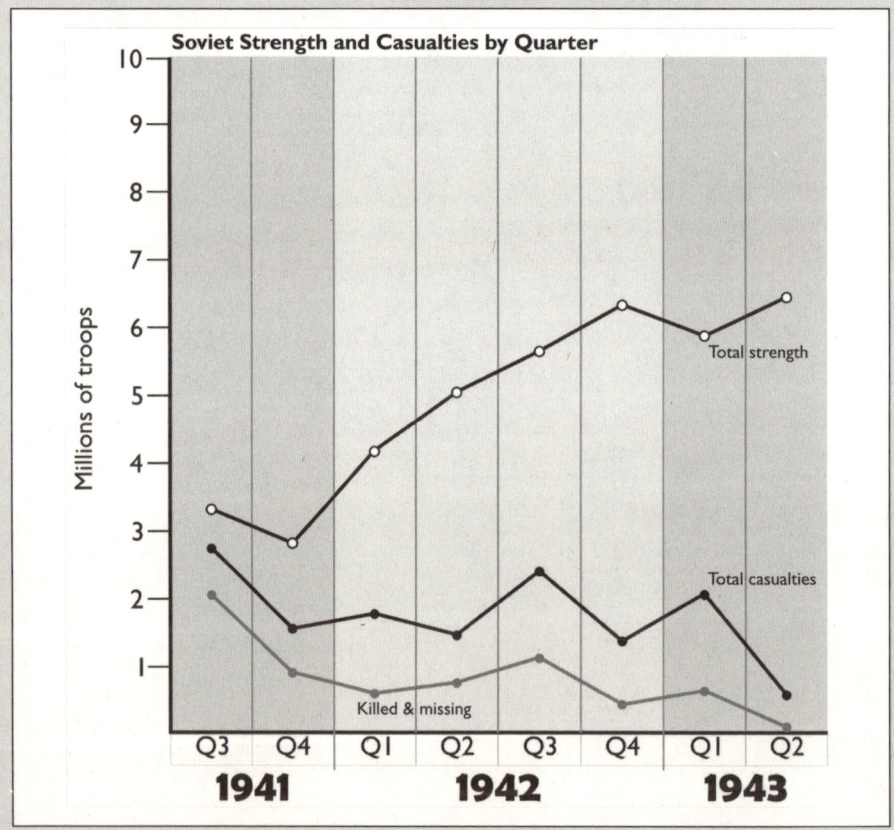

Chart 1 - Soviet Strength & Casualties by Quarter.

PROLOGUE

Comparative Losses

Even though there is concern that Krivosheyev's figures underestimate Soviet losses, especially for 1941, a comparison of German[46] versus Soviet losses by quarter is illustrative.

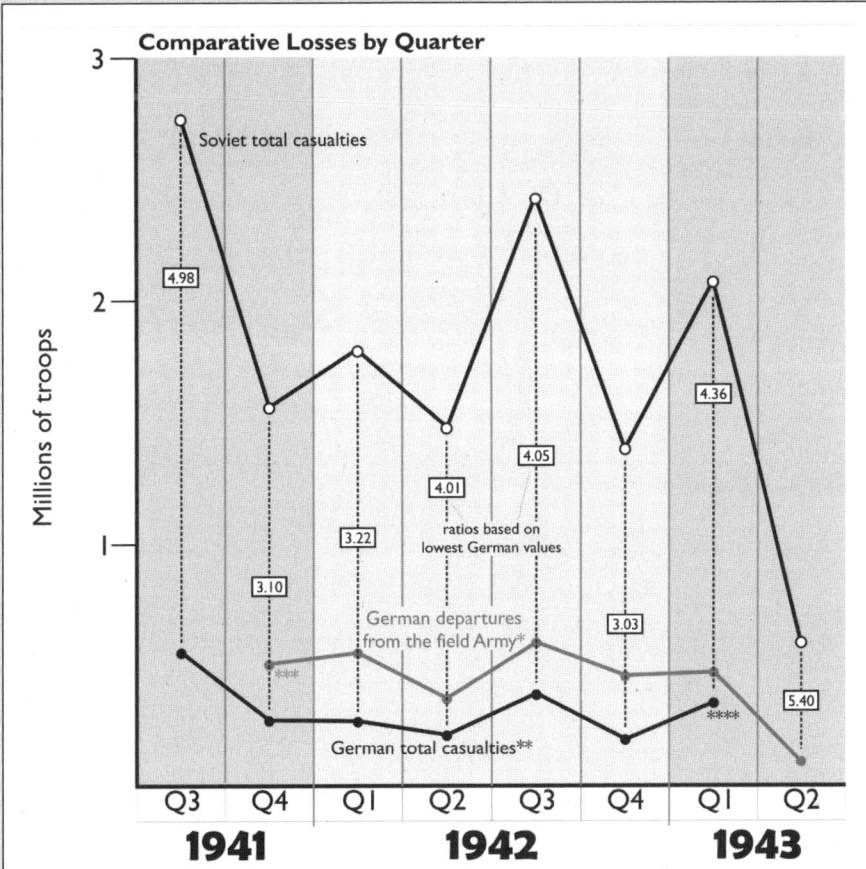

* This includes killed, missing, and evacuated with wounds or illness. It signifies departures from the field army, vice all casualties.
** This is drawn from BA-MA RW 6/v.552 and v.553, *Casualties on the Eastern Front 1941*. It covers from June 22 to the end of 1942. The June casualties (as the Krivosheyev figures do not appear to report these first nine days) are 41,084 and are included in the figures here; the ratio is 5.38 with this data not included. Data provided courtesy of Niklas Zetterling.
*** Data only provided for December (168,000). This figure was multiplied by three to produce a gross quarterly figure.
**** Data only covers January (260,080) and February (90,815). No attempt was made to estimate March.

Chart 2 - Comparative Losses by Quarter.

STRENGTHS

The Kursk Data Base assembled the strengths of every division and attached combat units. It did not attempt to determine how many non-combatant support personnel were with the armies and Fronts. Therefore, the strengths listed below should be considered the minimum strength of these formations, and in the case of armies and Fronts, they will be higher due to support personnel. These strength calculations do have the advantage that they are counting the same types of units for both sides.

From Kursk Data Base (see Appendix III of *Kursk: The Battle of Prokhorovka* for details)

	Personnel	Tanks[47]	Guns[48]	Mortars
Fourth Panzer Army	5,981	0	0	0
LII Corps	34,764	0	203	241
XLVIII Panzer Corps	91,924	650	677	472
SS Panzer Corps	71,446	601	560	256
Provisional Army Kempf	7,065	0	0	0
III Panzer Corps	79,202	416	612	290
Corps Raus	47,791	42	425	327
Total	338,173	1,709	2,477	1,586

	Personnel	Tanks	Guns	Mortars
Voronezh Front	15,178	31	139	0
Fortieth Army	75,412	119	927	1,278
Sixth Guards Army	85,849	150	1,053	1,221
Seventh Guards Army	80,767	239	873	1,102
First Tank Army	36,542	600	192	275
Sixty-ninth Army	46,865	0	482	853
XXXV Gds Rifle Corps	29,021	0	306	516
II Guards Tank Corps	11,451	187	56	97
V Guards Tank Corps	10,026	211	55	97
Total	391,111	1,537	4,083	5,439

PROLOGUE

According to other Sources
There are published figures available for these units. Some of them are listed below.

David M. Glantz's Figures[49]

	Personnel	Guns and Mortars	Tanks and SP Guns
Fourth Panzer Army	223,907		
Prov. Army Kempf	126,000		
German Total	397,900	3,600	1,617
committed	300,000		
Voronezh Front	625,591	8,718	1,704
Committed	466,236		
Thirty-eighth Army	60,000	1,168	106
Fortieth Army	77,000	1,636	113
First Tank Army			646
Steppe Front	573,195	8,510	1,639 or 1,551
Committed	295,000		900

Krivosheyev's Figures[50]

Voronezh Front	534,700		
Steppe Front	—		

Zetterling and Frankson's Figures[51]

Fourth Panzer Army	223,907	1,774	1,089
Prov. Army Kempf	108,000	1,073	419
Voronezh Front	625,591	9,751	1,704
Steppe Front	573,195	9,211	1,639

Lopukhovskii's and Zamulin's figures[52]

Army	Authorized	Actual	In Combat Portions
Thirty-eighth Army	87,348	76,882	61,100
Fortieth Army	99,767	91,676	75,807

Army	Authorized	Actual	In Combat Portions
Sixth Guards Army	118,244	100,257	79,653
Seventh Guards Army	110,834	94,157	76,831
Sixty-ninth Army	67,449	54,083	41,601
First Tank Army	48,101	41,648	28,248
Other Front forces*	153,104	138,222	54,211
Second Air Army	31,145	28,666	
Total	715,992	625,591	417,451

Army	Guns	Mortars	Tanks (/in repair)
Thirty-eighth Army	598	995	146/4
Fortieth Army	840	1,272	159/8
Sixth Guards Army	892	1,157	133/2
Seventh Guards Army	856	1,118	222/2
Sixty-ninth Army	380	851	
First Tank Army	192	264	556/6**
Other Front forces*	523	780	360
Second Air Army			
Total	4,281	6,437	1,576/22

Lopukhovskii relied upon a mix of archival and secondary sources for his Soviet figures. His columns for "authorized" and "actual" come from a secondary source from 1970 (probably the same one that Glantz used). He relied upon Zetterling and Frankson for his German figures.

* This includes the XXXV Guards Rifle Corps and its three divisions and the V Guards Tank Corps and II Guards Tank Corps.
** This does not include 24 assault guns (12 SU-76s and 12 SU-122s).

PROLOGUE

Notes

1. V. E. Tarrant, *Stalingrad, Anatomy of an Agony* (Leo Cooper, London, 1992), page 18.
2. See E.R. Hooton, *War over the Steppes: The Air Campaigns on the Eastern Front 1941-45* (Osprey Publishing, Oxford, 2016), pages 64-65: "ObdL. [German air command] calculated that between 22 June and 5 July the Russians lost 4,990 aircraft....Indeed, on 31 July the VVS staff calculated that 5,240 aircraft were 'unaccounted losses.' Russian strength returns for 22 and 24 June suggest losses of 3,922 aircraft, including some 2,000 on the first day, while force strength comparison of 1 June and 24 June suggests the loss of 47 per cent or 3,085 aeroplanes." Also see Von Hardesty and Ilya Grinberg, *Red Phoenix Rising: The Soviet Air Force in World War II* (University Press of Kansas, Lawrence, Kansas, 2012), page 9.
3. Soviet air strength before *Operation Barbarossa* is given as 7,133 aircraft with the Army Air Force (VVS – *Voyenno-Vozdushnye Sili*), 1,339 with the Long Range Bomber force (DBA or *Dahlnii Bombardirovochnaya Aviatsiya*), 1,445 with the Soviet naval air arm for a total of just under 10,000 aircraft, not counting auxiliary aviation. See Hardesty and Grinberg, page 27. These figures do not appear to include Home Air Defense (PVO or *Protivovozdushnaya Oborona*).

    Hooton, *War over the Steppes*, page 69 states: "By now [10 July] the VVS on the main front had only 1,679 aircraft, the DBA had 688 bombers and the PVO in the West had 1,179 fighters." This is a total of 3,546 planes. The Germans started the offensive with around 3,500 aircraft (2,500 combat aircraft) and their losses were lower. Von Hardesty has their strength as approximately 2,790 with 945 bombers, 345 dive-bombers, 1,036 single-engine fighters, 93 twin-engine fighters, 120 reconnaissance aircraft, and 252 transport and liaison aircraft. This comes out of 2,539 combat aircraft. See Clodfelter, page 815, Ellis page 233 and Hardesty and Grinberg, page 6.

    German losses to enemy action were 451 planes destroyed in July 1941 and 86 in December. Between 22 June and 31 December 1941 they lost 2,480 aircraft on the Eastern Front, of which 2,209 were "on operations." Of course, they regularly received replacements so as to maintain their strength. See Hooton, *War over the Steppes*, page 89.

    Soviet strength is given for 1 October 1941 as 1,540 aircraft with the main battle fronts, supported by 472 DBA bombers and 697 PVO fighters, for a total of 2,709 planes. See Hooton, *War over the Steppes*, page 92.

    German strength is given "on the main front" of 1,546 combat aircraft on 10 January 1942, 1,537 on 14 February 1942 and 1,550 on 14 March. See Hooton, *War over the Steppes*, page 97.
4. Tomas Polak with Christopher Shores, *Stalin's Falcons: The Aces of the Red Star* (Grub Street, London, 1999), page 9. Hardesy and Grinberg, pages 55-56 place the first raid on the night of 21/22.
5. The comparative strengths of the two forces "combat aircraft" over time is given by Ellis, page 233, as:

Date	German	Soviet
June 1941	2,139	8,100
Dec 1941	2,500	2,500
May 1942	3,400	3,160
Nov 1942	2,450	3,100
July 1943	2,500	8,300

Strength figures are also provided by Hooton, *War over the Steppes*, pages 69, 92, 97, 111, 115, 137, 147 and 164. They show:

Date	German	Soviet
10 July 1941		3,546
1 October 1941		2,709
10 January 1942	1,546*	
14 February 1942	1,537*	
14 March 1942	1,550*	
30 March 1942	1,766**	

1 May 1942	1,746***	5,528****
1 June 1942	2,324***	
1 July 1942		5,632
1 September 1942	2,142	
1 November 1942	2,034	
19 November 1942		6,769
1 February 1943	1,616	
April 1943	1,998	
June 1943	2,334	
1 July 1943		8,491*****

* "On the main front"
** "First-line strength"
*** Combat aircraft
**** 3,700 aircraft with the main battle front but only 3,146 pilots. The total includes the 329 ADD bombers, 1,051 PVO fighters and 448 VVS-KBF/ChF naval aircraft. This last category, naval aircraft, is not included in this previous totals. The figures for 1 July 1942 also included naval aircraft.
***** 8,491 on the main front on 1 July but only 5,732 aircrew. The total includes 740 ADD bombers, 1,079 PVO fighters, and 843 naval aircraft.

The following Soviet strength figures are provided by Hardesty and Grinberg, Appendix 4. These figures are from a Soviet-era source from 1962:

Date	Combat Aircraft
22 June 1941	7,133
10 July 1941	2,516
1 October 1941	1,716
5 December 1941	1,829
1 May 1942	4,038
19 November 1942	5,335
1 July 1943	8,826

The following German strength figures for the Eastern Front are provided by Dan Zamansky, pages 8-9, of his paper *How were German air force resources distributed between different fronts in the years 1941 to 1943 and what are the implications of this case study for understanding the political economy of the period?*: http://www.ww2.dk/Dan%20Zamansky%20-%20The%20Study.pdf

Date	Operational Aircraft	Combat Aircraft
8 November 1941	2,487	2,042
27 December 1941	1,936	1,571
10 December 1942	2,478	1,802
10 February 1943	2,425	1,671

These various totals are not consistent in their reporting nor is reporting based upon the same counting standards from report to report. The Soviet figures usually include their bomber command and the defensive fighter commands, and all aircraft, whether serviceable or they have pilots for. The Germans figures are often more tightly prescribed, making it a little bit of a comparison of apples and oranges. Note the differences in the figures between Ellis and Hooton and Hardesty.

6. Hooton, *War over the Steppes*, page 117 gives 308 for the South Front and 618 for the Southwestern Front.
7. Hooton, *War over the Steppes*, page 119.
8. Krasvoskii had been removed from command of the Second Air Army on 4 July 1942 and was only recently returned to command.
9. Hooton, *War over the Steppes*, page 137, has 1,714 Soviet aircraft assigned to the offensive while the German Fourth Air Fleet and the Romanians had 877 aircraft.

PROLOGUE

10. Micheal Clodfelter, *Warfare and Armed Conflicts* (McFarland & Company, Inc., Jefferson, North Carolina & London, 19992), page 824. Other figures have been noted, like 267,000 by Tarrant, *Stalingrad*, page 123, and 269,000 by Tarrant, *The Red Orchestra*, page 51. Forces surrounded included 20 German divisions, two Romanian divisions and a Croat regiment.
11. And this was supported by some German generals, including Marshal Erich von Manstein, who sent a report to OKH on 24 November 1942 stating that a breakout of the Sixth Army was not immediately necessary. See Williamson Murray and Allan R. Millett, *A War to be Won: Fighting the Second World War* (2000), page 288.
12. During the resupply efforts, the German Air Force lost 279 aircraft, included 174 Ju-52s. See Hooton, *War over the Steppes*, page 147. Hardesty and Grinberg, pages 142 and 163, give German losses as 488, but we are not sure of the time frame or operations. They specifically note 266 Ju-52s, 42 Ju-86s, 165 He-111s, 9 Fw-200s, 5 He-177s and 1 Ju-290. Hardesty and Grinberg, page 163, also report 2,000 Soviet aircraft lost during the defensive phase and 2,769 lost during offensive operations. If these figures cover the same time periods and operations, then this implies an almost 10 to 1 exchange ratio in favor of the Germans (1-to-9.77).
13. This offensive included the follow-up offensives: *Operation Gallup*, 29 January-18 February 1943, *Operation Star* from 2 February 1943, the *Ostrogzhsk-Rossosh Offensive*, 13 - 27 January 1943, the *Voronzezh-Kastornoye Operation*, 24-27 January 1932.
14. Richard Muller, *The German Air War in Russia* (The Nautical & Aviation Publishing Company of America, Baltimore, MD, 1992), page 106.
15. Cajus Bekker, *The Luftwaffe War Diaries* (Ballantine Books, New York, 1966), pages 430-431.
16. Richard Muller, page 106.
17. They had on 31 May 1943 2,113 aircraft in the west, 909 in Italy, 299 in the Balkans, and 1300 in rest and refit (Auffrischung) for a total of 8,036 aircraft. See T321, R154, page 62.

    For the Eastern Front this consisted of 300 short-range reconnaissance, 194 long-range reconnaissance, 547 fighters, 32 night fighters, 217 "destroyer" and ground attack, 580 bombers, 220 harassing, 434 Stukas, 223 transports, and 668 aircraft with the staffs. This is a total of 3,415 aircraft (1,728 with the Fourth Air Fleet), or 2,304 combat aircraft (1,134 with the Fourth Air Fleet), if one excludes the transports, harassing aircraft and those with the staffs.

    This matches well with the figure provided by E.R. Hooton, *Eagle in Flames, The Fall of the Luftwaffe* (Arms and Armour Press, London, 1997), page 171 for 30 June 1943 or 2,292 combat aircraft for the Eastern Front (612 fighters, 52 "destroyers," 552 bombers, 578 close support, 224 long-range reconnaissance, and 274 tactical reconnaissance aircraft). It does not appear that Hooton's figures include the harassment bombing aircraft. It also indicates that the air strength did not significantly change from 31 May to 30 June.
18. On 31 May 1943, the Fourth Air Fleet had 108 short-range reconnaissance, 69 long-range reconnaissance, 171 fighters, 17 night fighters, 166 "destroyers" (usually Me-110s) and ground attack, 329 bombers, 86 night harassment, 274 Stuka, 147 transport, and 361 miscellaneous aircraft. Figures are from Muller, pages 106 and 136, and T321, R154, page 62.
19. Hooton, *War over the Steppes*, page 162. A detailed order of battle is provided by Bergstrom, *Black Cross, Red Star*, pages 26-27.
20. Hooton, *War over the Steppes*, page 162. Bergstrom, *Black Cross, Red Star*, page 25, has their strength on 1 April at over 300 aircraft, including 63 Me-109s, 10 Me-110s, 86 Ju-87s, 35 He-111s, 41 reconnaissance planes and around 100 transport aircraft.
21. Bergstrom, *Black Cross, Red Star*, page 25 gives the count as 145 fighters, 136 bombers, 192 dive bombers, 83 ground attack aircraft, 19 long-range reconnaissance aircraft, 22 tactical reconnaissance aircraft and 100 transport planes (which we assume is an estimate).
22. Bergstrom, *Black Cross, Red Star*, page 59.
23. Bergstrom, *Black Cross, Red Star*, page 64. He has the sortie count as 446 Soviet sorties versus only 338 German sorties. He has the Soviet losses as 34 aircraft shot down (25 fighters and 9 Il-2s) and five that belly-landed with battle damage. The German lost one plane this day and two more that belly-landed with battle damage.
24. Hooton, *War over the Steppes*, page 162.
25. Bergstrom, *Black Cross, Red Star*, pages 77 and 88.
26. Bergstrom, *Black Cross, Red Star*, page 92.
27. Bergstrom, *Black Cross, Red Star*, page 109. There would have also been additional Soviet sorties in the area made by the Black Sea Navy air forces and by Long Range Aviation.

28. Hooton, *War over the Steppes*, pages 162-163. See Bergstrom, *Black Cross, Red Star*, pages 49-50 for a detailed order of battle.
29. Bergstrom, *Black Cross, Red Star*, page 128. The reports 197 sorties by bombers (mainly Pe-2s), 353 by Il-2s, and 876 by fighters. Not sure if these figures include Black Sea air forces and Long Range Aviation as a source is not given. There are no reported sortie counts for the Germans, but it was probably less. The Thirty-Seven and Fifty-Sixth Armies counted 1,047 German aircraft in the sky that day.
30. Bergstrom, *Black Cross, Red Star*, pages 130 and 131 reports 1,107 sorties on 27 May for the Fourth Air Army, 1,499 sorties on 28 May by the Fourth Air Army versus 733 German sorties that day, and 945 sorties on 29 May by Fourth Air Army versus 476 German sorties that day.
31. Bergstrom, *Black Cross, Red Star*, page 138 reports 788 sorties by the Fourth Air Army on 31 May.
32. The Long Range Aviation is reported to have flown 2,419 sorties between 17 April and 23 May, 1,141 against airfields and the remainder against enemy troops and defenses. See Hooton, *War over the Steppes*, page 163.
33. Hooton, *War over the Steppes*, page 163.
34. This is counting the 192 lost German aircraft compared to the 240 + 308 + 73 lost Soviet aircraft. This comes out of 1-to-3.23. The 132 German aircraft lost to accidents are not counted as some of them may have been lost outside of the Crimea and Taman peninsula area and also because we do not have similar totals for Soviet aircraft lost to accident. It was probably higher than the German total. Furthermore, the figures do not include the losses from the Soviet Long Range Aviation forces or the Black Sea air forces.
35. Ellis, page 233. Hardesty and Grinberg give a figure of 2,700, page 224, footnote 3 (on page 402).
36. Cajus Bekker, *The Luftwaffe War Diaries* (Ballentine Books, New York, 1966), page 432.
37. *Voyenno-Istroicheskii Zhurnal* [Military History Journal], 1968, Number 6. "Dokumentyi I Materialyi: Kurskaya Btva v Tsifrakh."
38. *Voyenno-Istroicheskii Zhurnal* [Military History Journal], 1968, Number 6. "Dokumentyi I Materialyi: Kurskaya Btva v Tsifrakh."
39. Bekker, page 432.
40. *Voyenno-Istroicheskii Zhurnal* [Military History Journal], 1968, Number 6. "Dokumentyi I Materialyi: Kurskaya Btva v Tsifrakh."
41. Glantz and House, *The Battle of Kursk*, page 390. This is as of 1 May 1943.
42. *Voyenno-Istroicheskii Zhurnal* [Military History Journal], 1968, Number 6. "Dokumentyi I Materialyi: Kurskaya Btva v Tsifrakh." This includes 881 with the Second Air Army, 735 with the Seventeenth Air Army, and 1,034 with the Sixteenth Air Army. There are additional airplanes in the area that may have been involved. The report footnotes note that these figures do not include about 480 night bombers from the Long Range Aviation and do not include the IX Fighter Corps and the 36th and 101st Fighter Division from the Air Defense Command. They also note that other Soviet secondary sources mention a total of 3,130 aircraft not counting Long Range Aviation, and 2,370 airplanes not counting Long Range Aviation and the neighboring Fronts. There is a reported figure of 550 aircraft for the Steppe Front from Dupuy and Martell, *Great Battles on the Eastern Front*, page 76, clearly taken from Soviet sources. These figures are not included in the above aircraft totals.

    Vasilevskii, Volume II, page 25, Konev, page 20, and Moskalenko give similar figures, in most cases having rounded them to the nearest hundred or thousand. Due to the centralized nature of Soviet historical writing and the tendency of generals to be assigned ghost writers, the consistency in the numbers between the various accounts in not surprising.

    See Konev, "The Great Battle at Kursk and its Historic Significances," *The Battle of Kursk* (Progress Publishers, USSR, 1974), page 20.
43. According to Hooton, *War over the Steppes*, page 165, as of 1 July 1943 they had 8,491 aircraft on the main front but only 5,732 aircrews.
44. Ellis, page 233.
45. Krivosheyev, pages 152–153, table 72.
46. German data is from the HERO Report: *German and Soviet Replacement Systems in World War II* (HERO, Dunn Loring, VA, July 1975), page 55. It was drawn from T78, R415, H1/182.
47. Tanks include tanks, flamethrower tanks, command tanks, artillery observation tanks, recovery tanks, assault guns, self-propelled antitank guns, and self-propelled artillery. A detailed listing by type is provided in Appendix III of *Kursk: The Battle of Prokhorovka*. Depending on a person's definition of a tank, this count can be lower by hundreds.

PROLOGUE

48. Guns include rocket launchers, and exclude 20mm, 37mm and 40mm AA guns. See Appendix III of *Kursk: The Battle of Prokhorovka* for details.
49. Glantz and House, *The Battle of Kursk*, pages 52, 60, 62 and 65.
50. Krivosheyev, page 188.
51. Niklas Zetterling and Anders Frankson, *Kursk 1943: A Statistical Analysis*, pages 18 and 20.
52. Lev Lopukhovskii, Prokhorovka: Bez Grifa Secretnosti (Eksmo, Yauza, Moscow, 2005), page 32, and Valerii Nikolayevich Zamulin, Prokhorovka: Neizvestnoye Srazheniye Velikoi Voinyi [Prokhorovka: the Unknown Battle in the Great War] (Tranzitkniga, Moscow, 2005), page 138. The first two columns are unique to Lopukhovskii's book, but the next four columns are the identical figures. Zamulin labels his column as "Total Personnel Strength" rather than "In combat portions," but their source is the same.

Chapter One

THE STRATEGIC AIR CAMPAIGN

The big air raid on Gorki the day before yesterday, which was also mentioned in the Wehrmacht report, was repeated yesterday by 128 machines with very great success. There are substantial flat fires as well as explosions and fires in oil storage. Only two machines were lost.

Reich Minister Joseph Goebbels dairy entry,
7 June 1943[1]

Both the German and the Soviet air forces primarily supported their ground operations, and as such were fundamentally structured to serve as tactical air forces. Little strategic bombing occurred on the Eastern Front. With the armies of these two nations locked in a life and death struggle, almost all air assets were focused on trying to win the ground war. In effect, strategic bombing was a luxury that neither nation could afford.

The German Air Force during April and May kept their operations somewhat limited, providing support where needed and occasionally striking at and interdicting the Soviet rail lines and rail yards. Mainly they were rebuilding so as to be ready for the offensive scheduled in May. With the offensive delayed, at the start of June the German Air Force took on its first real strategic air campaign on the Eastern Front. This focused on the rail yards around Kursk and on strategic bombing.

The Attacks on the Soviet Rail

Kursk was a lucrative target, as the rail lines from Voronezh to Kastornoye headed due west into the Kursk bulge and to the city of Kursk. Just east of the city, they turned north towards Maloarkhangelsk and south to Belgorod, and they also continued to the west. The rail lines were basically a cross in the middle of the bulge. As such, they provided rail to the north and south flanks of the Kursk bulge and to its western tip. This central hub supported the entire rail network of the Kursk bulge, and was a particularly vulnerable target.

Attacks against the Soviet railways started in mid-April, primarily by the Sixth Air Fleet (called the Air Command East at that time, it was renamed to the Sixth Air Fleet on 5 May 1943). These raids were carried out regularly, both day and night. They also organized several large-scale raids on the Kursk railway station. One of these occurred on 22 May with the Sixth Air Fleet flying 111 bomber, stuka, and attack sorties, along with fighter cover into the area

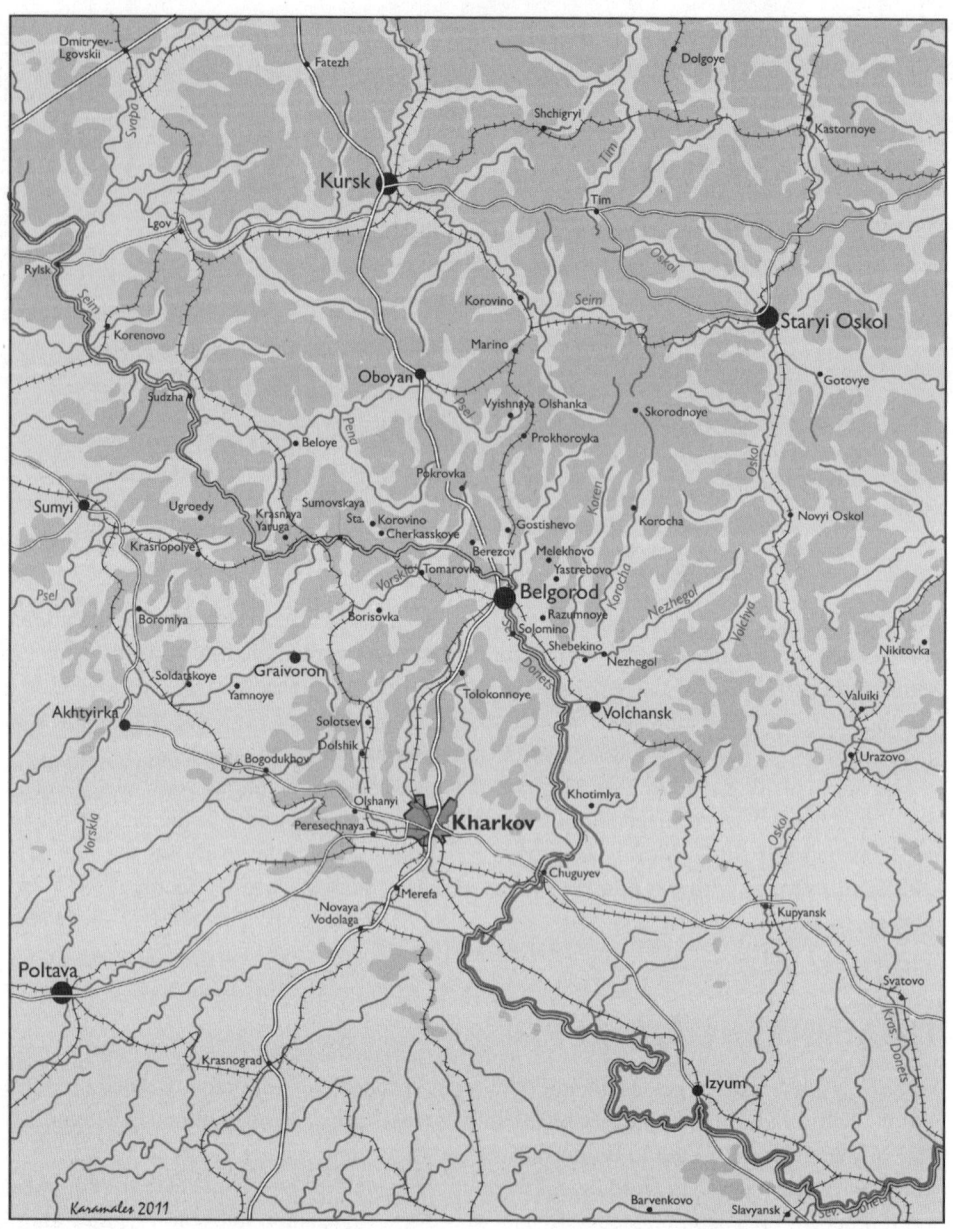

Kharkov, Belgorod and Kursk Map.

of Kursk.[2] The Soviets were notified of the raid by their front line observers and the railway officials were warned so that they could remove the cargo trains from the station. Defense was provided by scrambling Soviet aircraft and a considerable collection of antiaircraft guns, but with limited effect.[3] The German raid was able to penetrate but with losses.[4]

THE STRATEGIC AIR CAMPAIGN

The Soviets were able to bring the rail junction quickly back to working again, while the Germans conducted attacks by German or Hungarian aircraft on other parts of the rail lines including on 28 May, the night of 30/31 May and 1 June.[5]

On 2 June, the Germans organized a mass raid on the Kursk railway station using aircraft from the 1st Air Division of the Sixth Air Fleet and from the VIII Air Corps. The Sixth Air Fleet sent in 95 bomber sorties and 64 "destroyer" sorties (Me-110s) during the day, with heavy fighter cover (perhaps 280 fighters).[6] That night, they hit the Kursk area again with another 52 bomber sorties. The VIII Air Corps sent in 138 bomber missions during the day and 150 more during the night.[7] The Soviet defense against such raids was of limited effect.[8] These raids were opposed by 280 fighters of the Second and Sixteenth Air Armies and by 106 of the 101st Air Defense Division.[9] German losses connected with these raids were about 10 aircraft (2% losses).[10]

The German attack arrived over Kursk at 0439 (Moscow time). According to Soviet sources, the first wave consisted of 137 bombers and 30 fighters coming from the north and from the southwest. In response they sortied with 53 fighters from the Sixteenth Air Army and 42 fighters from the 101st Air Defense Fighter Division. The Soviets then observed three more waves of attacks coming in during the day. These German daytime attacks came at altitudes ranging from 1,500 to 7,000 meters. The fourth wave of attacks came in from the south with 106 bombers flying at 6,000 meters. The Second Air Army sent up 57 fighters to intercept them in the Oboyan area; and 13 fighters from the Sixteenth Air Army and 15 fighters from the 101st Air Defense Division to intercept them over Kursk. After about 1450 (Moscow time), activity quieted until the night raids, which were defended against using anti-aircraft artillery. While the damage caused to the railway junction was considerable, the tracks were mostly preserved. The Soviets were able to resume rail traffic through Kursk within 35 hours.[11]

This major attack with 499 bomber and "destroyer" sorties was followed up on 5 June with smaller raids that only had minimal VIII Air Corps participation.[12] These strikes were not followed up by similarly sized operations during the rest of the month.[13]

These raids did generate considerable losses for the German air forces. On 22 May the Sixth Air Fleet lost 11 aircraft and on 2 June they lost six, while the VIII Air Corps lost seven.[14] While it is not known if these losses actually occurred during the raid or other missions conducted that day, these daily loss reports are the highest daily losses in these formations from the beginning of May until the offensive started on 5 July. The Sixth Air Fleet never lost more than three planes on any other set of day or night missions until 5 July, while the VIII Air Corps never lost more than two planes in a day until 5 July. It would appear that most of these losses were suffered in these missions.

The Soviets defended the Kursk area in force, making extensive use of their fighters and bringing in considerable anti-aircraft assets. The Germans claimed they downed 17 fighters on 22 May, mostly around Kursk. For the raid on 2 June, the Sixth Air Fleet claimed 46 Soviet fighters downed, with another two at night, while the VIII Air Corps claimed 18 kills during the day.[15] This was the highest claim for June except for 8 and 10 June, when the Soviet air force attacked the Sixth Air Fleet airfields. Soviet losses are reported as 26 aircraft on 2 June.[16]

The value of these attacks was limited, in part because they were not sustained. It was hoped that because of the low density of Soviet rail and their limited reserve capacity that such a campaign could indirectly affect the Soviet fighting strength in the bulge. This may have been possible, but to achieve a permanent effect would have required a more concentrated and systematic effort. Instead, in the following days, the German Air Force switched to a strategic bombing campaign against their industry and never again struck the rail yards with anywhere near the same force. Still, before the offensive, the Germans managed to strike at the Yelets and other railway stations 10 to 18 times, the Liski station and the bridge across the Don 15 times, the small bridge at Cheremisinovo station 10 times, Kastornoye station 16 times, and the Kursk railway junction 15 times.[17] As such, the raids continued to disrupt and served as a constant drain on resources for the Soviets, but did not have any permanent impact.

Furthermore, the Soviet Army and civilian railway engineers were able to quickly repair and replace damaged stations, bridges, and sections of the lines. They concentrated repair teams near expected areas of attack, so they could get the damage fixed and the trains operating again within hours. Still, the Kursk railway junction was so badly damaged that they built a seven-kilometer detour line on the north side of the city. There had been continuous railroad work going on since Kursk had been recaptured on 8 February. Making use of local labor, through traffic on the Kastornoye-Kursk line was resumed on 17 March. At first the trains were limited to 15 kilometers an hour, but by June were allowed to go 40 kilometers an hour. Over the course of several months, the Soviets managed to build up the capacity of the trunk lines from about six trains each way per day to more than 24 a day. From April to June, 3,572 trains consisting of 171,789 cars were sent into the Kursk bulge. This included about 150,000 cars for supply.[18]

The value of such a campaign against the rail net was further degraded by its late start. The Soviet buildup before June was significant, with most of the units already in place. As such, an interdiction campaign with its high point in June was probably a little late to seriously degrade Soviet defensive capabilities. Without systematic follow-up, the overall effects of this effort were limited. Still, the Germans maintained regular attacks on the Soviet rail lines, many at night, throughout the month of June and also during the month of July. The Soviets primarily defended with antiaircraft guns, including antiaircraft guns mounted on armored trains.

The German Strategic Air Campaign

Immediately after the attacks on the Kursk rail junction, the Germans initiated the first serious strategic air campaign on the Eastern Front. It was at the instigation and under the overall command of Colonel General Robert Ritter von Greim, commander of the Sixth Air Fleet. The first target was Gorki (now called Nizhnyi Novgorod). Gorki was some 400 kilometers east of Moscow and almost 650 kilometers from the German lines. Gorki was home to the Molotov State Motor Vehicle Plant No. 1, the largest automotive plant in the USSR. It had been built between 1927 and 1932 with American assistance. This "Soviet Detroit" was estimated to produce 4,000 T-60 and T-70 light tanks a year. This was

THE STRATEGIC AIR CAMPAIGN

estimated to be 60% of the Soviet light tank production, and it was also believed to make T-34 components.[19]

All the bomber formations on the Eastern Front were now attached to the Sixth Air Fleet, although they continued to operate from their regular bases. This was a force of around 439 bombers.[20] In particular, the VIII Air Corps' 27th and 55th Bombardment Wings were now part of the Sixth Air Fleet's offensive. The first strike occurred during the night of 4/5 June with 168 bomber sorties.[21] There were 179 tons dropped on the Molotov Plant No. 1, with 70 people killed and 210 injured in the area of the factory.[22] The attack was effective. A Soviet report states that 80% of the production area was destroyed and an area of 11.4 thousand square meters laid in ruins.[23] This was at a cost of one or more German bombers.[24]

It was followed up the next two nights with 128 sorties and then 124 sorties. Finally, on the night of 7/8 June, a much smaller disruptive bombing run was made of 20 sorties. These four nights of bombing totaled 440 aircraft sorties and they dropped 636 tons of bombs.[25] The total civilian casualties from these raids were 233 killed and 542 injured.[26] There were some encounters with Soviet night fighters, at a cost of three Soviet fighters during these subsequent missions.[27] German losses for these subsequent raids were at least one plane.[28]

Over the next three days the Germans had their airfields attacked by the Soviet air force with little overall effect (see below), concentrating on those fields the bombers were operating from. The strategic bombing campaign then shifted to the synthetic rubber plant at Yaroslavl (250 kilometers northeast of Moscow) on the night of 9/10 June. There were 132 bombing sorties from the Sixth Air Fleet. Of those, 102 carried out the attack on Yaroslavl, 14 attacked mobile targets, and 16 had their operations cancelled due to technical problems. The Sixth Air Fleet reported their losses for the night as three He-111s, probably lost on the Yaroslavl raid.[29] It is claimed that six of the seven factory buildings were destroyed and there were 40 civilians killed.[30]

The next night, the Sixth Air Fleet flew another 126 bomber sorties, with 86 attacking Gorki yet again, 14 again attacked mobile targets and 26 had their operations cancelled due to technical problems. The Sixth Air Fleet reported their losses for the night as two He-111s, probably all lost on the Gorki raid.[31] The next night was much quieter with no strategic missions, while the night after that was spent hitting the rail around Yelets with 152 sorties, of which ten had their operations cancelled due to technical problems. This rail yard was outside the Kursk bulge but did link into the Voronezh-Kursk rail line. The night of 13/14 June the Sixth Air Fleet sent up another 118 sorties, with 92 sent to Gorki, 15 attacked mobile targets, and 11 had their operations cancelled due to technical problems. The 27th Bombardment Wing was part of the attacks on Gorki. Their losses were two He-111s, including Knight's Cross holder Captain Putz of the 27th Bombardment Wing. Weather halted activity for the next night and there were no more major night raids reported until the night of 19/20 June, when they again struck with 60 bomber sorties at the rail yards of Yelets, while two bombers went after mobile targets. There are other accounts of these operations that slightly disagree in times and details, and there were also at least two bombing raids on Saratov.[32] The Germans then ended their strategic air campaign with a second strike on Yaroslavl with the Sixth Air Fleet flying 112 bomber sorties on the night of 20/21 June. Of those 91 attacked Yaroslavl, 5 attacked mobile targets, and 16 had their operations aborted. The Germans reported three He-111 missing, assumed all from the Yaroslavl operation.[33] The Sixth Air Fleet then hit Gorki the following night flying 101 bomber sorties. Of those, 85 attacked Gorki, 10 attacked mobile targets, and 6 had their operations aborted. The Germans report one Ju-88 lost this night.[34] There were also four or so raids conducted against the oil refineries at Saratov between the 11th and the 15th.[35]

This was pretty much the entire German strategic air campaign for the middle of 1943. It consisted of at least nine major night raids of 31 to 168 bombers over 18 nights against only three major targets. They were primarily focused on attacking the armaments production facilities in an attempt to slow down the continued build-up of Soviet armaments. At the request of the army, this focused mostly on tank production, although the Luftwaffe also looked at industrial targets. It appears that the damage to the Molotov factory was extensive. The factory returned to full production on 18 August.[36] Still, for some reason, the Germans had not targeted the T-34 factory in Gorki. Even though it was estimated to have been responsible for 10–15% of Soviet T-34 production, it remained untouched.[37] Regardless of its effectiveness, the bombing campaign occurred too late to have any immediate impact on the defensive phase of the Kursk battle. Overall, the strategic bombing campaign in June involved 703 bomber sorties against Gorki, 193 bomber sorties against Yaroslavl, maybe an estimated 233 sorties against Saratov for an estimated total of 1,129 bombing sorties. There were at least 1,500 tons of bombs dropped.[38]

The missions included the 27th and 55th Bombardment Wings under the command of the Sixth Air Fleet. Most, if not all the planes used were He-111s and all the missions were unescorted night raids. The strategic bombing campaign was not as costly in aircraft as the rail yard campaign. The seven raids against Gorki probably resulted in the complete loss of six He-111s. The two raids against Yaroslavl may have lost three He-111s on each raid. The raids on Saratov may have been without loss.[39]

Because it was a two- and one-half-week air campaign conducted with an average of around 100 bombing sorties per raid, it probably did not seriously undermine the Soviet war effort. In comparison, in June, the US and UK flew 7,913 bomber sorties and dropped 17,601 tons of bombs on Germany![40] This German strategic bombing effort was brought to a halt by the preparations for the Kursk offensive. As it was the first strategic bombing offensive in the east, it did lead to plans for another campaign when the front was again quiet, including developing better intelligence and the creation of a target selection committee.

During that time, the Sixth Air Fleet also participated in a number of other efforts, including bombing other rail lines and rail areas, particularly Yelets. The VIII Air Corps, except for the participation of its bomber wings, was much less active during this period, although it also had its airfields attacked on 8 June. Both air forces continued night bombing, with the VIII Air Corps being surprisingly active. Both air units dropped hundreds of thousands of propaganda leaflets each night. The Sixth Air Fleet also participated in the largest German propaganda campaign of the war,[41] called *Operation Silver Streak* (Silberstreif), begun on 7 May and continuing up to the offensive. For example, between 7 May and 15 May, they dropped 84.5 million of these simple propaganda leaflets behind Soviet lines, in an effort to increase Soviet desertion.[42] On the night of 4/5 July, the Sixth Air Fleet dropped 760,000 propaganda leaflets. While figures have not been located for the VIII Air Corps, it was standard procedure for both sides to regularly drop such leaflets as part of their night bombing missions. In this particular case, though, a major reason for the missions was to advertise the new OKH Basic Order No. 13, which had been issued in April. The new order laid out a policy of preferred treatment for Russian deserters.[43] This attempt to suddenly try to win "hearts and minds" two years into what had been a very brutal war was probably comically doomed to start with. Still, it was pushed forward with considerable vigor, not only including leaflet drops announcing the new order, but also loud-speaker propaganda broadcasts at the front. How effective this was is hard to tell. While the number of deserters doubled in May compared to April, we would suspect that the desertion rate in May would naturally be higher than in April due to desertion rates tending to go up in anticipation of major combat action.[44]

Each of the German air fleets conducted extensive reconnaissance missions, often flying 50 reconnaissance sorties a day. The Sixth Air Fleet (called Air Command East at that time) conducted 1,638 reconnaissance sorties in April over the Kursk bulge.[45] There are no reports of the VIII Air Corps reconnaissance flights, but they had one short range reconnaissance group and were certainly flying dozens of reconnaissance sorties each day. The 10th NAG, which reported to the Sixth Air Fleet, but reported its activity separately, maintained six sorties a day to a high of 20 sorties on 3 July.[46] It was primarily supporting the Second Army. As the Soviet air force was active, many of these missions had to be escorted into Soviet air space.

All these various missions divided the efforts of an air force that was already not large enough for tasks being assigned to it. In addition, the German Air Force needed to rest up, rebuild, and improve its serviceability for the upcoming offensive. This last process was done better by the VIII Air Corps than the Sixth Air Fleet. From 28 May through 3 June (7 days), the VIII Air Corps flew 1,248 day missions (average of 178 a day) and 395 night missions (average of 56 a night) while the Sixth Air Fleet flew 2,817 day missions (average of 402 a day) and 300 night missions (average of 43 a night). With the strategic bombing campaign from 4 through 21 June, this comparison becomes even more imbalanced, in part because some of the VIII Air Corps' bomber wings were now reporting to the Sixth Air Fleet. During this period of 18 days, the VIII Air Corps flew 1,408 day missions (average of 78 a day) and 770 night missions (average of 43 a night) while the Sixth Air Fleet flew 4,248 day missions (average of 236 a day) and 2,314 night missions (average of 129 a night). After the strategic air campaign, and in the period leading up to the offensive, the Sixth Air Fleet still maintained considerably more activity than the VIII Air Corps. During this 12-day period, the VIII Air Corps flew 778 daytime missions (average of 65 a day) and 295 night missions (average of 25 a night) while the Sixth Air Fleet flew 1,811 day missions (average of 151 a day) and 449 night missions (average of 37 a night). The VIII Air Corps was the larger force.

One can see that the VIII Air Corps activity steadily declined as the offensive grew nearer. This was a deliberate attempt to give the crews rest and to bring the planes back up to serviceability. The VIII Air Corps was clearly focusing on being ready to provide ground support. The Sixth Air Fleet, along with the bombing groups borrowed from the VIII Air Corps, were involved in many other activities than just preparing for an offensive.

STRATEGIC BOMBING MISSIONS
June 1943

Sixth Air Fleet[47]

Night	Target	Sorties	Mobile Targets	Operations Cancelled	Total Sorties	Harassment Bombing	Other*	Losses
June 4/5	Gorki	168			230	29		2
June 5/6	Gorki	128	16	6	209	Kursk rail:18		2
June 6/7	Gorki	124	23	7	165			1
June 7/8	Gorki	20	8	3	39			0
June 8/9					98	Kochetovka rail: 91		0
June 9/10	Yaroslavl	102	14	16	138			3
June 10/11	Gorki	86	14	26	195	40	3	2
June 11/12	Saratov?	80?			89		3	0
June 12/13	Yelets rail	(142)		10	260	30	3	0
	Saratov?	69?						
June 13/14	Gorki	92	15	11	196		3	2
	Saratov?	69?						
June 14/15					5			0
June 15/16	?****	0?			15		3	0
June 16/17	Saratov?	15?			130	100	8 + 1**	0
June 17/18	included in the report of the previous day							
June 18/19					30	18	4	0
June 19/20	Yelets rail	(60)	2		157	50	6***	0
June 20/21	Yaroslavl	91	5	16	203	66	8***	3
June 21/22	Gorki	85	10	6	155	38		1
		896	107	101	2,314	371	151	16
Saratov		233?						

Yelets rail = 202
Kursk rail = 18
Kotchetovka rail = 91 (of which 9 aircraft attacked alternative targets)
Kastornoye rail routes = 29
Dive Bombing "Seletuchino" = 12

* Unless otherwise stated, the attacks consist of "railway chase" on the routes going to and from Kastornoye.
** On the night of 16/17 the Sixth Air Fleet claimed a kill by a night fighter, indicating at least one night fighter sortie that night.
*** There were six nighttime dive bomber missions on "Seletuchino."
**** Some sources say a raid on Saratov occurred this day, but there are only 6 to 12 planes available for such an effort.

THE STRATEGIC AIR CAMPAIGN

All these efforts before the battle were somewhat unfocused and did not result in any significant influence on the upcoming ground battle. The strategic bombing effort in June was too late to affect what was going to happen shortly in the field. The operations against the rail lines were too little, came into full force too late, and were not followed up. The reconnaissance effort was extensive and the Germans were kept well informed. While many of the other missions, like close air support, airfield suppression, and night bombing needed to be done, one wonders if more of an effect could have been achieved if the German air had concentrated its efforts on one set of targets, like the rail. A focused campaign for two months against the Kursk rail lines and supporting rail yards may have made some real difference. As it was, there was limited effect. Still, even with perfect management of resources, the fundamental weakness was that the German Air Force simply lacked the means to fulfill all the missions it was being called on for.

In the end, the Germans produced a rather haphazard and non-systematic rail interdiction and strategic bombing campaign. Fundamentally, the Luftwaffe, even with their extensive experience in bombing Britain, had not succeeded in working out an effective strategic bombing or interdiction strategy. As such, their efforts were wasted. What the Germans knew and did well was close-air support. Here the Luftwaffe was soon to be back into its element. On 30 June 1943 the Germans reported having 612 fighters, 52 "destroyers" (Me-110s), 552 bomber, 578 close support, 224 long-range reconnaissance and 274 tactical reconnaissance aircraft, or a total of 2,292 combat aircraft on hand in the Eastern Front.[48] This was the strongest this air force would be since the fall of 1942 and the strongest it had been at any point after that.[49] The German aircraft strength on 30 June was not significantly different than on 31 May.

The Soviet Strategic Air Campaign

In April, the Soviet Union also attempted a brief strategic air campaign. This was really not an organized campaign, but simply a series of raids, what the Soviet Air Force referred to as "morale bombings" of Germany cities. Over a period of two weeks in April, Soviet Il-4s and a few four-engine Pe-8s attacked Konigsberg, Tilsit and Danzig. Their biggest success was a night bombing of Tilsit on 20 April where 104 civilians were killed.[50]

The capital of Prussia was Koenigsburg (now called Kaliningrad), which translates as "King's mountain." Wilhelm I, the King of Prussia, became the first Emperor of the united German Empire in 1871. His son and grandson were the next German emperors. Even with the German army camped just outside of Leningrad, Koenigsburg was within range of Soviet bombers. On the night of 11/12 April 1943, the Soviet Long Range Aviation force (abbreviated as the ADD, Aviatsiya Dalnego Deistiviya) began bombing Koenigsburg. Over a month this bombing campaign flew 920 sorties against the city of 372,164 (in 1939) and dropped 788 tons of bombs. The bombing ended on the night of 13/14 May with little effect. It cost the Long Range Aviation force 14 aircraft.[51]

Konigsberg was an attractive "morale bombing" target as it was the capital city of Prussia. This city would be annexed by the Soviet Union at the end of the war and renamed Kaliningrad. It remains today as an isolated Russian enclave between Lithuania and Poland.

The Soviet Air Campaign

The Soviet air force had not been able to contend with the Germans for control of the sky since the beginning of the war. Even the German resupply of Stalingrad had been conducted with mostly unescorted transports. During its winter offensive and the German counterattack in March, the Soviet air force was never able to establish air superiority. During most of that period, the German Air Force was able to establish control over any space that it considered important.

Still, the Soviet air force continued to be built up and as such, was becoming a more dangerous and significant threat to German control of the air. First, the Soviet air force had grown larger. In particular, its fighter arm now outnumbered the Germans' on the Eastern Front. Second, they had continued to improve their aircraft and were now fielding planes almost as good as those the Germans manufactured. The Battle of Kursk was the first real attempt in two years to contest the Germans for control of the air.

The Soviet air force spent most of their time between March and July building up for the expected summer offensive. Still, they made a number of efforts to strike at the German rail and airfields. The German Army High Command War Diary notes that from the beginning of May, a series of heavy night attacks were made on important rail junctions, particularly in the Army Group Center area. They struck at the railway junction at Minsk on the night of 4 May with 109 bombers and also sent 109 bombers, including Pe-8s, to strike at the railway hub at Orsha (between Smolensk and Minsk).[52] The night strike on 4 May at Orsha resulted in the burning of 300 rail wagons, including three ammunition trains. The following night, the Soviets struck at Gomel, Bryansk, and Lokot, while for the night of 6 May, their night bombers hit the areas around Orel. These night attacks, often with more than 100 aircraft, continued throughout the months of May and June.[53]

The Soviet air campaign against the rail began on 4 April and continued until 4 July. It involved 9,400 sorties, of which 3,000 were against German targets opposite the Kursk bulge. Most of the missions were flown by Long Range Aviation with some support from the Sixteenth and Second Air Armies. While it was a large extended effort, its effect was limited.[54]

In addition to night harassing attacks on the German rail, the Soviets also launched two sets of airfield raids in an attempt to establish air superiority. This may have been at the instigation of the Voronezh Front command (Vatutin, Khrushchev and Major General Feodosii K. Korzhenevich), which suggested around 21 April that large air operations be mounted at once to destroy the German aircraft on their airfields so as to weaken the Germans before their offensive.[55]

The first set of airfield attacks was conducted from 6 to 8 May by six air armies (First, Second, Eighth, Fifteenth, Sixteenth, and Seventeenth) against 17 German airfields from Smolensk down to the Sea of Azov.[56] This was a 1,200 kilometer front with a depth of 200 kilometers. On the morning of 6 May this attack was initiated with 434 sorties.

The morning attacks were generally successful, with the Soviets achieving surprise at many of their targets and temporarily shutting down one large air base at Seshchinskaya.[57] But, the attack by the Second Air Army, organized by Lt. General Sergei Khudyakov, was not that successful.[58] Their attacks targeted four airbases around Kharkov and one at Poltava. The German Freya radar based in the area notified them of the incoming attack and the I/52nd Fighter Wing and II/3rd Fighter Wing were based in the area. These two fighter groups scrambled and intercepted the incoming Soviet missions with three or more Soviet planes shot down. The Soviet raids on Kramatorskaya and Dnepropetrovsk airfields by the Seventeenth Air Army also had problems. Some already airborne Romanian and German fighters intercepted their missions as they were arriving at Kramatorskaya airfield. The attacks by these two air armies on the airfields was not very effective.[59]

As a result of the morning attack by six Soviet air armies, they lost at least 29 planes. The Germans may have had 23 or more planes damaged or destroyed on the ground.[60] The delayed Soviet follow-up attacks in the afternoon and evening were not successful. Against an alerted Luftwaffe which already had two groups airborne, several formations were caught on the way to the target with high losses, in one case of an attack on Orel, it cost the Soviets more than two dozen aircraft.[61] South of the Kursk salient, the German's two fighter groups were again alerted by their Freya radar and again they scrambled to intercept the incoming Soviet fighters, costing the Soviets four La-5s. The Soviets did attack a German dummy airfield at Kharkov-Aleshki, with their escorting fighters losing four Yak-7Bs along with two Il-2s.[62]

There were additional operations towards the evening, including a strike at Kramatorskaya. The Germans were again waiting and that cost the Seventeenth Air Army another three Il-2s, one La-5 and one Yak-1. The Germans lost one Romanian Me-109 that belly-landed with combat damage.[63]

By the end of the day, the Soviets had lost 76 planes. Five axis (German and Romanian) fighters had been shot down, of which only one was a total write-off. The Germans had twenty-three planes damaged or destroyed on the ground, with maybe five of them destroyed.[64] So maybe a 76 to 10 exchange in aircraft for a 7.6-to-1 exchange ratio. The exchange ratio for pilots and aircrews was even more lopsided, with most German and all Romanian pilots surviving their downing.

The Soviets continued operations on the 7th, although having now lost surprise, they were again gutted as they were on the afternoon of the 6th. The Sixteenth Air Army, which had lost 40 aircraft the previous afternoon, lost 18 Il-2s and 7 fighters, while to their south, the Second Air Army lost 6 Il-2s and 9 fighters.[65] Soviet total losses for this day are not known, but the Germans claimed 60 victories this day with four planes shot down.[66] The Soviet losses were probably around 49 aircraft (see next paragraph). The following day, the Soviet air flew a few more missions, but without any significant accomplishments and with a loss of only 9 aircraft.

The three-day offensive was conducted with 1,392 sorties. The Soviets claimed 506 German losses for a cost of at least 122 planes according to Soviet-era secondary sources.[67] Their losses for the three days were 134 according to primary sources. This was 76 aircraft on 6 May, 49 aircraft on 7 May and 9 aircraft on 8 May.[68] Between 6 and 8 May the Luftwaffe registered no more than 23 aircraft lost.[69] The Soviet claims of German losses is certainly very much higher than what the Germans suffered.[70]

> ## THE BRITISH AND U.S. AIR CAMPAIGN IN THE WEST
>
> While the German strategic bombing campaign in the east in 1943 dropped at least 1,500 tons of bombs on the Soviet factories, this was a fairly low effort compared to the strategic air campaign the western allies were conducting against Germany. While the German strategic bombing campaign was being conducted against Gorki, Yaroslavl and Saratov, the allies were doing considerably more devastation in the west. This included the United Kingdom's devastating night bomber campaign in March 1943 called the Battle of Ruhr. That five-month effort, which involved over 1,000 bombers and some 18,506 sorties, attacked 26 different major targets. The United States joined into the effort, with 100 US bombers hitting the German port of Kiel on 14 May. More significant, it was a daylight raid, which by its nature, are much more accurate. On the night of 16/17 May the British bombers managed to destroy the Eder damns in the Ruhr. Finally, on the night of 24 July began the devastating bombing raids on Hamburg that continued until 3 August. It included four massive nighttime raids of 700-800 bombers and two daytime raids over 100 bombers.
>
> In all in the month of June the U.S. and the UK combined dropped 17,601 tons of bombs on Germany and it only got more devastating as time went on.[71] This was more than ten times the weight of bombs that the Germans used on the Soviet Union.[72] Whereas the German strategic air campaign was the only effort of its type in 1943 or for the rest of the war, the allied efforts in the west were steadily dropping over 15,000 tons a month on Germany, and getting heavier and more devastating each successive month.

This was the first of three Soviet attempts to strike at German air bases. They would try again on 8 to 10 June and then again on 5 July at the start of the Battle of Kursk. Their morning strike on 6 May was the single most successful of these strikes. Their subsequent raids were not very successful, mostly resulting in a lop-sided unfavorable exchange ratio with the Germans and rarely shutting down German airbases for long. Even then, the morning strike cost the Soviets 29 aircraft in exchange for 23 damaged and destroyed. Of those 23 damaged and destroyed, maybe only 5 were destroyed. So, this ended up being something like a six-to-one exchange against the Soviet attackers. It is debatable that they gained much from this effort, and this was their most successful of three raids.

A month later, the Soviets conducted a second airfield attack operation from 8 to 10 June using the First, Second, and Fifteenth Air Armies and their Long Range Aviation force. The Soviets attacked 28 airfields, focusing mostly on the bomber airfields. This decision to focus on the German bomber fields was probably in response to the German bombing of Gorki on 6 June.

The airfield attacks on 8 May occurred late in the day with at least 151 aircraft attacking at least three airfields during the day and another 264 aircraft from the Long Range Aviation force making night attacks on at least three airfields.[73] The attacks on 9 June were more limited because of weather with only around 160 planes from the Long Range Aviation going after Orel and Bryansk, probably as night attacks.[74] As the weather cleared on the 10th, more than 178 planes struck at least five fields, while the Long Range Aviation did additional night attacks.[75]

The Soviets claimed more than 220 German aircraft destroyed.[76] On the other hand, the German VIII Air Corps and Sixth Air Fleet only record a total of eight losses for these three days, although this probably does not include losses on the ground.[77] Ground losses were low due to the Germans being ready for such a strike, including have radar set up around Orel in addition to Kharkov.[78] It would appear that these two sets of raids in early May and early June mostly damaged the Soviet air force, resulting in high losses for themselves. At least 122 Soviet planes were lost in the May airbase attacks and at least 77 Soviet planes lost in June airbase attacks.[79] There were low losses for the Germans, perhaps as low as only seven to fourteen planes destroyed in May and eight or less planes destroyed in June.[80]

The German High Command War Diary claimed 2,304 Soviet aircraft destroyed in the air or on the ground from 29 April to 30 June. For May, the Germans claimed that 1,257 Soviet aircraft were destroyed, while they lost 143.[81] There is some doubt about the accuracy of the German claims but as discussed later, they tend to be more accurate than the Soviet claims.

Notes

1. Joseph Goebbels,, *Die Tagebucher von Joseph Goebbels* (The Diary of Joseph Goebbels) (K.G. Saur, Munchen, 1993), Part 2, Volume 8, page 433.
2. T312, R1234, Second Army air liaison officer reports 8 He-111s, 29 Me-110s, 64 Ju-87s and 10 Fw-190s ("jagdbomber"). Hardesty and Grinberg, page 236, claims it was 170 German bombers. Bergstrom, *Black Cross, Red Star,* pages 174-175 states that escort was provided by all available fighters from I/26 Fighter Wing and the 51st Fighter Wing. He references the 2nd Army air liaison reports, except the information on the escorts is not provided in the copies I have.
3. *The Battle of Kursk* (Progress Press Publishers), page 254. Page 252 provides the antiaircraft defense of the Kursk railway station as 64 medium and 24 light AA guns, 45 heavy machineguns and 26 searchlights. No date is given for these strengths.
4. T312, R1234, Second Army air liaison officer reports losses for the day of 9 Ju-87s, 1 He-111 and 1 Fw-190 out of a total of 397 sorties for that day. Bergstrom, *Black Cross, Red Star,* page 175, reports all 11 German planes were lost from this mission and five Soviet planes were destroyed and three severely damaged based upon Soviet sources.
5. T312, R1234, Second Army air liaison officer reports and Bergstrom, *Black Cross, Red Star,* page 175. It is a Soviet-era claim that says it took them 10 to 12 hours to bring rail junction back to working condition. The Second Army air liaison officer reports do not exist for 23-26 May 1943 so other raids during that time may have been missed. Also, on the days there are reports, the reports are very brief and possibly incomplete. For example, for 29 May there are 363 sorties reported for the Sixth Air Fleet but the mission and location is only provided for 124 aircraft sorties.
6. T312, R1234, Second Army air liaison officer report records 299 fighter sorties, of which the "mass" were for escort protection, although there were 19 hunting missions. This implies a rather hefty 280 fighter sorties for escort.
7. T312, R1234, Second Army air liaison officer reports. Hooton, *War over the Steppes,* page 200, states that the Germans flew 596 sorties on 2 June for *Unternehmen Carmen* and the following night attacked with 202 bombers. Hardesty and Grinberg, page 236, claim it was more than 400 bombers.

    Bergstrom, *Black Cross, Red Star,* page 176 provides a more detailed account of the operations. It includes German raids at 0400, 0540, 0730 and before 1100 with a total of 300 bombers and more than 85 escort fighters. Not sure how this account matches up with the reported figures from the Second Army air liaison officer reports of 95 and 138 bomber and 64 "destroyer" missions. He has the Sixth Air Fleet providing 299 fighters, although I believe the real figure was 280 or less. With 30 fighters in the first wave, and 55 fighters in the second and third waves, this would mean there were 195 fighters in the fourth wave. He claims the Soviets defended against the fourth wave with 205 fighters.

    Interesting enough, the VIII Air Corps does not claim to have sent fighters. They report flying 402 sorties that day, of which 138 were bomber sorties to Kursk and 91 stuka sorties on Oboyan. That leaves 173 sorties not accounted for. Yet they claim to have shot down 18 enemy fighters "in case of escort protection." This implies that there were fighter escorts from the VIII Air Corps.

    So we are looking at a situation where there were almost 200 German fighter escorts in the air facing over 200 Soviet fighters. Yet the reported German fighter losses for this day are one Fw-190 from Sixth Air Fleet and one Me-109 from the VIII Air Corps. This does raise some questions over the size and extent of the air engagements on this day. It also raises questions about the claims that the German bombing attacks were warded off or successfully fended off. One would expect to see heavier German fighter losses if they were being effectively intercepted, unless the Germans abandoned the attacks early on. In that case, one wonders why the rail traffic was shut down for 35 hours.
8. On the other hand, Bergstrom, *Black Cross, Red Star,* page 176, claims that for the first German wave that the Soviets "managed to tear apart and ward off the whole attack." For the second and third waves "Fifty-five German aircraft managed to break through to the target area, but they arrived singly or in small groups and their bombs fell scattered, hardly inflicting any serious damage to the rail installations." For the fourth wave "They were met by 205 Soviet fighters which once again succeeded in fending off the bombing raid." So, it appears by this account, only 55 scattered German bombers got through and

THE STRATEGIC AIR CAMPAIGN

the first and fourth wave were completely aborted. Yet, the rail traffic was shut down for 35 hours, which appears to be a significant shutdown if there were four failed German raids.

9. *The Battle of Kursk* (Progress Press Publishers), page 188.
10. VIII Air Corps lost 1 Hs-126, 1 Ju-87, 3 He-111s and 1 Me-109 during the day and 1 Ju-88 at night while the Sixth Air Fleet lost 4 Ju-88s, 1 Me-110 and 1 Fw-190 during the day and nothing at night. See T312, R1234. Hooton, *War over the Steppes*, page 200, states that the Germans lost 17 bombers to some 300 enemy fighter sorties. No source is given. Bergstrom, *Kursk*, page 21, states that "Seventeen of these aircraft were shot down and destroyed and another eight sustained severe battle damage." His source is the Luftwaffe quartermaster reports. Bergstrom, *Black Cross, Red Star*, page 176 gives German losses as "Twenty-nine of these were shot down, of which eighteen were written off. The losses included seven fighters, six Ju 88s from III./KG 1, and five Ju 97s from II./STG 77. The Soviet losses amounted to twenty-six aircraft. The German fighter pilots claimed thirty-eight victories."
    In contrast, the Soviets claimed to have shot down 104 German aircraft with their fighters and 41 with their antiaircraft artillery. See *The Battle of Kursk* (Progress Press Publishers), page 188. Hardesty and Grinberg, page 237, repeat the Soviet claims without crosschecking them to the German records. They also make the claim that the Soviets suffered a "modest loss" of 27 fighters.
11. *The Battle of Kursk* (Progress Press Publishers), pages 255–256 & 287. In all, the Soviets counted 424 bombers and 199 fighters sent against them during the day. The Germans report only 233 bomber sorties for this day and 64 destroyer sorties, along with up to 280 fighter sorties from the Sixth Air Fleet and probably some fighter sorties from the VIII Air Corps.
12. While writer #762 claims that "The Luftwaffe gave a very successful repeat performance of this raid on 5 June," the Sixth Air Fleet only flew a total of 249 sorties this day (compared to 402 on the 2nd), destination not stated. They only flew 18 bomber sorties at night at the train station at Kursk. The VIII Air Corps only flew 97 sorties on the 5th, with only three bomber sorties recorded as going to Kursk, and only eight bomber sorties recorded going to Kursk during the night. Losses were also very low, with only 1 Fw-190 lost by the Sixth Air Fleet on the 5th (and 12 kills claimed, 9 by air) and 1 Ju-88 lost over Kursk that night. The VIII Air Corps only lost 2 Ju-88s (and claimed only two kills). It is clear that the effort on 5 June was nowhere near the size of the attack on 2 June. See writer #762, *The "Zitadelle Offensive, Eastern Front, 1943, Luftwaffe Participation in the Area of the German OREL Armies* (T-26, page 157) and T312, R1234.
    Joseph Goebbels' diary (Minister of Propaganda) notes a mission on 3 June. Under the entry for 4 June, it lists yesterday's military actions, including over 200 bomber, "destroyer" and fighter bomber sorties on Kursk. See Joseph Goebbels, *Die Tagebucher von Joseph Goebbels* (The Diary of Joseph Goebbels) (K.G. Saur, Munchen, 1993). The Sixth Air Fleet flew 286 sorties this day and the VIII Air Corps flew 124. Both of them state that they patrolled their respective fronts without any mention of strikes on Kursk (T312, R1234). We suspect the Goebbels' reference is to the mission on 2 June or night missions for the night of 2/3 June.
    Bergstrom, *Black Cross, Red Star*, page 177 provides a more detailed description of this operation along with the claim that the German "attempt to break through to Kursk failed." This does not match with writer #762's claim or are accounted for by the German losses of this day, which are only reported as one Fw-190. Bergstrom does not provide losses for German operations during this day. This claim of "failure" may only apply to German night operations on 5 June, where 18 bomber sorties were sent to attack the rail station at Kursk at a reported loss of 1 Ju-88. Bergstrom reports only 3 Ju-88s attacking with two shot down along with one Fw-190 (we gather these loss reports are correct).
    The VIII Air Corps also sent three bomber sorties to the train station at Kursk with no reported losses, eight bomber sorties during the night with maybe one reported loss during that raid (T312, R1234).
13. Bergstrom, *Black Cross, Red Star*, page 176 claims that this is because of the failure of *Operation Carmen*, the German name of the series of air attacks against Kursk on 2 June 1943. He claims that "the Luftwaffe never again made any attempt at a large-scale air in daylight on the Eastern Front. From then on, German bomber units on the Eastern Front only operated in formations of relatively limited size in daylight and shifted all larger bomber operations to the hour of darkness." This is not what we see during the operations at Kursk from 4-17 July 1943.
14. These losses are at reported by the Second Army air liaison officer (T312, R1234). Christer Bergstrom, *Black Cross, Red Star*, page 176 report higher losses. This included 40 German planes lost on 2 June.

The specifics of these figures is somewhat mystifying. There is a claim that "Twenty-nine of these were shot down, of which eighteen were written off. The losses included seven fighters, six Ju 88s from III./KG 1, and five Ju 87s from II./StG 77." It is assumed that these losses are only for the last raid of the day (before 1100) but they may apply to all four raids of that day. Not sure if it includes or excludes losses from other missions conducted by the Sixth Air Fleet and VIII Air Corps that day. The sentence indicates that actually 11 planes were shot down and 18 planes returned to base that were later written off as destroyed. Do not know how his account then grows to 40 German airplanes shot down three paragraphs later.

15. Warning, these claims have not been cross-checked to reported Soviet losses.
16. Bergstrom, *Black Cross, Red Star*, page 176. This claim is from primary sources (unit records).
17. *The Battle of Kursk* (Progress Press Publishers), page 253.
18. *The Battle of Kursk* (Progress Press Publishers), pages 241–242 & 286.
19. Plant data from Muller, page 117, and is data drawn from German records.
20. Bergstrom, *Black Cross, Red Star*, page 188. These figures are as of 1 June 1943. Of those, 135 were Ju-88s (1st, 3rd and 51st Bombardment Wings) while 304 were He-111s.
21. This is in accordance with the Sixth Air Fleet reports provided by the Second Army air liaison officer. In all subsequent reports on strategic bombing missions, they list: 1) the number of bombers that attacked the target, 2) the number of bombers that attacked mobile targets (the figures on subsequent days being respectively 16, 23, and 8, and 14 on 9/10 June and 10/11 June, 15 on 13/14 June, two on 19/20 June, five on 20/21 June and 10 on 21/22 June) and, 3) the number of planes that did not complete the mission due to technical problems (6 on 5/6 June, 7 on 6/7 June, 3 on 7/8 June, 16 on 9/10 June, 26 on 10/11 June, 10 on 12/13 June, 11 on 13/14 June, 16 on 20/21 June and 6 on 21/22 June).

    If between 3 and 26 planes were unable to complete their missions because of technical problems in those subsequent nine reports, one wonders if some of the 168 bombers reported to have flown on 4.5 June also did not complete their missions.
22. Bergstrom, *Black Cross, Red Star*, page 190.
23. Bergstrom, *Black Cross, Red Star*, page 190.
24. This was at least one He-111. According the Second Army air liaison report for the night of 4/5 June (T312, R1234), the losses of the Sixth Air Fleet were one Ju-88 and one He-111. As is often the case, the losses reported were for the entire 230 sorties done that night by Sixth Air Fleet, not just specifically those on the attack on Gorki. On the following night, they report one He-111 lost in the attack on Gorki and one Ju-88 lost in the attack on Kursk, the second loss probably being from the 18 sorties sent to attack the train station at Kursk. On the night of 6/7 June they report one Ju-88 missing. On 7/8 June they provided a cumulative report that stated over the last few days there were 47 sorties against mobile targets, with two bombers missing. The total night losses from 4/5 to 7/8 July was only five planes, leading one to conclude from these reports that two He-111s were lost on the Gorki raids while two Ju-88s were lost from the attacks against mobile targets, and 1 Ju-88 was missing (possibly from attacks on mobile targets). Bergstrom, *Black Cross, Red Star*, page 190, claims that their losses were six planes. This is recorded as two each from KG 3 and KG 27 and one each from KG and KG 4 (3 Ju-88s and 3 He-111s).
25. Sortie count is the summation of all missions to Gorki from the records of the air liaison officer to the Second Army (T312, R1234). The records do report that 440 missions were on the tank works, and 47 were used to attack rail targets (with two planes reported missing). On the raid of 5/6 June, 128 sorties were on the tank works while 16 attacked mobile targets and 6 aborted their missions; on the raid of 6/7 June 124 sorties were on the tank works while 23 attacked mobile targets and 7 aborted their missions; on the raid of 7/8 June 20 sorties were on the tank works while 8 attacked mobile targets and 3 aborted their mission. The 168-sortie raid of 4/5 June does not provide a breakdown of targets, but according to the records, all planes attacked the tank works.

    The bomb tonnage is from Muller, page 117. He gives a figure of 420 planes involved, so the bomb tonnage figure may not be matched with the sortie count.

    Goebbels's dairy also mentions several of these raids. He reports on 7 June (for 5/6 June) a raid of 128 planes on Gorki with 2 losses and reports on 8 June (for 6/7 June) a raid of 123 planes on Gorki with 1 loss. In the diary entry on 8 June (for 7 June), he reports 200 tons of bombs dropped.
26. Bergstrom, *Black Cross, Red Star*, page 191. Bergstrom states that the losses were from "three raids." The raid on 7/8 June was only 20 planes, so it is either ignored or subsumed in these losses.

THE STRATEGIC AIR CAMPAIGN

27. Bergstrom, *Black Cross, Red Star*, page 190. Two Soviet fighters were shot down the night of 5/6 June and one fighter rammed an He-111 the night of 7/8 June. The Soviet pilot crash-landed and survived. The damaged He-111 made it back to base.
28. On the night of 5/6 June the Sixth Air Fleet reports 1 He-111 lost in the attack on Gorki (and one Ju-88 lost in the attack on Kursk). On the night of 6/7 June the Sixth Air Fleet reports 1 Ju-88 missing. Goebbel's diary records two planes lost on the raid on 5/6 June and one lost on the raid of 6/7 June.
29. Second Army air liaison officer records (T312, R1234). The 14 planes attacking mobile targets may not have flown to Yaroslavl, even though the structure of the paragraph in the records indicate that they did.
30. Bergstrom, *Black Cross, Red Star*, page 194. He also claims that 109 He-111s took part, which does not agree with the figures in the Second Army air liaison officer records.
31. Second Army air liaison officer records (T312, R1234). The 14 planes attacking mobile targets may not have flown to Gorki, even though the structure of the paragraph in the records indicate that they did.
32. Goebbels's diary paints a similar picture. On the 11th the diary records 100 sorties to Yaroslavl the previous day. It claims that 25% of the Soviet rubber production is there. It reports a raid on Gorki the following day. This all matches with the other German air reports we have.

    He provides no specific data for the following days until the 16th, when he reports that Saratov had the honor of another bombardment and that there was a strong attack on Yelets. This would indicate a bombing raid on 15/16 June if these are not delayed reports. Goebbels reports on the 17th that Saratov again underwent bombardment. On the 19th he reports 160 bombers hit Astrakhan with good effect. Fourteen bombers were used against the local channel that connected to the Volga. They sunk four vessels of 10,000 gross tones (German estimate).

    The Air Liaison officer reports for the Sixth Air Fleet indicate no major raids immediately after the night report of 13/14 June. They report only 5 sorties for the night of 14/15 June, 15 sorties for the night of 15/16 June, a more hefty 130 sorties for the two nights of 16/17 and 17/18 June, but 100 of these are Stoerkampfflugzeuge (night harassment bombing missions) and 8 were bombing missions aimed at the rails between Voronezh, Kastornoye and Yelets. The other 22 missions are unstated, but certainly included reconnaissance and at least one night fighter. There are 30 sorties the night of 18/19, of which 24 are reported on and then there is the report of 19/20, which reports 62 planes going after Yelets.

    We have not resolved the differences. The air liaison officer records clearly indicate no major raids between the night of 13/14(Gorki) and the night of 20/21 June (Yaroslavl). Based upon Goebbels's diary, there were two raids on Saratov during this period and a major raid on Astrakhan. This last raid was conducted by units other than the Sixth Air Fleet or VIII Air Corps and was not part of the strategic air campaign discussed here.
33. This is in accordance with the Second Army air liaison records (T312, R1234). Bergstrom, *Black Cross, Red Star*, page 195, says that seven bombers out of 88 were lost. The Sixth Air Fleet records show 91 bombers attacking Yaroslavl. He then states that the next night when 101 bombers flew against Gorki, two He-111s were shot down by night fighters. The Sixth Air Fleet records shows one Ju-88 lost. The records show 85 bomber missions against Gorki but 101 bomber missions total.
34. Goebbels also records on the 21st another strike on Saratov that is not discussed above. He notes a hit on a refinery, six major fires emerged and that a plane was lost. He also notes Luftwaffe attacks against ship targets in the Caspian Sea, with a claim of a steamer of 5,000 gross tons being sunk and several others damaged.

    On the 22nd Goebbels records heavy air attacks on Yelets, on the rubber factories in Yaroslavl, and on ship targets. All three attacks were carried out with very low loss. He picks up the attack on Gorki the following day, reports it with good effect. This matches the other records.

    On the 24th he records another "very effective" attack on the ball-bearing factory in Saratov on the 22nd that is not picked up by other sources. It was without losses and the Volga was "again" mined.
35. Muller, page 118, states there were four raids against Saratov on the 12th–15th of July which dropped 181 tons of bombs. The Sixth Air Fleet records 260 sorties the night of 12/13 June, of which 152 went to the rail lines around Yelets, and 33 other sorties are accounted for. This leaves 75 sorties unaccounted for. The night of 13/14 June records 196 sorties, of which 118 went to Gorki and 3 others are accounted for. This leaves 75 sorties unaccounted for. The night of 14/15 only had 5 sorties because of the weather, while the night of 15/16 only had 15. There may have been raids on the night of 12/13 and 13/14 June on Saratov with up to 75 sorties each night. Writer #762, page 159, notes that the Gorki tank factory was bombed seven times and Yaroslavl rubber plant twice. He makes no mention of Saratov.

Bergstrom, *Black Cross, Red Star*, page 195 states that the Germans bombed Saratov on the night of 11/12 June, and again on the nights of 13, 15 and 16 June. The Second Army air liaison officer records for the Sixth Air Fleet 89 sorties the night of 11/12, which 3 attacked the rail from Kastornoye to Yelez. The location of the other missions is not stated. The night of 13/14 the Sixth Air Fleet reports 196 sorties, with 118 reported as part of the attack on Gorki (92 attacked Gorki) and three attacked the rail from Kastornoye to Yelez. The night of 15/16 is only 15 night sorties and three of these were by Ju-52s. The night of 16/17 June and 17/18 June reports 130 sorties (for both nights?). Of those 100 are night harassment bombing missions and 8 were attacks on the rail from Voronezh to Kastornoye to Yelez. There was also at least one night fighter sortie.

These leaves 86 unaccounted sorties on the night of 11/12, 75 unaccounted sorties for the night of 12/13, 75 unaccounted sorties for the night of 13/14, 12 unaccounted sorties for the night of 15/16 and 21 unaccounted sorties for the two nights of 16/17 and 17/18. It is possible that raids were made on Saratov on the 11th, 12th, 13th, 15th and 16th, with the last two raids not being very large.

36. Hooton, *War over the Steppes*, page 200. Not sure of his source and cannot confirm the accuracy of this claim.
37. Horst Boog, Gerhard Krebs, Detlef Vogel, Derry Cook-Radmore (translator), *Germany and the Second World War: Volume VII: The Strategic Air War in Europe and the War in the West and East Asia, 1943–1944/5* (Oxford University Press, Oxford, 2006), page 385.
38. The bomb tonnage figure is from Muller, page 118, and is a summation of his figures for Gorki, Yaroslavl and Saratov. It is based upon 682 bombers raiding Gorki and 190 hitting Yaroslavl. The bomb tonnage figure does not match with the sortie figures from T312, R1234.

    Horst Boog, et al., page 385, have slightly different figures of 681 planes hitting Gorki seven times, and 192 planes hitting Yaroslavl in two raids.

    They give an overall figure of 1,553 aircraft and 2,690 tons of bombs. This includes 1,015 tons on targets in Gorki, 324 tons on Yaroslavl and 181 tons on the oil refineries at Saratov. (Muller provides these same figures for these three targets on page 118 but does not provide the overall figure of 2,690 tons dropped). Not sure what the other strategic targets the remaining 1,170 tons were applied to, apart from rail lines and rail yards.

    Hooton, *War over the Steppes*, page 200, says that the bombing campaign consisted of 1,813 sorties and that Factory 292 in Saratov, the prime producer of Yak-1s was hit. He states that "some sources state [the factory] was destroyed or severely damaged on 22/23 June." He also says that in defense the PVO (the Soviet home defense air force) flew 431 sorties and claimed 52 interceptions. He says that the Germans lost 20 aircraft in this bombing campaign.

    We do no think there were any bombing missions on Saratov on the night of 22/23 June. The Sixth Air Fleet reports 87 sorties that night, 19 to Kastornoye, 42 harassment bombing sorties and 26 not reported on.
39. Most likely all He-111s lost on the night the raids were conducted were during these raids. The records only clearly identify 3 He-111s as lost over Gorki.
40. John Ellis, *World War II: The Encyclopedia of Facts and Figures* (The Military Book Club, USA, 1995), page 234. It only got worse as the war went on. Horst Boog, et al., on page 385 report a higher figure of over 28,000 tons "over the same period" as the German air campaign in the east.
41. It was the "most ambitious German propaganda campaign of the war" according to Earl F. Ziemke, *Stalingrad to Berlin: The German Defeat in the East* (Center of Military History, the United States Army, Washington DC, 1987, originally published 1968), page 131. The Sixth Air Fleet's participation is noted in the Second Army air liaison officer's records.
42. Leaflet count from Muller, page 141, and appears to refer to the entire Eastern Front.
43. Zeimke, page 131.
44. According to one German army in the area there were 121 deserters reported in May, compared with 60 in March and 55 in April. Zeimke (page 131) reports that during the period of May and June, a total of 662 deserters came in, with less than half of them being a direct result of Silberstreif. Muller reports (page 141) that the number of deserters (across the entire Eastern Front?) in the month of May had doubled (compared to April?), totaling 2,424.
45. Muller, page 112.
46. Second Army air liaison officer records are the source of the sortie count. According to E. R. Hooton, *Eagle in Flames, The Fall of the Luftwaffe*, page 315, it consisted of the 2.(H)/10, 3.(H)/21, 2.(H)/31,

THE STRATEGIC AIR CAMPAIGN

5.(H)/32 armed with Fw-189s and Hs-126s. The plane designations from the Second Army air liaison officer records show Me-109s, Fw-189s and Hs-126s, although the Me-109s are last reported on 7 May.
47. All data from Second Army air liaison officer (T312, R1234) except where followed by a question mark, which is the author's guess as to what occurred.
48. Hooton, *Eagle in Flames*, page 171. These figures exclude seaplanes and transports and most likely exclude harassing bombers.
49. Hooton, *Eagle in Flames*, page 171, provides a strength of 1,766 aircraft for 30 March 1942, 2,690 for 30 June 1942, 2,324 for 30 September 1942, and then declining to 1,501 for 30 December 1942, and 1,993 for 31 March 1943. The figure for 30 September 1943 is 1,765, 31 December 1943 is 1,683 and 31 March 1944 is 1,785. These figures do not include transports or seaplanes.
50. Bergstrom, *Kursk*, page 18.
51. Hooton, *War over the Steppes*, pages 202-204.
52. Bergstrom, *Kursk*, page 18.
53. Jukes, page 56.
54. Hooton, *War over the Steppes*, page 201. Hooten has the ADD flying 15,328 sorties from January to July 1943 while the Sixteenth and Second Air Armies only join this campaign in early May and fly 1,909 sorties. The claim that it was of limited effect is from Army Group Center's rail transport officer and probably only applies to his zone. Still, there is little to indicate that this campaign was particularly effective.
55. Jukes, pages 50–51.
56. As there was one air army per Front, the Fronts from north to south were the Western (First Air Army), Bryansk (Fifteenth Air Army), Central (Sixteenth Air Army), Voronezh (Second Air Army), South Western (Seventeenth Air Army), and Southern (Eighth Air Army).
57. Bergstrom, *Black Cross, Red Star*, page 183.
58. Bergstrom, *Black Cross, Red Star*, page 184 states that Lt. General Sergei Khudyakov directed the strikes of the Second Air Army. Lt. General Sergei Khudyakov was a senior commander responsible for coordinating air operations of the Voronezh and Steppe Fronts during the Battle of Kursk and later during the Battle of the Dnieper. Lt. General Stepan Krasovskii was the commander of the Second Air Army (Voronezh Front), Lt. General Vladimir A. Sudets was the commander of the Seventeenth Air Army (Southwestern Front) and Major General Sergei K. Goryunov was the commander of the Fifth Air Army (Steppe Military District, on 9 July became the Steppe Front).

Sergei Khudyakov was originally born in January 1902 as Armenak Artem Khanferiants. He was of Armenian descent and was born in Boyuk Taghlar, an Armenian village in the Karabakh region of Azerbaijan. According to accounts, he gave himself the Russian name of Sergei Aleksandrovich Khudykov during the Russian Civil War in honor of a deceased friend of his. The original Sergei Khudykov, who was his commander, saved him from drowning when his steamer was sunk by a British gunboat and they had to swim to shore. That Sergei Khudykov later died during the Russian Civil War and Armenak Khanferiants adopted his name.

He was the Chief of Staff of the Soviet Air Force. He held other senior commands throughout the war. In the second half of 1943, his 14-year old son, who he had taken to the front with him, was killed in Kharkov. In February 1945, he was a military advisor to Stalin during the Yalta conference. He can be seen standing behind Stalin in the famous picture of Churchill, Roosevelt and Stalin at the Yalta conference. In December 1945 he was arrested and accused of being a spy for the British. He was executed in April 1950 and his wife, his younger son and his adopted son were exiled to Siberia from 1951-1953. The charges against Khudyakov were cancelled in 1954 and he was rehabilitated in 1965.

See: "Сталин и Берия не любили армян. А мне надо было взлететь" (nv.am) and Труд: Сбитый летчик (trud.ru)
59. Bergstrom, *Black Cross, Red Star*, page 184.
60. Bergstrom, *Kursk*, page 19. Bergstrom provides more detail on these attacks. He has 404 planes attacking between 0430 and 0600 in the morning. These attacks put 22 German aircraft out of commission, including eight from the 51st Fighter Wing, six from 4th Bomber Wing and six from 4.(F)/11 (a reconnaissance unit). A total of 21 Soviet planes were shot down on May 6.

Bergstrom, *Black Cross, Red Star*, page 184 has 23 German aircraft "put out of commission on the ground," at a cost of 29 Soviet aircraft.

ACES AT KURSK

Hooton, *War over the Steppes*, page 170 states that German losses were 5 aircraft destroyed and 20 damaged.

61. According to Bergstrom, *Black Cross, Red Star*, page 185, the Sixteenth Air Army lost at least 23 Il-2s and 3 escorting Yak-1s, while the opposing Germans lost two planes. The Germans (51st Fighter Wing) claimed 37 Il-2s and 6 fighters. The Sixteenth Air Army's losses for the day were 28 Il-2s, four Pe-2s, four Yak-1s, and four La-5s for a total of 40 planes lost.
62. Bergstrom, *Black Cross, Red Star*, pages 185-186. It includes a more detailed description of these operations.
63. Bergstrom, *Black Cross, Red Star*, pages 186-187.
64. Bergstrom, *Black Cross, Red Star*, pages 184 and 187. He notes that the Germans claimed 93 planes shot down for this day. Also see Hooton, *War over the Steppes*, page 170. He states that German losses were 5 aircraft destroyed and 20 damaged.

    The Sixteenth Air Army was the hardest hit with loses of 28 Il-2s, 4 Pe-2s, 4 Yak-1s and 4 La-5s (Bergstrom, *Black Star, Red Cross*, page 185, although it is stated in an account on page 187 that their losses were 27 Il-2s and 9 fighters).
65. Bergstrom, *Black Cross, Red Star*, page 187. Second Air Army losses were six Il-2s, four Yak-12s, three La-5 and two Yak-7Bs.
66. Bergstrom, *Black Cross, Red Star*, page 187. He notes that of the four German aircraft "shot down," only one was a write off.
67. Air Marshal Sergei Rudenko's article on "The Gaining of Air Supremacy and Air Operations in the Battle of Kursk" in *The Battle of Kursk* (Progress Press Publishers), page 188. Also see Hooton, *War over the Steppes*, page 170. Rudenko stated the Soviet claimed 500 German losses while Hooton states it was 506. Rudenko stated that the Soviets lost 125 planes while Hooton states it was 122 lost.
68. Bergstrom, *Black Star, Red Cross*, page 187, with footnotes referencing Soviet air unit records.
69. Bergstrom, *Kursk*, page 19. Bergstrom provides more detail on these attacks. He has 404 planes attacking between 0430 and 0600 in the morning. These attacks put 22 German aircraft out of commission, including eight from the 51st Fighter Wing, six from 4th Bomber Wing and six from 4.(F)/11 (a reconnaissance unit). The Soviets returned again with 372 aircraft between 1500 and 2000 hours. A total of 21 Soviet planes were shot down on May 6. The following two days, a total of 346 sorties were made against the German airfields, resulting in the Soviet Union losing 101 aircraft.

    Bergstrom, *Black Cross, Red Star*, page 184 has 23 German aircraft "put out of commission on the ground," at a cost of 29 Soviet aircraft. On page 187 he has twelve fighters shot down or severely damaged, with only two being total losses.

    Hooton, *War over the Steppes*, page 170 states that German losses were 5 aircraft destroyed and 20 damaged.
70. T312, R1232, the "Einsatzuebersicht Luftw. Kde. Ost am 7.5.43" reports only 1 He-111 lost this day while the NAG 10 reports none (as usual). Have not located German loss reports for the 6th and the 8th or for the Fourth Air Fleet, but there are no indications of heavy losses in any of the unofficial histories of the Luftwaffe. There is no reason to believe that the strike in May was significantly more successful than subsequent strikes.
71. Ellis, page 234 for June gives 15,271 tons for the Bomber Command and 2,330 tons for the US Eighth Air Force. For July it was 16,830 tons and 3,475 tons respectively.
72. It appears that the Germans dropped at least 1,500 tons and maybe as much at 2,690 tons. The 1,500 figures was used for this calculation, as we think the other bombing was targeted on rail lines and rail yards and other interdiction-like targets.
73. See Bergstrom, *Black Cross, Red Star*, pages 192-193. Attacking Orel 22 fighters as an advance force, 12 Il-2s and 9 La-5s. Attacking Seshchinkaya was an advance force of fighters, size not stated, 36 Il-2s and 22 fighters, and then a second wave of 26 Pe-2s. Attacking Poltava was 24 Bostons. The ADD sent 75 bombers to attack Orel, 87 to attack Bryansk and 102 to attack Seshchinskaya. I assume these were night attacks.
74. Bergstrom, *Black Cross, Red Star*, page 194. It was Il-4s, Mitchells and Li-2s.
75. Bergstrom, *Black Cross, Red Star*, pages 194-195. Attacking Sokolniki airfield near Kharkov and Mikoyanovka was 22 Il-2s, 8 Pe-2s and an unstated number of escorts, all from the Second Air Army. Attacking Seshchinskaya was 23 Il-2s, 36 Pe-2s and an unstated number of escorts. Attacking Bryansk was 24 Il-2, 9 Pe-2s and attacking Ozerskaya were 8 Il-2s. These two attacks were escorted by 48 fighters. There were also night attacks by the ADD.

THE STRATEGIC AIR CAMPAIGN

76. Air Marshal Sergei Rudenko's article on "The Gaining of Air Supremacy and Air Operations in the Battle of Kursk" in *The Battle of Kursk* (Progress Press Publishers), page 188. Hooton, *War over the Steppes*, page 170 states that they claimed 580 to 750 aircraft. This seems high even by Soviet claiming standards. He states that the Long Range Aviation flew 2,330 sorties for a loss of 25 planes.
77. T312, R1234. The VIII Air Corps for 8 June reports 1 Ju-87 lost due to flak and 1 Me-109 missing, and "no losses" for the night of 8/9 June; 1 Ju-87 missing for 9 June; and "no losses" for the night of 9/10 June, 10 June, or night of 10/11 June. The Sixth Air Fleet records "no losses" for the 8th of June, the night of 8/9 June, 9th of June. They report 3 He-111s lost for the night of 9/10 June (probably from the raid on Yaroslavl), and no losses of 10 June, and 2 He-111s (probably from the raid on Gorki) for the night of 10/11 June.

    Hooton, *War over the Steppes*, page 170 states that the Germans lost eight aircraft, half of them Storchs, while 11 were damaged. Not sure of the basis for his loss claims, probably the Luftwaffe quartermaster files.
78. Bergstrom, *Black Cross, Red Star*, pages 192-195. This account is not complete, but covers the daytime attacks on Orel, Seshchinskaya, and Poltava on 8 June, the night attack on Orel and Bryansk on 9 June, the daytime attacks on Sokolniki, Mikoyanovka, Seshchinskaya, Bryansk and Ozerskaya, and the night attack on Shatalovo. In those first three large raids no German planes were destroyed on the ground, and the subsequent attacks are said to be done with no effect, except for the night raid of 10/11 June in which nine German reconnaissance planes were "knocked out."
79. We do not have a good total for Soviet losses from 8 to 10 June 1943. Hooton, *War over the Steppes*, page 170 states that the Long Range Aviation flew 2,330 sorties for a loss of 25 planes. Bergstrom, *Black Cross, Red Star*, pages 192-194 reports Soviet losses on 8 June at Orel as 12 Il-2s and 8 fighters (including 5 Yak-7Bs), at Seshchinskaya as two Pe-2s, and at Poltava no losses. There are no reports of losses for 9 June. On 10 June is reported that the Second Air Army lost 3 Il-2s in their raids, the First Air Army lost 13 Il-2s, 11 Pe-2s and 6 fighters. Total Soviet losses appear to have been at least 77 planes and was probably higher.
80. The German VIII Air Corps and Sixth Air Fleet only record a total of eight losses for these three days in June, although this probably does not include losses on the ground. Not all of these may have been lost in the airfield raids. The Germans are reported to have had eight reconnaissance planes "knocked out" from an airfield night attack on 10/11 June.

    The German losses in May are discussed above. It appears that 5 planes were shot down (but only one written off) on 6 May and 5 destroyed on the ground. On 7 May 4 planes were shot down (but only one was written off) and none were lost 8 May.
81. Jukes, page 56. While these claims have not been verified, the Germans' low losses in May are partly confirmed by the Second Army air liaison officer records. There is not a complete set of reports for May, but the reports that we have usually show low losses for May. This includes reports for the Sixth Air Fleet for May 7th, 14th, 14/15th (a night report), 22nd, 27th, 28th, 28/29th, 29th, 29/30th, 30th, 30/31st, 31st and 31/1st; and for the VIII Air Corps for 28th, 28/29th, 29th, 29/30th, 30th, 30/31st, 31st and 31/1st. The German losses reported for these days are 1 Fw-189, 1 Fw-190, 3 He-111s, 2 Hs-126s, 10 Ju-87s, 1 Hungarian Ju-88, 1 Me-109, and 1 Me-110 for a total of 20 planes lost (five from VIII Air Corps). Making a straight line estimate from this limited data would produce a monthly loss figure of about 97.

    The German claims for Soviet air losses have not been verified. While the claims are very high, they are not out of line with claims that we have been able to verify for July.

Chapter Two

BOTH SIDES PREPARE

Our detractors used to say that the only reason we were able to defeat Paulus's colossal army at Stalingrad was that we had the Russian winter on our side.
They had said the same thing about our defeat of the Germans outside Moscow in 1941. Even since Russia turned back Napoleon's invasion, people claimed that winter was our main ally.
However, the Germans couldn't use this excuse to explain their defeat at the Battle of the Kursk Salient in 1943.
They fired the first shot; they chose the time, place, and form of the battle. All the cards were in the hands of Hitler and his cutthroats.
It was high summer.

Nikita Khrushchev ca. 1970[1]

Supporting the German Army Group Center and the German forces on the north side of the Kursk bulge was the Sixth Air Fleet under Colonel General Robert Ritter von Greim. Supporting Army Group South was the Fourth Air Fleet under command of General Otto Dessloch. The portion supporting the forces on the south side of the Kursk bulge was the VIII Air Corps under Major General Hans Seidemann. At this stage, there were over 700 aircraft in the 1st Air Division, Sixth Air Fleet, in the Orel bulge to support the attack in the north, and over 1,100 aircraft in the VIII Air Corps, Fourth Air Fleet, in the south to support that attack.[2]

The Fourth Air Fleet

The Luftwaffe formations in the Ukraine, including their antiaircraft units, were under the Fourth Air Fleet, commanded by General Otto Dessloch. General Dessloch had replaced the much-respected Field Marshal Wolfram von Richthofen in June. Richthofen was the German Air Force's close support expert. He had been the chief of staff of the Condor Legion in Spain and had commanded the VIII Air Corps since the campaign in Poland. He had commanded the Fourth Air Fleet since 18 July 1942 and led it through the Stalingrad and Caucasus Offensives, the attempts to resupply Stalingrad and the subsequent Soviet offensives and German counteroffensive. He had been transferred to command the Second Air Fleet in Italy a month before the Kursk offensive was to begin. This Richthofen was the cousin of the famous "Red Baron," the highest scoring ace in the First World War. The recently appointed General Otto Dessloch was the air fleet's antiaircraft commander, who while having served on the Eastern Front since the start of the invasion, had only taken over temporary command of the Fourth Air Fleet around 11 June 1943. This was all done under a cloud, as Manstein had made known his desire for Richthofen to stay in the east until the completion of *Citadel*, while Hitler and Goering felt they needed Richthofen in Italy to organize the air defense against the expected invasions of Sicily or Italy. The slated replacement for Richthofen was General Hans Jeschonnek, the chief of the Luftwaffe general staff, who had held that thankless job since 1 February 1939. Therefore, Dessloch was only temporarily appointed so as to provide a veteran officer for the offensive, while Jeschonnek was expected to take over the command sometime after the battle.

General Jeschonnek was caught in the unenviable position of being chief of staff under the dilettantish command of Goering while the Western allies were bombing Germany with increasing weight. With Goering's considerable absences, it was Jeschonnek who often had to bear the brunt of Hitler's criticisms, and his relations with both men declined. This led him to try to escape a miserable staff position for a command in the field. He had been the chief of staff over four years! Goering and Jeschonnek had tried to arrange for Jeschonnek and Richthofen to swap positions, but this plan fell through when Richthofen objected to taking over the chief of staff position. Instead, to mollify Manstein, who was concerned about command shifts before a major offensive, the experienced Dessloch was given temporary command of the Fourth Air Fleet, with Jeschonnek preparing to take command later. Meanwhile Jeschonnek had made several trips out east to familiarize himself with his new command, and was at its headquarters during Citadel, in anticipation of taking over.

Although the Fourth Air Fleet was under new leadership, the staff remained the same, and they had already done the planning for the operation. Under the air fleet were four air corps. The I Air Corps was in the Crimea and the Kuban, and supported Army Group A and the Seventeenth Army. This unit had originally been committed in the Kharkov area and was transferred to the Crimea in late March. The IV Air Corps was in the Mius and Donets sectors, up to Liman, 50 kilometers southeast of Kharkov. It was supporting the newly reconstituted Sixth Army and First Panzer Army. The Romanian Air Force Corps was also in the Mius sector, committed with the IV Air Corps.

Supporting the attack at Kursk was the VIII Air Corps, now under command of its former chief of staff, Hans Seidemann. Major General Hans Seidemann had originally been the chief of staff of the VIII Air Corps during the Polish Campaign. He took over command of the unit on 19 May 1943. He was certainly an experienced and knowledgeable commander. He also left a clear account of the corps activities at Kursk in a paper prepared for the U.S. in 1947. The corps headquarters was at Mikoyanovka, about twenty miles from the front. With him at the start of operations was Jeschonnek.

The VIII Air Corps was responsible for the area from 50 kilometers southeast of Kharkov (at Liman) to a line from Chernigov to Rylsk to Kursk to Svoboda (the towns were located in the Sixth Air Fleet area). North of that line, Sixth Air Fleet, supporting Army Group Center, took responsibility. The VIII Air Corps was to support Provisional Army Kempf and the Fourth Panzer Army. Its headquarters initially was in Poltava but was later moved to Kharkov, and just before the offensive, to Mikoyanovka. The majority of its aircraft were in the Kharkov area. The Royal Hungarian Air Division was also attached to it. The VIII Air Corps had been operating an airlift to supply the Kuban bridgehead, but was pulled from there towards the end of March and sent north to replace the I Air Corps.

The Fourth Air Fleet's antiaircraft was under command of the I Flak Corps under Lt. General Richard Reimann. It had three flak divisions with which to cover Ukraine.[3] The 10th Flak Division was responsible for the Luftwaffe antiaircraft units in the Kharkov area.

The winter fighting of 1942–43 had greatly weakened these formations. The numerous unit transfers and shifts required to cover a wide variety of locales along such an extended front had fatigued the personnel and reduced the readiness of the airplanes. The Luftwaffe flak units had also suffered. They had incurred high losses in ground fighting, primarily as a result of being used for antitank artillery. When the thaw set in, the Air Force stood down so as to conserve its materiel and give the troops an extended rest.

At this point, the strength of the air units was about 30% of their authorized strength, with the antiaircraft units being about 20 to 25% of their authorized strength. Fuel was extremely low.[4] The Fourth Air Fleet deliberately grounded most of its forces so as to build up fuel, ammunition, aircraft, and equipment reserves. By mid-April, the Fourth Air Fleet had around 870 aircraft.[5] Most of the formations were billeted in the I Air Corps and IV Air Corps areas.

The build-up in strength over the next three months was considerable, with Seidemann reporting the entire Fourth Air Fleet having about 1,556 planes at the start of the *Citadel* offensive. Just before the attack, most of the formations were to be transferred to the VIII Air Corps. Remaining in the south was the Romanian Air Corps of around 100 planes and the reconnaissance and harassing squadrons of the I Air Corps and IV Air Corps. All the other formations were attached to the VIII Air Corps before the offensive.

The Fourth Air Fleet was now left with a long-range reconnaissance group of 24 aircraft with its headquarters at Murafa (20 kilometers southwest of Bogodukhov).[6] In the Crimea, the I Air Corps had around 106 aircraft along with a Romanian formation of about 80 aircraft. The IV Air Corps had an estimated 234 aircraft, including 150 from the I Romanian Air Corps. Committed to the Kursk Offensive, under command of the VIII Air Corps, were an estimated 1,112 aircraft.[7] This put over 70% of the aircraft in Army Group South at the disposal of the VIII Air Corps. It was estimated by Seidemann that about 75% of these aircraft were ready for action on any given day.

The Kharkov airfields were not large enough to handle all the planned formations. Starting in May, the Germans began building a series of advanced airfields in the area north of Kharkov. New dumps were established to store the required fuel and ammunition. There were also a number of close-support fields prepared. There were plans to prepare airfields farther forward once the offensive progressed. These close-support fields were protected by mobile flak formations that could move forward as new airfields were built. By the end of May, the Luftwaffe was ready.

The German antiaircraft units had also been brought up to strength. With the exception of the Crimea, the antiaircraft units from the rest of the front were extensively depleted and the units were concentrated for the offensive under the 10th Flak Division. Six flak battalions were placed in the Corps Raus area and five battalions were placed with the III Panzer

Corps. They were up to strength, with sufficient ammunition and towing vehicles. The flak units were not under control of the VIII Air Corps.

The Soviet Air Force

The Soviet air force was not a separate service. Unlike the German Luftwaffe, it was still under command of the Soviet Army. Unlike the US Air Force in the Second World War, it was not under the nominal command of the army, but was instead very directly under the Soviet army commanders. Each Front had its very own air army that was part of it and reported directly to it. While this may appear to result in the distribution of the Soviet air assets equally across the front, in practice this was not the case. While every Front had an air army, and usually only one air army, the size of these air armies varied significantly from Front to Front. In the southern part of the Bulge, the Soviet Army had three air armies. The main one was the Second Air Army which was under command of the Voronezh Front. Its commander was Lt. General Stepan A. Krasovskii. Also significantly involved in operations some of the time was the somewhat smaller Seventeenth Air Army, under command of the Southwestern Front. It was commanded by Lt. General Vladimir A. Sudets. Finally, in reserve, not actively engaged and even smaller, was the Fifth Air Army, under command of Lt. General Sergei K. Goryunov. Its primary involvement in the defensive phase of the Battle of Kursk was to provide units to the other air armies. Later it was to directly participate in the offensive phase.

The Soviet air force was likewise in need of a breathing period to rebuild itself. As such, during the spring of 1943, the Soviet air activity was light, with most raids being on the immediate area of the front lines. There was no strategic bombing from these forces. As the time of the German offensive grew closer, Soviet air activity increased, in particular the nighttime nuisance bombing. The Germans were able to observe new airfields being built in the Valuiki, Staryii Oskol, and Kursk areas.

New Ground Attack Weapons

Just like for the ground battle, the Germans were now bringing into battle a number of new airborne weapons and armament schemes for the first time. This included the first large-scale use of the small one kilogram (2.2 pounds) fragmentation bombs. They were fundamentally an adaptation of a Soviet weapon, the "Molotov Bread Basket." They were dropped in bomb-shaped 250 and 500 kilogram delivery containers, with the 250 kilogram container called the SD1 and the 500 kilogram container the SD2.

Somewhat legendary, if not overrated, were the development of two special purpose tank-busting units used in this battle. The first was the tank busting Ju-87 used by the famous Lt. Hans-Ulrich Rudel of the 2nd Stuka Wing. The Ju-87 G-1s were armed with two 37mm cannon mounted under the wing, in addition to the plane's three machineguns. This was the German 37mm flak gun using a tungsten core round. The plane carried twelve rounds for each gun. It was potentially a very deadly antitank weapon. The additional weight made the Stuka, which was not a nimble or powerful aircraft, that much slower, making the aircraft extremely vulnerable.

In February 1943, after his 1,001st operational mission, Rudel was sent back to Germany to command the 1st Versuchstaffel, a special squadron armed with these experimental planes. This experimental squadron was then sent to the Crimea in April to field test. The unit suffered losses in its first attempt to attack tanks. This led it to develop the tactic of sending other Stukas in first to suppress the AA defenses with conventional dive-bombing attacks and then bringing in the specialized tank-buster Stukas. These Stukas were then used to target small boats in the Kuban. In May, at Rudel's request, he was returned to command his original squadron and brought one of the new Ju-87 G-1s with him.[8] As such, this aircraft was still unproven.

There was also a new antitank formation created from the five different Hs-129 squadrons that were brought in for this battle. They were placed under a tank hunter command as part of the 1st Ground Attack Squadron. The new B-2 models of the Hs-129s were armed with a 30-millimeter cannon. The Hs-129 was a two-engine ground attack plane. Its 30mm cannon was mounted below the fuselage and fired a round with a tungsten core penetrator. As such, it was capable of penetrating 80mm of armor. This gave the aircraft enough punch to serve as an effective antitank weapon. The Hs-129 had some limitations. Although its fuselage was armored, its two engines were not, and so it still had a significant vulnerability to ground fire. Its French-built engines were very susceptible to dust and dirt, and as such, especially with the extensive use of dirt airstrips, they had problems maintaining serviceability.

The Battle of Kursk was not the first use of the Hs-129s, as they had been engaged on the southern half of the Eastern Front since spring of 1942 and were used in May 1942 armed with the 30mm cannon. It was however the first time they had made use of them in mass. They had gathered together five squadrons, each with 10 to 17 Hs-129 B-2s or a mixture of B-1s and B-2s. It was these units that on 8 July 1943, under the operational command of Captain Bruno Meyer, would claim 40 tanks from a Soviet armored column (see Chapter Five).

This was the extent of the special purpose German aircraft for antitank use. The rest of the air forces had very limited ability to directly attack armor and were primarily used for direct support.

The Soviets had no such comparable capability, although they did have the sturdy Sturmovik (the Il-2), a very effective ground support airplane. With its 20mm cannon, it posed some armor threat but was primarily used for general ground attack. They did deploy for the first time at Kursk the new 2.5 kilogram antitank bomb (PTB). Each Il-2 would carry 312 of the bomblets.[9] Their effectiveness as an antitank weapon is hard to judge, as this is not noted in the German accounts.

The Harassment Bomber Squadrons

The Soviets, since early in the war, had deployed special squadrons to conduct harassment bombing at night. This usually consisted of obsolete aircraft like the U-2 (renamed Po-2 in 1944), dropping small bombs. While not particularly effective, their nightly harassment raids were a source of continued annoyance. There was also one all-female night bomber regiment in the Soviet Air Force, and some women also served in fighter and bomber units.

The female night bomber regiment was not at Kursk. The Soviets also used these missions to contact, insert, and resupply partisans behind the German lines.

Despite their limited effect, the Germans borrowed this idea from the Soviets and formed their first night harassing squadrons (Stoerkampfstaffeln) in late 1942. This "Stoerkamfgruppe Don" consisted of four squadrons of Ar-66s, Fi-156s, Fw-58s, He-46s, and Junkers W-34s.[10] This tactic was basically an attempt to make some productive use of the hundreds of obsolete aircraft, including training and liaison aircraft that were available to the Luftwaffe. These were not high priority formations, and as such, tended not to receive the pick of the pilots. National Socialism, with its social conservatism, did not make use of women in combat roles.

The Don Harassment Bomber Group would become the Fourth Air Fleet Harassment Bomber Group, in March 1943 consisting of six squadrons, with two new squadrons added. At about the same time, this idea was expanded to also create such groups for the First and Sixth Air Fleets.

German Night Fighters

The Germans did have some small night-fighter units in the Fourth Air Fleet area, having brought five night-fighter squadrons from the west. On 31 May 1943, the Fourth Air Fleet was reported to have 17 night-fighters. This was the largest German contingent of night fighters on the Eastern Front at that time. Their purpose was to intercept the Soviet night bombing attacks. This was to be done in conjunction with the mobile Freyja radar fixed to a rail car and the help of ground observers. A review of the night missions during 4–18 July indicates that they were either not present, not active, or were completely ineffective. The German daily reports of night action do not show any of these types of missions, nor do they claim any kills. The Soviets lost five U-2s and two R-5s over the 15 days of activity. All of these are reported as "failed to return," and could have been lost due to mechanical failure, accident, German antiaircraft, or German aircraft.

The Fighters

The German mainstay fighter was the Messerschmitt 109, version G. This plane, which was undergoing continued improvement, was the standard German fighter of the war. The Germans also had Focke-Wulf 190s in the 1st Ground Attack Wing, but these appeared to have primarily been used as a single-seater ground attack plane, not a fighter, even though many people judged it a better fighter than the Me-109.

The Soviets already had modern fighters in use and were continuing to upgrade them. The current collection of Yak-1s, Yak-7s, and La-5s were capable airplanes although a little down on power compared to the Me109s, with around .40 horsepower per kilogram of weight compared to .46 per kilogram for the Me-109. Otherwise the aircraft were similar in armament, size, weight and swept area to an Me-109. The Soviets also had the Yak-9, which had a little more power and was almost as capable as the Me-109. It had been in service since late 1942 and was being used in increasing numbers. Finally, for Kursk, they began deploying the

1,850-horsepower radial-engine La-5 FN version, which overmatched the Me-109 in power by almost 400 horsepower. The Soviet air force was not at a significant disadvantage in equipment.

Training and Experience

The fundamental difference between the two air forces was the degree of training and experience. The German Air Force had considerable combat experience, having been successfully and actively engaged in combat since late 1939. While these air operations entailed considerable losses, especially at the Battle of Britain, they were not high enough to deplete or damage the capability of the units. During the first year and a half of the war in Russia, the air fight had been very one-sided. As such, by the time they faced each other at Kursk, the German air units were manned by people with confidence, good training, considerable combat experience, and a high number of very successful aces.

Still, German training was in decline because of a failure to give it priority and due to increasing fuel shortages. By 1943 fuel shortages had reduced the average training time per pilot. Originally it was around 300 hours per pilot but was then cut to 260 hours.[11] In mid-1943, UK intelligence estimated that a German fighter pilot was receiving 250 hours of training. This quickly declined during 1943 to around 110 hours per pilot because of the need to replace growing losses, but this reduction in hours probably had little effect on the veteran formations at Kursk. The Germans were able to maintain an instructor-to-student ratio of one-to-five. Still, this was a good training program and compares favorably to the minimum of 140 hours that was given to the US pilots (although actual time was often much higher), and the ratio of instructors to students in both the UK and US air forces was the same as the Luftwaffe.[12]

In contrast, the Soviet air force did not have the depth or experience of personnel. The air force was pretty much swept from the skies in 1941 and had to be rebuilt. During this rebuilding process in 1942, the air force remained engaged and often with high losses. As a result, the air force had difficulty developing an experienced cadre of flyers. The Soviet formations at Kursk included a considerable number of new pilots and only a few seasoned veterans. The Soviet Union's most accomplished ace of the war would only score his first victories in this battle.

In addition, Soviet pilot training was not as extensive as the Germans'.[13] This is clear with the Fifth Air Army reports, and these indicate that the Soviet pilots may have been sent into battle with only a limited number of hours of training.[14] As such, the Soviets were operating at a major disadvantage, with their pilots having considerably less training, the units lacking seasoned pilots, and the units filled with a considerable number of newcomers.[15]

Radios

German aircraft were all equipped with two-way radios to allow the pilots to communicate with their bases and with each other. The Soviets on the other hand were very limited in their communication equipment. Only the flight leaders had two-way radios that allowed them to communicate with their base and other planes. Theirs also were the only planes with maps! Many of the planes had only receivers, so they could receive instructions, but could not communicate back. A large number of planes had no radios at all, including many of the night bombers, and this is probably part of the reason that so many Soviet planes were reported as simply "failed to return."

Soviet Intelligence

STAVKA, the Soviet Union's High Command, knew the Germans were attacking. They knew the name of the operation. In April their spy network had transmitted to them a copy of Hitler's Operations Order No. 6, issued 15 April 1943. This was the order that announced Hitler's final decision to conduct the Citadel offensive.[16] It stated the goal of this attack and the ultimate goals of the operation. The earliest the attack would be is 3 May 1943, and that from 28 April onwards that Army Group Center and Army Group South should be prepared launch their attack with six days' notice. It also provided brief instructions for the Luftwaffe.

They knew of the various postponements of the offensive. They knew it had been postponed from the first week in May. They knew that a new date of 12 June 1943 was set. They had received the technical characteristics of the new Panther tank, its monthly production figure and the location of its manufacturing plants. They knew of the meeting on 1 July 1943 by Hitler with his senior commanders. Most, if not all of this information was a result of the Lucy Spy Ring operating out of Switzerland. Their contact there, a German publisher named Rudolf Roessler living in Lucerne, was receiving information directly from a dozen people who held senior positions in the German armed forces. He was then passing this material to Soviet agents and radio operators in Switzerland. The Red Orchestra as they became known.

Information was also provided by the Briton John Cairncross, the fifth man in the infamous Cambridge spy ring that included Kim Philby, Guy Burgess, Donald Maclean, and Anthony Blunt. In 1943 Cairncross worked at Bletchley Park, the UK's main decryption facility. He took copies to London of the Ultra material on the Luftwaffe communications. He provided the Soviets with decoded German signals that disclosed the location of Luftwaffe units. The Soviet embassy then forwarded it to Moscow. This provided the Soviets with the data for which to plan their initial air strike on German airfields on 5 July.[17]

German and Soviet Reconnaissance

The German Air Force in the days before the battle maintained a steady reconnaissance over the area. During the day, they were flying about 40 to 80 sorties, of which the majority were probably reconnaissance missions. During the night, they were flying from 15 to 60 sorties, including a number of night harassment missions and five or six sorties to strike at the railroads. This was with over one thousand aircraft, which were mostly getting ready for action. The only German losses were a Ju-88 on 2 July, which was their first lost since 26 June, when the Hungarians had lost a Ju-88. This was the same rate of activity they had maintained for much of the previous month.

On the 3rd, the Germans did some preparatory strikes with 20 stuka sorties against the batteries southeast of Belgorod. With 78 sorties flown that day, it was the heaviest day of activity by the VIII Air Corps since 26 June, when they flew 140 sorties.

The Soviet Second and Seventeenth Air Armies were similarly quiet. Not wishing to reveal their degree of preparation or knowledge of the German attack, the Soviet air forces limited themselves during this time to reconnaissance flights and waited for the German offensive to start.

These operations were not without their drama, as Captain Nikolai Zakharchenko of the 288th Fighter Division recalls:[18]

> Our division was part of the Seventeenth Air Army. After Stalingrad, in May of 1943, we started flying our new fighters, La-5s. In the beginning of July the division commanders received the information about massive forces of tanks located to the west from Belgorod. My squadron received an order to determine the location of the tanks. I suggested that we should use only a couple of planes for that in order to be less visible. I flew out with Lieutenant Kozlov in another plane. We discovered the tanks very quickly. The tanks were camouflaged like bushes and haystacks. I decided to shoot at the haystack and set it on fire. The tanks immediately gave themselves away by firing back at us. The Germans shot antiaircraft artillery, which were exploding around our planes. It became clear to us that there was a whole tank unit there. We took off back up escaping from the fire. I noticed two "fokkers" to the right from us. We wanted to get to the clouds as soon as possible. The German planes were flying towards us. I noticed two more Fokke-Wulfs. The situation was getting worse. I reported to the ground about the location of the German planes as I was getting very close to the clouds. Then I noticed that two planes were attacking Kozlov's plane. I turned around and attacked one German fighter head on. I knew that the German pilots did not know how to deal with head-on attacks. The German plane went straight up and I fired at him the entire burst. I think I killed the pilot because the plane fell straight down. Taking advantage of the moment, Kozlov and I disappeared in the clouds. On the way to airport, I discovered an oil leak. Probably one of the German planes made a hole in the oil pipe. The oil was splashing on the windows of the cabin and onto my glasses. I tried to take my glasses off, but then the oil was splashing right into my eyes. "Kozlov, I cannot see anything, move ahead of me"—I said into the radio. He got in front of me and I could follow him to the airport.
>
> In this combat we saved each other's lives and completed a difficult task. Each of us got the Red Banner Order.

German Preparations

By late May, the German air units were in position and their communication network was in place with the help of two air force signal regiments. The airfields were set up to communicate via telephone, telegraph, and radio and were connected with the army. The lines were laid in a manner so as to permit their use by the army also. The air base commanders had been assigned labor forces from construction battalions and Reich Labor Service units. Maintenance platoons and workshops were at full strength and ready. There were sufficient replacement parts. They had assembled adequate quantities of bombs and machinegun and cannon rounds for the attack. "There was never a shortage in these items."[19] At each airfield was stored about ten sorties worth of fuel. Fuel trains were held in the rear area, ready to be quickly dispatched forward when needed. They had received additional aircraft, and the formations were able to maintain about 60% of their authorized strength ready-for-action. Seidemann, VIII Air Corps commander, claims that morale was good.

The VIII Air Corps had attached a number of liaison teams to the corps and divisions. These teams were to accompany the divisions onto the battlefield, where they could guide the dive-bombers and by radio direct the approaching Luftwaffe units to the targets designated by the ground unit commanders, including correcting their aim. They also provided reports on the local tactical air situation. The liaison teams reported to the VIII Air Corps every two hours about the ground situation, the air situation, and any other information.

Finally, the VIII Air Corps called their people back to duty. In the case of the 52nd Fighter Wing, one of its top aces, Guenther Rall, in early July was in an army hospital in Baden near Vienna due to a spinal cord injury, which intermittently caused him partial paralysis. It was here that orders reached him to return to the troops immediately and assume command of the III Group of the 52nd Fighter Wing at the Urgim airfield near Kharkov.[20] Germany's top ace at the time and a former 52nd Fighter Wing alumni, Hermann Graf, who had more than 200 victories at that time, was now in the west, and Gerhard Barkhorn, who had 137 victories at this time, was also not present.

In an attempt to achieve deception, many of the Luftwaffe elements were moved into position the evening preceding the attack.[21] The VIII Air Corps headquarters was moved to Mikoyanovka, southwest of Belgorod, on the night of 3/4 July. The four fighter groups and the ground attack wing were also brought into position on 3 and 4 July. The stuka wings and most of the Hs-129 squadrons were already in the area, but were shuffled around to different fields. Most of the bombers were already in position, operating from bases in Kharkov or Poltava (see "VIII Air Corps Base Locations and Transfers" in Appendix II for more details).

The German air bases were mostly clustered in two locations. About 20–22 kilometers to the southwest of Belgorod, connected by road and rail, was Mikoyanovka, the VIII Air Corps headquarters. Within a ten kilometer radius of this locale were airfields at Bessonovka, Urgim, Tolokonnoye, and Varvarovka. Both Bessonovka and Urgim were about eight kilometers north of Mikoyanovka and within 22 kilometers of the front. Bessonovka housed the III/3rd Fighter Wing, I/52nd Fighter Wing and the I & II/1st Ground Attack Wing. Urgim housed the III/52nd Fighter Wing. About five kilometers southeast of Mikoyanovka was Varvarovka, which housed all the Hs-129s, and Tolokonnoye, which held the 77th Stuka Wing.

The next collection of bases was around the Kharkov area, which was some 65 kilometers south-southwest of Belgorod. It housed the II/3rd Fighter Wing at Rogan, 15 kilometers east-southeast of the city and the 2nd Stuka Wing somewhere near Kharkov.

The bombers were scattered about, with the 3rd Bombardment Wing, I/100th Bombardment Wing and the 14th squadron of the 55th Bombardment Wing at Poltava, some 120 kilometers to the west southwest of Kharkov. At Dnepropetrovsk, some 270 kilometers from Belgorod and also 270 kilometers from most of the front line, were the I & II/27th Bombardment Wing while the III/27th Bombardment Wing was at KharkovVoitschenko. The 55th Bombardment Wing was primarily at Rogan.

VIII AIR CORPS ORDER OF BATTLE SUMMARY

Unit Name	Number of Planes
II & III/3rd Fighter Wing	65 Me-109
I, III & HQ/52nd Fighter Wing	80 Me-109
1st Ground Attack Wing	85 Fw-190
	16 Hs-123
	33 Hs-129
4th and 8th Sq./2nd Ground Attack Wing	27 Hs-129
Antitank Squadron/51st Fighter Wing	15 Hs-129
2nd Stuka Wing	111 Ju-87
77th Stuka Wing	120 Ju-87
3rd Bombardment Wing	73 Ju-88
27th Bombardment Wing	101 He-111
55th Bombardment Wing (-)	97 He-111
I/100th Bombardment Wing	38 He-111
VI Close-range Reconnaissance Group	34 aircraft
III Long-range Reconnaissance Group	35 Ju-88
Harassing Aircraft Group	60
VIII Air Corps Transport Squadron	13 Ju-52
Royal Hungarian Air Division[22]	90
Total Aircraft	1,093

Seidemann estimated the total strength to be 1,112. He estimated serviceability to be 75%, making around 900 aircraft (Seidemann's estimate) ready for action.

This author is still uncertain whether the 8th Squadron/2nd Ground Attack Wing, III Group/77th Stuka Wing, III Group/3rd Bombardment Wing or some reconnaissance squadrons were at this battle.

BOTH SIDES PREPARE

Soviet Preparations

The Soviet air forces, having been in place for three months, were well stocked for the upcoming operations. They had assembled 40,000 tons of fuel for their aircraft, which was enough for 7.5 sorties per plane. This could last for three or four days without resupply. The night bombers had plenty of fuel, with 596 tons of B-70 fuel. This would last for 20 sorties per plane. They had assembled a full range of demolition, fragmentation, and incendiary bombs, rocket rounds, and the new experimental antitank bombs. They had 6,850 tons of bombs, which were more than enough for the upcoming operations.

The Soviet air armies had built up considerable strength. The Second Air Army had a strength of 881 aircraft, while the Seventeenth Air Army had 735. The Fifth Air Army, sitting in reserve, had maybe 430 aircraft. In the north, facing the Sixth Air Fleet, was the Sixteenth Air Army with a strength of 1,034 combat aircraft.[23]

SECOND AIR ARMY ORDER OF BATTLE
(5 July 1943)

The Second Air Army was commanded by Lt. General S. A. Krasovskii. The chief of staff was Major General F. I. Kachev. The Deputy Commander of Political Affairs (effectively the Military Council Member) was Major General S. N. Ramazanov. The Chief of the Army Political Division was Colonel A. I. Asaulenko.

	On-hand, 1 July	Largest Number Flown in a Day
I Assault Corps	206 Assault	114 Il-2
	82 Fighters	60 Yak-1b
I Bomber Corps	117 Bombers	70 Pe-2
IV Fighter Corps	184 Fighters	38 Yak-1b,
		15 Yak-7b,
		65 La-5
V Fighter Corps	278 Fighters	26 Yak-1b,
		26 Yak-7b,
		100 La-5
291st Assault Division	100 Assault	48 Il-2
	28 Fighters	8 Yak-1,
		4 Yak-7b,
		3 La-5 or
		18 Fighters
208th Night Bomber Division	57 Night Bombers	27 U-2,
		4 R-5
50th Air Reconnaissance Regiment		7 Pe-2
454th Bomber Regiment	21 Reconnaissance	6 Bostons
272nd Independent Army Squadron		

SEVENTEENTH AIR ARMY FORCES
(5 July 1943)

The Seventeenth Air Army was commanded by Lt. General V. A. Sudets. The chief of staff was Major General N. M. Korsakov. The Deputy Commander of Political Affairs (effectively the Military Council Member) was Major General V. N. Tolmachev. The Chief of the Army Political Division was Colonel V. G. Tochilov.

	Base	Operational	Not Operational	Pilots
I Mixed Corps	Proyezzhaya			
288th Fighter Division	Starobelskaya	2 Yak-1		4
866th Fighter Rgt.	Peski	26 Yak-1	1 Yak-1	34
897th Fighter Rgt.	Peski	20 Yak-1	1 Yak-1	29
659th Fighter Rgt.	Polovinkino	22 Yak-1	2 Yak-1	31
5th Guards Assault Division	Ryibentsovo			
93rd Assault Rgt.	Novo-Pskov	26 Il-2	5 Il-2	35
94th Assault Rgt.	Mokartyatino	30 Il-2	1 Il-2	35
95th Assault Rgt.	Belokurakino	30 Il-2	2 Il-2	37
III Mixed Corps	Novo-Osinovka			
404th Ind. Squadron	Novo-Osinovka	5 U-2	1 U-2	9
207th Fighter Division	Aleksandrovka			
5th Guards Fighter Rgt.	Shchenyachye	21 La-5	1 La-5	33
814th Fighter Rgt.	Uchebnyii Sovkhoz	21 Yak-1/7b	3 Yak-1/7b	41
867th Fighter Rgt.	Bulatselovka	12 Yak-1/7b	3 Yak-1/7b	31
290th Assault Division	Kurilovka	1 Il-2		2
775th Assault Rgt.	Kurilovka	30 Il-2	2 Il-2	38
625th Assault Rgt.	Zatishnoye	33 Il-2	3 Il-2	34
299th Assault Rgt.	Manino	27 Il-2	5 Il-2	31
IX Mixed Corps	Pokrovskoye			
418th Ind. Squadron	Pokrovskoye	3 U-2		3
295th Fighter Division	Olshana	2 La-5		2
31st Fighter Rgt.	Budennovka	26 La-5	2 La-5	26

BOTH SIDES PREPARE

	Base	Operational	Not Operational	Pilots
116th Fighter Rgt.	Olshanyi	25 La-5	1 La-5	28
164th Fighter Rgt.	Nizhnyaya Duvanka	21 La-5	2 La-5	25
305th Assault Division	Nizhnyaya Duvanka	1 U-2		4
175th Assault Rgt.	Olshanyi	35 Il-2		36
237th Assault Rgt.	Pokrovskoye	30 Il-2	1 Il-2	31
955th Assault Rgt.	Rayevka	27 Il-2		29
306th Assault Division	Nizhnyaya Duvanka	1 U-2		1
672nd Assault Rgt.	Peschanka	34 Il-2		30
951st Assault Rgt.	Lantratovka	29 Il-2	2 Il-2	32
995th Assault Rgt.	Budennovka	28 Il-2	3 Il-2	33
244th Bomber Division	Rogovo	3 U-2		3
449th Bomber Rgt.	Mozhyakovka	24 TB-3		24
860th Bomber Rgt.	Shramovka	17 TB-3	1 TB-3	20
861st Bomber Rgt.	Rogovo	25 TB-3		32
260th Bomber Rgt.	Poddubnoye	10 TB-3	1 TB-3	20
262nd Night Bomber Division	Zapadnoye	2 U-2		3
719th Night Bomber Rgt.	Krinichnyii	8 R-5	1 R-5	22
97th Gds Night Bomber Rgt.	Kovalevka	19 U-2		24
370th Night Bomber Rgt.	Vasiltsevka	19 U-2		31
993rd Night Bomber Rgt.	Ponamarevka	14 U-2		29
39th Reconnaissance Rgt.	Velshanyi	18 Pe-2	1 Pe-2	14
50th Reconnaissance Rgt.	Velshanyi	2 Pe-2	1 Pe-2	4
403rd Ind. Squadron	Ivanovka	7 U-2	3 U-2	11
371st Transport Rgt.	Stepki	14 U-2		22
Totals		750	49	963

German Planning

Dessloch had assigned the VIII Air Corps to support the Fourth Panzer Army and Provisional Army Kempf. The VIII Air Corps was ordered to concentrate on supporting the main attack of the Germans and to only support the rest of the sectors in emergencies. This lead to most of the air support being provided to the XLVIII and II SS Panzer Corps, some to the III Panzer Corps, and almost nothing provided to the two supporting infantry corps. Furthermore, the German air units tended to not be distributed across the battlefield, but concentrated in the critical areas, at the expense of the rest of the battle. The German air, including their bombers, were to be used for tactical missions. The only strategic targets to be attacked were troop movements in the Oboyan and Kursk areas and the railway targets at Staryii Oskol and Valuiki.

The Germans chose not to start this battle with the customary strike against the Soviet airfields. Instead, the Germans were only to appear over the battlefield when the offensive started. This was in the hope that somehow Army Group South was going to achieve tactical surprise. This was a vain hope.

The Germans' foregoing of the initial strike against their enemy was unusual. Seidemann claimed in 1947 that even though such an attack would have been damaging, it "would have no long-range effect in view of the vast strength of Russian material which could soon make up losses inflicted by the Luftwaffe."[24] This reasoning is hard to explain. As this was a tactical operation that was expected to last for only a week or two, then the short-range effect of disrupting and depleting the Soviet air force would have certainly been useful. Furthermore, they were in a war of attrition. Still, the problem with such air operations was that if the German Air Force was concentrating on destroying the Soviet air force, then it was not providing ground support to the German Army on that day. The Germans could have launched the air attack a day or two early, which would have tipped off the Soviets, or they could have launched on the day of the attack, depriving the armed forces of their critical air support while they were trying to break through the fortified works. Of course, the "customary" air strike against the enemy air force is only useful if it catches the enemy unprepared. If the enemy is ready and warned, then it can turn out to be very ineffective. It is unknown whether these considerations played a part in the decision not to strike. The success of first strikes is somewhat checkered even though it succeeded outrageously well at the start of the Russian Campaign in 1941.

Still, there were some additional problems with striking at the Soviets. To start with, they had scattered their air forces across a lot more fields than the Germans had. Furthermore, they made use of camouflage, dummy fields, and dummy units at fields, and regularly moved planes from fields that had been attacked. As such, the Germans were facing a large number of poorly identified targets. German intelligence had identified at least 30 different airfields in the Voronezh Front area.[25] The Second Air Army had 24 airfields for its use, built with local labor.[26]

Furthermore, the Soviets had their own ground observer system to spot incoming strikes. While the Soviets did have a radar system with a range of 70 to 90 miles, and it was used at Kursk, it did not seem to play a role in the battle. It appears that they were positioned to help in the defense of the rail lines, and as the Germans did not conduct any daytime deep strikes to the rail or the airfields during the offensive, the Soviet radar did not play a major role. The Soviet air force also regularly kept fighters patrolling over their airfields. This last step was necessary due to the Soviets usually lacking radar and still not having a well integrated air defense system, which was often complicated by communication problems. We see throughout the Kursk battle Soviet aircraft regularly conducting defensive patrols. This was a necessary step to protect and defend their bases. In the face of these various measures, a German strike on Soviet air fields may have had limited success.

Regardless of the actual reasoning, the orders for the VIII Air Corps prohibited launching strikes before the battle "in the hope of ensuring tactical surprise (time and place of attack)."[27] In contrast, in the north the 1st Air Division (Sixth Air Fleet) had decided to start their battle with an air strike on the Soviet Sixteenth Air Army.[28] There is an obvious contradiction here.

Soviet Planning

Soviet planning often includes a "correlation of forces." In this case, it is interesting to examine as it shows a realistic appraisal of the German strength:

Type	Soviet	German
Fighter	389	405
Assault	276	60
Bombers	172	460
Night Bombers	34	–
Reconnaissance	10	32
Total	881	957

In contrast, the Soviets organized for air strikes on the German airfields to the south of the Kursk bulge for 5 July, with the Second Air Army, with help from the Seventeenth Air Army, going after the VIII Air Corps. They probably had a good idea of German locations, in part due to signal intelligence received from the British spy John Cairncross. The Second Air Army chose to do this by a series of concentrated blows and echeloned activities during the entire period. This approach may have been influenced by the use of the Seventeenth Air Army, which had farther to fly, making it more difficult to coordinate a massive strike. As it was, the counter-preparation operation did not occur as planned.

The German Air Strike on 4 July

The Second Air Army weather report for 4 July was mostly clear at night, with visibility for two to three kilometers. It was cloudy during the day, with visibility for eight to ten kilometers at 1,500–2,000 meters altitude.

ACES AT KURSK

The first part of the day was quiet, with the Soviets conducting reconnaissance, flying 159 sorties, including 10 on the night of 3/4 July. On the afternoon of the 4th, the Germans started the Battle of Kursk with a limited attack to help the XLVIII Panzer Corps clear off the Soviet outpost line. The Germans flew 224 sorties this day. The afternoon attack consisted of 28 Ju-88s that hit the area of Cherkasskoye and 132 Ju-87 sorties suppressing Soviet batteries, towns, and points of resistance in front of the XLVIII Panzer Corps attack. These were escorted by Me-109s. The Sixth Guards Army reported that at 1600 (Moscow time) 75 enemy Ju-88 and Ju-87 bombers, covered by 27 fighters, bombed the area of Butovo, height 230.8 (in meters on the map), and south of Krutoi gully. The Soviets claimed that during ten minutes, 2,500 aerial and fragmentation bombs were dropped on a front of one kilometer! The Sixth Guards Army also reported planes over Gertsovka, Bubnyi, Gostishchevo, Luchki, Lukhanino, and Dmitreyevka. The Seventh Guards Army reported German air patrolled their area, conducting occasional paired reconnaissance sorties. The Sixth Guards Army reported three to nine times as many overflights this day as the Seventh Guards Army did. Clearly the German effort was focused there.

This day's fighting resulted in the loss of two Ju-88s and an Me-109, while the V Fighter Corps (Second Air Army) lost three Yak-7bs which did not return from their intercept missions, while a Yak-1 was shot down by friendly AA fire! The Second Air Army reports four engagements this day, all by the V Fighter Corps. It was the most active unit, carrying out 118 sorties this day. The rest of the Soviet air limited their activities. One of the Bostons of the 454th Bomber Regiment was also attacked by an Me-109 at 7,000 meters (23,000 feet)! The three German aircraft lost this day may have been downed by air action, as neither the 26th Antiaircraft Division (Sixth Guards Army) or the 5th Antiaircraft Division (Seventh Guards Army) claimed any German planes shot down. The Germans claimed six kills for the day while the Second Air Army claimed 10 kills for the day.

That night, the Second Air Army's 208th Night Bomber Division conducted 44 sorties with 25 U-2s and four sorties with four R-5s. They dropped 270 bombs, ranging from 2.5 kilograms to 110 kilograms, and dropped 118,000 propaganda leaflets. The Southwestern Front's Seventeenth Air Army conducted no day or night sorties in the Belgorod area.

The Second Air Army weather report for 5 July was predominantly clear at night, with considerable haze, making for visibility of two kilometers. Also, considerable haze during the first part of the day, particularly at dawn, with visibility two to four kilometers. During the second half the visibility increased to six to seven kilometers.

The chart below shows the periods of light during the course of the battle, with the clear sections being daytime or moonlight, and the dark sections being night. As can be seen, sunrise on 5 July was a little after 0300 and sunset was a little before 2000 (8 PM). There was some light from the moon on the 5th, increasing during the course of the battle. This graphic is from German records.

BOTH SIDES PREPARE

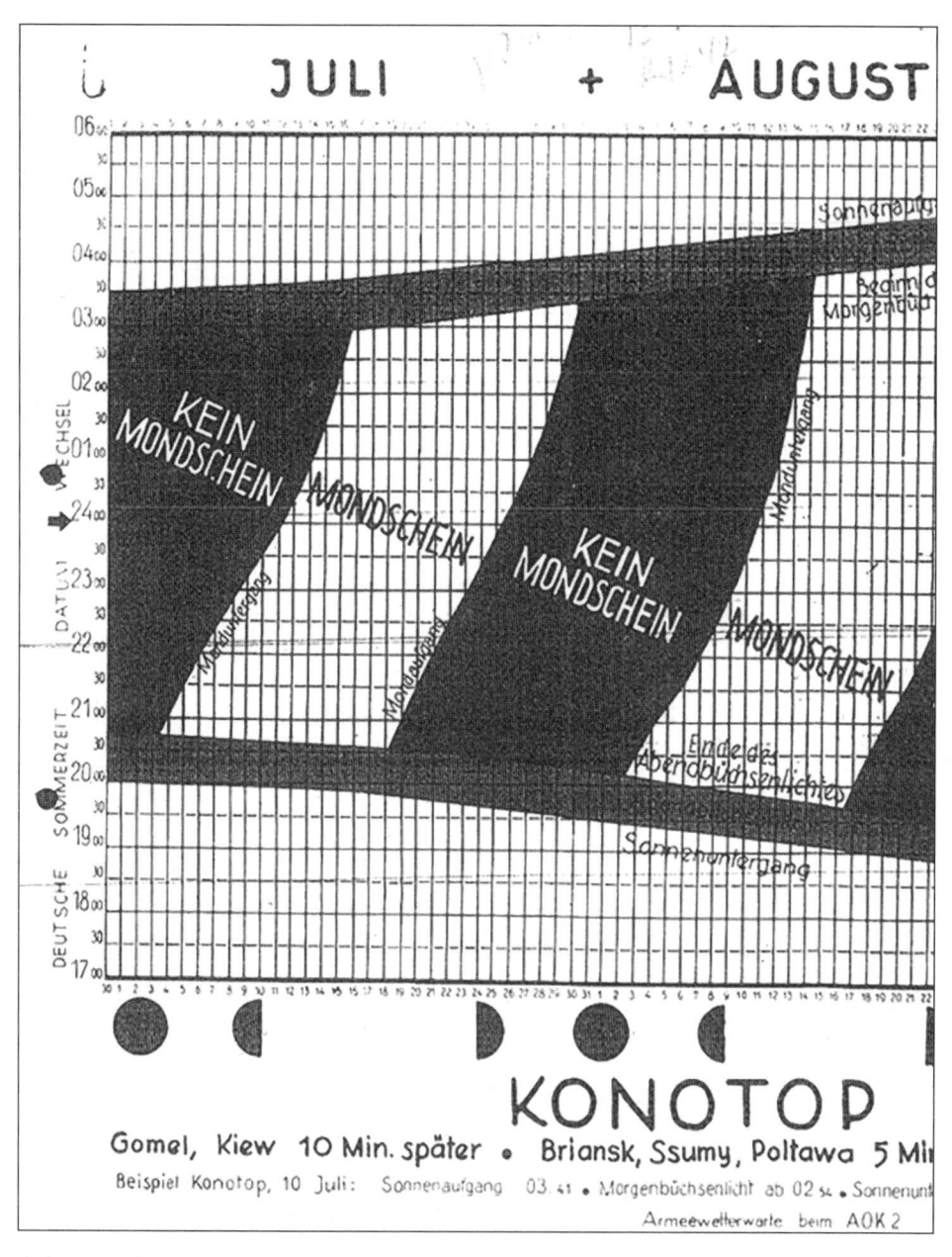

A German chart showing the times of sunrise, sunset, and the phases of the moon for Konotop.

GERMAN PLANES AT THE BATTLE OF KURSK[29]

The following planes were reported to be involved in the Battle of Kursk:

Ar-66: The Arado 66c was a trainer and communications aircraft. It was an open cockpit bi-plane with a two-man crew. It had a steel frame with a cloth covering. Its single 240 horsepower Argus As 10C engine powered it to a maximum speed of 210 kilometers per hour (130 mph) at sea level, with a cruising speed of 175 kilometers per hour (109 mph). It had a range of 715 kilometers (444 miles) and a service ceiling of 4,500 meters (14,675 feet). It could climb to 1,000 meters (3,280 feet) in 4 minutes and 6 seconds.

It entered service in 1933 and was the standard Luftwaffe trainer well into the Second World War. Many began to be modified starting in late 1942 for use as a night bomber, carrying two and four kilogram anti-personnel bombs (4.4 or 8.8 pounds). It had no guns. It was probably used in this role at Kursk, with one reported as lost on 13 July.

Do-215: The Dornier 215 B-4 bomber was identified in Soviet records as the plane they saw during the battle. The Soviets also identified Do-11D and Do-17s, but these were probably misidentifications. The Do-215s were most likely used by the VIII Air Corps as their long-range reconnaissance aircraft.

The Dornier 215 was a modern long-range reconnaissance plane and a medium bomber with a four man crew. It was originally an export version of the Dornier Do-17Z, "flying pencil," so named because of its long and narrow fuselage. It had two 1,075 Daimler-Benz engines which powered it to maximum speed of 525 kilometers per hour (326 mph) at 5,250 meters (17,220 feet). It had a maximum range of 2,500 kilometers (1,523 miles) and a service ceiling of 9,100 meters (29,850 feet). It could climb to 1,000 meters in two minutes.

It was armed with six 7.9mm MG 15s and carried a bomb load of 500 kilograms (1,102 pounds). The Do-17 originally entered service in 1937. There were 112 Do215s produced, of which 92 were reconnaissance versions (Do-215B-1 and Do-215B-4). They carried cameras.

Fieseler Storch: The Fieseler 156 C-2 Storch (Stork) was Germany's all-purpose small liaison plane. It was an overhead wing plane that could carry two men. Its single 240 horsepower Argus As 10C engine powered it to a maximum speed of 175 kilometers per hour (109 mph) at sea level, with a cruising speed of 128 kilometers per hour (80 mph). It had a range of 385 kilometers (239 miles) and a service ceiling of 5,090 meters (16,700 feet).

It entered service in 1936 and was the most common Luftwaffe liaison plane throughout the Second World War. It had one 7.9mm machinegun in the rear. It could carry a litter and many were used for medical evacuation during Kursk. There were also reconnaissance versions.

Fw-189: The Focke-Wulf 189 A-1 Uhu (Owl) was a reconnaissance and liaison airplane. It was a twin-boom plane with a three-man crew. Its two 485 horsepower Argus engines powered it to a maximum speed of 344 kilometers per hour (214 mph) at 2,500 meters (8,202 feet), with a cruising speed of 317 kilometers per hour (197 mph). It had a range of 940 kilometers (584 miles) and an initial rate of climb of 310 meters per minute (1,017 feet).

It first entered service in late 1940 and slowly replaced the Hs-126 as the standard Luftwaffe tactical reconnaissance plane. It was armed with two fixed forward firing 7.9mm machineguns and two flexible mounted rear firing 7.9mm machineguns. Its maximum bomb load was 200 kilograms (440 pounds).

Fw-190: The Focke-Wulf 190, although famous as a fighter, was used at Kursk as a ground attack plane, with the F-3 model. It was a modern single seat fighter-bomber. Its single 1,700 horsepower BMW engine powered it to a maximum speed of 525 kilometers per hour (326 mph) at sea level and 592 kilometers per hour (368 mph) at an altitude of 5,000 meters (18,045 feet). It had a normal range of 530 kilometers (330 miles). Its initial rate of climb was 645 meters (2,110 feet) per minute.

It was armed with two 7.9mm machineguns on the cowling, and two 20mm cannons on the wings. Its maximum bomb load was 250 kilograms (551 pounds). Its wing area was 18.3 square meters (196.98 square feet), its empty weight was 3,224 kilogram (7,328 pounds), and its maximum weight was 4,920 kilograms (10,850 pounds). This gave it a horsepower-to-weight ratio of .53 (.35 loaded) horsepower per kilogram and a weight-to-swept-area ratio of 176.17 (268.85 loaded) kilograms per square meter.

The Fw-190 made its combat debut in fall of 1941.

He-111: The Heinkel 111 H-16 was a twin-engine medium bomber with a crew of five. Its two 1,350 horsepower Junkers Jumo 211F-2 engines powered it to a maximum speed of 330 kilometers per hour (217 mph) at sea level and 405 kilometers per hour (252 mph) at 6,000 meters (19,685 feet). It had a range of 1,930 kilometers (1,200 miles) and a service ceiling of 8,500 meters (27,890 feet). It could climb to 6,000 meters in 42 minutes.

It entered service in late 1936 and was the one of the Luftwaffe's two major medium bomber designs in widespread use. It had a maximum bomb load, internal and external, of 3,250 kilograms (7,165 pounds). It was armed with a 20mm cannon, one 13mm machinegun, and up to five 7.9mm machineguns.

He-113: Identified in Soviet records as a plane the Soviets occasionally observed, this plane was in fact never produced. German propaganda did refer to the limited production Germany-based He-100 D-1 fighter as their latest operational fighter, the He-113, as a propaganda ploy.

Hs-123: The Henschel 123 A-1 was an open-cockpit dive bomber and ground attack biplane with a crew of one. Its one 880 horsepower BMW 132Dc engine powered it to a maximum speed of 342 kilometers per hour (213 mph) at 1,200 meters (3,940 feet). It had a cruising speed of 317 kilometers per hour (197 mph). It had a maximum range of 860 kilometers (534 miles) and a service ceiling of 9,000 meters (29,525 feet). Its initial rate of climb was 900 meters (2,950 feet) a minute.

This plane entered service in 1936. Production was terminated in 1938, but planes were used on the Eastern Front until mid-1944. There were even requests from the front to resume production of this obsolescent but effective support plane. About 40 Hs-123s operated on the Eastern Front. It had a maximum bomb load of 450 kilograms (992 pounds). It was armed with two 7.9mm machineguns and sometimes carried two 20mm cannons on under wing racks.

Hs-126: The Henschel 126 B-1 was an open-cockpit tactical reconnaissance biplane with a crew of two. Its one 850 or 900 horsepower BMW engine powered it to a maximum speed of 310 kilometers per hour (193 mph) at sea level and 356 kilometers per hour (221 mph) at 3,000 meters (9,840 feet). It had a normal range of 560 kilometers (360 miles) and a service ceiling of 8,230 meters (27,000 feet). Its time to 4,000 meters (13,130 feet) was 7 minutes and 14 seconds.

This plane made its operational debut in 1938. It was the Luftwaffe's primary tactical reconnaissance aircraft until it started being replaced by the Fw-189 in 1942. It had a maximum bomb load of 150 kilograms (331 pounds) and was armed with two 7.9mm machineguns.

Hs-129: The Henschel 129 B-2 was a twin-engine ground attack and antitank aircraft with a crew of one. Its two 700 horsepower French-built Gnome-Rhone engines powered it to a maximum speed of 407 kilometers per hour (253 mph) at 3,830 meters (12,570 feet). Its cruising speed was 315 kilometers per hour (196 mph). It had a range of 690 kilometers (429 miles) and a service ceiling of 9,000 meters (29,530 feet). Its initial rate of climb was 486 meters (1,595 feet) a minute.

This plane made its operational debut on 7 May 1942 in the Crimea. The main production B models using the Gnome-Rhone engines had considerable mechanical problems. The plane was heavily armored. It had a maximum bomb load of 350 kilograms (771 pounds) and was armed with two 7.9mm machineguns and two 20mm cannons. Specialized antitank versions included a 30mm cannon.

Ju-52: The Junkers 52/3m g7e was Germany's all-purpose transport plane. The Junkers tri-motor had an engine in its nose and one on each wing. Its three 830 horsepower BMW 132T-2 engines powered it to a maximum speed of 272 kilometers per hour (169 mph) at sea level, with a cruising speed of 257 kilometers per hour (160 mph). It had a range of 1,500 kilometers (930 miles) and a service ceiling of 5,500 meters (18,000 feet). Its time to climb to 3,000 meters (9,840 feet) was 19 minutes.

Originally built as a single engine civilian transport plane, the pre-war design became one of the most common transport planes in the world. It could accommodate 18 troops or 12 litters. It was armed with up to four 7.9mm machineguns. Bomber versions of the plane did exist but did not appear to be used in this role at Kursk. They were used extensively at Kursk for medical evacuation.

Soviet records also report seeing the four-engine Fw-200 Condor, but there is no confirmation that this large plane operated in the Belgorod area.

Ju-87: The Junkers 87 D-1 was the famous German gull-wing dive bomber with a crew of two. Its one 1,400 horsepower Junkers Jumo 211J-1 engine powered it to a maximum speed of 410 kilometers per hour (255 mph) at 4,100 meters (13,500 feet). It had a cruising speed of 185 kilometers per hour (115 mph). It had a maximum range of 1,535 kilometers (954 miles) and a service ceiling of 7,290 meters (23,900 feet). It could climb to 5,000 meters (16,400 feet) in 19 minutes and 48 seconds.

The prototype of this plane first flew in 1935 with its operational debut in spring of 1937. It became the Germans' primary dive-bomber and close support plane. It had a maximum bomb load of 1,800 kilograms (3,968 pounds). It was armed with three 7.9mm machineguns.

Although the word "stuka" is a German abbreviation for any type of dive-bomber aircraft, it has been almost universally applied as the name for the Ju-87.

Ju-88: The Junkers 88 A-4 was a twin-engine medium bomber with a crew of four. It was also designed to serve as a dive-bomber. Its two 1,340 horsepower Junkers Jumo 211J-1 or J-2 engines powered it to a maximum speed of 450 kilometers per hour (280 mph) at 6,000 meters (19,685 feet). It had a cruising speed of 370 kilometers per hour (230 mph). It had a maximum range of 2,730 kilometers (1,696 miles) and a service ceiling of 8,200 meters (26,900 feet). It could climb to 5,400 meters (17,716 feet) in 23 minutes.

It entered service in August 1939 and was one of the Luftwaffe's two major medium bomber designs in widespread use. It had a maximum bomb load, internal and external, of 3,600 kilograms (7,935 pounds). It was armed with two 13mm machineguns and three 7.9mm machineguns.

There were a large number of variants of this plane, including reconnaissance versions that were probably in use at Kursk.

La-5: There was one Soviet identification of this plane as an enemy aircraft. There is no other evidence that the Germans were flying captured Soviet La-5s at Kursk.

Me-109: The Messerschmitt 109 G-2 was the standard German fighter. It was a modern single seat fighter. Its single 1,475 horsepower Daimler-Benz DB 605A engine powered it to a maximum speed of 510 kilometers per hour (317 mph) at sea level and 653 kilometers per hour (406 mph) at an altitude of 9,000 meters (28,540 feet). It had a cruising speed of at least 483 kilometers per hour (300 mph). It had a range of 850 kilometers (528 miles) and a service ceiling of 12,000 meters (39,370 feet). It could climb to 2,000 meters (6,560 feet) in one minute and 30 seconds.

It was armed with two 7.9mm machineguns in the cowling, and one 20mm cannon firing through the propeller hub. Its wing area was 16.1 square meters (173.3 square feet). Its empty weight was 2,253 kilograms (4,968 pounds) and its maximum weight was 3,200 kilograms (7,055 pounds). This gave it a horsepower-to-weight ratio of .65 (.46 loaded) horsepower per kilogram and a weight-to-swept-area ratio of 139.94 (198.76 loaded) kilograms per square meter.

The first prototype flew in September 1935; it was used in Spain and was the standard German fighter throughout the war. The statistics for a G-2 are provided above, although the majority of Me-109s at Kursk were the G-6 versions, which had very similar performance statistics.

Me-110: Only a few Me-110 two-engine fighters were deployed in the Army Group South area. There were eight Me-110 G-3s with the 6th Close Range Reconnaissance Group, ten Me-110 E-2, F-4 and G-4s with the 5th Night Fighter Wing, and perhaps a few others with the 14th Close Range Reconnaissance Group. The statistics here are for the Messerschmitt 110 G-4 night fighter, although the plane had originally been developed as a fighter. It was a large twin-engine fighter with a three-man crew. Its two 1,475 Daimler-Benz DB 605B engines powered it to a maximum speed of 550 kilometers per hour (342 mph) at 7,000 meters (22,950 feet). It had a maximum range of 2,100 kilometers (1,305 miles) and a service ceiling of 8,000 meters (26,250 feet). Its initial rate of climb was 661 meters (2,170 feet) per minute.

Originally developed in May 1936 as a fighter, this plane was found wanting in that role during the Battle of Britain. Instead, it became a fighter-bomber and a night fighter. It was armed with four 7.9mm machineguns and two 20mm cannons firing forward and two 7.9mm machineguns in the rear cockpit in a flexible mount. Its wing area was 38.4 square meters (413.33 square feet) and its empty weight was 5,090 kilograms (11,220 pounds) and its loaded weight was 9,390 kilograms (20,700 pounds). This gave it a horsepower-to-weight ratio of .58 (.31 loaded) horsepower per kilogram and a weight-to-swept-area ratio of 132.55 (244.53 loaded) kilograms per square meter.

SOVIET PLANES AT THE BATTLE OF KURSK[30]

The following planes were reported to be involved in the Battle of Kursk:

Airacobra: The American-built P-39 Airacobra was a single mid-engine closed cockpit fighter built by Bell. It was a modern, aluminum skinned (often unpainted) fighter with a one-man crew. Its 1,150 horsepower Allison V-12 engine powered it to a maximum speed of

539 kilometers per hour (335 MPH) at 1,524 meters (5,000 feet altitude). It had a maximum range of 965 kilometers (600 miles) and a service ceiling of 8,840 meters (29,000 feet).

It was armed with two cowling-mounted .50 caliber (12.7mm) machineguns, four wing-mounted .30 caliber (7.62mm) machineguns and a nose-mounted 37mm cannon that fired through the propeller hub. It was designed to also carry one 227 kilogram (500 pound) bomb.

The Airacobra entered US service in 1941. Statistics provided here are from the P-39D version but later versions were not significantly different. There were 4,924 P-39s provided to the Soviet Union as a Lead-lease item. This was over half the P-39s manufactured. There were a few of these planes at Kursk as part of the Fifth Air Army and they were used primarily to patrol their airspace. Several sources claim that the 27th Fighter Regiment and Soviet aces Gulayev and Bobrov used the Airacobra at Kursk, but this was not the case.[31]

Boston: The American-built Havoc A-20B (known as the Boston to the British and Soviets) was a light bomber built by Douglas Aircraft. It was a modern, aluminum skin (unpainted) two-engine bomber with a crew of three. Its two 1,600 horsepower Wright engines powered it to a maximum speed of 563 kilometers per hour (350 mph) at 3,658 meters (12,000 feet). It had a cruising speed of 447 kilometers per hour (278 mph). It had a maximum range of 3,700 kilometers (2,300 miles) and a service ceiling of 8,717 meters (28,600 feet). It could climb to 3,048 meters (10,000 feet) in 5 minutes.

It was armed with two forward firing .50 caliber (12.7mm) machineguns, a flexible mounted .50 caliber (12.7mm) machine-gun and two flexible mounted .30 caliber (7.62mm) machineguns. Its maximum bomb load was 1,179 kilograms (2,600 pounds). The Havoc entered US service in 1941 and was provided as a Lend-lease item to the Soviet Union. There were only a limited number of these at Kursk and they appeared to be used primarily as a reconnaissance plane.

The statistics provided here are for the A-20B, which was the most common version sent to the Soviet Union. A total of 3,036 A-20s and DB-7 Havocs were provided to the Soviet Union by the US

Il-2: The Ilyushin Il-2 m3 was the Soviet Union's primary ground attack plane. It was a modern, heavily armored plane with a two man crew. Its 1,770 horsepower engine powered it to a maximum speed of 404 kilometers per hour (251 mph) at 1,500 meters (4,950 feet). It had a range of 765 kilometers (475 miles) and a service ceiling of 6,000 meters (19,690 feet). It could climb to 5,000 meters (16,405 feet) in 12 minutes.

It was armed with two forward firing 23mm cannons and two forward firing 7.62mm machineguns and had one flexible mounted 12.7mm machinegun in the rear. Its maximum bomb load was 600 kilograms (1,321 pounds) or it could carry eight 82mm or 132mm rockets. "Shturmovik" stood for "stormer" or a plane that storms (assault plane), but this name was often applied as the name for this aircraft. The single-seat version of this plane was in use at the start of the German invasion in mid-1941 but in autumn 1942, this particular two-seater version came into use. Although superior to the Stuka in many respects (speed, armor, climb), its bomb load was a fraction of the Stukas. It was a ground attack plane more in line with an Hs-129 than with the Ju-87 Dive Bomber.

La-5: The Lavochkin 5 FN was a closed cockpit fighter with a one-man crew. Its single 1,850 horsepower Shvetsov Ash-82FN radial engine powered it to a maximum speed of 648 kilometers per hour (403 mph) at an altitude of 6,400 meters (21,000 feet). It had a range of 765 kilometers (475 miles) and a service ceiling of 9,500 meters (31,116 feet). It could climb to 5,000 meters (16,400 feet) in four minutes and 42 seconds.

It was armed with two 20mm or 23mm cannons on the cowling. Its maximum bomb or rocket load was 300 kilograms (662 pounds). Its wing area was 17.59 square meters (189.34 square feet) and its empty weight was 2,605 kilograms (5,743 pounds) and its loaded weight was 3,360 kilograms (7,408 pounds). This gave it a horsepower-to-weight ratio of .71 (.55 loaded) horsepower per kilogram and a weight-to-swept area ratio of 148.10 (191.02 loaded) kilograms per square meter.

The La-5 was a development of the LaGG-3 and entered service in late 1942. The original La-5 with a 1,330 horsepower Shvetsov M-82F engine made its operational debut at Stalingrad. The La-5 FN version with its powerful 1,850 horsepower engine made its operational debut at Kursk. It is not known how many of the La-5s at Kursk had this engine. With this plane, the Soviets had a fighter that could match the Me-109.

Pe-2: The Petlyakov Pe-2 was the Soviet two engine dive bomber, similar to the original concept behind the Ju-88. It was a modern bomber with a three or four man crew. Its two 1,100 horsepower engines powered it to a maximum speed of 540 kilometers per hour (336 mph) at 5,000 meters (16,400 feet). It had a cruising speed of 428 kilometers per hour (266 mph). It had a range of 1,500 kilometers (932 miles) and a service ceiling of 8,800 meters (28,900 feet). It could climb to 5,000 meters (16,400 feet) in 7 minutes.

It was usually armed with two forward firing 7.62mm machineguns and usually had a flexible mounted 7.62mm machinegun in both the dorsal and ventral positions. Its maximum bomb load was 1,200 kilograms (2,645 pounds). The Pe-2 entered service in early 1941 and served throughout the war as the Soviets' primary tactical bomber. It was not inferior to the German Ju-88 or He-111 except that it did have a considerably smaller bomb load.

R-5: The Polikarpov R-5 was primarily a night reconnaissance plane and night bomber. It was an open cockpit biplane with two seats and a cloth covered frame. Its one 680 horsepower engine powered it to a maximum speed at sea level of 228 kilometers per hour (142 mph). It had a range of 800 kilometers (497 miles) and a service ceiling of 6,400 meters (20,997 feet).

It was armed with one fixed forward firing 7.62mm machinegun and one rear-firing 7.62mm machinegun and had a maximum bomb load of 400 kilograms (882 pounds). The R-5 was a design from the late 1920s and served as a trainer, liaison, night bomber, reconnaissance, partisan supply, partisan and agent insertion plane, and in numerous other roles.

TB-3: The Tupolev TB-3 was the Soviet four-engine heavy bomber. It was an older bomber design with a four to six man crew. Its four 970 horsepower engines powered it to a maximum speed of 288 kilometers per hour (179 mph). It had a range of 3,120 kilometers (1,939 miles) and a service ceiling of 7,740 meters (25,393 feet).

It was armed with six flexible mounted 7.62mm machineguns and had a maximum bomb load of 4,000 kilograms (8,818 pounds). The TB-3 was first flown in late 1930 and was in service well before the start of the Second World War. It served throughout the war as a bomber, transport and paratroop plane. A little slow, it did carry a large bomb load.

U-2: The Polikarpov U-2 VS, renamed as the Po-2 in 1944, was the Soviet Union's primary night bomber. It was an open cockpit biplane with two seats and a cloth covered frame. It's one 100 horsepower engine powered it to a maximum speed of 150 kilometers per hour (93 mph) at sea level. It had a range of 530 kilometers (329 miles) and a service ceiling of 4,000 meters (13,123 feet).

It was armed with one rear-firing 7.62mm machinegun and had a maximum bomb load of 250 kilograms (550 pounds). It could also be equipped to carry rockets. The U-2 was first flown in 1928 and served as a trainer, liaison, night bomber, and in numerous other roles.

Yak-1b: The Yakovlev 1 was a modern single seat fighter. Its single 1,100 horsepower Klimov engine powered it to a maximum speed of 500 kilometers per hour (311 mph) at sea level and 580 kilometers per hour (360 mph) at an altitude of 5,000 meters (16,400 feet). It had a cruising speed of 240 kilometers per hour (149 mph). It had a range of 850 kilometers (528 miles) and a service ceiling of 10,000 meters (32,810 feet). It could climb to 5,000 meters (16,400 feet) in four minutes and 30 seconds.

It was armed the same as the Me-109, with two 7.62mm machineguns in the cowling, and one 20mm cannon firing through the propeller hub. Its maximum bomb load was 200 kilograms (440 pounds). Its wing area was 17.15 square meters (184.6 square feet) and its empty weight was 2,300 kilograms (5,137 pounds) and its loaded weight was 2,820 kilograms (6,217 pounds). This gave it a horsepower-to-weight ratio of .48 (.39 loaded) horsepower per kilogram and a weight-to-swept-area ratio of 134.11 (164.43 loaded) kilograms per square meter.

The prototype I-26 first flew in early 1940 and entered service as the Yak-1 before the end of the year.

Yak-7b: The Yakovlev 7b was a modern single seat fighter. Its single 1,210 horsepower Klimov engine powered it to a maximum speed of 545 kilometers per hour (339 mph) at sea level and 613 kilometers per hour (381 mph) at an altitude of 5,000 meters (16,400 feet). It had a range of 825 kilometers (513 miles) and a service ceiling of 10,200 meters (33,464 feet). It could climb to 5,000 meters (16,400 feet) in four minutes and 55 seconds.

It was armed similar to the Me-109 with one 12.7mm machinegun in the cowling, and one 20mm cannon firing through the propeller hub. Its maximum bomb load was 200 kilograms (440 pounds). Its wing area was 17.15 square meters (184.6 square feet) and its empty weight was 2,480 kilograms (5,467 pounds) and its loaded weight was 3,010 kilograms (6,636 pounds). This gave it a horsepower-to-weight ratio of .49 (.40 loaded) horsepower per kilogram and a weight-to-swept-area ratio of 144.61 (175.51 loaded) kilograms per square meter.

The Yak-7 was a development from the Yak-1 and entered service in 1942.

Yak-9: The Yakovlev 9 was a modern single seat fighter. Its single 1,360 horsepower Klimov engine powered it to a maximum speed of 535 kilometers per hour (332 mph) at sea level and 602 kilometers per hour (374 mph) at an altitude of 2,000 meters (6,560 feet). It had a range of 1,410 kilometers (876 miles) and a service ceiling of 10,600 meters (34,775 feet). It could climb to 5,000 meters (16,400 feet) in five minutes and 42 seconds.

It was armed the same as the Yak-7 with one 12.7mm machinegun in the cowling, and one 20mm cannon firing through the propeller hub. Its maximum bomb load was 200 kilograms (440 pounds), but the bomb racks were a field installation, vice one done at the factory. Its wing area was 17.15 square meters (184.6 square feet) and its empty weight was 2,770 kilograms (6,107 pounds) and its maximum weight was 3,080 kilograms (6,790 pounds). This gave it a horsepower-to-weight ratio of .49 (.44 loaded) horsepower per kilogram and a weight-to-swept-area ratio of 161.52 (179.59 loaded) kilograms per square meter.

The Yak-9 was a development from the Yak-7 and entered service in late 1942. The statistics given above are for the Yak-9D, a long-range escort version.

The Germans also occasionally reported seeing LaGGs and LaGG-3s, but this was probably a misidentification.

Note: Soviet planes were usually named after their designers or the heads of their design bureaus: like Andrei Nikolayevich Tupolev (1888–1972), Vladimir Mikhailovich Petlyakov (1891–1942), Nikolai Nikolayevich Polikarpov (1892–1944), Sergei Vladimirovich Ilyushin (1894–1977), Semen Alekseyevkich Lavochkin (1900–1960), and Aleksandr Sergeyevich Yakovlev (1906–1989). While not untouched by the purges, none of these designers were completely removed from their work for long.

BOTH SIDES PREPARE

Notes

1. Nikita Khrushchev (translated and edited by Strobe Talbott), *Khrushchev Remembers* (Little, Brown and Company, Boston, 1970), page 208.
2. Cajus Bekker, *The Luftwaffe War Diaries* (Ballantine Books, New York, 1966), page 432.
3. These are identified by Klink, page 336, as the 10th Flak Division (motorized), the 17th Flak Division in the area of Kremenchug (on the Dnepr), and the 15th Flak Division in the area of Varenovka-Kamenka. Early in the year, the 9th Flak Division was at Stalingrad, but it was destroyed along with the rest of the Sixth Army.
4. This is from Seidemann, *The "Zitadelle" Offensive, Eastern Front, 1943: Luftwaffe Participation* (manuscript T-26, written in Newstadt, 1 November 1947 by Writer No. 737, General Seidemann), page 190, and has not been confirmed by other primary documentary sources.
5. This is from Seidemann, pages 190–191, and has not been confirmed by other primary documentary sources.
6. This is according to Seidemann, page 193. According to Klink, page 336, the Fourth Air Fleet had the 125th Long-range Reconnaissance Group, the 76th Weather Reconnaissance Squadron, a transport squadron, and a "sanitatsflugbereitschaft" (airborne ambulance flight).
7. This is from Seidemann, pages 192–193, and has not been confirmed by other primary documentary sources.
8. Hans Ulrich Rudel, *Stuka Pilot* (Bantam Books, New York, 1979, originally published 1958), pages 92, 98–99 clearly indicates that he only brought one Ju-87 G-1 with him to the Battle of Kursk, and only after it proved successful on or after 7 July, did they form an antitank squadron as part of the 2nd Stuka Wing.
9. A number of sources, including *The Battle of Kursk* (Progress Press Publishers), page 194, state 200.
10. Plane and squadron identification from Michael Holm in "Stoerkampfgruppe Luftwaffenkommando Don."
11. Hooton, *War over the Steppes*, page 167, states that "Despite shortages of both instructors and fuel, students still logged some 300 hours each during 1942…"
12. Hooton, pages 157–158 & 168. Also see, Hooton, *War Over the Steppes*, pages 46-48. On the other hand, Col. Raymond F. Toliver, and Trevor J. Constable, *Horrido! Fighter Aces of the Luftwaffe* (Bantam, New York, 1979), on page 25 states that US pilots received 450 hours of training.
13. Hooton, *War over the Steppes*, pages 165-166, provides some details of this. He states that the Soviet plans were to train 23,260 pilots in 1942 but they were only able to train 13,383. In 1943, the Soviet plans were to train 19,770 pilots but they were only able to train 12,277. The schools were only receiving from 52.5 (in 1943) to 55 Table II.20, a comparison of those percent ratings to the VIII Air Corps loss reports, is illuminating (in 1942) of their required personnel. In 1942 they flew 5,735,768 training sorties and in 1943 they flew less, 3,717,443 training sorties. "These flights averaged only 15 minutes duration or less."

    This does come out to an average of 303 (in 1943) to 429 (in 1942) sorties per pilot. If the average flight was 15 minutes (or less) then this comes out to an average of 76 to 107 hours or less per pilot.

    Hardesty and Grinberg, pages 230-231 paint a similar picture. To quote: "New pilots often had only minimal frontline training in combat aircraft—some with as little as fifteen to twenty hours, and others with as few as five to eight hours. Selecting commanders for small units also proved difficult in this context, as many pilots lacked extensive combat experience. Bomber crew often lacked proper navigational knowledge, the skill to coordinate missions with fighter escorts, and baseline experience in bombing targets with accuracy….Documents from the 293rd BAD, for example, reveal a whole range of inadequacies, mostly linked to the inferior training program: poor flying technique, inattention to proper radio communications, and lack of coordination with fighter escorts. According to this report, some aircrews were slow to follow orders and displayed a high degree of disorientation in the combat zones….Since staff training was minimal or nonexistent in some air units, there was no effective way to monitor performance. The proper coordination of air and ground action remained an elusive goal on many occasions."
14. See "Fifth Air Army Sortie Count," in Appendix II. It shows a total of 1,109 training sorties being done from over a 12-day period, with the average training sortie being less than an hour in length.
15. This point is also made by Bergstrom, *Black Cross, Red Star*, page 198. He states "Many new units had been formed, and these had been filled with novices straight from flight school, often with shortened training courses. In the Shturmovik units which took part in the Battle of Kursk, only 7% of the pilots had any combat experience at all prior to 5 July 1943. In fact, in the entire 9 SAK of 17 VA, only 672 ShAP of 306 ShAD had any combat experience."
16. A translation of the order is provided on pages 60-62 of my book *Kursk: The Battle of Prokhorovka*.

17. Information in part from Richard W. Stevenson, "John Cairncross, Fifth Briton in Soviet Spy Ring, Dies at 82," *New York Times*, 10 October 1995.
18. Nikolai Mitrophanovich Zakharchenko was a captain and squadron commander in the 288th Fighter Air Division at this time. He retired as a Colonel. He was interviewed 17 January 1999 by Col. Fyodor Sverdlov.
19. Seidemann, page 198.
20. From a letter sent to Maj.Gen. (ret.) Dieter Brand by Lt. General (ret.) Rall and an extended phone conversation with him on 9 July 1999.
21. Hans-Ulrich Rudel states that they received the order to move on 4 July and fly from Kerch-Bagerovo in the Crimea to Melitopol, the next morning they fly to an airfield just north of Kharkov, and the next morning (the 6th) they are flying operations. See Hans-Ulrich Rudel, *Stuka Pilot*, pages 94–95. The Second Army air liaison officer records clearly indicate that the 2nd Stuka Wing is operating on the 5th.
22. This figure may only have been around 63 aircraft. See Tables II.5 and Tables II.7.
23. The figure of 881 comes from the Second Air Army correlation of forces. The other figures come from *The Battle of Kursk* (Progress Press Publishers), page 189, but as they also use the 881 figure for the Second Air Army, and their strength figures for the Seventeenth Air Army are close to the archival figures we have, these figures appear to be correct. Page 194 gives a combined strength of 1,311 aircraft for the Second and Fifth Air Armies, from which one can derive a strength for the Fifth Air Army of 430 aircraft. This appears to match the archival records we have.

    The Voyenno-Istoricheskii Zhurnal [Military History Journal], 1968, Number 6. "Dokumentyi i Materialyi: Kurskaya Bitva v Tsifrakh" gives the following figures:

    Central Front: 1,034 planes (455 fighters, 241 Assault planes, 260 day bombers, 74 night bombers and 4 reconnaissance aircraft);

    Voronezh Front: 881 planes (389 fighters, 276 assault planes, 172 day bombers, 34 night bombers, 10 reconnaissance aircraft);

    Southwestern Front: 735 planes (218 fighters, 383 assault planes, 70 day bombers, 64 night bombers).

    Their footnotes note that these figures do not include about 480 night bombers from long-range aviation and do not include the IX Fighter Corps and 36th and 101st Fighter Divisions from the Air Defense command. They also note that other Soviet secondary sources mention a total of 3,130 airplanes not counting long-range aviation, and 2,370 airplanes, not counting Long Range Aviation and the neighboring Fronts. There is a reported figure of 550 aircraft for the Steppe Front from Dupuy and Martell, *Great Battles on the Eastern Front*, page 76, clearly taken from Soviet sources.
24. Seidemann, page 197.
25. See T312, R1253, pages 001010 & 001013, the Luftwaffe 1c reports for 17 July 1943.
26. *The Battle of Kursk* (Progress Press Publishers), page 290.
27. Quote from Muller, page 143
28. The plan of operations for the First Air Division is provided by Bergstrom, *Kursk*, page 35.
29. All technical data from Weal, Elke C., John A. Weal, and Richard F. Barker, *Combat Aircraft of World War Two* (Macmillan Publishing Co., Inc., New York, 1977), pages 100–127.
30. All technical data from Weal, Weal and Barker, pages 198 and 213–219.
31. See Seidl, pages 49 and 85.

Chapter Three

THE STRIKE AT DAWN
5 July 1943 (Monday)

I failed to shoot down the next Il-2 because both I and the Il-2 were subjected to fire from our own anti-aircraft artillery, although without hitting either of us.

Captain Josef Haiboeck[1]

While the Germans initiated their offensive in the south this morning with nine panzer and panzer grenadier divisions and five of their supporting infantry divisions, what occurred in the skies over this battlefield was equally violent. It was an air fight larger and bloodier than anything seen during the much more famous Battle of Britain.

The Strike at Dawn

If the real reason for not conducting a strike on the Soviet air force was their desire not to give up tactical surprise, then one wonders how the Germans expected to keep tactical surprise with most of the outpost line in front of the Fourth Panzer Army being forcefully cleared the day before. While the Germans chose to forego the option of launching a surprise air attack, the Soviets did not. Instead, they conducted the "customary" strike at dawn.

In the south, the Soviet counterblow was timed to strike early in the morning against five German airfields around Kharkov.[2] The attacking formations were from the Second and Seventeenth Air Armies. The Soviets had attempted such strikes in June, but with little success. On 8 and 10 June the Sixth Air Fleet had been attacked twice with a very favorable exchange rate for the Germans. A much smaller attempt was also made on the VIII Air Corps on 8 June, also with unfavorable results for the Soviets. The Germans with their communications networks, forward observers, radar systems and fighters ready to scramble were clearly prepared to meet such attempts. Why the Soviets thought that it would work now, when it had not worked in the past, is hard to explain.

Between the Second and Seventeenth Air Armies, the Soviets had at least 357 serviceable Il-2s, along with 70 Pe-2s and 38 TB-3s. They had at least 526 fighters available. If they were going to do an airfield strike, it would seem to have made more sense to use the entire force at their disposal for such a strike and to have concentrated on such a strike for most of the morning. Instead they started the day with a limited strike.

The Soviet Second Air Army went forward with groups of six to nine assault aircraft, escorted by the same number of fighters. Attacking the Pomerki and Sokolniki airfields just north of Kharkov were 48 Il-2s with fighter escort from the I Assault Corps while seven fighters from the IV Fighter Corps "blocked" the Pomerki airfield.[3] Attacking the Mikoyanovka airfield was the 291st Assault Division with 18 Il-2s escorted by 18 fighters, while 12 planes from the V Fighter Corps blocked the airfield.[4] They began bombing the German airfields in the area of Mikoyanovka, Sokolniki and Pomerki between 0425 and 0430 (Moscow time). These three locations were widely separated with three German fighter wings located around Mikoyanovka.

The German VIII Air Corps had already lined up their bombers on the airfields around Kharkov and were preparing them for take-off. Once the bombers were airborne, they were to form up and the fighters would then take off to join them as escorts. While the bombers were still taking off, the German aircraft warning service's radio monitors reported a sudden increase in the number of exchanges between Soviet air units, indicating that a major air operation was under way. Then the Freyja radar in Kharkov reported that several hundred aircraft were approaching.[5] This would be confirmed by listening stations and observers at the Germans lines.

The Freyja was the German mobile radar set, which they had been using since 1938. It sent out signals on a 240 centimeter wavelength and had a range of up to 160 kilometers (100 miles).[7] It could report direction and distance of a target, but not altitude. The unit in use by the VIII Air Corps was in Kharkov. Kharkov and a number of the German airfields (Osnovo, Rogan) were less than 30 kilometers from the front. As such, there was a second line of

SUMMATION OF TIMES AND ALTITUDES OF CLAIMED GERMAN KILLS 5 July 1943[6]

Time	3 JG	52 JG	Other
03:21–04:10	30	17	
04:13–05:03	1	1	1
05:25–05:53		4	
06:21–06:54	2	3	
07:10–07:58	11	8	
08:01–08:17		3	
09:10–09:57	6	6	
10:10–10:40	4	6	
11:15–11:45	2	3	
12:02–12:59	11	7	1
13:48–13:55	3		
14:00–14:35	4	3	
15:22–15:26	4	3	
16:18–16:42	5	1	
17:00–17:40	3		
18:00–19:10	22	27	1
	108	92	3

Altitude	3 JG	52 JG	Other
Tree level	15	11	
10–80	6	8	
100–400	33	20	
500–800	16	14	
1,000–1,800	18	11	
2,000–2,800	13	24	1
3,000–3,500	4	3	1
4,500		1	
5,000	1		
No height given	2		1
	108	92	3

THE STRIKE AT DAWN

warning, which were the sound stations that could hear planes flying. There were also visual observations. With the VIII Air Corps in communication with the front, there were several layers of warning against a Soviet first strike.

The Soviet strike was timed for just when the German operations would be starting. At the bases around Mikoyanovka, the German's 52nd Fighter Wing barely had time to clear the airfield before the Soviet aircraft arrived. Around Kharkov, the Germans were forced to halt bomber operations and instead sent their fighters of the 3rd Fighter Wing scrambling to take off. This included launching fighters through the lines of bombers that were readying to take off. Still, there was enough warning that when the Soviet air arrived, a very strong German fighter force of two fighter wings was waiting for them. Some of these forces may have been alerted in response to the earlier Soviet opening artillery barrage.[8]

One such aerial interception was of the Soviet 241st Assault Regiment (291st Assault Division) going to Mikoyanovka with 18 Il-2s. They were intercepted in route as they crossed the front lines just northeast of Belgorod by Me-109s of the III Group, 3rd Fighter Wing. Their escort of 18 Yak-7Bs from the 737th Fighter Regiment (also 291st Assault Division) joined the fight, as did two German squadrons from the 52nd Fighter Wing: the 2nd squadron led by 21-victory ace Sr. Lt. Paul-Heinrich Daehne and then the 7th squadron led by Lt. Erich Hartmann. The German pilots claimed six Il-2s and eight fighters. The 241st Assault Regiment is reported to have lost 7 Il-2s.[9] The 11 Il-2s continue to Mikoyanovka, where they found an empty airfield, which they bombed. The cost of this mission was seven Il-2s and three fighters.[10] The Soviet raid was launched at 0430 (Moscow time). The 291st Assault Division, which consisted of at least four regiments, reported their losses for the day as 15 planes, of which two Il-2s were shot down by AA and ten did not return from their missions, while three Yak-7Bs did not return. Also, four Il-2s and a Yak1b made forced landings on their own side of the lines.[11]

The Soviet attack on the Pomerki airfield was intercepted a little later in the morning. In this case, the II Group, 3rd Fighter Wing and I Group, 52nd Fighter Wing were "vectored" towards the Soviet 66th Assault Regiment and 735th Assault Regiment (266th Assault Division, I Assault Corps). These two German fighter groups had previously been fighting elements of the Seventeenth Air Army (see below). Eleven of fourteen Il-2s from these two Soviet regiments were shot down. Their attack on Pomerki, known to the Germans as Kharkov-North, failed to inflict any serious damage.[12]

Meanwhile the 820th Assault Regiment (292nd Assault Division, I Assault Corps) with 30 Il-2s managed to luckily waltz past most of the roving German fighter squadrons and bombed Sokolniki. It was with little effect as the airfield was already empty. The regiment lost 4 Il-2s on the mission.[13] The missions were launched between 0425-0430 (Moscow time) and the I Assault Corps lost 15 Il-2s this day, with 11 of them apparently lost from the attack on Pomerki.[14]

The Seventeenth Air Army had farther to fly but were scheduled to attack the Osnova, Rogan, Barvenkovo, and Kramatorskaya airfields between 0400 and 0530 (Moscow time). Again these were strikes in two widely separated locales, with Osnova being just south of Kharkov and Rogan being about 15 kilometers to its east, while Barvenkovo and Kramatorskaya were in the area of Izyum and Kramatorsk, some 135 to 180 kilometers to the southeast of Kharkov and well out of the Kursk battlefield area. The I Mixed Corps was to target the Kramatorskaya airfield. They sent eight Il-2s escorted by 18 fighters. This attack was conducted without loss to the Soviet forces. On the other hand, the I Mixed Corps claimed that up to 30 planes were burned at the airfield, including 18 Ju-87s and Me-109s. They also claimed to damage 25. These claims must be dismissed in light of the German reports about Ju-87 losses for this day. The VIII Air Corps reported none lost, while the Luftwaffe quartermaster reports show three lost and three damaged, all due to flak. The III Mixed Corps attacked the Barvenkovo airfield using 12 fighters. It made no claims for this attack.[15] In light of the transfers of aircraft just before the battle, these two airfields may have only been lightly manned by the Germans. The Soviet IX Mixed Corps attacked the Rogan and Osnovo airfields, with 16 Il-2s and probably an equal number of La-5s as escorts. They claimed four German planes burned on Osnovo airfield.[16]

The attack on Barvenkovo was conducted by the Fifth Guards Fighter Regiment. The regiment was commanded by the ace and Hero of the Soviet Union Vasili Aleksandrovich Zaitsev. Their report for 5 July states that from 4:21-5:50 twelve La-5s flew to block the airfield Barvenkovo with simultaneous bombing and ground attack. At 4:45 the group at a height of 1,000 – 1,200 meters bombed the parked aircraft and attacked German material for 12 minutes. In total, the crews were in the area of the airfield for 22 minutes. The crews observed in the caponiers[17] on the eastern side of the airfield ten single-engine aircraft with one aircraft standing in the open. There were no encounters with German air or anti-aircraft artillery over the aerodrome. On the flight back from Barvenkovo they were fired on by two medium-caliber anti-aircraft artillery battalions.[18] This account is interesting, as it clearly indicates that the German aircraft were protected and even when the airfield was undefended, it was hard to achieve any success.

The attack on Rogan airfield by the 237th Assault Regiment and 31st Fighter Regiment of the IX Mixed Corps was intercepted in route in the II Group of the 3rd Fighter Wing, with the Germans claiming victories as early as 0325 (Berlin time). The Germans were reinforced by the I Group of the 52nd Fighter Wing. As the Soviets continued to Rogan, they were also intercepted by the Hungarian fighter squadron 5/1 (first squadron, 5th Regiment). The 2nd Hungarian fighter squadron also scrambled at 0330 (Berlin time) and engaged with the 31st Fighter Regiment's La-5s. Only six Il-2s were able to get to and bomb Rogan, with little overall effect. This was at a cost of 13 Il-2s.[19] The Soviet IX Mixed Corps reports for this day five Il-2s shot down, and 45 Il-2s and seven La-5s that failed to return.[20] The IX Mixed Corps took about three-fourths of the Seventeenth Air Army's losses for this day.[21]

It was not difficult for the Seventeenth Air Army to reach and participate in the operations around Belgorod. The average flight time for all their missions for this day, which was mostly to the airfields and to the Corps Raus area, was just a little over an hour. With the Seventeenth Air Army having airfields less than a half hour away, they were in position to fully join the battle.

The Second Air Army tried to cover the assault aircraft by blocking the airfields, but it appears the German fighters were airborne when they arrived. The Soviet formations came under continual attack during their approach run and were then attacked again on their return flights. The Soviet fighters were supposed to cover them on the return flight. The IX Fighter Corps flew 50 such covering missions. The V Fighter Corps flew 24 missions to block the Mikoyanovka airfield and cover their assault aircraft on the return flight. In light of the heavy losses inflicted on the Il-2s, this was not a very successful cover. It does not appear that the Seventeenth Air Army flew blocking or covering missions.

WALTER "COUNT PUNSKI" KRUPINSKI

Walter Krupinski was born 11 November 1920 in Domnau East Prussia. He joined the Air Force in October 1939, went through fighter training and saw his first action in February 1941 at the Channel Coast. He then transferred to Russia with the 52nd Fighter Wing. Krupinski had a reputation for being reckless. In 1943, he was the commander of the 7th Squadron and was injured on 5 July when his plane flipped over while he was trying to avoid another rolling aircraft on the runway where he was landing. He had shot down two planes this day, now having 90 claimed kills.

In May 1944, he returned to Germany to participate in the Air Defense of the Reich. During the war he served in 52nd, 5th and 11th Fighter Wings and in JV-44, Adolf Galland's "squadron of experts" which flew the Me-262 jet fighter-bomber. He scored 177 victories on the Eastern Front and 20 on the Western Front. He flew over 1,100 sorties. He was shot down and bailed out five times and wounded four times.

He joined the West German Air Force when it was established in 1956, and was forced into an early retirement as a Lieutenant General in November 1976 as a result of his involvement in inviting Ju-87 pilot and neo-Nazi Hans Rudel to a veteran's reunion of the Immelmann squadron. He passed away 7 October 2000.

Overall, these Soviet strikes consisted of 90 Il-2s and around 117 fighters.[22] Opposing them were two wings of German fighters, potentially around 160 Me-109s. What transpired between Mikoyanovka and Kharkov was one of the largest air fights of the war, creating a spectacle of planes crashing and burning across an 80 kilometer battle area from Mikoyanovka to Kharkov.

The 3rd Fighter Wing claimed the first kills of the day with an Il-2 at 0321 (Berlin time). Over the next 16 minutes, the 4th, 5th, and 8th squadrons of this wing claimed 11 Il-2s and two fighters while the 2nd squadron of the 52nd Fighter Wing claimed two Il-2s and a fighter. The day's initial round of air battles continued until the last of the early morning German kill claims was made at 0410. In that 49-minute period, the two fighter wings had claimed 47 planes: 33 Il-2s and 14 fighters. In light of the Soviet losses for this day, these claims could not have been too far from the truth. Concentrated flak fire also inflicted heavy losses on the Soviet air. The Seventeenth Air Army's strikes had to pass though the antiaircraft defenses in the Corps Raus zone in addition to the antiaircraft defenses of the airfields.

There then appears to have been a moment of quiet across the battlefield, for the Germans made only three claimed kills between 0410 and 0525. From that point on, the Soviet losses continued at a rate of 3 to 19 planes an hour for most of the day.

This attack was a disaster for the Soviet air forces. Seidemann estimates that 120 Soviet aircraft went down in this raid, while the German losses were small. It appears that Seidemann's estimate is inflated. It appears that the actual Soviet aircraft losses in the morning airfield strikes were between 35 to 40 planes,[23] but it was still a disastrous start to a disastrous day for the Soviet air force.

Still, the strike had some effect. It delayed the morning ground support and caused the Germans some losses. The German 7th squadron of the 52nd Fighter Wing, based at Urgim, lost its squadron leader, Walter Krupinski, one of Germany's top aces. During the fighting, he was hit in the rear part of the fuselage. Having only partial rudder control, he had to come in for an immediate landing. As he was making his landing, an alerted flight was taking off across his front, forcing him to swerve. In the process, he applied the brakes too hard, the aircraft flipped and he fractured his skull. He was out of action for six weeks.[24]

Promoted on the spot to acting squadron leader was 21-year-old Lt. Erich Hartmann. Lt. Hartmann had spent June in Germany on leave at Wing Commander Major Hrabak's suggestion after Hartmann had collided in mid-air with an La-5 on 25 May and barely crossed back into German lines without power before making a forced landing. Hartmann had been flying on the Eastern Front since August 1942 and had 181 combat missions and 17 victories to his credit. Returning to the 52nd Fighter Wing for the upcoming offensive, he flew four missions this day. On the morning of the 5th he started with a scramble at 0323 (Berlin time), and claimed a victory on each of those four missions. It was his most successful day to date. Hartmann would eventually become the highest scoring ace in history.[25]

On the other side was Lieutenant Ivan Komarov, squadron commander of the 198th Assault Regiment, 227th Assault Division.[26]

> I was with this division since Stalingrad. I was a pilot, a flight commander, an Il-2 squadron commander. Unfortunately, I was in the Kursk battle for just one day, 5 July 1943.
>
> At three in the morning my squadron was waken up by an alarm. I got the order to attack the German fighters' aerodrome located to the southwest of Belgorod. We quickly took off and flew in the direction of the battle. When we were near the target, six Me-109 fighters attacked us from the right. We were grouped in a line of flights. I immediately ordered the right flight to drive off the "Messers" by any means. I was leading two flights (six planes) directly towards the target not changing the course by even one degree. Not paying attention to antiaircraft fire from below, our five planes attacked the enemy bombers with bombs and missiles four times and set more than ten enemy planes on fire. Unfortunately, one of our assault planes was destroyed by a fighter. We later destroyed this fighter. Another assault plane was shot during the air combat, but it managed to destroy one enemy fighter before it went down by directly attacking the plane from the front. The rest of the enemy planes flew away to the west, probably because they were low on fuel. I brought back seven planes. Near the front line we ran into six Messers.
>
> I ordered planes by squadron to regroup in a circle, to cover each other and fire at the fighters. We destroyed one of their fighters. It fell down to the ground on fire. One of the German pilots, probably the commander as he was more experienced, attacked my plane when he was at a long distance from me. I was wounded in the arm and leg by a shell fragment. Some fragments entered the motor and destroyed one control cable. My two wing men started firing at the fighter and drove him away. They flew to both sides of me and accompanied me back to the aerodrome. I even don't remember how I landed. I was unconscious when somebody took me from the cabin. They brought me to the hospital. I returned back to the division only at the Dnepr.

THE STRIKE AT DAWN

Air Support on the First Day (5 July)

The Germans, with their desire to concentrate all firepower on the decisive point, ended up assigning all the air support in the morning to the SS Panzer Corps, while the XLVIII Panzer Corps received the air support during the afternoon. The attacks this day flew forward of the two attacking panzer corps, with the targets including Soviet defensive points; artillery, antiaircraft, and antitank gun positions; tank assembly areas and vehicle columns.[27] They faced strong Soviet antiaircraft fire. This air support included 536 sorties by He-111s and Ju-88s, 1,071 stuka sorties and 335 ground attack sorties by Fw-190s and Hs-123s. The III Group of the 55th Bombardment Wing flew 82 He-111 sorties this day. Of those, 21 sorties went east of Luchki and 19 went to Byikovka. These strikes, well to the rear, came in at 2,600 to 4,000 meters (8,500 to 13,000 feet). The Luftwaffe ground observers claimed bloody Soviet losses and heavy material losses. Their "confirmed" claims included seven tanks, 30 guns, 70 vehicles, and nine ammunition or supply dumps.

The Second Air Army also started flying air support from the start of the battle, with the majority of it concentrated around the XLVIII Panzer Corps sector. Whereas over 80% of the German sorties this day were ground attack type sorties (1,942 sorties), the Soviets only had a little over 25% of their sorties as ground attack type sorties (334 sorties). There was considerably more weight to the German ground support effort than to the Soviet one.

The Second Air Army struck at the Donets River crossings using Il-2s with 17 sorties from the I Assault Corps. These strikes had little affect and in light of the high value of such targets, one is mystified why more effort was not made there. The main thrust of the Second Air Army air support effort was attacking German tanks and troops. Some 317 sorties were launched against them, including 173 from the Il-2s of the I Assault Corps and 29 from the Il-2s of the 291st Assault Division and 115 sorties by 70 Pe-2s of the I Bomber Corps. The Pe-2s flew in nine groups of nine to eighteen planes and bombed at heights of 2,300 to 2,900 meters, covered by the IV Fighter Corps. They attacked the areas of Butovo-Sybino-Rakovo and Kazatskoye-Tomarovka-Pushkarnoye. They encountered considerable German resistance, being involved in four engagements, of which two involved groups of 30 to 50 German fighters! The Germans claimed a number of Pe-2s this day, all at about the same time. Between 1245 and 1254, the 4th and 6th squadrons of the 3rd Fighter Wing claimed eight Pe-2s at altitudes between 2,200 to 3,000 meters while the 9th squadron of the 52nd Fighter Wing claimed three between 1251 and 1257 at altitudes of 2,000 to 2,500 meters. The Germans also claimed four Pe-2s during the morning, with two shot down around 0730 and two at around 0920. The Second Air Army reported losing four Pe-2s to dogfights this day while seven others simply failed to return. They also took losses to antiaircraft fire, which claimed four, and three other planes made forced landings on their side of the lines. With 18 Pe-2s down out of 70 that flew that day (26% losses), this was too high, and the I Bomber Corps would stand down for the next six days.

Lieutenant Andrei Lukyanets was in one of those Pe-2s. He recalls:[28]

> I had my first flight the morning of 5 July. I was leading an echelon, which was a part of the squadron, which was supposed to attack the enemy tanks. I don't remember exactly the area, but it was somewhere to the

southeast of Belgorod. As soon as we crossed the front line, two German Me-110s attacked my bomber, leading my echelon, from both sides. One of the engines caught on fire. I turned on an automatic fire extinguisher and immediately saw the German tanks on the ground. I pulled the bomb hatch control up and started bombing. The German fighters attacked me a second time and put my second engine and the fuel tank on fire. I heard the order of the commander "Everyone jump out!" I threw away the flashlight, jumped up from my seat, but the parachute straps got tangled around the machine-gun. My head bumped into something and I lost consciousness. As I was told later, the plane flipped upside down, the parachute straps got untangled and I fell down like a rock. At an altitude of about 2.5 kilometers, my consciousness returned, and I pulled the parachute ring. All of a sudden I saw two fighters flying at me. A bullet tore out a piece of the parachute. I was watching the hole getting larger and larger. I was thinking to myself how sad and unfortunate that I was going to die. I was falling down faster and faster, but I noticed that the hole in the parachute stopped growing. I fell on the ground on my side. There was fighting all around me. I heard several mine explosions next to me. I could not understand which territory I was in. I took my gun out of my pocket, loaded it and crawled to the east, orienting by the sun. I was very lucky that I ran into a group of our reconnaissance. They put a bandage on my wound and helped me get to my corps, fighting nearby. Colonel Dobyish [the air corps commander] was there. He gave me a hug and said "You returned from hell. It is good luck, now you will be alive until the victory." Luckily it turned out to be true. I was back fighting in five days.

There were also 20 daytime reconnaissance sorties, including six Bostons that carried out photographic reconnaissance. The Second Air Army reported having communications problems during the day, with their wire communications over the previous 24 hours having major interruptions which disrupted "normal" control of the air units. The radio communications, on the other hand, were fine.

The Seventeenth Air Army also contributed to the ground war, supporting the Seventh Guards Army. As the German air forces were not active over this area, then this effectively gave the Soviets air superiority over the Corps Raus and III Panzer Corps areas. The I Mixed Corps provided no support (as was also the case with the 244th Bomber Division). The III Mixed Corps sent 45 Il-2s with 62 fighter escorts to attack troops in the western Bezlyudovka and Ivanovka areas. The IX Mixed Corps sent 107 Il-2s with probably an equal number of La-5 escorts to attack German troop concentrations and crossings in the Solomino, Toplinka, Pristen, Pulyaevka, and Ivanovka areas. Most of these attacks were concentrated on Corps Raus, leaving the III Panzer Corps relatively unmolested.

During the day the Germans launched 1,942 ground attack type sorties compared to 486 ground attack type sorties by the two Soviet air armies.

The Air Superiority Fight

The majority of the Second Air Army sorties were by fighters, with 519 sorties to cover troops and 316 sorties to escort their bombers and assault planes. Escort duty was conducted by 60 Yak-1s of the I Assault Corps with 180 sorties, 18 Yak-1s and Yak-7s of the 291st Assault Division with 47 sorties, and the IV Fighter Corps for the Pe-2s of the I Bomber Corps with 89 sorties. Otherwise the IV Fighter Corps patrolled the Seventh Guards Army area in groups of eight to ten fighters with 89 sorties. The V Fighter Corps was heavily involved this day with 440 sorties, of which 220 sorties covered their troops and 160 sorties intercepted German aircraft.

This day was a disaster for the Second Air Army. In addition to the heavy losses in their dawn assault on the German airfields, they suffered losses steadily throughout the day with most of their formations. The German claims show particularly high Soviet losses of 19 claimed kills between 0710 and 0758 (including 10 Il-2s, seven fighters and two Pe-2s) and another 19 claimed kills between 1202 and 1259 (which included 11 Pe-2s). The highest number of claims was reserved for the end of the day, from 1800 to 1910, when the Germans claimed 50 kills (43 Il-2s and seven fighters), although this author is suspicious that some of these late-in-the-day reports are catch-up reports for the day. The German claims by individual pilots totaled 203 kills for this day, although this may not be all the claims.

The Second Air Army lost 114 airplanes while the Seventeenth Air Army lost 75. The Germans reported 19 aircraft lost this day. Of those, 12 were Me-109s. This is a ten-to-one exchange ratio!

In the case of the Second Air Army, they lost 27 Il-2s, 15 Pe-2s, one Boston and 48 fighters. Furthermore, 16 Il-2s, three Pe-2s and four fighters were damaged and forced to land on their side of the lines. The 208th Night Bomber Group had suffered no losses, which was typical for night groups. The I Assault Corps lost or force landed 27 Il-2s, including two lost from friendly AA fire and 13 which did not return from their missions. They also lost nine Yak-1bs.

TYPE OF PLANES CLAIMED BY THE GERMANS
5 July 1943[29]

Type	German Claims	Actual Soviet Losses
Il-2	113	109
LaGG	34	
LaGG-3	9	
La-5	22	7
MiG-1	2	
Yak-1	7	12
Yak-7		3
Fighter		39
Total of Fighter:	74	61
Boston III	1	1
Pe-2	15	18
Total Planes	203	189

The I Bomber Corps lost 18 Pe-2s, of which four were shot down in dogfights, four down by German AA fire, and seven failed to return from their missions. Three damaged Pe-2s were forced to land on their side of the lines. The IV Fighter Corps, patrolling over the Seventh Guards Army, got off relatively light with only eight planes lost, one due to antiaircraft, one by air combat, one forced landing and five that failed to return. They had only noted 15 engagements that day, as opposed to the V Fighter Corps which recorded a much more intense 46 engagements. These engagements cost the V Fighter Corps 31 fighters, with 11 shot down, one lost to antiaircraft and 19 not returning. The 291st Assault Division lost 16 Il-2s and four Yaks. The 454th Bomber Regiment also lost one of its Bostons. The 3rd Fighter Wing claimed a Boston at 0442 at 2,000 meters altitude.

This was a staggeringly lop-sided exchange. The Second Air Army fighters had managed 835 escort and air superiority sorties and were only facing a fighter force that conducted 371 Me-109 sorties this day. The German Fw-190s, a good fighter in its own right, played little role in the air combat with I Ground Assault Group claiming only one kill this day. Yet the Soviets lost 52 fighters, probably to air combat, while the Germans only lost 12 Me-109s and one Fw-190. This is around a four-to-one fighter exchange, and then the German fighters were probably able to bag another 56 assault aircraft and bombers, while the antiaircraft fire from both sides may have accounted for another eight Soviet planes. Most likely, the planes that "failed to return" were from air combat, not antiaircraft fire, which would rarely eliminate an entire flight and leave no reports.

The Seventeenth Air Army losses were less. The I Mixed Corps, which had only participated in a morning airfield strike on the southerly Kramatorskaya airfield, lost nothing. The III Mixed Corps, which had sent out 12 Yak-1s in the morning airfield strike, 45 Il-2s to attack German troops, and 62 escorting Yak-1s, had 16 Il-2s and two Yak-1s fail to return. It also had one other Yak-1 damaged in a dogfight. The IX Mixed Corps, which had sent out 16 Il-2s in the morning airfield strike, 107 Il-2s to attack German troops, and 124 escorting La-5s, had 45 Il-2s and seven La-5s that failed to return and five Il-2s shot down.

The IX Mixed Corps may have been the source of many of the German claims made between 1800-1910 (Berlin time) that day. The Germans claimsed that they shot down 50 aircraft at that time. According to one secondary source, late in the day General Sudets launched the Il-2s of the Seventeenth Air Army to attack the German pontoon bridges and ferries across the Donets. The author claims that for the remainder of the day (after 1500 Berlin time?) the "bulk of the air fighting took place over the Donets crossing."[30] According to individual German pilot accounts, elements of the I/52nd Fighter Wing took flight at 1820 and 1825 and intercepted them, shooting down many of Il-2s.[31] The Seventeenth Air Army does report that during the second part of the day the army had orders to launch assault aircraft and destroy the crossings over the Donets along the Solomino-Bezlyudovka sector.[32] This is the area where the 7th Panzer Division and the Corps Raus was crossing. The IX Air Corps losses this day were five Il-2s shot down and 45 Il-2s and seven La-5s that failed to return from their missions.

GERMAN KILLS AND LOSSES BY UNIT
5 July 1943[33]

	Total Claimed Kills	Losses, 5 July Destroyed	Seriously Damaged	Damaged
Staff II/3 JG	5			1
4/3 JG	24			1
5/3 JG	26	1		
6/3 JG	14			2
Staff III/3 JG	2	1		
7/3 JG	15	1		1
8/3 JG	11	1		1
9/3 JG	11	1		1
Staff/52 JG	3			
Staff I/52 JG	19		1	
1/52 JG	13	1		
2/52 JG	8	1		1
3/52 JG	5	1		
Staff III/52 JG	4	1		
7/52 JG	17		1	
8/52 JG	14	3		
9/52 JG	9	1	1	
I/100 KG	1	1		2
2/2 StG	1			
3/1 SG	1			
6 NAG				1
1/2 NAG				1
3(H)/32		1		
3 KG		1		2
27 KG		2		4
55 KG		2		2
2 StG		3	1	2
1 SG		2	2	7
	203	25	6	29

The 5th Guards Fighter Regiment, which reported to the III Mixed Corps, reports for 1828 that Il-2s bombed and assaulted the German troops on the eastern edge of the forest in the area Krutoi Log and Gremuchee (they probably mean Gremyachii). The aircrews observed at Solomino and Volkovo that the ferries were destroyed and noted in the Krutoi Log area and Shebekino up to 20 fires. They then state that when following a target in the Shebekino area, three Me-109fs were met. Two La-5s entered into battle with them. One Me-109f immediately left the battle, while a second German aircraft was hit but was able to fly to its own territory. Later, another four Me-109s approached and engaged two La-5s. "The fight was unsuccessful."[34] The III Mixed Corps reports that there were five dogfights, in which they claimed two Me-109s and one Fw-190s shot down and one Fw-190 damaged. Their losses were one Yak-1 damaged in a dogfight and 16 Il-2 and two Yak-1s that failed to return. No La-5s were reported as lost.

The 5th Guards Fighter Regiment also reports that from 1710-1815 eight La-5s escorted three Il-2s in the area of Solomino and Volkovo for bombing and assault on German forces. From 1805-1920 eight La-5s flew out and escorted seven Il-2s in the area of Solomino and Volkovo.

In the face of such heavy fighting, the German VIII Air Corps surprisingly reports no Stuka losses for the day, although the Luftwaffe quartermaster reports do indicate three lost and three damaged. Their losses, as reported by the VIII Air Corps, consisted of 12 Me109s, four He-111s, a Ju-88, an Fw-190 and an Hs-126. These appear to be permanent losses, and the number of planes damaged and disabled this day was higher. In addition to the noted ace Lt. Walter Krupinski being injured, the German ace Feldwebel (Technical Sergeant) Wilhelm Hauswirth (54 victories) of the 8th squadron was killed. He had claimed his 53rd victory on the 4th and his last on the 5th at 0503. He was then shot down by antiaircraft over the front lines. The III Group of the 52nd Fighter Wing had lost two major aces and four other pilots killed or injured this day.

The highest scoring German pilot on this day was Captain Johannes Wiese (133 career victories) of the staff I/52 JG. He claimed 12 Il-2s on this day but in return made five forced landings. Wiese claimed three Il-2s during the dawn attack (between 0347 and 0403), another two at 0751 and 0812 and another one at 0940. His next claim occurred in the afternoon at 1525 and then between 1830 and 1850 he claimed five more. The second highest scoring German pilot of the day was Sr. Lt. Joachim Kirschner (188 career victories) of the 5th squadron, 3rd Fighter Wing. He claimed eight kills this day.[35]

This day was a disaster for the Soviet air force and very clearly shows the downside of conducting the "customary" strike at dawn against a readied opponent. The Second Air Army claims that they destroyed 34 German planes at the airfields at Sokolniki and Pomerki, but these claims are not supported by the German records. The rest of the damage claims are very low (burned one hangar, two ammunition dumps blown up, four antiaircraft firing points suppressed, and one fuel tank burned). It appears that their airfield raids accomplished little.

More significant were the continued losses throughout the day. It would appear that there was a gross competency difference between the two air forces and because of this difference in tactical competence, the Germans were able to maintain a very favorable exchange ratio throughout the day.

PERSONAL KILL CLAIMS FOR THE DAY

These are claims for the top scoring pilots for the day:[36]

German pilots:
Captain Johannes Wiese, 1/52 JG	12
Sr. Lt. Joachim Kirschner, 5/3 JG	8
Sergeant Hans Gruenberg, 5/3 JG	6 or 7
Sr. Lt. Emil Bitsch, 8/3 JG	6
Lt. Johann-Hermann Meier, 1/52 JG	6

Soviet Pilots:
Sr. Lt. Nikolai Gulayev, 27 IAP	4
Jr. Lt. Ivan Shpak, 27 IAP	4
Sr. Lt. M.S. Vanin, 41 GIAP	4
Sr. Lt. O.V. Belikov, 88 GIAP	4

Some of these claims may be overstated. The Germans claimed 220 planes shot down in aerial combat this day, while the Second and Seventeenth Air Armies lost 189. Conversely, the Second Air Army claims 154 German planes shot down (76 of them by the 8th Guards Fighter Division) with 34 destroyed or damaged on the ground. Those 154 claimed included 25 Ju-88s, 22 He-111s, 20 Ju-87s, 66 Me-109s, 7 Do-215s, 8 Hs-126s, 1 Fw-189 and 5 Fw-190s. They also claimed 14 German aircraft damaged. The Seventeenth Air Army claimed 19 German planes shot down this day (13 Me-109s, 5 Fw-190s and 1 Fw-189) and 34 German planes destroyed on the ground.[37] The VIII Air Corps stated that they lost 19 this day, although the Luftwaffe quartermaster records indicate that they may have lost up to 27 from all causes and had 18 with severe or medium damage.[38]

The Seventeenth Air Army's attacks late in the day appear to have caused them considerable casualties. They lost at least 50 Il-2s in the attacks to bomb the German troops and crossing along the Donets.[39] Overall, the Seventeenth Air Army lost 75 planes this day.[40]

At the end of the day, the Soviets had lost 189 planes! Of those, 109 were Il-2s. This was 32% of the 337 Il-2s flown that day. The large number of them that simply "failed to return" indicates the nature of the fighting and the losses. It would appear that entire flights of these slow-moving aircraft were being eliminated. While the German VIII Air Corps over-estimated Soviet air losses at 220 in air battles and 40 due to flak, it does indicate that most of the Soviet planes were lost to air action, with up to 50 lost in the morning airfield raids (probably most from the Second Air Army) and at least 50 planes lost late in the day by the Seventeenth Air Army.

ACES AT KURSK

Overall, 2,387 German sorties were flown by the VIII Air Corps this day. This is more sorties than flown on any single day of the Battle of Britain (13 August to 31 October 1940), although with fewer planes. The two opposing Soviet air armies flew 1,778 sorties, which was more than the British Air Force ever put up during any day of the Battle of Britain and more than the Germans flew on all but one day of that battle. The bloodiest day in the Battle of Britain, "Black Thursday" (15 August) when the Germans lost 75 aircraft and the British 34, was not nearly as bloody as 5 July 1943, when almost twice as many aircraft were lost (206 airplanes). The air fight in the southern part of the Kursk bulge was of the same scale as the far more famous Battle of Britain, while, at the same time, there was a similar size operation occurring in the north!

TIME OF ACTIONS
5 July 1943

As there are not many surviving unit records for the Luftwaffe and we only accessed the Soviet air army records for the original Kursk Data Base project, there is some confusion over the timing of events for the day.

The day clearly started with a Soviet airstrike in the early morning. The Second Air Army reports indicate that they struck the German airfields from 0425 to 0430 (Moscow time). The Seventeenth Air Army states that their assault aircraft were to attack German airfields between 0400 and 0530 (Moscow time). The Germans claimed 47 planes were shot down between 0321 and 0410 (Berlin time). There were only three claims in the next hour.

After that there is no clear schedule of events. In my original Kursk book, we recorded the following air events for the ground units attached to the XLVIII Panzer Corps. They were deployed from west to east (or left to right): 332nd Infantry Division, Gross Deutschland Panzer Grenadier Division, 11th Panzer Division and the 167th Infantry Division. Action started early in the day with the 332nd Infantry Division reporting 10 Ratas over it while the Gross Deutschland reported five air attack, each with 8-12 aircraft before 0430. The XLVIII Panzer Corps reports that at 0705 the entire corps sector was under heavy attack by Soviet Il-2 ground attack planes and bombers. At 0750, the 339th Infantry Regiment (167th Infantry Division) reported that the 11th Panzer Division was suffering from an air-supported Russian counterattack. In the Gross Deutschland Division sector, it is reported at 0950 that the Soviet air force attacked the tempting concentration of tanks at the Berezovyii crossing. There were heavy losses, especially among the officers. The 11th Panzer Division reported recurring attacks on Butovo and the areas to the rear during the night and morning. The 11th Panzer Division reported seeing Soviet aircraft regularly during the morning. This included 10 aircraft between 0350-0440 and 25 Pe-2s between 0545-0725, which were attacking the vehicle assembly areas.

There were also attacks from close support aircraft from 0735 to 1003, consisting of 25 Il-2s and 16 Pe-2s. Four Soviet planes (Pe-2s and American-built Bostons) were claimed shot down by the 277th Army Flak Battalion and the 611th Motorized Flak Battalion (11th Panzer Division). Seven to ten more planes were observed by the Germans to be shot down by German fighters. The 167th Infantry Division observed three planes shot down. The Gross Deutschland Division reported that in the first half of the day (0430-1200) there were 8 to 11 aerial attacks by enemy bombers in groups of 9 to 12 aircraft (mostly Pe-2s) under fighter escorts, they bombed up to three kilometers deep. For the second half of the day (1200 to 2000) they reported air attacks in groups of 6 to 8 bombers, most escorted fighters. For the 332nd Infantry Division area they report that Soviet air activity was heavy during the entire day. The 11th Panzer Division reported during the day heavy friendly and enemy air activity. There were also reports of Soviet air activity at dusk. The left wing of the 167th Infantry Division came under heavy air attacking during the afternoon.[41]

There are similar but less complete reports for the SS Panzer Corps. They were deployed from west to east (or left to right): Adolf Hitler SS Division, Das Reich SS Division and Totenkopf SS Division. Lt. Macher with the Das Reich SS Division reported a low level air attack in the afternoon on his company. Private Kauffmann with the same division reported for the morning that the first low-level air attacks occurred by Il-2 on his antiaircraft battalion. These were a prelude to incessant air attacks on his battalion assembly area which resulted in one Il-2 shot down that as manned by only the pilot (as Kaufmann inspected the crashed airplane). The air attack let off considerably in his area during the afternoon. The SS Panzer corps reported lively Soviet air activity during the night of the 4/5th. The corps also claimed, in an unconfirmed report, that four centimeter capsules with irritant smoke candles were dropped on them. Their people had to temporarily put on gas masks. The morning attack on Berezov was preceded by an attack by 88 Stukas on those positions. Das Reich's attacks were further supported by Stuka attacks from 0700 to 0730 on the Zhuravlinyii woods and from 1100 to 1130 on the individual targets northeast of Berezov. At 1015, the VIII Air Corps sent a Stuka squadron to both the Das Reich and Adolf Hitler SS Division for employment as they directed.[42]

The Das Reich SS Division claimed eight aircraft down by its Flak Battalion (5 Il-2s and 3 Pe-2s). The Adolf Hitler SS Division reported a lot of air activity by both sides, while it received "splendid" support by stuka units. Totenkopf claimed lively Soviet air activity and strong friendly air activity too. It claimed the following shoot-downs: 1020 hours, one Il-2 by 88mm, 1030 hours, one Il-2 by 88mm, 1045 hours, one LaGG by 37mm and 1405 hours, one Il-2 by 37mm.[43]

To its right, the III Panzer Corps was deployed from north to south (or left to right): 168th Infantry Division, 6th Panzer Division, 19th Panzer Division and

7th Panzer Division. In the area of the 168th Infantry Division and 6th Panzer Division, the 6th Panzer Division reported that there were increasingly heavy Soviet air attacks along the front and the railroad. The 19th Panzer Division reported little Soviet air activity. The 7th Panzer Division, which was crossing at Solomino, reported heavy Soviet air activity with bombing attacks on the assault units during the morning. It is reported for the 7th Panzer Division that by the end of the morning, despite heavy Soviet air activity with bombing attacks on the assault units, the bridgehead was firmly established and the leading elements had advanced. Richard Rosen with the 3rd company of the 503rd Heavy Panzer Battalion, which was attached to the 7th Panzer Division, did not recall any Soviet air attacks.[44]

To the south of them was Corps Raus, consisting of only the 106th Infantry Division and the 320th Infantry Division, deployed from north to south (from left to right). The 106th Infantry Division reported that "during the whole day the sky was ruled by [Soviet] aircraft, and we suffered attacks from enemy fighters, dive bombers, and ground attack planes. The 320th Infantry Division had no air support this day, except for the called for ground attack support which arrived too late.[45]

Christer Bergstrom in his book on Kursk does indicate a partial timeline of the Soviet air actions. He has the Soviet Second Air Army conducting their early dawn attack (no specific times given). The Second Air Army then struck the XLVIII Panzer Corps area with Il-2 attacks at 0705 (Berlin time), notes air activity at 0900 (Berlin time) over the SS Panzer Corps, and then a relaxation of air activity over the XLVIII Panzer Corps at 1100 (Berlin time). At 1353 (Berlin time) there is renewed air activity over the Das Reich SS Division. At 1500 he has the 7th Panzer Division requesting fighter protection. At 1800 hours (not sure whose time) he has the Seventeenth Air Army "dispatch all available Il-2s." The German fighter group I/52nd Fighter Wing scrambled at 1820 (Berlin time) to intercept, with another plane from that group taking off at 1825.[46]

The air claims listed in the previous sidebar does not entirely support the above time line. They clearly show the dawn battle from 0321-0410 (Berlin time). They then show another round of increased German air claims from 0710-0758 (Berlin time). Whether this has anything to do with the Il-2 attacks in the XLVIII Panzer Corps area cannot be ascertained. There is also an increase in intensity from 1202-1259 (Berlin time). Finally there is clearly some very intense air activity from 1800-1910 (Berlin time). This was probably in response to the Seventeenth Air Army launching Il-2 attacks late in the day along the Donets River.

THE SOVIET MORNING AIR ATTACK ON THE XLVIII PANZER CORPS

In my original Kursk book, I noted the extensive air attacks reported by the Germans on the XLVIII Panzer Corps on the 5th. According to German accounts, the Soviet air started showing up early in the morning of the 5th. The 332nd Infantry Division reports 10 Ratas over it,[47] while Gross Deutschland reported five air attacks, each with 8-12 aircraft before 0430. At 0705 the XLVIII Panzer Corps that the entire corps sector was under heavy attack by Soviet Il-2 ground attack planes and bombers. They reported another series of attacks at 0950. The Gross Deutschland Division reported that in the first half of the day (0430 to 1200) there were 8 to 11 aerial attacks by enemy bombers in groups of 9 to 12 aircraft (mostly Pe-2s) under fighter escorts, they bombed up to three kilometers deep. For the second half of the day (1200 to 2000) they reported air attacks by groups of 6 to 8 bombers, most escorted by fighters. There were also reports of Soviet air activity at dusk.

Other reports included a report by the 332nd Infantry Division that Soviet air activity was heavy during the entire day and a report that after 0730, when the 11th Panzer Division and the 167th Infantry Division had jumped off their attack, they immediately came under heavy air attack. They requested air support. At 0750, the 339th Infantry Regiment, on the 167th Rifle Division's left, reported that the 11th Panzer Division was suffering from an air-supported Russian counterattack. The 11th Panzer Division reported recurring air attacks on Butovo and the areas to the rear during the night and morning. The 11th Panzer Division reported seeing Soviet aircraft regularly during the morning. This included 10 aircraft between 0350-0440 and 25 Pe-2s between 0545-0725, which were attacking the vehicle assembly areas. There were also attacks from close support aircraft from 0735 to 1003, consisting of 25 Il-2s and 16 Pe-02s. The 167th Infantry Division reported during the day heavy friendly and enemy air activity. In particular, during the afternoon the Soviets bombed the division left wing (339th Infantry Regiment). There was also a report by the Gross Deutschland Division that at 0950 the Soviet air force attacked the tempting concentration of tanks at the Berezovyii crossing. They reported that there were heavy losses, especially among the officers. Even with the air support the XLVIII Panzer Corps had in the afternoon, the left wing of the 167th Infantry Division came under heavy air attack during the afternoon.[48]

Four Soviet planes (Pe-2s and American-built Bostons) were claimed shot down by the 277th Army Flak Battalion and the 611th Motorized Flak Battalion (11th Panzer Division). Seven to ten more planes were observed by the Germans to be shot down by German fighters. The 167th Infantry Division observed three planes shot down. As the Second Air Army lost 114 planes on this day, it is hard not to accept these reports as being plausible.[49]

The German air was tangled up dealing with the Soviet air strikes against their bases and they had been assigned to support the SS Panzer Corps during the morning.

Therefore, there was little German air over the XLVIII Panzer Corps on the morning of the 5th. There was a lot of Soviet air over them though.

Other accounts have picked up on parts of this battle:

> The 291st ShAD operated efficiently and managed to halt the German 48th Panzer Corps....It would be safe to state that pilots from the 61st ShAP, the 291st ShAD, were the first to employ new PTAB-2.5-1.5 shape-charge bombs on the morning of 5 July when a group of Il-2s, led by Senior Lieutenant Dobkevich, managed to deliver a surprise air strike against an enemy convoy outside the village of Butovo.
>
> When recovering from run-ins, flight crew saw a great number of burning tanks and other vehicles and when retreating from the target, the group also successfully repulsed Messerschmitt attacks, shooting down one of them and taking its pilot as a prisoner of war. The divisional command decided to capitalize on the success, and air strikes delivered by aircraft from the 61st ShAP were followed by more attacks by groups from the 241st and the 617th regiments. Pilots reported killing up to fifteen enemy tanks; the use of the new bombs did not come unnoticed by the Voronezh Front command. General Vatutin noted in his night report to Stalin: "A group of eight Il-2s bombed concentrated enemy tanks with the help of new bombs. The efficiency of the bomb strike was high: twelve enemy tanks were set on fire immediately."[50]

Butovo was in the area of the 11th Panzer Division. The division at 0520 in the morning had requested more combat engineers to help clear the heavily mined areas about Butovo. At 0645 the 11th Panzer Division and the 167th Infantry division were ordered to be ready to jump off at 0730. Both divisions jumped off on schedule and immediately came under heavy air attack and requested air support. By 0900, two battalions of the 11th Panzer Division were advancing abreast toward the antitank ditches along the road south of the fork south of Cherkasskoye (between Chekasskoye and Butovo). At 0919, the II Battalion of the 110th Panzer Grenadier Regiment and the 911th Assault Gun Battalion reached the tank ditch east of the woods north of Butovo and crossed on a broad front under fire from Soviet antitank guns, mortars, artillery and automatic guns.[51]

It appears that the air attacks held up the 11th Panzer Division's advance in the morning for maybe an hour, up to an hour and a half. They lost around 13 tanks that day from all causes, including mines, breakdowns, anti-tank guns, mortars, artillery, enemy armor and of course, enemy aircraft. None were reported as totally destroyed.

There were also extensive attacks against the Gross Deutschland Division, which was tangled up in the gorge around Gertsovka. We have accounts of air activity against the Gross Deutschland. One additional account records:

THE STRIKE AT DAWN

> *Soviet air forces repeatedly attack the large concentration of tanks and infantry near the crossings at Berezovyy. There are heavy losses, especially among officers.* Grossdeutschland's *Command Post received a direct hit, killing the adjutant of the grenadier regiment and two other officers.*[52]

Bergstrom's account has a series of air combats occurring between 0730 and 1030 over the XLVIII Panzer Corps area.

These accounts seem to have generated a narrative that the XLVIII Panzer Corps was halted in the morning or considerably slowed down during the day by the Soviet air attacks. While there is no doubt that all this air activity had some effect, this is not a narrative you could determine from reading the German unit records. They do not indicate that they were halted by Soviet air attacks.

They were held up due to heavy defensive fighting at Gertsovka and Butuvo during the morning, and the continued fighting during the day trying to cross the Berezovyii ravine and to clear Cherkasskoye. The problem of mud in the Berezovyii ravine is mentioned as a significant factor is delaying the advance of the Gross Deutschland Division.[53]

There were considerable differences between the situation on 5 July 1943 faced by the XLVIII Panzer Corps and the neighboring SS Panzer Corps. Compared to the SS Panzer Corps, the XLVIII Panzer Corps had to deal with much less favorable terrain, including marshy gullies that were well defended. They did not have air support in the morning and they were being attacked by Soviet air. These were not conditions that the SS Panzer Corps faced. Yet, the argument is given that slower advance of the XLVIII Panzer Corps compared to the SS Panzer Corps was as a result of the Soviet air. The difference was, according to their figures, 16 kilometers advanced by the SS Panzer Corps compared to the 6-7 kilometers advanced by the XLVIII Panzer Corps.[54] These do not match our figures, which have the left flank of the SS Panzer Corps advancing 10.7 kilometers this day while the center of the XLVIII Panzer Corps advanced 6.3 kilometers.[55] This is not a significant difference considering that the XLVIII was in worse terrain while the SS Panzer Corps had air support in the morning. It is hard to say how much of an impact the Soviet air attacks had.

The XLVIII Panzer Corps losses for the day were similar to the SS Panzer Corps. Total losses for the three armor divisions and two infantry divisions that were part of the XLVIII Panzer Corps attack were 1,394 men killed, wounded or missing. Total losses for the three panzer grenadier divisions that made up the SS Panzer Corps was 1,220 men killed, wounded and missing.[56] While the air attacks against the XLVIII Panzer Corps were extensive, it is hard to determine their effectiveness.

In the afternoon the XLVIII Panzer Corps received German air support. Its effectiveness is also not discussed in the German records we have located.

Notes

1. Bergstrom, *Kursk*, page 33.
2. According to Hardesty and Gringberg, page 239, they attacked five airfields. Our list of airfields attacked include: 1) Pomerki, 2) Sokolniki, and 3) Mikoyanovka airfields by the Second Air Army and 1) Osnova, 2) Rogan, 3) Barvenkovo and 4) Kramatorskya airfields by the Seventeenth Air Army. The last two listed airfields attacked by the Seventeenth Air Army were in the area of Izyum and Kramatorsk, some 135 to 180 kilometers to the southeast of Kharkov.
3. According to Bergstrom, *Kursk*, page 26:

   "Further to the south-east, and around 100 kilometres to the east of the front lines at Belgorod, other *Shturmoviks* took off and formed up. At Glinev aerodrome near Novyy Oskol, 292 ShAD's 820 ShAP sent thirty Il-2s into the sky. At an airfield near Dubkiy, north-west of Valuyki, the ground personnel watched with excitement as eighteen Il-2s from 266 ShAD's 66 ShAP and 735 ShAP left the runway…

   "The 48 Il-2s of 2 VA's 266 ShAD and 292 ShAD, which were tasked to attack the two airfields Pomerki and Sokolniki north of Kharkov, were escorted by 40 Yak-1s of 247 IAP and 270 IAP.

   Dmitriy Khazanov, page 48, adds details to the account:

   "not every group reached its target at full strength—for instance, only six of the 12 Il-2s from the 735th ShAP, the 266th ShAD, took off from reasons unknown. The strength of the strike unit soon dwindled to four aircraft—one of the aircraft lost the group north-west of Kharkov when approaching the target, and another carried out an emergency landing in the friendly territory due to an engine failure.

   "A dozen attack aircraft from the 66th ShAP, flying a slight distance away, had also suffered losses over the airfield when two Il-2s had collided in mid-air. Thus, only eighteen of twenty-four aircraft from the 266th ShAD took off, and of those only fourteen reached their target."

   IAP = Fighter (Aviation) Regiment, ShAP = Assault (Aviation) Regiment, ShAD = Assault (Aviation) Division.
4. According to Bergstrom, *Kursk*, page 26:

   "At the airfield near Shumakovo, south-east of Kursk, eighteen Il-2s of 241 ShAP/291 ShAD took to the air and formed up their flight towards the south. Their target was the airfield at Mikoyanovka, some 56 kilometres south-west of Belgorod.

   "The northern attack force, 241 ShAP, was assigned with an escort composed of 18 Yak-7B from 737 IAP of the same 291 ShAD.

   "Simultaneously, twelve La-5s of 40 GIAP [V Fighter Corps] had taken off from Oboyan."
5. Also in the Kharkov area was a Wuerzburg radar (see Dmitriy B. Khazanov, *Air War Over Kursk: Turning Point in the East* (SAM Publications, Bedford, UK, 2010, page 47). This was a gun laying radar for use by their antiaircraft units. The final operational version, the Wuerzburg-Riese (Giant Wuerzburg) had a range of up to 70 kilometers (43 miles).
6. Records drawn from a listing of OKL Fighter Claims, Film C:2032/II. List was originally assembled by Tony Woods and is available through *The Luftwaffe, 1933-45* website.
7. According to Khazanov, page 47, both the Freyja and the Wuerzburg radars were capable of detecting individual aircraft at a range of 80-90 kilometers and large groups at a range of 130-150 kilometers.

   Hardesty and Grinberg, page 250, states that the: "German radar picked up the incoming Soviet aircraft at a distance of 80 to 93 miles (130 to 150 kilometers)." They also mention both the Freyja and Wuerzburg radars. They add the additional detail that: "The Germans challenged the Soviet attackers at 10,000 feet (3,000 meters), just before the later initiate their attack runs." We are not sure of the universal applicability of this last claim. See the sidebar "Summation of Times and Altitudes of Claimed German Kills, 5 July 1943."
8. Christer Bergstrom, *Black Cross, Red Star*, page 202 states that "The following air battle is well known but misunderstood in most historical accounts. It is commonly held that the German Freya radar stations,

THE STRIKE AT DAWN

which had been established at Belgorod and Kharkov in the spring of 1943, provided the Germans with an early warning which settled the fate for the Soviet airmen... Indeed, the Freya radar spotted some of the Soviet formations before the attack, and at Besonovka and Ugrim southwest of Belgorod, JG 52 was scrambled. But it was more due to the Soviet mistake to launch the Shtrumovik operations after the artillery onslaught had commenced, so that Fliegerkorps VIII had already sent out its aircraft to attack the Soviet artillery positions, That meant that fighters were also ordered into the air to cover the bombers. Thus at 0310 hours, II./JG 3 took off from Kharkov-Rogan for a free hunting missions [source: pilot's log book]. Fifteen minutes later, II. KG 55's He-111s took off from the same airfield for a bombing mission with SD 2 fragmentation bombs against Soviet artillery positions north of Belgorod [source: pilot's log book]. Oberstleutnant Walter Lehwess-Litzmann, the commander of KG 3 "Blitz," recalled, "I had just gathered by Gruppen commanders to give them the last instructions when I received an excited phone call which gave me revised orders. We were to take off immediately, although it was still dark, and attack the Soviet artillery positions." [source: book by Lehwess-Litzmann published in 1994]."

It is uncertain from Bergstrom's account if any of the 3rd Fighter Wing's two fighter groups had taken off in response to the artillery bombardment. It does not appear to have been the case with the two fighter groups of the 52nd Fighter Wing. It appears that the artillery bombardment did result in changed orders for the 3rd Bombardment Group. They were already readying for missions, so the phone call just changed their mission. So, the earlier Soviet artillery bombardment does not appear to have been a major factor in influencing the air battle on the 5th. I have also not located an account of a Freya radar set at Belgorod.

Bergstrom does states that it was "the Soviet mistake to launch the Shtrumovik operations *after* the artillery onslaught had commenced..." The artillery barrage was ordered by Marshal Zhukov, who was stationed with the Central Front, which did not conduct an air attack on German air installations that morning. It is generally considered that the bombardment occurred too soon and most of the German infantry had not yet moved forward to their attack positions, generating very few casualties (see Lawrence, *Kursk: The Battle of Prokhorovka*, pages 359-361.

9. Bergstrom, *Black Cross, Red Star*, page 202. Bergstrom's narrative is assembled from multiple sources. The 241st Assault Regiment loss report is from Soviet archival data.
10. Bergstrom, *Black Cross, Red Star*, page 203.
11. Second Air Army Operational Report #186, 2200, 5 July, 1943 (Fond: 2nd Air Army, Opis: 4196, Delo: 209, vol. 2, pages 383-389). The number of regiments in the 291st Assault Division is discussed in Table II.16. It appears that of their 20 losses this day, 12 were suffered on this mission.
12. Bergstrom, *Black Cross, Red Star*, pages 204-205. The source of losses is from unit records. Not sure it that is the total losses for the day or just the morning attack.

    Dmitriy Khazanov's book, page 48 notes that "only six of the 12 Il-2s from the 735th ShAP, the 266th ShAD, took off from reasons unknown. The strength of the strike unit soon dwindled to four aircraft—one of the aircraft lost the group north-west of Kharkov when approaching the target, and another carried out an emergency landing in the friendly territory due to an engine failure."

    He also notes that "A dozen attack aircraft from the 66th ShAP, flying a slight distance away, had also suffered losses over the airfield when two Il-2s had collided in mid-air. Thus, only eighteen of twenty-four aircraft from the 266th ShAD took off, and of those only fourteen reached their target."

    The Second Air Army records for this day record that the losses for the I Assault Corps were 22 aircraft, of which two Il-2s were downed by friendly AA fire and 13 did not return from their mission; two Yak-1s were shot down in dogfights and five did not return from their mission. Also, 12 Il-2s and two Yak-1bs made force landings on their side of the lines. The I Assault Corps consisted of nine regiments at this time.
13. Bergstrom, *Black Cross, Red Star*, page 205.
14. Second Air Army Operational Report #186, 2200, 5 July 1943((Fond: 2nd Air Army, Opis: 4196, Delo: 209, vol. 2, pages 383-389). The Second Air Army records for this day record that the losses for the I Assault Corps were 22 aircraft, of which two Il-2s were downed by friendly AA fire and 13 did not return from their mission; two Yak-1s were shot down in dogfights and five did not return from their mission. Also, 12 Il-2s and two Yak-1bs made force landings on their side of the lines.
15. Khazanov, page 49, has an account of the actions of the I and III Mixed Corps that states: "Attacks mounted by flight crews from the 17th Air Army on Barvenkovo and Kramatorskaya airfield, although not seeing any heavy losses, did not see any significant results. Some groups failed to reach their targets due to adverse weather and dropped their bombes on secondary targets, while other aircraft groups bombed dummies, set up by the Germans on the outskirts of the airfields in advance."

16. According to Bergstrom, Kursk, page 26:

    "Even further to the south, the air at Pokrovksoye was filled with noise as 17 VA's 305th ShAD sent eighteen Il-2s of 237 ShAP into the air. All sixty-six *Shturmoviks* flew against German airfields in the Kharkov area, En route to their targets, the Il-2s were joined by their fighter escort."

    "At Olshana, 25 kilomtres south-west of Porkhrovskoye, ten La-5s of 17 VA's 31 IAP took off and joined the 18 Il-2s of 17 VA's 237 ShAP which flew against Rogan air base south-east of Kharkov. This was the second early take-off that morning. Sixteen La-5s of 164 IAP had already left Olshana and, by this time, were already in the vicinity of the front lines."

    These numbers do not precisely match with my account. My account was assembled from the air records of the Second Air Army (Operational Report #186, 2200, July 5, 1943) and Seventeen Air Army (Operational Report #185, 2300, July 5, 1943). Files: Fond: Second Air Army, Opis: 4196, Delo: 29, vol. 2, Pages 384-389 and Fond: 370, Opis: 6518, Delo: 174, pages 7-8.

17. A caponier is a defensive structure.
18. Fond: 5GVIAR, Opis: 250507s, Delo: 1, list 296-351. This is one of the few regimental records we picked up during our research.
19. Bergstrom, *Black Cross, Red Star*, pages 203-204. This account was assembled from various sources.
20. Seventh Air Army Operational Report #185, 2300, July 5, 1943 (Fond: 370, Opis: 6518, Delo: 174, pages 6-8).
21. The I Mixed Corps reported no losses. The III Mixed Corps reported losing 16 Il-2s and two Yak-1s failed to return. The IX Mixed Corps lost 50 Il-2 and 7 La-5s.
22. It appears that the strength of the entire series of strikes by the Second Air Army was 143 planes: 48 IL-2s and 40 escorts (escort count from Bergstrom), 7 blocking fighters, 18 Il-2s with 18 escorts and 12 blocking fighters. The Seventeenth Air Army strengths were 64 planes (8 Il-2s and 18 escorts, 12 fighters attacking airfields, 16 Il-2s and 10 escorts (escort count from Bergstrom). The air army records did not provide a precise count of escorts in two cases, which is why the count from Bergstrom is used.

    Hardesty and Grinberg, page 239, give the strength of the strike as 296, with 100 Il-2s escorted by 94 fighters and 102 fighters blocking.

23. According to Khazanov, pages 48-49, in the morning strike the Second Air lost 20 attack aircraft while the Seventeenth Air Army lost about 15. According to accounts assembled from Bergstrom's two books, it does appear the Second Air Army's 291st Assault Division lost seven Il-2s and 3 Yak-7Bs in the morning, its 266th Assault Division lost 11 Il-2s and the Seventeenth Air Army's IX Mixed Corps lost 13 Il-2s in the morning, for a total of at least 31 Il-2s and 3 Yak-7Bs.

    According to Bergstrom, *Black Cross, Red Star*, page 205, the VIII Air Corps fighter pilots claimed 38 Soviet aircraft during their attempts to attack the German airfields at dawn. Also see the Summation of Times and Altitudes of Claimed German Kills, 5 July 1943 in this chapter which indicates that 47 Soviet planes were claimed shot down by the 3rd and 52nd Fighter Wings between 0321 and 410 (Berlin time).

    There were also other losses to the fighters. According to Khazanov, page 49, the 27th Fighter Regiment and the 40th [Guards] Fighter Regiment while they returning from their missions unexpectedly came across numerous large groups of German aircraft that were flying towards the front.

24. From Toliver and Constable, *The Blond Knight of Germany*, page 61. Obviously, some accident occurred, for the Quartermaster General of the Luftwaffe reports for 5 July that a Bf-109G-6 at Urgim flown by Krupinski "Uberschlag bei Landung infolge Ausweichen rollenden Flugzeug. Bruch 80%" (flipped over upon landing trying to avoid rolling aircraft). Krupinski was reported injured.

    On the other hand, in our interview with Krupinski in 1999, he stated that he cannot contribute anything regarding the events of 5 July, namely the warding off the Soviets' pre-emptive air attack. He says that he had been wounded on 4 July and did not participate in the sorties flown as part of *Citadel*.

    In contrast, the Senior Commander of Luftwaffe fighter claims shows Krupinski scoring a kill against a fighter at 0715 at 2,000 meters and another kill against a fighter at 1805 at 2,500 meters. An unpublished chronicle for the III/52nd claims Krupinski scored 11 kills on this day. To date, the author has not resolved this discrepancy.

    Toliver and Constable also claimed that this squadron lost six men killed or wounded this day but there is no confirming evidence in the Luftwaffe quartermaster loss reports. They record Krupinski as the only loss from the 7th squadron for the 5th (even though they record him with the 6th squadron). For this day though, the whole III Group shows three pilots killed, one missing and two injured. This may have been the basis for Toliver and Constable's claim.

THE STRIKE AT DAWN

25. Toliver and Constable, *The Blond Knight of Germany*, pages 59–62. These four kills are listed in the Senior Commander of Luftwaffe fighter claims as two Il-2s and two LaGGs. In contrast, Toliver and Constable list his kills on the 5th as four LaGGs on page 61 and as three Airacobras and a LaGG on page 297.
26. Col. (ret.) Ivan Danilovich Komarov was interviewed by Col. Fyodor Sverdlov on 19 November 1998. He remained in the war until the end, making 230 combat flights during the war. He was shot down and forced to bail out in 1944. He rose to corps commander and continued flying for five years after the war, retiring as a Colonel. He was rewarded with two Lenin Orders, two Red Banner Orders and a Red Star Order.
27. Hardesty and Grinberg, page 251, states that "At around 0500 hours, German artillery opened fire on the Soviet 6th Guard Army. Coincidental to this opening salvo, *Luftwaffe* bombers – in groups of sixty to seventy aircraft—appeared overhead, dropping explosives on the first and second lines of defense. These initial raids were intense, with perhaps as many as 400 sorties in the first hour."

    They continue with: "By 1100 hours, the II SS Panzer Corps moved forward, covered by elements of *Fleigerkorps* VIII. To challenge the *Luftwaffe* air cover, there were only two groups of VVS fighters from the 5th IAK; they offered spirited resistance, but to no avail." Some further detailed description of Soviet air actions follows. We cannot confirm the accuracy of these accounts.
28. Andrei Nikitovich Lukyanets was born in 1922 in the village of Zhulovka, Ukraine. He graduated from flight school in 1940 and started the war at the Don River as a navigator. He was interviewed 12 November 1998 by Major General G. G. Nessonov. The designation of Me-110s as the attacking plane may be in error.
29. Records drawn from a listing of OKL Fighter Claims, Film C:2032/II. List was originally assembled by Tony Woods and is available through *The Luftwaffe, 1933–45* website. Actual Soviet losses are from the Second and Seventeenth Air Armies' records.
30. Bergstrom, *Kursk*, page 33.

    The Seventeenth Air Army Operational Report #185, 2300, 5 July 1943 states that the I Mixed Corps was only involved in missions against the airfields and reconnaissance missions.

    It states that the III Mixed Corps attacked crossings and enemy troop concentrations in the Zapadnaya Bezlyudovko and Ivanovka area, in addition to attacking Barvenkovo airfield and doing reconnaissance. They flew 45 sorties for attacking enemy troops (probably all 45 Il-2 sorties flow that day) and had 16 Il-2s failed to return. The attack on Barvenkovo airfield (12 sorties) appears to have been done by fighters. They had 44 fighters conducting 93 sorties and 45 assault aircraft conducting 45 sorties. They listed for this day 12 reconnaissance sorties, 12 for attacking Barvenkovo airfield, 45 for attacking enemy troops, 62 for escort, and 9 for airfield cover (there is a math error of 2 sorties here).

    The IX Mixed Corps attacked Rogan and Osnova airfields in the morning. They flew 16 Il-2 sorties and according to Bergstrom, *Kursk*, page 34, they lost 13 Il-2s in the dawn operation. In the second half of the day they attacked enemy troop concentrations and crossing in the Solomino, Toplinka, Pristan, Pulyaevka and Ivanovka areas. They flew 107 sorties for attacking enemy troops (again, probably Il-2s). For the day they had 5 Il-2s shot down and 45 failed to return. If 13 were lost by the 305th Assault Air Division in the morning operation, then 37 may have been lost in these late afternoon operations. The Germans did claim between 1800-1910 to have shot down 50 planes and claim to have shot down another 16 planes between 1500-1800. It appears that the Seventeenth Air Army committed 152 Il-2 sorties against these crossings and troop concentrations along the Donets, losing up to 53 Il-2s in that effort. Some of these planes may have been lost on the airfield raids early in the morning or on other missions.
31. These were battle reports provided by Captain Josef Haiboeck of 1./52nd JG and Captain Johannes Wiese of 1./52nd JG. Wiese claimed six Il-2s and Il-7s (an incorrect designation) in this combat late in the day. The translated report is quoted by Bergstrom, *Kursk*, page 33. Also Obw. Walter Janke in his battle report claims the last kill of the day near Belgorod at 1910 (Berlin time). See Bergstrom, *Kursk*, pages 33-34.
32. Seventeenth Air Army Operational Report #185, 2300, July 5, 1943. Fond: 370, Opis: 6518, Delo: 174, pages 7-8. The actual wording of the sentence was: "During the second part of the day the army had orders to launch an assault aircraft attack, covered by fighters, against the enemy in the Solomino, Toplinka, Pulyaevka, Ivanovka, Ziborovka, Bezlyudovka area and destroy the crossings over the Northern Donets along the Solomino-Bezlyudovka sector."
33. Records drawn from a listing of OKL Fighter Claims, Film C:2032/II. List was originally assembled by Tony Woods and is available through *The Luftwaffe, 1933–45* website.

    The German losses are drawn from a list of German losses as reported by the Luftwaffe Quartermaster General files. This list was originally assembled by Christer Bergstrom of the *Black Cross, Red Star* series of books on the air war on the Eastern Front.

34. We gather the phrase "The fight was unsuccessful" means that no Me-109s were shot down as there are not reports from the III Mixed Corps of La-5s being shot down. The report is from 5th Guards Fighter Regiment records (Fond: 5GVIAR, Opis: 207616, Delo: 1, pages 297-301).
35. The claim is made in some books that Sr. Lt. Walter Krupinski (197 claimed kills) of the 7th squadron, 52nd Fighter Wing scored 11 kills on this day (for example see Robin Cross, page 182). This claim has not been confirmed and is hard to reconcile with his reported injury on this day.
36. Pilot claims are from Bergstrom, page 34, Khazanov, page 53, *Kursk: The Battle of Prokhorovka*, pages 1397 & 1398, and Second Air Army Operational Report #186. Gruenberg is listed as having 7 killed this day by Bergstrom and Khazanov. Vanin is listed the Second Air Army report as Guards Sr. Lt. Panin.
37. Second Air Army Operational Report #186, 2200, July 5, 1943 and Seventeen Air Army Operational Report #185, 2300, 5 July 1943. Files: Fond: Second Air Army, Opis: 4196, Delo: 29, vol. 2, Pages 384-389 and Fond: 370, Opis: 6518, Delo: 174, pages 7 - 8.
38. Bergstrom, *Kursk*, page 34.
39. This almost certainly includes 37 of the 50 Il-2s lost by the IX Mixed Corps and perhaps the seven La-5s that failed to return that day. It probably also includes 16 Il-2s from the III Mixed Corps. The III Mixed Corps also lost two Yak-1s that day.

    According to Bergstrom, *Kursk*, page 34, the Germans claimed 44 Il-2s over the Donets in the evening of 5 July, with another 12 claimed earlier in the afternoon. This is a total of 56 Il-2s shot down of which 45 "were confirmed" (under the German claiming procedures). He also states that the Seventeenth Air Army flew 200 sorties with 55 Il-2s shot down in the afternoon and evening. He gives their by unit: the 305th ShAD lost 13 Il-2s in the dawn operation, and lost 11 in the afternoon (9 from 175 ShAP and two from 955 ShAP). The 290th ShAD lost 16 out of 32 dispatched. The 306th ShAD recorded 28 aircraft and 19 crew lost.

    These figures are similar to those I have from the Seventeenth Air Army records. I have the III Mixed Corps with 16 Il-2 failed to return and the IX Mixed Corps with 5 Il-2s shot down and 45 failed to return. The 305th and 306th Assault Air Division's reported to the IX Mixed Corps, the 290th Assault Air Division reported to the III Mixed Corps.
40. The I Mixed Corps, which conducted the airfield attacks reports no losses, but does report that up to 25 planes were damaged. The III Mixed Corps report 1 Yak-1 was damaged in a dogfight.
41. Lawrence, *Kursk: The Battle of Prokhorovka*, pages 365, 370, 377, 385 and 387.
42. Lawrence, *Kursk: The Battle of Prokhorovka*, pages 391, 393 and 398.
43. Lawrence, *Kursk: The Battle of Prokhorovka*, page 398.
44. Lawrence, *Kursk: The Battle of Prokhorovka*, pages 403, 406, 407 and 410.
45. Lawrence, *Kursk: The Battle of Prokhorovka*, page 417.
46. Bergstrom, *Kursk*, pages 26-33.
47. This probably refers to night bombers, although it was also a nickname for the Polikarpov I-16 single wing fighter.
48. *Kursk: The Battle of Prokhorovka*, pages 365, 370, 377, 385 and 387.
49. *Kursk: The Battle of Prokhorovka*, page 387.
50. Khazanov, pages 51-52. This book is not footnoted nor does it have a bibliography, but the account appears to have been drawn from Soviet-era accounts. Bergstrom, *Kursk*, pages 31-32 makes a similar argument with Il-2 attacks occurring in the XLVIII Panzer Corps area at 0705, 0730 and 0900. We do not have a record of the 0900 attack.

    For the record, Bersgstrom's list of German planes and pilots lost on 5 July show four Me-109 pilots as captured or missing this day (see pages 129-130). This is Uffz. Heinz Luedtke, 8/3 JG, PQ 613, "Shot down by ground fire. Pilot later died of wounds"; Fw Emil Zibler, 9/3 JG, PQ 61182, "Belly-landed in hostile territory following air combat"; Uffz Hans Baumgart, 2/52 JG, Belgorod, "Air combat with 10 Il-2s"; and Fw Walter Knebs, 9/52 JG, Ugrim, "Shot down in air combat." Because of the areas of operations of the 3 JG compared with the 52 JG, and other accounts, if the Soviet kill claim is correct, it would most likely be Hans Baumgart, 2/52 JG.
51. See *Kursk: The Battle of Prokhorovka*, pages 377-385 and 388 for an account of the 11th Panzer Division's operations this day.
52. Bergstrom, *Kursk*, page 32. His source for this quote was author Niklas Zetterling.

53. See *Kursk; The Battle of Prokhorovka*, pages 370 and 375 for mentions of the problems of mud. For example, it states that "By 0945 only a few tanks of the Gross Deutschland Panzer Regiment had crossed the Berezovyii ravine when one Tiger broke down in the middle of the ravine and halted the entire crossing. Meanwhile, the engineers were working feverishly to construct a new crossing, but the construction material kept sinking in the deep mud" and "at 1735 the division's tanks crossing the Berezovyii ravine got stuck in mud again."
54. Bergstrom, *Kursk*, page 34.
55. See *Kursk; The Battle of Prokhorovka*, page 668. We have the LSSAH PzDrD advancing 10.7 kilometers while the GD PzGrD advances 6.3 kilometers. On the other hand, the DR SS PzGrD advanced 6.8 kilometers this day and T SS PzGrD advanced 6.7 kilometers.
56. *Kursk: The Battle of Prokhorovka*, pages 378, 388, 399 and 400.

Chapter Four

THE FIGHT FOR AIR SUPERIORITY
6 – 7 July 1943

The Russian pilot proved to be brave, but orthodox and not sufficiently skillful. One gained the impression that Russian flying crews were not sufficiently familiar with the technical aspects of flying and that they were inadequately trained. On the whole, however, the Red Air Force has caught up considerably, particularly as regards numbers. It had turned into a serious adversary.

Major General Hans Seidemann, 1947[1]

While the air fighting the previous day had definitely gone in favor of the Germans by a wide margin, you could not tell this by looking at the Secord Air Army unit records. Nor was it reflected in General Krasovskii's later post-war account.[2] The Second Air Army, which lost 114 aircraft the previous day, was claiming to have shot down 154 German planes. The Seventeenth Air Army report was far more realistic, for they claimed to have shot down only 19 planes although they had lost 75 on 5 July. While the commanders at the time probably had a more realistic understanding of the effectiveness of their forces then what was claimed, they bravely continued the fight over the next few more days.

The arrival of a cold front which brought low clouds resulted in the VIII Air Corps starting operations later in the morning than they had the previous day. The German Luftwaffe reappeared over the battlefield at around 0900.[3]

The Second Day (6 July)

During the night of 5/6 July the Soviet biplane bombers of the 208th Night Bomber Division, with the help of illumination bombs, attacked German troops in the Streletskoye-Butovo-Tomarovka area (XLVIII Panzer Corps) and in the Mikhailovka and Solomino sector (III Panzer Corps) in the area of the bridge crossings. The 208th Night Bomber Division flew 72 sorties, including a drop of 366,000 leaflets in the Tomarovka area. They were joined in their efforts by the 262nd Night Bomber and the 244th Bomber Division from the Seventeenth Air Army which attacked the areas of Ivanovka, Bezlyudovka and Korovino. They also bombed the German airfields at Rogan and Osnova. The night bomber division sent 71 sorties that hit the Germans along the Donets while 20 sorties reconnoitered and bombed the German airfields. The 244th Bomber Division sent 28 TB-3s to hit the Solomino and Ivanovka area, while four TB-3s reconnoitered German rail traffic and communications.

The Second Air Army reported that the weather that night was cloudy, with short periods of rain and a visibility of up to one kilometer. During the day it was less cloudy, with visibility up to ten kilometers.

During the day, the I Assault Corps attacked the German forces in the Streletskoye-Olkhovka-Kozmo-Demyanovka area (XLVIII Panzer Corps) and the Mikhailovka-Solomino sector (III Panzer Corps) in the area of the bridge crossings. The 291st Assault Division's Il-2s, escorted by their fighters, attacked the Germans in the Yerik-Gertsovka-Yamnoye area and the Butovo, Korovino and Vasilyevka areas. The assault units provided their own fighter escort. The I Assault Corps flew 189 Il-2 sorties and 132 Yak-1 escort sorties. This was done with 62 Il-2 and 54 Yak-1s, meaning that many planes were doing three or more sorties a day. They lost 18 planes, with 14 Il-2 and 4 Yak-1bs not returning from their missions. The 291st Assault Division flew 48 sorties with its 48 Il-2s while 16 fighters (3 Yak-1bs, 8 Yak-1s, and 3 La-5s) flew 52 escort sorties.

SOVIET SERVICEABILITY RATES

The Second Air Army provided in their correlation of air forces at the beginning of the operation a list of serviceable aircraft by type. This differs noticeably from the number reported on hand on 1 July. Just to compare:

Type	On hand, 1 July	Combat Ready, 5 July	Highest Number Flown (through 6 July)
Fighter	572	389	348
Assault	306	276	162
Bomber	117	172	70
Night Bomber	57	34	31
Reconnaissance	21	10	13
Total	1073	881	624

Readiness Rate	Based on Combat Ready Report	Based upon Number Flown
Fighter	68%	61%
Assault	90%	53%
Bomber	N/A	60%
Night Bomber	60%	54%
Reconnaissance	48%	62%
Average	82%	58%

The IV Fighter Corps patrolled in groups of six to ten aircraft in the Olkhovka-Ternovka-Gostishchevo and Teterevino-Vorskla-Kozmo-Demyanovka areas. The V Fighter Corps patrolled in the same areas and also covered their bases and troop concentrations in the near rear. The IV Fighter Corps flew 136 sorties this day with 48 La-5s, Yak-7bs and Yak-1bs. The larger V Fighter Corps flew 256 sorties this day with 92 La-5s, Yak-7bs, and Yak-1bs. The IV Fighter Corps only engaged in 15 fights this day, while the V Fighter Corps had 36. This was a more defensive posture than the previous day. Still, it ended up costing the IV Fighter Corps eight fighters that did not return from their mission while the V Fighter Corps lost 14 fighters, including two shot down in dog fights, two shot down by AA fire, and ten that did not return from their mission. Always optimistic, the V Fighter Corps claimed 60 German planes shot down while the IV Fighter Corps claimed 18. The Germans may have only lost two planes this day to enemy air.

The I Bomber Corps stood down this day while the 454th Bomber Regiment and 50th Air Reconnaissance Regiment conducted reconnaissance as far as Konotop and Kharkov with three A-20Bs and 7 Pe-2s. These missions were conducted without loss. The Second Air Army reported some minor breakdowns in cable communications.

The Seventeenth Air Army was active this day, focusing almost its entire effort against Provisional Army Kempf. The III Mixed Corps again hit the Corps Raus area and the German airfields. This included 53 Il-2 sorties with 88 fighter escort sorties against the German crossings and troops at Solomino, Ivanovka, Arkhangelskoye, Bezlyudovka, Krutoi Log and Maslova Pristan areas. Fourteen fighters struck at the Tolokonnoye airfield, claiming five planes burned and ten damaged, and at the Dudkovka airfield, claiming three Ju-52s burned and five damaged. These claims must be viewed with some suspicion. The Soviet air also attacked German vehicles along the Kharkov-Belgorod road, reconnoitered other German airfields, and four fighters tried to intercept German transport aircraft in the Kharkov area. Overall, they flew 53 assault sorties and 106 fighter sorties. This corps suffered low losses this day, losing only two Il-2s and two Yak-1s. They also lost one La-5 when their Shchenyachye airfield was bombed between 1350-1355 by four Ju-88s. Two Russians were killed and three were wounded in this raid.

The IX Mixed Corps also attacked the Solomino to Ivanovka area with some 116 Il-2 sorties and 59 fighter escort sorties. The corps aircraft also struck at Golovino airfield (five kilometers northeast of Mikoyanovka), claiming four German planes destroyed and four damaged. Again, these claims must be viewed with suspicion. This force did not get off so lightly as the III Mixed Corps, losing two La-5s and an Il-2 to German flak while 18 Il-2s did not return from their missions.

The 244th Bomber Division also used 36 of its TB-3s, with 27 fighters from the I Mixed Corps providing escort, to strike the Solomino to Bezlyudovka area.

The Soviet air force, after its heavy losses of the previous day, struggled to maintain a presence over the battlefield. Overall, the Second Air Army had managed to put up 823 sorties during the day, which was about 65% of what they did the previous day. The Seventeenth Air Army flew 462 sorties, of which at least 407 attacked targets in the VIII Air Corps area. They actually had more sorties on this day than the previous day.

SEVENTEENTH AIR ARMY ORDER OF BATTLE, 6 JULY 1943

	Base	Operational	Not Operational	Pilots
I Mixed Corps	Proyezzhaya			
288th Fighter Division	Starobelskaya	2 Yak-1		4
866th Fighter Rgt.	Peski	22 Yak-1	5 Yak-1	33
897th Fighter Rgt.	Peski	20 Yak-1	1 Yak-1	29
659th Fighter Rgt.	Polovinkino	22 Yak-1	2 Yak-1	31?
5th Guards Assault Division	Ryibentsovo			
93rd Assault Rgt.	Novo-Pskov	26 Il-2	5 Il-2	35
94th Assault Rgt.	Mokartyatino	30 Il-2	1 Il-2	33
95th Assault Rgt.	Belokurakino	32 Il-2		37
III Mixed Corps	Novo-Osinovka			
404th Ind. Squadron	Novo-Osinovka	5 U-2	1 U-2	9
207th Fighter Division	Aleksandrovka			
5th Guards Fighter Rgt.	Shchenyachye	18 La-5	4 La-5	33
814th Fighter Rgt.	Uchebnyii Sovkhoz	12 Yak-1/7b	9 Yak-1/7b	36
867th Fighter Rgt.	Bulatselovka	12 Yak-1/7b	3 Yak-1/7b	33
290th Assault Division	Kurilovka	1 Il-2		2
775th Assault Rgt.	Kurilovka	25 Il-2	2 Il-2	33
625th Assault Rgt.	Zatishnoye	18 Il-2	8 Il-2	23
299th Assault Rgt.	Manino	27 Il-2	5 Il-2	32
IX Mixed Corps	Pokrovskoye			
418th Ind. Squadron	Pokrovskoye	3 U-2	1 U-2	3
295th Fighter Division	Olshana	2 La-5		3
31st Fighter Rgt.	Budennovka	20 La-5	8 La-5	26
116th Fighter Rgt.	Olshanyi	22 La-5	6 La-5	24
164th Fighter Rgt.	Nizhnyaya Duvanka	13 La-5	5 La-5	20
305th Assault Division	Nizhnyaya Duvanka	1 U-2		4
175th Assault Rgt.	Olshanyi	24 Il-2		36
237th Assault Rgt.	Pokrovskoye	16 Il-2	1 Il-2	18
955th Assault Rgt.	Rayevka	15 Il-2		19
306th Assault Division	Nizhnyaya Duvanka			
672nd Assault Rgt.	Peschanka	33 Il-2	1 Il-2	35
951st Assault Rgt.	Lantratovka	27 Il-2	2 Il-2	32
995th Assault Rgt.	Budennovka	20 Il-2	3 Il-2	21

	Base	Operational	Not Operational	Pilots
244th Bomber Division	Rogovo	3 U-2		3
449th Bomber Rgt.	Mozhyakovka	24 TB-3		24
860th Bomber Rgt.	Shramovka	17 TB-3	1 TB-3	20
861st Bomber Rgt.	Rogovo	25 TB-3		32
260th Bomber Rgt.	Poddubnoye	10 TB-3	1 TB-3	20
262nd Night Bomber Division	Zapadnoye	2 U-2		3
719th Night Bomber Rgt.	Krinichnyii	8 R-5	1 R-5	22
97th Gds Night Bomber Rgt.	Kovalevka	19 U-2		24
370th Night Bomber Rgt.	Vasiltsevka	19 U-2		31
993rd Night Bomber Rgt.	Ponamarevka	14 U-2		29
39th Reconnaissance Rgt.	Velshanyi	18 Pe-2	1 Pe-2	14
50th Reconnaissance Rgt.	Velshanyi	2 Pe-2	1 Pe-2	4
403rd Ind. Squadron	Ivanovka	7 U-2	3 U-2	11
371st Transport Rgt.	Stepki	14 U-2		22
Totals		650	81	903

With the Soviet air force less present, the German VIII Air Corps was now free to concentrate on the second Soviet defensive line. They again provided all their support to the XLVIII and SS Panzer Corps, with the focus being on the SS Panzer Corps. The Soviet second echelon antitank gun and artillery concentrations were attacked continually. The III Group of the 55th Bombardment Wing sent 21 He-111 sorties against Novyiye Lozyi and 16 against Prokhorovka.

The German fighters and flak were again extremely successful, with the Soviet Second Air Army losing 50 aircraft, including 28 fighters and 22 Il-2s. The Seventeenth Air Army lost 30 aircraft this day, including 21 Il-2s. Of those, it appears that all but two were lost in the Belgorod area (an R-5 and an La-5 on the ground). The Germans lost only seven aircraft this day. Unlike the previous day, this included no fighters, but did include six Ju-87s and one Ju-88.[4] Five of the Ju-87s were lost to antiaircraft fire. With only two planes lost to enemy air, it appears that the Soviet air force was not very aggressive or effective on this day. The loss of 35 fighters without any fighter losses on the part of the Germans is a lop-sided result that is hard to explain. With 78 Soviet losses to seven German losses, it appears that the Germans maintained their ten-to-one kill ratio. The Germans claimed 74 kills for this day.[5]

The Germans conducted 1,686 sorties this day, which was only about 70% of what they had done on the 5th. There were 77 reconnaissance missions (104% compared to the 5th), 323 bombing missions (60% compared to the 5th), 793 stuka (74%), 240 assault (72%) and 253 fighter missions (68%).

THE FIGHT FOR AIR SUPERIORITY

During the day the Germans launched 1,356 ground attack type sorties on the 6th compared to 442 ground attack type sorties by the Soviets.[6]

The Soviet air ace, Nikolai Dunayev of the 279th Fighter Squadron (scored 24 kills during the war), killed his first fighter on this day, as he recounts:[7]

Our regiment was in air fights since the morning of 5 July, 1943. My squadron was there only from 6 July. To the north from Belgorod we started an air fight with five Messerschmitt 110s. It is hard to describe an air fight, because air fights are usually very short. It was the first time I destroyed a German fighter. I went straight on his front, firing constantly. I don't remember how I dodged it. When I returned back to the aerodrome, mechanics found three shell holes and twelve bullet holes in my Yak.

On 7 July our squadron intercepted a large group of German bombers. Our second squadron was supposed to take care of their bombers. The Germans achieved their objective but lost two Messerschmitts while our own losses were two planes. Our squadron managed to destroy four bombers. It was difficult to say during the combat who completed the destruction of a plane, or who destroyed one at once. We were too busy to notice that. We were low on gas and returned back to the aerodrome without further loss.

Our squadron had three or four more flights on that day. I must say that some German fighter pilots were trying to avoid one-against-one fights. They preferred to have three fighters attacking one of our planes. Sometimes they succeeded and our pilot got killed. More often three of our planes attacked this group of planes from different directions. Because of the impossibility of free maneuver, we attacked the German planes head on. We were trying to destroy bombers flying in large groups. Two of our planes tried to shoot the lead plane, which we often succeeded. After that the formation of bombers usually got destroyed and made it easier for us to pursue the remaining planes. It seems to me that during the first days of the battle (5–9 July) the number of the German fighters exceeded the number of our fighters, but the German fighters were not very tough. A lot of time they quickly dropped bombs at any random place (probably they were afraid of our antiaircraft) and returned back to the aerodrome in a hurry. During the air fights of 6–17 July, I gained good experience and learned the lesson: don't maneuver, don't look for a good position, just go straight onto the enemy. Following this rule, I destroyed nine German planes singularly and three planes together with the pilots of my squadron. On 17 July . . . a shell from a German fighter went into my left knee. I don't remember how I landed the plane. Then there was an amputation, hospitals, and demobilization. I worked at the electric shop for invalids for the rest of my life.

> "A Whole Soviet Tank Corps had been beaten back by Luftwaffe Attacks"

Christer Bergstrom, who has done some extensive research on the Eastern Front air war, makes the statement in his book for 6 July that "a whole Soviet tank corps had been beaten back by Luftwaffe attacks."[8] He details this operation in his narrative where he states in part: "The 2nd Guards Tank Corps struck in the evening...the Soviet corps mustered about 200 tanks....Major Alfred Druschel's SchG 1 scrambled against the Soviet armored columns. The Hs 129s of 4.(Pz)/SchG 1 and JG 51s Panzerjaegerstaffe dived down on the Soviet tanks. Meanwhile, I./SchG 1's Fw 190s...attacked the Soviet troops...These air attacks completely disrupted the intended counterattack and inflicted heavy losses on the 2nd Guard Tank Corps.[9]

The operations of the II Guards Tank Corps are discussed in depth in my book. On 6 July, the II Guards Tank Corps cross the Lipovyii Donets in the area of Novyiyi Lozyi at 1700 (Moscow time). They then attacked in the direction of Krapivinskiyi Dvoryi and the Smelo k Trudu Kolkhoz. According to the corps accounts, "Overcoming the resistance of superior enemy forces, and being subjected to intensive artillery and mortar bombardment, tank fire and enemy air attacks, the corps' units by 2000 drove the enemy out of Smorodino, Kamenskii, Glushinskii and the Smelo k Trudu Kolkhoz, where it occupied a circular defense and continued to trade fire with the enemy."

The Soviet advance succeeded in penetrating up to Smorodino and the ravine west of Soshenkov. The II Guards Tank Corps reported for the evening that it held the line from Smorodino to Glushinskii to the Smelo k Trudu Kolkhoz to three kilometers southwest of Soshenkov. According to the Soviet records, the II Guards Tank Corps lost 28 tanks this day (including 9 Churchills) and 191 men this day.

This advance forced the intervention of the armored battle groups of both the Das Reich and Totenkopf SS Divisions, and resulted in a German estimate of 11 Soviet tanks lost. As evening fell, the Soviet forces retreated from the German counterattack to the area of Soshenkov and Nepkhayevo. According to the Soviet records, this withdrawal was ordered by Vatutin (Voronezh Front commander) as a result of its exposed position. The corps was pulled back to the eastern bank of the Lipovyii Donets.[10] A map from the II Guards Tank Corps is provided opposite.

This is a far cry from a "whole Soviet tank corps...beaten back by Luftwaffe attacks." By their own account, the Soviet tank corps was subjected to "intensive artillery and mortar bombardment, tank fire and enemy air attacks. The German Das Reich and Totenkopf SS Divisions estimated they killed 11 tanks. The tank corps lost 28 tanks out of their initial strength of 187. The independent 96th Tank Brigade, with at least 51 tanks, was also involved in this attack, bringing their totals to above 200 tanks. The 96th Tank Brigade reported no losses for this day. There is no question that air power played an important part in this battle. The II Guards Tank Corps reports that German aircraft, in groups of 40 bombers, bombed the corps units continuously day and night. But it is clear that even with that, the Soviet tank losses due to German air attacks probably did not exceed a dozen. The Corps was not "beaten back by Luftwaffe attacks."

The air historian in question has done considerable, and often unique, research into the air war in the east. But these types of errors undermine the good work that he has done. The problem is that he consistently overrates and overemphasizes the effects of the air battle on the ground campaign. It is a bias that distorts his work. He states this bias with the statement early in his book "In recent years, certain accounts have attempted to downplay the accomplishments of aviation against armor during the Battle of Kursk. However, as this volume will show, that is an exaggeration just as large as the claims made by the anti-tank fliers."[11] Here we have seen this bias completely distort the account of a battle. The Battle of Kursk has suffered already from people distorting the true story for the sake of supporting some agenda. It would be best if people stuck with just the facts.

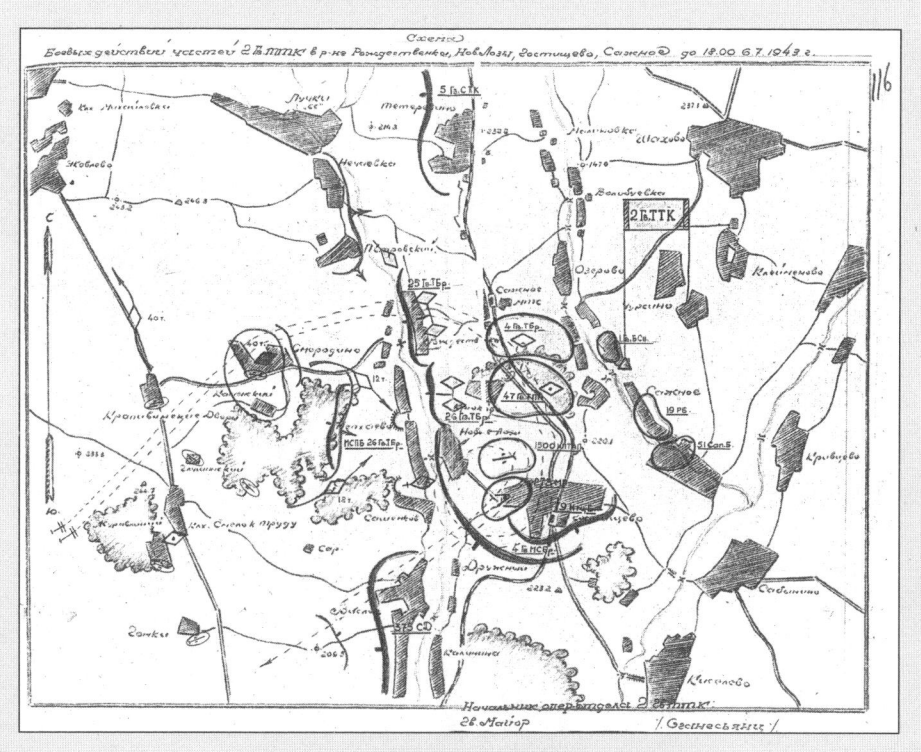

II Guard Tank Corps Map for 1800, 6 July 1943.

The major areas of dispute with Christer Bergstrom are:

1. The impact of the air attacks on the morning of 5 July 1943 against the XLVIII Panzer Corps
2. The air attacks against the II Guards Tank Corps on 6 July 1943.
3. The air attacks against the II Guards Tank Corps on 8 July 1943.
4. The air attacks against the III Panzer Corps on 9 July 1943.
5. Bombing raids against German airfields on 10 July 1943.
6. The air attacks against the V Guards Tank Army on 12 July 1943.

There are also a number of lesser disputes.[12] The usual procedure in history books is to simply state your case and ignore the other contradictory writings. But, as Christer Bergstrom's work is significant and done in considerable depth, I am unfortunately forced to address the major differences. Sometimes this is in a sidebar, sometimes it is in rather extended footnotes. This is unfortunate as Mr. Bergstrom has always been gracious and supportive in my interactions with him over the last two decades.

The Third Day (7 July)

The night remained the one time that both sides shared the airspace. During the night of 6/7 July the Luftwaffe conducted 64 sorties, making nuisance raids on Soviet reserves and road movements. They had six bomber sorties attack the railroad stations along the stretch from Kastornoye to Kursk and Volokonovka to Kastornoye. They claimed hits on four intermediate railroad stations. This nightly raid of around a half dozen bombers on the Soviet rail net would continue for almost every night of the offensive, with limited results. They also sent five bomber sorties which attacked a truck column in the area west of Prokhorovka, and 50 harassing bombers which attacked the villages and vehicle traffic to the southeast and east of Belgorod. The German night reconnaissance reported considerable convoy traffic.

NIGHT LANDING

Lieutenant Sergei Skvortsov of the 16th Guards Air Regiment of the long-range aviation recalls:[13]

> At night, on 6 July, 1943, when our regiment flew out to bomb the German tanks located to the south of Belgorod approaching the front from the reserve. According to the intelligence data, there were several kilometers to the target. I was lowering down and then I saw the tanks. We started

bombing. After the first attack three tanks caught on fire, after second and third attack—three more tanks caught on fire. We could not see if there were any destroyed tanks. When it was the time to fly back, a large antiaircraft shell hit the left engine of my plane. I thought that we could manage to get to our airport even using one engine. My plane could barely fly. I counted every second. The altitude and speed were dropping, but I could not do a thing about it. Then all of a sudden we came under fire from German antiaircraft artillery, the cabin was filling up with smoke. It would take one minute to fly to the front line. The German antiaircraft started shelling us again. The engine then stalled and the plane started falling down. Thud, noise, scratching sound of the fuselage against the ground . . . I and three other crew members got out of the plane. Only our navigator was wounded. The plane caught on fire. Carrying the navigator on our hands, we ran about 30 meters from the plane, the gas tanks exploded. We had our guns ready when we saw soldiers running towards us. It turned out that they were our soldiers, thank God! In two days we returned back to our airport. Our colleagues thought we were killed. In a day we took a spare bomber and flew out again. We could see the German tanks very well under the moonlight. Our strikes were precise. Our bombers set 12 tanks on fire and destroyed probably another dozen tanks. We returned back safely. One of our planes was destroyed by German fighters. During the battle I made several night flights with my squadron bombing the enemy's troops. I think we bombed the right places because there was massive antiaircraft fire at us. We flew up to high altitude and managed to dodge the fire.

SECOND AIR ARMY FORCES
7 July 1943

	On-hand, July 1	Largest Number Flown this Day
I Assault Corps	206 Assault	66 Il-2
	82 Fighters	54 Yak-1b
I Bomber Corps	117 Bombers	0 Pe-2
IV Fighter Corps	184 Fighters	30 Yak-7b, 36 La-5
V Fighter Corps	278 Fighters	11 Yak-1b, 17 Yak-7b, 48 La-5
291st Assault Division	100 Assault	59 Il-2
	28 Fighters	13 Yak-1, 13 Yak-7b, 4 La-5
208th Night Bomber Division	57 Night Bombers	26 U-2, 5 R-5, 1 Medium Bomber
50th Air Reconnaissance Regiment	7 Pe-2	
454th Bomber Regiment	21 Reconnaissance	3 Bostons
272nd Independent Army Squadron		

ACES AT KURSK

The Second Air Army continued its attacks in the XLVIII Panzer Corps area, with the 208th Night Bomber Division flying some 83 sorties and bombing in the area of Cherkasskoye-Streletskoye-Berezov and Vorskla-Byikovka-Voznesenki. The Seventeenth Air Army's 262nd Night Bomber Division continued its single plane attacks against the troops and crossings at Solomino, Toplinka, Pulyaevka, Orovino and Bezlyudovka. They also made night bombing attacks on Rogan airfield and conducted reconnaissance. The 262nd Night Bomber Division was making a major effort now, with its 45 U-2s launching more than three sorties a night (149 sorties) while the seven R-5s were flying two missions a night. They were again joined by the 244th Bomber Division which made 29 TB-3 sorties on the Solomino-Ivanovka-Bezlyudovka area, while five TB-3s reconnoitered the German rail traffic, station activity, and other rear targets.

There was also night bombardment provided by the Long Range Aviation force (the ADD), which are reported to have dispatched 163 bombers to attack the German rear areas north and northwest of Belgorod. These included the four-engine Pe-8s with their large bomb loads.[14] This would put them in the SS Panzer Corps and XLVIII Panzer Corps areas.

The Second Air Army reports the weather for the night as mostly clear, with clouds in some places. It was clear during the first part of the day, with some cloudiness during the second. Visibility was up to 15 kilometers.

The Soviet Second Air Army continued to focus its efforts on the XLVIII Panzer Corps and the Adolf Hitler SS Division. The I Assault Corps launched 120 Il-2 sorties, escorted by fighters, at German tanks in the Vorskla-Olkhovka-Byikovka area. These were certainly protected by the 123 Yak-1b sorties flown. There were also eight Il-2 sorties that conducted armed reconnaissance at dawn and dusk against the German tank concentrations near the Donets crossing in the Mikhailovka-Solomino sector (III Panzer Corps) and also the Butovo-Cherkasskoye-Dragunskoye area (XLVIII Panzer Corps).[15] The I Assault Corps appears to have maintained itself forward and in action, with some nine Il-2s and four Yak-1bs lost. These appear to have been mostly lost to German fighters.

The 291st Assault Division attacked the Gertsovka-Butovo-Cherkasskoye area (3rd Panzer Division) and Lukhanino-Berezovyi-Krasnyi Pochinok area (Gross Deutschland Division). This effort included 82 Il-2 sorties and 122 fighter escort sorties. They lost four Il-2s and six fighters this day.

One is left with the impression that the Soviet air efforts seemed to be obsessively concerned with attacking tank concentrations. While tanks are high value targets, they are also extremely difficult to kill from the air. On the other hand, other targets, such as bridges, convoy routes, and infantry forces, appear to have had a lower priority. Furthermore, unlike the German Air Force, there is not much indication that this air support was directed in coordination with the ground battle. Therefore, the shock and disruption effect of air attacks was not maximized. It was the close coordination of the German air with the ground attack that made it so valuable. The Soviet air, instead of being used as a close support weapon, appears to have been used for general disruption and attrition. This further weakened their value.

The IV Fighter Corps, in groups of 6 to 12 planes, covered the battle and the Soviet tank concentrations in the Dragunskoye-Belenikhino-Gostishchevo area (the II and V Guards

THE FIGHT FOR AIR SUPERIORITY

Tank Corps). This was a more passive and defensive role for the corps. Still, their losses were eight La-5s this day, the same as the previous day. The V Fighter Corps, in groups of six to ten planes, also covered the battlefield and the concentration of the Soviet tank corps in the Prokhorovka-Kochetovka-Belenikhino area (V Guards Tank Corps) and the Verkhopenye-Pushkarnoye-Dragunskoye areas (III Mechanized Corps). This more passive mission still resulted in the loss of 12 fighters, similar to their loses the previous day. Overall, the IV Fighter Corps flew 136 sorties this day with La-5s and Yak-7bs while the V Fighter Corps flew 238 mostly with La-5s. Even with their defensive missions, the two fighter corps reported 47 dogfights this day (compared to 61 on the 5th and 51 on the 6th) and claimed 85 German planes shot down (compared to 135 on the 5th and 78 on the 6th).[16]

The I Bomber Corps, like the previous day, did not engage in combat and remained in reserve. The Soviets were holding it back until they could properly protect it. The 454th Bomber Regiment continued its reconnaissance work with the Bostons while the 50th Air Reconnaissance Regiment used Pe-2s to check the approaches to the battlefield and check the location of German airfields. They continued to have minor communications problems with their cable communications. This would be the case for the following two days.

The Seventeenth Air Army continued to provide support for the Seventh Guards Army. The III Mixed Corps struck German airfields with 14 fighters, claiming a hard-to-believe 25 German planes destroyed on the ground. This effort included blocking the Tolokonnaya and Boldyirevka airfields and attacking the Rogan and Boldyirevka airfields. According to one account, due to a navigational error, the Il-2s attacked Varvarovka instead of Rogan.[17] They also launched 56 Il-2 sorties against German troops' escorted by 156 fighter sorties. These operations were with only five losses, including two Il-2s. The IX Mixed Corps again attacked the troops and crossings over the Donets in the Solomino, Ivanovka and Bezlyudovka areas, with 100 Il-2 sorties and 91 escort sorties. These attacks came throughout the day, as these 100 Il-2 sorties were generated with only 40 operational Il-2s. They also used 50 fighters to cover the Seventh Guards Army's troops and four fighters for reconnaissance up the Donets. The IX Mixed Corps again took the brunt of the losses with 26 Il-2s and four La-5s failing to return.

Their opponent appears to have been elements of 3rd Fighter Wing. Early in the morning Major Wolfgang Ewald, commander of III Group, along with a dozen or more Me-109s from the II and III Groups encountered a group of Il-2s. In a running battle that went from 0345 to 0414 (Berlin time) they claimed 12 shot down.[18]

The 244th Bomber Division again attacked during the day, with 34 TB-3s bombing Solomino, Toplinka, Pristen, Maslovka, and Maslova Pristen. They were again escorted by 43 fighters from the I Mixed Corps. The division lost three TB-3s. The I Mixed Corps also sent 40 fighters to cover the Seventh Guards Army. They lost three Yak-1s this day, probably due to flak fire.

The Soviet air force continued the contest the air space over the battlefield with limited success. The German VIII Air Corps flew 1,829 sorties this day. Their bombers, dive bombers and ground attack units attacked throughout the day ahead of the German armored spearheads in rolling waves of attacks. This was mostly in front of the SS Panzer Corps and elements of the XLVIII Panzer and III Panzer Corps. Their attacks also covered the east flank of the SS Panzer Corps. They struck at Soviet tank assembly areas, battery positions, and vehicle columns. This resulted in significant claims against the Soviet armor.

SEVENTEENTH AIR ARMY ORDER OF BATTLE
7 July 1943

	Base	Operational	Not Operational	Pilots
I Mixed Corps	Proyezzhaya			
288th Fighter Division	Starobelskaya	2 Yak-1		4
866th Fighter Rgt.	Peski	22 Yak-1	3 Yak-1	33
897th Fighter Rgt.	Peski	19 Yak-1	2 Yak-1	22
659th Fighter Rgt.	Polovinkino	22 Yak-1	2 Yak-1	31
5th Guards Assault Division	Ryibentsovo			
93rd Assault Rgt.	Novo-Pskov	26 Il-2	5 Il-2	35
94th Assault Rgt.	Mokartyatino	30 Il-2	1 Il-2	33
95th Assault Rgt.	Belokurakino	32 Il-2		37
III Mixed Corps	Novo-Osinovka			
404th Ind. Squadron	Novo-Osinovka	5 U-2	1 U-2	9
207th Fighter Division	Aleksandrovka			
5th Guards Fighter Rgt.	Shchenyachye	19 La-5	2 La-5	33
814th Fighter Rgt.	Uchebnyii Sovkhoz	20 Yak-1/7b	11 Yak-1/7b	39
867th Fighter Rgt.	Bulatselovka	4 Yak-1/7b	3 Yak-1/7b	30
290th Assault Division	Kurilovka	1 Il-2		2
775th Assault Rgt.	Kurilovka	15 Il-2	11 Il-2	32
625th Assault Rgt.	Zatishnoye	12 Il-2	10 Il-2	19
299th Assault Rgt.	Manino	27 Il-2	5 Il-2	32
IX Mixed Corps	Pokrovskoye			
418th Ind. Squadron	Pokrovskoye	3 U-2	1 U-2	3
295th Fighter Division	Olshana	1 La-5		2
31st Fighter Rgt.	Budennovka	19 La-5	8 La-5	26
116th Fighter Rgt.	Olshanyi	16 La-5	7 La-5	23
164th Fighter Rgt.	Nizhnyaya Duvanka	12 La-5	8 La-5	19
305th Assault Division	Nizhnyaya Duvanka	1 U-2		4
175th Assault Rgt.	Olshanyi	18 Il-2	6 Il-2	25
237th Assault Rgt.	Pokrovskoye	10 Il-2	4 Il-2	17
955th Assault Rgt.	Rayevka	8 Il-2	2 Il-2	17
306th Assault Division	Nizhnyaya Duvanka	1 U-2		2
672nd Assault Rgt.	Peschanka	19 Il-2	1 Il-2	21
951st Assault Rgt.	Lantratovka	20 Il-2	2 Il-2	23
995th Assault Rgt.	Budennovka	13 Il-2	3 Il-2	14

THE FIGHT FOR AIR SUPERIORITY

	Base	Operational	Not Operational	Pilots
244th Bomber Division	Rogovo	3 U-2		3
449th Bomber Rgt.	Mozhyakovka	24 TB-3		24
860th Bomber Rgt.	Shramovka	17 TB-3	1 TB-3	20
861st Bomber Rgt.	Rogovo	21 TB-3	2 TB-3	31
260th Bomber Rgt.	Poddubnoye	11 TB-3		22
262nd Night Bomber Division	Zapadnoye	2 U-2		2
719th Night Bomber Rgt.	Krinichnyii	6 R-5	3 R-5	22
97th Gds Night Bomber Rgt.	Kovalevka	19 U-2		24
370th Night Bomber Rgt.	Vasiltsevka	19 U-2		32
993rd Night Bomber Rgt.	Ponamarevka	14 U-2		14
39th Reconnaissance Rgt.	Velshanyi	17 Pe-2	2 Pe-2	14
50th Reconnaissance Rgt.	Velshanyi	2 Pe-2	1 Pe-2	4
403rd Ind. Squadron	Ivanovka	6 U-2	3 U-2	11
371st Transport Rgt.	Stepki	14 U-2		22
Summation		572	110	832

This was the first successful use of the Ju-87 G-1 armed with the 37mm guns against armor.[19] Hans-Ulrich Rudel decided that with the large tank engagements, this was a chance to try out this vulnerable plane, even though the Soviets were protected by antiaircraft. Rudel reasoned that the attacks he was making were close enough to the German lines, that unless he took a direct hit, he would be able to crash-land on his side of the lines. Using a flight of Stukas armed with bombs to support the attack and with him in one of the new tank-busting Stukas, Rudel claimed 12 tanks killed this day. This success led to a call for all the 37mm armed Stukas to be assembled for the Kursk battle and an antitank squadron of Ju-87 G-1s was formed and placed under Rudel's operational command. Meanwhile, as expected, the tank busting Ju-87 had to be repaired because of antiaircraft damage.[20] It is not known whether any other Ju-87 G-1s were used in combat during the offensive in the south, but this does not appear to be the case.[21]

Seidemann also claimed that the Germans destroyed an armored train at Teterevino. At this point, because of the problems the III Panzer Corps was having, some of the VIII Air Corps forces were diverted for the first time to support the III Panzer Corps. The III Group of the 55th Bombardment Wing sent 40 of its sorties to support the XLVIII Panzer Corps and 18 to support the SS Panzer Corps. This included operations over Krasnaya Dubrova and Malyie Mayachki, where they came under antiaircraft fire. In the afternoon, German reconnaissance identified extensive Soviet movement along the Belgorod to Kursk railway and in the woods and localities east of there. This may well have been observation of the II Guards Tank Corps, V Guards Tank Corps and Sixty-ninth Army.

The Soviet air force continued to resist on this day, resulting in continued high losses for them. The Second Air Army flew 839 sorties this day, while the 17th Air Army continued to bravely provide additional support with an additional 588 sorties. The Germans put up 297 fighter sorties this day while the two opposing air armies provided 999 cover and escort missions. Even in the face of this uneven odds fight, the Germans only lost 10 planes this day, including four Me-109s, while the Second Air Army lost 30 fighters and 13 Il-2s and the Seventeenth Air Army lost 28 Il-2s and six La-5s. This was an eight-to-one exchange, with the loss of 58 Soviet fighters for four Me-109s being hard to explain.

During this day the Germans launched 1,444 ground attack type sorties compared to 400 ground attack type sorties by the Soviets.

An Assessment of the Soviet Air Force

The Soviet air force, over the course of three days, had lost 342 airplanes compared to 36 German planes lost. Among the fighters, it was 16 German Me-109s lost compared to 193 Yak-1s, Yak-7s and La-5s. In defense of Soviet engineering, the Soviet fighters were good planes. They were certainly capable of providing a good fight for an Me-109. The Soviet Il-2s, of which 186 had been lost, were not slower nor more vulnerable than the Ju-87, of which only six had been lost. The difference here was not in weapon quality, but training and doctrine. The Germans were clearly dominating the skies over Russia with their superior skill and tactics.

AIR SUPPORT

Senior Lieutenant Ivan Kormiltsin, a squadron commander of the 610th Assault Regiment, 226th Assault Division, Second Air Army, recalls his story.[22] This strike at Syirtsevo could have occurred on either 6 or 7 July.

> Since June 1943, our regiment was at the field aerodrome located to the east from Kursk. When the massive German attack began on 5 July, my squadron flew three times to assault German tanks northwest of Belgorod. We had two air combats. Since fighters accompanied us, we successfully accomplished our tasks. I would like to tell about the combats that occurred on 6 July. On this day, as the regiment commander warned me, a column of about 200 tanks attacked our tank units along the road to the town of Oboyan. Our goal was to stop them. My squadron was supposed to attack the tanks to the south from the

large village of Syirtsevo. A fighter squadron accompanied us during our first flight. As we were approaching the target, 12 Messerschmitts attacked us. The fighters started the air fight with them, but about five Messerschmitts attacked the planes of my squadron. We fought back for about 15 minutes, lost two Il-2s, which I planned on using as a cover. Our fighters shot down two Messerschmitts. We managed to reach the targeted tank column, which was being followed by armored carriers. We fired at them with antitank missiles and bombs. I cannot say how many tanks we destroyed, because our second squadron was attacking ahead of us. However, I could clearly see some fire on the ground—it was burning tanks and armored carriers. We repeated the attack in two hours. We were lucky this time. We did not have the fighters with us this time. They were fighting near their aerodromes. Ten "Messers" attacked us. They destroyed two attack planes, as they say 'without a peep'. I arranged the remaining planes in a circle and we started a hard air fight. I went straight towards the leading fighter and destroyed it with a long burst of fire. I saw him dropping to the ground like a burning torch. My friends destroyed another fighter. The other Germans turned away, which allowed me to bring my seven planes to attack the tanks. I guess that the German antiaircraft was destroyed by our artillery, so our bombing was a success. Meanwhile, the enemy tanks moved a bit forward. This time I could clearly see that we put on fire four tanks and two armored carriers. On the way back to the aerodrome, my plane, which was the leading one, was attacked by two Fokke-Wulfs. The FokkeWulfs were new fighters, which had a very high speed and maneuverability. I had never encountered them before. I guess I destroyed one of them, but suddenly, I received a hail of lead on my plane and it caught fire. I jumped out of the plane with a parachute and landed on our territory. I was wounded. There were hard fights all around there. Hiding in grain fields and small ditches, I returned to my aerodrome in a day. Everyone there thought that I was already dead.

On the 9th of July, I took another plane and attacked the German tanks with a squadron of six planes in the area located to the northwest from the town of Syirtsevo. Later on in the evening we attacked southwest from Belgorod. Six fighters accompanied us. On my way to an enemy aerodrome, I was lightly wounded in my right side, a fragment from an anti-aircraft shell. I put a bandage on the wound, made from whatever I had on hand, and continued commanding my planes, clustering the fire on a group of Messers sitting on the ground. We put on fire at least 10 of them.

I stayed in combat. The regiment main staff said that from 5 July to the 10th my squadron made 250 combat missions, destroyed at least

> 20 German tanks and about 15 German planes. During one of my next flights an anti-aircraft shell hit the right side of my plane. The wing was partially destroyed; I could hardly handle the plane. I was thinking to myself if I should just drop it on the tank column. I jettisoned all the missile and bombs at once, but I felt another strike to the same side of the plane. The plane was almost impossible to handle, but somehow I dragged it to our aerodrome. The fighter who attacked me, decided probably to finish me, went around me to the back of the plane, but was destroyed by my friend's plane. My plane spun and fell on its wing on the ground while it was still spinning. A direct shock did not occur. Probably my skill helped—I was at war from the beginning of 1942. My gunner and I were thrown out of the plane by the shock of the landing. I was young and got well fast. As we say, everything healed like on a dog [meaning "quickly"]. I spent a week at the hospital and got back to combat by the beginning of our counterattack.
>
> I was at war until the victory. I have a "chest full of rewards," as they say. When I think about the combat, most often I think about our tank attacks near the town of Oboyan, and the true heroism of the pilots of my squadron. I treasure my pilot diary. It says that I destroyed 68 tanks, about 500 cars and 40 armored carriers during the war. I am very proud of it.

The Soviet air force had started this battle with well over 1,000 aircraft ready-for-action. With a quarter of them shot down, and certainly many more damaged and therefore not ready-for-action, the Soviet air power was beginning to fade. Their sortie rate per plane went up on this day, so they were able to maintain a similar level of activity with fewer planes, but this higher level of activity was certainly going to result in a further decline in serviceability. After three days of fighting, the Soviet air force had reached the limits of what it could do with its current strategy. On the first day, its loss rate per sortie was over 11%! On the 6th and 7th it shifted downwards to 6%, and from there on remained below 6% a day, with the Soviet aircraft taking a more conservative approach compared to the first day of the Battle of Kursk.

It appeared to Seidemann that the "great blood-letting" of 5 July had shocked the Soviet air force into a much more conservative stance. As Seidemann notes in 1947, "At any rate, the Russian aerial formations were rather reluctant. They frequently discontinued their raids when German fighters appeared and exhibited little fighting spirit. Intercepted radio messages indicate that Russian formations were at times instructed not to fight. In this manner German air superiority became evident on the very first day of the offensive. This state of affairs experienced little change during the entire 'Zitadelle' offensive."[23]

It appears that the Soviets, shocked by the high losses on the first day, and having been made clearly aware of German air superiority, chose to be much more selective and cautious for the rest of the battle. This effectively gave the Germans air superiority throughout most of the battle, although the Soviet air was always present, often providing ground support.

Still, according to Seidemann, the Soviet fighter pilots were better trained than before. He noted that a few of the Soviet fighter squadrons were well led and formidable opponents. One gathers that this was not the case with the majority of the Soviet fighter units. He did not consider their aircraft to be better than the German aircraft.

Seidemann referred to the Il-2s as "cumbrous, but heavily-armed" and noted that they frequently fell victim to the Messerschmitts. He also noted that the few US P-39 Airacobras that appeared distinguished themselves by their superior maneuverability and speed over the Il-2s. He also observed that the Soviet bombers were not that common and were limited to bombing the front lines or forward air fields. He stated that their results were not very good.

Seidemann observed that "The Russian pilot proved to be brave, but orthodox and not sufficiently skillful. One gained the impression that Russian flying crews were not sufficiently familiar with the technical aspects of flying and that they were inadequately trained. On the whole, however, the Red Air Force had caught up considerably, particularly as regards numbers. It had turned into a serious adversary."[24]

Lt. General Krupinski commented in 1999 that "The Russian fighters employed strange tactics, which have remained beyond my comprehension. If we encountered bomber formations with fighter support, the enemy fighters kept right on moving in their fixed formation. They always waited for us to attack before engaging in any dogfights. They never attacked on their own initiative. As a fighter pilot, however, one must have the grit to be the first to attack. So, we were always calling the shots, which surely helped manifest our notion of superiority."[25]

The Second Air Army analysis after the battle supports this picture:

"The following shortcomings were noted in our fighters' combat work:

a) A desire to engage in aerial combat over our territory, and a reluctance to attack enemy bombers on the approaches to their targets;
b) In certain circumstances the coordinated activities of fighter groups and pairs in combat were missing, and a tendency to engage in single combat. In these cases, our fighters suffered excessive losses;
c) Insufficient caution, particularly on the part of young pilots. There were instances when the enemy bombed our lines without resistance, even when our patrol groups were not far away, which caused deserved criticism of our fighters from the ground troops."[26]

Novikov's Inspection Teams

Major General Aleksandr A. Novikov was the commander of the Soviet air force, which was still a part of the Red Army. On 7 July, it is reported that he sent inspection teams to all air armies and air corps involved in the Kursk battle. They, of course, determined that the Soviet air units had suffered heavy losses, especially the Shturmovik or Il-2 regiments. A series of corrective actions were requested. These are discussed in the following chapter (under Novikov's Directive).[27]

THE VIII AIR CORPS SORTIE COUNT

According to the records of the Second Army air liaison officer, the VIII Air Corps flew the following sorties:

	Total Sorties	Recon	Stuka	Bombing (Harassing)	Ground Attack	Fighter
June 30	43					
Night	15					
July 1	57					
Night	57			11		
July 2	49					
Night	21			17 (11)		
July 3	78		20			
Night	No report					
July 4	224		132	28		
Night	No report					
July 5	2387	74	1071	536	335	371
Night	No report					
July 6	1686	77	793	323	240	253
Night	64			61 (50)		
July 7	1829	88	746	498	200	297
Night	57			52 (46)		
July 8	1686	77	701	493	186*	229
Night	28			26 (20)		
July 9	1621	97	699	384	183	258**
Night	No report					
July 10	682					
Night	18			14 (8)		
July 11	1039	62	447	197	157	176
Night	61			56 (49)		
July 12	654	52	150	13	248	191
Night	No report					
July 13	656	50	239	60	103	204
Night	28			23 (16)		
July 14	1452	83	510	486	135	238
Night	40			36 (23)		

THE FIGHT FOR AIR SUPERIORITY

	Total Sorties	Recon	Stuka	Bombing (Harassing)	Ground Attack	Fighter
				By Type		
July 15	706	33	191	282	68	132
Night	111			105 (93)		
July 16	499	76	191	30	57	145
Night	85			73 (45)		
July 17	138					
Night	27			25 (18)		
July 18	79	39				40
Night	18			17 (6)		
July 19	92	64				28
Night	18			18 (12)		
July 20	98	84				14
Night	21			21 (15)		
July 21	85	71				14
Night	0					
July 22	74	58				16
Night	6			5		
July 23	46	42				4
Night	30			29 (23)		
July 24	127	68		45		14
Summation	16,792	1,195	5,890	3,964	1,912	2,624
4–18 July	15,857	808	5,870	3,330***	1,912	2,534
				471 (368) Night Bombing Sorties		

   *   Of this number, 53 are tank hunter missions with Hs-129s armed with 30mm cannon.
  ** Corrected to match the daily total and the summary report for 5-9 July.
 *** Day bombing sorties.

THE III BOMBER GROUP OF THE 55TH BOMBARDMENT WING

The only surviving German air unit record is from one German bomber group. Its activities, which may or may not be typical, are shown below for illustration. It was armed with around 46 He-111s (2 He-111 H-6, 6 He-111 H-11, 26 He-111 H-11/R1, and 12 He-111 H-16, see Appendix II). The planes operating out of the Stalino base location were probably not involved in the Battle of Kursk.

Date	Air Base	Sorties	Weight of Bombs Dropped (kg)	Propaganda Leaflets Dropped
July 4	Stalino	6	11,070	180,000
July 5	Rogan	82	109,750	42 packs
	Stalino	6	11,070	288,000
July 6	Rogan	56	74,450	36 packs
	Stalino	10	17,270	456,000
July 7	Rogan	58	79,500	
Night	Stalino	10	20,650	480,000
July 8	Rogan	88	130,500	68 packs
Night	Stalino	6	13,470	288,000
July 9	Rogan	55	80,250	44 packs
	Stalino	7	15,845	336,000
July 10	Rogan	34	51,000	10 packs
	Stalino	7	13,215	336,000
July 11	Rogan	44	66,000	40 packs
	Stalino	9	17,365	432,000
July 12	no sorties			
Night	Stalino	10	21,555	480,000
July 13	Rogan	28	39,000	37 packs
Night	Stalino	10	19,650	480,000
July 14	Rogan	58	86,000	140 packs
Night	Stalino	10	18,510	480,000
July 15	Rogan	38	57,000	85 packs
Night	Stalino	11	17,966	528,000
July 16	Rogan	55	80,500	127 packs
Night	Stalino	5	9,225	
July 17	*	48	65,750	38 packs
Night	Stalino	9	18,015	308,000
July 18	Stalino	37	49,000	15 packs
Night	Stalino	10	20,050	480,000

* Report filed from "Rogan/Stalino"

THE FIGHT FOR AIR SUPERIORITY

Air Mission Details

Day	Height Flown (meters)	Take-off Times	Landing Times	Attack Times
5 July	2600–4000	03:20–14:10	04:26–15:35	04:07–15:12
6 July	1500–3500	09:45–17:45	10:42–19:25	10:25–18:49
7 July	2800–3500	08:10–15:35	09:20–16:35	09:07–16:35
8 July	2000–3600	05:20–18:40	06:35–20:00	06:25–19:25
9 July	2900–3500	08:45–16:57	10:10–18:25	09:44–17:52
10 July	1000–2900	06:52 & 10:16	07:39 & 18:00	07:20–17:20
11 July	2000–2800	08:40–18:20	09:45–19:55	09:19–19:25
12 July	no sorties			
13 July	3300–3500	05:04–16:55	06:30–18:25	06:00–18:10
14 July	3300–3700	07:12–16:30	08:35–17:55	08:07–17:25
15 July	3000–3800	14:10–17:20	15:35–19:29	15:00–18:57
16 July	3400–3800	03:30–16:50	05:15–19:43	04:46–18:22

SECOND AIR ARMY SORTIE COUNT

	Total Sorties	Recon	Ground Attack	Bombing	Escort	Cover & Intercept	Other
Night	10			9			1*
July 4	149	6		143			
Night	48		48				
July 5	1,296	14	202	115	316	531	17 & 19 & 66 & 16**
Night	72			72			
July 6	823	10	237		184	392	
Night	83			83			
July 7	839	10	210		251	368	
Night	96			96			
July 8	957	40	328		114	475	
Night	60			60			
July 9	658	57	217		114	270	
Night	69			68			1*
July 10	463	32	141		81	209	

Night	57	9		48				
July 11	540	8	133		75	324		
Night	109	8		101				
July 12	769	35	220	82	147	285		
Night	156	6		150				
July 13	666	21	222	86	187	150		
Night	200	8		192				
July 14	861	14	191	145	169	241	101***	
Night	151	5		146				
July 15	328	24	122		80	102		
Night	219	5		214				
July 16	723	15	143	159	253	145	8***	
Night	135	10		125				
July 17	486	34	159	52	154	87		
Night	199	8		190			1*	
July 18	435	9	94	93	182	57		
Summation:	11,657	388	2,619	732	2,307	3,779	230	
				1,602 night				

* Special Assignment.
** These are 17 Il-2 missions to attack bridge crossings, 19 fighter missions to block enemy airfields, 66 Il-2 missions to attack German airfields, and 16 unidentified fighter missions.
*** Ground attack by fighters and fighter-bombers.

SECOND AIR ARMY SORTIES BY PLANE TYPE

		U-2	R-5	Il-2	Pe-2	Boston	La-5	Yak-1	Yak-7b	Yak-9	Medium Bomber	Fighter
July 4	Number	6	4		3	3	36	14	38			
	Sorties	6	4		3	3	64	19	60			
July 5	Number	25	4	161	74	6	165	142	40			
	Sorties	44	4	285	123	6	395	372	115			
July 6	Number	27	4	110	7	3	75	88	41		1	
	Sorties	64	6	237	7	3	224	234	118		2	
July 7	Number	26	5	125	7	3	88	78	60		1	
	Sorties	73	8	210	7	3	237	206	176		2	

THE FIGHT FOR AIR SUPERIORITY

		U-2	R-5	Il-2	Pe-2	Boston	La-5	Yak-1	Yak-7b	Yak-9	Medium Bomber	Fighter
July 8	Number	28	4	143	10	3	79	89	34		3	
	Sorties	85	6	328	18	3	249	260	99		5	
July 9	Number	26	5	92	10	8	57	78	17		2	
	Sorties	51	5	217	19	8	165	217	32		4	
July 10	Number	24	5	66	2	3	51	51	30	10	3	
	Sorties	53	8	141	2	3	114	110	66	27	8	
July 11	Number	24	5	71	2		67	88	33	40	3	
	Sorties	45	9	133	2		126	158	53	68	3	
July 12	Number	40	4	102	82		19	83	42	80		
	Sorties	101	8	220	82		34	192	68	173		
July 13	Number	47	4	94	79	3	68					171
	Sorties	150	6	222	86	3	154					201
July 14	Number	52	3	82	99	5	56	89	22	29		
	Sorties	192	5	191	145	5	163	287	30	43		
July 15	Number	55	5	66	0	6	37	59	7	21		
	Sorties	146	5	122	0	6	50	115	14	21		
July 16	Number	58	3	86	103	5		34				167
	Sorties	214	5	143	159	5		102				314
July 17	Number	56	4	67	52	7		34			3	89
	Sorties	125	7	159	52	7		89			3	179
July 18	Number	58	6	59	84	5		48				99
	Sorties	190	9	94	93	9		98				141

SEVENTEENTH AIR ARMY SORTIE COUNT (TOTAL)

	Total Sorties	Recon	Ground Attack	Bombing	Armed Recon/ Airfield Attack	Escort	Patrol/ Airfield Cover	Intercept	Troop Cover
Night	26			26					
July 4	48	40						8	
Night	2			2					
July 5	448	43	152		36	204	13		
Night	123	24		99					
July 6	462	45	169	36	4	174	28	6	
Night	197	19		178					
July 7	639	40	156	41	14	290		8	90
Night	192	26		166					
July 8	228	20	76			118			14
Night	174	27?		121	26				
July 9	187	20	74		5	88			
Night	183	19		164					
July 10	71	22	17			24	8		
Night	149	8		141					
July 11	56	13	19			20	4		
Night	183	19		164					
July 12	134	15	52		8	57		2	
Night	164	34		130					
July 13	112	16	35			58		3	
Night	151	32		119					
July 14	168	23	57		10	76			2
Night	114	17		97					
July 15	35	19	4			2	10		
Night	146	19		127					
July 16	203	36	38		36	87			6
Night	144	45		34	65				
July 17	721	29	349		24	102			217
Night	172	26		88	58				
July 18	871	37	373	18	12	39		8	384
Summation 6,503									

THE FIGHT FOR AIR SUPERIORITY

SEVENTEENTH AIR ARMY SORTIE COUNT
(Only Those That Were in the Belgorod Area or Attacked the VIII Air Corps)

	Total Sorties	Recon	Ground Attack	Bombing	Armed Recon/ Airfield Attack	Escort	Patrol/ Airfield Cover	Inter-cept	Troop Cover
Night	–								
July 4	–								
Night	–								
July 5	392		152		36	204			
Night	123	24		99					
July 6	407	24	169	36	4	174			
Night	197	19		178					
July 7	588	4	156	34	14	290			90
Night	192	26		166					
July 8	216	8	76			118			14
Night	147			121	26				
July 9	170	8	74			88			
Night	183	19		164					
July 10	61	20	17			24			
Night	149	8		141					
July 11	48	9	19			20			
Night	183	19		164					
July 12	118	3	52		8	55			
Night	164	34		130					
July 13	101	5	35			58		3	
Night	151	32		119					
July 14	141	4	57		10	70			
Night	114	17		97					
July 15	8	4	4						
Night	146	19		127					
July 16	171	4	38		36	87			6
Night	144	45		34	65				
July 17	0								
Night	58				58				
July 18	12				12				
Summation:	4,384	355	849	70	269	1,188	0	3	110
				1,540 Night					

HARTMANN & RALL

The three highest scoring aces in the history of aviation were serving with Jagdgeschwader 52 (52nd Fighter Wing) and two of them were present at Kursk. They were Erich Hartmann, with 352 claimed kills, and Guenther Rall with 275 claimed kills. Gerhard Barkhorn, with 301 claimed kills, was part of the II Group of the 52nd Fighter Wing, and as such, was not at Kursk. Almost all of these pilots' victories were scored on the Eastern Front.

Guenther Rall: At the time of the Battle of Kursk, Guenther Rall was one of Germany's leading aces, becoming the third ace to score 200 victories in August 1943, after Hermann Graf and Hans Phillip.

Rall was born in Gaggenau in Baden (in southern Germany) on 10 March 1918. His father was a merchant and Rall grew up primarily in Stuttgart. He joined the German Army as a cadet in December 1936. He was encouraged by a friend to join the Luftwaffe, entering pilot school in the summer of 1938 and was promoted to Lieutenant in September 1938. He was posted to the II Group of the 52nd Fighter Wing in 1939 and flew patrol missions along the French-German border.

After transferring to the newly formed III Group of the wing, he scored his first victory in May 1940. After France, he was posted to the English Channel and participated in the Battle of Britain. Due to the attrition of squadron commanders, Rall was promoted to head the 8th Squadron when he was 22 years old. This unit was withdrawn from combat in October 1940 and sent to Romania. From there he participated in the German operations in the Balkans, Crete, and the invasion of Russia. The 52nd Fighter Wing would remain operating in southern Russia for the next three years. He had scored 36 kills when he was shot down on 28 November 1941 and severely injured. He spent Christmas with a broken back and wrapped in body cast. He was grounded for the next nine months, although during that time he met his future wife, the Austrian-born Hertha Schoen. She was one of his doctors and eight years his senior.

In August 1942, he had returned to his squadron, which by this time was scoring an impressive number of kills against the poorly trained and poorly armed Soviet air forces. Rall competitively joined the hunt and in three months had pushed his personal score to 101 kills. This was an average of about two kills every three days for a three month period. These kills secured him the Knight's Cross in September and the Oak Leaves to his Knight's Cross in December. He took advantage of the trip back to Germany for the award ceremony with Hitler to get married on 11 November 1942. His wife had been under observation by the Gestapo (German secret police) for having helped some Jewish friends leave Vienna for London in 1938.

He continued operations in the south throughout this period and in April 1943 he was promoted to Captain. By the time the Battle of Kursk started, this very seasoned veteran pilot was credited with 145 victories. He was given command of the III Group

THE FIGHT FOR AIR SUPERIORITY

of the 52nd Fighter Wing on 6 July 1943, returning from Germany after convalescence treatment because of his previous injuries. Under his command would be Hartmann, Krupinski (when he returned) and others.

Rall continued serving with the 52nd Fighter Wing, scoring his 200th kill on 29 August 1943 after 555 combat missions and was awarded Swords to his Knight's Cross the following month. Rall was then transferred to the Western Front on 18 April 1944 to become commander of the II Group of the 11th Fighter Wing. On 12 May 1944, he was shot down and forced to bail out. The injuries and subsequent infections from his wound kept him out of action until November. He then took command of a training school and then command of the 300th Fighter Wing in March 1945, ending the war with the rank of Major.

During his career, Rall was awarded 275 victories, all but three from the Eastern Front. He was shot down eight times during the war, crash landing seven times and bailing out once. He was wounded three times and spent 15 months in hospitals. He flew 621 combat missions. He had the reputation of being a very good shot. He would later almost be killed in a car accident in 1968.

He surrendered to the Americans. After his release, he looked into studying medicine but ended up working for Siemens as a representative and later as an administrator at a medical school. In 1956 he returned to flying and joined the West German Air Force. He eventually rose to become the chief of staff of the German Air Force from 1970–74. He retired in 1975 with the rank of Lt. General, resigning amid a scandal over a trip to South Africa. After retirement, he went into private industry. His wife passed away in 1985, survived by two daughters. Guenther Rall passed away at home on 4 October 2009 at the age of 91.

His list of claims during Kursk is provided below:[28]

Victory Number	Date	Time	Aircraft Type	Location	Details
146	7 July	1146	LaGG-3/La-5[29]	PQ 35 Ost 62742	east of Pawlowka[30] 10 km west of Prochorowka
147	7 July	1152	LaGG-3/La-5	PQ 35 Ost 61131	north of Jilinskij 15 km southwest of Oboyan
148	8 July	0751	LaGG-3/La-5	PQ 35 Ost 62842	south of Wyshnaja 10 km west of Prochorowka
149	8 July	1346	LaGG-3/La-5	PQ 35 Ost 62793	west of Kotschetowka 10 km east of Prochorowka
150	8 July	1416	LaGG-3/La-5	PQ 35 Ost 61221	south of Prochorowka 15 km northwest of Prochorowka
151	8 July	1835	LaGG-3/La-5	PQ 35 Ost 61132	south of Kotschetowka 20 km north of Prochorowka

Victory Number	Date	Time	Aircraft Type	Location	Details
152	9 July	0712	LaGG-3/La-5	PQ 35 Ost 62872	northwest of Prochorowka 15 km northwest of Prochorowka
153	9 July	1533	LaGG-3/La-5	PQ 35 Ost 62791	Orlowka 10 km north of Prochorowka
154	9 July	1543	LaGG-3/La-5	PQ 35 Ost 62871	Wessilij 10 km north of Prochorowka
155	11 July	0959	LaGG-3	PQ 35 Ost 62812	Rshewtschik 20 km east of Oboyan
156	11 July	1743	LaGG-3/La-5	PQ 35 Ost 62843	Korytnoje 20 km north of Prochorowka
157	12 July	1645	La-5	PQ 35 Ost 62762	east of Snowilow 15 km southeast of Oboyan
158	14 July	1907	LaGG-3	PQ 35 Ost 64363	southwest of Michailowka No location given
159	15 July	1503	LaGG-3	PQ 35 Ost 64381[31]	North of Bokhov Near Zmiyckka
160	17 July	1908	LaGG-3	PQ 35 Ost 54613	west of Bolkhov No location given
161	17 July	1916	LaGG-3	PQ 35 Ost 54631	east of Bokhov northeast of Orel

The locations on this listing clearly establish that the III Group, 52nd Fighter Wing was still operating in the Belgorod area as late as 12 July and had moved to Orel area by 15 July. Bolkhov is 56 kilometers (35 miles) from Orel. The place names in this listing are using the transliteration from German, so differ slightly from the transliteration used elsewhere in this book. The coordinate system is from the Luftwaffe *Planquadrat* maps, which put the location in a grid square of 3 by 4 kilometers.

The interesting aspect of the second set of listed locations is that most of the claimed kills were done on the Soviet side of the lines. As Erich Hartmann was the 7th squadron commander (starting 6 July) in Rall's III Group, the locations of their kills should be similar. Regardless, for both pilots, all actions are in the Second Air Army's area of operations.

Erich "Bubi" Hartmann: Erich Hartmann was the youngest of Germany's three highest scoring aces. Born in 1922 in Stuttgart, he lived for a while in China during the 1920s where his father, who was a physician, was practicing. His mother, Elisabeth Machtholf, was one of Germany's early women aviators. Hartmann, because of his mother, learned to fly gliders in his teens and was a fully qualified glider instructor in 1938 at the age of 16. He joined the Luftwaffe on 15 October 1940 and began flight training in March 1941. In August 1942 he was posted to

THE FIGHT FOR AIR SUPERIORITY

the 7th squadron of the 52nd Fighter Wing in Russia. He saw action on his third sortie, lost orientation and ran out gas, having to force land. He scored his first kill on 5 November 1942 on his 19th mission, an Il-2, but again damaged his plane and crash landed. His second kill occurred almost three months later on his 41st combat mission. By the end of May 1943 Hartmann had 17 kills and took leave in June.

During the Battle of Kursk, between 5 and 17 July he claimed 22 kills, including seven kills on 7 July. Hartmann became the acting squadron commander for the 7th squadron of the III/52nd Fighter Wing when his mentor Krupinski was injured on 5 July. He was shifted over to command the 9th squadron in August. By the end of August 1943, Hartmann had 90 victories (compared to 200 by Rall at that time). He became operations officer of the III Group in April 1944 when Krupinski was transferred to the west. He became the III Group's commander after Barkmann was transferred. In 1944, he married Ursula Paetsch, who he had known since a teenager, and they had a son and a daughter.

Hartmann flew 1,400 missions during the war, seeing combat about 800 times. He scored 352 victories during the war, with 345 of them against the Soviet Union. He was never wounded although he was brought down sixteen times, at least eight from the debris of the planes he was shooting down. He had the reputation of coming in extremely close to his targets during his attacks. He was forced down behind Soviet lines on 20 August 1943, briefly captured, but was able to escape and returned to his lines after four days.

At the end of the war, he was ordered to leave his group behind in Czechoslovakia by General Seidemann and fly out to surrender to the British. Instead, he, along with the famous German ace Hermann Graf (212 kills), disobeyed the order and marched with the III Group to the American zone and surrendered. As his unit had been in the Soviet zone at the time of the surrender of Germany, he and the rest of the group were handed over to the Soviets that same month. He then spent ten and a half years in Soviet prisons before being repatriated back to West Germany, during which time his young son had died. He joined the West German Air Force in 1956 and retired in 1973 as a Colonel. He then worked at a flight training school. His original intention of becoming a doctor, like his father, was never fulfilled. Erich Hartmann passed away on 20 September 1993 at the age of 71.

A list of his victories during Kursk, as drawn from his personal log book, is provided below:[32]

Victory Number	Sortie Number	Date	Time	Aircraft Type
18	182	5 July	0323–0420	Il-2
19	183	5 July	0648–0744	LaGG
20	184	5 July	1345–1445	Il-2
21	185	5 July	1735–1845	La-5

Victory Number	Sortie Number	Date	Time	Aircraft Type
22	191	7 July	0306–0405	Il-2
23	191	7 July	0306–0405	Il-2
24	192	7 July	0545–0645	Il-2
25	192	7 July	0545–0645	La-5
26	194	7 July	1707–1805	La-5
27	194	7 July	1707–1805	La-5
28	194	7 July	1707–1805	La-5
29	195	8 July	0820–0932	La-5
30	195	8 July	0820–0932	La-5
31	198	8 July	1742–1845	La-5
32	198	8 July	1742–1845	La-5
33	204	10 July	0633–0730	La-5
34	206	11 July	1620–1718	La-5
35	213	15 July	1334–1436	La-5
36	214	15 July	1704–1745	La-5
37	216	16 July	0646–0736	La-5
38	217	16 July	1400–1434	La-5
39	233	17 July	1845–1945	La-5

A slightly different listing is provided from other sources:[33]

Victory Number	Date	Time	Aircraft Type	Location	Details
18	5 July	0340	Il-2 m.H.	PQ 35 Ost 61663	10 km north of Vovchansk
19	5 July	0710	LaGG-3	PQ 35 Ost 61151	10 km north of Krasny-Liman
20	5 July	1400	Il-2 m.H.	PQ 35 Ost 61333	10 km north Tomarovka
21	5 July	1815	LaGG-3	PQ 35 Ost 61124	Bogatoje
22	7 July	0350	Il-2 m.H	PQ 35 Ost 61183	Krasny-Liman
23	7 July	0352	Il-2 m.H	PQ 35 Ost 61154	10 km north of Krasny-Liman
24	7 July	0605	Il-2 m.H	PQ 35 Ost 61331	10 km north of Tomarovka
25	7 July	0610	LaGG-3/La-5[34]	PQ 35 Ost 61182	vicinity of Krasny-Liman
26	7 July	1715	LaGG-3/La-5	PQ 35 Ost 61214	southwest of Prokhorovka
27	7 July	1720	LaGG-3/La-5	PQ 35 Ost 62872	10 km northwest of Prokhorovka

THE FIGHT FOR AIR SUPERIORITY

Victory Number	Date	Time	Aircraft Type	Location	Details
28	7 July	1730	LaGG-3/La-5	PQ 35 Ost 62792	15 km northwest of Prokhorovka
29	8 July	0905	LaGG-3/La-5	PQ 35 Ost 61223	10 km east of Prokhorovka
30	8 July	0910	LaGG-3/La-5	PQ 35 Ost 61221	10 km south of Prokhorovka[35]
31	8 July	1805	LaGG-3/La-5	PQ 35 Ost 62872	10 km north of Prokhorovka
32	8 July	1825	LaGG-3/La-5	PQ 35 Ost 61134	10 km northwest of Prokhorovka
33	9 July	0725	Il-2 m.H	PQ 35 Ost 61272	
34	9 July	0910	LaGG-3	PQ 35 Ost 62871	10 km north of Prokhorovka
35	9 July	0920	LaGG-3	PQ 35 Ost 62844	20 km north of Prokhorovka
36	10 July	0705	LaGG-3/La-5	PQ 35 Ost 62872	10 km north of Prokhorovka
37	11 July	1655	LaGG-3/La-5	PQ 35 Ost 62883	20 km northeast of Prokhorovka
38	15 July	1720	LaGG-3/La-5	PQ 35 Ost 54562	southwest of Bolkhov
39	16 July	1415	LaGG-3/La-5	PQ 35 Ost 54661	west of Bolkhov
40	17 July	1925	LaGG-3/La-5	PQ 35 Ost 54497	west of Zubkovo

The locations on this listing clearly establish that the 7th Squadron, III Group of the 52nd Fighter Wing was still operating in the Belgorod area as late as 11 July and had moved to Orel area by 15 July. Bolkhov is 56 kilometers (35 miles) from Orel. The place names in this listing are using the transliteration from German, so differ slightly from the transliteration used elsewhere in this book. The coordinate system is from the Luftwaffe *Planquadrat* maps, which put the location in a grid square of 3 by 4 kilometers.

Note that the two lists are fundamentally in agreement with times and plane type shot down except for claims number 33-35 on this list for 9 July, which is not on the first list and claims 35 and 37 on the first list that is not on this second list. Not sure why these lists differ.

Comparison to Soviet Losses

Date	Rall's Claims	Second Air Army Losses	Seventeenth Air Army Losses
7 July	2 La-5s	18 La-5s	6 La-5s
8 July	4 La-5s	16 La-5s	–
9 July	3 La-5s	14 La-5s	1 La-5
11 July	2 LaGG-3s/La-5s	9 La-5s	–
12 July	1 La-5	2 La-5s	–
14 July	1 Lagg-3	5 La-5s	–

Date	Hartmann's Claims	Second Air Army Losses	Seventeenth Air Army Losses
5 July	2 Il-2	43 Il-2s	66 Il-2s
	1 LaGG, 1 La-5	39 fighters	7 La-5s
7 July	3 Il-2s	22 Il-2s	21 Il-2s
	4 La-5	18 La-5s	6 La-5s
8 July	4 La-5s	16 La-5s	–
9 July	1 Il-2	15 Il-2s	8 Il-2a
	2 LaGG-3	14 La-5a	1 La-5
10 July	1 La-5	6 La-5s	–
11 July	1 La-5	9 La-5s	–

It would appear that all 17 or 20 of Hartmann's claims from 5 to 11 July are possible. It would appear that all 13 of Rall's claims from 5 to 14 July are possible. Because of the high Soviet air losses, it is hard to find a day where a single German claim is not possible. The total claims made by all the Germans may exceed the total Soviet losses, as happened on 5 July 1943.[36]

KOZHEDUB, GULAYEV & YEVSTIGNEYEV[37]

Four of the six highest scoring aces of the Soviet Union (and of the allies during the Second World War) flew at the Battle of Kursk. Due to the continued level of intensity of combat in the southern part of the Eastern Front from the middle of 1942 to almost the end of the war, it is not by accident that many of the most famous aces from both sides would face each other over Kursk and other battlefields in the southern Soviet Union. It was the largest, most extended air campaign in history, and as such produced high-scoring aces for both sides.

Ivan Kozhedub Ivan Nikitovich Kozhedub was born in the Sumy area on 8 June 1920. He joined the Soviet air force in 1940 and became a pilot a year later. He then spent some time as a flight instructor before being transferred to the 240th Fighter Regiment on 13 March 1943 to fly La-5s.

His first kill came four months later at the Battle of Kursk, on 6 July 1943, when he was a Junior Lieutenant. According to his personal log, this was a Ju-87.[38] The Germans lost a Ju-88 and one Ju-87 due to air combat (and five Ju-87s lost due to antiaircraft fire) on the 6th. Kozhedub also claimed a Ju-87 on 7 July and two Me-109s on 9 July.[39] It would appear that Kozhedub's claim of 7 July must be incorrect, as the Germans report losing no Ju-87s on that day.[40] On 9 July, the Germans lost seven Me-109s. During the Battle of Kursk, these were his first four claimed kills. He was awarded his first Order of the Red Banner on 22 July 1943.

THE FIGHT FOR AIR SUPERIORITY

After Kursk Kozhedub became a squadron leader and in the summer and fall of 1943 continued scoring, reaching his 20th kill on 29 October, qualifying for his first Hero of the Soviet Union. The year of 1944 saw him in a competitive scoring race with his squadron mate Kirill Yevstigneyev. He was then posted as the deputy commander of the 176th Guards Fighter Regiment and switched to flying Yak-7s. He continued flying and scoring until the end of the war.

His total for the war was 62 victories, making him not only the highest scoring Soviet ace but the highest scoring Allied ace of the war.[41] He flew 330 combat sorties and had 120 encounters with enemy aircraft. He was wounded at least once. He was one of only three people to win the Hero of the Soviet Union three times (the other two were Marshal Zhukov and Lt. Colonel Aleksandr Ivanovich Pokryishkin, the Soviet number two ace). Kozhedub claimed that his personal total was actually in excess of 100.[42] He ended the war as a Major.

After the war, he graduated from the Air Force Academy in 1949 and commanded the 324th Fighter Division in the Korean War, which was engaged with US and United Nations' aircraft. He scored no kills during this time. He continued service in the Soviet Air Force, graduating from General Staff Academy in 1956 and rising to the rank of Marshal. He passed away in August 1991.

Nikolai Gulayev: Nikolai Dmitriyevich Gulayev was born in the Rostov area on 26 February 1918. He joined the Soviet air force in 1938 and completed his pilot training two years later. He was assigned to the Stalingrad Front in April 1942 where he joined the 27th Fighter Regiment and conducted his first combat missions. He followed the regiment when it was deployed to the Voronezh Front, and on 14 May 1943 claimed one or two Ju-87s and successfully rammed another one after having run out of ammunition.[43] Gulayev was forced down near elements of the 52nd Guards Rifle Division.

At Kursk he was able to add a dozen claimed kills to his score, resulting in him being recommended for a Hero of the Soviet Union, which was awarded 28 September 1943.[44]

He became deputy squadron leader and by 28 September had scored 27 victories.[45] He was promoted to Captain and squadron leader but was shot down and wounded in early 1944. He returned to duty shortly and continued scoring. His fighting career ended in June of 1944 when he was wounded in a dogfight and crash landed. At this point, he was leading ace in the Soviet air forces.

Gulayev's total for the war was 55 victories and five shared victories.[46] He was the fourth highest scoring Soviet ace and may have become the highest if he had not been wounded. He flew 248 combat sorties and had 69 encounters with enemy aircraft. He was wounded at least twice and rammed enemy aircraft twice. He was twice awarded the Hero of the Soviet Union.

After the Second World War, he continued with the Air Force, graduating from the Air Force Academy in 1950 and the General Staff Academy in 1960. He retired in 1967 as a Colonel General and passed away 27 September 1985.

Kirill Yevstigneyev: Kirill Alekseyevich Yevstigneyev was born in the Kurgan area on 17 February 1917. He enlisted in the Soviet Army on 21 September 1938 and passed through flight school three years later. He was then sent to the Far East to train pilots and later transferred to Moscow. At his request, he was transferred to the front, and sent to the 240th Fighter Regiment on 17 March 1943, just after Kozhedub had arrived. He first flew La-5s in the Kharkov area and started scoring immediately, running up five kills before being shot down and wounded in both legs.[47] He returned to his unit before Kursk.

At the Battle of Kursk, Yevstigneyev claimed another seven kills (2 shared). On 7 July he claimed a Ju-87 and on 8 July claimed three more.[48] Yevstigneyev described his claimed triple kill on 8 July:

> *"I was assigned on a front line patrol encountering a heavy layer of clouds at 5,000 meters. Captain Podorozhnyi's attack group consisting of six fighters was flying below so as to intercept enemy bomber formations while three comrades were assigned as top cover to engage any fighters that might appear. Once over the front the first bombers were spotted going in to hammer our ground forces. Podorozhnyi immediately ordered the attack and bounced one Junkers from astern teaming with his number two to destroy it on his first pass. Flying slightly behind him I hit the left-hand aircraft with a burst from starboard at 50 meters range and saw it blow up and hit the ground. While this was going on, a second enemy bomber force was spotted. I swept down and went through their formation, and back around for a second pass, downed one of them as they were breaking formation and trying to race away just above the ground. I pulled in behind another and started to pour fire into him at 50–60 meters range and saw him crash for my third victory of the day."*[49]

On 8 July, the VIII Air Corps records 2 or 6 Ju-87s lost among the 5 or 8 aircraft lost that day.[50] Yevstigneyev was credited with killing Me-109s on 9, 13, and 16 July. The VIII Air Corps records 7 Me-109s lost on 9 July but none on the 13th and 16th.[51]

In August, Yevstigneyev was promoted to squadron leader and scored heavily during the latter half of 1943. He then got into a scoring duel with Kozhedub in the spring of 1944. He continued flying and scoring until the war's end, having been promoted to Major and serving as deputy commander for the 178th Fighter Regiment. Most of his fighting had been done with a La-5, although towards the end of the war, he was flying La-7s.

During the war he claimed 53 kills, three shared kills, flew 283 sorties and had 109 combat engagements. He was awarded Hero of the Soviet Union twice. He was the Soviet Union's fifth highest scoring ace.

He remained in the Air Force after the war, graduating from the Air Force Academy in 1955 and the General Staff Academy in 1960. He retired in 1972 as a Major General and passed away 29 August 1996 in Moscow.

CAPTAIN JOHANNES WIESE

Captain Johannes Wiese was the acting commander of the I Group, 52nd Fighter Wing. He claimed 12 kills on 5 July 1943. They are recorded as:

Time	Plane	Location	Note
0347	Il-2 m.H.	PQ 35 Ost 61891	20 km south-southwest of "Bilyi Kolodiaz"
0355	Il-2 m.H.	PQ 35 Ost 60123	
0403	Il-2 m.H.	PQ 35 Ost 60193	
0750	Il-2 m.H.	PQ 35 Ost 61321	
0812	Il-2 m.H.	PQ 35 Ost 61321	
0940	Il-2	PQ 35 Ost 61352	
1525	Il-2 m.H.	PQ 35 Ost 61812	
1830	Il-2	PQ 35 Ost 61622	3 km south of Polyana
1833	Il-2 m.H.	PQ 35 Ost 61622	4 km south of Polyana
1840	Il-2 m.H.	PQ 35 Ost 61624	3 km northeast of Volkhovo
1845	Il-2	PQ 35 Ost 61651	3 km southwest of Volkhovo
1850	Il-2	PQ 35 Ost 61651	2 km northeast of Toplinka
1855	Il-2	vicinity of Toplinka	Unconfirmed kill

This is 12 confirmed kills and one unconfirmed kill for the day.[52] It would appear that he flew at least four sorties this day and perhaps more. The last sortie, where he claimed five kills, was in the area of the Soviet Seventh Guards Army. The locations given are to the south and southwest of the 7th Panzer Division's crossing at Solomino and to the east of the crossing points of the German 106th Infantry Division. Volkhovo and Toplinka are on the west bank of Donets River in the area of the German 320th Infantry Division (see 1:50000 scale map M37-50C).[53] Polyana is ten kilometers to the east of the Donets River (see 1:50000 scale map M37-50D). Three of the five kills appeared to have been made over Soviet lines.

His other kills for the Battle of Kursk are:

Date	Planes	Note
6 July	two La-5s	Time and locations given[54]
7 July	seven Il-2s	Listed as not confirmed in the Matthew and Foreman listing.[55]
16 July	two Il-2s	Both 10 km southwest of Prokhorovka at 0525 and 0530
17 July	four Il-2s	Time and locations given.[56]
18 July	two Yak-1s	Time and locations given.[57]
20 July	one Il-2	
22 July	one Yak-1	
23 July	one Yak-1	
27 July	two Il-2s	

He has no other claimed kills until October. His claimed victories of 27 July 1943 were in the vicinity of the Kalinovka, indicating that the I Group, 52nd Fighter Wing was still operating near Belgorod at this time (meaning it had not been transferred out of the area). Of his 30 confirmed and unconfirmed claims from 5 to 18 July, two of them cannot be correct according to Soviet loss reports (the two Yak-1s claimed on 18 July).[58] He ended the war with 133 confirmed kills, all from the Eastern Front.[59]

Johannes Wiese was born 7 March 1915 in Breslau. His father was a minister. He joined the German Army in 1934 and transferred to the air force in 1936. He claimed his first aerial victory on 23 September 1941. He earned the nickname the "Lion of Kuban" for his actions in the Kuban bridgehead before Kursk. He was awarded the Knight's Cross in January 1943 and in March 1944 the Oak Leaves to the Knight's Cross. Transferred to the west to command a fighter wing, he was shot down by a British Spitfire, bailed out and injured in December 1944.

He spent over four years in Soviet prisoner of war camps after the war, and then returned to West Germany, where he joined the German Army in 1956. He retired as a Lt. Colonel and passed away in 1991.

Comparison to Soviet Losses

Date	Wiese's Claims	Second Air Army Losses	Seventeenth Air Army Losses
5 July	12 Il-2s, 1 unconfirmed	43 Il-2s	66 Il-2s
6 July	2 La-5s	12 La-5s	3 La-5s
7 July	7 Il-2s	13 Il-2s	21 Il-2s
16 July	2 Il-2s	6 Il-2s	2 Il-2s
17 July	4 Il-2s	13 Il-2s	–
18 July	2 Yak-1s	–	–

It would appear that 28 out of 30 of Wiese's claims from 5 to 18 July are possible

THE FIGHT FOR AIR SUPERIORITY

Notes

1. Seidemann, page 201.
2. Aviation Marshal S. A. Krasovskii, *Zhizn v Aviatsii* [A Life in Aviation] (Moscow, 1960). For example, Marshal Kravsovskii claimed on page 165 that they inflicted a "crushing blow on the enemy" shooting down 217 Hitlerite bombers on 6 July 1943.
3. Bergstrom, *Kursk*, page 56.
4. The Luftwaffe quartermaster reports on the other hand, show four Ju-87s, one Fw-190 and an Me-109 completely destroyed this day. Bergstrom, *Black Star, Red Cross*, pages 226, makes the argument that the Ju-87 were left unprotected because most of the fighters had been assigned to cover Provisional Army Kempf. He states that resulted in the 77th Stuka Wing having ten planes shot down or severely damaged and the 1st Assault Wing lost four aircraft, including three Fw-190s. This narrative and losses simply do not match with the VIII Air Corps report of five Ju-87s lost to antiaircraft fire and only two planes lost to air. This issue is discussed further in the next footnote.

   He does give revised German losses for 6 July as 11 aircraft destroyed and 11 aircraft damaged (page 227). These are higher losses than derived from the quartermaster reports we have seen, provided to us by Christer Bergstrom in 2002. See Table II.20.

5. While I do not want to get into the habit of disputing the accounts of every book written on Kursk, I do have to contend with two accounts for this day in Christer Bergstrom's *Black Cross, Red Star*, page 223.

   First there is the claim that on 5 July the Soviet Il-2 strikes "had a decisive impact, allowing the Soviet defenders on the ground to halt 6th Panzer Division at the Mikhailovka Bridgehead just east of Belgorod, even though they were up against a twofold German numerical superiority. Of significant importance was that they put the 24-ton bridge that German engineers had built across the Donets at the Mikhailovka Bridgehead out of action." The footnote to this paragraph references page 401 of my first book on Kursk. There is little discussion of air support for this defense in my book. As I note on page 410, "The 6th Panzer Division reported increasingly heavy Soviet air attacks on the front and the railroad. The [neighboring] 19th Panzer division reported little Soviet air activity. "

   The defending 81st Guards Rifle Division was well-entrenched, deployed across only 10.2 kilometers, in two echelons. This unit's frontage was the narrowest of any of the ten Soviet divisions in the first echelon. Furthermore, it had the 262nd Tank Regiment attached with dug-in tanks, along with an anti-tank regiment and four artillery, Katyusha and mortar regiments. It was partly protected by marshlands and the Donets River, the towns of Staryii Gorod and Chernaya Polyana (held by 375th Rifle Division) were heavily fortified. Elements of the division were deployed on higher ground. This was a strong position that was initially attacked by elements of the 417th Infantry Regiment of the 168th Infantry Division.

   The bridges for this bridgehead included at least one 24-ton bridge. As noted at page 402 of my book, *Kursk: The Battle of Prokhorovka,*, this bridge could not be completed before the scheduled time of the attack. The attack by the 417th Infantry Regiment was then stopped because a section of the 24-ton bridge at Mikahilovka collapsed when an assault gun was crossing, which precluded the assault guns from supporting the attack. It is also reported that between 0225 and 0600 the 24-ton bridge the 11th Panzer Regiment (6th Panzer Division) was to cross took a direct hit and the regiment had to use another bridge. It is not certain of the source of this hit, but there is a mention in the German records of a 24-ton bridge having been hit by artillery. There are no reports of bridges in the Mikhailovka Bridgehead being hit by air.

   Alfred Rubbel, who was with the attached Tiger tank company, notes in his interview (on page 403 of *Kursk: The Battle of Prokhorovka*), "All in all, it was impossible to continue to attack the enemy's prepared position and his massive artillery fire using the forces available on our side. Quite appropriately, the attack was called off after a short time." It does not appear that the Il-2s had a "decisive impact" in helping the 81st Guards Rifle Division's defense, if they helped at all.

   The second area of concern is the statement in the following paragraph that says "In consequence, Generalmajor Seideman, the C-in-C of Fliegerkorps VIII, directed most of his fighters to cover Army Detachment Kempf on 6 July." Again, I have nothing to support that statement. I do note that the Second Air Army lost 50 planes this day including 28 fighters, while the Seventh Air Army lost 28 planes in the area, including only five fighters. This would argue against "most of his fighters" covering Provisional Army Kempf on this day. The 291st Assault Division from the Second Air Army, which is referenced in Bergstrom's discussion, did report conducting missions to Yerik-Gertsovka-Yamnoye and Butovo-Korovino-Vasileka area. These areas are both in the XLVIII Panzer Corps area, not the III Panzer Corps area. The I Assault Corps on the other hand, did send missions to attack the III Panzer corps area.

Bergstrom, in his detailed accounts of actions drawn from a variety of sources (see pages 223-225) does put the 7th Squadron of the 52nd Fighter Wing over Solomino in the morning along with elements the II and III Groups of the 3rd Fighter Wing, while elements of 9th Squadron/52nd Fighter Wing scrambled to intercept. In the late afternoon the Il-2 missions were intercepted by I Group of 1st Assault Wing flying Fw-190s.

6. Bergstrom, *Black Cross, Red Star*, page 225, states in his account that "To the troops of XLVIII Panzer Corps on Hoth's left flank, it appears as though the Soviets had achieved air superiority." This appears to be an overstatement as are several other claims made on this page.

    The 332nd Infantry Division reported that air sorties were minimal compared to the day before but does report some Soviet bombing missions. The 3rd Panzer Division reports that it suffered from continuous bombing and strafing by Soviet aircraft despite strong German fighter presence (which was weaker than on previous day). The 3rd Panzer Division counted 63 Soviet sorties on the 6th and reported two aircraft shot down. The Gross Deutschland Division stated that Soviet air activity was weaker than the previous day. The 11th Panzer Division reported that there was moderate air activity on both sides. They recorded only penetrations by four bombers and four low flying aircraft in their sector. They reported there was strong Soviet air activity over the entire combat area, especially at the bridge east of Berezovyii. The Germans reported that the bombing and strafing attacks did little damage. The 167th Infantry Division reported that there was little Soviet air activity. See Lawrence, *Kursk: The Battle of Prokhorovka*, pages 439, 463 and 465.

7. From an account written by Nikolai Panteleevich Dunayev and provided by Col. Fyodor Sverdlov in 1999. Dunayev was born in Moscow in 1923 and was a squadron commander of the 270th Fighter Regiment. During the war he scored 24 personal victories and 9 shared credits. He was awarded the Hero of the Soviet Union on 2 September 1943 for 13 kills.

8. Bergstrom, *Black Cross, Red Star*, page 227.
9. Bergstrom, *Black Cross, Red Star*, page 225.
10. Lawrence, *Kursk: The Battle of Prokhorovka*, pages 474-475.
11. Bergstrom, *Black Cross, Red Star*, page 22.
12. This includes when Rudel first used the Ju-87 G1 in combat and many elements of the ground battle. For example, in *Black Cross, Red Star*, page 244, Christer Bergstrom states that "Farther to the west, all Soviet efforts to crush the bridgehead across River Psyol which had been established by Division "Totenkopf" on the previous day, were blown to pieces by Luftwaffe attacks." Now, I have described this engagement in some depth in my books, *Kursk: The Battle of Prokhorovka*, pages 747-752, 759, and 761; and in *The Battle of Prokhorovk*a, pages 160-163, 172 and 174. At no point did I ever get the sense that the Soviet attacks were being "blown to pieces by Luftwaffe attacks." Does Bergstrom have additional evidence or did he simply extrapolate that conclusion from his readings of the battles?
13. Sergei Ivanovich Skvortsov retired as a colonel. He was interviewed by Col. Fyodor Sverdlov in 1999.
14. Christer Bergstrom, *Black Cross, Red Star*, page 227. He states it was 163 "bomber crews." We never accessed the Soviet ADD records for the Kursk Data Base project.
15. Armed reconnaissance is an air mission flown with the primary purpose of locating and attacking targets of opportunity.
16. Second Air Army records for 5 July 15 dogfights and 17 German planes shot down for the IV Fighter Corps and 46 dogfights and 118 Germans shot down for the V Fighter Corps. The I Assault Corps reported 17 dogfights and 12 German planes shot down. The 291st Assault Division claimed six dogfights and six German planes shot down. The I Bomber Corps reported four dogfights, on which six German planes were shot down. They record 81 dogfights total for the army and 154 German planes shot down by for the air army. Note that the totals from the individual units are higher than the combined report given by the air army.

    For 6 July they record 15, 18, 36, 60, 18, 21, 6, 6, 0, 0, and 64 and 105 respectively. For 7 July they record 12, 25, 35, 60, 20, 24, 7, 3, 0, 0, and 74 and 112 respectively. Needless to say, these claim figures are absurdly high.

    The IV Fighter Corps flew 229 sorties on the 5th with 13 losses. On the 6th they flew 136 sorties with 8 losses. The V Fighter Corps flew 404 sorties on the 5th with 31 losses and 256 sorties on the 6th with 14 losses.

THE FIGHT FOR AIR SUPERIORITY

17. Bergstrom, *Kursk*, page 61 and *Black Cross, Red Star*, page 230. Still, these were very small missions (total of 14 Il-2s for both airfields) and according to Bergstrom the attack was done in the afternoon. He identifies the Il-2s as being from the 237th Assault Air Regiment (IX Mixed Corps) and the 775th Assault Air Regiment (III Mixed Corps). Escort was provided by the 5th Guards Fighter Aviation Regiment, which according to Bergstrom prevented any Il-2 losses but lost 4 La-5s in an engagement with Me-109s of II Group, 3rd Fighter Wing.

    The 5th Guards Fighter Regiment reports that from 1050 to 1140 four La-5s flew to explore the approach of German reserves to the front line in the areas of Belgorod, Kharkov, Martovaya, Volchansk and Razumnoye. They report observing from an altitude of 3,000 meters 15 single-engine aircraft at Rogan airfield and they detected no aircraft at Chuguyev. They then reported that at 1730 to 1835 eight La-5s flew to bomb and attack the Rogan airfield. Crews observed up to 50 enemy bombers on the western, eastern and southern borders of the airfield, among several transport aircraft were the Ju-52 and Fw Kurier (4-motor); at the same time 12 Ju-88s and 6 He-111s approached for landing and one Ju-52 took off. Crews dropped bombs from a height of 1500 to 700 (1,700?) meters. As a result, 6 Ju-88s were smashed and the Courier was lit up. After the bombing, the Soviet planes attacked German planes coming in for landing and coming in from Chuguyev. Lieutenant Yaremenko, at an altitude of 3000 meters, lit up one Ju-88, which fell on the Rogan aerodrome. Jr. Lt. Glinkin lit up one He-111, the German aircraft fell into a ravine at Kamennaya Yaruga. Captain Dmitriyev attacked a Ju-52 taking off and shot it down. At the time of the Soviet bombing attacks, 12 Me-109Gs attacked the Soviet fighters. They had to engage in battle by dragging the German fighters into Soviet territory.

    As Rogan airfield had the II/3rd Fighter Wing (with Me-109s) and III/55th Bombardment Wing (with He-111s), then it is possible that the Soviet aircraft did indeed attack Varvarovka or elsewhere. It is not clear from the regiment's records if there were Il-2s involved in the operation and there may have been less than 14 fighters. It is hard to reconcile the differences with the army records. The army records do not report any airfield attacks by the IX Mixed Corps and they report only 14 sorties for dive-bombing enemy airfields by the III Mixed Corps. But from the mix of sorties and missions flown listed in the III Mixed Corps report, they had to be conducted by fighters. The Seventeenth Air Army records for this day that the losses in the III Mixed Corps were two La-5s, 1 Yak-1 and two Il-2s, all which failed to return.

18. Bergstrom, *Kursk*, page 60.
19. Rudel does not say exactly which day this was done, but one can infer that it was probably done on the either 7 or 8 July.
20. Rudel, pages 98–99. The Luftwaffe quartermaster files report no damaged Ju-87 G-1s at this time (reconfirmed in email with Christer Bergstrom, 10 July 2020, listing all Ju-87 losses on the Eastern Front on 7 and 8 July 1943 according to the Luftwaffe quartermaster files). The dating of this event as 7 July is drawn from other secondary sources (i.e., Robin Cross, page 190). Rudel's book only indicated that it occurred shortly after he arrived (7 or 8 July?) and that he left the area for Orel in the second half of the month. The only source for this story appears to be Rudel's book, and no confirming or supporting evidence has been located.
21. The 10.(Pz)/St.G.2 was formed from the 2./Versuchsstaffel on 17 July 1943. As of 1 July, this unit had 8 Ju-87 D-1s and 11 Ju-87 D-3s. During the month all of these planes were transferred out of the unit, so that by 1 August, the unit was reporting having no planes. It then received 8 Ju-87 G-1s during the month of August. The only Ju-87 G-1s reported available in July were with the 1./Versuchsstaffel, which on 1 July reported 1 Ju-87 D-1, 3 Ju-87 D-3s and 8 Ju-87 G-1s. It lost one Ju-87 G-1 to enemy action during the month. This unit was used to create 10.(Pz)/ St.G.1, again on 17 July 1943.
22. Ivan Vasilyevich Kormiltsin retired as a colonel. Interview conducted by telephone in Moscow on 15 November 1998 by Major General G. G. Nessonov. Seidl, pages 236–241, provides a list of "top Sturmovik aces." There are only six listed who scored as many or more tank kills than Kormiltsin. Seidl does not list Kormiltsin but his list is not exhaustive. Because of the nature of the combat, one must view claims of tank kills with much greater suspicion than aerial kill claims.
23. Seidemann, page 202.
24. Seidemann, page 201.
25. Interview with Maj.Gen. (ret.) Dieter Brand on 20 April 1999.
26. Fond: Second Air Army, Opis: 4196, Delo: 39, page: 1.

ACES AT KURSK

27. Aleksandr Novikov (1900-1976) was erased from the early Soviet histories of the war as he was arrested on spurious charges and imprisoned from 1946-1953. He returned as the Chief Marshal of Aviation under Khrushchev and retired in 1958.
28. Source is the Wikipedia article on Guenther Rall. Their list is drawn from Matthews and Foreman, *Luftwaffe Aces – Biographies and Victory Claim*s (Red Kite, Walton on Thames, 2015) and supplemented by Prien, Stemmer, Rodeike and Bock, *Die Jagdfliegerverbände der Deutschen Luftwaffe 1934 bis 1945* (Struve-Druck, Eutin, Germany, 2012).
29. According to the Wikipedia list, Matthews and Foreman claim that these planes were listed as La-5s.
30. Two locations are given. The first is from Prien, et al, 2012. The second listed location is from Matthews and Foreman, 2015. These two sets of locations often do not match.
31. This is probably a typo and the coordinate number should be 54381.
32. The list of victories is from Colonel Raymond F. Toliver and Trevor J. Constable, *The Blond Knight of Germany*, pages 297– 298. Toliver and Constable claim that the first three planes killed on the 5th were Airacobras. Yet on page 61 of the same book, they report that Hartmann downed four La-5s this day.

    The P-39 is a very distinctively different looking plane, being an unpainted silver, with a mid-engine and a different body shape than any other Soviet aircraft. The Soviet Fifth Air Army had 28 of these (the 304th Fighter Division, 69th Guards Fighter Regiment), but they were not in action on the 5th. Two Airacobras flew out at 1107 to intercept a Ju-88 reconnaissance aircraft in the Khlebnoye area, but did not encounter the German because he changed course and disappeared. The Second Air Army clearly identifies their sorties by plane type and their losses by plane type in a summary report. They neither flew nor lost Airacobras. The Seventeenth Air Army reports losses on this day by plane type, provides on-hand reports on 5 July and 25 July and a list of irreplaceable losses by 25 July. None of these show P-39s.

    This is almost certainly incorrect, and the quartermaster claims for type of plane killed on 5 July has been inserted for these three claimed Airacobras. The times of the kills in all three cases are within the frame of the times given for the missions.
33. Source is the Wikipedia article on Erich Hartmann. Their list is drawn from Matthews and Foreman, *Luftwaffe Aces – Biographies and Victory Claim*s (Red Kite, Walton on Thames, 2015) and supplemented by Prien, Stemmer, Rodeike and Bock, *Die Jagdfliegerverbände der Deutschen Luftwaffe 1934 bis 1945* (Struve-Druck, Eutin, Germany, 2012).
34. According to the Wikipedia list, Matthews and Foreman claim that these planes were listed as La-5s.
35. One of these two La-5s shot down may have been the 40th Guards Fighter Aviation Regiment commander and ace with 22 victories Hero of the Soviet Union Major Moisei Stepanovich Tokarev (1913-1943). See Bergstrom, *Kursk*, page 64. The V Air Corps lost 31 planes this day.
36. The VIII Air Corps claimed 220 Soviet planes shot down in aerial combat and 40 shot down by flak. The Soviet Union lost 189 planes that day in their units facing the VIII Air Corps.
37. Relied primarily on Hans D. Seidl, *Stalin's Eagles, An Illustrated Study of the Soviet Aces of World War II and Korea* (Schiffer Military History, Atglen, PA, 1998) for the biographies. Claims are cross-checked to the Second Army air liaison officer reports from the VIII Air Corps.
38. The listing from Kozhedub's log book comes from the web site for *Black Cross/Red Star* by Christer Bergstrom and follow-up discussions between this author and Christer Bergstrom in May 2002. It was drawn from his personal list. Also see Hans D. Seidl, *Stalin's Eagles*, page 114.
39. These claims are in accordance with the Russian Red Falcons website: *Nasheyi Rodinyi Krasnyie Cokolyi [Our Homeland Red Falcons]*: http://www.airaces.ru/asy-velikojj-otechestvennojj-vojjny/kozhedub-ivan-nikitovich.html#footnote_0_5121. The source given for the Kozhedub claim list is M. Yu. Byikov, *Vse Asyi Stalina 1936-1953 [All the Aces of Stalin, 1936-1953]*. The site specifically lists his claims as:

1. 06.07.1943	Ju-87	west of Zavidovka
2. 07.07.1943	Ju-87	Gostishchevo station
3. 09.07.1943	Me-109	Krasnaya Polyana
4. 09.07.1943	Me-109	east of Pokrovki

    On the other hand, Christer Bergstrom's website *Black Cross, Red Star: Air War Over the Eastern Front* has a victory list at http://www.bergstrombooks.elknet.pl/bc-rs/koz.html. This site lists a Ju-88 shot down on 6 July (instead of a Ju-87), another Ju-88 shot down on the 8th and three (not two) Me-109s shot down on 9 July.

THE FIGHT FOR AIR SUPERIORITY

Other sources remain equally confusing with Seidl listing only 1 Me-109 shot down on the 9th. See Hans D. Seidl, *Stalin's Eagles, An Illustrated Study of Soviet Aces of World War II and Korea* (Schiffer Military History, Atglen, PA, 1998). Polak and Shores lists the four kills from 6-9 July, but then mentions that he has his eighth victory on 16 July 1943. See Tomas Polak with Christopher Shores, *Stalin's Falcons: The Aces of the Red Star* (Grub Street, London, 1999). The Russian War Heroes website records the four kills the same as the Russian Air Aces website. See *Geroi Stranyi [Country's Heroes]*: http://warheroes.ru/hero/hero.asp?Hero_id=403. The Wikipedia article on Kozhedub just listed the four kills from 6 to 9 July 1943. The source for their listing is given as Mikhail Bykov, *Stalin's Falcons*.

40. The Germans report no Ju-88s lost of 8 July, which contradicts those lists that give Kozhedub credit for such a kill on this day.
41. Polak and Shores, page 179, claim 62 planes shot down. Some accounts credit him with 64 kills. This includes the listing in the Russian Red Falcons website and the kill listing in Wikipedia (their source is also Byikov). Some accounts (Seidl, Bergstrom and Wikipedia) credit him with 62 kills and two American P-52s shot down on 17 April 1945. Wikipedia questions the claim of two P-52s shot down. This author also questions the validity of this claim. The Russian Red Falcons website claims 64 kills and two P-52s shot down.
42. Seidl, *Stalin's Eagles*, page 117.
43. According to Seidl, page 85, he shot down two Ju-87s and rammed a third one. The Russian Red Falcons website http://airaces.narod.ru/all1/gulaev.htm shows two Ju-87s shot down on 14 May with the note "one shot down by a battering ram."
44. According to War Heroes website, the count given for the end of July was 95 combat missions, with 13 planes shot down and 5 shared kills. This was the basis for the award of his first Hero of the Soviet Union awarded 28 September 1943. According to 129th Guards Fighter Regiment records, he was awarded the Hero of the Soviet Union because of 16 kills while assigned to the Voronezh Front (Fond: 129 GVIAP, Opis: 518635-s, Delo: 1, pages 5-6).

According to Seidl, page 85, he had 13 kills by 11 July and he downed a Ju-88 by ramming on 9 July. However, the VIII Air Corps does not record losing any Ju-88s on the 9th. The quartermaster report does note one Ju-88 written off as destroyed on 9 July, but it is not reported in the air liaison officer files. See Appendix II, Tables II.20 and II.21.

The Red Falcons website http://airaces.narod.ru/all1/gulaev.htm shows a claim list with 17 kills by 11 July, including two shared kills. It also does not show a Ju-88 as rammed and downed on 9 July, but instead shows a Ju-87 as downed from ramming on 12 July. On the other hand, in the text of the website it makes the same claim of 13 kills and 5 shared kills "as of July." It is also claimed in the text that on 9 July Gulayev made his second ram near Belgorod and landed safely by parachute. So the Red Falcons website disagrees with itself on the same page. The claims for 9 July are probably incorrect. The 27th Fighter Regiment lists only an Me-109 downed on the 9th by the regiment. There is no mention of Gulayev ramming an aircraft, going down or parachuting in any of the regiment records we have.

There is a picture on the website of Gulayev and his plane in the winter of 1944. The plane shows 32 kill markings on the side. As of the end of 1943, the claim list shows him with 34 kills, including 3 shared kills. He claimed two kills on 17 December 1943 and two kills on 8 January 1944.

His list of claimed kills is provided by the Red Falcons website at http://airaces.narod.ru/all1/gulaev.htm. It gives the following claims through the end of July:

1.	3 August 1942	He-111	Novokhopersk	
2.	24 August 1942	Ju-88	Korotoyak	
3.	14 May 1943	Ju-87	Gostishchevo	
4.	14 May 1943	Ju-87	Gostishchevo	One downed by ramming
5.	22 May 1943	Ju-88	area Gryaznoye	
6.	22 May 1943	Me-109	area Gryaznoye	
7.	8 June 1943	Me-109	Pokrovka	
8.	22 June 1943	Me-109	Khotmyizhsk	
9.	5 July 1943	Ju-87	Verkhopenye	
10.	5 July 1943	Me-109	Prokhorovka	
11.	5 July 1943	Ju-87	Korovino	

12. 5 July 1943	Me-109	Dragunskoye		
13. 6 July 1943	Fw-190	west Verkhopenye		
14. 7 July 1943	Ju-87	Belenikhino		
15. 7 July 1943	Hs-126	south Belenikhino	shared victory (1/3)	
16. 7 July 1943	Fw-189	NW Gostishchevo	shared victory (1/3)	
17. 8 July 1943	Me-109	south Belenikhino		
18. 12 July 1943	Ju-87	Prokhorovka		
19. 12 July 1943	Ju-87	Prokhorovka	One downed by ramming	
20. 12 July 1943	Me-109	Prokhorovka*		

*This claim is an Fw-190 according to the 27th Fighter Regiment records. See Appendix II.

This list counts a total of 60 claimed kills (5 shared), in 250 sorties and 49 air battles. Note that the Ju-87 downed by ramming on 12 July 1943 is reported in the 27th Fighter Regiment records as simply brought down. No mention is made of ramming in the unit record for 12 July (see Fond: 22GVIAD, Opis: 1, Delo:12, page 165).

45. This is from Seidl, page 85. Other sources state otherwise with the Red Falcons website http://airaces.narod.ru/all1/gulaev.htm showing 20 planes (two shared) by the 12th of July and showing no more claimed kills until October.
46. Sources differ on his count of victories. He either had 57 claimed kills and 3 shared kills (Seidl, Polak and Shores, Wikipedia) or 55 claimed kills and 5 shared kills (War Heroes website, Red Falcons website, and also Wikipedia). We assume it was the latter. If he had 57 claimed solo kills, then he would be the third highest scoring ace of the Soviet Union, not fourth.
47. Wikipedia specifically states that the kills were:

1. 28 March 1943: one Me-109 near Urazovo,
2. 28 March 1943: one Ju-87
3. 12 April: one Me-110
4. 6 May: one Ju-88
5. 6 May: one Me-110

Their source is not given but this matches with other reports we have found. Seidl, page 224, states it was nine kills, but we suspect this is incorrect. The wounding in both feet is stated in Wikipedia as occurring on 5 August 1943.

48. Seidl, page 224, gives that date of these kills at June and states that only two Ju-87s claimed on 8 June.
49. Quoted from Seidl, page 224, who gives the event as occurring on 5 July. VIII Air Corps records no Ju-87s lost among the 19 aircraft lost that day.
50. The air liaison officer reports two Ju-87s lost this day, while the quartermaster report records 6 as 100% damaged. The difference here may be planes that were able to return to their airfield and then were written off. See Appendix II, Tables II-20 and II.21.
51. Footnote reads: There is a kill list for Yevstigneyev in the Soviet Hammer blog at http://soviethammer.blogspot.com/search?q=yevstigneyev dated 24 February 2015. The claim listing is in French. It states:

1. 28 March	Me-109	In the area of Urazovo	
2. 28 March	Ju-88	In the area of Urazovo	shared victory
3. 12 April	Me-110	In the area of Urazovo	
4. 6 May	Ju-88	Valcuyki	
5. 6 May	Me-110	Valcuyki	
6. 7 July	Ju-87	Byikovka	shared victory
7. 8 July	Ju-87	Belenikhino	
8. 8 July	Ju-87	Belenikhino	
9. 8 July	Ju-87	Belenikhino	
10. 9 July	Me-109	Kochetovka	
11. 13 July	Me-109	Vasilyevka-Belenikhino	
12. 16 July	Me-109	Streletskoye	

Note that the list on the Soviet Hammer blog only mentions 55 kills (3 shared), not the 56 he is usually credited with.

THE FIGHT FOR AIR SUPERIORITY

There is a similar listing on at http://airaces.narod.ru/all1/evstign.htm. That list reads:

1. 28 March	Me-109	Titovka	
2. 12 April	Me-110	southwest of the area of Urazovo	
3. 6 May	Me-110	SW Velikii Burluk	
4. 6 May	Ju-88	Velikii Burluk	
5. 7 July	Ju-87	Byikovka	shared victory (1/6)
6. 8 July	Ju-87	Krasnaya Polyana	
7. 8 July	Ju-87	Krasnaya Polyana	
8. 8 July	Ju-87	Krasnaya Polyana	
9. 9 July	Me-109	East Kartashovka	
10. 13 July	Me-109	SW Prokhorovka	shared victory (1/2)
11. 16 July	Me-109	West Byikovka	

This listing also only records 55 kills (3 shared).

According to the Russian War Heroes site, Yevstigneyev was recommended for a Hero of the Soviet Union award based upon 70 combat missions, participation in 18 air battles and shooting down 10 planes and 2 shared victories. The recommended award was downgraded to an Order of Suvorov, 3rd degree.

52. Source is the Wikipedia article on Johannes Wiese. The list is drawn from Matthews and Foreman, *Luftwaffe Aces – Biographies and Victory Claim*s (Red Kite, Walton on Thames, 2015) and supplemented by Prien, Stemmer, Rodeike and Bock, *Die Jagdfliegerverbände der Deutschen Luftwaffe 1934 bis 1945* (Struve-Druck, Eutin, Germany, 2012). Although the two lists disagree in a number of details, both listings agree on Wiese's claims for July 1943 with the exception of the seven kills on 7 July. The Prien*, et al*, list shows 133 confirmed kills and 7 unconfirmed kills. The Matthews and Foreman list shows 118 confirmed kills and 28 unconfirmed kills.
53. These 1:50000 scale maps are available in both of my previously published Kursk books, *Kursk: The Battle of Prokhorovka* and *The Battle of Prokorovka*.
54. First claimed kill was at 1815 either in the vicinity of Leski (Prien, et all, 2012) or 10 km south of Prokhorovka (Matthew and Forman, 2015). Second kill was at 1815 south of Luchki (Prien, et al, 2012).
55. The first kill is listed as occurring at 0927 at PQ Ost 61253. The other six do not have a time or location given.
56. First claim was at 0540 at 5 km northeast of Bagatoje. Second claim was at 0541 at either west of Alisowka (Prien) or 10 km south of Oboyan (Matthews and Forman). Third was at 0545 3 km west of Oboyan and the fourth was at 0550 5 kilometers south of Oboyan. These were clearly all claimed during the same sortie.
57. First claim was at 17:52 either south of Marinovka (Prien) or in the vicinity of Kalinovka (Matthews and Foreman). Second was at 17:53 in the same areas.
58. Note that 5 Yak-1s were lost from the I Mixed Corps of the Seventeenth Air Army. These units were involved in operations outside of the area of the Battle of Kursk. Wiese's two claims were at PQ 34 Ost 88256, south of Marinovka, in the vicinity of Kalinovka. This is the Second Air Army area of operations and they did not record losing any Yaks on 18 July (see Table II.27).
59. Matthews and Foreman only record 118 confirmed claimed kills for him.

Chapter Five

THE AIR WAR CONTINUES
8–9 July 1943

After 20 July [the 1944 assassination attempt on Hitler] everything came out, things I had considered impossible. It was precisely those circles against me who had profited most from National Socialism. I pampered and decorated them. And that was all the thanks I got. I ought to put a bullet in my head. I lacked hard fighters. Model and Dietrich are such. And Rudel [the Stuka pilot]. Now there's a successor for me. Intelligence. What are his views on art and culture?

Adolf Hitler, 1945?[1]

The First Air Transfers (7–9 July 1943)

At this point, the problems in the Orel sector were about to influence the battle in the south. In the north, Model's Ninth Army had only advanced twelve kilometers and had yet to break the Soviet second defensive line. According to Seidemann, the VIII Air Corps was ordered on the evening of 7 July to transfer an estimated 270 aircraft to the 1st Air Division of the Sixth Air Fleet. Seidemann claimed that the forces sent north were the two groups of the 3rd Fighter Wing (with an estimated 80 aircraft), the three groups of the 2nd Stuka Wing (with an estimated 120 aircraft) and two groups of the 3rd Bombardment Wing (with an estimated 70 aircraft).[2]

It appears that most of these units were transferred much later. The number of German sorties did not noticeably decline on 8/9 July. The 3rd Fighter Wing appears to have remained in the Belgorod-Kharkov area until at least 16 July.[3] The 2nd Stuka Wing appears to have remained in the Belgorod-Kharkov area until 15 July.[4] Only in the case of the 3rd Bomber Wing was there no evidence that it was in the south after 7 July. Therefore it is assumed that it was transferred north sometime between the 7th and the 9th.[5]

Seidemann then claims that the Hs-129s were ordered to transfer to the 1st Air Division at Orel on 9 July, further reducing the ground attack force by an estimated 60 aircraft. Again, this does not appear to have been the case, as it would appear from the quartermaster reports that the five squadrons of Hs-129s were not transferred to Orel until around 15 July.[6]

THE AIR WAR CONTINUES

However large this transfer initially was, it did not seem to take the steam out of the German air effort, for on the 6th and 7th, they flew 1,686 and 1,829 sorties respectively, while on the following two days, they flew 1,686 and 1,621 sorties. It was only on the 10th that the sortie rate declined to 682 sorties in one day. As the Soviets only opened their offensive on the north side of the Orel bulge on the 12th, then the transfer was probably done later to support the defense, as that was the German contingency plan. Still, for these next two days, the German Air Force was able to remain active and effective at its old sortie levels and most likely at close to its starting strength.

Soviet Air Transfers

On the Soviet side throughout the battle, the Second Air Army was transferring units and receiving reinforcements. The first transfer occurred on the 7th, when the 183rd Fighter Regiment from the IV Fighter Corps sent 18 planes to the 291st Assault Division. Six were based at the 617th Assault Regiment's airfield at Solntsevo and the other 12 at the 61st Assault Regiment's airfield at Maksimovo.

Reinforcements were periodically received during the battle, with 172 new planes being sent to the Second Air Army during the month of July. They also received aircraft from other units, a total of 152 during the month of July, although many of these probably arrived after the German offensive ended. There were a small number of planes under repair (eight during the month of July). As such, the strength of the Soviet air units remained in flux throughout the battle as planes were lost, new planes were received, and units were transferred in or out.

Novikov's Directive

Marshal Aleksandr Aleksandrovich Novikov was the Commander of the Red Army Air Force and Deputy to the People's Commissar of Defense of the USSR for Aviation. On 7 July 1943 he issued a directive. It noted a significant number of shortcomings in recent Soviet air combat. The directive noted that combat missions were frequently vague and without specific goals. As a result, there was a reduced sense of responsibility among air commanders at all levels. The directive noted that aviators were more concerned with flying sorties than accomplishing a mission. It also noted that operational planning was far from ideal. The directive mentioned a lack of creative approaches and a tendency to use standard means and methods, like the same altitudes, directions and attack methods. It noted a lack of pre-strike reconnaissance of targets and their air defenses. It also noted that radio vectoring did not satisfy the requirements of modern air combat. The radio network was not wide enough and its personnel did not possess the necessary qualifications.

The directive encouraged the development of "free hunting" using the best pilots, similar to the German Air Force. It noted that fighter units rarely engaged in "free hunting" over German territory or the destruction of German aircraft during the approach to the front lines. The rigid linking of patrolling fighters to specific areas prevented Soviet pilots from active offensive air engagement. The directive wanted more cohesiveness and coordination among "flying pairs" during combat. These "flying pairs" had to be permanent. It was felt that this would increase the wingmen's responsibility for the actions of their leaders. He also called for the ability to create numerical superiority by using the radio to call for reinforcements during engagements. It was noted that this is similar to how the Luftwaffe operated.

The directive called for increased initiative among division and regiment commanders, providing them with greater flexibility in the planning of combat operations. It also called for strike groups to utilize compact formations and for increased self-defense by creating a high density of defensive fire, as well as coordinating with fighter escorts and antiaircraft artillery.[7]

July 8

The nighttime activity of 7/8 July continued unabated by both sides. The Germans flew 57 sorties during the night, with six bombing missions again going against the railroad from Kursk to Kastornoye, with three breaks in the railroad claimed. There were 46 harassing sorties made to the east of Belgorod, in the Koren River area. Night reconnaissance reported considerable Soviet movement in the area of Korocha and northeast and north of Prokhorovka.

The Second Air Army's 208th Night Bomber Division increased its activities, making 96 sorties during the night. Their sortie rate had increased, so that their 28 U-2s were able to carry out 85 sorties. They bombed in the area of Kozmo Demyanovka-Olkhovka-Zadelnoye. The Seventeenth Air Army's 262nd Night Bomber division continued to maintain a sortie rate of over three sorties per plane, and sent out 163 night sorties. They sent out 38 U-2s on 140 bombing sorties and 7 U-2s and 7 R-5s on 23 reconnaissance missions. Their targets along the Donets were the same as the previous day. They now bombed both Rogan and Osnova airfields around Kharkov. They continued to be assisted by the 244th Bomber Division which added another 29 sorties by 15 TB-3s. Twelve of them conducted 26 bombing missions and three planes conducted reconnaissance. These missions were focused on the Solomino-Ivanovka area and the Rogan and Osnova airfields.

The Soviet Long Range Aviation force sent 66 bombers to conduct night attacks on the ferries across the Donets and to attack a pontoon bridge the Germans were building in the Lukhanino area.[8]

The Second Air Army reported that the weather at night was mostly clear, with scattered clouds and thick haze, and visibility from one to three kilometers. During the first part of the day there was slight cloudiness, with visibility up to ten kilometers. In the second part of the day there were thick clouds and heavy haze, with visibility two to four kilometers.

The Second Air Army continued the fight, but at a lower loss rate than before. The I Assault Corps continued to sortie its Il-2s at a rapid rate, with its 84 Il-2s carrying out 218 sorties. They struck in the areas of Pogorelovka-Kozmo, Demyanovka-Vorskla, and Teterevino-Solonets-Dubrova. Their 46 Yak-1s carried out 150 sorties with 74 of these sent as escort. Flying in groups of 10 aircraft they also patrolled the battlefield, with 76 sorties in the Krasnyii Oktyabr-Aleksandrovka-Belenikhino area. The 291st Assault Division sent groups of 6 to 12 Il-2s for massed attacks against German tanks and concentration areas in

THE AIR WAR CONTINUES

the Pogorelovka-Dubrova-Pokrovka area. The 59 Il-2s carried out 110 sorties while being escorted by 44 fighter sorties. This unit took heavy losses of seven Il-2s and three fighters, while the I Assault Corps lost 9 Il-2s and five Yak-1bs.

The two fighter corps patrolled and covered the area of Krasnyii Oktyabr-Belenikhino-Aleksandrovka. The IV Fighter Corps made 109 sorties and the V Fighter Corps with 59 planes flew 190 sorties. The IV Fighter Corps also sent 115 fighters for reconnaissance and armed reconnaissance. Pairs of fighters were sent out against the columns along the Belgorod-Myasoyedovo road. The two fighter corps lost 11 planes each.

This activity displayed a real change of emphasis by the Soviet air force. It was no longer concentrating on the XLVIII Panzer Corps area and the forces advancing on Oboyan, but instead was focusing its attention on the eastern flank of the German penetration. Fighters were also providing cover for the area leading to Prokhorovka and for their armored formations in the Donets triangle. It would appear that this was done to try to support and help cover II Guards and X Tank Corps' armored counterattacks on 8 July.

The I Bomber Corps was again inactive, sending up only ten reconnaissance sorties in the Kharkov area. The 454th Bomber Regiment and 50th Air Reconnaissance Regiment also sent up reconnaissance sorties.

The Seventeenth Air Army continued its support of the Seventh Guards Army, with the I Mixed Corps sending 60 Il-2s to strike the Germans in the Yastrebovo, Belovskoye, Razumnoye and Krutoi Log areas and German tanks in the Olkhovka-Byikovka area. The corps' 50 active fighters flew 90 escort sorties and 14 sorties covering the Seventh Guards Army. They lost one Yak-1 and eight Il-2s this day. This was the first ground support activity by the I Mixed Corps. They had flown only eight Il-2s on the 5th for an air strike and only two Il-2s on the 6th for an interception attempt. The sudden appearance of 60 Il-2s was probably reinforcements, most likely transferred from the IX Mixed Corps.

The III Mixed Corps made strikes on Sevryukovo, Yastrebovo, Byikovka, Razumnoye, Solomino, Maslova Pristan and the Krutoi Log area with only 16 Il-2s. Their 19 fighters conducted 28 escort sorties and eight reconnaissance sorties. They lost five Il-2s.

The Seventeenth Air Army also reconnoitered at the Barvenkovo and Kramatorskaya airfields. We have no reports of the IX Mixed Corps activities this day and it does not appear that they flew. Their losses over the previous three days had been horrendous. On 5 July they lost 50 Il-2s and 7 La-5s. The next day they lost 19 Il-2s and two La-5s. On the 7th they lost 26 Il-2s and four La-5s. This loss of 95 Il-2s, in addition to those damaged, probably stripped the IX Mixed Corps of almost all their operational Il-2s. As such, they withdrew from the Battle of Kursk, and would only conduct very limited operations for the next week.

The Seventeenth Air Army's support was now waning. It had gone from conducting 176 Il-2 sorties on the 5th to 169 Il-2 sorties on the 6th, to 156 Il-2 sorties on the 7th, to only 76 Il-2 sorties on this day. This was partially due to losses, for the army had lost 118 Il-2s since the start of the operations. They had lost 66 Il-2s in the first day of the operation, but the following day still managed to fly the same number of sorties, probably by using reserve planes and other pilots. On the 7th they still maintained a high number of sorties, as clearly the planes were averaging better than two sorties a day. On this day, the 8th, they appear to have gone back to one sortie per plane, and with the greatly reduced number of planes, this caused the overall number of sorties to drop. After spending three days making more than 150 strikes a day to the Provisional Army Kempf sector, the Seventeenth Air Army effort now declined.

The German air continued to be very active with 1,686 sorties. They continued with strong bomber, dive bomber, and ground assault attacks throughout the day. These were conducted in rolling waves along the whole Fourth Panzer Army front. In particular, they continued to concentrate on the SS Panzer Corps' flanks where there were strong Soviet tank concentrations. Soviet tanks were engaged to the northeast of Belgorod in the III Panzer Corps area and forward of the SS Panzer Corps, south of Prokhorovka. The III Group of the 55th Bombardment Wing again split its effort between the two attacking corps of the Fourth Panzer Army. This included sending 22 sorties to Kochetovka and 23 to Verkhopenye. Again, it appears that the He-111s were being used for ground attack strikes on the Soviet second echelon and on the Soviet reserves. The German daytime reconnaissance revealed the assembly of a major Russian tank force around Prokhorovka. This was probably the X Tank Corps.

The Second Air Army losses for the day were 47 planes, including 16 Il-2s and 30 fighters. This was a slightly lower loss rate than the previous days. The German losses declined to five planes but casualties included an Fw-190, two Hs-129s and two Knight's Cross winners in Ju-87s! Lost due to flak east of Verkhopenye was Knight's Cross winner Captain Bernhard Wutka, while lost due to Soviet aircraft was Knight's Cross winner Senior Lt. Karl Fitzner.[9]

It was on this day that the 240th Fighter Aviation Regiment, which included future top aces Kozhedub and Yevstigneyev, jumped a group of Stukas with at least nine La-5s. According to Soviet accounts they shot down five Ju-87s and a Me-109. Lt. Kirill Yevstigeneyev was personally responsible for three of those claims.[10] The Germans lost only one Ju-87 to air action this day according to the air liaison report, but the quartermaster report shows 6 Ju-87s with 100% damage this day. There was one Me-109 100% damaged this day according to the quartermaster report, but no Me-109s lost according to the air liaison report (see Appendix II: Tables II.20 and II.21).

During the day the Germans launched 1,380 ground attack type sorties on the 8th compared to 404 ground attack type sorties by the Soviets. Among the people shot down this day was Lt. Ivan Filin, squadron commander with the 147th Assault Aviation Regiment, 294th Assault Aviation Division.[11] He recalled:

> I arrived at the regiment in the middle of June, 1943. On the day of my arrival, we started fighting with German bombers to the northwest of Belgorod, to protect our troops. On a sunny day it is very difficult to see the enemy planes. First, I saw two Me-109 fighters above us, then two more planes behind them. As it turned out later there were 10 German planes there. I commanded "Attack!" and took my Yak-7B right up, having no doubt that the rest of our planes were following me. The distance between my plane and the German planes was quickly getting shorter. The battle broke into three groups. All of a sudden, I saw that the leader of the group behind me caught on fire. I became furious. I understood that it was dangerous because an Me-109 had a gun in the front, but I attacked it right to its front and in a second opened

fire. I saw two or three of my shells explode in the cabin of the German pilot. I realized that this was the end of him. Then me and my wingman flew up, turned around and from both sides attacked another "Messer." He wanted to fly up also, but he did not have time. Our two rounds got into his cabin and damaged his motor. He dropped like a stone. Unfortunately, the battle with the other two groups did not end so successfully. They lost two planes and damaged only one Me-109. But we did fulfill our task; we did not let the German fighters attack our troops.

During the battle, we did 3–4 flights a day, mostly to attack German bombers. The number of German bombers seemed countless. Honestly speaking, for three days from 5 until 7 July we destroyed only two planes, but we almost all the time forced them to turn around, drop their bombs and fly back. Sometimes their bombs would drop on their own troops.

In the morning, on 8 July, I had a fiasco. Our regiment flew out to cover our tank troops, which were being attacked along the Belgorod-Oboyan highway by massive German tank forces. German bombers were flying protected by a large number of fighters. For the first time, I got scared— it was such a massive number of German planes. I received the order from the regiment commander: "We are fighting the bombers, you should attack the fighters." I calmed down and led my six planes to the attack. I always knew that the best defense is offense in an air battle. My wingman was protecting me, and I managed to destroy one Me-109. I got so involved in the attack that I was always looking ahead, which is an unforgivable mistake. The joy of victory makes you euphoric. At that moment a shell hit my plane followed by gun fire. My first thought was "where in the hell was my wingman. . . ." Then I understood that I was wounded in the side and I felt blood in my boot. But there was still strength in my arms. I looked back, my wingman was dropping. My plane was damaged (probably one panel and the control cable). I bit my tongue until it bled, getting weaker and weaker, but trying to fly the plane back to the airport. When I reached the airport, I did not have any energy to land the plane. Instead I lowered down the plane and dropped it on the ground. As my friends told me, I was thrown out from the cabin. I regained consciousness only in the evening, in the hospital.

Tank Busting

Early in the morning on the 8th, Captain Bruno Meyer was conducting a reconnaissance of the woods around Gostishchevo with a section of Hs-129s. Meyer was the commander of the antitank group attached to the 1st Ground Attack Wing. Below him, moving out of the woods into attack positions was at least one brigade of Soviet armor along with their supporting infantry. This was part of the II Guards Tank Corps' attack into the SS Panzer Corps' flank. Meyer, on his own initiative, ordered his Group by radio to immediately scramble and join him in attacking the Soviet tanks. Flying out of Mikoyanovka, the first squadron arrived 15 minutes later and began attacking the advancing Soviet armor as it moved in the open. The Hs-129s, with their 30mm guns, would come in low and attack from the side or rear. Attacking by squadrons, within an hour, the entire Group was able to unload on the tanks below, while Fw-190s led by Major Alfred Druschel bombed the supporting infantry. According to German accounts, forty tanks were destroyed and the tank brigade retreated back into the woods.

CAPTAIN BRUNO MEYER AND THE HS-129

Captain Bruno Meyer was the commander of the antitank command of the 1st Ground Attack Wing at the Battle of Kursk. It was the first use of the tank-busting Hs-129 B-2s in a formation the size of a group.

Bruno Meyer had been involved in antitank aircraft since the early days of the war when he was part of the only antitank group in the German Air Force. This was the II Group of the 2nd Training Wing (a combat unit) and was mostly armed with He-123 biplanes and some Me-109s. As a squadron commander in the summer of 1941, First Lt. Bruno Meyer gained fame for scattering an attacking force of Soviet tanks by repeatedly diving on them, even though he had no bombs left. On 21 August 1941, he was awarded the Knights Cross, having flown over 200 combat missions.

In spring of 1942, this unit was merged into the First Ground Attack Wing and in the summer of 1942, the II Group consisted of Hs-129s. These were armed with 20mm cannons, machineguns, and had an armored cockpit, making them an effective ground attack weapon.

The Germans on an experimental basis assembled a few dozen of the Hs-129s armed with 30mm cannons to be used as antitank weapons. This squadron was first used in May 1942 against the Soviet offensive around Kharkov. The Germans kept two squadrons in use throughout 1942 while they further developed the system. In early 1943, with the bugs worked out, they finally formed their first antitank group for use at Kursk. This group initially consisted of four squadrons from three different air groups: the 4.(Pz)/Sch.G.1, 8.(Pz)/Sch.G.1, 4.(Pz)/Sch.G.2, and the Panzerjaegerstaffel/JG51. In August the 8.(Pz)/Sch.G.2 was added to his command.

On 18 October 1943, this group of five squadrons was designated the IV Antitank Group of the 9th Ground Attack Wing (IV.Pz)/SG9) in Kirovograd. Meyer continued as their commander until 1 October 1944. He took over command of the I Group of the 104th Ground Attack Wing on 24 October 1944 until 3 March 1945.

Bruno Meyer was born in Jeremie, Haiti, on 13 November 1915. He joined the German Army 4 April 1934, but switched to flying by 1937. He served in Poland, France, the Balkans, the Soviet Union, Africa, and back to the Soviet Union. He had flown 1,000 combat missions by 1 May 1944, and it is claimed that he killed 183 tanks in his career. He passed away in 1974.

THE AIR WAR CONTINUES

The reports of heavy Soviet tank losses due to German air first appeared in the German records for 7/8 July. The VIII Air Corps claimed seven tanks on the 5th of July, but on the 7th (the day Rudel claimed 12 tanks) they claimed one tank platoon and 44 tanks destroyed and one tank platoon and 32 tanks damaged. On the 8th, they claimed 84 tanks destroyed, including 11 burned, and 21 tanks damaged. These attacks on the 8th were noted by Seidemann, who reported that "The German antitank ground attack aircraft were exceptionally successful. In the afternoon, the German air reconnaissance identified a powerful Soviet tank attack aimed at the extended flank of the II SS Panzer Corps and issuing from woods east of GOSTCHEVO [sic] Station. The antitank ground attack aircraft of the IV Group, 9th Antitank Ground Attack Wing [sic], were ready for service, fortunately. In a short time they were on their way to meet the enemy force. The Russian tank attack was smashed after about one hour. The remainder of the enemy force discontinued the attack and turned around. Approximately 40 enemy tanks had been knocked out."[12] The VIII Air Corps reported that "The initial action by the antitank aircraft squadron was quite effective. Given the number of burning [enemy] tanks reported, it must be assumed that there was an even greater number that were just knocked out (more than 6 hits reported). Especially in the late afternoon attack from the northeast against SS Reich and the evening tank battle, the Russians were stopped and driven back."[13] The antitank squadrons were clearly engaged during this period, as two of the Hs-129s were lost on the 8th and one on the 9th.

The only major armored formation around Gostishchevo on the 8th was the II Guards Tank Corps. The Soviet brigade that came under attack was the 26th Tank Brigade (see Chapter Eleven of *Kursk: The Battle of Prokhorovka* and the II Guards Tank Corps map for the 8th) which was attacking from Visloye at 1200 (Moscow time). Visloye is at the northwest tip of the large woods south of Gostishchevo. This attack drove onto height 209.5, two kilometers southwest of Visloye. The brigade reported being attacked by 40–50 planes during the German counterattack (1210 Berlin time). To its north was the 4th Guards Tank Brigade attacking at Nepkhayevo while the corps' other tank brigade remained in the rear. The neighboring 96th Tank Brigade was attacking to the southeast this day against the III Panzer Corps and the II Guards Tank Corps' 47th Heavy Tank Regiment (with Churchills) was already engaged with the III Panzer Corps seven to twelve kilometers south-southeast of Gostishchevo. Therefore, there is not much question that this was the attack being referred to by the Germans.

The 26th Tank Brigade as of 0700 on 8 July had 26 T-34s and 15 T-70s. The corps reported losing 8 T-34s and 3 T-70s for the day, with effectively only two of its brigades engaged. The 26th Tank Brigade attack also included one regiment from the 4th Guards Motorized Brigade, which may have included up to 20 Bren Gun Carriers. The brigade reported at 0700 on 10 July having 22 T-34s and 12 T-70s. The corps reported only Churchills lost for the 9th. From 0700 on the 8th to 0700 on the 10th, the 26th Guards Tank Brigade shows a decline of 4 T-34s and 3 T-70s ready-for-action, while the 4th Guards Tank Brigade shows a decline of 2 T-34s and 2 T-70s. The 25th Guards Tank Brigade's tank strength actually increased during this time. The corps did have a corps reserve of 20 T-34s and 10 T-70s located at Bubnovo on the 8th. This unit is no longer mentioned and may have been used on the 10th or 11th. As the 4th Guards Tank Brigade clearly took casualties, this all points to the actual losses of the 26th Tank Brigade being around nine tanks. Assuming some were lost to German armor, antitank guns, and infantry (both during the attack and during the German counterattack) then it would appear that the claim by the VIII Air Corps of "more than 6 hits" may in fact be high. The claim of 40 tanks "killed" appears to be off by an order of magnitude. While it is not in the least unusual for ground kill claims by air forces to be grossly over inflated, this claim of 40 or 50 kills has been repeated in other sources without critical analysis.[14]

HANS RUDEL

Hans-Ulrich Rudel was born 2 July 1916, and grew up in Silesia. His father was a Lutheran minister. Rudel became seriously devoted to athletics and did not drink alcohol.

Rudel joined the Luftwaffe in December 1936. Although his desire was to serve with the fighters, he volunteered for the dive-bombers in response to a false rumor that his entire class was to be assigned to bombers. He began flying Ju-87s in June 1938. Having not impressed his superiors, in January 1939 he was assigned to reconnaissance training and became an observer.

Lt. Rudel served during the Polish Campaign with Distant Reconnaissance Squadron 2F 121. Rudel was then transferred to an adjutant position in a training regiment and did little flying. After continual requests, Rudel was finally transferred back to stuka training in May 1940 but missed the French Campaign and most of the Battle of Britain. When his squadron was transferred to the Balkans, Rudel was sent back for more training, having again failed to impress his superiors. He was sent back to his squadron as a replacement after Greece, but was grounded by the commander due to his past poor performance. Rudel missed the invasion of Crete and was sent back to Germany. He rejoined his squadron unannounced shortly after the Soviet Union was invaded and flew his first combat mission on 23 June 1941.

Once airborne, Rudel quickly established himself as a competent and determined pilot. He first operated in the Army Group Center area and then moved up to Leningrad, where on 23 September he was personally credited with sinking the Battleship *Marat*. For this and other actions he was awarded the Knights Cross on 15 January 1942.

Rudel was then shifted back to the Army Group Center to support the attack on Moscow and on 24 December 1941 he flew his 500th operational sortie. He was then sent back to Germany in early 1942 to conduct training. It was at this time that Rudel married. The squadron was then sent to the Crimea for further training and in June Rudel began flying operational missions in the Crimea, the Caucasus, Stalingrad, and eventually the retreat from Stalingrad. In September 1942 he was made commander of the 1st squadron of the 2nd Stuka Wing.

In February 1943, after his 1001st operational mission, Rudel was sent back to Germany to take command of an experimental squadron of Ju-87 tank-busting aircraft armed with two 37mm guns. This unit was then sent to the Crimea in April to field-test

THE AIR WAR CONTINUES

the aircraft. In May, at his request, Rudel was transferred back to command of his old squadron, taking one of the experimental Ju-87s with him. He was awarded the Oak Leaves for the Knight's Cross on 14 April 1943.

His unit was then shifted up to Kharkov for the Kursk offensive in July. During the Battle of Kursk, he lost a cousin in an He-111 that he saw go down. He made the first effective combat use of this new cannon equipped Stuka on 7 July, when he claimed 12 tanks. This led to the experimental squadron being attached to the II Stuka Group with Rudel effectively in command of both his old Stuka squadron and the experimental squadron. He was then transferred with his Wing to help defend the Orel bulge in the second half of July. He was made group commander on 19 July after the previous commander, Walter Krauss, was killed the night of 16/17 July during an attack by Soviet U-2 planes on the Orel-Northern airfield. The wing was later shifted back to Kharkov.

After Kursk, Rudel continued flying in the south. On 25 November, he was awarded the Swords to the Knight's Cross and had claimed around 100 tanks killed. He reached his 1,500 operational sortie in March 1944. Very much the darling of the Nazi leadership, Rudel was awarded the Diamonds to his Knight's Cross, the highest award Germany had (only 27 awarded), on 29 March 1944. He then retreated with his squadron through Romania in the summer of 1944, having now flown over 2,000 sorties. He then served in the Baltics, Hungary and the retreat back to Germany. He was presented on 1 January 1945 the newly created highest award and only such award minted, the Golden Oak Leaves of the Knight's Cross. At the beginning of February 1945 he lost his right leg below the knee in action. He returned to action before the war's end. He ended the war as a colonel and a wing commander of the 2nd Stuka Wing, the unit he had served in throughout the war. Even though Rudel's primary demonstrated talent was in killing tanks, Hitler thought highly of him, mentioning him in passing once as a possible successor.

It is claimed that during the course of the war, Rudel destroyed 519 tanks, 80 self-propelled guns, a battleship, one or two cruisers, a destroyer, 70 assault boats, 800 or 1,000 vehicles, 150 artillery pieces, four armored trains and scored nine or eleven air victories (about 400 of his sorties were in an Fw-190, from which these air victories were claimed). These claims have not been confirmed. He was shot down over thirty times, several behind enemy lines, and was wounded five times. On six or eight occasions he landed behind enemy lines to rescue a downed Stuka crew. He flew 2,530 operational sorties, which may be the all-time record number of combat sorties flown by any pilot.[15]

He surrendered to the Americans and was released in April 1946. In 1948 he moved to Argentina where he was involved in organizing a Nazi-like political party and wrote political books in 1951 that clearly delineated his views (including the need for Lebensraum or "living space" in the East). He returned to Germany in 1953 where he was an unsuccessful candidate for an ultraconservative party. He published his memoirs in 1958, and his memoirs always show Hitler in a good light. Rudel died of a brain hemorrhage on 18 December 1982 at the age of 66.

To the northeast of the Das Reich SS Division was the V Guards Tank Corps, which reported losing 37 tanks on the 8th, and probably lost around 49 tanks. Also in the area were the II and X Tank Corps, neither of which reported tank losses on this day. Overall, these four units lost 48 or more tanks on this day. As two of the tank corps were attacking against two different German divisions, certainly a number of these were to German ground units.

The Effectiveness of German Air Against Armor

This brings up a bigger issue, which is how effective was German air against armor (or Soviet air against armor, for that matter)? The broadest ranging report we have on this subject is from the First Tank Army, which reported that they lost a total of 648 tanks between 4-18 July, of which 84 were due to artillery, 11 due to air, 471 were "burned" and 82 were technical breakdowns.[16] While it is not known how many of the "burned" were due to air attacks, some certainly were. Still, this report does not lead one to conclude that air attacks were a major cause of tank losses. These figures are not out of line with other reports from other theaters of the war.[17]

The 86th Tank Brigade reported that between 8th and 11 July, the brigade lost 9 T-34s to enemy planes, 19 T-34s to artillery and 1 T-60 to a mine. Enemy aircraft also destroyed 10 cars, 1 76mm gun, 60 rifles, 7 antitank rifles, 8 light machineguns and one heavy machinegun. The brigade still had 16 T-34s, 5 T-70s and 6 T-60s ready for action.[18] This is 31% of the tank losses due to air power, or 16% of the unit's armor strength being attrited due to air power. This is the worst recorded case located, although in only a few cases do the records provide a cause for the losses.

The claims made that the Hs-129s on 8 July halted a Soviet tank attack "by air power alone" are clearly not correct and probably resulted in six or fewer tanks being damaged or destroyed by air attacks. There are other individual reports of tank losses due to air attack. Operating by itself the air was certainly responsible for some attrition, but there is no case that we have observed where airpower alone halted a brigade-size or larger unit. However, operating as support for a ground attack and as part of a combined arms attack, it was responsible for helping defeat the II and V Guards Tank Corps on this day as well as in many other cases.

With the data being spotty, it is hard to determine what percentage of the Soviet tanks were knocked out due to German air, but there is not much reason to believe that it was responsible for more than 20% of the Soviet tank losses, and the real figure is probably noticeably less than that. While this is still a significant contribution, it is not always the impression one gathers from descriptions of the battle. In general, the picture one sees is that while German air power played a major role in softening up positions, it was not, in and of itself, capable of halting an attack. This also applies to the specialized tank-busting aircraft.

There is even less data on the effectiveness of Soviet air. One is left with the conclusion that this is probably because it was less effective. That the Soviet air tended to be used for general attack and attrition, as opposed to coordinated close air support probably further limited its effectiveness. In the end, the real value of airpower was as part of a combined arms attack, and it did not, by itself, dominate any section of the battlefield.

July 9

The Germans flew only 28 sorties the night of 8/9 July, with the same six bomber sorties against the railroad stations between Kursk and Kastornoye and 20 harassment bombing sorties east of Belgorod in the Koren River area. According to Seidemann, they reported that additional Soviet motorized units were moving up to the front from the direction of Kursk. It is uncertain which Soviet formations were being referred to here.

The Second Air Army and Seventeenth Air Army continued their nighttime activities unabated. The 208th Night Bomber Division sent 60 sorties to bomb the Olkhovka-Byikovka-Yakovlevo area and the roads leading to the front. The 262nd Night Bomber Division attacked the crossing on the Severnyii Donets and German troops in the area of Razumnoye-Krutoi Log-Solomino-Bezlyudovka. The 244th Bomber Division attacked the Rogan and Osnova airfields with 26 sorties and conducted three reconnaissance sorties with 17 TB-3s.

SECOND AIR ARMY FORCES
(8–9 July)

	Largest Number Flown in a Day
I Assault Corps	84 Il-2, 46 Yak-1b
I Bomber Corps	6 Pe-2
IV Fighter Corps	30 Yak-1b, 15 Yak-7b, 44 La-5
V Fighter Corps	14 Yak-1b, 16 Yak-7b, 32 La-5
208th Night Bomber Division	28 U-2, 5 R-5, 3 Medium Bombers
291st Assault Division	59 Il-2, 6 Yak-1b, 3 Yak-7b, 3 La-5
50th Air Reconnaissance Regiment	6 Pe-2
454th Bomber Regiment	8 A-20 Bostons
272nd Independent Army Squadron	

SEVENTEENTH AIR ARMY FORCES
(8–9 July)

	Largest Number Flown in a Day
I Mixed Corps	64 Il-2, 50 Yak-1
III Mixed Corps	16 Il-2, 27 fighters, 1 La-5
IX Mixed Corps	0 Il-2, 0 La-5
244th Bomber Division	17 TB-3
262nd Night Bomber Division	45 U-2, 7 R-5
39th Air Reconnaissance Regiment	
48th Air Reconnaissance Regiment	
50th Air Reconnaissance Squadron	

During the day, the I Assault Corps sent out 134 ground attack sorties with their 54 operational Il-2s, striking in the area of Greznoye-Komsomolets Sovkhoz-Krasnaya Polyana-Yakovlevo-Pokrovka-Verkhopenye. The 28 operational Yak-1s carried out 81 escort sorties and sent 25 sorties to patrol and reconnoiter in the area of Tomarovka-Olkhovka-Byikovka. These operations continued to result in high Il-2 losses, with nine of them along with one Yak-1b failing to return from their mission. The 291st Assault Division attacked troops and tanks in the Greznoye-Gremuchii-Verkhopenye area and in Krapivinskiye Dvoryi-Smorodino-Luchki area. Their 38 Il-2s conducted 83 ground attack sorties, supported by 33 escort sorties. This formation continued to be attrited, with six Il-2s lost and two Yak-1s.

The IV and V Fighter Corps continued to provide ground cover. The IV Fighter Corps sent up 128 sorties in groups of six to ten planes over Krasnyii Oktyabr, Kochetovka, and Belenikhino and four pairs of fighters reconnoitering the Belgorod-Igumenka road. The V Fighter Corps with 124 sorties sent groups of six to 12 planes over Krasnyii Oktyabr, Novoselovka, and Greznoye. They sent 15 sorties on paired reconnaissance of German tank concentrations in Belenikhino, Kochetovka, and Verkhopenye. It is clear that the Soviets were keeping a good eye and appraisal on the state and focus of the German advance. The two fighter corps lost 17 fighters this day.

The I Bomber Corps continued to stand down, as it had since the 5th. The corps, along with the 454th Bomber Regiment and the 50th Air Reconnaissance Regiment, only conducted reconnaissance flights.

The Seventeenth Air Army only flew 187 sorties this day. The I Mixed Corps sent 64 Il-2s to Razumnoye-Krutoi Log-Maslova Pristan-Solomino, escorted by 37 Yak-1s flying 68 sorties. There was very little enemy air activity in this sector, with only one engagement reported. Still, the corps lost one Il-2, and six others did not return but were assumed to have made forced landings. The III Mixed Corps hit in the same areas, Krutoi Log to Maslova Pristan to Ivanovka, but with only 10 Il-2s. They were escorted by 20 fighters, and eight fighters conducted reconnaissance. Each plane only flew one sortie this day. They lost an La-5 and an Il-2. The IX Mixed Corps remained inactive, while the III Mixed Corps' activity was minimal. Like the IX Mixed Corps the previous day, the III Mixed Corps had also been stood down. While it had not suffered as much as the IX Mixed Corps, it was also a smaller formation, having contributed on 5 July 45 Il-2s and 44 Yak-1s to the battle. It lost 14 Il-2s and two Yak-1s on that first day. Over the next three days it only lost nine Il-2s, three La-5s, and three Yak-1s. Its contribution on this day was minimal. This was the last day it would contribute to the Voronezh Front's defense. Its assault aircraft were probably transferred to the I Mixed Corps.

The I Mixed Corps was now carrying the burden of activity. Overall, we are now seeing a decline in the level of activity of the Soviet air, as casualties, damage, serviceability and fatigue reduced their activity. While still fully participating in the night battles, the Seventeenth Air Army was now reduced to providing support with only one of its three mixed corps.[19]

The Germans maintained their presence at their previous levels, including 97 reconnaissance sorties and 258 fighter sorties. There were 384 bomber sorties flown in support of the III Panzer Corps, Totenkopf SS, Adolf Hitler SS, 11th Panzer and Gross Deutschland

THE AIR WAR CONTINUES

Divisions. They attacked assembly areas, battery positions and tank concentrations. The III Group of the 55th Bombardment Wing sent 21 sorties west of Verkhopenye to height +1.3, 21 sorties to Kalinovka and 13 to Zorinskiye-Dvoryi. There were 699 stuka sorties concentrated on supporting the SS Panzer Corps and the 11th Panzer Division, while 183 ground attack plane sorties struck retreating Soviet forces in front of the SS Panzer Corps and XLVIII Panzer Corps "with good effect." The Germans suffered high losses this day, with 11 planes downed, including an Hs-129. This included 7 Me-109s lost this day, the first time since the 5th that the Germans had suffered significant fighter losses. This was in exchange for 22 Soviet fighters downed.

Three of these Me-109 losses were due to an early morning weather reconnaissance mission by III Group, 52nd Fighter Wing that went astray and resulted in the loss of the German aces Edmund Rossmann, Siegfried Seyler and Erst Lohberg. This is discussed in more depth in a sidebar.

ROSSMANN AND SEYLER AND LOHBERG

Edmund "Paule" Rossmann was born 11 January 1918 in Caaschwitz Kreis Gera in Thuringia. He joined the 7th Squadron of the 52nd Fighter Wing on 1 March 1940. Rossmann fought in the Battle of Britain, where he scored six kills. He then steadily scored on the Eastern Front so that by 29 November 1942 he had 80 victories and had been awarded a Knight's Cross in March 1942. For much of Erich Hartmann's early career, he was the wingman of Rossmann.

Rossmann has 88 victories at the start of the Battle of Kursk. From 5 to 8 July 1943, he claimed five more. Early on the morning of 9 July the commander of the III Wing, Guenther Rall, sent out four planes at 0300 (Berlin time) to do weather reconnaissance. The flight initially consisted of Sergeant Rossmann, Lt. Siegfried Seyler (five claimed kills, all in July) and Sergeant Ernst Lohberg (25 claimed kills). The fourth plane of the flight was delayed for eight minutes because of problems starting the plane. Fifty minutes into the flight, radio messages indicate that Lohberg has flown away from Rossmann and Seyler. Rossmann then instructed everyone to assemble a thousand meters over Belgorod. Their three planes never showed up there.[20]

According to post-war accounts, Lt. Siegried Seyler had mechanical problems and was forced to land on the Soviet side of the lines. Rossmann landed his plane nearby to pick him up. In the ensuing scuffle with nearby Soviet infantry, Seyler was shot and fatally wounded (1923-1943) and Rossmann was captured.[21] Their fate was not known in Germany until 1949 when Rossmann was released by the Soviet Union.

Rossmann scored a total of 93 claimed kills in his career, six of them in the west, and flew 640 combat missions. He was released from Soviet prison in October 1949 and returned to West Germany. He passed away 4 April 2005 at the age of 87.

Guenther Rall, at this time the highest scoring ace on the Eastern Front, claimed six planes shot down between 7/9 July, all of them La-5s. He was himself shot down on 9 July but managed to crash-land the airplane between German and Soviet lines. He was then recovered by a tank crew of an SS armored unit.[22]

During the day the Germans launched 1,266 ground attack type sorties on the 9th compared to 291 ground attack type sorties by the Soviets. This was the last day of heavy German air presence over the battlefield, although they maintained air superiority for several more days.

Changing Exchange Ratios

The first four days of the air battles had been horrific for the Soviet Union. On 5 July the exchange ratio was 10-to-1 in favor of the Germans, while on 8 July it was 12-to-1 in favor of the Germans. On this day, the exchange ratio declined to 4.2-to-1, still in favor of the Germans but nothing like it was before. It would continue at this lower rate for the rest of the battle. The Germans suffered heavily this day with 11 planes lost (including seven fighters), while the Soviet losses were not insignificant with 46 planes lost (including 22 fighters). But even the fighter exchange was at a more favorable three-to-one ratio favoring the Germans, which is still lower than on previous days.

Table 5.1: Intensity of Combat

Date	Total German Daytime Sorties	Soviet Daytime Sorties	Total German Daytime Losses	Soviet Daytime Losses	Exchange Ratio
4	224	149	3	4	1-to1.33
5	2,387	1,688	19	189	1-to-9.95
6	1,686	1,230	7	77	1-to-11
7	1,829	1,427	10	86	1-to-8.60
8	1,686	1,173	5	60	1-to-12
9	1,621	828	11	46	1-to-4.2

Air historian Christer Bergstrom does put forth the theme that because of changes to their tactics, the Soviet air force had become more successful this day. Specifically, he states that "it was evident that the Soviet airmen operated with considerably higher effectiveness than previously" and "The new and improved Soviet fighter escort methods showed clear results" and "Many Soviet airmen who returned from their missions on this day reported a tendency among the German aircraft to show increased caution. Previously, small groups of German fighters had boldly attacked larger groups of Soviet fighters, but now they often engaged in combat only when they enjoyed a tactical or numerical superiority. The German fighters also scaled down their free hunting missions and began to provide their bombers and close support aircraft with stronger fighter escort."[23] As there are virtually no surviving operational air records from the German side, these points are a little hard to determine with any certainty.

THE AIR WAR CONTINUES

The Soviet airmen did achieve a more favorable exchange ratio this day, being down to only around 4.2-to-1 or 2.4-to-1 against them (depending on which figures are preferred). This last ratio is Christer Bergstrom's calculation for this day. It relies on a comparison of the losses from the German quartermaster reports to the reported Soviet air losses for his comparisons. This is a little bit of comparing apple to oranges, and it does tend to overstate German losses relative to Soviet losses.[24]

I do think there is some validity to some of these points. But the number of Soviet daytime sorties was noticeably lower, whereas the number of Germans sorties did not drop. This would make the argument that the lower Soviet casualties was indeed due to them being extremely more careful as to when and where they were flying. Their caution appears to have been what was driving the reduced Soviet losses, not German caution.

Of course, one must ask the question, after two years of warfare, why were the Soviet tactical and operational changes suddenly being addressed on 9 July 1943. It is not like they had not have plenty of exposure to German tactics and operations before then. They had the extended campaign in Kuban during April and May, and they had certainly had multiple air operations during 1942. Furthermore, General Novikov had been in his position since the Spring of 1942. So it does seem odd after over twenty-four months of air warfare that this week was now the time that the Soviet air force decided to start changing and adjusting tactics, and this achieved an immediate effect.

The Fifth Air Army

The Fifth Air Army was attached to the Steppe Front. As such, it was a reserve force that remained in the rear and trained throughout this battle. It was to be ready for the counteroffensive and as such played no role in the fighting in the defensive phase. This air army had at the start of the offensive 470 planes ready-for-action. While this seems like a useful force that could have been thrown into the fighting, most likely its state of training and readiness were worse than the Second or Seventeenth Air Armies.

The army consisted of five corps in various states of readiness. The VII Mixed Corps had only one division of Pe-2 bombers, the VII Fighter Corps had only one regiment of US built P-39 Airacobras, while the III Fighter Corps had neither planes nor pilots. The Airacobras were used for interception while the Pe-2s trained. The Fifth Air Army's main strength was the VIII Mixed Corps of three divisions and the X Fighter Corps of two fighter divisions. The VIII Mixed Corps had a complete complement of Il-2s, along with a half-dozen Il-2 trainers. It had a regiment of Yak-7s and two regiments of Yak-9s. These three fighter regiments would be transferred to the Second Air Army on the 9th. The X Fighter Corps appears to have been held well to the rear. The Fifth Air Army also had the 511th Independent Reconnaissance Regiment. It had about twenty Pe-2s and they also spent most of their time training.

A look at the nature of the training missions is enlightening, for the army appeared to be spending time conducting some very basic type take-off-and-landing training. For example, on 11 July one Pe-2 trainer flew 28 sorties and on 12 July, one Il-2 trainer flew 22 sorties. From the 4th through the 6th the army mostly trained, with a few interception missions that did not encounter anything.

FIFTH AIR ARMY ORDER OF BATTLE, 1 JULY 1943

The Fifth Air Army was commanded by Lt. General Sergei K. Goryunov. The Chief of Staff was Major General N. G. Seleznyov. The Deputy Commander of Political Affairs (the Military Council Member) was Major General V. I. Alexeyev. The Chief of the Army Political Division was Colonel N. M. Protsenko.

	Ready Planes	**Not Ready**	**Pilots**
VII Mixed Corps	94 Pe-2s	3	92
202nd Bomber Division			
18th Bomber Regiment			
36th Bomber Regiment			
797th Bomber Regiment			
VIII Mixed Corps			
256th Fighter Division	33 Yak-9s	19	62
	28 Yak-7bs	13	32
32nd Fighter Regiment			
91st Fighter Regiment			
728th Fighter Regiment			
4th Guards Assault Division	88 Il-2s	6	93
90th Guards Assault Regiment			
91st Guards Assault Regiment			
92nd Guards Assault Regiment			
264th Assault Division	86 Il-2s	7	99
235th Assault Regiment			
451st Assault Regiment			
809th Assault Regiment			
X Fighter Corps			
201st Fighter Division	22 Yak-1s	0	22
	23 La-5s	0	23
236th Fighter Regiment			
437th Fighter Regiment			
235th Fighter Division	50 La-5s	0	50
3rd Fighter Regiment			
181st Fighter Regiment			
239th Fighter Regiment			
VII Fighter Corps			
259th Fighter Division	No planes		No pilots
304th Fighter Division	24 P-39s	4	29
69th Guards Fighter Regiment			

THE AIR WAR CONTINUES

	Ready Planes	Not Ready	Pilots
III Fighter Corps			
265th Fighter Division	No planes		No pilots
287th Fighter Division	No planes		No pilots
511th Reconnaissance Regiment	22 Pe-2s	0	21

The Fifth Air Army began to shift air units on the 7th to help cover the initial approaches of the Soviet ground units being sent to reinforce the fighting at the front. They sent 14 Yak-9s from the 32nd Fighter Regiment and 13 Yak-7s from the 728th Fighter Regiment to the Voronezh Front area, while 25 Yak-9s from the 91st Fighter Regiment were moved to the Zemlyansk airfield (northwest of Voronezh).

On the 7th, the Fifth Air Army covered the march of the Fifth Guards Tank Army units in the Ostrogozhsk to Chernyanka area, and the IV Guards Tank Corps (referred to as the IV Tank Corps in Fifth Air Army report) in the Zemlyansk to Livnyi area. The IV Guards Tank Corps was heading northwest to support the Central Front. It sent up 43 Yak-9 and 30 Yak-7 sorties to cover the Fifth Guards Tank Army while 62 Yak-9 sorties covered the IV Guards Tank Corps. The following day, it covered the Fifth Guards Tank Army in the Chernyanka area with 5 Yak-9s and 4 Yak-7bs from 0400 to 0700 and the IV Guards Tank Corps in the area of Livnyi with 22 Yak-9s from 0400 to 1100. This was done by the airplanes from the three regiments that had been shifted. After these missions were completed, the three regiments were moved back to their main airfields.

On the 9th, the first permanent transfer was made when the 256th Fighter Division, consisting of the 32nd Fighter Regiment, 91st Fighter Regiment and 728th Fighter Regiment, was shifted to the Staryii Oskol airfield and became part of the Second Air Army. This probably added at least 55 planes to the Second Air Army, including at least 38 Yak-9s.[25]

The units that remained in the Fifth Air Army continued training. On the 11th, the X Fighter Corps was operationally subordinated to the Fifth Air Army (although it was already listed in its order of battle on 1 July). It consisted of the 201st Fighter Division with 45 Yak-1s and La-5s and the 235th Fighter Division with 50 La-5s. They were located well to the rear with the division headquarters at Voronezh and Markovka.

There was no other major activity in the Fifth Air Army besides training and an occasional intercept mission which rarely encountered anything. On the 18th, the I Assault Corps and the IV Fighter Corps were transferred to them from the Second Air Army, and in return they transferred the VIII Mixed Corps, with more than 160 Il-2s, and the X Fighter Corps, over to the Second Air Army.

During the period of 1 to 18 July, the Fifth Air Army conducted 1,883 sorties, of which 178 were used for troop cover, 45 for interceptions (usually in pairs) and 1,660 for training. On average, 46 planes flew a day, for a total of 1,094 flying hours. They claimed two encounters during this period, which resulted in a single engagement. They lost four planes during this time, probably all due to accidents (one Yak-9 and three Pe-2s).

FIFTH AIR ARMY ORDER OF BATTLE, 18 JULY 1943

	Ready Planes	Not Ready	Pilots
IV Fighter Corps			
294th Fighter Division	58 Yak-1s	35	105
183rd Fighter Regiment			
427th Fighter Regiment			
515th Fighter Regiment			
302nd Fighter Division	49 La-5s	24	65
193rd Fighter Regiment			
240th Fighter Regiment			
297th Fighter Regiment			
I Assault Corps			
292nd Assault Division	18 Il-2s	36	83
667th Assault Regiment			
800th Assault Regiment			
820th Assault Regiment			
266th Assault Division	22 Il-2s	26	46
66th Assault Regiment			
673rd Assault Regiment			
735th Assault Regiment			
203rd Fighter Division	37 Yak-1s	22	78
247th Fighter Regiment			
516th Fighter Regiment			
270th Fighter Regiment			
202nd Bomber Division	91 Pe-2s	4	91
18th Bomber Regiment			
36th Bomber Regiment			
797th Bomber Regiment			
511th Reconnaissance Regiment	19	1	19

This large reserve of training aircraft gave the Soviet air command significant strategic depth, something that the Germans did not have. As such, the Soviets were able to transfer at least 55 aircraft to the Second Air Army on the 9th and then later on the 18th, when the Soviet Army was on the offensive, replace two of the Second Air Army's air corps with two new fresh air corps. In addition, the other units of the Fifth Air Army were used to supply additional Soviet forces elsewhere on the front.

THE KURSK MAGNETIC ANOMALY

The Kursk, Belgorod and Voronezh oblasts are rich in iron ore. This has created the largest magnetic anomaly in the world. It affects all the compasses in the region so that precise navigation by compass was difficult.

It clearly had an impact on aircraft operations. On 28 June 1942, a Hungarian Heinkel fabric-covered He-46 reconnaissance plane sent to observe Don River crossing points had disappeared. Some speculate that it may have been because of the magnetic anomaly effect on their compass.[26]

THE STORY OF LIEUTENANT MOISEI LVOVICH KOROBKOV

The commander of a flight of the 617th Assault Aircraft Regiment of the 219th Assault Aircraft Division of the Second Air Army.

> In March 1942 I was called up to the army. I was a sportsman-gymnast, had fine health and therefore was sent to the famous Borisoglebsk School of Airmen (Voronezh region), for the Department of Assault Aircraft. In September 1942 the School was evacuated to the East, just before that we finished studying and became airmen. I took part in air battles during the Stalingrad counteroffensive, received the Orders of the Red Banner and Red Star.
>
> In March 1943 our 219th Assault Aircraft Division was redeployed from the Seventeenth Air Army of the Southwestern Front to the Second Air Army of the Voronezh Front. Just at that time Lieutenant-General of Aviation Krasovskii became the commander of the Second Air Army.
>
> He was my commander during the entire war, until Berlin, and during that time I grew from a pilot-lieutenant to a commander of an assault aircraft regiment, a Lieutenant Colonel. Never was wounded, though took part in combat, without any breaks, from July 1943 until the end of the War.
>
> During the Battle of Kursk I was a commander of a flight (4 assault airplanes), a Senior Lieutenant. It is written in my flight book that from 4 July until 23 August 1943 I conducted 84 battle sorties as part of a pair, flight or squadron. When the weather was good, flights took place two to three times a day. During that time our flight damaged, hit and burned 15 enemy tanks and about 60 trucks with infantry. We took part in air battles, too, brought down 3 enemy airplanes. The hardest battles

were during the enemy's offensive from 5 until 20 July 1943. Mainly I attacked tanks and infantry in trucks as the head of a flight or two flights. As a rule, we supported tank armies. In the First Tank Army and from 9–10 July in the Fifth Guards Tank Army we had two our officers with wireless radios. They called the commander of our division, Major General Vitruk, and relayed to him information from the staffs of the tank armies. After that assault airplanes appeared over the battlefield. The division commander defined the quantity of airplanes himself, taking into account our possibilities. Besides those efforts, by order of the staff of the Second Air Army, we reconnoitered and attacked trains with ammunition at the railway stations (2–3 planes, not more). Possibly, such a system of managing was not ideal because we often got contradictory orders.

I remember some successful attacks. 8 or 9 July I and the commander of the squadron, Senior Lieutenant Nikolaev, blew up a railway bridge somewhere to the south from Belgorod. During the same time, leading a group of 7 assault planes, we successfully attacked a tank column of the enemy that tried to break the defense of the First Tank Army near a highway. I remember that attack very well, because we burned a minimum of 4 tanks and because an antiaircraft shell hit my plane. Simultaneously we were attacked by 2 German fighters. But two comrades guarded us and we reached our aerodrome. I was not wounded but for the first time I thought: "Finished, I'll fall down."

I remember, too, the 12th of July. On that day our regiment, headed by the commander of the regiment, Lieutenant Colonel Kryukov, attacked German tanks in front of our tank corps (I don't remember its number) of the Fifth Guards Tank Army. We supported that corps the next day, too. The commander of our division was together with the commander of one of the tank corps and gave all orders. Such a system was effective and therefore was used in other battles, especially at the main directions of offensives.

I remember a flight when our troops pressed the enemy to the south—it was about 20 July. My partner and I flew a free hunting mission. We found a long column of trucks with infantry. It was without antiaircraft defense—that was not typical. We attacked the column four to five times at a low height while using all of our ammunition. A lot of trucks caught fire, Germans had serious losses. But usually some of our airplanes attacked antiaircraft artillery, while others attacked the main target. If enemy fighters appeared, but our fighters were absent, we formed a circle and covered each other. Our planes had two men in them—pilot and gunner. Gunners shot at German fighters. We had losses but brought down German fighters, too. In July my flight brought down 3 German fighters. At the same time, one of my pilots was brought down and perished.

I gained battle experience and bravery (without boasting) quickly enough. After the Battle of Kursk I fought until the end of the war.

After the war I served seven more years in assault aviation. After that I was an instructor in a Military School. In the middle of 1950s the half-wit Khrushchev ordered the reduction of aviation. The School was disbanded, I was retired.

I worked at an aviation factory in Kharkov. I was already married, had two sons. My wife's parents had a little house in Malakhovka (it was a "Jewish district"). In the end of 1980s the parents died, we moved here. I am 75 already. My sons in 1995 moved to Israel (with their families). Both of them are aviation constructors. I can't decide about moving to Israel. I have a lot of friends here, we meet from time to time, remember the past. Live for pension, it is enough for life.

Orders? A lot! I fought two years without any break: Order of Lenin, three of the Red Banner, one of Alexander Nevskii (received in Berlin), three of the Patriotic War; a lot of medals. Here they are, on my uniform. I put it on two years ago, when I took part in a parade of veterans.[27]

Notes

1. Nicolaus von Below, *At Hitler's Side: The Memoirs of Hitler's Luftwaffe Adjutant 1937-1945* (Greenhill Books, London, 2001), page 223.
2. Seidemann notes that this transfer was the equivalent of a 40% reduction in fighter strength, a 50% decrease in ground attack formations and a 30% reduction in bomber strength. According to a count generated from Seidemann's work, this transfer would have reduced the available German planes for the southern fight by about 25%.

    The account by writer #762 on air operations in the north does not note this transfer. It seems that these units are incorrectly included in his order of battle of 5 July, although he does note that some of the units, including the IV Group of the 9th Ground Attack Wing, may have or did arrive after 5 July. This transfer is also not noted in the Luftwaffe air liaison officer records.
3. The 3rd Fighter Wing shows losses in the 4th squadron at Kharkov-Rogan on 16 July, the 5th squadron at coordinate 61223 on 16 July, the 6th squadron at Kharkov on 13 July, the 7th squadron at coordinate 61183 on 14 July and the 9th squadron at Belgorod on 9 July and coordinate 6136 on 14 July and the staff of III at coordinate 61922 on 14 July. Clearly, some, if not much of JG3, remained in the area until 16 July.
4. The 2nd Stuka Wing shows losses in the II Group at Kharkov North on 15 July, 1st squadron at coordinate 61212 on 11 July, 2nd squadron at Kharkov North on 11 July, 3rd squadron at coordinate 6251 on 9 July, 5th squadron at Kharkov North on 13 July and at coordinate 6122 on 14 July, 7th squadron at coordinate 6125 on 13 July, 8th squadron at north of Kharkov on 9 July, 9th squadron East of Verkhopenye on 8 July and at coordinate 6288 on 14 July. Clearly, some, if not much of StG 2, remained in the area until 15 July.

    Rudel notes the transfer to Orel, but one could infer from his book that it occurred in the second half of July. See Rudel, pages 100–101.
5. The 3rd Bombardment Wing shows no losses past the 7th.
6. The 4th squadron, I Ground Attack Group shows losses at coordinates 61242, 61218 and Yasnaya Polyana on 12 July and losses at coordinate 63527 and Orel-West on 17 July. The 8th squadron, I Ground Attack Group shows losses at coordinate 61564 on 12 July and losses at coordinate 41255 on 14 July and 54653 on 16 July. The antitank squadron shows losses at coordinates 61242 and 61187 on 12 July and coordinates 63537, 63584 and Orel-West on 15 July.
7. Hardesty and Grinberg, page 258, describes the directive in some detail.

    Hooton, *War over the Steppes,* pages 175-176, states that Novikov "dispatched inspection teams to all air armies and air corps on 7 July and soon discovered that they had suffered heavy losses, often through ignoring doctrine…" The Second and Seventeenth Air Army records clearly, and it appears accurately, report losses each day.

    He then states: "on the second day of the offensive, units seem to follow Novikov's demand that they operate in large formations and that rear-gunners retain a third of their ammunition for the return flight. Both measures helped cut 'Ilyusha' losses." We cannot confirm from the unit records that they operated in any larger formations after 7 July (which would have been the fourth day of the offensive). Their losses did decline, but there appears to be multiple reasons for this.

    Hooton also claims that Novikov demanded that air armies delegate mission planning to division commander, who could use their initiative to respond to changing conditions. To improve fighter performance, they replaced defensive regiment-sized patrol missions with pairs of fighters operating over enemy lines.

    Bergstrom, *Kursk*, pages 58-59, picks up the same theme, stating that "Meanwhile, in the VVS headquarters, the air operations were carefully analysed, leading to an important conclusion: one of the dominant reason for the grievous *Shturmovik* losses during the first two days was the tactic of dispatching the Il-2s piecemeal, in small formations which could easily be hacked to pieces by the German fighters which operated in groups of four to eight aircraft.,…*General-Leytenant* Krasovskiy, 2 VA's command, instructed his *Shturmovik* units to form such large groups in the air during the operations the next day." This adjustment by Lt. General Krasovskii would have occurred a day before Novikov's directive.

    Il-2 losses as a percentage of sorties flown did decline after 5/6 July. On 5 July it was 43 Il-2s lost out of 202 ground attack sorties or 21%, on 6 July is was 22 Il-2s lost out of 237 ground attack sorties or 9%, on 7 July it was 13 Il-2s lost out of 210 ground attack sorties or 6%, on 8 July it was 16 Il-2s lost out of 328 ground attack sorties or 5%, on 9 July it was 15 Il-2s lost out of 217 ground attack sorties or 7%.

THE AIR WAR CONTINUES

8. Bergstrom, *Black Cross, Red Star*, page 231. Bergstrom states that they were attacking "the pontoon bridge which the Germans were building across the Pena river to the 3rd Panzer Division's bridgehead on the northern side of this river...the Soviet night bomber crews...succeeded in destroying the pontoon bridge across the Pena and even managed to force the 3rd Panzer Division to abandoned its forward positions...This was a significant tactical setback to the XLVIII Panzer Corps as it prepared to reopen its attack toward Oboyan."

   The 3rd Panzer Division was stalled on the south bank of the Pena River on 6 July (see Lawrence, *Kursk: The Battle of Prokhorovka*, page 434). They then shifted to their east and crossed a branch of the river at Lukhanino in the late afternoon of the 6th (see pages 505-506). Heavy Soviet resistance and air attacks coupled with extensive minefields had prevented the construction of a bridge over the Pena. As of 2310, the division was still reporting fierce Soviet resistances in the northern part of Lukhanino. Repeated Soviet air attacks on the southern part of the town (night attacks) were hampering the construction of the bridge.

   The much larger Gross Deutschland Panzer Grenadier Division also had a foothold across the Pena at Lukhanino and bridgehead at Dubrova. By 0600 in the morning the tanks and forward infantry elements of the Gross Deutschland Panzer Regiment had overcome the antitank ditches near Dubrova and, after refueling, were ready for further advance.

   It appears that Christer Bergstrom overstates the impact of these 66 Soviet night bombers, as the primary attack of the XLVIII Panzer Corps was being led by the Gross Deutschland Division and the 11th Panzer Division. Neither were significantly held up by Soviet air operations, although the Gross Deutschland was dealing with Soviet armored counterattacks and its Fusilier Regiment was detached to help the 3rd Panzer Division at Lukhanino. We also suspect that the pontoon bridge in the 3rd Panzer Division area was not "destroyed." We are not aware of any pontoon bridges that were "destroyed" by aerial or artillery bombardment during the German offensive phase of the Battle of Kursk. According to the account that Bergstrom quotes, "the division ordered the forward positions to be vacated temporarily during the shelling." This is not the same as the air attacks forcing "the 3rd Panzer Division to abandoned its forward positions." The 3rd Panzer Division was delayed this morning in its attack, but this delay was caused by much more than just the Long Range Aviation night bombing missions. The 3rd Panzer Division's two infantry regiments were more than capable of crossing what was a creek (the Pena river) without a pontoon bridge.

9. Rudel claims that during the Kursk battle his training school friend, Flight Lieutenant Wutka, commander of the 8th squadron, was killed. Rudel indicates that the loss may have been as a result of a short circuit when the bomb release was operated, possibly as a result of sabotage. See Rudel, pages 96–97.

   The Luftwaffe quartermaster records do record Captain Wutka's death and the loss of his Ju-87 D-3 on 8 July, but they are listed as being from the 9th squadron. The cause of loss is listed as "crashed due to explosion." They also record Sr. Lt. Karl Fitzner's death and the loss of his Ju-87 D-3 from 5/StG 77. The cause of loss is listed as "exploded in the air."

   The Second Army air liaison officer records (T312, R1243, page 000095) list them both by name and as Knight's Cross Winners. It does list Wutka as "Captain Wuka," but this is clearly a typo. Bernhard Wutka was awarded the Knight's Cross on 16 November 1942 as a Sr. Lt. with 8./Sturzkampfgeschwader 2. The various listings of Knight's Cross records we have do not list a Captain Wuka. Karl Fitzner was awarded the Knight's Cross on 27 November 1942 as a Lt. with 1./Sturzkampfgeschwader 77.

10. See Bergstrom, *Kursk*, pages 62-63, Bergstrom, *Black Cross, Red Star*, page 235, and Seidl, page 224. Seidl dates the action as 5 July. The accounts also differ as to the specifics of the combat.

11. Lt. Filin was a Russian born in 1923. He was interviewed by Col. Valerii Akimov in 1999.

12. Seidemann, page 204.

13. T312, R1242.

14. For example, see Cross, pages 198–199; Glantz and House, *The Battle of Kursk*, page 135; Bergstrom, *Kursk*, page 66; or Paul Carell, *Scorched Earth*, pages 69–71. Robin Cross claims six tanks "within a few minutes" and 50 tanks "in the space of an hour." According to Cross this attack occurred "As the morning mist cleared, sixty T-34s and their supporting infantry emerged from the wood and moved west against Hausser's deep flank, aiming to cut the Belgorod-Oboyan highway and II SS Panzer Corps' supply route. The tanks rumbled forward in a huge wedge preceded by dense blocks of infantry, like a medieval army on the march."

   In light of the German records reporting at 1145 of a Soviet attack with 20–40 tanks and weak infantry units through the ravine from Visloye and Ternovka to the west against the defenses at the Belgorod-Kursk highway, one wonders how this story grew to 60 T-34s as the morning mist cleared.

ACES AT KURSK

Bergstrom, *Black Cross, Red Star*, page 232, also repeats this story, although he should have been wary of these accounts. He references page 1022 of my book *Kursk: The Battle of Prokhorovka* claiming that I state that the II Guards Tank Corps lost 30 tanks on the 8th. The page he referenced does not report the II Guard Tank Corps losses. The losses of the II Guards Tank Corps are reported in my book for this day as 11 tanks (see pages 635 and 643). These losses come from the II Guards Tank Corps records. Bergstrom also ignores my discussion of this event on pages 557-558, which rather strongly disputes the story he repeats. He also ignores my discussion of the II Guards Tank Corps losses from 6 to 8 July on pages 637 to 641.

Bergstrom does state (page 232) about the II Guards Tanks Corps that "This unit has been severely mauled by SchG 1's anti-tank aircraft two days previously, and most of its tanks were of obsolescent models." He then recounts a second alleged mauling of the tank corps on 8 July. As I note in my book (page 635) for the 8th "At this point, the II Guards Tank Corps still had 94 T-34s and 61 T-70s (down to 95% and 85% of starting strength respectively). On page 638 I provide a comparison of the losses from 4 to 8 July for the six Soviet tank and mechanized corps that had been seriously engaged. The II Guards Tank Corps at 83% of it starting strength was in better shape than any other five corps. This was after being "mauled" by air attacks on the 6th and the 8th according to Bergstrom.

The popular version of this story was probably originally from Paul Carell, who claims there were 68 "brand new" Hs-129s. This is probably also incorrect as the Hs-129 B-2 had been in service since spring of 1942, and even though there were 50 to 75 of them in the five squadrons on 1 July, the VIII Air Corps only records 53 sorties for the 30mm armed Hs-123s for this day.

The claims made by Glantz that "a tank attack was halted by air power alone" is incorrect, and in fact contradicted at the beginning of his paragraph with his reference to the Totenkopf SS Panzer Regiment.

15. Various claims exist but not all match exactly. For example, in Hans Ulrich Rudel, *Stuka Pilot* (Bantam Books, New York, 1979, originally published 1958), it states that he flew 2,530 operational flights (page ix) and is credited with over 500 tanks destroyed (page 288). Gunther Just, *Stuka Pilot Hans-Ulrich Rudel* (Schiffer Military History, Atglen, PA., 1986) notes the 519 tanks, 150 artillery guns, 800 vehicles, the various ships and 9 aircraft shot down.

16. Fond: 299, Opis: 3070, Delo: 226, page: 16. This report covers the III Mechanized Corps, VI Tank Corps, XXXI Tank Corps, 180th Tank Brigade, 86th Tank Brigade, 203rd Independent Tank Regiment from the 4th–10th, and the 192nd Tank Brigade.

17. See Richard C. Anderson, Jr., "Artillery Effectiveness versus Armor," *The International TNDM Newsletter*, Volume I, Number 6, pages 26–29.

18. Fond: 3304, Opis: 1, Delo: 24, pages 93–96. Note these figures are also subsumed in the figures presented for the 86th Tank Brigade in the First Tank Army report, which records 27 T-34s, 1 T-70 and 3 T-60s as irreplaceable losses for 6 - 13 July. This strongly indicates that a number of the "burned" and "irreplaceable losses" in the First Tank Army report were from airpower.

19. In Bergstrom, *Black Cross, Red Star*, page 240, there is a claim that "But the situation for Soviet Seventh Guards Army was saved by 17 VA's Shturmovik units…"

There was a major offensive push conducted by the III Panzer Corps that was pushing to the north and suffered to total of 108 tanks lost that day. Bergstrom notes this with the notation that the XXV Guards Rifle Corps commander "sent his gratitude to 17 VA for the successful action by its Shturmoviks, which…had destroyed 47 German tanks."

Now, obviously as we have already seen, aerial claims of enemy tanks are often inflated by an order of magnitude, whether made by Germans or Soviets. Added to that, Soviet kills claims just tend to be inflated. So, while they were no doubt helpful, the actual German tank losses from air power are probably much lower.

Bergstrom reports 74 Il-2s providing this support. Our records (daily reports from the Seventeenth Air Army) show that the I Mixed Corps sent 64 Il-2s to Razumnoye-Krutoi Log-Maslova Pristan-Solomino area while the III Mixed Corps sent 10 Il-2s to the same area. Most of this area is in Corps Raus area, a German infantry corps of three divisions, not the III Panzer Corps, which was now mostly moving to the north. Only the 7th Panzer Division, which was holding the flank, remained in this area. It was being relieved this day by the newly arriving 198th Infantry Division assigned to Corps Raus. The XXV Guards Rifle Corps was on the flank of the III Panzer Corps, to their east. Their 15th and 94th Guards Rifle Divisions were facing the 7th Panzer Division. This German panzer division is recorded as losing five panzers this day from all causes (see *Kursk: The Battle of Prokhorovka*, page 773). It was the reinforced 6th Panzer Division which

THE AIR WAR CONTINUES

lost 97 tanks this day from all the elements under its command (see page 772). It was facing the reinforced 92nd Guards Rifle Division and the 305th Rifle Division, which both reported to the XXXV Guards Rifle Corps of the Sixty-Ninth Army. They were reinforced by the 96th Tank Brigade among other units. On the other hand, the III Panzer Corps did report heavy Soviet air activity in the corps zones during the day.

Still, it does not appear that air power played a significant part of the 6th Panzer Division attack that day. It does appear that the Soviet claim of 47 tanks destroyed was off by at least a factor of 10 and probably only applied to operations against the 7th Panzer Division and Corps Raus (which did have assault guns attached). Neither Corps Raus nor the 7th Panzer Division conducted any major offensive operations this day. Soviet losses in the divisional level engagements against this this day was less than 400 casualties in each of these engagements (see pages 773, 793 and 794). The 106th Infantry Division, which was just south of the 7th Panzer Division did report heavy Soviet air activity over the division, but less than on previous days. They report numerous Soviet air attacks with bombs and other weapons, especially on the division's left. Two attacks by seven Ils took place against Polyana and positions to the south. The 320th Infantry Division (to the south of the 106th Infantry Division) reports that during the day there were frequent air attacks on the front line, although it was less Soviet air activity than on previous days. This all points to the Seventeenth Air Army's attacks going against the right flank of the German attack and Corps Raus and were not significantly involved in German attack to the north (which was going away from the XXV Guards Rifle Corps).

20. Gunther Rall, *My Logbook: Reminiscences 1938-2006* (NeunundzwanzigSechs Verlag, Moosberg, Germany, 2006).
21. A different story is provided by Christer Bergstrom, *Kursk*, pages 67-68. Almost all sources say Rossmann landed to rescue Seyler. Bergstrom states it was Lohberg based on his interview with Rossmann. This is from an email exchange between Christopher Lawrence and Christer Bergstrom in March 2019.

    In his book Bergstrom states that at 0300 hours Guenther Rall (the III Group commander) dispatched a *Schwarm* (4 planes) on a weather reconnaissance mission in the Oboyan area. The pilots were Rossmann, Sgt. Lohberg, Lt. Puls and Lt. Seidel. Rossmann's wingman, Seidel, disappeared into the overcast and then Rossmann saw an open parachute about 100 meters above the ground. Rossmann and Lohberg dived towards the parachute while Russian soldiers were approaching him. They held the Russian soldiers at bay with several low-level attacks by machineguns. Then Lohberg's aircraft starting pouring smoke and it belly-landed in a field about 20 kilometers to the west of Oboyan. Rossmann saw Lohberg climb out of his aircraft and wave at him. Rossmann turned around and landed next to his Messerschmitt. Lohberg raced towards his aircraft, but just as he climbed onto the wing, he bent forward and fell to the ground. Rossmann unstrapped himself and jumped out to help him. He was then hit by a blow from a Russian soldier's rifle butt and captured. Much of Bergstrom's account is based upon interviews with Rall and Rossmann.

    There is a list of pilots lost in the 52nd Fighter Wing in 1943. It is here: http://www.denkmalprojekt.org/verlustlisten/jg52_vl_1943.htm

    This list shows Rossmann as captured on 9 July 1943, while both Seyler and Lohberg are listed as missing on 9 July. Puls is shown as killed on 17 August 1943 while there is no listing for a Seidel. Most likely the interviewer or interviewee confused Seyler with Seidel.

    According to one on-line database, Ernst Lohberg was missing in action on 9 July 1943 at Belgorod, Ugrim, cause unknown. He is credited with 25 kills. Rossmann was taken prisoner trying rescue Siegfried Seyler. See http://www.aircrewremembered.com/KrackerDatabase/?q=seyler

    Dmitriy B. Khazanov, *Air War Over Kursk: Turning Point in the East* (SAM Publications, Bedford, UK, 2010), page 38, states that "Feldwebel E. Lohberg" was shot down on 7 July and became a PoW.
22. Letter from Lt. General (ret.) Rall to Maj.Gen. (ret.) Dieter Brand and phone conversation on July 9, 1999. This shoot-down is not recorded in the Luftwaffe quartermaster files.
23. Bergstrom, *Black Cross, Red Star*, pages 237, 239-240. The statement at the start of discussion of the air operations of 9 July that "the day…would make a turning point in the air war…" is somewhat of an overstatement, as the Germans maintained air superiority until around the 15th, when they had withdrawn most of their planes.
24. By using German quartermaster reports, they pick up not only those planes that were shot down, but also those planes that were in accidents and those planes that returned to base and were later written off as destroyed. These last two categories of losses are not necessarily always reported in the Soviet air army

daily reports that we have accessed. So, comparing German quartermaster reports to Soviet loss reports is not a direct comparison. That said, there is a justifiable suspicion that the air liaison loss reports sometimes understate German losses for that day.

So, for example, our comparison of losses for 9 July was 4.2-to-1 in favor of the Germans. This was based upon 46 Soviet plane losses compared to 11 German plane losses. Bergstrom has the exchange ratio for the 9th as 2.4-to-1, still in favor of the Germans. This is based upon 46 Soviet planes lost compared to 19 German plane losses.

25. According to Khazanov, page 60, the 256th Fighter Division consisted of 96 fighters, 53 Yak-7bs and 43 Yak-9s. Khazanov states that Vatutin and Khrushchev had been requesting from Stalin additional air reinforcements for the Second Air Army since 8 July. They asked for two fighter corps and another assault corps from the reserves of the Supreme High Command, but this one division was all that Stalin would authorize. Bergstrom, *Kursk*, page 75, provides the same plane counts for the 256th Fighter Division.
26. Gyula Sarhidai, Gyorgy Punka and Viktor Kozlik, *Hungarian Eagles: The Hungarian Air Forces 1920-1945* (Hikoki Publications, Aldershot, UK, 1996), pages 22-23.
27. Lieutenant Colonel Moisei Lvovich Korobkov was born in 1924 in Malakhovka, Moscow Region. Interview taken by Major General G. G. Nessonov in 1998.

Chapter Six

A LESS INTENSE AIR WAR CONTINUES
10–11 July 1943

> *I did not like it when some pilots would brag "I have destroyed two German tanks," "I got three tanks." We were bombing the enemy tanks by flying two to four times over them. Sometimes entire squadrons or the regiment was firing. The tanks were on fire, but it was impossible to say who exactly set a tank on fire. When you are bombing in a flight, it was not possible to say who destroyed what.*
>
> Col. Semen Isaakovich Gurvich, 1998[1]

From 5 July through the 9th, the Germans had flown between 2,387 and 1,621 daytime sorties each day. The opposing Soviet Second and Seventeenth Air Armies had flown between 1,688 and 828 daytime sorties a day. Starting with the 10th, the rate of activity declined noticeably for the Germans, with them flying only 682 sorties on this day. Between 10-16 July, they would fly an average of 817 daytime sorties a day compared to their average of 1,842 for the first five days of the offensive. For the Soviets there was a similar decline, as they flew an average of 714 daytime sorties a day over the next week compared to 1,269 for the first five days of the offensive. The intensity of the air war had clearly declined.

This decline in activity by the Germans was caused by the weather. The results of their transfer of aircraft to Orel would not play a major part in this decline until around the 15th.[2] This decline in activity for the Soviets was caused by the weather, their high losses, and the shifting of most of the Seventeenth Air Army away from supporting the battles around Belgorod. In the case of the Second Air Army, it continued flying sorties at about two-thirds of its previous rate. Both sides were probably affected by the general reduction in readiness and serviceability caused by the heavy action of the previous five days.

A weather front had moved in. It had been mostly a clear day on 7 July. The first half of 8 July was clear, but clouds moved in during the day. There was rain the night of 8/9 July and cloudiness the following day. It rained during the night of 9/10 July and for 10 July the Second Air Army was reporting that it was cloudy with a visibility of eight to ten kilometers, with rain in some areas. The number of daytime sorties by the Second Air Army dropped from 658 on the 9th to 463 on the 10th. The opposing German VIII Air Corps had a much more dramatic drop off, going from 1,621 daytime sorties on the 9th to only 682 on the 10th. The following day the Second Air Army reports that it was cloudy during the night and day, with intermittent rain and storms. The Second Air Army put up 540 daytime sorties on the 11th while the VIII Air Corps put up a more energetic 1,039 daytime sorties. On the 12th, the weather in the morning was poor but got better as the day developed according to a number of sources.[3]

Furthermore, the balance of air support was no longer as favorable to the Germans. Instead of flying almost 50% more sorties than the Soviets, as they had at the start of the offensive, the Germans were now flying a roughly equal number. Still, this does not mean that the Soviets were contesting or regaining control of the skies. The Soviet loss rate per sortie continued to decline throughout this period and remained lower than it was in the first five days of the offensive. They suffered an average of 6.81% losses in the first five days as opposed to 3.57% over the next week. In contrast, German losses went up, to a daily loss average of .55% in the first five days, as opposed to .88% over the next week. In actual count of losses, the Germans lost about the same (52 aircraft from 5 to 9 July compared to 50 from 10 to 16 July). In contrast, the Soviet losses declined noticeably (456 losses from 5 to 9 July compared to 176 losses from 10 to 16 July).

This decline in losses for the Soviets appears to have primarily been caused by their more cautious and selective approach to their missions. Or, perhaps more correctly, high losses of the first five days were a result of an overly aggressive and headstrong approach that was beyond the capabilities of this force. The almost 9-to-1 exchange ratio achieved by the Germans in the first five days of the air battle was certainly attributable to the nature of the operations of the two Soviet air armies. Once they took a more cautious and cost-effective approach, the exchange of casualties declined noticeably to a 3.5-to-one exchange ratio (still very much favoring the Germans). While this was not good, it was much better. Although the overall ratio of daytime sorties was now more favorable to the Soviets, this does not seem to have been a major factor in their reduced loss rates, for the average number of fighter sorties flown by the Germans declined from 282 a day to 181 a day (64%) while the average number of Soviet fighter sorties declined from 826 a day to 435 a day (53%). So in all reality, over the course of the battle, the force ratios in the air superiority fight actually became more favorable for the Germans. This just further reinforces the point that the high Soviet casualties during the first five days of the operations were as a result of an overaggressive approach, certainly one beyond the means of the Soviet air force, and that with a more thoughtful approach, casualties could be reduced. Obviously, the Soviet air force was not in position to achieve a favorable exchange ratio, as the differences in experience and training were too great. See Table 6.1.

The night action continued much as before. The Germans maintained an average of 50 sorties a night while the Soviets actually increased their activity from an average of 244 sorties a night in the first five days to 297 sorties a night in the following week. This increase was as a result of more activity by the Second Air Army.

A LESS INTENSE AIR WAR CONTINUES

Table 6.1: Intensity of Combat

Date	Total German Daytime Sorties	Soviet Daytime Sorties	Total German Daytime Losses	Soviet Daytime Percent Losses	German Percent Losses per Sortie	Soviet Losses per Sortie
4	224	149	3	4	1.34%	2.68%
5	2,387	1,688	19	189	.80	11.20
6	1,686	1,230	7	77	.42	6.26
7	1,829	1,427	10	86	.55	6.03
8	1,686	1,173	5	60	.30	5.12
9	1,621	828	11	46	.68	5.56
10	682	524	3	25	.44	4.77
11	1,039	588	14	19	1.35	3.23
12	654	887	11	31	1.68	3.49
13	656	767	5	27	.76	3.52
14	1,452	1,002	9	30	.62	2.99
15	706	336	5	11	.71	3.27
16	499	894	3	33	.60	3.69
17	138	486	5	16	3.62	3.29
18	79	447	1	6	1.27	1.34
Total	15,338	12,426	111	660	.72	5.30

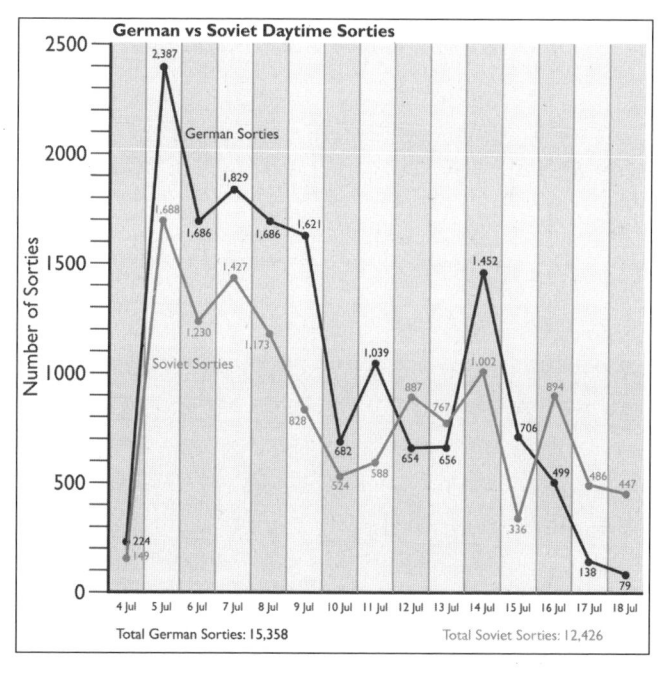

Chart 14.4 - Soviet vs German Daytime Sorties.

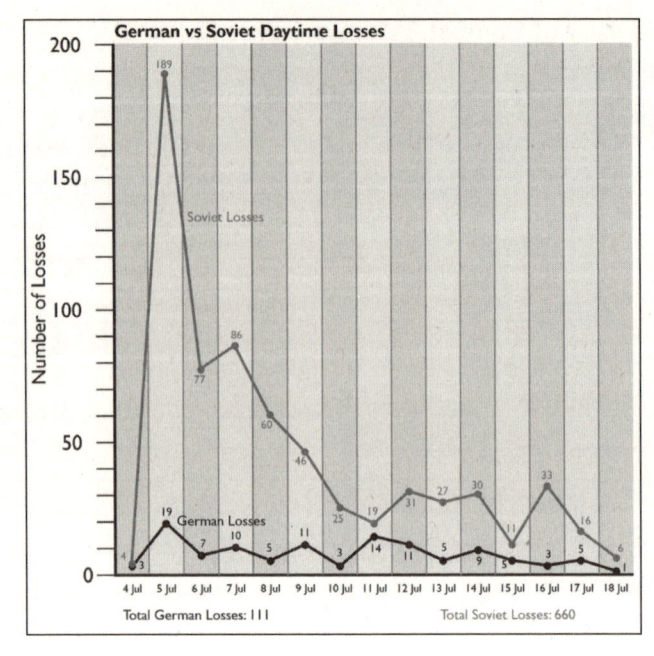

Chart 14.5 - Soviet vs German Daytime Losses.

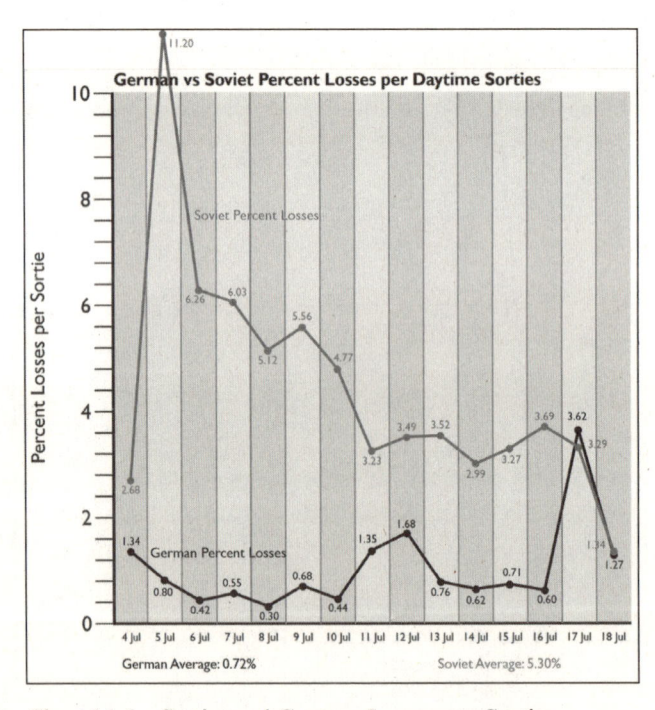

Chart 14.6 – Soviet and German Losses per Sortie.

A LESS INTENSE AIR WAR CONTINUES

10 July

During the night of 9/10 July, the 208th Night Bomber Division sent 69 sorties to the Malyie Mayachki, Luchki, Pokrovka, Ryilskii, and Krasnaya Polyana areas and reconnoitered along the Belgorod-Graivoron and Murom-Kharkov areas, and along the roads leading to the front. The Seventeenth Air Army continued its active night bombing campaign with 156 bombing sorties by the 262nd Night Bomber Division against the Donets crossings and along the Razumnoye-Belovskaya-Krutoi Log-Maslova Pristan-Solomino-Bezlyudovka sector. The 244th Bomber Division hit the same area with 24 bomber sorties by TB-3s and also conducted three reconnaissance sorties. There are no reports for the Germans for this night and because of the weather, they may not have flown.

The Soviet Long Range Aviation force sent 174 bombers to conduct night attacks against German troop concentrations. This did not appear to have had much impact.[4] It does appear that these night bombing runs by the Soviet Long Range Aviation were a fixture in the south for every night of the battle. They are first reported in secondary sources for the night of 6/7 July, and periodically reported after that. We suspect they were sending missions of 66 to 174 bombers every night to attack the German southern offensive (in addition to attacks against the northern offensive). In the Soviet General Staff Study they record a total of 2,082 bombing attacks against ground targets by Long Range Aviation during the Battle of Kursk. Of those 778 were in support of the Sixteen Air Army against the German offensive in the north from 5 – 12 July 1943. This leaves 1,304 attacks against ground targets that are not reported. In the south we report 403 of them on the nights of 6, 7 and 9 July. This leaves 901 not accounted for that may have occurred on other nights (or other areas).[5] If they all went to attack the southern offensive, this would average over 100 bombing sorties on each of the seven nights, counting through to 15 July.

FIRST COMBAT

Lt. Semen Isaakovich Gurvich saw his first combat at Kursk with the 226th Guards Assault Aviation Regiment, 4th Guards Assault Aviation Division:[6]

> In March 1943 after I graduated from the Military Aviation School, I was sent to the division of Major General G. Baidukov of the Fifth Air Army. Baidukov was a famous pilot who made a non-stop flight to America with V. Chkalov. My first baptism under fire was in the defensive fighting to the east of Belgorod. Starting from 5 July 1943, I flew two to three times a day, as a part of the squadron or sometimes as a part of the regiment, to assault the enemy tanks trying to get to the north towards Kursk. I don't want to brag, I did not have much experience and I was a bit scared. We were fighting enemy fighters every single day. I quickly learned the tactics of mutual aid of our

wonderful Il-2s. The Germans called them "black death." My cabin was armored in the back, where German fighters were usually shooting. Soon I learned antiaircraft maneuvers and I felt braver to fly lower and bomb and fire from the lower altitude, which increased the accuracy. I did not like it when some pilots would brag "I have destroyed two German tanks," "I got three tanks." We were bombing the enemy tanks by flying two to four times over them. Sometimes entire squadrons or the regiment was firing. The tanks were on fire, but it was impossible to say who exactly set a tank on fire. When you are bombing in a flight, it was not possible to say who destroyed what.

Approximately on 10 July, I was in one of four Il-2s attacking an enemy artillery battalion. I could clearly see that my missiles destroyed one and then another gun, but you don't want to celebrate too quickly during combat. Mortal danger is lying in wait for you every minute. My plane was hit by a shell. Two "Messers" literally attacked me hoping to finish me. My bravery saved me. I flew directly at the front of one plane. The German pilot could not stand it and dodged up. I started a steady fire with bullets and shells. He fell down like a rock. The second plane flew around me at my tail. I heard one shell penetrate into the body. I could smell smoke. I thought to myself "This is the end." I wanted to live. I quickly dropped altitude, flew very low, just above the ground, then above the woods and then turned. The German pilot probably thought that he had destroyed me and turned away. My colleagues went back to the airport but did not say that I was shot down. It was a tradition to wait until the last minute. Even though my plane was damaged, I managed to fly to another airport and landed. They immediately called my commander to let him know where I was. The commander sent a car for me and sent two technicians. They worked for two days almost without any rest and fixed my Il-2. I flew back to my regiment. Starting from 12 July, I made at least three flights a day as part of the squadron supporting the offensive of our tanks. There was very heavy fighting. When I looked down, I could observe literally a sea of fire, but our tanks kept moving forward. We supported them well.

I had more air combats. The successful offensive was inspiring me. I gained more experience. We reached Kharkov more than a month later. I made more than 100 combat flights during this time. I made over 200 combat flights over the course of the year. I was awarded the Hero of the Soviet Union in July 1944 for these flights and for the damage caused to the enemy. Before we got to Berlin, I made the same amount of combat flights.

A LESS INTENSE AIR WAR CONTINUES

The Second Air Army reported that the weather at night was cloudy, with rain and storms, with visibility of one to two kilometers. During the day the weather was cloudy, with visibility eight to ten kilometers. There was rain in some areas.

This was the first day that the number of sorties by the VIII Air Corps declined considerably, down to 682 for the day. According to the corps, this was because of the poor weather. As the VIII Air Corps was able to raise their sortie count noticeably on the 11th and 14th, any transfers over the last few days had apparently not hamstrung the VIII Air Corps effort. On this day, the XLVIII Panzer Corps received most of the air support, for German air reconnaissance had noted the large Soviet motorized and tank formations moving to the front in this area. Some support was also given to the SS and III Panzer Corps on this day, dissipating the German air strength. The III Group of the 55th Bombardment Wing limited itself to only 34 sorties this day. It struck at Staryii Gorod with 14 sorties and Shlyakhovo with 20 sorties.

The Second Air Army continued as before. The I Assault Corps sent 83 Il-2 sorties to strike in the area of Greznoye, Komsomolets Sovkhoz, Veselyii, Krasnaya Polyana, Malyie Mayachki, Kochetovka, Verkhopenye, height 251, Sukho-Solotino, Tavrovo, and Neckuchonoye. They were escorted by 47 Yak-1 sorties. The 291st Assault Division hit the same area, Bolshiye Mayachki, Verkhopenye, Krasnaya Polyana, Gremuchii and Ilinski with 58 Il-2 sorties and escorted with 34 fighter sorties. The Il-2s and fighters of both units maintained an average of more than two sorties per plane per day. The 291st Assault Division lost another five Il-2s while the I Assault Corps lost seven Il-2s and two Yak-1bs.

The two fighter corps continued their defensive patrols, with their IV Fighter Corps in the area of Vladimirovka, Kruglik and Verkhopenye, while the V Fighter Corps patrolled in Pokrovka, Kruglik, Verkhopenye, Kochetovka, Orlovka, and Zorinskiye Dvoryi. The IV Fighter Corps flew 107 sorties with five losses. One of those was claimed to be an La-5 that had rammed an Me-109! The V Fighter Corps flew 129 sorties with six losses. This corps, for the first time, showed up in battle with the new Yak-9s! It flew 27 sorties that day with ten Yak-9s. One failed to return from its mission while another was shot down in a dogfight. These were recently arriving reinforcing aircraft that had been sent into battle.

The Soviet air force had also begun to rotate its units on the front with units of the Fifth Air Army in the rear. In the case of the V Fighter Corps, the 205th Fighter Division may have been withdrawn around the 10th and replaced with the 256th Fighter Division.[7] This included the 27th Fighter Regiment, which had in its complement at Kursk the soon to be top aces of Nikolai Gulayev (55 claimed kills and 5 shared kills), Vladimir Bobrov (43 claimed kills and 24 shared kills) and Fyodor Arkhipenko (30 claimed kills and 14 shared kills). Accordingly the Fifth Air Army, the 256th Fighter Division, with its 32nd, 91st and 728th Fighter Regiments, was shifted to the Staryii Oskol airfield as part of the Second Air Army.[8]

The I Bomber Corps and the 454th Bomber Regiment continued reconnaissance, as probably did the 50th Reconnaissance Regiment.[9] The IV and V Fighter Corps' communications with the Air Force staff broke down this day.

SECOND AIR ARMY FORCES
(10 July)

	Largest Number Flown in a Day
I Assault Corps	41 Il-2, 26 Yak-1b
I Bomber Corps	2 Pe-2
IV Fighter Corps	16 Yak-1b, 12 Yak-7b, 27 La-5
V Fighter Corps	3 Yak-1b, 17 Yak-7b, 10 Yak-9, 21 La-5
208th Night Bomber Division	24 U-2, 5 R-5, 3 Medium Bombers
291st Assault Division	25 Il-2, 6 Yak-1b, 1 Yak-7b, 3 La-5
50th Air Recon. Rgt.	0 Pe-2
454th Bomber Regiment	3 A-20 Bostons
272nd Ind. Army Sqd.	

SECOND AIR ARMY FORCES
(11 July)

	Largest Number Flown in a Day
I Assault Corps	49 Il-2, 36 Yak-1b
I Bomber Corps	2 Pe-2
IV Fighter Corps	44 Yak-1b, 8 Yak-7b, 32 La-5
V Fighter Corps	2 Yak-1b, 25 Yak-7b, 40 Yak-9, 34 La-5
208th Night Bomber Division	24 U-2, 5 R-5, 3 Medium Bombers
291st Assault Division	22 Il-2, 6 Yak-1b, 0 Yak-7b, 1 La-5
50th Air Recon. Rgt.	0 Pe-2
454th Bomber Rgt.	0 A-20 Bostons
272nd Ind. Army Sqd.	

SEVENTEENTH AIR ARMY FORCES
(10–11 July)

	Largest Number Flown in a Day
I Mixed Corps	21 Il-2, 32 Yak-1
III Mixed Corps	0 Il-2, 6 fighters
IX Mixed Corps	0 Il-2, 8 La-5
244th Bomber Division	33 TB-3
262nd Night Bomber Division	44 U-2, 8 R-5
39th Air Recon. Rgt.	
48th Air Recon. Rgt.	
50th Air Recon. Sqd.	

A LESS INTENSE AIR WAR CONTINUES

The Seventeenth Air Army effectively ceased to contribute to the fight in the north. The I Mixed Corps again attacked the crossing over the Severnyii Donets in the Yastrebovo-Belovskaya-Bezlyudovo area with 21 Il-2 sorties and 32 fighter sorties. The operations were unusual this day, in that this produced only 17 ground attacks, 12 reconnaissance and 24 escort sorties. They used four Il-2s for reconnaissance or escort duty. The planes only flew one sortie this day and had no encounters with German aircraft and no losses. The III Mixed Corps used eight fighter sorties and six fighters to reconnoiter in the Provisional Army Kempf area, without action. That was their only activity for the day. The IX Mixed Corps also flew eight sorties, covering the Velikii Burluk railroad station. They also had no encounters. The 244th Bomber Division conducted two reconnaissance sorties. For all practical purposes, the Seventeenth Air Army had ceased active participation in the daytime battle.

During the day the Germans probably launched around 500 ground-attack type sorties on the 10th compared to 158 ground-attack type sorties by the Soviets.

German "Strength"

On 10 July, the Soviets estimated German strength as follows:

Airfield	Total	Fighters	Bombers	Unknown
Rogan	50	10	40	
Osnovo	100	15	85	
Tolokonnoye	100	64	36	
Bessonovka	36	36		
Pomerki	30			30
Akhtyirka	6		6	
Kramatorskaya	42	20	22	
Sokolniki	75	61	14	
Total	439	206	203	30

This is intelligence data gathered from reconnaissance flights, and as such should always be viewed with considerable suspicion. It appears that at this stage in the battle, the Germans had 700 or more aircraft operational. These Soviet estimates, however, miss a number of German airfields (Mikoyanovka, Barvenkovo, Varvarovka, Urgim, Dudkovo and Golovino).

11 July

This night only saw 18 German sorties, including six bombing missions on the Staryii Oskol railroad station, which left lots of material burning, and eight harassing missions southeast of Belgorod. The Soviets maintained their heavy night attacks, with the 208th Night Bomber Division carrying out 57 sorties in the area of Malyie Mayachki, Luchki, and

Ryilskii and the adjacent ravines. The 262nd Night Bomber Division sent 116 sorties into the area of Polyana Sovkhoz, Solomino, Ivanovka and Maslova Pristan. The 244th Bomber Division sent 33 TB-3s to hit Razumnoye-Krutoi Log-Bezlyudovka. Two of these TB-3s also struck at Rogan airfield.

The weather was not good this day. The Second Air Army reported that it was cloudy during the night and day, with intermittent rain and storms.

Although hindered by the poor weather, the Germans picked up the action today with some 1,039 sorties. The bombing was again concentrated mostly in support of the Fourth Panzer Army with most of the Stukas directed to their targets (Leitverkehr or control station traffic). The III Group of the 55th Bombardment Wing supported the III Panzer Corps with 11 sorties at Sabyinino, eight at Sheino, six at Shlyakhovo and 19 at Gostishchevo. The VIII Air Corps only flew 176 fighter sorties this day and took heavy losses, some 14 planes, including four Me-109s. The high losses were reported to be because of the poor weather. Furthermore, the Germans were unable to assess the effects of their attacks due to the poor visibility.

The VIII Air Corps may have also accidently attacked their own troops this day. A post-war interview states that some supporting Stukas hit elements of the Leibstandarte SS Adolf Hitler Division as they were advancing towards Prokhorovka. They hit Major Joachim Peiper's III Panzer Grenadier Battalion and elements of Captain Rudolf von Ribbentrop's 6th Panzer Company, which was being held in reserve. The Luftwaffe air liaison officer's armored vehicle was stationed next to the battalion's staff vehicle.[10]

With this poor weather, the level of Soviet activity and losses remained low, with the Second Air Army only putting up 539 sorties this day. The Second Air Army losses were only 18 aircraft this day, including 13 fighters. The army did report 31 engagements this day but that is lower than on previous days.

The I Assault Corps sent another 49 Il-2s to fly 92 sorties against the area of Yakovlevo-Luchki (south) to Teterevino-Kalinin-Ozerovskii-Luchki (north) to Bolshiye Mayachki-Pokrovka-Krasnaya Polyana. They were escorted by 36 Yak-1s conducting 62 sorties at a cost of one Il-2 and two Yak-1s. The 291st Assault Division sent 22 Il-2s on 41 sorties to strike the area of Syirtsevo-Krasnaya Polyana-Ilinskii-Verkhopenye. They were escorted by seven fighters conducting 13 sorties. This light escort did not seem to adversely affect them, as they lost the same as the I Assault Corps.

The two fighter corps continued their patrol over their lines, with the IV Fighter Corps covering the Aleksandrovskoye-Belenikhino-Krasnyii Oktyabr area with 160 sorties while the V Fighter Corps covered the Orlovka-Kalinina-Krasnaya Polyana-Kochetovka area with 170 sorties. The IV Fighter Corps lost 10 planes this day while the V Fighter Corps lost only three.[11]

The I Bomber Corps only flew two reconnaissance missions, while the 454th Bomber Regiment did not fly because of the weather. The Second Air Army headquarters continued to have communication problems by cable, so most of the communications during the day were by radio.

The Seventeenth Air Army continued with only the most tepid support during the day. The I Mixed Corps attacked the Krutoi Log and Polyana Sovkhoz areas with 19 Il-2s escorted by 20 Yak-1s. One of the Il-2s and eight of the Yak-1s also flew reconnaissance sorties in the area of Solovyev Kolkhoz-Batratskaya Dacha and Myasoyedovo. The rest of the Seventeenth Air Army operations were out of the battlefield area.

Seidemann claimed in 1947 that "the Soviet air force began to take an increasing part in the fight. The German advance had considerably shortened the length of the approach run Soviet formations had to make in order to get to the front lines. The German fighters were no longer able to sweep the skies of Soviet aircraft at all times. For this reason, the VIII Air Corps began to move its fighter and ground attack formations forward into the area southwest of Prokhorovka. Two air fields were prepared north of Luchki, but there was no chance to occupy these however."[12]

During the day the Germans launched 801 ground-attack type sorties on the 11th compared to 152 ground-attack type sorties by the Soviets.

Strengths

One source gives the strengths of the Soviet air before the famous Battle of Prokhorovka as 472 serviceable aircraft (half of them fighters) for the Second Air Army and 350 for the Seventeenth Air Army.[13] These seem like reasonable figures although they may be a little high.

On 11 July the Second Air Army was able to put up 292 or 293 aircraft flying 539 to 542 daytime sorties.[14] Of those, 437 of the daytime sorties were flown by 219 fighters. The air army also flew 109 sorties the night of 11/12 July 1943 using 44 aircraft. So they had at least 336 operational aircraft on 11 July (vice the 472 serviceable aircraft claimed).

Their level of activity on the 12th was higher with 759 to 761 daytime sorties flown by 408 aircraft and 156 nighttime sorties flown by 51 aircraft. This included 224 fighters flown that day. So it does appear that they had at least 459 operational aircraft on 12 July 1943.

On 11 July the Seventeenth Air Army only flew 56 sorties using 47 aircraft. They also flew 183 night sorties, using 67 aircraft. On 12 July their level of activity remained low with 134 daytime sorties flown and 151 nighttime sorties. All of the night sorties are counted as being flown into the area of the Belgorod offensive.

The German VIII Air Corps strength was still probably more than 900 aircraft with maybe up to 675 serviceable.[15] They started the battle with an estimated 1,093 – 1,112 aircraft. According to the VIII Air Corps reports they had lost 74 planes from 4 - 11 July 1943. The quartermaster reports indicate that 82 planes were 100% destroyed in that period and another 8 planes were 80-95% destroyed.[16] They had 72 aircraft 20% to 75% damaged (see Table II.20). They had probably transferred at least one wing of aircraft (maybe 20-30 aircraft) elsewhere. On 11 July they flew 1,039 sorties in the day and 61 at night.

Notes

1. See interview of Lt. Semen Isaakovich Gurvich under "First Combat."
2. Seidemann, page 204, complains that the combat strength of the VIII Air Corps had waned to about one-third of its original strength. This appears to be grossly incorrect.
3. See Hardesty and Grinberg, pages 255-256. They state that on the morning of the 12th all Soviet Shturmovik units were grounded. After 1000 hours (Moscow time) on the 12th the weather improved slightly to allow 142 Il-2 sorties.

    Bergstrom, *Kursk*, page 78, states for 12 July that "The whole region was covered by thick clouds that hung low. This compelled Krasovskiy to delay 1 BAK's opening attack by four hours. At 03.30 (04.30 German time), around seventy Soviet bomber crews who had already climbed into their Petlyakovs, were ordered out of their aircraft of their aircraft just seconds before the planned take-off. Seidemann was less cautious. As usual, a few Bf 109s were sent out on early dawn fighter sweeps over the front area. Apparently, some VVS fighters also were airborne...."
4. Bergstrom, *Black Cross, Red Star*, page 241.
5. What we reported: 6 July (night of 6/7): 163, 7/8 July 66 and 9/10 July 174. Bergstrom, *Black Cross, Red Star*, page 225, states that there were heavy attacks by ADD on the night of July 5 (night of 5/6), which is not surprising. He does not source most of his reports, but we gather they come from Russian secondary sources.
6. Col. Semen Isaakovich Gurvich was interviewed 16 December 1998 by Col. Fyodor Sverdov. In addition to Hero of the Soviet Union, he was awarded four Orders of the Red Banner, two first degree Orders of the Great Patriotic War and two Orders of the Red Star. His family, parents, wife and son, were killed during the war in Rostov-on-the-Don.
7. Bergstrom, *Kursk*, pages 74-75. Bergstrom states that it occurred on the 10th and included the 27th Fighter Regiment. Gulayev's claim list shows three planes downed on the 12th at Prokhorovka. It appears that the 205th Fighter Division, with the 27th Fighter Regiment remained with the Second Air Army.

    According to Bergstrom the 27th Fighter Regiment had lost 11 Yak-1s and 8 pilots in the fighting to date. The entire 205th Fighter Division, which included the 27th, 438th and 508th Fighter Regiments, was shifted to the rear and its Yak fighters were handed over to the arriving 737th Fighter Regiment and 256th Fighter Division. The 256th Fighter Division mustered 96 fighters, including 53 Yak-7bs and 43 of the new Yak-9s. The Yak-9s equipped the 91st Fighter Regiment and parts of the 32nd Fighter Regiment. The division commander was Colonel Nikolai Gersimov, Hero of the Soviet Union who by the end of the war was credited with 14 kills and 10 shared kills.
8. HQ, Fifth Air Army, Operational Report #367, 2000, July 9, 1943 (Fond: 5th Air Army, Opis: 4999, Delo: 66).

    The backfield shuffle at the Fifth Air Army continued over the next couple of days. On 11 July, the X Fighter Corps was operationally subordinated to the air army, although its corps headquarters was well in the rear at Voronezh. It consisted of the 201st Fighter Division (HQ was in Voronezh) and 235th Fighter Division (HQ was in Markovka).

    On 1 July the Fifth Air Army consisted of the VII Mixed Corps, the VIII Mixed Corps, the X Fighter Corps (!), the VII Fighter Corps (the 259th Fighter Division had no planes on hand) and the III Fighter Corps (whose two fighter divisions had no planes on hand). On 18 July the army consisted of the IV Fighter Corps and the I Mixed Corps. (Fond: 5th Air Army, Opis: 499, Delo: 33).
9. According to Second Air Army records two Pe-2s reconnoitered the enemy reserves moving up to the front line in the Belgorod-Tomarovka area. They state there was no encounters with enemy aircraft and no losses (see Fond: 2nd Air Army, Opis: 4196, Delo: 29, vol. 2).

    Bergstrom, *Kursk*, page 74 has on 10 July a group of Pe-2s escorted by La-5s, including Ivan Kozhedub, attacking the German airfield at Varvarovka. That does not appear to have occurred on this day and we have no record of it occurring during the Battle of Kursk. His source is Kozhedub's Soviet-era autobiography, which provides the date. The mission may have occurred on a later date, 12 July (82 sorties), the 13th (86 sorties), the 14th (145 sorties) or later. On the 10th and 11th the I Bomber Corps flew only two reconnaissance sorties each day according the Second Air Army records.

    In his later book, *Black Cross, Red Star*, page 241, he has added to that account with an attack on the airbases at Kharkov-Rogan and Mikoyanovka by 48 Il-2s from the 266th and 292nd Assault Divisions covered by the same number of fighters from the IV Fighter Corps. He also has 28 La-5s sent out in

A LESS INTENSE AIR WAR CONTINUES

advance to prevent the German fighters at Rogan from taking off. The paragraph detailing a German hangar destroyed at Rogan and two ammunition depots burned out at Mikoyanovka is footnoted as being from the Soviet archives, the file is given as "TsAMO, f.20043, op. 000---1, d. 011). The name of the file is not given.

Our daily accounts for the Second Air Army (Fond: 2nd Air Army, Opis: 4196, Delo: 20, Vol. 2, Operational Report #191, 2200, 10 July, 1943) does not give any of those accounts. They report for the I Bomber Corps only 2 Pe-2 flights for reconnaissance. They record for the 291st Assault Division only 25 Il-2s today conducting 58 sorties, bombing the enemy tanks and motorized infantry. They had 10 fighters conducting 34 sorties with one dogfight in the Kochetovka area, but without result. They did have five Il-2s failed to return from their mission. The 266th Assault Division, which is part of the I Assault Corps, is not specifically reported on. The I Assault Corps reports that 41 Il-2s conducted 83 sorties and 26 Yak-1s conducted 47 sorties. Again, the area of operations did not include German airfields and they reported attacking enemy tanks and men. The IV Fighter Corps intercepted enemy aircraft and covered ground troops in the area of Vladimirovka, Kruglik and Verkhopenye. Among all their 107 fighter missions, they had 27 La-5s conduct 53 sorties. They do note that one La-5 rammed an Me-109.

There is either a significant gap in the Second Air Army reports, or unreported missions, or Bergstrom's accounts of airfield attacks have been assigned to the wrong day. It is most likely the later.

10. Bergstrom, *Kursk*, page 75. It is from an interview with LSSAH member Willi Rogmann. Rogmann is the author of *Meine Kriegserlebnisse: Einzelkaempfer der Leibstandarte, Traeger der Nahkampfspange in Gold* (Bethge Verlag, Bad Lobenstein, Germany, 2009).
11. According to Bergstrom, *Kursk*, page 81 (source is not given), a formation of ten Yak-9s from the 256th Fighter Division became lost and five of them ran out of fuel. They had to perform emergency landings in the countryside. If this happened on this day, then they were able to recover and return some of the planes to action the following day.

    The Second Air Army reported no Yak-9s lost on the 11th. On 12 July both the IV and V Fighter Division were able to fly 40 missions with their Yak-9s. The 256th Fighter Division had 43 Yak-9s according to Bergstrom, *Kursk*, page 75.
12. Seidemann, pages 205–206.
13. Hooton, *War over the Steppes*, page 177.
14. There are some minor math errors in the records. For example, Second Air Army says 539 sorties but the totals given by plane in the next paragraph equals 542 sorties.
15. This assumes 75% serviceable, based upon Seidemann's estimate for the start of the battle. It was probably lower at this stage of the battle.
16. Apparently 81-99% destroyed means "Totally destroyed, crashed in German-controlled area." See Bergstrom, *Kursk*, page 131. Bergstrom, *Black Cross, Red Star*, page 245, gives German losses in the south as 96 aircraft from 5 July to 11 July. This is clearly based upon the quartermaster reports, from which we show at least 90 lost.

Chapter Seven

THE AIR BATTLE TO SUPPORT THE OFFENSIVE NORTH OF KURSK
5–11 July 1943

H-Hour was 0330. Everyone feverishly awaited that hour. The attack began with a fierce barrage by the German artillery, and our Stukas pounded the Soviet positions with incredible fury. Our Ferdinands moved off into this inferno, and the Soviet defenses then began to open up with a withering barrage.

Unteroffizier Heinz Leuschen[1]

The German offensive at the Battle of Kursk consisted of two parts. The large attack in the south that is the focus of this book, and a smaller attack in the north. That attack in the north was about two-thirds the size of the attack in the south, both on the ground and in the air. The Soviet defenders in the north were similar in strength to those in the south. Therefore, the northern attack by the German XLI (41st) Panzer Corps only had penetrated 11 kilometers into Soviet lines, stalling after 7 July 1943 at the village of Ponyiri.[2] The XLVII (47th) Panzer Corps to the west of Ponyiri penetrated a little deeper, 15 kilometers. It was a three-day offensive conducted primarily by two German corps, followed by four days of hard back and forth fighting that did not move the lines.

The primary reason this book focuses on the southern offensive part of the Battle of Kursk is that this work was funded by the US Army Concepts Analysis Agency (CAA). As such, we have an extensive two-sided collection of data from the unit records of both sides. This was not a small research effort and would be difficult to recreate for both sides for the north. To date, none of the other books written on the northern attack have been fully developed from the unit records of both sides. Therefore, we will limit ourselves to only briefly discussing the northern attack and will not discuss larger Soviet offensive north of Kursk that started on 12 July or the larger Soviet offensive to the south of Kursk that started on 3 August. These two counteroffensives went until 18 and 23 August 1943, respectively. As the Battle of Kursk is the largest battle of the Second World War, these should to be addressed in a separate book. So, while the events in the north are no less

THE AIR BATTLE TO SUPPORT THE OFFENSIVE NORTH OF KURSK

important, as this was a pincher attack, they will only be dealt with in this book in a most general manner.

The Northern Attack

The northern attack was to be conducted by General Walter Model's Ninth Army. It consisted of five corps. They were, from west to east: the XX (20th) Corps, XLVI (46th) Panzer Corps, the XLVII Panzer Corps, the XLI Panzer Corps, and the XXIII (23rd) Corps. The XX Corps was not actively involved in the attack, but was holding the line in the northwestern part of the bulge opposite the Soviet Sixty-fifth Army and connected with the Second Army, which was the German army on the west face of the bulge. It consisted of four infantry divisions (from west to east: the 251st, 137th, 45th, and 72nd). Attached to the corps was one artillery battalion, an engineer battalion, an observation battalion and various bridging units. Opposing it was the Soviet Sixty-fifth Army, which had almost the same east and west boundaries as the XX Corps. That army consisted of nine rifle divisions, a rifle brigade, and four tank regiments and had a frontage of 82 kilometers.

The next corps, the XLVI Panzer Corps, did not have any panzer divisions in it. It also consisted of four infantry divisions (from west to east: the 102nd, 258th, 7th, and 31st). Its armor consisted of the 909th Assault Gun Battalion and Group von Mantueffel, consisting of the 9th, 10th, and 11th Jaeger Battalions. This Group von Mantueffel was placed into the line between the 102nd and 258th Infantry Divisions. This corps' total armored assets included around 31 assault guns and 9 tanks.[3] This corps was supported by three artillery battalions, a nebelwerfer battalion, an artillery company, and two platoons (effectively adding up to five supporting battalions). There was one engineer battalion, an artillery observation battalion, and various bridging and construction troops.

The main attack was carried out by the two panzer corps in the center, consisting of six panzer divisions. The westernmost of these armored corps was the XLVII Panzer Corps consisting of the 20th Panzer Division and the 6th Infantry Division on the front and the 2nd Panzer Division and the 9th Panzer Division in the rear ready to exploit the attack. They also had the 21st Panzer Brigade, with the 505th Heavy Panzer Battalion (Tiger) and the 312th Panzer Company (with small radio controlled mine-clearing demolition tanks, the Goliaths). Also with this corps were two assault gun battalions (904th and 245th). Their attached artillery consisted of one battalion with a platoon detached, two artillery companies, one artillery platoon, and one nebelwerfer regiment (effectively adding up to 5 artillery battalions). There also were two engineer battalions and various bridging troops.

The next panzer corps, the XLI Panzer Corps, consisted of only the 18th Panzer Division and two infantry divisions, the 292nd and 86th. The two infantry divisions were in the front with the panzer division behind them ready to exploit the attack. This corps also had the 656th Panzer Jaeger Regiment, consisting of the 653rd Panzer Jaeger Battalion and the 654th Panzer Jaeger Battalion (each with 45 Ferdinands). Other armor included three assault gun battalions, the 177th and 244th, both with Sturmgeschuetz IIIs, and the 216th Sturmpanzer Battalion with 45 new 150mm Sturmpanzers. Also attached were the 313th and 314th Panzer Companies (with small radio controlled mine-clearing demolition tanks, the Goliaths). Their attached artillery consisted of four artillery battalions, two companies and a platoon, and a nebelwerfer regiment and another nebelwerfer battalion (effectively nine artillery battalions). They had one attached engineer battalion and various bridging and construction troops.

Well behind them, and ready to exploit the attack, was Gruppe von Esebeck with the remaining two panzer divisions (12th and 4th) and the 10th Panzer Grenadier Division. This panzer grenadier division was not the same as the large powerful formations that existed in the south. This was effectively a motorized infantry division, with limited armored assets, as they had no tanks or assault guns.[4] These forces were only partially committed to the attack and by 12 July, most of the 12th Panzer Division still had not been committed to the attack.

The XXIII Corps was another infantry corps consisting of three deployed divisions from west to east: the 78th Assault Division, the 216th, and the recently raised 383rd. They also had the 87th Infantry Regiment (36th Infantry Division) with two battalions, and well to the rear, as a reserve, the rest of the 36th Infantry Division. Corps armor consisted of two assault gun battalions (185th and the 189th, the last of which was part of the 78th Assault Division) and two jaeger battalions (8th and 13th). Their artillery included six battalions, two companies, four platoons, and a nebelwerfer regiment (effectively ten battalions). There were two engineer battalions, two engineer companies, an artillery observation battalion, and limited bridging troops.

Under control of the army were an additional two engineer battalions, a large number of bridging and construction troops, a security battalion, and other command and support troops. Overall, this army consisted of six panzer divisions, one panzer grenadier division, and 14 infantry divisions, of which four were clearly not part of the attack. They were supported by a tank battalion, two panzer jaeger battalions, eight assault gun battalions, and three tank companies. They had the equivalent of 29 artillery battalions and nine battalions of engineers. Overall, this force of 17 attacking divisions was similar in size to the 17-division effort in the south although with only around half the tanks and less hitting power.[5]

This whole effort was supported by the Sixth Air Fleet, whose 1st Air Division consisted of around 730 planes. The Sixth Air Fleet was able to put up 2,088 sorties on the 5th of July as opposed to the 2,387 sorties done by the VIII Air Corps that same day.

Just to compare the two forces:

	South	North
Large Panzer Grenadier Divisions	4	0
Pz Division with two armored battalions	3	0
Pz Division with one armored battalion	2	6
Regular Panzer Grenadier Division	0	1

THE AIR BATTLE TO SUPPORT THE OFFENSIVE NORTH OF KURSK

	South	North
Infantry Division	7	1
Infantry Division with two regiments	1	9
Attached Panzer Battalions	3	1
Attached Assault Gun Battalions	2	7[6]
Attached Panzer Jaeger Battalions	0	2
Attached Artillery Battalions	25	29
Attached Engineer Battalions	9	9
Summation		
Total Armored and Assault Gun Battalions	26	17
Total Recon Battalions	14	10
Total Infantry and Jaeger Battalions	102	102
Total Engineer Battalions	25	26
Total Artillery Battalions	72	90[7]

Opposing them in the North was the Central Front under command of General Rokossovskii with Marshal Zhukov serving at the senior commander overseeing operations from Stavka. The engaged forces were less than those of the Voronezh Front.[8] They consisted of the Seventieth Army and the Thirteenth Army, with the Second Tank Army in Front reserve, which was quickly committed. The Seventieth Army had eight rifle divisions while the Thirteenth Army had a massive twelve rifle divisions in three echelons. The Second Tank Army had two tank corps and quickly picked up two more tank corps that were part of the Front reserve. The Central Front also had three other armies under its command that did not participate in the fighting directly, which were the Forty-eighth Army, the Sixty-fifth Army, and the Sixtieth Army.

Overall, the forces in the two armies facing the German attack, the tank army, and Front reserves consisted of:

Tanks Corps	4
Tank Brigades	1
Tank Regiments	8
Rifle Divisions	20 (including Guards)
AT Artillery Brigades	3
AT Artillery Regiments	2
Artillery Corps	1 (3 divisions)
Artillery Division	1
Mortar Regiments	2
Antiaircraft Regiment	1

The Seventieth and Thirteenth Armies occupied a frontage of 94 kilometers, with the very powerful Thirteenth Army concentrated into only 32 kilometers with its twelve divisions in three echelons. The entire Central Front occupied a frontage of 308 kilometers.

The Central Front's Sixtieth Army was opposite the German Second Army, while the Sixty-fifth Army was opposite the German XX Corps. They were both to the left of the battle, well inside the part of the bulge to be encircled. To the right of the battle was the Forty-eighth Army, consisting of seven rifle divisions, three tank regiments, and one antitank artillery brigade, and occupied 40 kilometers of front. It was opposite part of the XXIII Corps, although they did not engage, and was also opposite part of the Second Panzer Army.

The area where the Germans were going to attack was much denser than it was in the south. Looking at the number of artillery gun tubes per kilometer of front for 4 July provides a good illustration of this:[9]

Unit	Frontage (in kilometers)	Artillery Tubes per kilometer
Seventh Guards Army	55	26.7
Sixth Guards Army	60	27.9
Fortieth Army	50	32.7
Thirty-eighth Army	80	11.3
Sixtieth Army	92	9.8
Sixty-fifth Army	82	14.5
Seventieth Army	62	25.6
Thirteenth Army	32	86.4
Forty-eighth Army	40	24.8

Actual Tube Count[10]

Unit	82mm & 120mm Mortars	45mm, 57mm, 76mm AA & AT Guns	76mm, 122mm, 152mm & 203mm Divisional Artillery & Reinforcing	Total Tubes
Seventh Guards Army	779	418	477	1,674
Sixth Guards Army	653	426	391	1,470
Fortieth Army	869	393	371	1,633
Thirty-eighth Army	551	159	194	904
Sixty-ninth Army	590	309	155	1,054
First Tank Army	249	20	68	337
II & V Gds Tank Corps	190	40	48	278
XXXV Gds Rifle Corps	362	184	112	658
Front Reserve	180	40	128	348

Unit	82mm & 120mm Mortars	45mm, 57mm, 76mm AA & AT Guns	76mm, 122mm, 152mm & 203mm Divisional Artillery & Reinforcing	Total Tubes
Voronezh Front (Totals)	4,423	1,989	1,944	8,356
Sixtieth Army	508	219	178	905
Sixty-fifth Army	544	392	251	1,187
Seventieth Army	768	411	406	1,585
Thirteenth Army	1,325	587	854	2,766
Forty-eighth Army	487	321	183	991
Front Reserve	155	152	36	343
Central Front (Total)	3,787	2,082	1,908	7,777

The German Air in the North

Supporting the Ninth Army attack on the north side of the Kursk bulge was the Sixth Air Fleet, consisting of the 1st Air Division, the 12th Flak Division and the 10th Flak Brigade. Reporting directly to the Sixth Air Fleet was a night fighter group, night bomber group and a long range reconnaissance group. The 1st Air Division, under command of Major General Paul Deichmann, also had three short-range reconnaissance groups reporting to it.

Under the 1st Air Division were parts of nine wings consisting of 16 groups. They had elements of four bombardment wings with a total of seven groups. There was one incomplete fighter wing and a group from another fighter wing for a total of four fighter groups and one Spanish squadron. There were one complete stuka (ground attack) wing and a group from another wing for a total of four stuka groups. There were elements of a "destroyer" (Me-110) wing with one group and an antitank squadron, which were primarily used for ground attack. There were also elements of three reconnaissance groups.

Under direct command of the Sixth Air Fleet was a night fighter group, a night bomber group (harassment bomber group), five reconnaissance squadrons, and three transport groups and several other transport and liaison squadrons.

Overall, this amounted to around 730 planes.[11] On the first day of the Battle of Kursk, this force was able to fly 2,088 sorties. Its rate of sorties declined in the following days, and it averaged 1,274 flights a day. From the 5th through the 11th, inclusive, the force flew a total of 8,917 daytime sorties, which was 82% of the number flown in the same time period by the VIII Air Corps.

This does not fully reflect the difference in air support levels. The VIII Air Corps was literally flying only half the reconnaissance missions that the Sixth Air Fleet was flying, and flew about the same number of fighter missions. If one just compares the number of stuka missions, bomber missions and "hunting" or "destroyer" missions, which are the ground attack missions, then one discovers that the Sixth Air Fleet flew a total of 4,198 ground attack sorties while the VIII Air Corps flew 7,388 from the 5th through the 9th (there is no sortie breakdown for the VIII Air Corps for the 10th). This puts the Sixth Air Fleet flying only 57% of the ground attack type missions that were flown by the VIII Air Corps.

The antiaircraft units attached to the Sixth Air Fleet consisted of the 12th Flak Division with three regiments and the 10th Flak Brigade with five or six flak battalions and two searchlight batteries.[12]

The Soviet Air in the North

Opposite them was the Soviet Sixteenth Air Army that was attached to the Central Front. Around the rest of the Orel bulge was the Fifteenth Air Army (Bryansk Front) and the First Air Army (Western Front). Without looking into the records and details of their operations, it is difficult to determine how much opposition the Sixth Air Fleet faced from them. It certainly was fully engaged with the Soviet Sixteenth Air Army (Central Front) during Operation Citadel. The degree that the First Air Army (Western Front) and the Fifteenth Air Army (Bryansk Front) were involved was certainly much less. For example, the Sixth Air Fleet's losses from the 5th through the 11th were recorded as 39 airplanes over the seven days, never losing more than 13 planes a day (compared to 69 planes lost by the VIII Air Corps in the same period). Starting with the 12th, the Sixth Air Fleet's losses went up precipitously, to 61 airplanes over the next four days (compared to 30 planes lost by the VIII Air Corps in the same period). These losses were certainly due to the offensives initiated by the Western and Bryansk Fronts on the north face of the Orel bulge, and their supporting air operations. The Sixth Air Fleet was not only responsible for supporting the Ninth Army, but also the Second Army and the Second Panzer Army. On the 12th, the Second Panzer Army came under attack by the Soviet Western and Bryansk Fronts as part of the Soviet counterstroke. In contrast, German air losses in the south declined after the 12th of July.

The Correlation of Opposing Air Forces at Beginning of German Offensive

The Soviet General Staff did a study on the Battle of Kursk early 1944. Their analysis was based upon their own unit records, their estimates of enemy actions, intents, and strengths, and included some post-battle analysis based upon their one-sided understanding of what occurred. This study included the following table on correlation of forces:[13]

	16th Air Army	2nd Air Army	17th Air Army	Totals	Enemy Aircraft
Fighters	455/71	389/85	163/43	1,007/199	600
Assault	241/28	276/23	239/27	756/78	100
Day Bombers	260/14	172/18	76/2	508/34	1,000
Night Bombers	74/2	34/15	60/1	168/18	–
Recce	4/2	10/8	–	14/10	150
Totals	1,034/117	881/149	538/73	2,453/339	1,850

Note: The larger number to the left of the slash represents operational aircraft, and the lower number to the right is the count of aircraft in disrepair.

THE AIR BATTLE TO SUPPORT THE OFFENSIVE NORTH OF KURSK

SOVIET AIR STRENGTHS

We have the air strength of the Second and Seventeenth Air Armies based upon research into their unit records that *The Dupuy Institute* conducted in the 1990s. We do not have archival records for the Sixteenth Air Army because that was not part of the original Kursk Data Base project. Still, there are a number of Soviet-era secondary sources that give us such strengths. The following table from a book by Trevor Dupuy and Paul Martell reported these air strengths for 1 July 1943.[14]

Soviet Air Strength
1 July 1943

	Central Front	Voronezh Front	Southwestern Front	Total
Corps				
Fighter	1	2	–	3
Ground Attack	–	1	–	1
Bomber	1	1	–	2
Mixed	1	–	3	4
Total	3	4	3	10
Divisions				
Fighter	6	5	3	14
Ground Attack	2	3	4	9
Bomber	4	3	2	9[15]
Total	12	11	9	32
Aircraft				
Fighters[16]	455	389	218	1,062
Ground Attack	241	276	383	900
Day Bombers	260	172	70	502
Night Bombers[17]	74	34	64	172
Reconnaissance	4	10	–	14
Total	1,034	881	735	2,650

This book was published in 1982. A lot of the research was done by Paul Martell using published Soviet era secondary sources. Still, we can check the accuracy of this table for the Second and Seventeenth Air Armies. The count of air corps is correct and the count of air divisions is correct for both air armies. The airplane strength of 881 for the Second Air Army matches the number of operational aircraft given for the correlation of forces in the Soviet General Staff study. The division by fighters, assault, day bombers and night bombers also match the correlation of forces. Neither of these tables exactly match the count of aircraft we obtained from the Second Air Army records.

Our count from those records is a total of at least 1,080 aircraft on-hand.[18] This is at least 50 planes more than the count of 881 operational aircraft and 149 in repair (last figure from the correlation of forces report). The mix of planes is close, but not quite the same, with the various Soviet secondary sources reporting 389 fighters versus 572 from the Second Air Army records, 276 ground attack aircraft versus 306, 172 day bombers versus 117, 34 night bombers versus 57 and 10 reconnaissance versus at least 28 in the Second Air Army records. The Second Air Army report was from a report in their unit records summarizing the movements of planes in and out of their aircraft park for July (including losses).[19]

The number actually operational appears to be in some question. For example (see Chapter Two), the I Assault Corps has 206 Assault aircraft and 82 Fighters. Yet the total flown on 5 July by that corps was only 114 Il-2s (55%) and 60 Yak-1bs (73%). So the Second Air Army reports 1,080 planes on 1 July, yet only flies 624 sorties on 5 July (58%). So it does appear that readiness of these units may not have been stellar, as they flew less than 60% of their aircraft, even though the correlation of forces report implies a readiness of 86%.

The airplane strength for the Seventeenth Air Army of 735 is not far from our total of 750 operational and 49 not operational for a total of 799 for 5 July 1943 (see Chapter Two). The Soviet General Staff study only reports 538 operational and 73 in repair, while Dupuy and Martell more accurately have the count as 735. This is probably a figure for operational aircraft based upon the comparisons to the reports on the Second Air Army.

Both sets of figures are noticeably higher than the figure of 538 operational and 73 in repair given for the Seventeenth Air Army in the Soviet General Staff study correlation of forces. They either left out one of the mixed air corps in their correlation or just got the numbers wrong. Other Soviet era sources also use the figures of 1,034 for the Sixteenth Air Army, 881 for the Second Air Army and 735 for the Seventeenth Air Army.[20]

The mix of planes is close, but not quite the same, with Dupuy and Martell reporting 218 fighters versus 198 operational and 16 not operational from the Seventeenth Air Army records, 383 ground attack aircraft versus 360 operational and 24 not operational, 70 day bombers versus 76 operational and 2 not operational, 64 night bombers versus 60 operational and 1 not operational and no reconnaissance aircraft reported versus 20 operational and 2 not operational in the Seventeenth Air Army records and at least 34 operational and 4 not operational other U-2s attacked to mixed divisions and in independent and transport regiments. The Seventeenth Air Army records also included a report that matches this total of 735 operational aircraft.[21]

THE AIR BATTLE TO SUPPORT THE OFFENSIVE NORTH OF KURSK

> This does give us some confidence that the figures for the Sixteenth Air Army are reasonable, especially as the figure of 1,034 matches the figures in the correlation of forces given in the 1944 Soviet General Staff study. Still, there is clearly a need for someone to access the Soviet archives and compare these figures with the reports of the Sixteenth Air Army.
>
> Paul Martell was a cover name for a Soviet-era Polish army officer who defected to the United States and later worked for Trevor Dupuy at his companies. He did write a book of his experiences and his defection under his real name, Colonel Pawel Monat.[22]

This correlation of forces is not dated, but may have been prepared around 1 July 1943. It shows 1,034 to 1,151 aircraft in the north and 1,419 to 1,641 aircraft in the south. Their estimate of German aircraft is good as the Germans had around 730 aircraft in the north and around 1,100 aircraft in the south. Their estimates of plane type is off, with the number of fighters overestimated.

This overestimation of fighter strength does seem to be part of some odd attempt to justify the exchange rates. While the Soviet records show the Germans losing more fighters than the Soviets did, it was probably understood by command that this was not really the case, although they may not have understood how unfavorably lopsided the exchange rates were. As they note in their staff study "The enemy had the advantage in aviation basing.... To a considerable degree, such a basing of enemy fighter aviation made it possible for him to maintain a balance of forces in the air during the first days of the operation, despite our more than 1.5-fold superiority in fighters."[23]

They estimated that the Germans had 600 fighters, both south and north. In fact, the Germans had deployed for these operations eight fighter groups among their four fighter wings. Each fighter group had 40 or less planes. So, while the Soviets had 1,206 fighters, the Germans only had around 320 fighters, probably around 331.[24] Now, the Germans also deployed Fw-190s in the south as ground attack aircraft and Me-110s in the north for ground attack, so this could add another 140 fighters to the count.[25] This does add up to 471, except around 30% of these planes were not used as fighters. Regardless the Soviet estimation of German fighter strength was off, and appears to have been off by a factor of two. This is not surprising in light of the lop-sided exchange ratios.

In the south, the Germans were able to maintain around a six-to-one kill ratio. It appears to have been even worse in the north. The difference of basing probably did not influence the results of the air battle "to a considerable degree." There were other more significant factors involved that the Soviet General Staff study does not seem to want to grapple with.

It does show for the Sixteenth Air Army a readiness rate of 90% and for all three air armies, an average readiness rate of 88%. This does seem a little high. The estimate by the VIII Air Corp commander, General Seidemann, was that German readiness was around 75%. As shown by the number flown each day for the Second and Seventeenth Air Armies, it does not appear that Soviet readiness rate was actually much above 80%.

In the book *Kursk 1943: The Northern Front* by Robert Forczyk there is a table of plane strengths that is similar to other reports, but slightly lower.[26] They record the planes by type:

Soviet Operational Aircraft Strength

Type	Model	Number Serviceable (estimated)
Fighters	Yak-1/7/9	300
	La-5	110
	P-39	40
Day Bombers	Pe-2	175
	A-20	85
Ground Attack	Il-2	241
Total		951

These figures are close to the other figures, in that the Soviet General Staff study reports 455 fighters while there are 450 reported in this table. The totals do match for ground attack and day bombers (A-20s are Bostons). This table leaves out the night bombers and reconnaissance aircraft. This table probably comes from Soviet-era sources, but the source has not been identified.

The German Strike in the North

Of interest, and in contrast to the Soviet air strike in the south, was the German strike in the north by the 1st Air Division. As in the south, the last elements moved up to their respective operational fields on the evening of 4 July. They then struck at first light, crossing the front lines at about 0330 (Berlin time) on the 5th. They attacked the Soviet airfields around and west of Kursk.[27] At the same time, other German formations attacked Soviet artillery concentrations around Maloarkhangelsk.

The Soviet air force did not attempt such a strike in the north, and only made their presence known rather late in the morning, around 1000. They did not maintain a strong presence at first, leading the Germans to conclude that they had obtained tactical surprise. Soviet ground attack planes did not begin appearing over the battlefield until around noon. Writer #762 estimates that a total of about 110 Soviet aircraft were shot down on the 5th.[28] The Air Liaison officer reports claim 163 Soviet planes shot down by air and two by flak. The Sixth Air Fleet only lost 13 planes this day, including 2 Fw-190s from the fighter wings and 1 Me-110. Out of 2,088 sorties, they had flown 168 Me-110 sorties and 522 fighter sorties (in contrast to 371 fighter sorties in the south). This much stronger fighter presence certainly played a part in maintaining control of the air in the north, but by the same token, the ground forces in the south had much better air

THE AIR BATTLE TO SUPPORT THE OFFENSIVE NORTH OF KURSK

support on the first day, with 1,942 stuka, bomber and ground attack sorties compared to 1,397 in the north.

It is hard to tell whether launching the first strike was the better strategy. In the north it may have initially reduced the Soviet air presence and resulted in lower casualties. In contrast, by letting the Soviets make the first strike in the south, it appears that the VIII Air Corps was able to seriously attrite the Soviet air force. In the face of a noticeably less capable opponent, all strategies yield good results.

The German Sortie Count

The German Second Army air liaison officer kept a daily record of the number of sorties flown by the Sixth Air Fleet and the VIII Air Corps during this time. The neighboring Second Army was unengaged at this time and positioned to the west of Kursk. This is the only record of the number of sorties and missions flown by the German Air Force at Kursk. He also tracked the number of losses. This is one of two loss reports for the German Air Force at Kursk, the other being the Luftwaffe quartermaster files.

The Second Army Luftwaffe liaison officer reports the following for the Sixth Air Fleet:

Table 7.1: The Sixth Air Fleet Sortie Count[29]

(while supporting the German offensive north of Kursk 5 to 11 July 1943)[30]

	Total Sorties	Recon	Stuka	Bombing (Harassing)	"Destroyer"*	Fighter	Transport
June 30	108						
Night	9						
July 1	114						
Night	29			(19)			
July 2	67						
Night	0						
July 3	182					7	
Night	111			86 (13)			
July 4	No report						
Night	**						
July 5	2,088	141	647	582	168	522	28
Night	15			4			
July 6	1,023	139	289	164	93	317	21
Night	92			36 (44)[31]			
July 7	1,687	195	582	454	123	307	26
Night	134***			54 (58)			

	Total Sorties	By Type					
		Recon	Stuka	Bombing (Harassing)	"Destroyer"*	Fighter	Transport
July 8	1,173	100	378	274	73	291	57
Night	6						
July 9	877	164	181	138	52	255	87
Night	22			3			
July 10	1,136	134	375	220	66	266	75
Night	51			6 (36)			
July 11	933[32]	111[33]	249	226	20	283[34]	44?
Night	21						
Daytime Sorties from 5 through 11 July 1943						
Summation	8,917	984	2,701	2,058	595	2,241	338?
Nighttime Sorties from 5 through 11 July 1943						
Summation	341						

* "Destroyer" missions are usually missions by Me-110s. They could be fighter missions, ground attack or other types of missions, or some combination of the three. Another air liaison record and the standard usage at this time indicates that they were probably used for ground attack.
** 760,000 pamphlets as part of Operation *Silberstreif* in front of the Second Army.
*** 496,000 pamphlets in front of the Second Army.

Table 7.2: The Sixth Air Fleet Loses

(according to the Second Army air liaison officer)

	Total	Ju-88	He-111	Ju-87	Me-110	Fw-190	Ar-66	Me-109
June 30	1	1						
Night	0							
July 1	0							
Night	0							
July 2	0							
Night	0							
July 3	0							
Night	0							
July 4	No report							
Night	–							
July 5	13	1	1	8	1*	2**		
Night	–							
July 6	6	3	–	1	1	1		

THE AIR BATTLE TO SUPPORT THE OFFENSIVE NORTH OF KURSK

	Total	Ju-88	He-111	Ju-87	Me-110	Fw-190	Ar-66	Me-109
Night	1						1***	
July 7	3	2	1					
Night	–							
July 8	2	–	–	1	–	1****		
Night	0							
July 9	5	–	–	1	–	3	–	1
Night	0							
July 10	7	–	2	1	2	2		
Night	0							
July 11	2	–	–	1	–	1*****		
Night	0							
Summation (for 5 through 11 July 1943)	39	6	4	13	4	10	1	1

* Labeled as Me-110 (Zerstroyer) which implies that this plane was operating as a fighter.
** Labeled as Fw-190 (Jager) which implies that these planes were operating as fighters.
*** Labeled as Ar-66 (Storkampfflugzeuge) which implies that these planes were doing harassment bombing.
**** Note after the Fw-190 says "Sergeant Stasal missing, 25 kills on 6 + 7 July."
***** Note in the report says "Knight's Cross Major Resch, 91 air victories."

Table 7.3: The Sixth Air Fleet Claimed Kills

	Claimed Kills Total	By Fighters	By Flak	By Air Combat	Other
June 30	2	2			
Night	1		1		
July 1	4	3	1		
Night	0				
July 2	1		1		
Night	0				
July 3	6			6	
Night	0				
July 4	No report				
Night	–				
July 5	165		2	163	
Night	–				
July 6	130		12	118	
Night	1				1*
July 7	81		7	74	

	Claimed Kills Total	By Fighters	By Flak	By Air Combat	Other
Night	–				
July 8	73		6	67	
Night	0				
July 9	85		18	67	
Night	0				
July 10	75		15	60	
Night	0				
July 11	42		5	37	
Night	1				1**
Summation (for 5 through 11 July 1943)	653		65	586	2

* "durch Aufklarer" or through reconnaissance.
** By night fighter

Table 7.4: The 10th Near Reconnaissance Group Missions

The 10th Near Reconnaissance Group (Nahaufklarungs Gruppe 10 or NAG 10) missions were reported separately from the Sixth Air Fleet mission in the Second Army air liaison records. The NAG 10 reported to the Sixth Air Fleet. Their missions are listing below:

	Total Sorties	Fw-189	Hs-126	Ordnance dropped:*		Pamphlets
				SD 50	SC 10	
July 1	11	5	6	10	20	430,000
July 2	11	5	6	10	20	384,000
July 3	20	12	8	14	30	457,000
July 4	16	10	6	6	20	353,000
July 5	12	6	6	10	30	366,000
July 6	11	6	5	6	30	307,000
July 7	13	6	7	6	60	466,000
July 8	12	6	6	12	60	537,000
July 9	13	6	7	12	30	656,000
July 10	10	5	5	10	50	352,000
July 11	10	6	4	-	30	576,000
July 12	7	3	4	-	30	312,000
July 13	5	3	2	-	10	180,000
July 14	15	6	9	-	60	655,000
July 15	9	5	4	-	20	336,000
July 16	14	6	8	4	30	588,000

THE AIR BATTLE TO SUPPORT THE OFFENSIVE NORTH OF KURSK

	Total Sorties	Fw-189	Hs-126	Ordnance dropped:* SD 50	Ordnance dropped:* SC 10	Pamphlets
July 17	12	6	6	15	40	468,000
July 18	9	5	4	10	10	312,000
July 19	12	7	5	14	30	420,000
Night	2	2	-	8	-	70,000
July 20	11	5	6	10	30	396,000
July 21	8	4	4	8	20	142,000
July 22	7	3	4	6	30	114,000

* The SD 50 was a thick-walled fragmentation bomb weighting 55 kilograms (121 pounds). The SC 10 was a thin-cased high explosive bomb weighing 12 kilograms (22 pounds).

The reconnaissance group does not report any losses and does not claim any kills. It appears to have had about a dozen operational aircraft.

The Soviet Sortie Count

We do not have the daily sortie count from daily unit records for the Sixteenth Air Army, such as we were able to assemble for the Second and Seventeenth Air Army. Still, there is some material on the count of sorties in various secondary sources. The Soviet General Staff study on Kursk, written in early 1944, provided the following table:[35]

Sorties by Air Army (1-4 July)

	Total Sorties	Recce	Attacking Forces	Attacking Rail Targets	Protecting Installations	Intercepting Enemy Aircraft	Accompanying Assault Aircraft
16th Air Army	464	178	114	17	23	44	71
2nd Air Army	434	111	63	–	–	260	–

The narrative notes the German operations began at 0425 (Moscow time) on 5 July with German bombing raids. They then note that only 520 sorties were flown by the Sixteenth Air Army before 1200 hours (Moscow time) on 5 July. They state that the plan for combat employment of the aviation was put into effect at 0930 (Moscow time) and at that time intensive air combat operations began. They also note that during the day assault aircraft flew 225 sorties, which was less than one flight for each operable aircraft, and the bombers flew only 105 sorties, which is less than a half sortie per operable aircraft. They claim that this was because of a lack of available escort aircraft.[36]

The Soviet General Staff study on Kursk does provide a count of Soviet sorties flown each day for 5 through 12 July 1943. This is presented in the table below.[37]

Air Operations on Both Sides, 5 – 12 July

Date	Fighter	Assault	Day Bomber	Night Bomber	Total	LRA	Enemy Aviation Total	Night
5.7	817	225	105	102	1,249	17	2,257	24
6.7	779	225	122	469	1,595	269	1,162	32
7.7	731	219	235	422	1,607	210	1,203	41
8.7	613	130	170	342	1,255	169	933	58
9.7	448	152	175	181	956	36	350	16
10.7	419	79	173	250	921	77	955	5
11.7	218	80	3	176	477	–	680	11
12.7	25	71	1	236	333	–	72	7
Total	4,050	1,181	984	2,178 [38]	8,393	778	7,612	194

The Soviet estimates of German sorties have them flying 2,257 daytime sorties on 5 July, while the German air liaison officer reports 2,088 sorties flown that day (28 were transport missions). For the 5th through the 11th, the Soviets estimate the Germans flew 7,540 daytime sorties while the Germans reported flying 8,917 sorties during that time. Of those, it appears that 338 were transport missions, which by their nature were usually behind German lines and therefore most likely not observed and counted by the Soviet air force. Therefore, we are looking at a Soviet estimate of 7,540 daytime sorties compared to 8,579 German daytime combat sorties flown. The Soviet estimate is within 14% of the German reported sortie count.

On the 12th, the Soviet count of German sorties, which have been reasonably accurate up to now, is only recording 72 sorties while the Sixth Air Fleet is reported to have flown 1,111 daytime sorties. The difference is clearly that many of the German sorties were flow outside of this Kursk-Ponyiri battle area and were instead flown in support of the German forces defending elsewhere on the Orel bulge. On the 11th the Germans flew 933 sorties while the Soviet General Staff study reports 680 sorties flown. On the 12th the Germans flew 1,111 sorties while the Soviet General Staff study reports only 72 sorties flown.[39] It is clear that the German forces around Ponyiri did not receive much air support on the 12th.

They also have a report of cumulative daytime sorties by army. No date is given for the report but they report 9,804 daytime sorties for the Second Air Army.[40] Our records from the Second Air Army clearly report that they flew 9,844 daytime sorties from 5 to 18 July. The close correlation of these figures does increase our confidence in daily sortie counts provided above by the Soviet General Staff study. Therefore, this is assumed to be the same time scale for all three air armies in this report, although they may have limited the count for the Sixteenth Air Army to only cover from 5 through 12 July 1943.

THE AIR BATTLE TO SUPPORT THE OFFENSIVE NORTH OF KURSK

	Second Air Army	17th Air Army	16th Air Army	Total
Day sorties	9,804	2,808	6,151	18,763
For troop cover	3,683	165	1,800	5,648
To accompany assault aircraft and bombers	2,226	1,216	2,057	5,499
To attack airfields	85	70	–	155
To achieve air superiority				
Sorties	5,994	1,451	3,857	11,302
Percentage	61	52	62	60

These figures do seem to indicate that there were only 2,294[41] sorties flown by the Sixteenth Air Army for ground support and reconnaissance. If these figures cover 5-18 July, that is only 164 sorties a day, and this includes reconnaissance flights in addition to ground support. If it was only for the 5-12 July (the period covered by table is not certain), then it is 287 sorties a day. Calculated from these statistics, the Sixteenth Air Army provided only 44% of the ground attack sorties and reconnaissance sorties that were used in the south by the Second and Seventeenth Air Armies.

There is a table in the Soviet General Staff study that directly addresses this. It shows the following.[42]

	Sortie counts			Of these			
Missions	Second Air Army	Seventeenth Air Army	Sixteenth Air Army	LRA	Total	Day	Night
Attacking ground forces	5,042	2,962	3,453	2,082	13,539	6,484	7,055
Air superiority	5,994	1,451	3,857	78	11,380	11,302	78
Attacks on enemy rail transport	–	–	–	139	139	–	139
Recce	422	298	241	–	961	961	–
Totals	11,458	4,711	7,551	2,299	26,019	18,747	7,272

There are a number of interesting aspects to this table. First the "attacking ground forces" sortie count is not particularly meaningful, as over half the sorties are at night (usually done with U-2 and R-5 biplanes). The effectiveness of these sorties at ground attack is a fraction of what is provided by a daytime sortie.[43] Still given these gross totals, it appears that Sixteenth Air Army, counting both day and night sorties, provided only 43% of the ground support compared to what was provided by the Second and Seventeenth Air Armies.

The presence of Long Range Aviation (the LRA column) of 2,082 ground attack sorties is of interest. This was under a separate and higher command than the air armies, and as such, was completely independent of them. According to the previous table, the Long Range Aviation provided 778 sorties between 5-12 July in support of the Sixteenth Air Army.

These appear to be nighttime sorties. This leaves 1,304 sorties not otherwise accounted for from the previous table. It could well be that most or all of them were nighttime sorties.[44] There does appear to have been one or more night missions done by Long Range Aviation during this time consisting of 78 fighters and 139 bomber sorties. These unaccounted - for 1,304 sorties could include sorties from 1-4 July, they could include sorties after 12 July, they could include sorties to other parts of the Orel bulge, they could include sorties in support of the Voronezh Front defense in the south, and they may have been mostly nighttime sorties. We do not know and do not currently have access to the Long Range Aviation records. This would be useful to know for a complete picture of Soviet air operations, although if the majority of the unaccounted Long Range Aviation sorties are nighttime sorties, their impact on the fighting is limited.

Soviet Losses and Loss Claims

According to the Soviet staff report for 5 July, 106 enemy aircraft, of which 72 were fighters and only 34 were bombers, were shot down in 76 air battles. On 6 July, they declared that combat was more intense with 113 German aircraft shot down in 92 air battles. They report 90 of their own planes shot down on 6 July.[45] The German Sixth Air Fleet reported losing 13 planes on the 5th and six planes on the 6th. The Germans claimed 165 Soviet airplanes shot down on the 5th and 130 on the 6th.

The Soviet General Staff study supports these claims, along with their claim of improved control and management of their air planes starting on 7 July, with the following table:[46]

Air Battles: 5-8 July

Days	Air Battles	Destroyed Enemy Aircraft	Our* Losses	Average Losses of Aircraft Per Air Battle (Enemy)	Average Losses of Aircraft Per Air Battle (Ours)
5-6 July	168	219	188	1.3	1.12
7-8 July	125	185	87	1.5	0.70

* This is a Soviet table, so "our" or "ours" means Soviet. "Enemy" means German and German allies.

The Luftwaffe liaison officer reports for the German Sixth Air Fleet record their losses from 5 and 6 July as 13 and 6 respectively. They record their losses from 7 and 8 July as three and two respectively (and one plane lost the night of 6/7). They claim 165 kills on the 5th, 130 on the 6th, 81 on the 7th and 73 on the 8th (and claimed a kill the night of 6/7). The German claims are 163% of the Soviet losses. The Soviet claims are 1,683% of the reported German losses. From 5-8 July 1943, the Germans reported losing 24 aircraft while the Soviets report 275 lost. This is a 11.46-to-1 exchange ratio.

German losses as reported by the quartermaster reports are higher. According to historian Christer Bergstrom, there were 18 planes lost on the 5th, 11 planes lost on the 6th, six planes lost on the 7th and two planes lost on the 8th for a total of 37 planes lost. Using these figures,

THE AIR BATTLE TO SUPPORT THE OFFENSIVE NORTH OF KURSK

from 5-8 July 1943 the Germans are now counted as losing 37 aircraft compared to the Soviet reported totals of 275 lost. This is still a 7.43-to-1 exchange ratio.

Now there are problems with the loss reports of the Luftwaffe liaison officer and the quartermaster reports. The Luftwaffe liaison officer reports are probably conservative in their daily totals of losses. So actual German losses will be the same or higher than what is reported. The Luftwaffe quartermaster reports is a record of planes damaged and destroyed, regardless of cause - whether the plane is lost due to enemy action, accidents, crashes on returning, or a catastrophic mechanical failure. These are not always losses due to combat action. Non-combat losses of aircraft is not an insignificant number. If a plane conducted an emergency landing on their side of the battlefield and cannot later be recovered, then this may be a case where the plane is written off as destroyed in the quartermaster reports but not recorded as such by the Luftwaffe liaison officer report. This may have been the case for three German planes on the 7th. Furthermore, if a plane returns from a mission and is subsequently written off due to damage or mechanical issues, then it is counted as a lost plane in the quartermaster reports, even though it would not have been recorded as such in the Luftwaffe liaison officer report. It is clear that the count of planes lost from the quartermaster reports cannot be compared directly with the loss reports from the Soviets, unless those Soviet loss reports include all planes lost from all causes and severely damaged planes that may not be unrepairable. I do not think that is the case with the Soviet General Staff study loss reports, especially as it does appear to slightly under-report their losses when compared to other reports (this is discussed later).

The exchange ratios achieved are similar to what was occurring to the south of Kursk except both sides are over-reporting claims at a higher level than they were doing in the south, and the exchange ratio in the north was even more favorable for the Germans than it was in the south.

Of course, the figures for "average losses of aircraft per air battle", if based upon reported German losses as compared with inflated Soviet estimates, provides a figure for 5-6 July of 0.11 against 1.3 and for 7-8 July of 0.04 against 1.5. This would argue against any improvement over time in combat effectiveness and, in fact, demonstrates the reverse. The exchange ratio for 5-6 July was 19 reported German planes compared to 188 Soviet planes or a 9.89-to-1 exchange ratio in favor of the Germans. The exchange ratio for 7-8 July was five reported German planes compared to 87 Soviet planes or a 17.40-to-1 exchange ratio in favor of the Germans. Both of these ratios are much higher than the 5.95-to-1 exchange ratio for the fighting in the south, although the VIII Air Corps did achieve a ten-to-1 exchange ratio on the 5th (9.95-to-1). Now, these German calculations are based upon their reported losses by the Luftwaffe liaison officer records, and these losses may be lower than their actual combat losses. But the differences in losses between those reported by the air liaison officer and in the Luftwaffe quartermaster records are usually not that significantly different.

It does appear that either the 51st and 54th Fighter Wing in the north was more effective than the 52nd and 3rd Fighter Wings in the south, or that the Sixteenth Air Army was less effective than the Second and Seventeenth Air Armies. My suspicion is that all four of these German fighter wings were roughly similar in capability (even though the 51st and 54th Fighter Wing rearmed with the newer Fw-190s). I suspect the difference was in the capabilities of the Second and Seventeenth Air Armies, which has been at Stalingrad, and

179

then the Kuban and then were at Kursk. They simply had a little more hands-on combat experience. The Sixteenth Air Army was formed during the Battle of Stalingrad and participated in the counteroffensive and the subsequent counteroffensives across the front, but in the interim did not participate in the extended air campaign around the Kuban.

As this was reported from the internal Soviet General Staff study, then it appears that this gross misrepresentation of the combat situation, as exemplified by the gross over-reporting of enemy kills, flowed from the lower levels up to the highest levels of command.

The Daily Battle Narrative

Not having access to Soviet primary sources for this battle, we will limit the narrative to a simple overview of events that we can comfortably support. There are several more detailed narratives on these operations, although our confidence in them is not absolute because of the lack of either Luftwaffe or Soviet primary records to cross-check the accounts to.[47]

5 July
The offensive started on the morning of the 5th with an attack by the German XLVII and XLI Panzer Corps, with support on the right by the XXIII Corps. It initially was an attack by eight infantry divisions and one armored division (20th Panzer Division). In the morning, it appears the German air initially had a free hand with the Soviet air only arising in mass to fight later in the morning.[48] This may have been because of the Soviet operational plan, which was to commit only about a third of their attack aircraft to flying combat missions at the request of front-line units, while holding the rest of the attack air aircraft and all available bombers in reserve to be employed in massive strikes against any penetrating German units.[49] This split of resources probably also applied to their fighters.

The Soviet General Staff study states that only 520 sorties were flown by the Sixteenth Air Army before 1200 hours (Moscow time) on 5 July. They state that the plan for combat employment of the air force was put into effect at 0930 (Moscow time) and at that time intensive air combat operations began. This was probably the reported order given by Rokossovskii to Rudenko to commit 200 fighters to regain air control and 200 bombers to attack the German spearheads.[50]

As the day developed, the Soviets began delivering air strikes in the early afternoon, claiming to have used around 150 Pe-2 and Bostons.[51] The count of sorties from the Soviet General Staff study has the Sixteenth Air Army flying only 105 bomber sorties this day.

The Germans flew 2,088 sorties this day while the Soviets only flew 1,147 daytime sorties. German ground support included 647 stuka sorties, 582 bombers sorties and 168 "destroyer" sorties (Me-110s). Soviet ground support was much less with 225 assault aircraft sorties (Il-2s) and 105 bomber sorties. So, this is a difference of at least 1,397 ground support sorties to 330 sorties or more than 4-to-1.[52] Certainly, as demonstrated by the losses, most of the German sorties got through to their targets, whereas many of the Soviet sorties did not. The Soviet sorties counts were again surprisingly low. They flew 225 assault aircraft sorties this day using some 241 operational assault aircraft and a

THE AIR BATTLE TO SUPPORT THE OFFENSIVE NORTH OF KURSK

total of 269 assault aircraft. This is less than a sortie per aircraft, although we suspect the Soviet General Staff study overestimates the number of operational aircraft. They also flew only 105 bomber sorties this day, which is less than one sortie for every two operational aircraft.[53] They claim that this was because of a lack of available escort aircraft.[54]

The air superiority fight was much more even with 522 German fighter sorties compared to 817 Soviet fighter sorties. It is estimated that the Germans had 186 fighters, while the Soviets had 455 operational fighters and a total of 526 fighters. This would mean that the Germans were conducting an average of 2.81 sorties per aircraft while the Soviets were only doing 1.80 sorties per aircraft. There is reason to believe the Soviet General Staff study over-reported the number of operational planes. On subsequent days, the German count of fighter sorties was much less, ranging from 255 to 317.

Still, the exchange ratio was lopsided with the Germans reporting 13 planes lost this day (or 18 total losses according to the Luftwaffe quartermaster reports)[55] while the Soviets are reported to have lost 100 on 5 July.[56] This is a 7.7-to-1 exchange ratio using the air liaison figure.[57] This is similar to the exchange ratio for the first day in the south, which was 10-to-1. On the other hand, using the total loss figure of 18 from the Luftwaffe quartermaster files, produces a 5.6-to-1 exchange ratio in favor of the Germans.[58]

Now there is not as much confusion over the Soviet losses. It is reported that the Sixteenth Air Army conducted 76 air engagements for this day.[59] It is reported that they lost either 98 planes or 100 planes: 83 fighters, 16 Il-2s and one Boston.[60] The Germans claimed 165 planes this day, 163 in air battles. According to one source this figure was later reduced to 120.[61] As a result of the air fighting, the Austrian born Hubert Strassl of III/JG 51 claimed 15 victories this day.[62]

By the end of the day, the two attacking German panzer corps had advanced around eight to ten kilometers. They had effectively cleared the first of three Soviet defensive belts. The Germans had only committed two panzer divisions to the offense (the 20th Panzer Division and elements of the 18th Panzer Division). Moving up late in the day to join the offensive were the 2nd and 9th Panzer Divisions.

Stalin's Evening Call

That evening, Joseph Stalin called Rokossovskii, commander of the Central Front, to ask if he had managed to establish air superiority. The commander of the Sixteenth Air Army, General Sergei Rudenko was with Rokossovskii during that call. Rokossovskii provided an evasive response so Stalin asked "Will Rudenko be able to cope with the task?" Rokossovskii then promised to establish air superiority as early as the following day.[63]

The story reported by Rudenko is: "When darkness fell, I reported the results of the day to the Front commander. I specified how many enemy aircraft had been shot down and emphasized that the fight had been severe. Suddenly a phone call was made. I.V. Stalin called K. K. Rokossovskiy. They used to hold telephone conversations each day, but previously I had not been present. This time, however, I heard everything."

"Rokossovskiy began by reporting the results of the day, but he was interrupted by Stalin; '*Have we gained control of the air or not?*'

"This proved to be his main interest! Rokossovskiy replied *"Comrade Stalin, it is impossible to tell. There have been very hard combats in the air and both sides have suffered heavy losses."* But Stalin just retorted: *'Tell me precisely, have we won in the air not? Yes or no?'* Rokossovskiy looked at me, and after a short pause he answered: *"I will consult him."* [...]

"A short while later, Zhukov arrived and turned to me and said: *"Stalin just phoned and his first question was regarding the domination of the air. What do you think?"*

"I explained and showed that our plan for the use of fighters was correct. But since the enemy possessed such large forces, it was impossible to destroy them all at once. The operations of the enemy aviation during the battle had immediately been met by counteraction from our side. Powerful groups of fighters had risen to the air. The commanders had led the operations with great vigour and in due time increased the forces. It has been necessary to employ bombers and *Shturmoviks* to attack strong enemy forces."[64]

After this day's lop-sided exchange, it is clear that the Soviet air force was not going to achieve air superiority. It is harder to determine if Rudenko and Rokossovskii thought they could.

6 July

The day began overcast and there were scattered showers throughout the day. Meanwhile, the Soviets attempted to conduct a major counterattack in the morning with some of their rifle divisions and parts of the Second Tank Army. The Central Front had four tank corps. They planned a counterattack in the morning with the XIX, XVI, and III Tank Corps. This did not come together as a coordinated attack, with only XVI Tank Corps attacking in the morning. The other tank corps were still moving up with the XIX Tank Corps not becoming seriously engaged until later in the day and the III Tank Corps only engaging on the following day. The morning attack was initiated by a barrage by the Soviet IV Artillery Corps at 0450 and followed by Soviet multiple air attacks throughout the morning.

The Soviet counterattacks petered out as the morning went on and at around noon, the Germans went back on the offensive, pushing forward with six infantry divisions and now four armored divisions. The XLVII Panzer Corps moved forward their 2nd and 9th Panzer Divisions to join the fight. The Ninth Army now had four panzer divisions engaged this day (20th, 2nd, 9th and 18th). This was not as hard-hitting an attack as that to the south of Kursk, where Army Group South deployed nine panzer and panzer grenadier divisions to initiate their offensive on the 5th. The offensive developed slowly on the 6th as the two panzer corps continued pushing through the layers of Soviet defenses.

Today was a more equal fight in the air with the Germans putting up 1,023 daytime sorties while the Soviet air force put up 1,126 daytime sorties, close to the same count as the previous day. The Germans still had the edge in the ground campaign with 289 stuka stories, 164 bomber sorties and 93 "destroyer" sorties. The Soviet air support was more active with another 225 assault aircraft sorties and 122 bomber sorties. This is a difference in ground support of only about 1.6-to-1 based upon sortie counts.

THE AIR BATTLE TO SUPPORT THE OFFENSIVE NORTH OF KURSK

According the Rudenko's post-war account, he concentrated his air attacks so as to make "one devastating strike." To explain this in his own words: "I concluded that it would be more expedient to deal one devasting strike against a large force of enemy troops, so for this end I decided to dispatch our aircraft in massive strength. The idea also was that this massing of our aircraft would suppress the enemy's air defence and thus reduce our own losses. Moreover, we would not only cause great material damage on the enemy, but also render a major moral impact on the ground troops."[65]

Not sure how this actually matches up with what occurred on the battlefield. Seriously doubt if he meant a single strike. Suspect he meant several large strikes instead of a larger number of smaller strikes. Other discussions indicate the waves of escorted bombers attacked German positions throughout the morning.[66] These attacks appear to have focused on the German Second Panzer Division that was part of the XLVII Panzer Corps attack and were done in support of the counterattack that morning by the XVII Guards Rifle Corps and XVI Tank Corps. This developed into a major air battle as the German fighters had scrambled in response. This apparently was due to German interception of Soviet messages and German fighters being sortied to intercept. It does not appear that the German air force conducted offensive operations until around noon, when they started their offensive. They may have also been trying to conserve and rest their forces this day, with the overall sortie count being half of what it was the previous day.

Still, even with Soviet air support, the Soviet morning counter-attack ground to a halt and at one point some of their advancing elements were even bombed by their own bombers.[67] As the day developed the Germans went back over to the offensive, and did so with considerable Stuka support. A late afternoon counter-attack by the Soviet XIX Tank Corps was partly countered by German air.[68]

The air superiority fight also did not go in favor of the Soviet air force even though they put up a healthy 779 fighter sorties compared to the 317 fighter sorties by the Germans. The Germans reported six planes lost this day (or 11 lost according to the Luftwaffe quartermaster reports),[69] while the Soviets lost around 91 planes this day for a 15-to-1 exchange ratio, or an 8-to-1 exchange ratio using the losses derived from the Luftwaffe quartermaster figures. The Soviets reported 92 air engagements for this day, which was more than the previous day.[70] German ace, Hubert Strassl is credited with four more for this day.[71]

The Fifteenth Air Army, on the north side of Orel bulge, also conducted some fighter operations to distract the Germans and this drew a response from the Sixth Air Fleet, reportedly the 51st Fighter Wing.[72]

By the end of the day, the two attacking German panzer corps had advanced another four or so kilometers. The Germans decided to commit the 4th Panzer Division to the attack, along with a battle group from the 12th Panzer Division.

The Soviet activity at night grew considerably. The night of 5 July they put up 102 nighttime sorties along with 17 sorties from Long Range Aviation. These are assumed to also be nighttime sorties. This night they put up 469 nighttime sorties along with 269 sorties from Long Range Aviation.[73] The actual effectiveness of these nighttime sorties had to be considerably less than the effectiveness of daytime sorties, as discussed earlier.

At this point, with Soviet losses of a least 191 planes over the first two days of battle, the majority of them being fighters, Rudenko requested that the 234th Fighter Division from the Fifteenth Air Army be transferred to the Central Front. As these were the forces slated from the upcoming Soviet counteroffensive, this request had to go from Zhukov up to Stalin. Also during the evening, the commander of the Soviet air force, Major General Aleksandr A. Novikov issued his directive (see Chapter Five).

As Soviet losses were less on the 7th and 8th than they were on the 5th and 6th, some sources credit this directive or some of Rudenko's operational changes as having a positive effect. In the south, it was clear that the intensity and frequency of engagements declined, resulting in lower losses for both sides. In the north, we suspect the same occurred. A less aggressive posture leads to less combats which leads to lower losses. In the south, the VIII Corps commander, Hans Seidemann, commented about the lower level of aggression by the Soviet pilots after the first couple of days of battle, and it is natural to expect that the same would have occurred here.

WEATHER REPORTS

The XLI Panzer Corps weather reports are summarized below. These reports refer to the area that included Ponyiri.[74]

5 July: Almost cloudless until late morning, then overcast and some rain. Temperature in morning of 15° Celsius [59° Fahrenheit], reaching 21° Celsius by noon [70° Fahrenheit].

6 July: Sunny and fine with intermittent showers. Temperature at 0700 hours was 15° Celsius, reaching 20° Celsius at noon.

7 July: Sunny, very dry and dusty with scattered clouds. Temperatures ranged from 13° Celsius in the morning [55° Fahrenheit] to 25° Celsius at noon [77° Fahrenheit].

8 July: Sunny with scattered clouds. Temperatures ranged from 20° Celsius in the morning to 32° Celsius in the afternoon [90° Fahrenheit].

9 July: Cloudy with scattered showers. Temperatures ranges from 20 to 25° Celsius.

10 July: Cloudy with occasional showers. Roads and paths, however, remained passable.

11 July: Cloud, windy with isolated showers that made the roads greasy and sometimes difficult to traverse.

THE AIR BATTLE TO SUPPORT THE OFFENSIVE NORTH OF KURSK

7th of July

The weather was better today, which may partly explain the increased German air presence over the battlefield. The Germans were still advancing on the 7th, but the advance only continued forward slowly. The advance of the XLI Panzer Corps stalled at the village of Ponyiri, with the Germans occupying half of the village. This turned into an extended multi-day fight over the village and train station. To the west of the XLI Panzer Corps, the XLVII Panzer Corps did continue to push forward ever so slowly, advancing south towards Olkhovatka.

The Germans put up 1,687 sorties this day, the second most active day of the offensive. The Germans were able to put up 2,088 sorties on the 5th with 730 aircraft and 1,687 sorties this day, probably with less operational aircraft. It does appear that they flew multiple sorties for the Stukas and bombers on 5 and 7 July, but not on the 6th.

The Soviet air force continued its effort with 1,185 daytime sorties on the 7th. It is a strange dynamic where the Germans put up over twice as many sorties as the Soviet air force did on the first day of battle, then on the second day of battle the German level of effort declined to that of the Soviets, and now the German effort once again increased to give them an edge. The Soviet effort had been relatively steady over these three days, with 1,034 to 1,151 aircraft on hand, they rather consistently put up 1,147, 1,126 and 1,185 sorties over those three days.

There is no clear explanation for this odd shift back and forth. It appears that the Germans put up their planes for multiple sorties on the 5th and then relaxed and rested the crews some on the 6th. They were not flying many early morning missions on the 6th when the Soviet air force started their waves of attack that morning. The German Air Force then scrambled to contest with the Soviet air forces. The weather was also not great on the 6th. On the 7th, the Sixth Air Fleet appears to have increased their level of effort in line with the renewed German offensive on the ground.

Considering that the Soviets had the option of flying multiple sorties in a day, it is odd that their sortie counts are relatively low over these three days. In the south, on the first day, the Second Air Army flew 1,296 daytime sorties with a plane count of 881 planes.[75] The lower sortie count might have been because the Sixteenth Air Army was being more cautious in their selection of missions, and only doing missions that could be properly escorted. Still their loss and exchange ratios with the Germans were similar to the Second Air Army in the south, although their losses in assault planes and bombers were considerably less. On 5 July, the Second Air Army lost 91 planes with another 23 damaged and forced to land on their side of the lines. This is between 10.3% and 12.9% losses for one day. The exchange ratio for the Second and Seventeenth Air Army against the Germans was almost ten-to-one against them, although this was heavily influenced by the 66 Il-2s lost by the Seventeenth Air Army on this day. The Sixteenth Air Army lost 100 planes this day, or between 9.7% and 11.5% losses for one day. Their exchange ratio was better, being 7.7-to-one against them using the Luftwaffe air liaison figures.

There was one significant difference between the fighting in the north and the fighting in the south. In the north, over three-quarters of the Soviet planes lost were fighters, while in the south, the losses were split between the fighters and the assault planes and bombers. For example, on the first day in the north, 83 of their 100 losses were fighters. In the south on the first day 61 of their 189 losses were fighters or 32% of their losses. Now, some of these high losses among assault aircraft were driven by the Seventeenth Air Army operations, which was further from their targets and clearly sent out a number of unescorted Il-2 flights. So, on the first day the Seventeenth Air Army lost 9 fighters and 66 assault planes, while the Second Air Army lost 52 fighters, 19 bombers and 43 assault aircraft. But it is clear from the mix of plane types lost between the Sixteenth Air Army (83% were fighters), the Second Air Army (46% were fighters) and the Seventeenth Air Army (12% were fighters), that the operations in the north were conducted differently, resulting in higher fighters losses (both as a percentage and in absolute numbers) and considerably lower losses among assault planes and bombers. The forces in the south may have provided more air support from the ground forces during the first couple of days of the battle, but it was at considerable cost.

In the north, the two sides' air forces were engaged around 0500 (Berlin time) on the 7th. The Germans still had the advantage in the ground campaign with 582 stuka sorties, 454 bomber sorties and 123 "destroyer" sorties during the day. The Soviet air support remained active with 219 assault aircraft sorties and 235 bomber sorties. The number of Soviet bomber sorties flown this day was more than twice what it was on the previous days. This included Pe-2s for the III Bomber Corps, which had not been used yet against this offensive. Even with the increased Soviet presence, the increase in the number of ground attack sorties by the Germans was greater than the previous day. The end result was the Germans had more than twice the air support than the defending Soviet forces. The difference in ground support is 2.6-to-1 based upon sortie counts.

The accounts of this day seem to indicate a heavily contested air space, but the losses on both sides tend to tell another story. The air superiority fight had clearly wound down. The Soviet lost 30 or 43 planes this day,[76] compared to 91 the day before, while the German losses were reported to have been as low as three planes, with the Luftwaffe quartermaster indicating eight planes lost. According to one source, six Fw-190s were shot down, with three of them managing to return to their own territory for emergency landings.[77] This comes out to between as high as a 14-to-1 exchange ratio or as low as a 5-to-1 exchange ratio, depending on what figures you choose to use. Among the German losses for this day was Knight Cross winner Captain K. A. Pape of the III Group of the 1st Stuka Wing. He was shot down in a Ju-87 D-3 at Krasavka, 20 kilometers west of Ponyiri.[78]

The German ace Hubert Strassl claimed six kills this day.[79] Still, on this day, the German Air Force in general was claiming twice as many kills as they actually made. They claimed 81 kills this day, 74 by fighters and 7 by flak. In general, unlike the VIII Air Corps claims, the Sixth Air Fleet rather consistently overclaimed the number of kills each day.

The Soviet General Staff study reports losing 87 planes for 7/8 July. If they lost 43 planes on the 7th, then their losses for the 8th would be 44. For the Soviets, it is reported that they lost 49 planes on the 8th based upon Sixteenth Air Army records. They also report 11 planes that made emergency landing due to battle damage.[80] The total provided for these two days in the Soviet General Staff study report may be low.

The Germans continued to advance slowly this day, gaining only one or two kilometers, with a three-kilometer advance in the 9th Panzer Division area.

THE AIR BATTLE TO SUPPORT THE OFFENSIVE NORTH OF KURSK

The Soviet night activity continued at a high level, with 422 nighttime sorties and 210 sorties from Long Range Aviation. In contrast the Germans had put up 15, 92 and 134 sorties over the three nights since the 5th. This was the last night of any significant German night activity, with the Germans limited to 6 to 22 sorties on four of the next five nights.

8 July

On this day the Germans renewed the offensive with 4th Panzer Division added to the battle. There were now five panzer divisions committed to this offensive. The Soviets again conducted a series of counter-attacks on the ground that tangled up, engaged and stymied the German efforts for this day.

The Germans again responded, similar to they did on the 6th, to Soviet deployments and again sent up fighters to intercept the missions. This was primarily done in both cases by their radio intercept work, where they intercepted and translated Soviet messages and then ordered up intercepting flights accordingly.

In the air, both sides' level of activity declined. This may have been influenced by worsening weather, with rain showers in the afternoon. The Germans put up 1,173 sorties this day, including 378 stuka, 274 bomber, 73 "destroyer" and 291 fighter sorties. The Soviets put up 913 sorties this day, 130 assault aircraft, 170 bomber and 613 fighter sorties. There may have also been another 157 sorties from the Fifteenth Air Army supporting these defensive operations.[81] This was a 2.4-to-1 ratio of ground support sorties. The German air support was prioritized to support the XLVII Panzer Corps attacks in the morning.

In part this lower activity was due to poor weather, as there was rain and heavy cloud cover, especially in the afternoon, where dark clouds covered the sky. Still, air operations continued until late in the afternoon, when Hubert Strassl claimed three more kills at 1700 (Berlin time). This ran his total claims to five for the day and 30 kills for the entire battle. He was then shot down to the south of Ponyiri, flying an Fw-190 A-4 with the number "Black 4."[82] His parachute failed to open in time when he bailed out. He was awarded the Knight's Cross posthumously.

The Germans claimed they only lost two planes this day, while the Luftwaffe quartermaster report records only nine damaged (two were not because of enemy operations) and two shot down.[83] This is a whole lot less than the Sixteenth Air Army's claim of 88 shot down this day. The Sixteenth Air Army reported 49 of their own planes shot down and another 11 having to make emergency landings due to battle damage.[84] This is a 25-to-1 exchange ratio for planes lost, not counting those that made emergency landings. The German claims were also higher than Soviet losses with 67 claimed in aerial combat and six by flak.

The German advance for this day was a kilometer or less across the front. By the end of the day the 4th Panzer Division had taken parts of Teploye on the right flank of the advance and held half of Ponyiri on the German left flank.

Soviet night activity remained high with 342 night sorties and 169 Long Range Aviation sorties.

9 July

With the Soviet attacks of the previous day defeated, the Germans returned to the offensive, but made little progress. The XLVII Panzer Corps intended to launch a coordinated attack with the 2nd, 4th and 20th Panzer Divisions and supported by Stukas, but this attack never materialized. Instead they ended up advancing only hundreds of meters in some areas of the battlefield, but in most areas they were stymied.

The Soviets opened the day with a poorly escorted series of large bomber raids. This was 110 Pe-2s from the III Bomber Corps and 62 Il-2s from the 299th Assault Division. The raid was concentrated against the XLVII Panzer Corps rear area at Saborovka.

Some of the escorts were provided by the newly arriving 234th Fighter Division. This was an inexperienced unit and probably not adequately trained. The weather this day was poor, as a low-pressure front had arrived the previous day that brought rain, fog and low cloud cover. The inexperienced 234th Fighter Division suffered for operating in this poor weather, with ten fighters having to make emergency landings after running out of fuel, while two went missing. The fighters failed to find the Il-2s they were supposed to escort nor reported any encounters with German aircraft. The unescorted Il-2s were found by the German fighters, which claimed to have shot down six of them. Another group of a dozen escorts IL-2s, that were escorted by six Yakovlevs, were later intercepted by the 51st Fighter Wing, which claimed five Il-2s and one Yak.

The Pe-2s of the 241st Bomber Division was able to strike and return home with the loss of only one plane. The escorted Pe-2s of the 301st Bomber Division were intercepted by the 51st Fighter Wing, and lost maybe six Pe-2s (German claims) and its escorting 192nd Fighter Regiment lost two La-5s (again German claims).[85] We do not have reports of Soviet losses this day from their side.

The air battle continued throughout the day, while on the ground the XLVII Panzer Corps made a limited offensive against the Soviet positions. The Soviets had reduced air support after this initial morning strike. They reported 175 bomber and 152 assault aircraft sorties for the day. The morning strike consisted of 110 of those bomber sorties and 62 of the assault aircraft sorties, leaving 155 ground attack sorties to support the defense for the rest of the day. The Germans ended the day with their own large deep strike sending almost a 100 He-111s from the 4th and 53rd Bomber Wings. This would leave the Germans with around 271 ground attack sorties for the rest of the day. The effectiveness of these large bomber raids is hard to evaluate. As they tended to strike in the rear of units, they did not have an immediate effect on the ground battle.

The Germans put up only 877 sorties this day, including 181 stuka, 138 bomber, 52 "destroyer" and 255 fighter sorties. The Soviets put up 755 sorties this day, 152 assault aircraft, 175 bomber and 448 fighter sorties. This was around a 1.1-to-1 ratio of ground support sorties. We do not have reports of Soviet air losses for this day, the Germans air losses are reported to be five, and they claimed 85 kills this day, which is probably an overestimate.[86] The Soviets claimed 52 victories for this day, which is clearly an overclaim. The German quartermaster reports record 8 aircraft destroyed and two severely damaged.[87]

THE AIR BATTLE TO SUPPORT THE OFFENSIVE NORTH OF KURSK

Night activity declined, with the Soviets putting up 181 nighttime sorties and only 36 sorties from Long Range Aviation. It does appear with Long Range Aviation not under direct command of the Central Front, that their priorities and targets had shifted. Still, they conducted attacks directly on German airfields around Orel at a cost of four Il-4s, their two-engine heavy bombers.[88] It is not known whether this raid was part of the 36 night sorties credited to the front by Soviet General Staff study, but it may not have been.

The Reinforcements

On around the 9th and 10th, both sides received reinforcements. In the case of the Sixteenth Air Army, they requested the 234th Fighter Division from the Fifteenth Air Army around the 6th but it was not committed to action in force until the 9th. Being an unexperienced and not fully trained unit, its first day of battle was not successful. It may not have been that successful of an addition, perhaps adding only 67 combat ready fighters to the fray. There were some other units added to the Sixteenth Air Army, leading them to receive 200 aircraft total, at least 107 of them were fighters.[89]

The Germans also shifted up some planes from the south. How many and who is not known. The amount shifted up north around the 9th does not appear to have been that significant (see Chapter Five: The First Air Transfers (7-9 July 1943)).

The Soviet's air forces had been attritted. The following table of strengths of the Sixteenth Air Army on 10 July compared to 5 July drives that point home.[90]

Change in Strength of Sixteenth Air Army between 5 and 10 July 1943

	As of 5 July 1943		As of 10 July 1943	
Aircraft type	Aircraft Total	Serviceable	Aircraft Total	Serviceable
Fighters	526	455	440	311
Attack aircraft	269	241	168	119
Day bombers	274	260	251	197
Night bombers	76	74	75	71
Reconnaissance planes	6	4	11	8
Total	1,151	1,034	945	706

The Sixteenth Air Army was reinforced with 200 aircraft, including 107 fighters. It is stated that 67 of the fighters were in combat-ready condition, meaning their serviceability was 62.6%, assuming that the definitions of "combat-ready" and "serviceable" are the same. Irreplaceable losses from 5 – 9 July were 330-340 aircraft according to one source. Our estimated count is 328 (see below). The Sixth Air Fleet scrapped about 80 to 90 aircraft at that time with a significant number damaged and out of action. Fighters accounted for half of those scrapped. Our count of German losses between 5 – 9 July was 30 to 47 (see below). The 51st Fighter Wing had lost 37 Fw-190s and were reinforced by its II Group, which came down from the Leningrad area. On the morning of 10 July, the strength of the German air force was estimated by one source to be around 650 aircraft (excluding transports, liaison planes and other auxiliary aircraft).[91]

Now the serviceability rates seemed high for the reports for 5 July. Let us look at the subject now.

Aircraft type	As of 5 July 1943 Serviceability Percent	As of 10 July 1943 Serviceability Percent
Fighters	86.5%	70.7%
Attack aircraft	89.6%	70.8%
Day bombers	94.9%	78.5%
Night bombers	97.4%	94.7%
Reconnaissance planes	66.7%	72.7%
Total	89.8%	74.0%

Even a 74% serviceability seems high, considering the number of planes that were damaged and had to be repaired. It makes you wonder what was considered to be serviceable.

10 July

At 0700 in the morning, the XLVII Panzer finally got it's three panzer division attack going assisted by ground support aircraft. This attack allowed the 4th Panzer Division to take all of Teploye by the end of the day (by 1800), but required the commitment of two panzer divisions for even this small gain. They also brought up the 10th Panzer Grenadier Division to relieve German infantry units. Even though this offensive was not breaking through Soviet positions, they needed to maintain pressure as Army Group South was having some success with its offensive south of Kursk. Otherwise, their advances this day were limited.

The Sixteenth Air Army again conducted a major concentrated air strike in the area of Kashara, a village about 2 miles (or over 3 kilometers) north of Olkhovatka. This time it was 106 Pe-2s from III Bomber Corps, 65 Bostons from the 221st Bomber Division and 37 Il-2s from the 2nd Guards Assault Division. The VI Fighter Corps provided fighter escort with everything they had ready for action. German air resistance was limited, perhaps because they were caught off guard by this raid.[92]

The Germans still put up a healthy 1,136 sorties this day, including 375 stuka, 220 bomber, 66 "destroyer" and 266 fighter sorties. The Soviets put up only 671 sorties this day, 79 assault aircraft, 173 bomber and 419 fighter sorties. This was a 2.6-to-1 ratio of ground support sorties. We do not have reports of Soviet air losses for this day, the German air losses are reported to be seven,[93] while they claim 75 kills for this day, also suspected of being an overestimate.

The German fighter pilots submitted claims for 43 Soviet fighters. One German ace, Lt. Gunther Scheel of 2/54 JG, claimed five kills this day. The 234th Fighter Regiment lost 11 planes this day.[94]

THE AIR BATTLE TO SUPPORT THE OFFENSIVE NORTH OF KURSK

Night activity was 250 nighttime bombing sorties and 77 from Long Range Aviation. Based upon the reports from the Soviet General Staff study, these were the last sorties from Long Range Aviation for the rest of the defensive phase of the battle. German night activity increased to 51 sorties compared to 22 or 21 on the previous or subsequent days.

Command Issues

Needless to say with the heavy losses taken over the last five days, some of the Soviet air units had become more cautious. There were reports that fighters were conducting their patrols ten kilometers behind the front line, leaving the German aircraft with control of the skies over the front.[95] The commander of the Sixteenth Air Army ended up threatening punishment for any fighter pilot who showed "cowardice," including being sent to penal battalions or even executed. He also replaced the VI Fighter Corps commander, Major General Andrei Yumashev (1902-1988) with experienced Major General Yevgenii Yerlyikin (1910-1969).

Andrei Yumashev was the co-pilot of the second record-breaking non-stop flight over the north pole from Moscow in 1937. This one went all the way to San Jacinto, CA setting a new world distance record for a flight. They flew 6,700 miles in 62 hours and 12 minutes in a single-engine ANT-25 and landed in California on 14 July 1937. Yevgenni Yerlykin was leading the VII Fighter Corps in the Leningrad area and had been a fighter pilot in the Spanish Civil War with two claimed kills and three shared claims.

Many of the Soviet air units were given a break the following day, leading to an usually low number of sorties.

11 July

The German advance on Olkhovatka by the XLVII Panzer Corps remained stalled while the XLI Panzer Corps held around Ponyiri (the XLI Panzer Corps). There were no major offensive actions by either side on this day.

The level of air activity was also lower for both sides, and considerably lower for the Soviets. The Germans put up only 933 sorties this day, 249 stuka, 226 bomber, 20 "destroyer" and 283 fighter sorties. The Soviets put up only 301 sorties this day, 80 assault aircraft, three bomber and 218 fighter sorties. This was almost a 6-to-1 ratio of ground support sorties, with Soviet ground support being particularly light this day. We do not have reports of Soviet air losses for this day, the German air losses are reported to be only 2, or 3 according to the quartermaster reports, with their claims reduced down to 42.[96] The main loss to the German air this day was the commander of IV Group, 51st Fighter Wing, Major Rudolf Resch, was shot down. He had 94 claimed kills to his name (one from the Spanish Civil War). According to one source, he was probably shot down by Senior sergeant Kirov of the 234th Fighter Division over Maloarkhangelsk.[97] Another source has him flying a Fw-190 A-5 and shot down to the north of Yudinka, four kilometers southwest of Maloarckhangelsk.[98]

Soviet night activity was 176 nighttime sorties and there was no support from Long Range Aviation.

12 July
On this day little happened in this corner of the Battle of Kursk. The Germans did not advance and had little air support. They flew 1,111 sorties this day, but the Soviet Sixteenth Air Army only reports seeing 72 enemy sorties this day. There is no strong reason to doubt this report, so most likely the German Air Force put up less than a hundred sorties in this area. This may have also been partially the case the previous day, when the Germans put up 933 sorties, but the Soviets only observed 680.

The Soviet Sixteenth Air Army only put up 97 daytime sorties this day (and 236 nighttime sorties). This includes 71 assault aircraft, one bomber and 25 fighter sorties. Clearly there was very little air action over the battlefield on this day.

This was the end of the German offensive in the north. Their penetration of Soviet positions was around 15 kilometers, taking the village of Teploye in the west. They had not taken Olkhovatka and held only half of Ponyiri in the east. It was 77 kilometers to Kursk from their start line, and they had advanced at best 15 kilometers. They had advanced only about a fifth of the way to Kursk. They halted operations with permission from Hitler and waited to see how the other battles developed. In the south, the Germans were still attacking, including around Prokhorovka. Meanwhile new fronts opened that fully drew the attention of the Sixth Air Fleet.

Losses in the Air Battle North of Kursk

For 5 July we have two reports for German losses, the air liaison officer report of 13 planes lost and the Luftwaffe quartermaster reports showing that 18 planes were scrapped that day. For the Soviets we also have two reports of losses, the report of 98 or 100 planes lost taken from primary source records (the Sixteenth Air Army?) and a report of 188 planes lost on the 5th and 6th taken from Soviet General Staff study. The comparison of various reports indicates that the total for those two days was at least 191. The reports of losses for the 6th through the 8th are reported from the same sources.

For 9-11 July we have a problem in that we have no clear reporting of losses for the Soviets. There is a report for the campaign of 391 total losses with 48 damaged aircraft written off as destroyed.[99] With losses from 5-8 July calculated as 283, this means that there were at least 108 aircraft lost from 9 through 11 July.

The Germans lost from 5 to 11 July 39 aircraft according to the liaison officer count and 57 destroyed and 34 receiving severe or medium damage according to the quartermaster reports.[100] During that same period, they recorded 26 aircraft destroyed or damaged in accidents. One source estimates German losses in the north for 5-11 July 1943 as between 110-120 irreplaceable and 70-80 repairable.[101] There does not appear to be any basis for this estimate and it appears to be incorrect. The Sixteenth Air Army claimed 517 German aircraft shot down,[102] which appears to be an overestimate by a factor of 10. Real German combat losses were somewhere between 39 and 57.

According to one source, irreplaceable losses from 5-9 July were 330-340 aircraft. Our estimated count is 328 (see below). Another source states that the Sixteenth Air Army

THE AIR BATTLE TO SUPPORT THE OFFENSIVE NORTH OF KURSK

between the 5th through the 12th lost 391 aircraft in combat.[103] This was 262 fighters, 90 assault planes (Il-2s) and 39 bombers. They also report 48 damaged written off as destroyed for total losses of 439 aircraft.[104]

This is summarized in the following table:

	German losses		Soviet Losses	
Date	Air liaison Officer	Quartermaster Files	Reports	Estimated[105]
5 July	13	18	100	
6 July	7	11	91	
7 July	3	8	43	
8 July	2	2	49 + 11[106]	
9 July	5	8	–	45[107]
10 July	7	7	–	40
11 July	2	3	–	23
Total	39	57	391 or 439	

Therefore, the loss exchange ratio of planes reported lost at that time is 39 compared to 391 to 1-to-10. The lost exchange ratio of destroyed planes is 57 to 439 or 1-to-7.7. The exchange ratio in the first two days of the battle (based upon liaison officer reports) is 20 to 191 or 1-to-9.6. The exchange ratio for the next five days of battle is 19 to 200 or 1-to-10.5. This argues against any Soviet claims of improvement in operations over times. The exchange rate is worse than what we see in the south with the Second and Seventeenth Air Armies after the first day of the battle. The exchange ratio in the south for the first day was around 1-to-10 (1-to-9.95). The exchange ratio for the first five days in the south was around 1-to-9. It then declined to around 1-to-3.5. The exchange ratio for the entire fight in the south from 4 to 18 July 1943 was 1-to-5.95. It is hard to tell which Soviet air army was performing better, but it does appear that the Second Air Army did if you ignore their disastrous first day of combat which included their failed strike at the German airfields by the Second and Seventeenth Air Armies.

A Comparative Analysis Between the Air Fight in the North and the Air Fight in the South

As the fight in the north effectively ended after the 11th and moved into a new stage, let's take this moment to compare the differences between the two operations north of Kursk and south of Kursk. In the north it was the German Sixth Air Fleet versus the Sixteenth Air Army, which received some reinforcements during the battle from the Fifteenth Air Army. In the south it was the German VIII Air Corps versus the Second Air Army and parts of the Seventeenth Air Army, with reinforcements from the Fifth Air Army.

First is a comparison from 5 to 11 July 1943 between the German Sixth Air Fleet to the north of Kursk and the VIII Air Corps to the south of Kursk.

Comparison of Sixth Air Fleet to the VIII Air Corps

	Sixth Air Fleet	VIII Air Corps	Ratio
Estimated number of planes	730	1,093+	0.67
Total daytime sorties 5-11 July	8,917	10,930	0.82
Total nighttime sorties 5-11 July	341	228+	1.50
Average number of sorties per plane (over 7 days)	12.68	10.00	1.27
Highest number of daytime sorties in a day	2,088	2,387	0.87
Highest number of nighttime sorties in a day	134	64	2.09
Average number of daytime sorties per plane (5 July)	2.86	2.18	1.31
Total fighter sorties*	2,241	1,584	
Percent fighter sorties	25%	15%	
Total stuka sorties*	2,701	4,457	
Percent stuka sorties	30%	43%	
Total bombing sorties*	2,058	2,431	
Percent bombing sorties	23%	24%	
Total ground attack sorties*	0	1,301	
Percent ground attack sorties	0	13%	
Total other sorties*	1,917	475	
Percent other sorties	21%	5%	
Total ground attack type sorties**	5,354	8,189	0.65
Percent ground attack type sorties	60%	80%	
Total planes lost, daytime (5-11 July)	39	69	0.57
Percent planes lost	5.34%	6.31%	
Percent per planes lost per sortie, daytime (5 – 11 July)	0.44%	0.63%	
Total fighters lost (5-11 July)	11 ***	27****	0.41
Percent losses that were fighters	28%	39%	
Total planes claimed in aerial combat	586	508	1.15
Planes claimed per fighter sortie	0.26	0.32	

* there is no detailed breakdown of sorties for 10 July for the VIII Air Corps. The percentages are calculated with the 682 sorties of 10 July not counted.
** Stuka, bombing, "destroyer" and ground attack missions. Does not include sorties counts of 10 July for the VIII Air Corps.
*** 10 Fw-190s and 1 Me-109.
**** Me-109s only.

Then there were three Soviet air armies engaged between 5 to 11 July in the Battle of Kursk. This was the Sixteenth Air Army in the north, and the Second and Seventeenth Air Armies in the south. The Seventeenth Air Army was only partly engaged, while the Fifth Air Army was attached to the Steppe Military District and only became engaged until well after the 11th.

Stuka in flight, by Buschel, 19 July 1943.

Fighter on the ground, by Laux, 14 July 1943.

Yak-9 at war memorial, northwest of Yakovlevo, Belgorod-Oboyan road. (Photo by Christopher A. Lawrence, 1995)

La-7, Kursk Battle Museum, Belgorod. There were no La-7s at Kursk, which was a development and refinement of the La-5. (Photo by Christopher A. Lawrence, 1995)

Above: The Donets River, south of Belgorod, showing Maslova Pristan and at the top, Krutoi Log, 2 June 1943. Toward the top is the area of the Solomino crossing used by the 7th Panzer Division.

Right: Solomino, the Southern Donets over 70 years ago. (Photo and markings courtesy of Rainer Prill)

Belgorod, 3 July 1943.

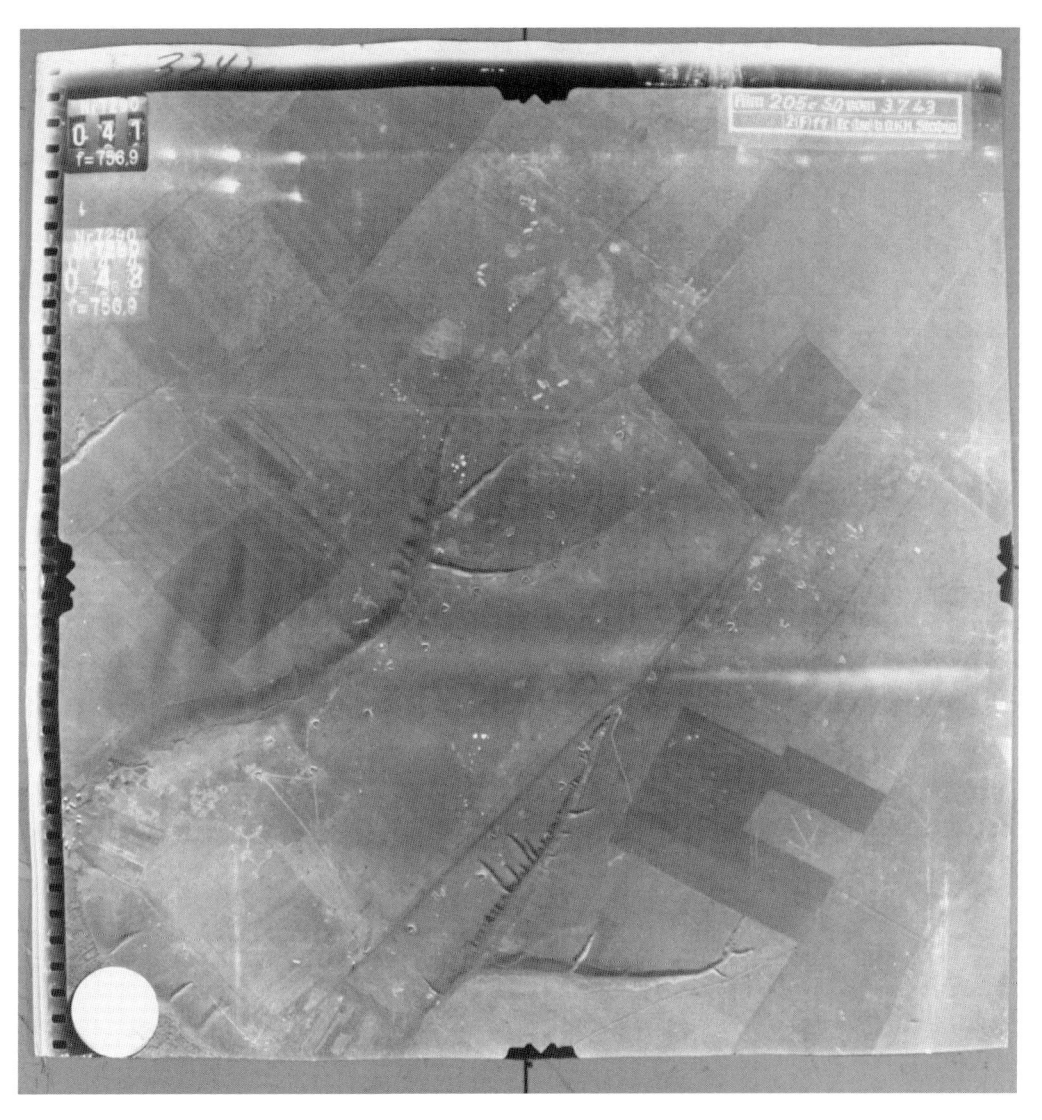

Close-up photo of a Soviet airfield east of Kochetovka, 3 July 1943. Note the revetments and the 10 airplanes on the runway.

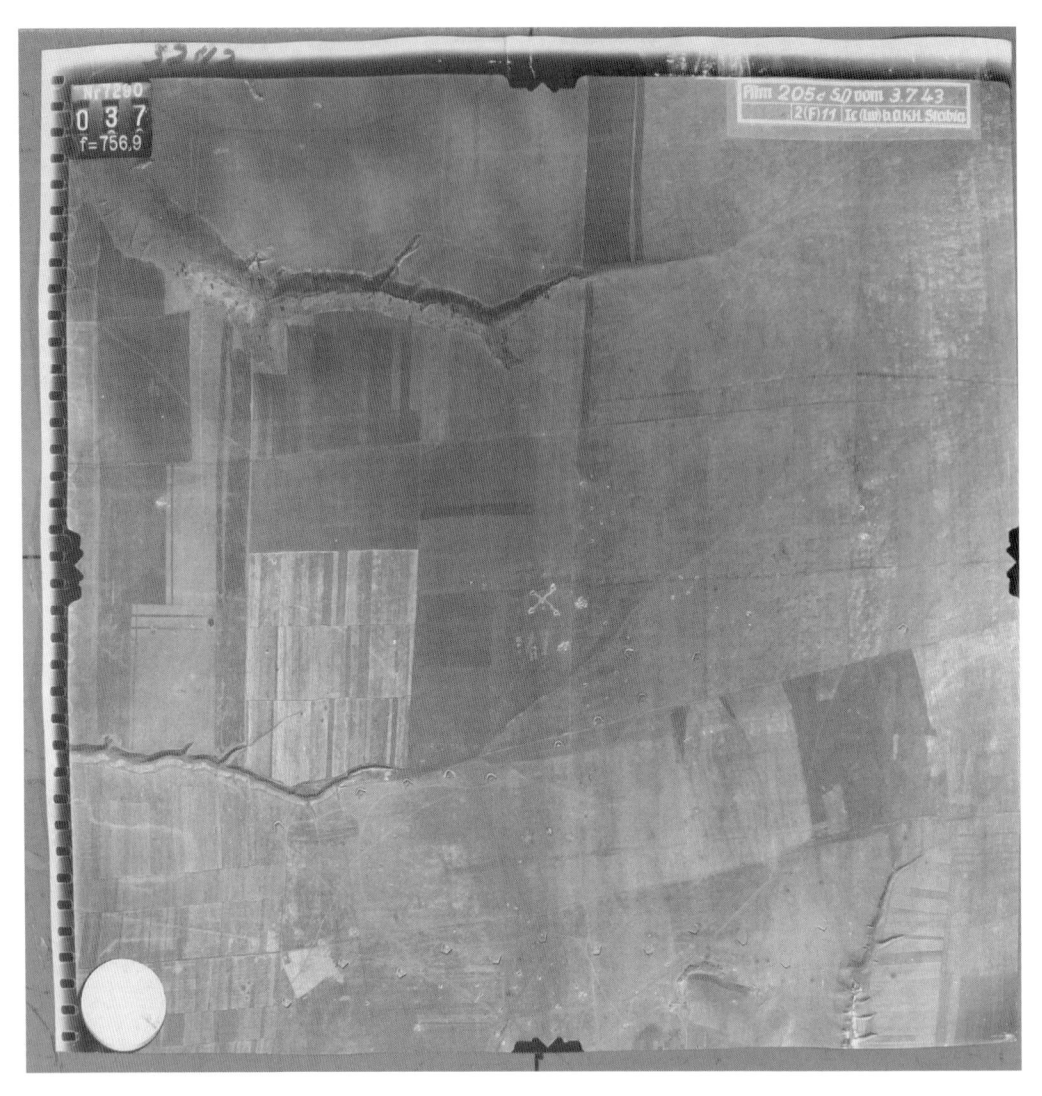

Close-up photo of a Soviet airfield east of Prokhorovka, 3 July 1943. Note the revetments and the 6 airplanes on the runway. Later photos on 16 July show it unoccupied.

Prokhorovka, 2 June 1943.

Looking northeast toward Prokhorovka along Yakovlevo-Prokhorovka road at crest near Prelestnoye-Prokhorovka road intersection. (Photo by Christopher A. Lawrence, 1995)

Looking northeast (zoomed shot) at Prokhorovka monument. (Photo by Christopher A. Lawrence, 1995)

German Air Commanders

Above left: General Otto Dessloch (Fourth Air Army), 18 May 1944.

Above right: Colonel General Hans Jeschonnik, 20 August 1943. (date of photo file, photo is certainly earlier)

Above left: Jeschonnik, 20 March 1941.

Above middle: Major General Hans Seidemann (VIII Air Corps), around September 1944.

Above right: Seidemann, 30 November 1944.

German Flyers and Aces

Above left: Major Barkhorn 1944, photo by Hans Hoffman, 11 March 1944.

Above right: Captain Alfred Druschel I/S.G. 1.

Below left: Major Dietrich Hrabak (52nd Fighter Wing), 22 April 1943.

Below right: Hrabak, 27 November 1943.

Above left: Colonel Hartmann (52nd Fighter Wing), Sept. 1944.

Above right: Walter Krupinski (52nd Fighter Wing), undated.

Below left: Captain Wilhelm Lemke (3rd Fighter Wing), 27 November 1943.

Below right: Captain Kirchner (3rd Fighter Wing). (Photo by Hans Hoffman, undated)

Above left: Guenther Rall (52nd Fighter Wing), 3 November 1942.

Above right: Major Hans-Ulrich Rudel, before July 1944.

Below left: Rudel, 27 November 1943.

Below right: Colonel Hans-Ulrich Rudel, 1945.

Above: Major Rudel and Adolf Hitler. (Photo by Hans Hoffman, March 1944)

Right: Captain Bernhard Wutka (2nd Stuka Wing), 11 May 1943.

Below: Hitler and his pilots. From left to right: Colonel Walther, Major Buehlingen, Jabs, Jope, Seiler, Boettcher, Captain Ademiet, Major Wiese, Staff Sergeant Petersen, Major Dr. Otte and Sr. Lt. Krupinski. (Photo by Hans Hoffman, March 1944)

Soviet Air Commanders

Above left: Stepan Akimovich Krasovskii (Second Air Army), 1943. (With thanks to Col. Fyodor Sverdlov)

Above right: Krasovskii. Later photo from Wikipedia.

Below left: Vladimir Aleksandrovich Sudets (Seventeenth Air Army), 1945. (With thanks to Col. Fyodor Sverdlov)

Below middle: Sudets. Post-war photo from Wikipedia.

Below right: Sergei Kondratyevich Goryunov (Fifth Air Army), 1943. (With thanks to Col. Fyodor Sverdlov)

Soviet Aces

Above left: Ivan Nikitatovich Kozhedub, 1949. (Photo from Wikipedia)

Above right: Nikolai Dmitriyevich Gulayev, 1944. (Photo from Wikipedia)

Right: Kirill Alekseyevich Yevtigneyev, 1945. (Photo from Wikipedia)

Right: Grave of Ivan Nikitovich Kozhedub (1920-1991), the top Soviet ace and thrice Hero of the Soviet Union. (Photo by Natalia Guseva)

Below left: Bust of Nikolai Dmitriyevich Gulayev (1918-1985), Soviet ace and twice Hero of the Soviet Union. (Photo from Geroi Stranyi website at www.warheores.ru)

Below right: Grave of Kirill Alekseyevich Yevstigneyev (1917-1996), Soviet aces and twice Hero of the Soviet Union. (Photo from Geroi Stranyi website at www.warheroes.ru)

THE AIR BATTLE TO SUPPORT THE OFFENSIVE NORTH OF KURSK

Comparison of Soviet Air Armies

	Sixteenth	Second	Seventeenth*	Ratio
Estimated number of planes	1034 (vice 1151)	881	735	0.64
Plane types:[108]				
Fighters:	455	389	218	0.75
Assault Planes:	241	276	383	0.37
Bombers;	260	172	70	1.08
Night Bombers:	74	34	64	0.76
Reconnaissance:	4	10	–	0.40
Total daytime sorties 5-11 July	6,118	5,576	2,091	0.80
Total nighttime sorties 5-11 July	1,942	546	1,201	1.11
Average number of daytime sorties per plane (over 7 days)	5.92	6.58	3.12	
By Plane Type:				
Fighters:	8.85	9.61	5.27	
Assault Planes:	4.61	5.62	1.73	
Bombers:	3.78	0.67	1.10	
Night Bombers	26.24	16.06	18.77	
Reconnaissance:	–	17.10	not sure	
Highest number of daytime sorties in a day	1,147	1,296	639 (on the 7th)	0.59
Highest number of nighttime sorties in a day	469 (on the 6th)	109 (on the 11th)	197 (on the 6th)	1.53
Average number of daytime sorties per plane (5 July)	0.90	1.53	0.67 (448)	
By plane type				
Fighters:	1.80 (817)	2.27 (882)	1.16 (253)	
Assault Planes:	0.93 (225)	1.03 (285)	0.40 (152)	
Bombers:	0.40 (105)	0.67 (115)	0 (0)	
Night Bombers:	1.38 (102)	2.12 (72)	1.55 (99)	
Reconnaissance:	–	1.40 (14)	not sure (67)	
Total fighter sorties	4,025	3,739	1,148	0.82
Percent fighter sorties	66%	67%	55%	
Total Assault sorties	1,110	1,551	663	0.50
Percent Assault sorties	18%	28%	32%	
Total bombing sorties	983	115	77	0.20
Percent bombing sorties	16%	2%	4%	
Total reconnaissance sorties	–	171	203	

	Sixteenth	**Second**	**Seventeenth***	**Ratio**
Percent reconnaissance sorties	–	3%	10%	
Total ground attack type sorties	2,093	1,666	740	0.87
Percent ground attack type sorties	34%	30%	35%	
Total planes lost, daytime (5-11 July)	391	336	170	0.77
Percent planes lost	38%	40%	25%	
Percent per planes lost per sortie, daytime (5 – 11 July)	6%	6%	8%	
Total fighters lost (5-11 July)	–	192	28	
Percent losses that were fighters	–	57%	16%	
Total planes claimed in aerial combat	517	708**	see Second Air Army	0.73
Planes claimed per fighter sortie	13%	14%	see Second Air Army	

* Sortie data is from the table "Seventeenth Air Army Sortie Count (Total)" and includes sorties not in the Belgorod offensive battle area. Those sorties are listed in the following table "Seventeenth Air Army Sortie Count (Only Those That Were in the Belgorod Area or Attached to the VIII Air Corps)".

** This is the total claims for the both the Second and Seventeenth Air Armies.

One can make a few observations from these charts. In the case of the Germans, the Sixth Air Fleet in the north was about two-thirds the size of the VIII Air Corps in the south and provided about two-thirds of the ground support as the VIII Air Corps did. This was even though the Sixth Air Fleet flew more sorties per plane than the VIII Air Corps. While the Sixth Air Fleet lost only 57% of the planes that the VIII Air Corps did (and only 41% of the fighters), they claimed more planes. This was mostly due to overclaiming on the part of the Sixth Air Fleet.

In the case of the Soviets, the Sixteenth Air Army in the north was about two-thirds the size of the Second and Seventeenth Air Armies in the south. Still, this is not a very good direct comparison, as the Seventeenth Air Army was only partly committed to the defensive battles between Belgorod and Prokhorovka, and there were considerable reinforcements that arrived in the south during that time. The Sixteenth Air Army managed to put up over 80% of the sorties that the two air armies in the south did and almost 90% of the ground attack sorties. The nature of the ground support was different. The south put up almost twice as many Il-2 sorties as the Sixteenth Air Army put up, while the Sixteenth Air Army made up this deficit with bomber sorties. Still, these are not the same. An Il-2 sorties tends to be more directly aimed at equipment on the ground and often more accurately delivered. Therefore, they tend to have more influence on the immediate battle. Bomber sorties tended to strike a little further back from the front line and at a higher altitude. On the other hand, the bombers carried a larger load (600 kilograms for an Il-2 compared to 1,200 kilograms for an Pe-2). But bomber attacks tended to be on more rear area targets and may have not had much immediate effect on the battle. It is hard to say which is better, but most people tend to value close air support in a combat scenario.

THE AIR BATTLE TO SUPPORT THE OFFENSIVE NORTH OF KURSK

COMPARATIVE GERMAN AIR REPORTS

In the Second Army air liaison officer records, there were several reports that compared the differences between operations of the Sixth Air Fleet with those of the VIII Air Corps. The first report dated 10 July 1943 shows the following:[109]

Air force deployment of the Sixth Air Fleet (Ninth Army) and VIII Air Corps (Fourth Panzer Army) from 5 to 9 July 1943
From that:

	Total Sorties	Recon	Bombing	Stuka	Ground Attack	Fighter	Transport
Sixth Air Fleet	6,848	739	1,612	2,077	509	1,692	219
VIII Air Corps	9,209	413	2,234	4,010	1,144	1,408	–
Total	16,057	1,152	3,846	6,087	1,653	3,100	219

This count of sorties, when compared to the daily reports for that same period, produces the same figures. They are clearly a total of their daytime sorties. The 509 "ground attack" sorties listed for the Sixth Air Fleet match the 509 "destroyer" (Me-110) sorties listed in the daily reports of the Sixth Air Fleet. This would argue that the Me-110s were primarily being used for ground attack, not air superiority. Also, this report does not note any transport flights for the VIII Air Corps. It is hard to believe that there was none.

These totals indicate that during this time the Sixth Air Fleet flew only 74% of the sorties as the VIII Air Corps and provided only 57% of ground attack type sorties (bombing, stuka and ground attack) as the VIII Air Corps.

That same report also records:

	Kills		
	Air Battle	Flak	
Sixth Air Fleet	489	45	
VIII Air Corps	471	40*	
Total kills	960	85	1,045

* Destroyed by flak in the Fourth Panzer Army area from 6 to 9 July not included.

Now, the VIII Air Corps report for 5 July claims of 40 Soviet planes shot down by flak is probably an over-estimate based upon comparisons with the Soviet records. We also have no AA claims by the VIII Air Corps after 5 July. The total claimed by the VIII Air Corps for 5 July was 220 by air and 40 by flak, while the actual documented Soviet losses were 189.

Finally, there is a listing of their own losses (probably covering 5 to 9 July. The total matches with the added daily totals for 5 to 9 July for the VIII Air Corps but not the Sixth Air Fleet, which reports 23 planes lost from 5 to 7 July, and 7 more lost July 8 and 9):

Lost	Recon	Bomber	Stuka	Ground Attack	Fighter	
Sixth Air Fleet	1	7	6	2	7	23 planes
VIII Air Corps	1	9	10	9	23	52 planes
	2	16	16	11	30	75 planes

They also note:

"With a total of 16,057 sorties, there were 75 losses (0.05%)."

"In air combat and by flak, 1,045 enemy aircraft (5.5% of the number of units deployed) were shot down. Of the 3,100 fighter missions (escort, protection and free hunting) they shot down 960 enemy aircraft (32% of the operational number) with 30 losses (1%)."

The record was signed by a captain (probably the air liaison officer).

There is also a report that states:

"On 7.7 until 10:30 AM, against strong opposing air force deployment, up to this time the Sixth Air Fleet had about 30 kills and the VIII Air Corps had about 35 kills."

"Preliminary Report of the Air Force deployment on 5 and 6 July."

	Sorties	Shot down	Losses
Sixth Air Fleet	3,111	295	13
VIII Air Corps	4,087	330	19*
Total about	7,198	625	32

* Losses of the VIII Air Corps on 6 July not yet included."

The VIII Air Corps losses on the 6th were 7 planes according to the reports of the air liaison officer. This report was signed by the same captain.

The combat effectiveness of the Second Air Army in the south appears to have been better than the Sixteenth Air Army in the north. The exchange ratio in the north was 39-to-391 or 1-to-10 in favor of the Germans. The exchange ratio in the south was 69-to-506 or 1-to-7.33. This is based upon the German liaison officer's reporting of German losses. The two Soviet southern air armies caused the Germans 77% more air casualties (and 2.45 times more fighter casualties) than the Sixteenth Air Army did while suffering only 29% more casualties in the south. There is also reason to suspect that the losses of the Sixteenth Air Army are under-reported by 20 or 30%.[110]

Still the nature of the operations was different. In the south the German VIII Air Corps was causing .32 Soviet casualties per fighter sortie, while the Sixth Air Fleet in the north was causing only .17 Soviet casualties per fighter sortie. Conversely, in the south, the two Soviet Air Armies were causing 0.014 German casualties per fighter sortie while in the north the Sixteenth Air Army was causing 0.010 German casualties per fighter sortie. It does appear that over 90% of combat losses were caused by enemy fighters. So it appears that the VIII Air Corps was more effective at shooting down enemy aircraft than the Sixth Air Fleet while the Second Air Army was more effective at shooting down enemy aircraft than the Sixteenth Air Army. It does appear that the Sixteenth Air Army was more conservatively commanded, although their losses per sortie were about the same as the Second Air Army and better than the Seventeenth Air Army (0.064 versus 0.060 versus 0.081). One of the problems with these statistical comparisons is that the Second and in particular the Seventeenth Air Army lost a considerable number of Il-2s on the first day of the battle, many not properly escorted. It also does appear that the Sixth Air Fleet fighters were not as effective or aggressive at protecting their charges. In the north, 28% of German losses were fighters while in the south 39% were fighters.

The overall impression that this author draws from this comparison is that Soviet air units in the south were more experienced, probably because of the experience in the Kuban. The German air units in the south may have also been more experienced. This argument is certainly reinforced by the number of famous aces located in the 52nd Fighter Wing.

Finally, there is the issue of the overclaiming of kills by the German Sixth Air Fleet. The VIII Air Corps claimed 508 planes shot down between 5-11 July 1943 while the Second and Seventeenth Air Army lost 506 aircraft during this time. The Sixth Air Fleet claimed 586 planes shot down between 5-11 July 1943, and probably shot down around 391 (with 48 damaged aircraft written off as destroyed). This would appear to be overclaiming by around 50%, assuming the Soviet figures are correct. It could be that Soviet loss figures as drawn from the sources used are simply too low by 50%. It could be a combination of the two factors. It is suspected that the Soviet loss figures are low and there are reasons to suspect the Sixth Air Fleet is overclaiming kills. Without direct access to the Sixteenth Air Army records, this is difficult to resolve.

The Soviet Counteroffensive

On 12 July, the Soviet Army launched *Operation Kutuzov*. It initially consisted of the Western Front and the Bryansk Front attacking the German Second Panzer Army (which had no panzer divisions) and Model's Ninth Army. The defending Central Front would not join the offensive until the 15th. This offensive added the attached Soviet First and Fifteenth Air Armies to the battle, seriously taxing the German Sixth Air Fleet. This is the start of the next phase of this battle, ending the German offensive. Although the German offensive in the north was cancelled after 12 July, the German offensive in the south continued.

SIXTH AIR FLEET ORDER OF BATTLE[111]

Sixth Air Fleet – Colonel General Robert Ritter von Greim

Unit	Airfield	Commander	Aircraft Type	Aircraft Available 1 July 1943
IV/5th Night Fighter Wing	Seshchinskaya, Bryansk, Roslavl	Capt. Heinrich Prinz zu Sayn Wittgenstein	Ju-88, Me-110, Do-217	42
FAGr 2		Maj. Oskar Otolsky		
2. Night Recon Sqn (F)	Orel-west, Orsha-south		Ju-88, He-111, Do-217	11
4.(F)/11			Ju-88	10
4.(F)/14	Smolensk-north		Ju-88	14
1.(F)/100	Orel-west, Orsha-south		Ju-88, Ju-86, Ar-240	16
4.(F)/121	Seshchinskaya		Ju-88	11
Sixth Air Fleet Harassment Bomber Group				30*
1/Harassment Bomber Group			Ar-66, He-46	see above
2/Harassment Bomber Group			Go-145	see above
3/Harassment Bomber Group			Ar-66, Fw-58	see above
Staff/3rd Transport Wing		LtC. Fritz Schroeder	–	–
I/3rd Transport Wing		Capt. Hans-Hermann Ellerbrock	Ju-52	52
II/3rd Transport Wing		Maj. Otto Baumann	Ju-52	52
Staff/4th Transport Wing		LtC. Richard Kupschus	Ju-52	–
II/4th Transport Wing		Maj. Ludwig Beckmann	Ju-52	52
Sixth Air Fleet Transport Sqn			Ju-52	11
Liaison Command (S) 5			He-111, Do-17, Hs-126, DFS-230	?

THE AIR BATTLE TO SUPPORT THE OFFENSIVE NORTH OF KURSK

Unit	Airfield	Commander	Aircraft Type	Aircraft Available 1 July 1943
Sixth Air Fleet Readiness Unit			Fi-156	?
Medical Readiness Unit 4			Fi-156, Ju-52	?
Total number of Aircraft: 301**				

* This is the total for the harassment bomber group.
** Total excludes Liaison Command (S) 5, Sixth Air Fleet Readiness Unit, and Medical Readiness Unit 4.

1st Air Division – Major General Paul Deichmann

Unit	Airfield	Commander	Aircraft Type	Aircraft Available 1 July 1943
III/1st Bombardment Wing	Orel-west	Capt. Werner Kanther	Ju-88 A and C	25
Staff/4th Bombardment Wing		LtC. Werner Klosinski	He-111 H	2
II/4th Bombardment Wing	Seshchinskaya	Maj. Reinhard Graubner	He-111 H	39
III/4th Bombardment Wing	Karachev	Maj. Kurt Neumann	He-111 H	42
Staff/51st Bombardment Wing	Bryansk	Maj. Hanns Heise	Ju-88 A	2
II/51st Bombardment Wing	Bryansk	Maj. Herbert Voss	Ju-88 A	44
III/51st Bombardment Wing	Bryansk	Capt. Wilhelm Rath	Ju-88 A and C	21
Staff/53rd Bombardment Wing	Olsufyevo	LtC. Fritz Pockrandt	He-111 H	6
I/53rd Bombardment Wing	Olsufyevo	Maj. Karl Rauer	He-111 H	35
III/53rd Bombardment Wing	Olsufyevo	Maj. Emil Allmendinger	He-111 H	28
Staff/1st Stuka Wing	Orel-north	LtC. Gustav Pressler	Ju-87 D, Me-110	10
I/1st Stuka Wing	Orel-east	Maj. Helmuth Krebs[112]	Ju-87 D	32

Unit	Airfield	Commander	Aircraft Type	Aircraft Available 1 July 1943
II/1st Stuka Wing	Orel-east	Capt. Frank Neubert[113]	Ju-87 D	42
III/1st Stuka Wing	Orel-east	Capt. Friedrich Lang	Ju-87 D	43
III/3rd Stuka Wing	Konevka	Capt. Eberhard Jacob [114]	Ju-87 D	39
Staff/1st Destroyer Wing		LtC. Joachim Blechschmidt	Me-110 G	4
I/1st Destroyer Wing	Ledna-east	Capt. Wilfried Hermann	Me-110 E, F and G	37
Antitank Staff/1st Destroyer Wing	Ledna-east		Me-110	14
Staff/51st Fighter Wing		Maj. Karl-Gottfried Nordmann	–	
Staff squadron/51st Fighter Wing	Orel	Sr. Lt. Diethelm von Eichel-Streiber	Fw-190 A	16
I/51st Fighter Wing	Orel	Maj. Erich Leie	Fw-190 A	40
III/51st Fighter Wing	Orel	Capt. Fritz Losigkeit	Fw-190 A	36
IV/51st Fighter Wing	Orel	Maj. Rudolf Resch	Fw-190 A	38
15 (Spanish)/51st Fighter Wing	Orel	Comandante Mariano Cuadra Medina	Fw-190	18
I/54th Fighter Wing	Orel	Capt. Reinhard Seiler	Fw-190 A	38
Staff/NAGr 4 (AOK 9)		Maj. Toni Vinek	Me-109 G	3

THE AIR BATTLE TO SUPPORT THE OFFENSIVE NORTH OF KURSK

Unit	Airfield	Commander	Aircraft Type	Aircraft Available 1 July 1943
1./NAGr. 4			Me-109 G	15
2./NAGr. 4			Me-109 G	13
3./NAGr. 4			Me-110	8
NAGr 10 (AOK 2)		Sr. Lt. Werner Stein	–	
1./NAGr. 10 – 3.(H)/21	Stanovka		Hs-126 B	9
2./NAGr. 10 – 2.(H)/31			Fw-189 A	9
Staff/NAGr 15 (Pz AOK 2)	Kuznetsy	Maj. Hubert Correns	–	–
1.(H)/11	Oserskaya		Fw-189 A	10
11.(H)/12	Kuznetsy		Fw-189 A	8
Total Number of Aircraft: 726				

SIXTEENTH AIR ARMY ORDER OF BATTLE – LT. GENERAL SERGEI IGNATYEVICH RUDENKO

Headquarters: Ukolovo[115]

Unit	Divisions	Airfields*	Regiments	Aircraft	Commander
VI Fighter Corps	273rd Fighter Division	Limovoye	157th	Yak-1, Yak-7B, Yak-9	Maj. Viktor Volkov
MG Andrei B. Yumashev	Col. Ivan E. Fyodorov	Novoselki	163rd	Yak-7B, Yak-9	LtC. Pavel Pologov
HQ: Yarishche		Yarishche	347th	Yak-9	Capt. Pavel Dankevich
	279th Fighter Division	Mokhozoye	92nd	La-5	Maj. Boris Solomatin
	Col. Fyodor N. Dementyev	Kolpnyi	486th	La-5	Maj. Pelipets
III Bomber Corps	241st Bomber Division	Chernovo-	24th	Pe-2	
MG Afanasii Z. Karavatskii	Col. Ivan G. Kurilenko	Pyatnitskaya	128th	Pe-2	LtC. Mikhail Voronkov
HQ: Yelets			779th	Pe-2	LtC. Afanasii Khramchenkov

203

ACES AT KURSK

Unit	Divisions	Airfields*	Regiments	Aircraft	Commander
	301st Bomber Division	Voronets	34th	Pe-2	
	Col. Fyedor M. Fedorenko		54th	Pe-2	LtC. Mikhail Krivtov
			96th Gds	Pe-2	Aleksandr Yakobson
VI Mixed Corps	221st Bomber Division	Pelets	8th Gds	A-20B	LtC. G. S. Kucherkov
MG Ivan D. Antoshkin	Col. Sergei F. Buzyilev	Zadonsk	57th	Boston III	Maj. Bebchik
HQ; Khmelnets			745th	Boston III	
	282nd Fighter Division	Kunach	127th	Yak-1	
	Col. A. M. Ryazanov [116]		517th	Yak-1	
			774th	Yak-1	
1st Guards Fighter Division		Rzhava	30th Gds	Airacobra	Maj. Ivan Khlusovich
Col. Aleksandr Utin**		Fatesh	53rd Gds	Yak-1	Maj. Ivan P. Motornyii
HQ: Rzhava			54th Gds	Yak-1	LtC. Yevgenii Malnikov
			55th Gds	Yak-1	Maj. Vasilii Shishkin
			67th Gds	Airacobra	LtC. Aleksei Panov
283rd Fighter Division		Mokva	56th Gds	Yak-1	Maj. Stephan Chirva
Col. Sergei P. Denisov			176th	Yak-1	Maj. Geogii Makarov
HQ: Mokva			519th	Yak-7	Maj. Kirill Murga
			563rd	Yak-1	
286th Fighter Division		Zyibino	165th	La-5	
Col. Ivan I. Ivanov			721st	La-5	
HQ: Zyibino			739th	La-5	
			896th	Yak-1	

THE AIR BATTLE TO SUPPORT THE OFFENSIVE NORTH OF KURSK

Unit	DIVISIONS	Airfields*	Regiments	Aircraft	Commander
2nd Guards Assault Division		Ryishkovo	58th Gds	Il-2	Maj. Yevgenii Koval
Col. Georgii I. Komarov		Shchigri	59th Gds	Il-2	Maj. Maksim Sklyarov
HQ: Ryishkovo			78th Gds	Il-2	Maj. Aleksandr Nakonechnikov
			79th Gds	Il-2	Maj. I.D. Borodin
299th Assault Division		KR. Zariya St.	41st	Il-2	
Col. Ivan V. Krupskii			217th	Il-2	
HQ: Kr. Zariya St.			218th	Il-2	Maj. Nikolai Lyisenko
			431st	Il-2	Maj. Gavrilov
			874th	Il-2	Maj. M. G. Volkov
271st Night Bomber Division		Kazanka	44th Gds	U-2	
Col. Konstantin P. Rasskazov			45th Gds	U-2	
HQ: Kazanka			372nd		LtC. Nikolai Chernenko
			714th		Maj. Fyodor Sushko
			970th	U-2	Maj. Nikolai Pushkaryov
16th Reconnaissance Regiment				Boston III, Pe-2	Maj. D. S. Sherstyuk
98th Guards Reconnaissance Regiment				Pe-2[117]	Maj. Semyon Berman***
11th UTA Regiment					LtC. M. M. Kuzmin

* Airfields are listed for the division; they are not listed for the regiments.
** Khazanov, pages 129 and 131, lists the commander as LtC. I. V. Krupenin.
*** Khazanov, pages 129, lists the commander as LtC. B. P. Artemyev.

GERMAN LOSSES ON 5 JULY IN ACCORDANCE WITH THE QUARTERMASTER REPORTS[118]

Plane	Percent Damaged	Notes
He-111 H-11	35	Shot down by fighters and flak
Fw-190 A-5	20	Belly-landed after running out of fuel
Me-109 F-2	90	Crashed immediately after take-off. Pilot wounded.
Me-109 G-4	100	Shot down by fighter. Pilot bailed out. Pilot wounded.
Fi-156 C-5	50	Technical failure. Pilot is wounded.
Me-109 G-4	100	Cause unknown. Pilot is Missing
Me-110 G-2	30	Crash landed due to technical failure
Me-110 G-2	80	Belly landed following engine failure
Me-110 D-3	20	Crash landing
Ju-87 D-3	80	Force landed after getting hit by Flak. One crew wounded.
Ju-87 D-3	60	Collided with Ju-87 during landing
Ju-87 D-3	60	Collided with Ju-87 during landing
Ju-87 D-3	100	Hit by flak. Crew are missing.
Ju-87 D-3	100	Engine failure. Crew KIA.*
Ju-87 D-3	100	Hit by flak. Crew are missing.
Ju-87 D-3	80	Crashed following engine failure. One KIA, one wounded.*
Ju-87 D-1	90	Hit by flak. Crew wounded.
Ju-87 D-3	30	Force landed
Ju-88 A-4	30	Belly landed after getting hit by Flak
Ju-88 A-4	70	Crash landed after getting hit by Flak. One crew wounded.
Ju-88 A-14	100	Mid-air explosion, 3 crew KIA, 1 missing.
Ju-88 A-4	60	Belly landed after getting hit by Flak. One crew wounded
He-111 H-16	40	Hit by AAA.
He-111 H	?	Wounded by fire from Soviet fighter. One crew KIA.
He-111 H	?	Wounded by fire from Soviet fighter. Three crew wounded.
He-111 H-16	90	Shot down by fighter.
He-111 H-16	100	Shot down by fighter. one crew wounded, four missing.
Fw-190 A-4	20	Crash landing

THE AIR BATTLE TO SUPPORT THE OFFENSIVE NORTH OF KURSK

Plane	Percent Damaged	Notes
Fw-190 A-4	100	Air combat with fighter. Pilot bailed out. Pilot is missing.
Fw-190 A-5	100	Crashed following air combat. Pilot KIA.
Fw-190 A-5	20	Hit by AAA.
Fw-190 A-4	15	Technical failure.
Fw-190 A-5	30	Hit by ground fire.
Fw-190 A-4	100	Crashed following air combat. Pilot bailed out over hostile territory. Pilot KIA.
Fw-190 A-5	80	Hostile fire.
Fw-190 A-5	100	Force landed following air combat with LaGG-3. Pilot wounded.
Fw-190 A-5	15	Hostile fire.
Fw-190 A-5	100	Hostile fire.
Fw-190 A-5	100	Hostile fire.

* If the plane was lost due to engine failure, then "killed in action" does not appear to be due to enemy action.

This is a total of 39 planes listed as damaged and destroyed. Of those 16 are clearly destroyed (90% - 100% damaged), which is close to the overall loss figure provided by the air liaison officer report. Of those 16 planes, two to four were not lost due to enemy fire. Of those four, one "crashed immediately after take off," one had "engine failure," one had a "mid-air explosion" (which may or may not have been combat related), and one was "cause unknown" (which may or may not have been combat related). We are not able to determine which other two planes were counted as down to get to Christer Bergtrom's reported total of 18, perhaps the two of the four reported as 80% damaged.

There are four planes reported as 80% damaged, one at 70% damage and three at 60% damage. This is defined as "Write-off category, Certain parts could be used as spare parts for other aircraft." Of those eight aircraft, only four were damaged by enemy fire.

So the Luftwaffe liaison officer reports 13 planes shot down on 5 July. From the quartermaster report one could make the argument that the real figure is either 12 or 14 or 16 or 18 or 20 or 22 or 24. It is dependent on what counting criteria one uses.

The other fifteen damaged planes are reported at 50% damage or less. Of those, eight are due to enemy fire. Overall, it would appear that 15 of the 39 damaged and destroyed planes were not due to enemy fire, or could not be confirmed as being due to enemy fire (there are two cases in question).

TOP GERMAN ACES AT BATTLE OF KURSK (NORTH)

Name	Unit	Rank	Kills	Combat Missions	Remarks
Ofw. Otto Kittel	I/JG 54	4th	267	583	KIA 1945
Sr. Lt. Joachim Brendel	1/JG 51	18th	189	950	
Uffz. Guenther Josten	1/JG 52	22nd	178	420	
Sr. Lt. Horst-Guenther von Fassong	10/JG 51	44th	136		
Sr. Lt. Karl-Heinz Weber	III/JG 51	44th	136	500+	
Capt. Adolf Borchers	11/JG 51	52nd	132	@ 800	
Sr. Lt. Franz Eisenach	3/JG 54	57th	129	319	Wounded 8 July
Ofw. Rudolf Rademacher	1/JG 54	60th	126		
Maj. Erich Leie	I/JG 51	71st	118	500+	KIA 1945
Maj. Reinhard Seiler	I/JG 54	105th	100 + 9 SCW	@ 500	Wounded 6 July
Capt. Diethelm von Eichel-Streiber	JG 51		96		
Heinrich Hoefemeier	1/JG 51		96		
Capt. Rudolf Resch	IV/JG 51		93 + 1 SCW		KIA 11 July 1943
Lt. Gerhard Loos			92		KIA 1944
Uffz. Oskar Romm	1/JG 51		92		Half Jewish
Sr. Lt. Hans Goetz	2/JG 54		82	600	KIA 4 August 1943
Fw. Rudolf Wagner	10/JG 51		81		KIA 11 December 1943
Sr. Lt. Hermann Luecke	9/JG 51		78		KIA
Lt. Guenther Scheel	2/JG 54		71	70	At least 24 kills during Kursk, KIA 16 July 1943[119]
Capt. Fritz Losigkeit	III/JG 51		68	@ 750	
Capt. Herbert Findeisen	1/NAGr 4		67		
Fw. Hubert Strassl	8/JG 51		67	221	30 kills during Kursk, KIA 8 July 1943

THE AIR BATTLE TO SUPPORT THE OFFENSIVE NORTH OF KURSK

Name	Unit	Rank	Kills	Combat Missions	Remarks
Capt. Gerhard Homuth	I/JG 54		63		KIA 2 August 1943
Fw. Peter Bremer	1/JG 54		40		
Capt. Herbert Wehnelt	7/JG 51		36		

Ranking is based upon the list of aces in Wikipedia, which appears to be the most comprehensive list available. Still, for example, it left Adolf Borchers (132) off the listing even though there is a personal Wikipedia page for him. Herbert Wehnelt was also not in the Wikipedia listing. The rankings have been adjusted accordingly.

SCW = Spanish Civil War (1936-1939)

TOP SOVIET ACES AT BATTLE OF KURSK (NORTH)

Name	Fighter Regiment	Kills	Shared Kills	Sorties	Combats	Remarks
Andrei Ye. Borovykh	157th	32	14	475	113	HSU 24 Aug 43 and HSU 23 Feb. 45
Vladimir N. Zalevskii	157th	23	17	300+		HSU 30 Jan. 43. KIA 5 July 1943
Stepan K. Koleschenko	519th	21	4	135	27	HSU 2 Sep. 43, KIA 30 Aug. 1943
Victor F. Volkhov	157th	17	8[120]	290	75	HSU 1 July 44. Regiment CO.
Ivan D. Sidorov	92nd	16	7	400	130	HSU 2 Sep. 43, KIA 5 or 6 July 1943
Nikolai M. Tregubov	721st	16	3	461		HSU 13 April 44.
I. V. Kuznetsov	30th Gds	12	15	356		HSU 22 March 91.

HSU = Hero of the Soviet Union

OBERFELDWEBEL HUBERT STRASSL

Sergeant Hubert Strassl (24 May 1918 – 8 July 1943) was an experienced Luftwaffe pilot who had gone on a kill streak in the six weeks before his death. He claimed 13 victories in 1942, the first on 6 July 1942. He was then transferred to Germany. Returning to the Eastern Front in May 1943 he claimed 24 victories between 30 May and 3 July 1943. According to one listing during the Battle of Kursk, he claimed 15 victories on the 5th, 4 victories on the 6th, 6 victories on the 7th, and 5 victories on the 8th. He was then shot down, bailed out at low level but his parachute failed to deploy. He was credited with 67 kills in 221 mission. In light of the possible overclaiming by 50% by Sixth Air Fleet during the Battle of Kursk, then his actual count may be less. He was awarded the Knight's Cross posthumously.

The list of his claims during this time is provided below:[121]

38	5.7.1943	3:48	MiG-3	8./JG 51	63 651 at 1.500m
39	5.7.1943	3:50	MiG-3	8./JG 51	63 631 at 2.500m
40	5.7.1943	7:18	MiG-3	8./JG 51	63 651 at 1.800m
41	5.7.1943	7:25	MiG-3	8./JG 51	63 613 at 2.000m
42	5.7.1943	7:28	MiG-3	8./JG 51	63 652 at 1.200m
43	5.7.1943	10:34	LaGG-5	8./JG 51	63 543 at 2.000m
44	5.7.1943	10:36	LaGG-5	8./JG 51	63 544 at 1.800m
45	5.7.1943	10:42	Il-2	8./JG 51	63 542 at 1.000m
46	5.7.1943	10:46	LaGG-5	8./JG 51	63 551 at 1.200m
47	5.7.1943	10:49	Boston	8./JG 51	63 564 at 1.000m
48	5.7.1943	10:51	LaGG-5	8./JG 51	63 552 at 1.200m
49	5.7.1943	18:24	Il-4	8./JG 51	63 562 at 800m
50	5.7.1943	18:27	Il-4	8./JG 51	63 621 at 800m
51	5.7.1943	18:31	Il-4	8./JG 51	63 551 at 100m
52	5.7.1943	18:33	Il-4	8./JG 51	63 522 at 100m
53	6.7.1943	12:34	LaGG-5	8./JG 51	63 654: at 2.500m
54	6.7.1943	12:37	MiG-3	8./JG 51	63 652: at 2.600m
55	6.7.1943	12:40	LaGG-5	8./JG 51	63 653: at 2.800m
56	6.7.1943	19:35	MiG-3	8./JG 51	63 582: at 2.500m
57	7.7.1943	4:20	MiG-3	8./JG 51	63 751: at 3.800m
58	7.7.1943	4:25	Il-2	8./JG 51	63 527: at 300m
59	7.7.1943	9:10	LaGG-5	8./JG 51	63 561: at 700m
60	7.7.1943	9:24	LaGG-5	8./JG 51	63 583: at 2.500m
61	7.7.1943	9:26	LaGG-5	8./JG 51	63 573: at 2.000m
62	7.7.1943	18:36	LaGG-5	8./JG 51	63 714: at 1.800m
63	8.7.1943	12:20	MiG-3	8./JG 51	63 387: at 3.000m
64	8.7.1943	12:27	Boston	8./JG 51	63 675: at 2.500m
65	8.7.1943	17:38	LaGG-3	8./JG 51	63 584: at 2.000m
66	8.7.1943	17:50	LaGG-5	8./JG 51	63 582: at 2.100m
67	8.7.1943	17:51	LaGG-5	8./JG 51	63 582: at 2.100m

GERMAN ACES NORTH OF KURSK

Otto Kittel – Sergeant Otto "Bruno" Kittel was born 21 February 1917 in the Sudetenland, then part of the Austro-Hungarian Empire. He joined the Luftwaffe in 1939 and the 54th Fighter Wing in the spring of 1941. His first kills were on 24 June 1941, on the third day of the Eastern Front campaign and all his kills during the war were on the Eastern Front. Sergeant Kittel started the Battle of Kursk with 55 claimed kills to his credit.

On 5 July he claimed four more kills. Two days later he claimed three more kills. Two were claimed to be P-40s, but there were no P-40s in the Sixteenth Air Army. He claimed two Il-2s on 9 July and two fighters on 10 July for a total of 11 airplanes from 5-11 July.[122]

He then claimed another 28 kills between 13 July and 5 August, during the defensive phase of the Battle of Kursk. He was awarded the Knight's Cross in October 1943 for having shot down 120 aircraft and was promoted to an officer on 1 November. He was awarded Oak Leaves in April 1944 after 152 victories and Swords in November 1944.

On his 583rd combat mission, he was shot down around 14 or 16 February 1945 in Latvia by a gunner of Shturmovik (Il-2). He was 27, married and had a son.

With 267 claimed kills, he had become the 4th highest scoring ace in the German Air Force and the highest scoring ace not to survive the war. He was only outscored by Erich Hartmann (352 claimed kills), Gerhard Barkhorn (301 claimed kills) and Guenther Rall (275 claimed kills), all of 52nd Fighter Wing.

Walter Nowotny – Walter Nowotny was the fifth highest scoring ace in the German Air Force and the first ace to claim 250 kills. He was not at the Battle of Kursk. He claimed his 124th victory on 24 June 1943 and then went on home leave.[123] He did not make claim another kill until 12 August 1943. He died 8 November 1944 fighting against US fighters. He had claimed 258 kills.

Rudolf Resch – Captain Rudolf Resch, born 7 April 1914, was shot down by Soviet fighters during the Battle of Kursk on 11 July 1943. He was credited with 1 kill during the Spanish Civil War and 93 kills on the Eastern Front. He was awarded the Knight's Cross in September 1942.

Hugo Broch – Sergeant Hugo Broch was born on 6 January 1922 and entered service wih the Luftwaffe in 1939. The young sergeant (unteroffizier) arrived on the Eastern Front in January 1943 and two months later claimed his first victory. He would go on to claim 81 victories in 324 missions, all on the Eastern Front. He was awarded the Knight's Cross in March 1945. Born on 6 January 1922, he was still alive in 2020.

ACES AT KURSK

Guenther Scheel – Lt. Guenther Scheel was born 23 November 1921. He was posted from training school to the 54th Fighter Wing in January 1943.[124] In his first 50 missions he claimed 30 kills! On the opening day of the Battle of Kursk he claimed eight victories and followed it on the 7th with seven more claims. He ended up claiming at least 24 kills between 5 - 11 July. On 16 July 1943, during the Soviet offensive against Orel, he collided with a Yak-9 about 12 kilometers north of Bolkhov, near Orel, and was killed in the crash. He flew around 70 combat missions and is credited with 71 kills.[125] He was awarded the Knight's Cross posthumously. On 1 August 1944 he was officially listed as missing in action and there were reports of him being a prisoner of war in 1946-1948.[126]

Hubert Strassl – Sergeant Hubert Strassl, born 24 May 1918 in Linz Austria, was credited with shooting down 67 planes in his career. He had served with the 51st Fighter Wing since 1941 and by March 1943 had accumulated 19 victories. He then was posted to France to serve as a fighter instructor under Major Hermann Graf, the top scoring German ace at that time. He returned to service in late May of 1943 and before 5 July had run his tally from 19 up to 38. He then opened the first day at Kursk with 15 claimed kills and between 5 and 8 July 1943 had claimed a total of 30 aircraft.[127] He was shot down on 8 July 1943 and died when his parachute did not open in time. He was awarded the Knights' Cross posthumously. A listing of his 30 kills is provided in the sidebar in this chapter.

SOVIET ACES NORTH OF KURSK

Andrei Borovykh – Lt. Andrei Yegorovich Borovykh was the top Soviet ace north of Kursk. He was born in Kursk 30 October 1921, graduated from the 7th class (effectively 7th grade) in 1936 and graduated from the Kursk aeroclub in 1937. He joined the army in 1940 and graduated from the Chuguveysk Military Air College in January 1941. After graduation he continued on there as an instructor. In December 1941 he was posted to the 728th Fighter Regiment and claimed his first victory in February 1942. He transferred to the 157th Fighter Regiment in September 1942, where he remained for the rest of war, and during the summer of 1943 he became a squadron leader. He became a member of the Communist Party in 1943.

During the Battle of Kursk, he claimed eight victories although he was shot down on one occasion. We do not have a listing of kill claims, so some may have occurred during the period of the counteroffensive. He was promoted to a senior lieutenant on 10 July 1943.

He continued in the war all the way to Berlin in 1945, having been promoted to a major. He claimed a total of 32 individual kills and 14 shared kills. This was in

475 sorties and 113 combats.[128] He won the Hero of the Soviet Union twice, in August 1943 and February 1945.

After the war, he remained in the air force, rising to the rank of Col. General (equivalent to a US Lt. General) and retired in 1988. He died of a stroke in 1989 at the age of 68. He was buried in the prestigious Novodevichy Cemetery in Moscow and there was a bronze bust to him placed at his hometown of Kursk and a street there was named after him.

Vladimir Zalevskii – Captain Vladimir Nikolayevich Zalevskii was also in the 157th Fighter Regiment, which also included Andrei Borovykh (32 solo and 14 shared kills) and regiment commander Major Victor F. Volkhov (17 solo and 8 shared kills). Three of the five top aces involved in the northern defensive phase of the Battle of Kursk were from the 157th Fighter Regiment.

Vladimir Zalevskii was born on 15 July 1918 in Dekanskaya in the Donetsk region. He graduated from Junior High School and graduated from the flying club in 1937. He joined the army in 1937 and graduated from the Chuguyevsk Military Aviation School in 1940. At the start of the war, in June 1941, he was serving with the 157th Fighter Regiment, operating near Leningrad (now St. Petersburg). He is credited with destroying a Ju-88 by a double ramming strike on 27 August 1941 with his I-16. He was able to return to his airbase with his damaged plane. By April 1942 he had flown 149 sorties, conducted over 30 air battles and shot down 11 enemy aircraft. He was shot down one time behind enemy lines, was captured and escaped, killing his guard.[129] He was awarded the Hero of the Soviet Union on 30 January 1943.

At the start of Kursk, Captain Zalevskii was a deputy squadron commander. He was killed on the first day of the Battle of Kursk, 5 July 1943. He was credited with two kills that day before he was shot down in his Yak-7B. He had 23 solo kills to his credit and 17 shared victories, having flown over 300 sorties.

Stepan Kolesnichenko – Lt. Stepan Kalinovich Kolesnichenko was born 24 December 1913 in Grigoriopol, Odessa Oblast in what is now Moldovia. He worked as a tractor driver before he was drafted into the army in 1935 and choose to remain. In 1939 he graduated from the Odessa Aero Club, served in the Baltics in 1940 and then attended the Odessa Military Aviation Pilot School. When the war started he was evacuated to Kyrgystan, becoming a pilot later in 1941. In the spring of 1942 he was posted to the 519th Fighter Regiment on the West Front in April. Flying a Yak-7B at Kursk he claimed two victories on 5 July 1943 (an Me-110 and Fw-190) or three victories on the 6th (two Fw-190s and a Ju-88), depending on the source.[130] On 8 July he may have been the pilot who shot down German ace Hubert Strassl.[131] According to another source it was Captain Sulikov who shot him down.[132]

By mid-July he had claimed a total of 20 kills (four shared) in 114 sorties and 24 engagements, though he may have flown 135 sorties, 27 air battles, with 21 personal and 4 group kills by the time he was killed in action on 30 August 1943.[133] He was awarded the Order of the Red Banner and was posthumously awarded the Order of Lenin and Hero of the Soviet Union in September 1943.

Ivan Sidorov – Captain Ivan Dmitriyevich Sidorov was born 24 September 1916 in village of Svetlii Yar, near Stalingrad. He graduated from the 7th grade and joined the army in 1934. In 1937 he graduated from the 7th Stalingrad Military Aviation Pilot School and joined the Communist Party in 1941.

He was involved in the war since the beginning. At Kursk, he was a squadron commander. On 5 July he is credited with three kills, but his plane caught fire and he then rammed a German fighter.[134] He parachuted out but his parachute lines burned and he was killed. He was posthumously awarded the Hero of the Soviet Union on 2 September 1943. He was credited with 16 solo and 7 shared kills in 130 air battles and 400 sorties. A street was named after him in Stalingrad.

THE AIR BATTLE TO SUPPORT THE OFFENSIVE NORTH OF KURSK

Notes

1. Quote from Martin Nevshemal, *Objective Ponyri: Defeat of the XXXXI. Panzerkorps at Ponyri Train Station* (Leaping Horseman Books, Sydney, Australia, 2015), page 41. Time given in the original source was 0315.
2. The more common transliteration is Ponyri, with the "ы" in the Cyrillic alphabet transliterated as just a "y". See Appendix I for transliteration conventions.
3. Zetterling and Frankson, page 28. This count does not include Marders.
4. Zetterling and Frankson, page 28.
5. According to Robert Forczyk, *Kursk 1943: The Northern Front* (Osprey Publishing, Oxford, 2014), pages 24 and 29, the Ninth Army had 800 tanks and assault guns. Also see page 33. We have not done an independent tank count for the Ninth Army. According to our counts for the Army Group South attack, it started the offensive 1,426 tanks and assault guns; or 1,707 tanks, assault guns and tank-like armored fighting vehicles depending on how they are counted.
6. The 78th Assault Division also had an assault gun battalion.
7. Most of these were based upon three-gun batteries, vice the four-gun batteries in the south.
8. Krivosheyev reports that the Central Front strength was 738,000, with the report based upon the strength of 41 rifle divisions and four tank corps. Yet, the combat in the north was primary fought against 20 rifle divisions and the four tank corps. Krivosheyev reports the Voronezh Front strength as 534,700, but provides no strength for the Steppe Front. The Voronezh Front strength is based on 35 rifle divisions, one mechanized corps, four tank corps and six tank brigades, but this clearly includes the Thirty-eighth Army, which was only peripherally involved in the fighting. The Kursk Data Base records a total Soviet committed strength of 391,111 for the Voronezh at the start (4 July), but this is based upon a summation of the strength of all combat units and may not be directly comparable to the Krivosheyev figures. There were significant additional units added to the fight. See Krivosheyev, page 188.
9. This data is from a chart in the 1944 Soviet General Staff Study, Glantz and Orenstein (1997), page 183. While this author has not checked the veracity of the numbers, it serves to illustrate the difference, as it is assumed the Soviet staff officers used the same method of calculation for all the armies. The number of guns used for the calculations are shown and include 82mm and 120mm Mortars, 45mm, 57mm and 76mm antiaircraft and antitank guns, and 76mm, 122mm, 152mm and 203mm divisional artillery and "reinforcing guns." The chart also provides densities for the "enemy offensive front" for the Voronezh Front (100 kilometer front covering all of the Sixth Guards Army and most of the Seventh Guards Army with 50.6 tubes per kilometer) and for the Central Front (a 45–50 kilometer front covering the Thirteenth Army and parts of the Seventieth Army and Forty-eighth Army with 95 tubes per kilometer). These densities are higher than the densities for any of the armies as they include army second echelon and Front reserve artillery.
10. Glantz and Orenstein (1997), pages 180–182 and 185–189.
11. Hooton, *Eagle in Flames*, page 195. Bergstrom, *Kursk*, page 123, provides a 1 July 1943 calculation of 726. A lower figure of 686 "combat aircraft" is provided by Forczyk, pages 26 and 33. His figures are similar to Bergstrom's, less the Hs-126s and Fw-189s. They also disagree slightly in their total count of Ju-87s and Me-110s.
12. This part of the Sixth Air Fleet order of battle was drawn from Klink, page 335, and has not been cross-checked.
13. David M. Glantz and Harold S. Orenstein, translators and editors, *The Battle for Kursk 1943: The Soviet General Staff Study* (Routledge, New York, 2013), page 240.
14. T. N. Dupuy and Paul Martell, *Great Battles of the Eastern Front: The Soviet-German War, 1941–1945* (Bobbs-Merrill Company, Indianapolis, IN, 1982), page 82. Footnotes in this table are from the original table.
15. Includes three divisions (208th, 262nd and 271st) of night bombers.
16. Fighters of the IX Fighter Corps and the 26th and 101st fighter air division of the Air Defense of the Country also participated.
17. Participating night bombers of Long Range Aviation are not shown.
18. The actual count is 1,073 but there are no on-hand reports for the 50th Air Reconnaissance Regiment or the 272nd Independent Army Squadron. On 5 July, the 50th Air Reconnaissance Regiment flew 7 Pe-2s, to the total count of planes had to be at least 1,080.

ACES AT KURSK

19. From the report "Condition and Movements of Second Air Army's Aircraft Park, July, 1943. They list by unit the planes on-hand as of 1 July 1943. Fond: Second Air Army, Opis: 4196, Delo: 39, pages 15-16.
20. For example, see the chapter by Air Marshal Sergei Rudenko "The Gaining of Air Supremacy and Air Operations in the Battle of Kursk" in *The Battle of Kursk* (Progress Press Publishers, USSR, 1974), page 189.

    Sergei Rudenko was the commander of the Sixteenth Air Army during the Battle of Kursk. Many of these types of article were ghost written by staff or professional Soviet-era historians and the involvement of the senior commander in research and preparation varied widely. As such, the statistics and stories presented in these accounts are often consistent across various sources. For example, see the claims of German sortie counts on page 193.
21. This is the "Movement of 17th Air Army's Units, July 5-25, 1943." It provided a count of on-hand aircraft for 5 July 1943 of 735 and a count of on-hand aircraft from 25 July, 1943 of 529. Fond: Second Air Army, Opis; 6518, Delo: 28, page 89.

    Comparing this particular report to the more detailed order of battle in Chapter 2: they record 70 TB-3s with the 244th Bomber Division vice 76 TB-3s and 3 U-2s, 64 planes (8 R-5s and 56 U-2s) with the 262nd Night Bomber Division vice 62, 172 planes (69 Yak-1s and 103 Il-2s) with the I Mixed Corps vice 156, 162 planes (49 Yak-1s, 21 La-5s, 92 Il-2s) with the III Mixed Corps vice 150, and 267 planes (79 La-5s and 188 Il-2s) with the IX Mixed Corps vice 262. Their total is 735 (which matches Dupuy and Martell) vice the 750 given in the order of battle presented in Chapter 2.

    This July summary report does not record the 41 Pe-2s and U-2s with the two reconnaissance regiments, the 403rd Ind. Squadron or the 371st Transport Regiment. The July summery report also does not record the 11 U-2s with the III Mixed Corps, IX Mixed Corps and 244th Bomber Division.
22. Pawel Monat with John Dille, *Spy in the U.S.* (Berkley Publishing Corporation, New York, 1963, originally published in 1961 by Harper and Row). His name Paul Martell was derived from Charles Martel (Charles the Hammer), the Frankish leader famous for winning the Battle of Tours in 732 AD.
23. Glantz and Orenstein (2013), pages 240-241.
24. We have the II and III/3rd Fighter Wing with 65 Me-109s, the I, III and HQ/52nd Fighter Wing with 80 Me-109s, the HQ, I, III, IV/51st Fighter Wing with 148 Fw-190s and the IV/54th Fighter Wing with 38 Fw-190s for a total of 145 fighters in the south and 186 fighters in the north.
25. We have the 1st Ground Attack Wing with 85 Fw-190s. There were 55 Me-110s in the north in the "destroyer" wing. There were also at least 18 Me-110s in the south. This was 8 Me-110s with the 6th Close Range Reconnaissance Group and 10 Me-110s with the night fighter group in the south. In the north there were 8 Me-110s and 31 Me-109s in the reconnaissance squadrons. There were also some Me-110s in the night fighter group in the north.
26. Forczyk, page 34.
27. According to Bergstrom, *Kursk*, page 37, and *Black Cross, Red Star*, page 214, the German Air Force cancelled the opening air strike in the north, even though it was planned for and this planning is documented (see page 35 of *Kursk*). This is in accordance with a post-war interview conducted with Gerhard Beaker, a captain with III/1st Bomber Wing.

    According to Writer #762, an opening air strike was conducted. Writer #762 has been identified as Major General Friedrich Kless, who during the battle was the Chief of Staff of the Sixth Air Fleet: see page xiii, Steven H. Newton, *Kursk: The German View* (Da Capo Press, Cambridge, MA, 2002). Also see pages 162-163 for an account of the actions on 5 July. The German records on these air operations are sparse.

    It is possible that this strike was not particularly large and effective. Being hit with a first strike is not discussed in Soviet-era or recent Russian secondary sources. This probably needs to be thoroughly checked with Russian primary sources.
28. Writer #762, page 174.
29. Note that for the 11th through the 18th of July for both the Sixth Air Fleet and the VIII Air Corps, the sortie count is listed at "Feindfluge," meaning enemy sorties. We believe that this is repeated typo and they are indeed reporting their own sorties, along with some details on them. Especially as some of these more detailed listing includes count of dive bombing sorties (and the Soviet air force did not use dive bombers) and "destroyer" sorties (also not used by the Soviet air force, and reports of bombing attacks in Soviet held areas. The format for these reports are the same as the previous reports. The report for 12.7 actually provides a date of "12.6" in a report dated 13 July 1943. Obviously, another typo.

    See the NARA files for the Second Army T312, R1242, starting page 732.

THE AIR BATTLE TO SUPPORT THE OFFENSIVE NORTH OF KURSK

30. This Sixth Air Fleet's area of operation covered the entire Orel bulge, not just the area of the offensive operation. Some missions listed here obviously were outside of the areas of the German offensive, especially the reconnaissance missions.
31. The figure of "36" is almost unreadable on my copy and this may be an incorrect reading.
32. The total for the given missions is only 889, which is 44 less than the total that they give (which is incorrectly labeled "Feindfluge"). Most likely there were 44 transport missions unreported.
33. Note in the report states "65 with a bomb"
34. Note in the report states "13 Jabo"
35. Glantz and Orenstein (2013), page 247. The total number of sorties provided for the 16th Air Army adds up to only 447, vice the 464 reported. This is an error in the original 1944 Soviet General Staff study.
36. Glantz and Orenstein (2013), pages 257-258.
37. Glantz and Orenstein (2013), page 260.
38. Khazanov, page 135, lists the number of combat sorties flown "north of Kursk area" from 5 to 11 July. While the number of daytime sorties by Sixteenth Air Army agrees with the Soviet General Staff study figures, as does the number of Long Range Aviation Sorties, the number of night time sorties is about half of what is reported in the General Staff study. He reports for night times sorties respectively 85, 200, 212, 173, 145, 173 and 176 for a total of 1,164 (vice 1,942). The reason for this difference is not known.

    For 9 July he reports 956 daytime sorties for the Sixteenth Air Army while the total number of day and nighttime sorties is reported here at 956. This appears to be typo on their part.

    For the German Sixth Air Fleet, his report of daytime sorties agrees with the data in Table 7.1. His nighttime sorties in his table is off by a day. So for example, the Germans flew 15 sorties on the night of 5/6 July, he lists their nighttime sorties for 5 July as 0 and their nighttime sorties for 6 July as 15. Furthermore, for the night of 8/9 July, the Germans report flying 6 sorties while he has them flying 0 sorties for the night of 9 July. For the night of 9/10 July the German report flying 22 sorties (3 listed as bombing and harassing) while he has them flying 3 sorties for the night of 10 July.
39. The actual day-by-day comparison for daytime sorties is:

Date	Sixth Air Fleet Report	Soviet General Staff Study Report	Difference (Soviet/German)
5 July	2,088 – 28 = 2,060	2,257	1.10
6 July	1,023 – 21 = 1,002	1,162	1.16
7 July	1,687 – 26 = 1,661	1,203	0.72
8 July	1,173 – 57 = 1,116	933	0.84
9 July	877 – 87 = 790	350	0.44
10 July	1,136 – 75 = 1,061	955	0.90
11 July	933 – 44? = 889	680	0.76
12 July	1,111 – 0 = 1,111	72	0.06

    A similar comparison for the night action (5 July = night of 5/6 July):

Date	Sixth Air Fleet Report	Soviet General Staff Study Report	Difference (Soviet/German)
5 July	15	24	1.60
6 July	92	32	0.35
7 July	134	41	0.31
8 July	6	58	9.67
9 July	22	16	0.73
10 July	51	5	0.10
11 July	21	11	0.52
12 July	15	7	0.47
Totals	306	194	0.63

40. Glantz and Orenstein (2013), page 263.
41. 1,800 (for troop cover) and 2,057 (to accompany assault aircraft and bombers)
42. Glantz and Orenstein (2013), page 266.
43. For example, the maximum bomb load of an Il-2 is 600 kilograms. The maximum bomb load of a U-2 is 250 kilograms. Then there is the difference in effectiveness of a ground attack mission in the day, where it can see the potential targets and identify the best areas of attack compared to the night. Then there is actual accuracy of the day time bombing compared to nighttime bombing. Finally, daytime

bombing often tends to occur more near the front line in the area of combat, whereas nighttime bombing tends to occur against positioned resting units. As such, their effect on the combat is different. Furthermore, daytime bombing often catches units in the open or on the move, while nighttime bombing tends to catch units in prepared positions where they are encamped for the night. The difference in overall effectiveness is significant. The main advantage of nighttime bombing is its harassment value, in that it keeps people awake and has some impact on morale and fatigue.

44. There are a total of 2,082 LRA sorties. Of all sorties done by the other armies, 52% were nighttime sorties (7055/13,539 = .5211). Assuming the same split applies to the LRA, then it might be 997 daytime sorties and 1,085 nighttime sorties. We have not located any reports for daytimes sorties at this time by Long Range Aviation.
45. Glantz and Orenstein (2013), page 258.
46. Glantz and Orenstein (2013), page 259.
47. Three accounts that go into more depth for each day is Bergstrom's *Kursk: The Air Battle: July 1943* (1995), pages 34-55 and 70-73; Khazanov (2010), pages 18-34, and Bergstrom's *Black Cross, Red Star, Volume 5* (2020), pages 214-221 and 251-269.
48. See Bergstrom, *Kursk* (1995), pages 38 and 39.
49. See Khazanov, page 22.
50. Forczyk, page 49.
51. Claim is according to Khazanov, page 22. There is some doubt about the accuracy of these claims.
52. On page 24 of Khazanov, he claims that the Germans dropped 1,500 tons of bombs on the Soviets while Soviet aviation dropped a little more than one-twelfth of that amount on the Germans. Not sure what data was used to make this comparison.
53. Khazanov, page 24, provides a somewhat different ratio of sorties per plane. He states that "the number of combat sorties per each serviceable attack aircraft amount to less than one on the first day of battle, while day bombers featured a ratio of one combat sorties per two serviceable aircraft." There were 105 bombing sorties and according to the Soviet General Staff study 260 operational bombers. He also states that "The average number of combat missions flown by a serviceable German fighter that day amounted to three and a half sorties, while and average Soviet fighter flew just over two missions." These sortie rates seem high and cannot be recreated from the figures that I have. We can only assume he is using a different (lower) count of serviceable aircraft than provided by the Soviet General Staff study, but have not identified where that count is from.

    He also states that "Each combat-ready He 111 or Ju 88 in service with the German 1st Air Division conducted three to four sorties, and each Ju 87 carried out at least four to five sorties." Again, we cannot confirm the accuracy of these calculations.
54. Glantz and Orenstein (2013), pages 257-258.
55. See Bergstrom, *Kursk* (1995), pages 41. These are taken from the Luftwaffe quartermaster files and show 29 aircraft "put out of commission due to either unknown reasons or hostile action on 5 July 1943, and of those, 18 were total losses."
56. The losses for the 5th and 6th were reported as 188 planes according to the Soviet General Staff study. Christer Bergstrom, from the records he drew from the archives on the Sixteenth Air Army, reports 100 planes lost on the 5th and 91 lost on the 6th.

    The report of a 100 aircraft lost by Sixteenth Air Army includes the breakdown of 83 fighters, 16 Il-2s and one Boston. They also report that the VI Fighter Corps lost 51 fighters this day. This is drawn from Bergstrom, *Kursk*, page 40, who draws these two reports from "TsAMO, f. 16 VA, op. 6476, d. 169", meaning from the Sixteenth Air Army's archival records. He reports that the Sixteenth Air Army lost 91 planes on the 6th, 22 Il-21s, 9 Bostons and 60 fighters.

    The report from the Soviet General Staff study of 188 planes lost on 5/6 July is probably a little lower than actual losses based upon our comparison with the losses of the Second Air Army records to the claimed losses in the Soviet General Staff study (see Glantz and Orenstein, Table 28 from page 253). The staff study gives the total losses for the 5th - 18th as 371: 172 fighters, 31 bombers, and 168 assault. We have the Second Air Army's losses for 5 - 18 1943, taken from their daily reports, as 481 (See Table II.27 of this book). This includes 248 fighters, 48 bombers, 180 assault and 5 night bombers. So actual losses of the Second Air Army were 28% higher than what was reported in the Soviet General Staff study.

    One does wonder about the process where even the internal classified post-operation staff studies understate their losses (in additional to many other errors). They did have the unit records available to

THE AIR BATTLE TO SUPPORT THE OFFENSIVE NORTH OF KURSK

them. In particular, the table is vastly off on 5 July when the Second Air Army lost 114 planes and the Soviet General Staff study reports only 78, but it consistently underreports for every single day. They also do not report the losses for the Seventeenth Air Army, which according to our count was another 182 or 221 planes lost (see Tables II.29 and Tables II.30). This does argue that the reported losses for the Sixteenth Air Army may be low compared to reality.

The figure of 91 aircraft lost on the 6th is from Bergstrom, *Kursk*, page 48, who draws this report probably from "TsAMO f. 16 VA, op. 6476, d. 169," the same as the previous references. Khazanov, page 26, reports the same figure. Based upon these reports the Soviet losses for the 5th and 6th were 191 planes, which is three greater than Soviet General Staff study figures. These higher figures were used.

Khazanov reports that the VI Fighter Corps lost only 45 aircraft this day (see Khazanov, page 24) compared to the claim of 51 fighter lost given by Bergstrom. He also reports for the 6th that the VI Fighter Corps lost a total of 81 aircraft and 58 pilots from the start of the battle, meaning for the 5th and the 6th (page 27).

57. Based upon the Luftwaffe air liaison officer's claim of 13 lost planes. It could have been as high as 29 planes "put out of action" from all causes based upon the Luftwaffe quartermaster reports, which would still give an exchange ratio of around 4-to-1. The figure of 29 "put out of action" is from Bergstrom, *Kursk*, page 40.
58. Khazanov, page 24, gives the German losses as 13 aircraft shot down "behind the front line", and 33 more sustained heavy damage, with 22 of them being written off later on. This estimate of 35 planes lost appears high.

These figures look like an attempt to integrate the air liaison reporting with the quartermaster reporting. It does appear to overstate German losses and may be adding the losses reported by the air liaison officer and the quartermaster together. As shown in Appendix II, these reports do not always integrate well. This does lead to the odd statement that "Given the fierce resistance offered by the Soviet anti-aircraft artillery; the ratio of irreplaceable losses suffered in air engagements can be assessed as 4:5." I do not think there is much validity in this conclusion.

59. Khazanov, page 24.
60. The claim of 98 is from Khazanov, page 24, while the claim of 100 is from Bergstrom, *Kursk*, page 40. I gather both figures come from primarily Soviet sources. Khazanov has the VI Fighter Corps losing 45 aircraft while Bergstrom has them losing 51 fighters.
61. This reduction in German claims is according to Khazanov, page 24. He does state that "the Luftwaffe aces" claimed 166 air victories.
62. Bergstrom, *Kursk*, page 40, has him with 15 victories this day. Khazanov, page 24, also has him with 15. This count of 15 is also provided in the list in the *Aces of the Luftwaffe* webpage by Petr Kacha (http://www.luftwaffe.cz/).
63. Khazanov, pages 25-26.
64. Quote from Rudenko directly from Bergstrom, *Kursk*, page 40. It is taken from Rudenko's book, *Kryliya Pobedyy*, page 163. This book was published in the Soviet Union in 1976. Needless to say, there were limits as to what they could write. The different spelling of Rokossovskii is due to differing transliteration conventions.
65. Quote from Rudenko directly from Bergstrom, *Kursk*, page 42. It is taken from Rudenko's book, *Kryliya Pobedyy*, page 164.
66. For example, see Bergstrom, *Kursk*, page 42 and Khazanov, page 26. Khazanov has an initial strike of 25 Bostons from 221st Bomber Division escorted by the same number of Yaks from the 282nd Fighter Division. He has this as "the first of four strikes" against the German XLVII and XLI Panzer Corps. He has additional strikes also conducted by attack aircraft from the 2nd Guards Assault Division and 299th Assault Division, escorted by fighters from the 283rd and 286th Fighter Divisions.

Bergstrom, *Kursk*, pages 42-44 has four waves. The first was the 221st Bomber Division escorted by 282nd Fighter Division. The second wave was the 2nd Guards Assault Division escorted by the 283rd Fighter Division. He reports that the 2nds Guards Assault Division lost 15 Il-2s in their morning attack. The third wave comes in after 0500 (Berlin time). It appears to consists of again the 221st Bomber Division escorted by the 282nd Fighter Division. The next wave arrived after 0700 (Berlin time) and consisted of the 299th Assault Division and the 286th Fighter Division. This last wave apparently encountered little resistance.
67. Bergstrom, *Kursk*, page 44. Khazanov, page 26 states that "in a number of cases such bomb strikes managed to hit friendly troops," implying that is occurred more than once.

68. Bergstrom, *Kursk*, page 48.
69. Quartermaster claims are from Bergstrom, *Kursk,* page 48.
70. This figure is from Bergstrom, *Kursk*, page 47 and Khazanov, page 26.
71. Bergstrom, *Kursk*, page 47, has him with three kills but this may not be a complete accounting for the day. Khazanov, page 27, has him with ten kills. The list from *Aces of the Luftwaffe* webpage by Petr Kacha shows 4 kills this day.
72. Bergstrom, *Kursk,* page 47.
73. Bergstrom, *Kursk*, page 49, has Long Range Aviation doing 495 sorties with 238 crews. His source is N. S. Skripko, *Po tselyam blizhnim i dal'nim*. Moscow: Voyenizdat, 1981.
74. Nevshemal, pages 37, 63, 79, 93, 105, 119, and 125.
75. The Seventeenth Air Army, which was further away and only partially engaged, flew 448 daytime sorties on 5 July with a plane count of 735 and lost 75 planes this day.
76. See Bergstrom, *Kursk*, page 53, who states "The air fighting on 7 July…cost 16 VA a loss of 30 aircraft." Later on the page he states "Both sides greatly exaggerated the enemy's losses in the air in the air on 7 July…compared with 16 VA's actual losses of 43 aircraft."
77. See Bergstrom, *Kursk,* page 53.
78. Shot-down from Khazanov, page 141.
79. This is based upon the list from *Aces of the Luftwaffe* webpage by Petr Kacha. It shows 15 victories on the 5th, 4 victories on the 6th, 6 victories on the 7th, and 5 victories on the 8th.

    Khazanov, page 24, credits him with 15 kills on the 5th and on page 27 with 10 kills on the 6th. Bergstrom, *Kursk*, on page 40, also states that he shot down 15 planes on the 5th, on page 40 reports at least 3 victories, and on page 53 records him with 7 victories on the 7th and implies he scored 5 victories in the 8th. But in the next paragraph Bergstrom states (on page 53) "On the first day of Operation *Zitadelle*, he [Strassl] is credited with 11 kills, followed by three on 6 July and six on the seventh (These figures are based on the RLM victory register at the Bundesachiv/Militararchiv; other figures in other printed sources appear to be based on second-hand sources).
80. Bergstrom, *Kursk,* page 55.
81. Fifteenth Air Army sorties are from Bergstrom, *Kursk*, page 55.
82. Plane identification and location of shoot down from Khazanov, page 141.
83. Bergstrom, *Kursk*, page 55.
84. Bergstrom, *Kursk*, page 55, claims and losses both drawn from Sixteenth Air Army records.
85. This account of the bombing missions on Saborovka is drawn primarily from Bergstrom, *Kursk,* page 70.
86. The Soviets reported losing 188 planes on the 5th and 6th while the Germans claimed 295 from aerial combat and flak (14 from flak) for those two days. The Soviets reported losing 87 planes on the 7th and 8th while the Germans claims 154 from aerial combat and flak (13 from flak) for those two days. These two estimates overestimate Soviet losses by a factor of 1.6 and 1.8 respectively.
87. Bergstrom, *Kursk*, page 71.
88. Bergstrom, *Kursk*, page 71, the source of this report is credited to N. S. Skripko, *Po tselyam blizhnim i dal'nim*. Moscow: Voyenizdat, 1981.
89. Khazanov, page 31. Specifically, 107 fighters were delivered to the 234th Fighter Division, of which 67 were in "combat ready condition." Do not know the source of his data.
90. Chart is from Khazanov, page 31. His source is not known, but the first two columns of the chart matches the figures provided by the Soviet General Staff study.
91. All these statistics are from Khazanov, page 31.
92. Bergstrom, *Kursk*, page 71. The actual timing of the raid is given as "shortly before noon" and a report from Second Tank Army is says "In the afternoon of 10 July…"
93. Both the Luftwaffe liaison officer and the Luftwaffe quartermaster report records seven losses. From the liaison officer report it is 2 He-11s, 1 Ju-87, 2 Me-110s and 2 Fw-190s. The quartermaster report (source: Bergstrom, *Kursk*, page 73) lists 2 He-111s, 2 Me-110s and 3 Fw-190s.
94. Bergstrom, *Kursk,* page 71.
95. See Bergstrom, *Kursk*, page 73 and Khazanov, page 31.
96. Quartermaster report from Bergstrom, *Kursk*, page 73.
97. Khazanov, page 33. He says "must have been" shot down by Kirov.
98. Khazanov, page 141.

THE AIR BATTLE TO SUPPORT THE OFFENSIVE NORTH OF KURSK

99. This figure of 391 was provided by both Bergstrom, *Kursk*, page 73 and Khazanov, pages 33 and 72.
100. Quartermaster reports are from Bergstrom, *Kursk*, page 73.
101. See Khazanov, page 72. His estimates are not footnoted. He also overestimates German losses in the south.
102. Bergstrom, *Kursk*, page 73. Source of the Soviet claim is given as Prussikov, page 100. This is either G. K. Prussikov, *16-ya vozdushnaya: Voyenno-istoricheskiy ocherk o boyevom puti 16-y vozdushnoy armii 1942-1945*. Moscow, Voyenizdat, 1973 or *Doletim do Odera*. Moscow: Voyenizdat, 1985.
103. This figure of 391 was provided by both Bergstrom, *Kursk*, page 73 and Khazanov, pages 33 and 72. Without access to the Sixteenth Air Army records, it is hard to confirm. We suspect the real number is probably a little higher than this figure. Khazanov does estimate irreplaceable Soviet losses in the south at 371 for the Second Air Army and over 200 for the Seventeenth Air Army. Our counts, based upon their records are 485 (including four planes on 4 July) for the Second Air Army and 182 or 221 for the Seventeenth Air Army depending on which set of figures are used. See Tables II.27, II.29 and II.30 of this book.
104. The report for 5-9 July is from Khazanov, page 31. The report for 5-12 July is from Khazanov, page 33 and from Bergstrom, *Kursk*, page 73. His source is Khazanov and Gorbach: D. B. Khazanov and V. G. Gorbach. *Aviatsiya v bitve nad Orlovsko-Kurskoy dugoy*. Moscow, 2004.
105. Total lost is given as 391 with 48 damaged aircraft written off as destroyed for a total loss of 439. There were 283 aircraft reported as lost between 5-8 July. That leaves 108 aircraft lost for 9-11 July. The Germans claim 450 aircraft shot down in air combat, by flak and in night operations from the 5th through the 8th. This is 1.59 as many as the Soviets report losing (a 59% overclaiming). They claim 85 planes for the 9th, 75 planes for the 10th and 42 planes for the 11th. This is 202 claims kills compared to 108 losses, or an overclaiming of 1.87 times. Therefore, it was decided to simply distribute the 108 losses across those three days in the same ratio as the German kill claims.
106. They report 11 planes that made emergency landing due to battle damage. These are not counted in the totals below.
107. The Soviets claimed 52 German kills this day. Soviets often claim more kills than they lose.
108. *The Voyenno-Istoricheskii Zhurnal* [Military History Journal], 1968, Number 6. "Dokumentyi i Materialyi: Kurskaya Bitva v Tsifrakh."
109. T312, R1243, page 97
110. We did do a comparison of the losses from Second Air Army records to the claimed losses in the Soviet General Staff study (see Glantz and Orenstein, Table 28 from page 253). The staff study has the total losses for the 5th - 18th as 371: 172 fighters, 31 bombers, and 168 assault. We have the Second Air Army's losses for 5 to 18 July 1943, taken from their daily reports, as 481 (See Table II.27 of this book). This includes 248 fighters, 48 bombers, 180 assault and 5 night bombers. So actual losses of the Second Air Army were 28% higher than what was reported in the Soviet General Staff study.

    One does wonder about the process where even the internal classified post-operation staff studies understate their losses (in additional to many other errors). They did have the unit records available to them. In particular, the table is vastly off on 5 July when the Second Air Army lost 114 planes and the Soviet General Staff study reports only 78, but it consistently underreports for every single day. They also do not report the losses for the Seventeenth Air Army, which according to our count was another 182 or 221 planes lost (see Tables II.29 and Tables II.30). This does argue that the reported losses for the Sixteenth Air Army may be low compared to reality.
111. This order of battle is taken primarily from Bergstrom, *Kursk*, page 123. Some German nomenclature were translated into English. Khazanov, page 129, was used to identify the variants of the planes (i.e. Hs-126 B vice Hs-126). The rank of Major Nordmann was changed to reflect that he was not promoted to Lt. Colonel until 1 August 1943.
112. Bergstrom has the unit commanded by Capt. Helmut Krebs. Khazanov, page 129, has the leader of I/StG 1 as Major H. Kaubisch. According to the website Luftwaffe Officer Career Summaries by Henry L. deZeng IV and Douglas G. Stankey, Major Helmuth Krebs commanded I/StG I from 17 June to 15 July 1943.
113. Khazanov, page 129, has the leader of II/StG 1 as Major O. Ernst. According to the website Luftwaffe Officer Career Summaries, Capt. Frank Neubert was in commander of the II/StG 1 from 2 October 1942 to September 1943.
114. Bergstrom has the unit commanded by Major Bernhard Hamester. Khazanov, page 129, has the III/StG 3 as Capt. E. Jacob. According to the website Luftwaffe Officer Career Summary Hamester was

in command of St.G. 102 at this time. The website has Capt. Eberhard Jacob appointed provisional commander of III/StG 3 from 17 June to 18 October 1943.

115. This order of battle is taken primarily from Bergstrom, *Kursk*, page 126. Some Soviet abbreviations were translated into English. Some of the names were expanded (usually adding their middle initial) based upon the order of battle provided in Khazanov, page 129.
116. Khazanov, pages 129 and 131 lists the commander as Col. A. M. Ryazanov, with the note that LtC Yurii M. Berkal took over from 17 July 1943. Bergstrom, *Kursk*, page 126 has the commander as "Col. Yurii Berkal."
117. This plane type is from Khazanov, pages 129 and 131. It is not listed in the Bergstrom order of battle.
118. This listing it taken from Bergstrom, *Kursk*, pages 130-131. The analysis of it is our own.
119. Bergstrom, *Kursk*, pages 40, 50, 53, 54, 71 and 73 indicate at least 24 kills, 8 on 5 July, 7 on 7 July, 1 on 8 July, 5 on 10 July and 3 on 11 July. There may have been other claims during this time period. Because of the Sixth Air Fleet habit of overclaiming kills by 50%, some of these claims are suspect. It does appear that at least three of the claims on 7 July are not correct (see Bergstrom, *Kursk*, page 50).
120. Shore, page 329, states that by March 1944, Volkhov had 23 victories (8 shared). This claim of 8 shared is also mention in http://www.warheroes.ru/hero/hero.asp?Hero_id=4038 of him having by March 1944 shot down 15 aircraft and 8 shared. That same site says that by the end of the war, he had personally shot down 17 enemy aircraft (but does not mention the shared kills).
121. http://www.luftwaffe.cz/strassl.html. This listing is from the *Aces of the Luftwaffe* webpage by Petr Kacha (http://www.luftwaffe.cz).
122. Claims are based upon the listing in Wikipedia: Otto Kittel, as drawn from the work of air historians Matthews and Foreman, and cross checked to air historians Prien, Stemmer, Rodeike and Bock.
123. "Home leave" is according to Bergstrom, *Kursk*, page 53.
124. *The Luftwaffe, 1933-1945* website (www.ww2.dk) records him with the 2/JG 54 on 9 February 1942.
125. Bio mostly drawn from Bergstrom, *Kursk*, pages 40, 50, 53, 54, 71, 73, 87, 88, 92 and 103.
126. This is from *The Luftwaffe, 1933-1945* website (www.ww2.dk). They also note that he had "c.70 combat missions" vice exactly 70.
127. Mostly drawn from Bergstrom, *Kursk*, page 53. Bergstrom, *Kursk*, page 53, states that he had 42 victories by 4 July. There is a contradiction here, for it he had scored 42 victories by 4 July, and 30 victories between 5-8 July, then how is his career total 67? Bergstrom does state on page 40 that he scored 15 victories on 5 July and states on page 53 that he claimed 11 kills on 5 July, 3 of 6 July and 6 on 7 July.
128. This is in accordance with the War Heroes website: http://www.warheroes.ru/hero/hero.asp?Hero_id=253. According to Polak, page 95, he flew nearly 600 sorties and had 150 engagements.
129. Source is War Heroes website: http://www.warheroes.ru/hero/hero.asp?Hero_id=559
130. Polak, page 166 and Seidl, page 107. Also see the Order of Battle for the Sixteenth Air Army.
131. For one description of the air battle see Bergstrom, *Kursk*, page 55
132. Khazanov, page 29, provides a more detailed description of the air battle but credits the kill to Captain Sulikov. I have not any further data on Captain Sulikov.
133. Polak, page 166 and Seidl, page 107. Polak reports the claims for the 5th while Seidl reports the claims for the 6th. The total claims reported in Seidl account exceeds 20 kills. They are 6 kills through 30 October 1942, 12 kills and 3 shared kills in April 1943, 4 Fw-190 destroyed in ground attacks, 3 kills on 16 May 1943, 3 kills on 6 July 1943 and 1 kill on 8 July 1943 for a total of 25 kills, 3 shared kills and 4 planes destroyed on the ground. The War Heroes website has either 16 personal and 4 group kills; or 135 sorties, 27 air battles, 21 personal and 4 group kills.
134. Note that Shores, page 294, claims he brought one German plane down by ramming but was killed doing so. The War Heroes website (http://www.warheroes.ru/hero/hero.asp?Hero_id=379) claims that his plane had been hit and then rammed a German fighter.

Chapter Eight

THE SOVIET COUNTEROFFENSIVES
12–14 July 1943

> *To hurry with the counterblow, when the situation has not yet ripened for it, means to prematurely exhaust all one's opportunities for continuing the struggle while it is still going on and has not yet reached its culmination point. This may often place the entire defense under danger of a complete defeat.*
>
> Brigade Commander Georgii S. Isserson, 1938[1]

On the morning of 12 July 1943 the Soviets launched a counteroffensive along the entire German line in the south. At the same time, they launched an offensive by the Western Front and the Central Front on the German positions north of Orel.

The offensive in the south was conducted across the entire front. In the far south, the Seventh Guards Army attacked the German Corps Raus, now with three infantry divisions, and the German III Panzer Corps. In the center the Soviet Sixth Guards Army, the Sixty-Ninth Army, the newly arriving Fifth Guards Army and the Fifth Guards Tank Army attacked the III Panzer Corps and the SS Panzer Corps. On the Soviet right, to the west, the Sixth Guards Army and the First Tank Army attacked the German XVIII Panzer Corps.

These attacks started in the morning at different times across the front, with some major Soviet attacks in the center starting around 0830 (Moscow time). The weather across the front in the morning was poor, so the nature and degree of air support was initially limited. The weather did clear some during the morning so there was more activity in the afternoon. Still, much of the initial Soviet offensives that day were resolved before the afternoon, so it is hard to say how much air was initially involved in the fighting that morning between the SS Panzer Corps and the Fifth Guards Army and the Fifth Guards Tank Army.

That said, the level of German air support on 12 July was lower than it has been for any other day of the battle. On the 5th the VIII Air Corps flew 2,387 sorties, on the 11th they flew 1,039 sorties. Yet for the 12th, they reported flying only 654 sorties during the day. This was the lowest number of sorties they had flown in a day since the offensive began.

Soviet air support was also restrained. On the 5th the Second and Seventeenth Air Armies flew 1,688 sorties. On the 11th they flew only 588 sorties into the battle area. For the 12th, they reported flying 887 sorties in the battle area during the day, 769 by the Second Air

Army and only 118 sorties by the Seventeenth Air Army. This was the first day since the start of the battle that the Soviet air armies had flown more sorties into the battle area than the VIII Air Corps.

But the nature of the Soviet sorties was such that there was limited ground support. There were 495 fighter sorties, and only 354 ground attack type sorties. In contrast the Germans had 191 fighter sorties and 411 ground attack type sorties (150 stuka, 13 bombing and 248 ground attack). Although the Soviet army was on the offensive in the south, the Germans had more support from their ground attack type aircraft.

While the fighting on the ground on 12 July was some of most intense and bloody fighting of the battle, the fighting in the air was much less so.

12 July

The night leading up to the famous Battle of Prokhorovka was unexceptional. The Germans flew 61 sorties. This included the nightly attack on the rail, now done by seven bomber sorties. They attacked the Staryii Oskol railroad station, which they claimed was left burning and the rails were broken. They also flew 49 harassing bomber sorties against villages and vehicle traffic in the Koren River area.

The Soviets continued their night bombing activity as before, with the 208th Bomber Division bombing the area of Pokrovka-Gremuchii-Bolshiye – Mayachki-Yakovlevo-Dubovoye-Pogorelovka-Malyie – Mayachki-Ryilskii-Krasnaya – Polyana-Luchki (north) and the adjacent ravines, with 101 U-2 sorties while conducting reconnaissance with eight R-5 sorties. The 262nd Night Bomber Division attacked in the area of Belovskaya, Razumnoye, Krutoi Log and Maslova Pristan as well as the river crossings along the Solomino-Bezlyudovka area. This totaled another 140 U-2 bombing sorties and 16 R-5 reconnaissance sorties. They continued to be assisted by the 244th Bomber Division, which hit the Verkhnyii Olshanets-Razumnoye-Kazachye area with 24 TB-3 bombing sorties. As they did the previous night, they also flew three reconnaissance sorties.[2]

According to secondary sources, there were no night bombing attacks by Long Range Aviation in the Belgorod-Prokhorovka area as their bombers were assigned to conduct raids against the areas north of Kursk and Orel in preparation of the Soviet counteroffensive.[3]

The Second Air Army reported that the weather was cloudy at night with intermittent rain, and visibility of six to ten kilometers. It was also cloudy during the day, with visibility of four to ten kilometers, and rain. Some authors claim that the weather in the morning was particularly poor and therefore the Second Air Army was unable to sortie until 1000.[4] We do not have supporting data to clarify those claims, but as the Fifth Guards Army and the Fifth Guards Tank Army both initiated their attacks at 0830 in the morning, it would mean that the first hour and a half of fighting was done without air support by either side.

During the day, the Germans flew only 654 sorties. They were only able to fly 13 bomber sorties because of the weather. Instead, their air support was provided by 150 stuka sorties and 248 ground attack sorties. This was the lowest level of air support that the Germans had provided to the army since the start of the offensive. This, on the day of the highest drama! This effort was capped with only 191 fighter sorties and again the Germans took heavy losses, 11 aircraft, although the air liaison records do not record the losses by type. The quartermaster records only report 6 planes lost, 1 Ju-52, 1 Fw-189, 1 Fw-190, 2 Hs-129s and 1 Me-109.[5]

The Soviet air was still active this day, although most of the strikes occurred well behind the front line. The I Assault Corps launched massed strikes with Il-2s in the Yakovlevo-Luchki (south)-Kalinin-Malyie – Mayachki-Veselyii-Sukho-Solotino-Krasnaya – Polyana-Pokrovka-Shlyakhovo-Melekhovo-Verkhnyaya Olshanka area. They sent up 72 Il-2s to conduct 142 sorties and 38 Yak-1s to provide 101 escort sorties. This increased effort was at a cost of eight Il-2s and a Yak-1. The 291st Assault Division attacked the area of Pokrovka-Yakovlevo-Bolshiye Mayachki-Luchki-Verkhopenye-Syirtsevo-Dmitrievka-Novo-Cherkasskoye and the woods south of Dubrava-Lukhanino-Gremuchii. They sent up 30 Il-2s to conduct 78 sorties and 16 Yak-1s to provide 46 escort sorties. This was at a cost of four Il-2s.

AIR SUPPORT OVER THE TANK FIELDS OF PROKHOROVKA

The legend of Prokhorovka includes not only a swirling tank battle on the ground, but an equally swirling air battle overhead, amid the majesty of overcast skies and dramatic thunderclouds and lighting. This is the scene displayed in the diorama in the Belgorod Museum. It is correct as far as the weather goes.

The German and Soviet air battle over the battlefield at Prokhorovka on 12 July was limited. On 5 July, the Germans flew 1,942 ground attack type sorties (stuka, assault, bombing and ground attack sorties). On the 12th they flew only 411. On 5 July, the Soviet Second and Seventeenth Air Army flew 486 such ground attack type sorties, which is the most they did during the German offensive. On the 12th they flew 354 (see Table 10.1). So, while the Germans flew four times as many ground attack sorties as the Soviets did on 5 July, by the 12th, the level of activity had declined to being almost equal. For the Germans this was certainly being driven by weather conditions, as on the 14th they flew 1,131 ground attack sorties. On 12 July, German ground attack sorties were the lowest they had been since the start of the offensive, which had produced more than 1,200 ground attack sorties a day for the first five days of the offensive. The weight of German air support on the 12th was a fraction of what it had been on previous days.

Of the German 411 ground-attack type sorties this day, 150 were stuka sorties. As two stuka groups supported the Germans' morning defense, this could lead to the conclusion that the Stukas only sortied in mass once during this day. The reports from the other sectors of the battlefield records little German air activity (by either side). Therefore, it would appear that on this day the SS Panzer Corps received the lion's share of the German air support. Still, with the large number of complaints about German air and the high Soviet sortie counts, one cannot rule out the possibility that the German VIII Air Corps report for this day did not record all the sorties flown.

We do need to take a moment and look at the entire battlefield. Engaged south of Kursk were five attacking German corps and seven defending Soviet armies. The tank fields of Prokhorovka cover only the actions of part of three German divisions and one Soviet tank army. To its west were four Soviet armies engaged with two German corps and the majority of the Totenkopf SS Division.

On 12 July there were 97 sorties noted by the Sixth Guards Army, which at this point was mostly facing the German XLVIII Panzer Corps. The opposing German forces noted that the Soviet attacks were accompanied by considerable Soviet air activity, with bombing and strafing. The 11th Panzer Division noted that there was some German air activity during the day, but more Soviet, including some dive bomber attacks.

In the area of the Psel River bend to the west of Prokhorovka the Fifth Guards Army was holding. The Fifth Guards Army reported that a group of aircraft bombed the positions of the 95th Guards Rifle Division and the 9th Guards Airborne Division at 0530. The 9th Guards Airborne Division more specifically reported that at 0540, 28 bombers bombed the 23rd Guards Airborne Regiment, which was in the Petrovka area (as were elements of the 95th Guards Rifle Division). The Fifth Guard Army did note, "Our fighter aviation did not securely cover our ground forces. The XXXIII Guards Rifle Corps reports that German aircraft in groups of up to 100 Ju-88s bombed their units. The Totenkopf SS Division was facing them and at 0910, the VIII Air Corps notified the SS that it had dispatched two stuka groups to strike at the forces moving southwest from Petrovka. These forces moving southwest was probably a reference to the XVIII Tank Corps attack which was moving southwest down the Psel.

So it would appear that west of Prokhorovka, there may have been 120 German sorties or more, including Ju-88 sorties attacking infantry early in the morning, including escorting fighters and including maybe 60 stuka sorties later in the morning. Those 60 stuka sorties may well have attacked the XVIII Tank Corps, one of the two attacking Soviet tank corps that morning.

On the actual tank fields of Prokhorovka, the units of the Fifth Guards Tank Army were reporting devastating German air attacks. The Fifth Guards Tank Army reported that German aircraft in groups of up to 25-50 planes uninterruptedly bombed the army starting at 0530 (Moscow time), From 0530 until 1700, the army reported 1,500 sorties. On this day, the Germans flew only 654 sorties and not all of them were to areas the Fifth Guards Tank Army was fighting over.

The XVIII Tank corps reported up to 1,500 German sorties over their lines. The XVIII Tank Corps reported that "lacking necessary support from our fighter aviation and suffering heavy casualties from enemy artillery fire and bombing – by 1200 enemy aircraft had conducted 1,200 sorties – moved slowly forward".[6]

The XXIX Tank Corps and the II Guards Tank Corps reported heavy German aerial bombardment during their attacks. The XXIX Tank Corps was also attacked by their own aircraft. The 32nd Tank Brigade was attacked at 1300 by Soviet assault aircraft and also by the neighboring 170th Tank Brigade. Meanwhile shortly after

THE SOVIET COUNTEROFFENSIVES

1400 (Moscow time) the 31st Tank Brigade had reached the northeastern outskirts of Oktyabrskii Sovkhoz, where the brigade was delayed by German artillery and mortar fire and by the "ceaseless" German air attacks. During the day it is claimed that the Germans launched 240 air sorties over the 31st Tank Brigade's units. The 25th Tank Brigade was reported to have taken significant casualties from air and artillery fire (this is Rotmistrov's claim). The brigade reported that they had suffered heavy personnel and equipment casualties from German air and artillery during their attack in the direction of Stalinskoye Otdeleniye Sovkhoz. In the afternoon the 53rd Motorized Rifle Brigade was forced to abandon the Komsomolets Sovkhoz under pressure from German ground forces and air attack.

To the south of the tank fields of Prokhorovka were most of the Das Reich SS Division, two other German corps, and two Soviet armies. South of Prokhorovka the II Guards Tank Corps was attacking the Das Reich SS Division. At 1210 the SS division requested close air support to attack the estimated 25 attacking Soviet tanks. This German air support and a counterattack from tanks from the Das Reich SS Division caused the Soviet attackers to veer south. The II Guards Tank Corps reported that its 25th Guards Tank Brigade attack was met with heavy artillery and mortar fire, and from hull-down tanks. They also reported the Germans were well-supported by a large number of aircraft. The Sixty-ninth Army reported that 32 Ju-87s bombed Shakhovo, which would have been in the II Guards Tank Corps area. They also reported that 6 Me-109s staffed ground units in the area of Kuzminka and Prokhorovka and two He-111s and a Ju-88 conducted reconnaissance around Korodnoye, Korocha and Klenovets.

The daily report for the SS Panzer Corps notes at 1835 that there had been strong enemy air activity but that because of bad weather, their own air forces could only intervene with weak forces. The Totenkopf SS Division reported heavy air activity by both sides, including bombing and strafing. The Adolf Hitler SS Division reported heavy enemy air activity in the morning. The Das Reich reported at 0710 that 34 Soviet bombers hit the area north of Luchki (north).

Further south, in the III Panzer Corps area, the 19th Panzer Division reported that Soviet close air support was very active early in the day and again around noon, bombing division artillery positions. The Luftwaffe had only light reconnaissance and fighter activity. The 6th Panzer Division reported that the Soviet air activity was at its usual level.

Well south of them was Corps Raus with three infantry divisions. The 106th Infantry Division, in its defense of Polyana, reported that the Luftwaffe sent "obsolescent" tank destroyer aircraft (probably the Hs-123s) and Stukas to bolster their defense. No other Luftwaffe support was provided although the Germans provided the 198th Infantry Division with aerial reconnaissance during the day.

So, to the west of Prokhorovka, the Fifth Guards Tank Army was reporting 1,500 German sorties this day while the Germans only flew 654. Furthermore, it was clear that some of those German sorties were not flown in the areas contested by the Fifth Guards Tank Army. To its west the Sixth Army reported 97 sorties.[7] The Fortieth Army, the First Tank

Army and the Fifth Guards Army records we have do not report sorties. This is also the area where Guenther Rall of the III Group, 52nd Fighter Wing was engaged this day. The Fifth Guards Army, just to the west of the Fifth Guards Tank Army, also was attacked by Ju-88 or Ju-87s. In addition to attacking Ju-88s and Ju-87s, there were escorts. So probably around 60 or more of the 654 sorties went into this area. It appears that 60 stuka sorties may have attacked the XVIII Tank Corps. It is not clear whether they had escorts.

To the south of that battlefield was the Sixty-ninth Army which reported 41 sorties in their 1900 report and for their 0700 report the next day they reported 15 sorties. The Seventh Guards Army reported 87 sorties.[8] Only a few ground support missions were sent to support the Germans, one to Das Reich SS Division and two to the 106th Infantry Division at Polyana. There was also a reported attack on Shakhovo by 32 Ju-87s. This probably accounts for at least another 68 ground attack type sorties, in addition to at least 6 escorts.[9]

The Second Air Army, which covers the entire area the Voroezh Front was fighting in, reported 519 German sorties this day, of which 265 were by Ju-87s, 132 by Ju-88s, 64 by He-111s, nine by Do-215s, 17 by Me-110s, 32 by Me-109s, two by Hs-126s, three by Hs-123s, two by He-113s and six by Fw-189s. These counts by plane total 532, compared with their given total of 519. As the Second Air Army estimates cover the entire battlefield and are consistently close in count to the actual German sortie count, then this argues strongly the Fifth Guards Tank Army estimate of 1,500 sorties is grossly inflated. As history has shown, it would not be the only grossly inflated report out of Rotmistrov's command.

The Seventeenth Air Army, which primarily was providing support to the Seventh Guards Army with one of its air corps, reported 60 German reconnaissance sorties this day. This does not appear to be a complete record of what they faced this day as they reported four dogfights with Me-109s and Fw-190s. This may have included some sorties from units attached to other German air units.

There is also a summary from the Red Army Air Force Command, which states that "Enemy aviation with daylight operated in groups of 9 to 30 bombers against the combat formation of our forces, concentrating their effort on the Prokhorovka axis, where up to 400 of the total number of 546 sorties were counted."[10]

So, 654 German sorties flown minus a guestimated 60 flown to the west of Prokhorovka (half assumed to be ground attack type sorties) and minus at least 74 flown south of Prokhorovka (at least 68 ground attack sorties) would equal maybe 520 sorties flown over and around the Fifth Guards Tank Army. Most of those were probably in the area of the attack by the XVIII Tank Corps and XXIX Tank Corps. Of those 520 sorties, then maybe 313 were ground attack type sorties. Probably less than half of them were stuka sorties and the rest were Fw-190 ground attack sorties.[11] This is still a significant amount of air support, but nothing like some Soviet-influenced accounts have implied or indicated.

On the Soviet side we are looking at 769 sorties flown by the Second Air Army, including 302 ground attack type sorties. We are looking at 118 sorties flown by the

THE SOVIET COUNTEROFFENSIVES

> Seventeenth Air Army, including 52 ground attack type sorties. The Seventeenth Air Army sorties clearly operated well to the south of the Prokhorovka battlefield, as they had been during the entire battle. According to the Second Air Army records, the I Assault Corps (142 Il-2 sorties), the 191st Assault Division (78 Il-s sorties) and the I Bomber Corps (82 Pe-2 sorties) all bombed to the rear of the front line and appears to have favored operations in the German XLVIII Panzer Corps area. That leaves only the IV and V Fighter Corps flying over the battlefield area, and neither were heavily engaged this day (14 engagements reported and 12 planes lost). It would appear that there was little direct support over the tank fields of Prokhorovka. According to some sources, there were no Soviet aircraft flown until after 1000 (Moscow time).
>
> That said, there clearly was some. Both the Totenkopf and Das Reich SS Divisions reported Soviet bombing and strafing attacks and the shooting down of an Il-2 and a Martin (Boston?). The XVIII and XXIX Tank Corps reported that they were attacked at Oktyabrskii Sovkhoz at 1330 (Moscow time) by their own Il-2s. So clearly there were some Soviet ground attack type sorties in the area, but we gather not many.

The two fighter corps continued patrolling, with the IV Fighter Corps covering the Aleksandrovskoye-Leski-Vasilyevka area with 157 sorties. The IV Fighter Corps now had 40 Yak-9s flying. The V Fighter Corps covered the Voznesenovka-Ivnya-Fedchevka-Kruglik-Prokhorovka-Vasilyevka-Belenikhino-Maloye Yablonovo area with 163 sorties. It also had 40 Yak-9s flying. This put both of the fighter corps over the tank fields of Prokhorovka. Although the Soviet close-air support aircraft were not reported in this area, both the Totenkopf and Das Reich SS Divisions reported Soviet bombing and strafing attacks (see Chapter Sixteen of *Kursk: The Battle of Prokhorovka*) and the shooting down of an Il-2 and a Martin (Boston?). Still, the level of air combat activity on this day was low, with the IV Fighter Corps reporting only three engagements and three losses. Of those, one was due to antiaircraft. The V Fighter Corps reported only 11 engagements, with a loss of nine planes, including two Yak-9s.

Finally, after a six-day hiatus, the Second Air Army felt it was safe to sally forth with their Pe-2s again. The I Bomber Corps flew 82 sorties in groups of nine to 26 Pe-2s. These were escorted by the fighters from the IV and V Air Corps. Due to the weather, 14 of the Pe-2s were not able to locate their escorts and so aborted, returning to their airfields with full bomb loads.[12] The weather also affected the 454th Bomber Regiment, which did not send up any sorties this day. The remaining Pe-2s struck the Germans in the area of Bolshiye Mayachki-Pokrovka-Yakovlevo – the woods two to four kilometers east of Yakovlevo. Considering the large number of significant targets on the battlefield, this rear area strike was of limited value to the immediate battlefield. This same tendency appears with the Il-2 strikes. Even though they were ground attack planes, one notices that the areas they were attacking were consistently well to the rear of the front line. As such, it is clear that the Soviet air, unlike the VIII Air Corps, was not conducting close air support. Thus, the use of Soviet air in the Battle of Kursk was more for harassment and attrition. What it did not do, which the Germans did well, was to concentrate on the critical points on the battlefield, in conjunction with the armor and artillery, so as to be able to suppress and take areas with minimal casualties.

The Second Air Army was only supported by the I Mixed Corps of the Seventeenth Air Army during the day. They sent 52 Il-2s on 52 sorties to Verkhnyii Olshanets, Novo-Oskochnoye, Kazachye, Razumnoye, Krutoi Log and the crossings over the Severnyii Donets around the Nizhnyii Olshanets-Solomino area. They also flew 54 Yak-1s to provide 55 escort sorties, eight armed reconnaissance sorties, and three reconnaissance. They lost three Il-2s.

The Second Air Army continued to have communication problems. For the second day in a row it reported that its headquarters and the 208th Night Bomber Division had no cable communications. The day before that (the 10th), the IV and V Fighter Corps had no connections with the staff. The main means of communication between the subordinate units and the headquarters was by radio. They also were using the 272nd Independent Communications Squadron to deliver messages for the army air staff. The Second Air Army would continue to have communications problems on the following days, reporting problems through the 15th and on the 17th, and with minor breaks on the 18th.

Overall, the Soviets lost 31 planes this day, while the Germans claimed only 16 kills in aerial combat. One is left with the impression that the area over the Fifth Guards Tank Army's attack was not seriously contested. Both sides are reported to have flown in that area, with the Fifth Guards Tank Army counting some 1,500 German sorties. The Fifth Guards Army was vocal about its lack of air support (again, see Chapter Sixteen of *Kursk: The Battle of Prokhorovka*). It does not appear that the Soviets provided much direct air support for their attack. Instead the I Assault Corps and 291st Assault Division concentrated on the rear areas of the two attacking panzer corps. The German air was in operation for the German defense and for their counterattacks in the afternoon.

During the day the Germans launched 411 ground-attack type sorties compared to 354 ground-attack type sorties by the Soviets. This was the lowest level of support provided by the VIII Air Corps since the start of the offensive and considerably lower than the daily average of 1,478 ground-attack type sorties provided in the first five days of the attack. On the other hand, after two days of limited support, the Soviet air forces were making their presence felt again at almost the same level they provided in the first four days of the German offensive. Overall, the influence of air on the fighting this day was low, certainly lower than it had been during the first four days of the offensive. Much of this was due to the weather. It clearly suppressed the German operations and the degree of close air support. It also reduced the Soviet ground attacks. It also appears to have dampened the intensity of the aerial combat. The plane losses for both sides during this day appear to have been from weather and antiaircraft, with limited losses due to air combat.[13]

Fratricidal attacks this day

The Soviet air effort was further undercut by the large number of fratricidal attacks they conducted this day against their own troops. There were five such incidents this day that we have identified:

THE SOVIET COUNTEROFFENSIVES

Date	Unit	Attacker	Location	Notes
12 July	XVIII & XXIX Tank Corps	Il-2s	Oktyabrskii Sovkhoz	At 1300 (Moscow time)
12 July	11th Gds Mechanized Brigade	25 Il-2s	Ryindinka	At 1211 (Moscow time)
12 July	11th Gds Mechanized Brigade	30 Il-22	Ryindinka	At 1230 (Moscow time)
12 July	II Guards Tank Corps	Il-2s and bombers	Kalinin	1700-1800 (Moscow time)
12 July	11th Gds Mechanized Brigade	1 U-2	Ryindinka	night attack

Therefore, of the 302 ground attack sorties conducted by the Soviet Second Air Army, it would appear that 75 or more of them ended up being conducted against their own troops. The Germans would have two reported fratricide incidents the following day. This was not something unique to the Soviet air force.

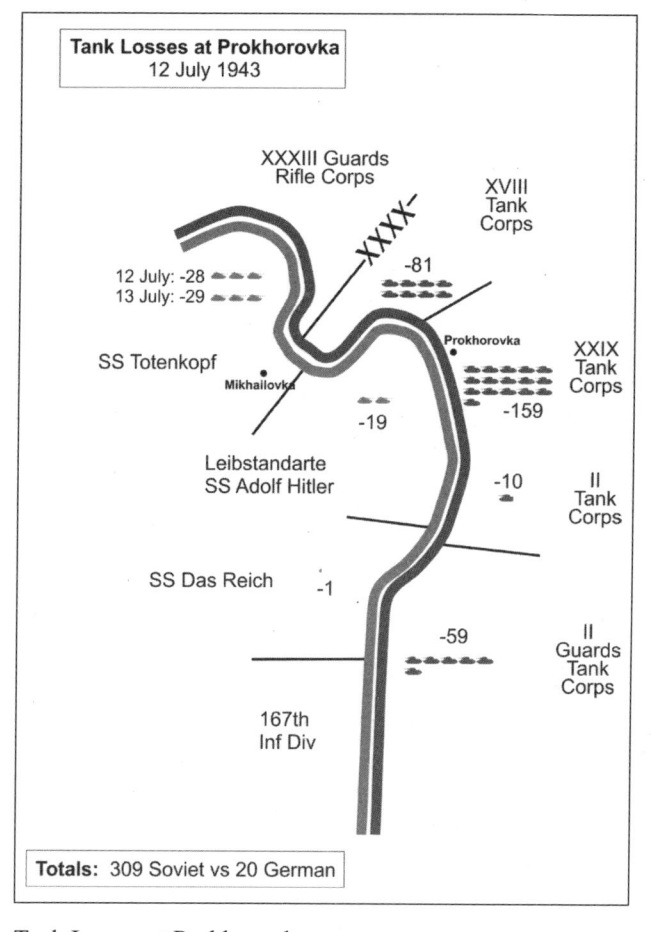

Tank Losses at Prokhorovka.

TIMING OF ATTACKS ON 12 JULY 1943

The timing of the fighting around the tank fields of Prokhorovka is not always clear. The timing of the air that supported and countered these operations is even less clear. Below is a listing of the events during this day for which we have times reported, as extracted from my previous books on the battle. Berlin time is one hour before Moscow time at this time of 1943.

The attacks by both the V Guards Tank Army and the V Guards Army (an infantry army of seven divisions) were to start at 0830 (Moscow time). On the Fifth Guards Army's right flank, their forces were moving forward with the 97th Guards Rifle Division having advanced to the line from height 183.1 to Ilinskii by 0900 (Moscow time). At 0930, its 289th Guards Rifle Regiment had captured height 209.3 and by 1200 had reached the southeastern outskirts of Kochetovka (see 1:50000 scale map M37-25D).[14]

In the area north of the Psel where the Totenkopf SS Division was engaged, they reported Soviet attacks on the barracks northwest of Klyuchi at 0330 and 0730 (Berlin times). At 0630, Totenkopf was complaining about the Soviets conducting a slow infiltration on the flank positions at the barracks west of Klyuchi along with heavy artillery and Katyuska fire. At 0400 (Berlin time) Totenkopf took the panzer battalion that had crossed over the river the previous day and began advancing against the barracks (at Klyuchi?). They reported taking them at 0715. The 52nd Guards Rifle Division reported a German attack at 0500 (Moscow time) while the 95th Guards Rifle Division reported a German attack at 0525 that pre-empted their efforts to take over the positions of the 52nd Guards Rifle Division. At 0830, the 153rd Guards Rifle Regiment of the 52nd Guards Rifle Division advanced in the direction of Polezhayev, but it was repulsed and fell back to the area east of Polezhayev.

Still, the Totenkopf SS Division was still deploying when the Soviet Fifth Guards Tank Army launched its attack. They report that the last elements for the SS attack finally crossed into the bridgehead at 0900, and at 0930 (Berlin times) the armored group jumped off from hill 226.6 to the northeast. The Fifth Guards Army reported the Germans launched an attack with up to 100 tanks at 1215 (Moscow time) in the direction of height 226.6. The political officer of the 11th Motorized Rifle Brigade, which was holding on top of hill 226.6, also reported that the Germans launched an attack at 1200 (Moscow time).

As the fighting continued towards noon, the Soviets tried to maintain pressure on the northern flank of the Totenkopf SS Division with more attacks at 1110 (Berlin time) south of Veselyii and Ilinskii. But what temporarily diverted Totenkopf's drive to the northeast was its decision at 1115 (Berlin time) to turn its armor south to cross the Psel at Mikhailovka and move in behind the Soviets south of the Psel.

Near the open fields to the southwest of Prokhorovka were the Soviet XVIII and XXIX Tank Corps primarily facing the German Adolf Hitler SS Division. At 0830

THE SOVIET COUNTEROFFENSIVES

(Moscow time), following a short artillery preparation, the Fifth Guards Tank Army moved into the attack.

At 0500 (Berlin time), the Adolf Hitler SS Division reported that after a notably quiet night, they were hearing numerous tank noises along their front and heavy enemy air activity. They reported that the Soviets then launched an attack at 0515 (Berlin time) with 40 tanks from Yamki to Stalinskoye Otdeleniye Sovkhoz. This would have been the 25th Brigade of the XXIX Tank Corps. They launched another attack from Prokhorovka with 35 tanks on both sides of the Prokhorovka-Teterevino road, which would have been the XXIX Tank Corps' 32nd Tank Brigade and 25th Tank Brigade. They also reported a third attack with 40 tanks from Petrovka along the road one kilometer south-southeast of Oktyabrskii Sovkhoz. This would have been the XVIII Tank Corps. The Germans reported that the Soviet attack was well supported by artillery and "proceeded at great speed." They also reported that another Soviet attack in regiment strength at 0600 over the line Prokhorovka-Petrovka was stopped by combined artillery concentrations before it reached the front line. This would have also been from the XVIII Tank Corps. The times given by the Germans for these attacks seem too early.

The Totenkopf SS Division, sitting on the higher ground on the north side of the Psel, could see the Fifth Guards Tank Army attack developing. They noted the gathering enemy forces as early as 0705 (Berlin time). At 0745 the Totenkopf SS Division noted two Soviet regiments and about 40 tanks from the northwest entering Mikhailovka and the hills to the southeast. The 95th Guards Rifle Division's 287th Guards Rifle Regiment was located along the line from Mikhailovka and Prelestnoye to Petrovka. It reported at 1000 (Moscow time), that the units of the 42nd Guards Rifle Division and tanks from the Fifth Guards Tank Army attacked through them.

At 0910 (Berlin time), the VIII Air Corps notified the SS that it had dispatched two stuka groups to strike the forces moving southwest from Petrovka. The Totenkopf SS Division also reported an attack on Vasilyevka from 0950 to 1100. This attack penetrated to the center of Vasilyevka in heavy house-to-house fighting. A counterattack by Totenkopf drove the Soviets from Vasilyevka. At 1110 they reported a Soviet attack from Vasilyevka to the southwest. This was probably elements of the Soviet tank force that turned south from the Psel valley and succeeded in breaking through Adolf Hitler's thin flank security and drove through its artillery positions.

The XVIII Tank Corps' attack down the Psel River by noon (Moscow time) had stalled. Rotmistrov reported that at 1330 (Moscow time), the first echelon brigades of the XVIII Tank Corps were fired on by 13 Tiger tanks from the area of height 226.6, which were moving in the direction of the northwest outskirts of Mikhailovka. These were certainly Totenkopf's advancing armor that was diverted from its drive to the northeast at 1115 (Berlin time). The Totenkopf SS Division was now conducting offensive operations against the XVIII Tank Corps, and as of 1330 (Berlin time) German aerial reconnaissance report that Totenkopf was advancing up the valley. At

1445 (Berlin time), Totenkopf reported that it took the west edge of Andreyevka in an attack. Totenkopf at 1455 launched an eastward attack from Vasilyevka that by 1530 had penetrated into the western part of Andreyevka and by 1645 had reached the northeast edge of Andreyevka. At 1500 (Berlin time) the Totenkopf armored group was now two kilometers northwest of Polezhayev, having returned to its original objective for the day after having been diverted in the early afternoon towards Mikhailovka.[15]

Captain Rudolf von Ribbentrop, the commander of the 6th panzer company of the Adolf Hitler SS Division, was located with his unit near height 252.2. He indicates in his narrative that he noticed maybe as late as half past five in the morning the "somewhat unquiet front line." The XXIX Tank Corps also initiated its attack at 0830 (Moscow time). In the center of the battlefield, around height 252.2, the only time reported was at 1115 (Berlin time) the Germans reported that a "local modest breakthrough" at 252.2 was resolved by an armored counterattack. A Russian secondary source stated that between 1030-1045 (Moscow time), the attack was halted on hill 252.2 and the Oktyabrskii Sovkhoz.

By 1300 (Moscow time), the 32nd and 31st Tank Brigades of the XXIX Tank Corps had gone over to the defensive. The 32nd Tank Brigade went over to the defense

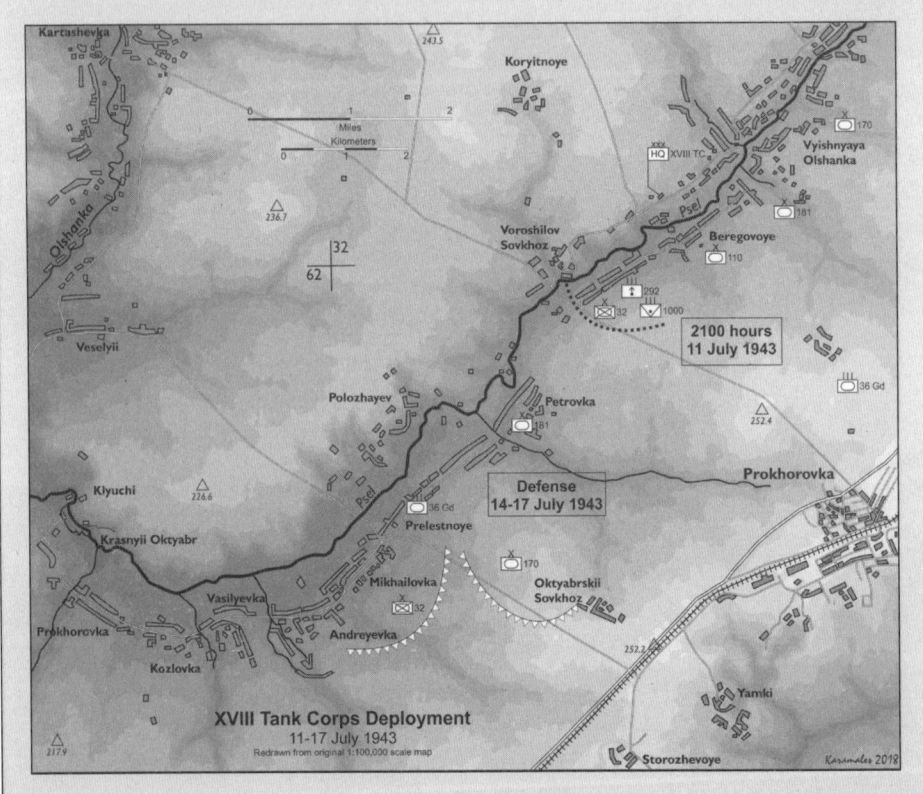

Map 1 - XVIII Tk Corps Deployment, 12 July 1943.

at Oktyabrskii Sovkhoz with what appear to have been very heavy losses. At 1300, it was also attacked, along with the neighboring 170th Tank Brigade (XVIII Tank Corps), by Soviet assault aircraft. Deployed in echelon, it is reported that the 31st Tank Brigade attacked behind the 32nd Tank Brigade and by 1400 (Moscow time) had reached the area one kilometer northeast of Oktyabrskii Sovkhoz. The Fifth Guards Tank Army also reports that after "fierce fighting," by 1400 (Moscow time), they were able to take Komsomolets Sovkhoz.

On the other side of the railroad track, the 25th Tank Brigade, with two batteries of the 1446th Self-Propelled Artillery Regiment attacked through Stalinskoye Otdeleniye Sovkhoz and by 1400 (Moscow time) they had taken Stororzhevoye and overcome the German fire resistance from Ivanovskii Vyiselok and the groves 1.5 kilometers northeast of Yasnaya Polyana. They also are reported to have taken significant casualties from air and artillery fire. Supporting the XXIX Tank Corps attack was the 9th Guards Airborne Division. Its 28th Guards Airborne Regiment did move forward to join the attack south of the railroad and by 1400 (Moscow time) its I and II Battalions had reached the middle of the woods northwest of Storozhevoye.

The Soviet attacks continued into the afternoon. A renewed effort by the XVIII Tank Corps helped the XXIX Tank Corps break into the north portion of the Oktyabrskii Sovkhoz at 1300 (Moscow time). At 1400 (Moscow time), the XVIII Tank Corps reported that the 181st Tank Brigade had occupied the Oktyabrskii Sovkhoz and was fighting along the line from Andreyevka to height 241.6.

According to the Adolf Hitler SS Division's daily report, "thanks to the defense against this massive armored attack, the enemy made little progress, there being during the entire day just the small penetration east of Storozhevoye." The situation in that sector was restored at 1330 (Berlin time). At 1401 (Berlin time), the Germans reported that the Soviets launched an attack along the line from the east edge of Yamki to the road bend one kilometer west of Prokhrovka. The entire attack was stopped by combined artillery fire before it contacted the German front line.[16]

There was also continued action on the south side of the railroad tracks that split the battlefield. The Das Reich SS Division reported at 0700 (Berlin time) that the II Battalion, Der Fuehrer SS Regiment, repulsed an attack by Soviet infantry and seven tanks, and at 0830 a battalion-sized attack made local penetrations at Yasnaya Polyana. This location is around nine kilometers southwest of height 252.2 The division also reported in the morning an attack against the small forest east of Ivanoskii Vyiselok with 18 to 20 tanks and against its defenses west of Storozhevoye with infantry and tanks. It reported at 1140 Soviet attacks with tanks and infantry against the II Battalion, Deutschland SS Regiment. After this attack was defeated, at 1255 the battalion attacked Storozhevoye. They also reported that at 1205, the Russians attacked the left wing of the II Battalion, Der Fuehrer SS Regiment just north of Kalinin (12 kilometers southwest of height 252.2) with

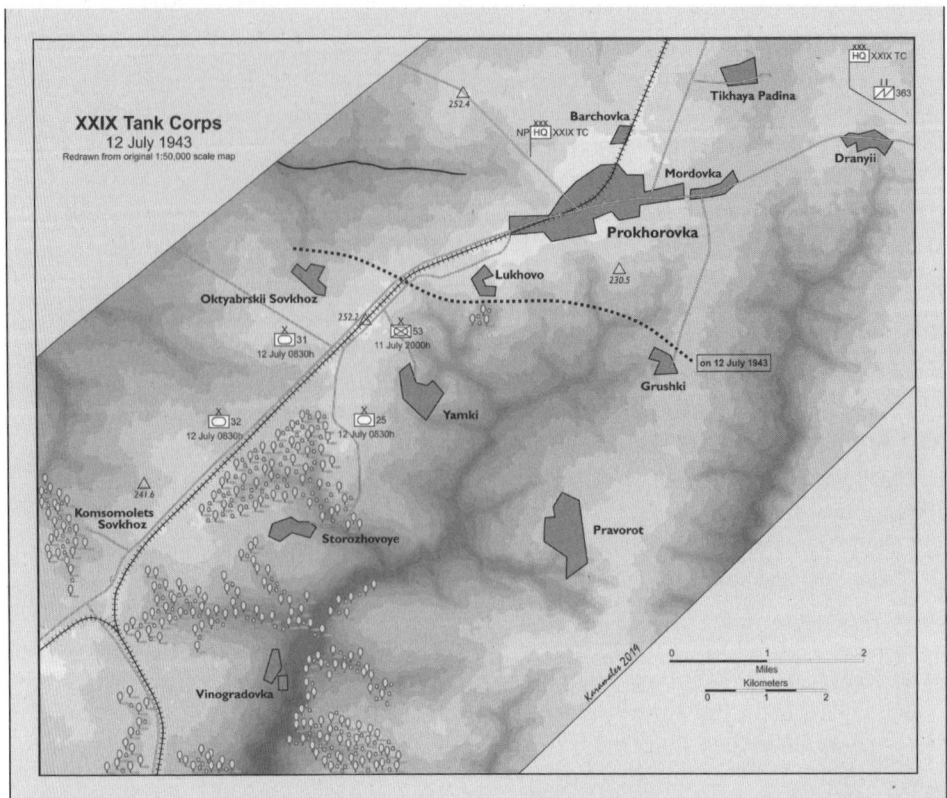

XXIX Tk Corps, 12 Jul 1943.

40 tanks from Belenikhino and also attack the battalion's right wing with 10 tanks. At 1340, the II Battalion then took the south part of Storozhevoye as well as the little woods south of there. At 1505 (Berlin time), the battalion was in the north part of Storozhevoye attacking to the east.

To the south of the Das Reich SS Division, at 1015 (Berlin time), news of the massive Russian tank attack against the Adolf Hitler SS Division and the Das Reich SS Division reached the 167th Infantry Division's command post. This is one of the few clear references in the German records of a "massive Russian tank attack." The Das Reich was tangled up this day in an extended fight with the Soviet II Guards Tank Corps. At 1220, the division requested close air support to attack the estimated 24 attacking Soviet tanks. This German air support and a counterattack from tanks from the Das Reich SS Division caused the Soviet attack to veer south. By 1320, the 339th Infantry Regiment (167th Infantry Division) reported that many Soviet tanks were destroyed in front of its left flank, but still the Soviet attack went forward, penetrating the positions of the III Battalion, 339th Infantry Regiment at Petrovskii at 1445. By 1450, the 167th Infantry Division was reporting that the penetration in the north wing

THE SOVIET COUNTEROFFENSIVES

had been forced out and another penetration on the heights of Rozhdestvenka had been mopped up.[17]

The only timed events we have of German aerial activity is the statement that the V Guards Army was being attacked at 0530 (Moscow time) and its 9th Guards Airborne Division reported that they were attacked at 0540 (Moscow time), with 28 bombers bombing the 23rd Guards Airborne Regiment, which was in the Petrovka area (as were elements of the 95th Guards Rifle Division). These attacks were probably to soften up enemy positions in preparation of the attack by the Totenkopf SS Division. The Fifth Guards Tank Army also reported that German aircraft in groups of up to 25-50 planes uninterruptedly bombed the army starting at 0530 (Moscow time). From 0530 until 1700, the army reported 1,500 German sorties. The XVIII Tank Corps also reported after the battle that "lack the necessary sport from out fighter aviation and suffering heavy casualties from enemy artillery fire and bombing – by 1200 enemy aircraft has conducted 1,200 sorties – moved forward slowly."

At 0910 (Berlin time), the VIII Air Corps notified the SS that it had dispatched two stuka groups to strike at the forces moving southwest from Petrovka. Now, we can't be sure how long it took for the planes to take off, form up in the air or to fly to their target; or whether the VIII Air Corps message was sent before or after they had all taken off, but it is probably a reasonable guess to say that they probably did not arrive on target until after 0930 (Berlin time, 1030 Moscow time). This means they would arrive two hours after the Fifth Guard Tank Army initiated its offensive.

The other reported attacks include the Das Reich reported at 0710 (Berlin time) that 34 Soviet bombers hit the area north of Luchki (north). At 1410, they reported several Soviet aircraft bombed and strafed the highway at Luchki (north). They reported shooting down a Martin bomber (Boston?) and an Il-2 during the day. At 1300 (Moscow time) the XVIII and XXIX Tank Corps were attacked by their own Il-2s at Oktyabrskii Sovkhoz. There were also two other fratricidal type attacks against the 11th Guards Mechanized Brigade at 1211 (Moscow time) and 1230 (Moscow time). These were both at Ryindinka, well south of the Prokhorova battlefield. The first strike was with 25 Il-2s, the second with 30 Il-2s. Then there was another strike between 1700-1800 (Moscow time) at Kalinin. This was Il-2s and bombers against the II Guards Tank Corps. These areas (Ryindinka and Kalinin) were away from the tank fields of Prokhorovka but were still part of the larger Battle of Prokhrovka.

There were other operations in the area after 1500 (Berlin time) but for the sake of this analysis, we will end this discussion at 1500.

The day started with probably at least 13 sorties attacking Soviet positions (the Soviets reported at least 28 bombers). As the Germans only conducted 13 sorties by their bombers this day, it is assumed to have been this mission. There appeared to be little other air activity by either side in the morning. The reports for this day would indicate that there was virtually no aircraft over the area of the tank fields of Prokhorovka from the period of 0830 to 1030 (Moscow times). It was a modern battle fought without air support from either side. This was probably the case for most of the other areas of the German southern offensive.

After 1030 (Moscow time), maybe 60 Stukas arrived in support. As the day developed the level of air activity increased. Between 1211 (Moscow time) and 1410 (German time) were four reported Soviet air strikes in the Prokhorovka area and to its south. Other strikes are reported between 1700-1800 (Moscow time). Probably most sorties on both sides occurred in the afternoon, after the initial Soviet attack had stalled.[18]

So, a tentative schedule of aerial events would indicate (times are in Moscow times):

0530-0540:	Guestimated 13 German bomber sorties over Petrovka area.
0540-0810:	Nothing reported.
0810:	Reported 34 Soviet bombers hit Luchki (north)
0810-1030:	No significant air activity by either side.
Around 1030:	120 Stuka sorties arrive in two groups. Not sure if they were escorted.
1030-1211:	No significant air activity by either side.
1211-1510:	Significant air activity by both sides. Maybe up to 180 German Fw-190 sorties (see below) and at least 65 Soviet Il-2 sorties and maybe two dozen other bomber and Il-2 sorties.
1510-1700:	Nothing reported
1700-1800:	At least two dozen Il-2 and bomber sorties versus Kalinin.

So, an estimated 520 German sorties this day that went into the area. Of those, it is estimated that 313 were ground attack type sorties, with less than half of them being stuka sorties. If we assigned the 13 bomber sorties conducted this day to the reported bombings of Petrovka and 120 Stukas to the two groups that were attacking around 1030 (Moscow time) in the morning, then we are left with 180 other ground attack sorties, mostly Fw-190 and some Hs-129s.

So, 13 bomber sorties before the Soviets initiate their main attack, maybe 120 Stukas around 1030 (Moscow time) conducted during their main attack that morning, and 180 ground attack sorties in the afternoon, after the Soviet attacks had been stalled and when the Germans were counterattacking. This examination can be expanded with some more research. For example, there were 16 German victory claims this day.[19] The times of these claims might help supplement this narrative of events. One historian notes: "Although the German fighter pilots were continually in the air over the battlefield, they reported no Soviet aircraft shot down in this sector [meaning Prokhorovka area] during the first seven hours of the battle."[20]

As it is, Guenther Rall claimed one kill at 1645 (Berlin time) over Oboyan (almost 35 kilometers northwest of height 252.2) and was taken down by a collision with a Russian fighter at 1700 (Berlin time).

THE SOVIET COUNTEROFFENSIVES

Identification Friend or Foe

The changing weather conditions over the battlefield affected visibility. The newer La-5s had a radial engine, unlike the Yaks and the LaGG-3 which were powered by inline engines. As such, they resembled the Fw-190s, and this mistaken identity almost cost Guenther Rall his life. As he tells it:[21]

> On 12 July I went up for a free chase with my adjutant late in the afternoon. The sun stood in the west, a humongous cumulus cloud rose up in the east, which was drenched in glowing red sunlight. We flew at an altitude of about 4,500 meters (15,000 feet) so that I did not notice what went on in terms of intense fighting on the ground that day. I then noticed two dots in front of the glowing red cloud. We attacked immediately, having the sun in our rear. Upon approaching I became unsure whether these were really enemy planes or whether they could be two of the newly commissioned Fw-190 chase planes. I was aware that a squadron with that new type had been sent to the front for Citadel, but I had never seen this airplane before. So I pulled up just before the other airplanes in a turn, and that is where I saw the red star on the wing. I immediately commenced the attack, and—coming from the side—I flew directly towards one of the enemy airplanes. Then occurred what is termed a "mid-air collision." While my propeller cut off the enemy's wing, his propeller slit my plane open from underneath. The enemy plane immediately fell out of the sky, while I was able to retain lift. The damaged propeller and the hull that was slit open was causing such severe vibrations, though, that I felt the engine would be torn out of the airplane any minute. But I managed to get behind my own lines where I made another crash landing.

SHOT DOWN TWICE

Captain Guenther Rall was the top ace active on the Eastern Front in July 1943. Before the start of the Battle of Kursk, he was credited with 145 kills. He was convalescing in Austria when he was called back to duty. He returned back to his unit on 6 July and took over command of the III Group, 52nd Fighter Wing.

He certainly had an eventful week on his return, claiming two fighters on the 7th, four on the 8th, and three on the 9th, two on the 11th and one more on the 12th. All claims were LAGGs.[22]

In return, he was taken down on the 9th and the 12th. On 9 July Rall was shot down at 0730 and according to one source came down in no-mans land near Novoselovka. This was in the XVIII Panzer Corps' area of operations. He was then recovered by a German tank commander.[23] According to another source he force-landed "near Petrovka" (which I cannot find on a map) north of Belgorod.[24] Rall's interviews indicate that he was picked up by members of the SS after he crash-landed in a forest. He stated in a post-war interview that it was the first time he had ever met someone from the SS.[25]

Some claim that the pilot who shot him down was indeed Ivan Kozhedub, who would eventually become the top scoring Soviet and allied ace of the war. Ivan Kozhedub, flying an La-5, states that he spotted two Messerschmitt Bf-109s positioning for an attack. Kozhedub turned head on towards the leader and says that "I was the first to shoot. I held the firing button, squeezed and blasted away a long burst, and it was sufficient! The leader turned over from his steep dive and I saw him hit the ground."[26]

Rall crash-landed. Kozhedub did claim two Me-109s this day, one shot down near Krasnaya Polyana and one east of Pokrovki. Rall indicates that he went down in the SS Panzer Corps' area of operation. Krasnaya Polyana on 9 July was just inside the SS Panzer Corps' western boundary (see the map on page 724 of *Kursk: The Battle of Prokhorovka*). I have found no village named Pokrovki. It might be Pokrovka, just inside the SS Panzer Corps' western boundary, or it could be the smaller village of Pokrovskii (just west of Krasnaya Polyana but outside of SS Panzer Corps area). Whether one of these Me-109s shot down was Guenther Rall is hard to say for certain. If he came down near Novoselovka, then it is not.

The next time he was taken down was due to a collision three days later. According to Rall's account, at around 5:00 pm (1700) he was flying east with two Me-109s at 15,000 feet. He saw two planes coming towards them, but behind them was a large cumulus cloud lit up by the setting sun, making them just black silhouettes, hard to identify. With this distorted view he mistook the planes for the new German Fw-190s. So he held his fire. He turned and pulled above them. Suddenly recognizing they were Russian, he dove on one plane, even though they were only 165 feet beneath him. Diving and firing, he then had to pull up suddenly to avoid collision. The plane stalled and fell back down on the Soviet plane, colliding with it. The Soviet plane's propeller sliced into the bottom of the fuselage of Rall's plane, cutting it open. The Soviet plane right wing was cut off by Rall's plane and went into a spin and crashed. Flying the seriously vibrating plane home he landed the plane in a field near his base.[27]

Guenther Rall was shot down about eight times during the war, seriously wounded three times and spent 15 months in the hospital. In 1941 he had broken his back in three places, the eighth and ninth thoracic vertebrae and the fifth lumbar vertebra.[28] He went through therapy to be able to walk again. In 1943, he married one of his doctors, Dr. Hertha Schoen of Vienna.

The Yak-9

This day is noted for the first extensive appearance of the Yak-9 over the battlefield during the Battle of Kursk. In the V Fighter Corps, they would have been from the newly arriving 256th Fighter Division, which had moved up on 9 July from the Fifth Air Army area and put themselves under command of the Second Air Army. The division had 43 of the new Yak-9s, assigned to two of its three regiments, along with 53 Yak-7bs. They apparently also had some Yak-1bs handed over to them by the withdrawing 205th Fighter Division.[29] The V Fighter Corps reports that 40 Yak-9s conducted 72 sorties this day while the IV Fighter Corps also reports that 40 Yak-9s conducted 101 sorties this day. The V Fighter Corps had two Yak-9s shot down. The Yak-9 first saw combat in late 1942 at Stalingrad, so this was not their first appearance.

Air Support

There was some Soviet air support over the battlefield this day, and more from the Germans. The Das Reich reported at 0710 that 34 Soviet bombers hit the area north of Luchki (north). At 1410, they reported several Soviet aircraft bombed and strafed the highway at Luchki (north). They reported shooting down a Martin bomber (Boston?) and an Il-2 during the day.

The XVIII Tank Corps reported up to 1,500 German sorties over their lines. The XXIX Tank Corps and the II Guards Tank Corps reported heavy German aerial bombardment during their attacks. The Fifth Guards Tank Army reported that German aircraft in groups of up to 25–50 planes uninterruptedly bombed the army starting at 0530 (Moscow time). From 0530 until 1700, the army reported 1,500 German sorties. On this day, the Germans flew only 654 sorties. It is not known how many were sent in support of these battles. The Germans reported flying 411 ground-attack type sorties this day, of which 150 were stuka sorties. As two stuka groups supported the Germans' morning defense, this could lead to the conclusion that the Stukas only sortied in mass once during this day. The reports from other sectors of the battlefield recorded little German air activity (by either side). Therefore, it would appear that on this day the SS Panzer Corps received the lion's share of the German air support. Still, with the large number of complaints about German air and the high Soviet sortie counts, one cannot rule out the possibility that the German VIII Air Corps report for this day does not record all the sorties flown.

The Fifth Guards Army reported that a group of aircraft bombed the positions of the 95th Guards Rifle Division and the 9th Guards Airborne Division at 0530. The 9th Guards Airborne Division more specifically reported that at 0540, 28 aircraft bombed the 23rd Guards Airborne Regiment, which was in the Petrovka area (as were elements of the 95th Guards Rifle Division). The Fifth Guards Army did note, "Our fighter aviation did not securely cover our ground forces."

13 July

There is no German report for this night. Seidemann claimed that nighttime reconnaissance again showed heavy traffic on the roads to the battle area from Kursk and Staryii Oskol.

The 208th Night Bomber Division flew 156 sorties, bombing the Germans in the area of Olkhovka, Melekhovo, Dalnyaya Igumenka, Verkhnyii Olshanets, Shlyakhovo, Olkhovatka, Byikovka, and Vorskla. The 262nd Night Bomber Division, with 39 U-2s flying 100 sorties, hit the area of Belgorod, Belovskaya, Mikhailovka, Razumnoye, Krutoi Log and Maslova Pristan. Two U-2s and eight R-5s flew 30 reconnaissance missions. The 244th Bomber Division with 13 TB-3s flying 26 sorties attacked Maslova Pristan-Solomino-Bezlyudovka while four TB-3s flying eight sorties performed reconnaissance.

The Second Air Army reported the weather at night as cloudy, but clearing towards the morning, with rain in places. Visibility was four to ten kilometers. It was cloudy during the day, with light rain in places and visibility six to ten kilometers.

The VIII Air Corps sent up 656 sorties today despite inclement weather. There were again only limited (60 sorties) bombing attacks. These included 28 from the III Group of the 55th Bombardment Wing, which sent 22 of them to Veselyii. This unit suffered its first losses for the battle when two He-111s collided with each other in the clouds over the airfield. While two crew members were able to parachute out of one of the stricken planes and save themselves, the two planes and the other eight crew members went down. The VIII Air Corps reported losing two He-111s this day on their own side of the lines. The VIII Air Corps provided Stuka support to the III and XLVIII Panzer Corps with 239 sorties. Seidemann noted the participation in the XLVIII Panzer Corps battles on this day. It was here that the value of the air liaison officers attached to the panzer divisions was again demonstrated. Still, the Luftwaffe was unable to have these officers accompany all divisions, riding in tanks or armored halftracks. Their cumbersome SdKfz 305s (a special purpose 3-ton Opel Blitz truck) were frequently unable to follow the attacking units. Whenever the liaison officer rode with the unit commander in his command tank, however, it was possible to direct German air attack to the most dangerous targets.

The German ground attack planes also flew 103 sorties, attacking strong points and Soviet attack groups in front of the XLVIII Panzer Corps and SS Panzer Corps. Because of the thick clouds and poor visibility, the results could be observed for only a few attacks. Still, they claimed 25 Soviet tanks destroyed this day.

Seidemann reported that at this stage the operational strength of flying formations remained at about two-thirds of reported morning strength. He claimed the Soviet air operated primarily over Prokhorovka and the sector south of Oboyan.

The Soviet I Assault Corps continued to strike behind the front line with 163 sorties striking at Pokrovka-Yakovlevo-Luchki-Bolshiye Mayachki-Malyie Mayachki-Krasnaya Polyana and in the ShlyakhovoMelekhovo-Dalnyaya Igumenka-Verkhnyii Olshanets area. They were escorts by 112 Yak-1 sorties. The 291st Assault Division sent 59 Il-2 sorties against Greznoye, height 255, Malyie Mayachki, Luchki, Bolshiye Mayachki and northwest of Ozerovskii. They were supported by 42 escort sorties.

THE FAMOUS FRATRICIDE INCIDENT AT RHZAVETS

On 12 or 13 July occurred the most famous of the fratricide incidents during the battle, and there were several of them on both sides. During the night of 11/12 July, a column of German tanks from the 6th Panzer Division, along with some Tigers, had made a night march to take a crossing near Rzhavets. This nighttime coup de main was successful and allowed the IIII Panzer Corps to finally establish bridgeheads across the Donets River to the south of Prokhorovka. At 1020 (Berlin time on the 12th or 13th), He-111s bombed the bridgehead, mistaking the Germans for a Soviet armored formation.[30] The bombs hit a conference of staff officers and unit commanders being held by Major General Walter von Huenersdorff next to his command vehicle. Fifteen Germans were killed and 49 wounded. Major Rogalla von Bieberstein, commander of the 114th Panzer Grenadier Regiment, was killed. Among the wounded were Colonel Oppeln-Bronikowski, the panzer regiment commander, and General Huenersdorff. Huenersdorff would continue to command, only to meet his fate a day or two later. Oppeln was replaced by lightly wounded Major Baeke.[31]

If this count is correct, the division had lost two regiment commanders on the 12th. Other German records, on the other hand, indicate that this event occurred on the 13th. On the 13th, the Tiger Battalion at Rzhavets reported being attacked by friendly aircraft, which caused heavy losses of men and material. This very effective German air attack accounted for five German officers and 15 NCOS and enlisted killed, and seven officers and 49 NCOs and enlisted wounded.[32] Because of the similarities in casualty figures, the author remains suspicious that this was the same air attack as other authors (Cross, Kurowski, Bergstrom) claim occurred on the 12th. The author had not located any references to the air attack on the 12th in the unit records. The Germans only reported 13 bombers missions for 12 July while they conducted 60 for 13 July.

What caused this fratricide incident is also in question. Most accounts of this incident state that it was because the Luftwaffe had not been informed that the Germans had seized the bridgehead. According to one account, this incident may have been caused by the SdKfz 305 of the Luftwaffe liaison officer breaking down in route.[33] Therefore the air force did not know and could not notify its units about the sudden advance that had been made in the III Panzer Corps area. According to an VIII Air Corps staff report compiled the evening of 13 July, the bombing by a squadron of He-111s was due to poor weather conditions, limited visibility and poor navigation. They became lost and bombed the Rzhavets area. It was investigated at 1635 the same day (the 13th?) and the investigation determined that no one should be accused of criminal negligence since all precautionary measures have been observed.[34] This second explanation is more likely if the attack occurred on 13 July, not the 12th.

This was one of many fratricide incidents caused by German and Soviet aircraft during the battle. A list of those this author is aware of is provided in a subsequent sidebar.

LIST OF FRATRICIDE INCIDENTS DURING KURSK

Unfortunately, air forces are notorious for accidently attacking their own troops. This occurred multiple times during the battle by both the German and Soviet air forces. A list of fratricide incidences we have identified is provided below:[35]

Date	Unit	Attacker	Location	Notes
4 July	11th Panzer Division	Ju-88s	Butovo	5 killed, 7 wounded
4 July	One Yak-1	Soviet AA		Shot down
5 July	Two Il-2s	Soviet AA		Lost
6 July	Das Reich AA Bn	Hs-123s	Luchki	no casualties?
9 July	183rd Rifle Division	60 Il-2s		
9 July	II Tank Corps	58 Il-2s		
11 July	LSSAH PzGr Division	Stukas		caused casualties
12 July	XVIII & XXIX Tank Corps	Il-2s	Oktyabrskii Sovkhoz	At 1300 (Moscow time)
12 July	11th Gds Mechanized Brigade	25 Il-2s	Ryindinka	At 1211 (Moscow time)
12 July	11th Gds Mechanized Brigade	30 Il-22	Ryindinka	At 1230 (Moscow time)
12 July	II Guards Tank Corps	Il-2s and bombers	Kalinin	1700-1800 (Moscow time)
12 July	11th Gds Mechanized Brigade	1 U-2	Ryindinka	night attack
12 or 13 July	6th Panzer Division	6 He-111s	Rzhavets[36]	20 killed, 56 wounded
13 July	3 He-126s damaged	German AA	SS Corps area	

The IV Fighter Corps covered the area of Aleksandrovka-Belenikhino-Vasilyevka-Maloye Yablonovo with 61 sorties, and provided 41 sorties for escorts of the Pe-2s in the Prokhorovka-Vasilyevka-Belenikhino-Maloye Yablonovo area. They also conducted six reconnaissance missions. The V Fighter Corps covered the area of Aleksandrovskii-Vasilyevka-Belenikhino-Maloye Yablonovo with 89 sorties and sent out four reconnaissance sorties.

The I Bomber Corps flew 86 sorties, bombing Verkhnyii Olshanets and Shlyakhovo-Melekhovo and conducting some armed reconnaissance missions with single planes. They lost two Pe-2s this day when they crashed into each other over the Ilovskoye airfield.

Both planes burned and their crews died. The dangers of flying in difficult weather were demonstrated this day with both the Germans and Soviet bombers suffering similar types of accidents. The 454th Bomber Regiment sent three Bostons on reconnaissance missions but ended the missions early due to the weather. They lost one Boston.

The I Mixed Corps continued attacking in the Seventh Guards Army area, sending 35 Il-2s to strike at Novo-Oskochnoye, Verkhnyii Olshanets and Kazachye. The corps had 37 fighters conduct 58 escort sorties, five reconnaissance sorties and three interception sorties. They had one Il-2 fail to return.

During the day the Germans launched 402 ground attack type sorties on the 13th compared to 343 ground attack type sorties by the Soviets.

14 July

During the night, the VIII Air Corps sent up another 28 sorties, including seven bombers to the railroad station at south Kastornoye and 16 harassing sorties in the Koren and Korocha area.

The Soviets continued to make good use of the night, with the 208th Night Bomber Division sending out 102 bombing sorties and five reconnaissance sorties. The U-2s bombed Kazachye-Shlyakhovo-Olkhovka-Verkhnyii Olshanets-Novo-Oskochnoye-Raevka-Dalnyaya Igumenka-Melekhovo. The 464th Bomber Regiment also flew three of their Bostons that night to reconnoiter and look for the arrival of German reserves. The 262nd Night Bomber Division again bombed the area of Razumnoye-Krutoi Log-Maslova Pristan with 107 U-2 bombing sorties and also conducted 30 reconnaissance sorties. They flew 40 U-2s and 8 R-5s this night. The 244th Bomber Division again attacked in the area of Razumnoye-Krutoi Log and the Donets crossing in the Maslova Pristan-Solomino sector. Twelve TB-3s bombed while two others reconnoitered.

The Second Air Army reported the weather as cloudy at night, with visibility up to three kilometers. During the second half of the night, it was cloudy in the area northeast of Belgorod, with thunderstorms in places. During the day there were brief rains, with visibility up to ten kilometers.

The VIII Air Corps ratcheted up the intensity this day. Seidemann noted that while he received orders on this day discontinuing the offensive, it did not mean an end to the VIII Air Corps actions. They flew some 1,452 sorties this day, the highest level of activity since the 9th. In the late morning, they sent strong bomber units to strike in front of the Gross Deutschland.[37] In the afternoon, they changed the focus of these attacks to the Totenkopf and Das Reich SS Divisions. They flew 486 bomber missions this day. The III Group, 55th Bombardment Wing flew 58 sorties, sending 21 to Avdeyevka and 37 to around Veselyii. Rolling attacks by Stukas were used to try to break the Soviet resistance in front of Gross Deutschland, Das Reich and III Panzer Corps. These 510 stuka attacks were claimed to have opened the way for the ground troops and resulted in heavy losses in men and material. There were 135 ground-attack sorties used to continually support the attacking spearheads and cover the troops. There were 238 fighter sorties this day, but it does not appear that the German Air Force was seriously contested. Even though they lost nine planes this day, three were to flak and one to a bomb explosion. There were only three Me-109s lost this day.

It also does not appear that the Germans were seriously contesting the Soviet airspace, for the Soviets were able to fly Pe-2 sorties throughout the day with relative impunity.

The Second Air Army recorded its highest level of activity since the 5th, and the highest daytime activity since the 8th. The I Assault Corps launched another 124 Il-2 sorties in the area of Kazachye-Verkhnyii Olshanets-Novo-Oskochnoye-Shlyakhovo-Melekhovo and in the area of Lukhanino-Berezovka-Butovo-Rakovo-Cherkasskoye-Syirtsevo. These last locales were clearly to the rear and attacks there would have had little direct influence on the fighting, unlike the German Stuka strikes around Tolstoye Woods. These planes were escorted by 40 Yak-1s which flew 199 sorties this day. The 291st Assault Division flew 67 Il-2 sorties to Novo-Oskochnoye-Verkhnyii Olshanets and to the Syirtsevo-Lukhanino-Gremuchii area. They were escorted by 41 fighter sorties.

The IV Fighter Corps patrolled the area of Bogoroditskoye-Pravorot-Shakhovo and escorted the planes from the I Bomber Corps. They launched 209 sorties this day. The V Fighter Corps patrolled the area of Bogoroditskoye-Belenikhino-Shakhovo-Pravorot and the area of Vladimirovka-Verkhopenye-Berezovka-Kruglik with 154 sorties.

SECOND AIR ARMY FORCES
(12–13 July)

	Largest Number Flown in a Day
I Assault Corps	72 Il-2, 56 Yak-1b
I Bomber Corps	82 Pe-2
IV Fighter Corps	22 Yak-1b, 10 Yak-7b, 40 Yak-9, 0 La-5
V Fighter Corps	7 Yak-1b, 32 Yak-7b, 40 Yak-9, 19 La-5
208th Night Bomber Division	47 U-2, 4 R-5, 0 Medium Bombers
291st Assault Division	30 Il-2, 16 Yak-1b, 0 Yak-7b, 0 La-5
50th Air Recon. Rgt.	0 Pe-2
454th Bomber Rgt.	3 A-20 Bostons
272nd Ind. Army Sqd.	

SEVENTEENTH AIR ARMY FORCES
(12–15 July)

	Largest Number Flown in a Day
I Mixed Corps	52 Il-2, 54 Yak-1
III Mixed Corps	0 Il-2, 18 fighters
IX Mixed Corps	0 Il-2, 0 La-5
244th Bomber Division	17 TB-3
262nd Night Bomber Division	44 U-2, 8 R-5
39th Air Recon. Rgt.	
48th Air Recon. Rgt.	
50th Air Recon. Sqd.	

THE SOVIET COUNTEROFFENSIVES

The I Bomber Corps, in groups of 9 to 18 Pe-2s, bombed in the Verkhnyii Olshanets-Novo-Oskochnoye-Kazatskoye area and the Syirtsevo-Lukhanino-Dubrovo area. A total of 99 Pe-2s flew 145 sorties. This major bombing effort resulted in the loss of four of them, three due to antiaircraft fire.

The I Mixed Corps attacked the Germans in the Kazachye-Novo-Oskochnoye-Verkhnyii Olshanets area with 57 Il-2 sorties by 47 Il-2s. The corps' 49 active fighters flew 70 escort missions, 10 armed reconnaissance and four reconnaissance missions. They lost three Il-2s and three Yak-1s.

This increase in activity by both sides did not see a corresponding increase in losses. The Germans lost nine planes this day, of which only five could have been due to aerial combat. The Second Air Army lost 20 planes this day. This included six planes lost to antiaircraft fire. Loss rates remained low for both sides on this day and it appears that the two sides were managing to attack each other's ground forces without too much conflict in the air.

During the day the Germans launched 1,131 ground attack type sorties on the 14th compared to 401 ground attack type sorties by the Soviets.

VIII AIR CORPS LOSSES AND CLAIMS

Date	German Losses	German Claims
June 30	0	5
Night	0	0
July 1	0	0
Night	0	0
July 2	1	1
Night	0	0
July 3	0	5
Night		
July 4	3	6
Night		
July 5	19	260 (220 by air, 40 by AA)
Night		
July 6	7	74
Night	0	0
July 7	10	96
Night		
July 8	5	43

Date	German Losses	German Claims
Night		
July 9	11	38
Night		
July 10	3	14
Night	0	0
July 11	14	23
Night	0	0
July 12	11	16
Night		
July 13	5	21
Night	0	0
July 14	9	24
Night	0	0
July 15	5	8
Night	0	0
July 16	3	24
Night	0	0
July 17	5	10
Night	0	0
July 18	1	1
Night	0	0
July 19	0	1
Night	0	0
July 20	0	0
Night	0	0
July 21	0	0
Night	0	0
July 22	2 Hungarian	1
Night	0	0
July 23	0	0
Night	0	0
July 24	1	4

SECOND AIR ARMY COMBAT LOSSES, JULY 1943

Shot Down in Air Combat

	Total	Pe-2	A-20	Il-2	La-5	Yak-1	Yak-7	Yak-9
I Assault Corps	44			32		7	5*	
I Bomber Corps	12	12						
IV Fighter Corps	12				3	8	1	
V Fighter Corps	59				31	4	14	10
208th Night Bomber Div.	–							
291st Assault Division	35			27	1	4	3	
454th Bomber Regiment	2		2					
Total	164	12	2	59	35	23	23	10

* The I Assault Corps did not fly any Yak-7s through 18 July, so this figure is probably post-Kursk offensive activity.

Shot Down by Antiaircraft Fire

	Total	Pe-2	A-20	Il-2	La-5	Yak-1	Yak-7	Yak-9
I Assault Corps	35			27	2	4	2*	
I Bomber Corps	9	9						
IV Fighter Corps	4				1	2	1	
V Fighter Corps	18				8	3	7	
208th Night Bomber Div.	–							
291st Assault Division	41			36	1	2	2	
454th Bomber Regiment	1		1					
Total	108	9	1	63	12	11	12	

* The I Assault Corps did not fly any Yak-7s through 18 July, so this figure is probably post-Kursk offensive activity.

Not Returned from Mission

	Total	Pe-2	A-20	Il-2	La-5	Yak-1	Yak-7	Yak-9	U-2
I Assault Corps	20			12	1	2	5*		
I Bomber Corps	15	15							
IV Fighter Corps	45				4	28	13		
V Fighter Corps	40				14	7	12	7	
208th Night Bomber Div.	3							3	
291st Assault Division	34			28	1		5		

ACES AT KURSK

	Total	Pe-2	A-20	Il-2	La-5	Yak-1	Yak-7	Yak-9	U-2
454th Bomber Regiment	1		1						
Total	158	15	1	40	20	37	35	7	3
Total of all causes	430	36	4	162	67	71	70	17	3

* The I Assault Corps did not fly any Yak-7s through 18 July, so this figure is probably post-Kursk offensive activity.

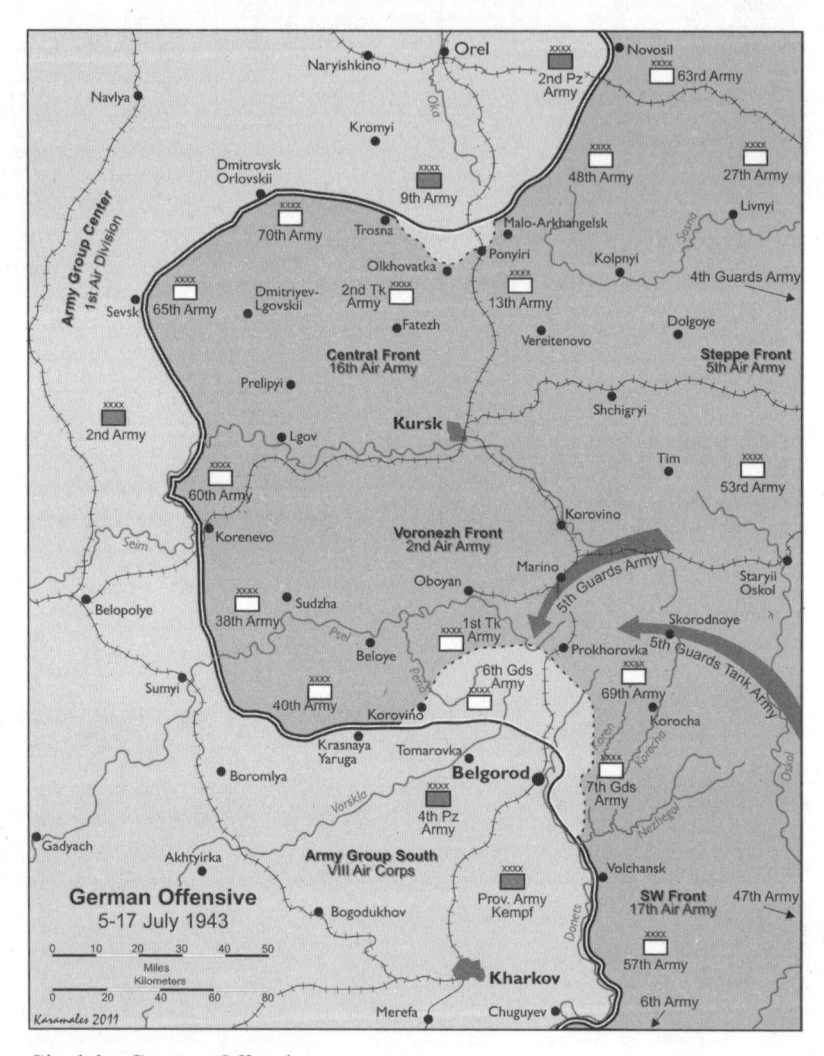

Citadel – German Offensive.

THE SOVIET COUNTEROFFENSIVES

Notes

1. Isserson, *Osnovyi Oboronitelnoi Operatsii* [Fundamentals of the Defensive Operation], published in 1938 by the RKKA General Staff Academy, page 54. Translation provided by Dr. Richard Harrison.
2. Our data is taken from their respective air army records. Bergstrom, *Black Cross, Red Star*, page 245 has similar figures also taken from Soviet unit records, possibly the regiment records. He has the 208th Night Bomber Division conducting 126 sorties compared with our report of 109 sorties and the 262nd Night Bomber Division conducting 183 sorties against our report of 156 sorties. His account does not pick up the 24 TB-3 sorties and three reconnaissance sorties flown this night by the 244th Bomber Division, unless he lumped them in with the 262nd Night Bomber Division sortie count.
3. Bergstrom, *Black Cross, Red Star*, page 245.
4. Khazanov, pages 60-61 states: "In addition to heavy losses, aviation activities were considerably interfered with by adverse weather conditions on 12 July especially in the morning. General S. A. Krasovskiy had to cancel take-offs of most attack aircraft squadrons until 10:00 hours, but later on Soviet aviation operated extremely intensively, making 759 combat sorties by nightfall."

    Hardesty and Grinberg, pages 255-256, state that on the morning of the 12th all Soviet Shturmovik units were grounded. After 1000 hours (Moscow time) on the 12th the weather improved slightly allow 142 Il-2 sorties.

    Similar descriptions are provided by Bergstrom, *Kursk*, page 78, which states: "But the weather continued to be adverse. The whole region was covered by thick clouds which hung low. This compelled Krasvskiy to delay 1 BAK's opening attack by four hours. At 03:30 hours (04:30 German time), around seventy Soviet bomber crews who had already climbed into their Petlyakovs, were ordered out of their aircraft just seconds before the planned take-off."

    "Seidemann was less cautious. As usual, a few Bf 109s were sent out on early dawn fighter sweeps over the front area. Apparently, some VVS fighters also were airborne. II./JG 3's Fw. Hans Grünberg returned from one of those early missions with a claim for a La-5, which was recorded as his 50th victory. But in general, the skies were relatively calm during the first hours of the day."

    One does note that the Adolf Hitler SS Division reported at 0500 (Berlin time) that they were hearing numerous tank noises along their front and heavy enemy air activity. The Fifth Guards Tank Army reported that German aircraft in groups of up to 25-50 planes uninterruptedly bombed the army starting at 0530 (Moscow time). The Das Riech SS Division reported at 0710 (Berlin time) that 34 soviet bombers hit the area north of Luchki (north). At 0910 (Berlin time), the VIII Air Corps notified the SS that it had dispatched two stuka groups to strike at the forces moving southwest from Petrovka, which is opposite the Totenkopf SS Division. See *Kursk: The Battle of Prokhorovka*, pages 929, 931 and 952.

    It does appear that aviation activity was severely restricted by both sides until after 0900 (Berlin time) or 1000 (Moscow time).
5. Bergstrom, *Black Cross, Red Star*, pages 248-249 states that "On this July 12, SchG 1 and its subordinate Pazerjaegerstaffel.JG 51 recorded eleven aircraft put out of commission -- of which six Hs-129s were total losses. All these were due to ground fire." On page 250 he states that 19 German aircraft were put out of commission. "Put out of commission" is a not the same as "shot down."
6. "Account of XVIII Tank Corps' Combat Activities, July 12-24, 1943" (Fond: XVIII TC, Opis: 1, Delo: 48, page 7).
7. In Operational Report #144 for 1900 12 July 1943 the Sixth Guards Army reports 62 German sorties from 0500-1700. The Guards Sixth Army Combat Report #73 from 12 July 1943 reports 97 German sorties.
8. The Seventh Guards Army Operational Report #370 for 1900 12 July 1943 reports 64 sorties since 0500. The Seventh Guards Army "Short Description of Combat Activities" for 12 July reported 87 sorties.
9. The estimation of 68 was based upon the 32 Ju-87s that hit Shakhovo, the airstrike in support of the Das Reich SS Division and the two airstrikes that hit in the area in front of the 106th Infantry Division. It is estimated these strikes consisted of at least 12 Ju-87s or Hs-123s each. There are escorts (only 6 counted) and also reconnaissance flights over the area (not counted). So, 32 +12 + 12 + 12 = 68 and 6 escorts. The real count may be higher.
10. Zamulin, *Demolishing the Myth*, page 328. The report was "Operations of Aviation in the Belgorod Defensive Operation." Using intelligence reports to indicate an enemy's action is fraught with problems. In this case, their total sortie count (546 sorties) is close to the reported count of German sorties (654) for this day.

ACES AT KURSK

11. There were 150 stuka sorties this day, only 13 bomber sorties and 248 ground attack sorties. Note that this does not match the Second Air Army estimates, which was 265 Ju-87 sorties, 132 Ju-88 sorties, 64 He-111 sorties and none by Fw-190s.
12. This is also described in Hardesty and Grinberg, pages 255-256, with apparently added drama. They state that: "Seventy-eight Pe-2s of Polbin's 1st BAK were unable to influence the ground battle. Another fourteen bombers were unable to take off due to the weather. Six bombers were lost, and the rest barely managed to return home at treetop level in conditions of poor visibility."

    This appears to be an overstatement, as the Second Air Army reports 82 sorties conducted by 82 Pe-2s that day, mostly Pe-2s escorted by fighters that attacked the enemy (single aircraft carried out reconnaissance). They provide a list of ordnance dropped (14 205-kg, 350 100-kg and 70 50-kg demolition bombs, 245 10-kg, 469 8-kg and 408 2.5-kg fragmentation bombs, 24 AG-2 bombs, 1,040 20mm rounds, and 800 armor-piercing shells). Furthermore, they report that of those 82 sorties, 14 were ineffective because they could not meet their fighter escorts due to the poor weather. They also report two dogfights and claim four Me-109s were shot down. Their losses are reported as three Pe-2s "failed to return" from their missions. Our source: Second Air Army Operational Report #193, 2200, 12 July 1943 (Fond: 2nd Air Army, Opis: 4196, Delo: 29, vol. 2, page 415).
13. Bergstrom, *Kursk*, page 81 and *Black Cross, Red Star*, page 250, notes the same with the claim that it appears that only one German plane was shot down by Soviet fighters in the south flank of the Kursk Bulge on 12 July. This was a Ju-52 intercepted as it flew wounded men from the battle zone.
14. These 1:50000 scale maps are available in both of my previously published Kursk books, *Kursk: The Battle of Prokhorovka* and *The Battle of Prokorovka*.
15. This is only a partial description of the battle focusing only on given times of engagement. For the complete description see Lawrence, *The Battle of Prokhorovka*, pages 306-312.
16. This is only a partial description of the battle focusing only on given times of engagement. For the complete description see Lawrence, *The Battle of Prokhorovka*, pages 312-335.
17. This is only a partial description of the battle focusing only on given times of engagement. For the complete description see Lawrence, *The Battle of Prokhorovka*, pages 329-336. This description also deliberately leaves out of the operations of the II Tank Corps, the II Guards Tank Corps and the XLVIII Rifle Corps, which were part of the offensive, but are not critical for this discussion.
18. We find ourselves in general agreement with the account of the air battle on 12 July 1943 given by Bergstrom, *Black Cross, Red Star*, pages 245-250. We do think the German fratricidal bombing raid on Rzhavets occurred on the 13th and we also think that Rudel used his Ju-87 G-1 for armor attack before 12 July, not on 12 July. We do not agree with his descriptions of some of the fighting on the ground, especially in the III Panzer Corps area. We also do not completely support claims like "It is not too little to say that the Luftwaffe's decisive contribution to the famous Battle of Prokhorovka has been underestimated in most published accounts." We do not think the German air contribution was decisive, as the initial Soviet attacks had been primarily stopped by an array of weapons.
19. Nine of these claims include: 1) one La-5 by Sgt. Hans Gruenberg in the morning, 2) one La-5 by Sr. Sgt. Alfred Surau after 0630 around Prokhorovka, 3) one La-5 by Lt. Johannes Bunzek at 1345 over Prokhorovka, 4) three Il-2s by Sr. Lt. Ernst-Heinz Loehr and one Il-2 by Sgt. Walter Steinhans after 1540 in Provisional Army Kempf area, 5) one claim by Guenther Rall at 1645 over Oboyan, 6) one Yak-1 by Sr. Lt. Joachim Kirschner at 1658 over Bogoroditskoye or 15 km NW of Prokhorovka. Claims are taken from Bergstrom, *Black Cross, Red Star*, pages 246, 248, 249 and 250 and from kill listings for the individual aces posted in Wikipedia.

    There are also some reports of the times of Soviet kill claims. They include 1) two Ju-87s by Captain Chepinota between 0953-1103 (Moscow time), 2) two Ju-87s and one Fw-190 by Sr. Lt. Gulayev between 0953-1103 that fell in the area of Prokhorovka, 3) one Ju-87 by Sr. Lt. Karmin between 1128-1230 that fell in the area of Rozhdestvenka, 4) one Ju87 by Jr. Lt. Ivanov between 1128-1230 that fell in the area of Kochetovka, and 5) one Me-109 by Sr. Lt. Sechin at 1925 in the area of Mukhanovka.
20. Bergstrom, *Black Cross, Red Star*, page 248. He then notes that at 1345 Lt. Johannes Bunzek of 7/JG 52 claimed an La-5 over Prokhorovka.
21. Letter from Lt. General (ret.) Rall to Maj.Gen. (ret.) Dieter Brand and phone conversation on 9 July 1999. This accident is also not recorded in the Luftwaffe quartermaster files.
22. The claim in some sources (like Wikipedia) that the three Yak-1s mentioned in *the Soviet General Staff Study* are a result of Hartmann and Rall's work is probably incorrect. See Bergstrom, *Kursk*, page 67.

THE SOVIET COUNTEROFFENSIVES

23. Bergstrom, *Kursk*, pages 68-69.
24. See Wikipedia article on Guenther Rall. They reference Prien, et al. 2012. There is a Petrovka on the Psel near the tank fields of Prokhorovka, but this is clearly not it.
25. Jonathan Glancey, "Hitler's Decent Warrior," *The Guardian*, 20 December 2004. See https://www.theguardian.com/culture/2004/dec/30/1. It is assumed to reference this incident, as on the 12th he force landed near Ugrim airfield.
26. Ralph Wetterhan, "Kursk: The greatest tank battle in history might have ended differently had it not been for the action in the air," *Air & Space Magazine*, May 2015. See https://www.airspacemag.com/military-aviation/kursk-180954670/#d0wcoYm3BsyRkER5.99. Also see Bergstrom, *Kursk*, pages 67-68. Bergstrom says that the Me-109 came down in the Novoselovka area, just sixteen kilometers from Prokrovka. This was in the XVIII Panzer Corps' area of operations.
27. This account is from letters and interview with Guenther Rall, 9 July 1999 (see section "Identification Friend or Foe" in Chapter Six); and from his authorized biography published in 2002, Jill Amadio, *Guenther Rall: A Memoir: Luftwaffe Ace & NATO General* (Tangmere Productions, Santa Ana, CA, 2002), pages 159-161. There are slight differences in the two accounts. The location of where he landed is from Bergstrom, *Kursk*, page 81.

    Bergstrom, *Kursk*, page 81 has Rall's wingman identified as his adjutant, Sr. Lt. Rudolf Trepte and has them taking off from Ugrim airfield at 1600. The fight is somehow identified as the "last air combat over Prokhorovka" even though Rall claimed an La-5 shot down at 1645 at 15 kilometers southeast of Oboyan and was probably not operating near Prokhorovka at the time. Bergstrom does note that the seriously damaged Me-109 is not claimed in the lost lists of the Luftwaffe quartermaster reports, leading one to question either the accuracy of the quartermaster reports or whether this incident occurred on the 12th.

    On the 12th of July, Rall was credited with one La-5 at 1645 at PQ 35 Ost 62762, east of Snowilow, 15 km southeast of Oboyan.
28. *Aviation History: Interview with World War II Luftwaffe Ace Guenther Rall* dated 6/12/2006. Article was written by Colin Heaton and originally appeared in the September 1996 issue of *World War II* magazine. See https://www.historynet.com/aviation-history-interview-with-world-war-ii-luftwaffe-ace-gunther-rall.htm
29. Bergstrom, *Kursk*, pages 74-75.
30. The time of the attack comes from Zamulin, *Demolishing the Myth*, page 419. It is from an VIII Air Corps staff report compiled the evening of 13 July.
31. Cross, page 209, and Kurowski, *Panzer Aces*, pages 62-63. Kurowski claims it was one errant He-111. Khazanov, page 66, states it was 6 Heinkels and has the losses being 5 officers, 15 *Unteroffiziers*, and 56 servicemen, including killing battalion commander and Knight's Cross holder Captain Jeckel. I cannot find a Captain Jeckel on a list of Knight Cross recipients.

    On the other hand, Franz Kurowski, *Panzer Aces 2*, pages 547-548 claimed that Oppeln's command vehicle was hit by a Soviet antitank gun when he chose to take a shortcut through the Soviet positions after being told to report to the wounded Huenersdorff. This directly contradicts the account he provides in *Panzer Aces*.
32. See *Kursk: The Battle of Prokhorovka*, page 996.
33. Bergstrom, *Kursk*, page 78.
34. Zamulin, page 419. He records the incident as occurring on 13 July, based upon the secondary source: V. Gorbach and D. Zhazonov, *Aviatsiia v bitve nad Orlovsko-Kursk dugoi* [Aviation in the battle over the Orel-Kursk bulge] (Moscow, Moskva 2004), page 169.
35. See Lawrence, *Kursk: The Battle of Prokhorovka* for detailed descriptions of most these actions. The incidents with the 11th Guards Mechanized Brigade on 12 July are in Lawrence, *The Battle of Prokhorovka*, page 390. Also see Bergstrom, *Kursk*, page 75, for more details of the attack on 11 July.
36. This incident is discussed a number of accounts although they disagree on details. A group of He-111s hit a conference of staff officers and unit commanders being held by Major General Walter von Huenersdoff (6th Panzer Division commander) next to his command vehicle. Fifteen Germans were killed and 49 wounded. Major Rogalla von Bieberstein, commander of the 114th Panzer Grenadier Regiment was killed. Among the wounded were Colonel von Oppeln-Bronikowski, the panzer regiment commander, and General Huenersdoff. Huenersdorff would continue to command, only to meet his fate a day later. The division lost two regiment commanders on the 13th. See *Kursk: The Battle of Prokhorovka*, pages 988-989 and 996. The event probably occurred on the 13th of July although many sources place it on the

12th. Khazanov, page 66, states it was 6 Heinkels and has the losses being 5 officers, 15 *Unteroffiziers*, and 56 servicemen,

37. According to Bergstrom, *Kursk*, page 99, based upon the logbook of Hansgeorge Baetcher, the He-111s of I/KG 100 dropped masses of AB 70 bomb containers and SD 50 fragmentation bombs in repeated mission against Soviet 183rd Tank Brigade at Novenkoye, in front of the 3rd Panzer Division.

    For the 14th of July I have the 183rd Tank Brigade (X Tank Corps) in the southeastern edge of the Tolstoye Woods at 1900 (Moscow time). Novenkoye was three kilometers northwest of Tolstoye Woods and occupied by the VI Tank Corps. German aerial reconnaissance confirmed in the morning that there were strong Soviet concentrations at Novenkoye. See Lawrence, *Kursk: The Battle of Prokhorovka*, pages 1053 – 1056.

Chapter Nine

WINDING DOWN
15–24 July 1943

Thus has been exploded the legend that the German summer offensives are always successful and that the Soviet forces are always compelled to retreat.

Joseph Stalin, 24 July 1943[1]

The Soviet offensive operations were primarily on July. While they were supposed to continue offensive operations on the 13th, most of the units remained in place or sent out only limited reconnaissance attacks. Still, there were multiple division-size Soviet attacks at various points along the line on the 13th, especially against the German's right flank.

The Germans did continue their offensive on the 13th, with the Totenkopf SS Division in the center conducting a failed attack to the north of Prokhorovka. To the south of Prokhorovka was the "Donets Triangle", the Soviet held area south of Prokhorovka that extended almost to Belgorod. On the 13th the III Panzer Corps continued to push north towards Prokhorovka and to clean up this triangle. In the west, the XVIII Panzer Corps was attacking to the west trying to clean up its penetrated flank.

The following day consisted of a failed attack to the south of Prokhorovka by the Das Reich SS Division that continued through the 15th. The III Panzer Corps ended up finally clearing out the Donets Triangle, especially when the Soviet Sixty-Ninth Army and other forces there decided to withdrawn from there on the 15th.

This ended German offensive operations. By the 15th, the German attacks had stalled in front of Prokhorovka, the Donets triangle had been cleared, and the Soviets had withdrawn from the penetration of the German left flank at Tolstoye Woods. The German offensive had ended on the 15th.

The battlefield then sat quiet for two days (16th and 17th) while Manstein (Army Group South) prepared for a limited offensive towards the west, and then all German offensives were cancelled. On the 18th, the Soviets started a limited counteroffensive, while the Germans on subsequent days conducted an organized withdrawal. By 24 July, the German Army had pulled back to near the positions they occupied at the start of the offensive.

The Big Transfer (15–17 July)

Sometime around the 14th or just after, the VIII Air Corps was again called on to shift more forces up to the north. At this point, not only had the Ninth Army's attack failed, but the Second Panzer Army was becoming unhinged by the incessant Soviet attacks on the north side of the Orel bulge. Major formations were now shifted north to cover this critical situation. This resulted in the VIII Air Corps being stripped of the 52nd Fighter Wing, 1st Ground Attack Wing, the five Hs-129 squadrons, the 2nd Stuka Wing (starting the 12th?), the 77th Stuka Wing, and possibly several bombardment groups of the 27th and 55th Bombardment Wings.[2] This was at about the limit of what Sixth Air Fleet could accommodate and service, so the remaining formations stayed with the VIII Air Corps. This left primarily the Royal Hungarian Air Division to provide air support at Kursk.

This transfer probably involved 500 or more planes, reducing the VIII Air Corps to below 500 planes, or less than half of its initial strength. Air losses from the 4th through the 14th had been at least 97 aircraft.

The VIII Air Corps maintained a healthy 1,452 sorties on the 14th, so it is expected that most of the transfers occurred the following days. The air corps reported only 706 sorties on the 15th. At that point, the ability of the VIII Air Corps to maintain air superiority was severely compromised. The VIII Air Corps would only fly 499 sorties on the 16th and only 138 on the 17th and less than a hundred a day until the 24th.

15 July

The VIII Air Corps flew 40 sorties this night, having now sent 13 bomber sorties to the Staryii Oskol station and the unloading point at Stretenka (15 kilometers due west of Staryii Oskol). They report train cars and station buildings set on fire. There were also 23 harassing sorties in the Koren and Korocha areas.

The 208th Night Bomber Division attacked the German forces in Komsomolskii, height 255, Yasnaya Polyana, Ozerovskii, Teterevino, the woods west of Belenikhino, Verkhnyii Olshanets, Olkhovatka, Raevka, Kazachye, Rzhavets, Novo-Oskochnoye, Shlyakhovo, and Melekhovo. The 262nd Night Bomber Division hit the area of Razumnoye-Krutoi Log-Maslova Pristan-Solomino. There were 40 U-2s that flew 77 bombing sorties and eight R-5s that flew 15 sorties. The 244th Bomber Division attacked the area of Razumnoye-Maslova Pristan-Krutoi Log-Solomino and reconnoitered. There were 14 TB-3s which flew 20 bombing sorties and two reconnaissance sorties.

The Second Air Army reported that it was cloudy at night with rain and thunderstorms in places, with visibility of one to three kilometers. It was cloudy during the day, with rain and visibility of two to three kilometers.

During the day, the VIII Air Corps flew 706 sorties, which was half of what they had done the previous day. This much reduced level of effort included only 132 fighter sorties. There were still a significant number of bomber sorties—282—flown this day. This serious commitment of the entire bomber and dive bomber force, as well as continuing ground attack aircraft support, was focused in the Donets triangle, where the spearheads of the Das

Reich SS Division and the III Panzer Corps were converging. In the case of the III Group, 55th Bombardment Wing, they only flew their sorties in the afternoon, with 19 near Marino and Prokhorovka and the other 19 completely outside the Belgorod area. The German air was also used to cover the flank of this movement from strong Soviet tank forces coming from the north (possibly the V Guards Mechanized Corps).

For the first time since the start of the offensive, the German air effort was diverted from the Kursk battles, possibly with the entire bomber force and two close assault groups sent against villages and railroad stations in the Izyum area and striking at the Soviet preparations area. They claim these raids caused heavy losses in Soviet personnel and material. At this point, with possibly over 200 bombers still on-hand, it is estimated that such a raid resulted in at least 100 bombing sorties and at least 40 assault sorties heading south to deal with the latest developing threat from the Soviet Army.[3]

The Second Air Army effort was noticeably reduced because of the weather (as was probably also the case with the German VIII Air Corps). The I Assault Corps was not very active because of the weather. They still managed to send up 46 Il-2s on 97 sorties along with 39 Yak-1s for 65 sorties. This attack struck at PokrovkaTomarovka-Shepelevka-Leski-Kalinina-Lukhanino area and the Belenikhino-Leski-Kalinina-Ivanovka-Greznoye area. They lost four Il-2s and two Yak-1s this day. The 291st Assault Division sent up 320 Il-2s on 25 ground attack sorties and 10 Yak-1s on 18 escort sorties. They also suffered the loss of four Il-2s.

The IV Fighter Corps from 0600 to 1600 (Moscow time) covered the area from Aleksandrovka-Pravorot and from 1600–2300 (Moscow time) covered the area from Pravorot to Shakhovo. In all, 37 planes flew 58 sorties. They were not heavily engaged, reporting only one engagement and no losses. The V Fighter Corps also covered troops, with 52 planes flying 59 sorties, with also little activity, reporting only six engagements and the loss of only a single Yak-9.

Because of the weather, the I Bomber Corps did not conduct any missions, but the 454th Bomber Regiment sent six Bostons to reconnoiter as far as the line from Tomarovka to Belgorod, also dropping bombs.

The I Mixed Corps conducted almost no operations this day due to the poor weather, including rain and low cloud cover. It sent four Il-2s to attack Kazachye-Novo-Oskochnoye-Verkhnyii Olshanets area and four fighters to conduct meteorological reconnaissance. It reported two engagements, but no losses.

During the day the Germans launched 541 ground attack type sorties on the 15th compared to 126 ground attack type sorties by the Soviets. Still, 150 to maybe more than 300 of these German ground attack type sorties may have been outside the battle area. The weather also clearly played its part in reducing the level of activity of both air forces.

16 July

This was also a quiet day in the air, but not nearly as quiet as on the ground. The German night air activity increased considerably, with 111 sorties flown. Twelve bombing sorties struck at Kupyansk railroad station (a little over 100 kilometers east southeast of Kharkov) while 93 harassing sorties struck at Malinovka, Gavrilovka and Andreyevka. All of this was now well out of the Kursk battlefield area and again focused on the developing threats in the south. The 111 sorties flown this night were the highest recorded night activity for the VIII Air Corps since the offensive began.

During the night, the 208th Night Bomber Division again attacked Belenikhino, Yasnaya Polyana, Kalinin, Ozerovskii, Luchki (north), Kazachye, Kurakovka, Novo-Oskochnoye, Verkhnyii Olshanets, Vyipolzovka and Rzhavets. It conducted a rather hefty 214 sorties with 58 U-2s and five sorties with three R-5s. The 262nd Night Bomber Division was also active, with 42 U-2s launching 100 bombing sorties in the area of Novo- Oskochnoye-Verkhnyii Olshanets-Dalnyaya Igumenka and seven R-5s flying 16 reconnaissance missions. The 244th Bomber Division also attacked the area of Verkhnyii Olshanets and Blizhnyaya Igumenka with 12 TB-3s and 27 bombing sorties while two TB-3s flew three reconnaissance sorties.

This day was the last day of any significant air activity in support of the German attack on Kursk. The VIII Air Corps flew 499 sorties during the day, including 191 stuka sorties. It attacked Soviet tanks and assembly areas in front of the Fourth Panzer Army. The corps only flew 145 fighter sorties this day, complaining that with their depleted numbers, the air corps could no longer completely defend against enemy air attacks, even though the Stuka attacks were restricted to the morning and evening hours. The German fighters escorted the Stukas and conducted free-hunting missions. The VIII Air Corps bomber units were now committed to action in the south with the IV Air Corps. As such, the VIII Air Corps only reported 30 bombing sorties for this day. The III Group, 55th Bombardment Wing recorded 55 sorties this day, including 19 sorties to Krasnyii Oskol. The rest were out of the Belgorod area. These were the last sorties they did in support of this operation. The following day, the entire unit was operating out of Stalino, far to the south.

During the day, Soviet assault aircraft continued to work over the battlefield, with the I Assault Corps flying 104 ground attack sorties with 47 Il-2s and 102 escort sorties with 34 Yak-1s. They attacked Belenikhino, Ozerovkskii, Ivanovka, Leski, Shakhovo, Verkhopenye, Syirtsevo, Berezovka and Rakovo. The 291st Assault Division hit the woods east of Leski, the ravines west of Maloye Yablonovo,[4] Maloye Yablonovo, the Yamnoye-Gridin-Shakhovo road, Shakhovo and the ravines to the west of Shakhovo, the woods and the ravines southeast of Krasnyii Uzliv, and the woods northeast of Chapayev. This was done with 39 Il-2 sorties and 34 sorties from the escorting fighters.

The I Bomber Corps was again active after a two-day hiatus, with 103 Pe-2s launching 159 bombing sorties at Belenikhino, Kalinin, Ivanovka, Ozerovskii, Byikovka, Streletskoye, Krasnyii Uzliv and Chapayev. This was a bloody series of missions which resulted in the loss of 11 Pe-2s. The IV Fighter Corps provided escort for 12 groups of Pe-2s and also patrolled the Gnezdilovka-Pravorot-Shakhovo-Shchelokovo areas. They lost five Yak-1s, probably on the escort missions. The V Fighter Corps also escorted Pe-2s and patrolled the same area as its compatriot fighter corps, with a loss of seven planes, including three Yak-9s. Five of those planes failed to return from their mission, again leading one to conclude that the majority of fighters lost were on escort missions. The 454th Bomber Regiment reconnoitered in the area of Tomarovka-Belgorod.

WINDING DOWN

The Seventeenth Air Army was beginning to get more active. After having effectively stood down two of its three mixed corps for a week, all three began flying again. The I Mixed Corps bombed around Verkhnyii Olshanets using 33 Il-2s in 38 sorties. They used 40 Yak-1s to provide 42 escort sorties, six sorties to cover ground troops and four reconnaissance sorties. These operations were with light losses, losing only two Il-2s.

The III Mixed Corps sent eight Il-2s to strike at Kramatorskaya airfield. As they had tried before, 10 fighters blocked the airfield beforehand while 22 provided escort. There were also 11 other fighters that conducted reconnaissance unrelated to the Battle of Kursk. They claimed two German planes destroyed and four damaged at the airfield. On the way home, the mission ran into an estimated 60 Ju-88, He-111 and Me-110 bombers (?) escorted by 25 Me-109s and Fw-190s. The German fighters attacked, resulting in a fight. Still, this was not bloody, with only one La-5 failing to return from this mission. The 244th Bomber Division struck at the Rogan airfield this day using 18 TB-3s. The IX Mixed Corps flew 23 fighters as escort for these missions, along with six reconnaissance sorties. They also had an La-5 fail to return.

During the day the Germans launched 278 ground attack type sorties on the 16th compared to 340 ground attack type sorties by the Soviets.

17 July

The Germans continued their heavy night action with another 85 sorties, including 28 bombing sorties at Kastornoye station with a claim of good results, and 45 harassing sorties again in the Koren and Korocha areas.

The Soviets continued to respond with their heavy night bombing campaign. The 208th Night Bomber Division put up 132 sorties. They bombed the Verkhopenye, Spitsyin, Shepelevka, Alekseyevka, Lukhanino. Syirtsevo, Berezovka and Rakovo areas. The 262nd Night Bomber Division expanded its targets to include the VIII Air Corps airfields. They sent only 34 sorties to bomb the Razumnoye-Maslova Pristan-Solomino area and the crossing over the Severnyii Donets along the Solomino-Maslova Pristan sector. They did 39 reconnaissance sorties. Sixteen sorties were sent to strike at Rogan airfields while 20 were sent to bomb the Kramatorskaya airfield. The 244th Bomber Division went after the Sokolniki airfield with 15 TB-3 sorties, the Osnova airfield with 14 TB-3 sorties and sent six sorties on reconnaissance missions. The effectiveness of this new night bombing effort on the airfields was probably minimal. The Second Air Army's 454th Bomber Regiment also sent up three medium bombers for reconnaissance during the night.

The Second Air Army reported that the weather was cloudy at night with visibility of six to ten kilometers. The clouds increased during the day, but visibility remained at six to ten kilometers.

The German VIII Air Corps put up a rather anemic 138 sorties this day. The VIII Air Corps action in support of Provisional Army Kempf and the Fourth Panzer Army consisted of only some close assault and fighter sorties, as most of the remaining German units of the VIII Air Corps were now operating in the area of the IV Air Corps around Izyum. The Royal Hungarian Air Division had to cover the gap created by all the German transfers, and this is shown by them taking three of five losses this day. The Germans flew no stuka missions this day.

SECOND AIR ARMY FORCES
(14–18 July)

Largest Number Flown in a Day

I Assault Corps	52 Il-2, 40 Yak-1b
I Bomber Corps	103 Pe-2
IV Fighter Corps	37 Yak-1b, 0 Yak-7b, 0 Yak-9, 30 La-5 or 91 fighters
V Fighter Corps	0 Yak-1b, 7 Yak-7b, 21 Yak-9, 24 La-5 or 73 fighters
208th Night Bomber Division	58 U-2, 6 R-5, 0 Medium Bombers
291st Assault Division	39 Il-2, 16 Yak-1b, 0 Yak-7b, 2 La-5 or 34 fighters
50th Air Recon. Rgt.	0 Pe-2
454th Bomber Rgt.	7 A-20 Bostons, 3 Medium Bombers
272nd Ind. Army Sqd.	

SEVENTEENTH AIR ARMY FORCES
(16 July)

Largest Number Flown in a Day

I Mixed Corps	33 Il-2, 40 Yak-1
III Mixed Corps	8 Il-2, 43 fighters
IX Mixed Corps	0 Il-2, 29 fighters
244th Bomber Division	14 TB-3
262nd Night Bomber Division	42 U-2, 7 R-5
39th Air Recon. Rgt.	
48th Air Recon. Rgt.	15 planes (TB-3s and Pe-2s)
50th Air Recon. Sqd.	

SEVENTEENTH AIR ARMY FORCES
(17–18 July)

Largest Number Flown in a Day

I Mixed Corps	0 Il-2, 0 Yak-1, 41 planes
III Mixed Corps	79 Il-2, 46 fighters
IX Mixed Corps	103 Il-2, 70 fighters
244th Bomber Division	33 TB-3
262nd Night Bomber Division	41 U-2, 10 R-5
39th Air Recon. Rgt.	
48th Air Recon. Rgt.	11 planes (TB-3s and Pe-2s)
50th Air Recon. Sqd.	

WINDING DOWN

With the German effort now minimal, and the weather clearer than on previous days, the Soviet air force took over the skies and made their presence felt. The Second Air Army put up 486 sorties during the day. The I Assault Corps struck in the Verkhopenye-Berezovka-Syirtsev-Rakovo-Komsomolets Sovkhoz-Pokrovka area and the Sukho-Solotino-Krasnaya Polyana-Malyie Mayachki area with 115 Il-2 sorties supported by 89 escort sorties. Still, the corps took considerable losses this day, possibly from flak, as they report two Il-2s shot down from antiaircraft fire, and 11 Il-2s force-landed on their side of the lines. The 291st Assault Division attacked the southern outskirts of the woods north of Dolgii, the ravines east of Rakovo, southeast and northeast of Berezovka, south of Zavidovka, Cherkasskoye, Dubrova, and Butovo. This was done with 21 Il-2s which flew 44 sorties escorted by 10 fighters which flew 36 sorties. For some reason, this division decided to drop some 2,000 leaflets this day. This was a small effort compared to the 214,000 leaflets dropped during the night by the 208th Night Bomber Division.

The I Bomber Corps sent 52 Pe-2s to bomb the area of Verkhopenye-Berezovka-Syirtsevo. They were escorted by the IV Fighter Corps, which also patrolled and covered its airfields. They flew 58 sorties with 44 planes. The V Fighter Corps patrolled and covered the Soviet troops in the Vladimirovka-Kruglik-Novenkoye-Melovoye area. They carried out 85 sorties with 35 fighters.

The 454th Bomber Regiment sent up seven Bostons for daytime reconnaissance, looking out to a line from Vorozhba to Sumyi to Akhtyirka to Poltava to Kharkov.

The Seventeenth Air Army, except for its night bombing, had now withdrawn from this battle. The I Mixed Corps did not fly this day, while the III and XI Mixed corps, while very active, were now operating farther south, along the Izyum sector in support of the Soviet offensive initiated in that area on 17 July (the Izyum-Barvenkovo Offensive).

It was a quiet day, with the Germans conducting only 138 sorties this day, in contrast with the 486 sorties from the Second Air Army. The Second Air Army only reported 13 engagements this day and lost only six planes downed, of which two were shot down by antiaircraft fire. The Soviets were still not reaping the full benefit of the German surrender of the air. It is clear that with a concerted push, the Soviets could establish air superiority, and this in the face of a German withdrawal on the ground.

The Germans may not have provided any daytime ground attack missions on the 17th compared to 211 ground attack type sorties by the Soviets.

18 July

During the night, the VIII Air Corps sent up only 27 sorties, with seven bombers hitting Kastornoye railroad station and 18 harassing sorties in the Koren and Korocha areas.

The Soviet night activity remained high with 199 sorties. The 208th Night Bomber Division hit the Olkhovka-Novo-Cherkasskoye-Dmitrievka-Trirechnoye-Cherkasskoye-Butovo-Kazatskoye area and the Pokrovka-Yakovlevo area and along the Yakovlevo-Belgorod road. They also conducted reconnaissance and photo reconnaissance missions. They also sent an R-5 on a "special assignment" from which it did not return. Most likely, these various solitary "special assignment" night missions that occurred on the nights of 3/4, 9/10 and 17/18 were to insert agents behind German lines or fly aid to partisans.

The Seventeenth Air Army now withdrew from the night battles around Belgorod and flew no bombing sorties in this area. It did continue its night bombing of the German airfields, with 33 U-2 sorties hitting Kramatorskaya airfield and 25 TB-3 sorties hitting the Sokolniki and Osnova airfields.

The Second Air Army recorded the weather at night as cloudy, with occasional rain and visibility of two to five kilometers. The Second Air Army was the only air force active during the day. On this day, the Germans only conducted 79 sorties: 40 fighter sorties and 39 reconnaissance sorties. This low level of activity was partially a result of the weather.

The I Assault Corps sent out 53 Il-2 sorties to hit the retreating Germans along the roads in the Yakovlevo, Gostishchevo, Butovo, Streletskoye and Tomarovka areas. They were escorted by 47 Yak-1 sorties, but did not encounter any enemy aircraft and suffered no losses. The 291st Assault Division sent 41 Il-2 sorties to attack Verkhopenye, Gremuchii, Olkhovatka, Lukhanino, Cherkasskoye, Butovo, Greznoye, SukhoSolotino, and the Malyie Mayachki areas. They were escorted by 16 Yak-1bs flying 51 sorties. They reported only one engagement with no losses from that engagement, but they did lose three Il-2s.

The I Bomber Corps hit the areas of Pokrovka, Yakovlevo, Dubrova, Solonets, Olkhovka, Luchki, Streletskoye and Gostishchevo. They flew 93 Pe-2 sorties with 84 Pe-2s, but nine of those sorties were aborted because of the weather. They were again covered by the IV Fighter Corps, which also covered the fuel at Slonovka Station (southwest of Novyii Oskol). The V Fighter Corps continued covering ground troops. The 454th Bomber Regiment conducted reconnaissance with its Bostons. None of these units encountered any German aircraft.

The Seventeenth Air Army was very active this day, with all three mixed corps flying, but it was all in support of operations in the south except for 12 TB-3 sorties against the Kramatorskaya airfield.

There was little air combat this day, with the Second Air Army reporting only one engagement and losing only seven aircraft, probably all due to antiaircraft or mechanical breakdown. The Germans lost one Me-109, shot down and burned by its own flak from the SS Panzer Corps.

The Germans did not provide any daytime ground attack missions on the 18th compared to 187 ground attack type sorties by the Soviets.

The Rest of the Withdrawal

The German sortie rate for the rest of the withdrawal remained less than 100 during the day, and less than 20 during the night. The daytime missions were mostly reconnaissance and a lesser number of fighter missions. There were no more daytime bombing or ground support missions except for bombing missions on the 24th, although the Stukas of the 77th Stuka Wing did return on the 25th to provide support. The Germans continued sending handfuls of bombers at night to attack the railroad station at Staryii Oskol and on harassing raids in the Koren and Korocha areas. On the 19th, the remaining bombers, Stukas, and ground assault aircraft units were transferred to the IV Air Corps in the Izyum area. The German troops around Belgorod were effectively on their own. The VIII Air Corps was now limited in the day to reconnaissance missions, with some fighter support. They had no bomber, ground attack, or Stuka support. With the Seventeenth Air Army reinforced but diverted to the south, they also played no further role in these battles. The Second Air Army now reduced its effort to a lower level. The Fifth Air Army remained well to the rear. The Soviet air force may have been able to assert control over the air at this point, but it does not appear that either side was interested in serious further conflict. As such, the Soviet Il-2s and Pe-2s were free to bomb where they wished during the withdrawal, but were not as active as they had been in the past.

THE AIR ARMY WEATHER REPORTS

We do have scattered weather reports from various ground units on both sides and have systematic weather reports from the Second, Fifth and Seventeenth Air Armies records. Let us summarize the Second Air Army weather reports as they are the most relevant to coverage of the battle area. Their headquarters was located at Zavodnyii throughout the battle.

Report Date	Report
4 July 1943, 2200 hours	Mostly clear at night, with visibility two to three kilometers.
	Cloudy during the day, with visibility eight to ten kilometers at 1,500-2,000 meters altitude.
5 July 1943, 2200 hours	Predominantly clear at night, with considerable haze (or mist), making for visibility of two kilometers.
	Considerable haze during the first part of the day, particularly at dawn, with visibility two to four kilometers. During the second half visibility increased to six to seven kilometers. Cloudiness five to seven points, height 1,000-1,500 meters. In the second half of the day, an increase in cloudiness to nine points.
6 July 1943, 2200 hours	Cloudy at night, with short periods of rain, and visibility up to one kilometer. Cloudiness ten points, height 500-700 meters.
	During the day it was less cloudy, with visibility up to ten kilometers. In the first half of the day cloudiness five to seven points, height 200-1000 meters. In the second half of the day cloudiness was six to seven points, height 500-800 meters.
7 July 1943, 2200 hours	The weather was mostly clear at night, with cloud in some places. Cloudiness six to eight points, height 600-1,000 meters.
	Clear during the first part of the day, with some cloudiness during the second, and visibility up to 15 kilometers. Cloudiness three to five points.

Report Date	Report
8 July 1943, 2200 hours	The weather at night was mostly clear, with scattered clouds and thick haze, and visibility from one to three kilometers. During the first part of the day there was slight cloudiness, with visibility up to ten kilometers. In the second part of the day there were thick clouds and heavy haze, with visibility two to four kilometers. Cloudiness one to three points, height 2,000–3,500 meters. In the second half of the day cloudiness was ten points.
9 July 1943, 2200 hours	Cloudy at night, with slight rain in places. Cloudiness ten points, height 600-1,000 meters. Less cloudy during the day, with rain in spots and visibility up to five kilometers. Cloudiness five to nine points, height 1,000-1,500 meters.
10 July 1943, 2200 hours	Weather at night was cloudy, with rain and storms, and visibility one to two kilometers. Cloudiness eight to ten points, height 600-1,000 meters. During the day the weather was cloudy with visibility eight to ten kilometers, with rain in some areas. Cloudiness nine to ten points, height 800 meters.
11 July 1943, 2200 hours	Cloudy during the night and day, with intermittent rain and thunderstorms. Cloudiness six to ten points, height 600–1,000 meters, in some places up to 300 meters, south wind three to five meters per second.
12 July 1943, 2200 hours	Cloud at night with intermittent rains and visibility of six to ten kilometers. Cloudiness six to ten points, height 600–1,000 meters. East wind is five to eight meters per second with it weakening to three to four meters per second. [eight meters per second is 28.8 kilometers per hour or 17.9 miles an hour] Cloudy during the day, with visibility four to ten kilometers and rain. Cloudiness ten points, height 600-800 meters, in places down to 100 meters. When it rains [visibility is] two kilometers, the wind is southern and three to five meters per second.
13 July 1943, 2200 hours	Cloudy at night, with clearing towards morning, with rain in places. Visibility was four to ten kilometers. Cloudiness six to ten points, height 600-1,000 meters. South wind two to four meters per second. Cloudy during the day, with light rain in places and visibility six to ten kilometers. Cloudiness six to ten points, height 300-600 meters, South quarter wind three to seven meters per second.
14 July 1943, 2000 hours	Cloudy at night, with visibility up to three kilometers. During the second half of the night it was cloudy in the area northeast of Belgorod, with thunderstorms in places. Cloudiness six to ten points, height 600-1,000 meters. During the day there were brief rains, with visibility up to ten kilometers. Cloudiness three to nine points, height 1,500-2,000 meters.

WINDING DOWN

Report Date	Report
15 July 1943, 2200 hours	Cloudy at night, with rain and thunderstorms in places, with visibility one to three kilometers. Cloudiness six to ten points, height 1,000-1,500 meters. Cloudy during the day, with rain, and visibility two to three kilometers. Cloudiness ten points.
16 July 1943, 2200 hours	No report
17 July 1943, 2200 hours	Cloudy at night, with visibility six to ten kilometers. Cloudiness five to nine points, height 600 meters, west wind three to five meters per second. Cloudier during the day, with visibility six to ten kilometers. Cloudiness nine to ten points, height 600 meters.
18 July 1943, 2200 hours	Cloudy at night, with occasional rain, haze, visibility two to five kilometers. Cloudiness seven to ten points, height 1,000-2,500 meters.

The Seventeenth Air Army also provides daily weather reports, including the temperature. Their headquarters was located in Rovenki through 12 July. This town is around 180 kilometers to the east-southeast of Belgorod. On the 13th the headquarters reported from the town of Pokhrovskoye. We believe this is located around 150 kilometers to the southwest of Belgorod.[5]

Report Date	Report
4 July 1943, 2300 hours	Cloudy at night, with visibility four to ten kilometers. Temperature was ten degrees [50 degrees Fahrenheit]. Cloudiness seven to nine points, height 600-1,500 meters, west wind two to four meters per second. Cloudy during the day, with visibility 10-15 kilometers, and a temperature of 25 degrees [77 degrees Fahrenheit]. Cloudiness four to nine points, height 600-1,000 meters, west wind three to eight meters a second.
5 July 1943, 2300 hours	Cloudy at night, with brief rains; temperature 11 degrees. Cloudiness six to ten points, height 600-1,000 meters, West wind two to four meters per second. Cloudy during the day, with visibility 10-15 kilometers. Cloudiness five to eight points, height 1,000-1,500 meters.
6 July 1943, 2300 hours	Cloudy at night, with rain; visibility four to ten kilometers and a temperature of 12 degrees. Cloudiness six to ten points, height 600-1,000 meters, west wind zero to two meters per second. Cloudy during the day, with visibility 10-15 kilometers and a temperature of 23 degrees. Cloudiness five to nine points, height 600-1,000 meters, west wing four to eight meters per second.

Report Date	Report
7 July 1943, 2300 hours	Light clouds at night, with visibility four to six kilometers and a temperature of ten degrees. Cloudiness three to six points, height 600-1,000 meters, wind three to five meters per second. Partly cloudy during the day, with visibility 10-15 kilometers. Cloudiness three to six points, height 1,000-1,500 meters, southeast wind three to six meters per second.
8 July 1943, 2300 hours	Partly cloudy at night, with visibility four to ten kilometers and a temperature of ten degrees. Cloudiness zero to five points, height 1,000-1,500 meters, primarily west wind zero to three meters per second. Scatter clouds during the day, with visibility four to ten kilometers. Temperature of 31 degrees [87.8 degrees Fahrenheit]. Cloudiness two to three points, height 1,000 meters, south and southeast wind three to eight meters per second.
9 July 1943, 2300 hours	No report
10 July 1943, 2300 hours	No report
11 July 1943, 2300 hours	Partly cloudy at night, with rain and visibility four to ten kilometers. Cloudiness three to seven points, height 600-1,000 meters, Southeast wind five to eight meters per second. During the day it was cloudy, with intermittent rains and visibility two to four kilometers and a temperature of 19 degrees. Cloudiness seven to ten points, height 600-1,000 meters, Southeast wind six to twelve meters per second.
12 July 1943, 2300 hours	Cloudy at night, with rain and thunderstorms. Visibility was two to four kilometers, with a temperature of 13 degrees. Cloudiness six to ten points, height 600-1,000 meters, southeast wind two to eight meters per second. Cloudy during the day, with rain. Visibility was four to ten kilometers and a temperature of 22 degrees. Cloudiness seven to ten points, height 800-1,000 meters, south wind three to seven meters per second.
13 July 1943, 2300 hours	No report
14 July 1943, 2300 hours	Weather at night was cloudy, with visibility four to ten kilometers, and the temperature 12 degrees. Cloudiness five to eight points, height 600-1,000 meters, During the day it was less cloudy, with visibility 10-20 kilometers, and a temperature of 30 degrees. Cloudiness zero to five points, height 1,000-1,500 meters, southwest wind of three to seven meters per second.

WINDING DOWN

Report Date	Report
15 July 1943, 2300 hours	Weather was cloudy at night, with visibility up to ten kilometers, with a temperature of 17 degrees. Cloudiness five to ten points, height 600-1,000 meters, southwest wind zero to three meters per second. Cloudier during the day, with rain and visibility four to ten kilometers, with a temperature of 22 degrees. Cloudiness seven to ten points, height 300-600 meters, west wind one to five meters per second.
16 July 1943, 2300 hours	Moderate cloudiness at night, with visibility four to ten kilometers and a temperature of 11 degrees. Cloudiness three to seven points, height 600-1,500, west wind one to four meters per second. Cloudy during the day, with visibility ten kilometers and a temperature of 24 degrees. Cloudiness three to nine points, height 600-1,000 meters, southwest wind two to five meters per second.
17 July 1943, 2300 hours	The weather at night, with visibility of two to four kilometers and a temperature of 11 degrees. Cloudiness five to eight points, height 1,000-1,500 meters, west wing two to five meters per second. Cloudy during the day, with visibility four to ten kilometers, with a temperature of 22 degrees. Cloudiness five to ten points, height 600-1,000 meters, west and southwest winds, three to seven meters per second.
18 July 1943, 2300 hours	The weather at night was cloudy, with visibility four to ten kilometers and a temperature of 12 degrees. Coudiness three to seven points, height 600-1,500 meters, southwest wind zero to three metes per second. Weather during the day was cloudy, with visibility 10-15 kilometers, and a temperature of 30 degrees. Cloudiness five to ten points, height 600-1,000 meters, southwest wind two to six meters per second.

The Fifth Air Army also submitted daily weather reports. It was well to the rear, behind the Seventeenth Air Army. On 19 July 1943, 0800 its records state that during the period 0800 on 17 July to 0800 on 18 July, the air army headquarters moved from Petropavlovka to a place ten kilometers northwest of Chernianka. Petropavlovka is over 300 kilometers east of Belgorod.

Report Date	Report
4 July 1943, 2000 hours	Cloudy, with light rain and thundershowers in places. Visibility is 10-15 kilometers, with temperatures from 21-24 degrees. Cloudiness four to six points, height 1,000 meters, west wind (of the quarter) four to seven meters per second.
5 July 1943, 2000 hours	Cloudy, with light rain in places. Visibility is 10-20 kilometers, with temperatures from 20-24 degrees. Cloudiness five to eight points, height 1,000 meters, southwest wind five to seven meters per second.

Report Date	Report
6 July 1943, 2000 hours	Weather is cloudy, with brief rains and thunderstorms in some areas. Visibility is ten kilometers, with temperatures from 18-22 degrees. Cloudiness six to eight points, height 1,000 – 2,000 meters, west wind five to eight meters per second.
7 July 1943, 2000 hours	Cloudy, with visibility 10-20 kilometers. Temperature from 22-25 degrees. Cloudiness five to seven points, height 1,000 meters, west wind four to seven meters per second.
8 July 1943, 2000 hours	No report
9 July 1943, 2000 hours	Cloudy, with visibility 10-15 kilometers. Temperatures from 28-32 degrees. Cloudiness four to six points, height 1,000 meters, southwest wind three to six meters per second.
10 July 1943, 2000 hours	Weather was cloudy, with visibility four to ten kilometers. Light rain in some areas, with temperatures from 21-26 degrees. Cloudiness six to ten points, height 1,000 meters, south wind three to six meters per second.
11 July 1943, 2000 hours	Weather is cloudy, with rain and thunderstorms in places. Visibility is ten kilometers, with temperatures from 28-33 degrees. Cloudiness six to eight points, height 1,000 meters, southeast wind eight to ten meters per second.
12 July 1943, 2000 hours	Weather is cloudy, with rain in places. Visibility is ten kilometers, with temperatures from 22-24 degrees. Cloudiness six to eight points, height 1,000 meters, southeast wind four to six meters per second.
13 July 1943, 2000 hours	Weather is cloudy, with brief rains and thunderstorms with reduced cloud cover up to 300 meters. Visibility is more than ten kilometers, with temperatures from 20-23 degrees. Cloudiness four to eight points, height 1,000 meters, south wind four to ten meters per second.
14 July 1943, 2000 hours	Weather is cloudy, with brief rains and weak thunderstorms. Visibility is four to ten kilometers with temperatures from 19-23 degrees. Cloudiness six to eight points, height 600 meters, south wind four to six meters per second.
15 July 1943, 2000 hours	The weather is cloudy, with brief rains and thunderstorms. Visibility is four to six kilometers, with temperatures from 20-23 degrees. Cloudiness six to eight points, height 600-1,000 meters, southwest wind two to five meters per second.
16 July 1943, 2000 hours	Weather is cloudy, with brief rains and thunderstorms in places. Visibility is 10-15 kilometers, with temperatures from 22-24 degrees. Cloudiness six to eight points, height 1,000 meters, west wind five to seven meters per second.
17 July 1943	No report
18 July 1943	No report
19 July 1943, 0800 hours	The weather is cloudy, with visibility 10-15 kilometers. Brief rain in places, with temperatures from 14-16 degrees. Cloudiness four to six points, height 1,000 meters, weak wind.

Notes

1. From the official order of the day hailing the Kursk victory. This line was personally added by Stalin. See Georgii K. Zhukov, *Marshal Zhukov's Greatest Battles*, page 200.
2. Seidemann claims that the VIII Air Corps was stripped of another one or two fighter groups, the three groups of the 77th Ground Attack Wing, Rudel's Antitank Group, and several bombardment groups of the 27th and 55th Bombardment Wings, in addition to claiming around the 7th of July that they had transferred the 3rd Fighter Wing, the 2nd Stuka Wing, the 3rd Bombardment Wing and the Hs-129s. According to Hooton, *Eagle in Flames*, page 196, Col. Helmut Bruck's 77th Stuka Wing was transferred to the 1st Air Division in the north on the 16th of July.

    The VIII Air Corps flew no stuka sorties from the 17th through the 24th, flew no ground attack sorties from the 18th of July through the 3rd of August, no bomber sorties from the 18th through the 23rd, and less than 30 fighter sorties a day from the 19th through the 24th.
3. We note that the only unit record we have, the III/55th Bombardment Wing, sent half of their flights to the Kursk battlefield and half to the Izyum area. Obviously the "entire bombing force" did not strike in the Izyum area. There were 282 bombing sorties that day.
4. Almost certainly "log Sukhaya Plota."
5. We believe they are referring to the modern village of Pokhrovske in Voroshilovgrad Oblast or Lugansk Oblast (now Luhansk Oblast in Ukraine), which is around 50 kilometers closer to the front line than Rovenki.

Chapter Ten

THE LAST AIR OFFENSIVE

Much to their disenchantment I had written my parents already back in 1942 that we could not possibly win this war.
Lt. Gen. (ret.) Walter Krupinski, 1999[1]

Never, never will we win this war. What a mistake and what a waste.
Dr. Alfred Hartmann to his son, Lt. Erich Hartmann, June 1943[2]

This war is finished.
Captain Guenther Rall to his wife, September 1943[3]

Summation

This was the last large air offensive the Luftwaffe staged over the battlefield area until the failed Operation Bodenplatte (Baseplate) offensive on 1 January 1945 that was launched during the Ardennes Campaign (Battle of the Bulge). Somewhat ignored by air historians, this was a very large air battle. In the 15 days from 4 July to 18 July, the Germans flew 15,857 sorties, or an average of 1,057 a day. The two Soviet air armies flew 16,041 sorties into the Belgorod area or against the VIII Air Corps, or 1,069 sorties a day. That was 11,657 sorties by the Second Air Army and 4,384 sorties by the Seventeenth Air Army.

To again look at the Battle of Britain analogy, during the month of August 1940, the Germans flew only 4,779 sorties and dropped 4,636 tons of bombs. During the month of September 1940, the Germans flew 7,260 sorties and dropped 7,044 tons of bombs, and during the month of October 1940, the Germans flew 9,911 sorties and dropped 9,113 tons of bombs.[4] As the area fought over was smaller than the area of the Battle of Britain, the shorter distances to be traveled by the opposing sides resulted in higher sortie rates.

The tonnage of bombs dropped at Kursk by the VIII Air Corps is not known. The Second Air Army reported that it dropped 1,244 tons of bombs and estimates that the Germans dropped 7,000 tons. In light of the total of 11,641 ground-attack type sorties flown by the Germans and only 4,295 ground-attack type sorties flown by the Soviets from the 4th through the 18th, this estimate of German bomb weight appears to be reasonable. The Germans flew at least 5,870 stuka sorties, at least 3,330 daytime bomber sorties, and at least 1,912 ground attack sorties. Considering that the maximum bomb load of a Stuka was 1,800 kilograms, of an He-111 was 3,250 kilograms, and for an Hs-123 was 450 kilograms, then one is looking at a maximum weight of 22,248.90 metric tons that could have been dropped. In all reality, these aircraft rarely carried their maximum bomb load. For example, the total weight of bombs dropped by the 644 He-111 H-11R sorties from Rogan for the III/55th Bombardment Wing from 4 to 17 July was 919.7 metric tons, or an average of 1,428.11 kilograms per sortie. Still, it would appear that the Soviet estimate of 7,000 tons of German bombs dropped may have been low and the actual figure could have been around 10,000 to 12,000 tons.

The Soviet air forces flew 3,485 Il-2 ground attack sorties, 732 Pe-2 daytime bombing sorties, 70 TB-3 daytime bombing sorties, and 109 ground attack sorties by fighters and fighter bombers during the offensive. With the maximum bomb load of Il-2s at 600 kilograms, the Pe-2 at 1,200 kilograms, the TB-3 at 4,000 kilograms, and the La-5 FN at 300 kilograms, then the maximum weight of bombs that the Soviets could have dropped during the daytime was 3,282.10 tons, about one-seventh of what the Germans could have done. Most of the sorties were from the Second Air Army, with the Seventeenth Air Army contributing 849 Il-2 sorties and the 70 TB-3 sorties. With 3,142 night attack sorties and a 250 kilogram capacity for a U-2, then we are looking at a maximum figure of around 785.5 tons for the night. These were roughly split evenly between the two Soviet air armies. Of this combined figure of 4,067.60 tons, the Second Air Army made up 2,893.20 tons (compared to 1,244 actually reported as delivered) of this figure and the Seventeenth Air Army made up a maximum of 1,174.40 tons (28.87% of the total figure). Assuming the same proportion of delivered bombs to maximum bomb-carrying capacity, then we are looking at around 1,748.96 tons of bombs delivered by both the Second and Seventeenth Air Armies.

The overall daytime losses for this air campaign were 111 German planes and 660 Soviet planes (and a total of 667 Soviet planes lost). This lopsided 5.95-to-one exchange ratio is hard to explain, as the Soviets' equipment was as good as the Germans'. It clearly shows the differences in training and experience between the two air forces. In light of the heavy losses the Soviet air force took, no one can question their bravery.

What Were German Losses During the Battle?

According to VIII Air Corps reports their losses from 4-18 July 1943 totaled 111 aircraft. This was from a report kept by the Luftwaffe liaison officer assigned to the unengaged German Second Army, located to the west of Kursk. VIII Air Corps files did not survive the war.

This report probably under-records German losses. It probably only reports battle losses that day and probably does not report losses due to accidents and other operational issues. The German Luftwaffe quartermaster records contain detailed records of German planes damaged and destroyed. These reports provide a slightly higher total. They report 104 planes totally lost (recorded as 100%) and 10 planes 80-95% lost. The definition of 81% lost is "Totally destroyed, crashed on German-controlled area."[5] Therefore, this would mean at least 114 planes lost, and we gather this would include losses from accidents, mechanical problems and other operational issues. This is not a big difference, although there is some difference by day. A comparison of these two reports is provided in Table II.20.

Some other sources give higher losses for the Germans. One source claims that "From 5 – 31 July….Seidemann lost 192."[6] He does not footnote his sources, but most likely this figure is drawn from the quartermaster reports. Still, VIII Air Corps losses after 18 July 1943 were low, and many units had been transferred out, and the VIII Air Corps was reduced to flying less than a hundred sorties a day. So this difference is certainly not accounted for by the different time periods used. If the units suffered additional losses after that time, it was because of losses taken outside of the fighting in the southern part of the Battle of Kursk. Perhaps he counted all planes 60% or more damaged (see Table II.20). Planes that are 60% damaged are "write-off category. Certain parts could be used as spare parts for other aircraft." There were 23 planes recorded in the 60-75% category, for a total of 137. This is still short of 192.

How Effective Were the Two Air Forces in Supporting the Ground Troops?

The Germans flew 11,641 ground-attack type sorties during the day and at least 471 bombing sorties during the night. Of those, there were 368 harassing sorties. As the German harassing aircraft primarily dropped two and four kilogram bomblets, the effectiveness of these harassing missions was probably extremely limited.

The Soviets flew 4,396 ground-attack type sorties during the day and 3,142 bombing (harassing) sorties during the night. Their harassing sorties carried more tonnage of bombs than the Germans, as each U-2 could carry 250 kilograms of bombs.

A simple measurement of effectiveness for this air campaign is the volume of bombs dropped by each side. The Second Air Army states that it dropped 1,244 tons of bombs and estimated that the Germans dropped 7,000 tons. Assuming the estimate of German tonnage is reasonable, then this demonstrates a 5.6-to-one difference in weight of bombs dropped by the two sides. The number of daytime ground attack sorties flown was 2.6 times more for the Germans. The weight of bombs delivered per sortie tended to be higher for the Germans due to their more extensive use of two-engined bombers and their higher bomb-load capacities. Just looking at maximum capacity weight each side could have dropped with their sorties, then the Germans could have delivered 6.8 times as many tons of bombs during the day. With the Soviets delivering an estimated 1,750 tons of bombs and the Germans delivering an estimated 10,000 to 12,000 tons, the actual German tonnage figure was probably around six or seven times higher than the Soviet tonnage figure.

One must not forget the German Air Force was more experienced and better trained. The differences in training and capability between the two air forces that were clearly displayed in the air superiority fight certainly also existed in the ground support effort. As such, not only did the Germans provide more sorties and higher bomb weight, but their attacks were certainly better coordinated, better directed and possibly more on target. Also, the Soviet air forces, not having control of the skies and suffering very high losses, were probably under more pressure and haste when conducting their ground attack operations. Overall, the degree of ground attack support received by the German Army was certainly multiples higher than for the Soviet Army. It could be comfortably claimed that the German Air Force provided their ground troops at least ten times the support that the Soviet air force provided to theirs.

Before the battle, the Soviets had stored up in the Second Air Army alone 6,850 tons of bombs. It was clear that they were well prepared for this operation. As it was, because of their inability to maintain control of the air, their high losses, and the limited sorties conducted by their bombers, they only used 18% of their available bomb supply. In the case of the I Bomber Corps, which spent most of the offensive grounded, they were the only planes that delivered the 250 kilogram bombs. "The I Bomber Corps light activity and the insufficient activity of the I Assault Corps is explained by the fact that the fighters assigned to escort these units were busy fighting the enemy aircraft."[7] As the report points out, this led to the actual number of bombs dropped on the Germans being much less than were dropped on them.

The Soviet Army clearly was not getting effective support from their air force. On the other hand, the Second Air Army did pepper the battlefield with 90,000 of the 2.5 kilogram antitank bombs (225 tonnes). This was 64% of their original supply issue of these bombs. The effectiveness of these bombs as an antitank weapon was limited. No reports have been located of any German tanks lost to them, although certainly some were immobilized or otherwise damaged.

The Second Air Army after-action report singled out the fighters as having worked the hardest of all. They singled out the 737th Fighter Regiment (291st Assault Division) for having carried out five or six sorties per combat-ready plane on some of the most intense days. They also singled out the 8th Fighter Division of the V Fighter Corps for being almost as busy as the 737th Fighter Regiment and from the first day of the operation, took upon itself the full weight of fighting the German bombers.

Table 10.1: Summation of Daytime Ground Attack Type Sorties (Stuka, Assault, Bombing, and Ground Attack Sorties)

Date	German	Soviet	Ratio
4	160	0	N/A
5	1,942	486	4.00
6	1,356	442	3.07
7	1,444	400	3.61
8	1,380	404	3.42
9	1,266	291	4.35
10	529*	158	3.35
11	801	152	5.27
12	411	354	1.16
13	402	343	1.17
14	1,131	401	2.82
15	541	126	4.29
16	278	340	.82
17	?	211	N/A
18	0	187	N/A
Total	11,641	4,295	2.71

* Estimated

So What Drove the Soviet Air Loss Claims?

One surprising feature of the Soviet records is the very large number of claimed kills as compared to the actual German losses. A comparison is displayed in chart 10.1 below.

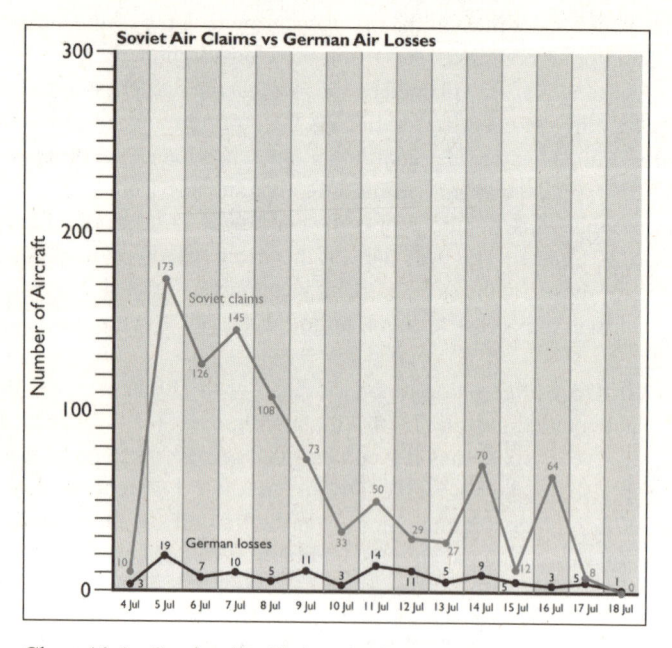

Chart 10.1 - Soviet Air Claims vs German Losses.

This comes out to a total of 840 claimed kills by the Second Air Army and 88 claimed kills by the Seventeenth Air Army. This does not address the claimed kills by the Soviet ground units. This compares poorly to actual German losses of 111 planes. The Soviets claimed more than eight times what the Germans actually lost.

The reverse tendency is not displayed by the Germans. A comparison of their claims to actual Soviet losses is provided in chart 10.2, overleaf.

This comes out to a total of 658 claimed kills by the VIII Air Corps compared to 660 actual losses by the Second and Seventeenth Air Armies. It would appear that at least for this two-week period, German reporting of air claims was reasonably accurate while the Soviet claims were outrageously high. Also bothersome is that the Soviet claims do not appear to have been related to the German casualties. Instead, if one compares Soviet losses to Soviet claims of German losses, one does find a fit.[8]

The pattern is fairly clear, the Soviets always claimed more casualties than they lost.[9] With the Soviets losing 660 planes, and claiming 928 German kills, we are looking at the Soviets claiming about 40% more kills than they lost. This over-claiming is fairly consistent from day to day, and as shown elsewhere, is not a problem unique to the Soviet air force. The Seventeenth Air Army, possibly as a result of its lower level of activity, did a little bit better in regard to accuracy in its claims.

THE LAST AIR OFFENSIVE

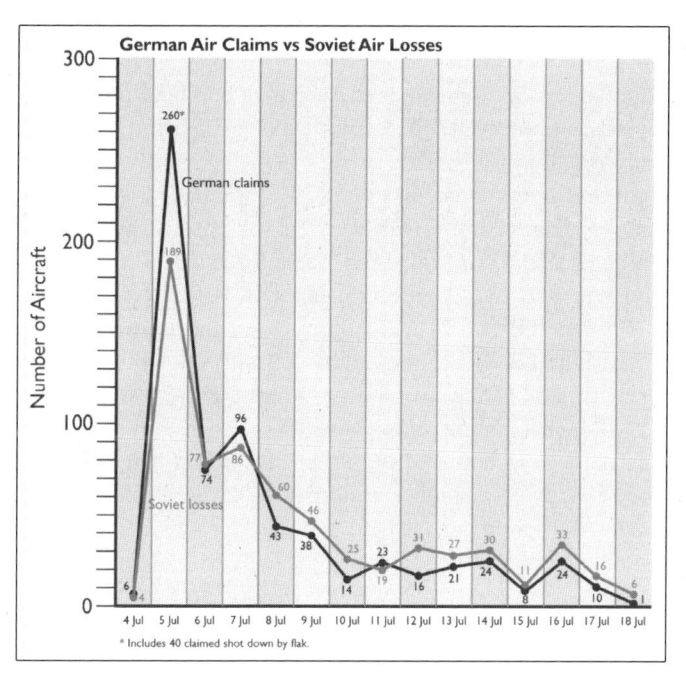

Chart 10.2 - German Air Claims vs Soviet Losses.

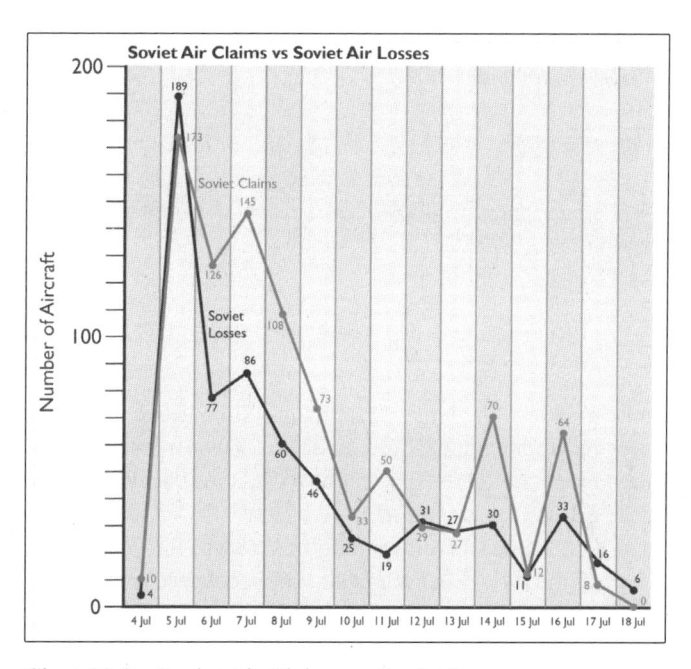

Chart 10.3 - Soviet Air Claims vs Soviet Losses.

The Long Range Aviation

During the war the Soviet Union maintained a separate bombing force called Long Range Aviation (abbreviated as the ADD, Aviatsiya Dalnego Deistiviya) under command of General Aleksandr Ye. Golovanov. This force, consisting mostly of bombers, conducted daytime and nighttime operational and strategic bombing strikes in critical areas of the battlefield and especially in the rear areas. It was also involved in supporting and supplying partisan and NKVD operations. It was a force of 700 to 800 planes in 1943.[10] They were armed with the two-engine Ilyushin DB-3s, the two-engine Tupolev SBs, the four-engine Tupolev TB-3s, the Petlyakov Pe-2s, the four-engine Petyakov Pe-8s (originally designated the TB-7), the two-engine Yermolyaev Yer-2s, the Lisunov Li-2s (a license-built Soviet version of the two-engine Douglas DC-3), and American lend-lease two-engine B-25 Mitchells, among other planes.

Their files were not accessed as part of our research effort. During the Battle of Kursk it appears that they conducted a number of deeper strikes into the rear areas but were not otherwise involved in the fighting on the battlefield, as far as we know. The majority of their aircraft were committed to the north of Kursk, especially with Soviet offensive against Orel that started 12 July 1943.[11] We have not explored their operations in any depth.

THE ACE FACTOR

It has been discussed in many sources that in aerial combat, and in combat in general, a small number of people do a large share of the killing.[12] A quote from Major General Dmitrii P. Galunov, commander of the V Fighter Corps, reinforces this point:

"A relatively small number of pilots regularly shoot down several enemy aircraft. For instance, only 37 pilots of the corps (who score five or victories) shot down 183 aircraft, which amounted to 40% of all aircraft shot down in the course of the Belgorod operation."[13]

Conclusion

The Battle of Kursk produced the largest continuous air confrontation since the beginning of the war between the German and Soviet air forces. Over two-thirds of the German Air Force on the Eastern Front was there. This was also the largest deployment of Soviet aircraft since the start of the war in the summer of 1941.

But the Battle of Kursk consists of four parts. There was the German offensive around Belgorod from 5 to 17 July 1943, which is all that is covered in this book. There was a smaller German offensive to the north of Kursk which ran from 5 to 12 July 1943. There were then two massive Soviet counteroffensives. One started north of Kursk on 12 July while the counteroffensive south of Kursk did not start until 3 August. They went on

THE LAST AIR OFFENSIVE

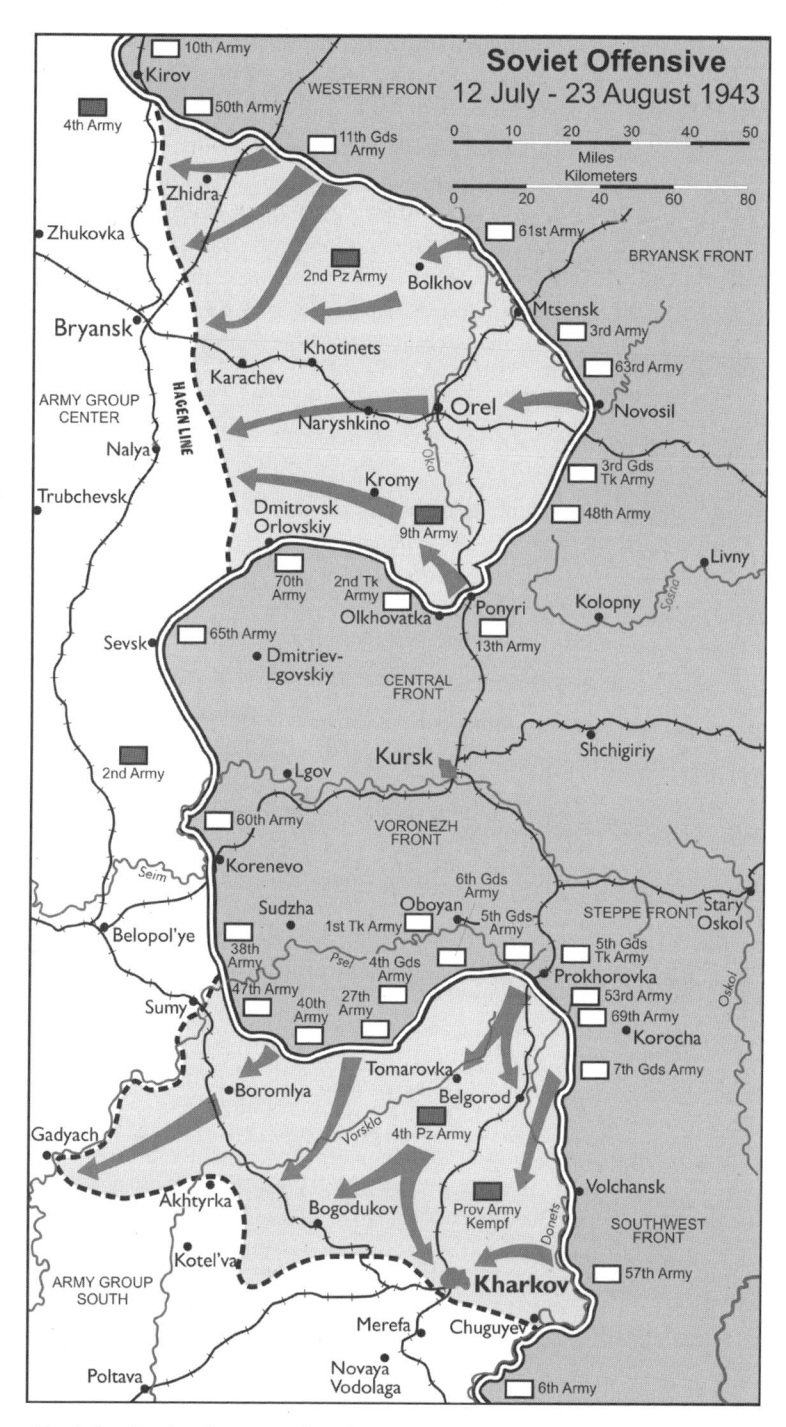

Citadel – Soviet Counteroffensive.

until 23 August, re-taking Orel and Kharkov. During the defensive phase (5 to 12 July 1943) the Soviet Union flew 28,161 sorties both north and south of Kursk. In the counteroffensive phase, from 12 July to 18 August, they flew 79,272 sorties.[14] Still, the levels of intensity during the German offensives resulted in the Soviet air force flying almost twice as many sorties as they did later when they were on the offense.[15]

After August 1943, the two air forces would never again confront each other in such strength.[16] With the German air force withdrawing forces to deal with their fighting in Italy and focused on defending Germany from the Allied bombing campaign, never again would the German Air Force directly confront the Soviet air force in such numbers.[17] The Battle of Kursk was the largest air battle of the Second World War that fielded forces roughly equal in size.

Post-Mortem

General Hans Jeschonnek's attempts to escape to the field by taking over command of the Fourth Air Fleet had failed. After the British bombing of Hamburg on 24/25 July, Goering decided that Jeschonnek would remain as chief of staff. Trapped in an impossible job, Jeschonnek was also affected by the recent loss of his father, brother, and brother-in-law. On the night of 17 August, the RAF bombed the missile base at Peenemuende.[18]

Jeschonnek had already displayed considerable sensitivity, having almost had a nervous breakdown in November 1941 and spending three days in bed after General Udet (the famous First World War ace) had committed suicide and General Wilberg and the famous ace Major Moelders had been killed in separate air crashes while flying to Udet's funeral. He had also previously attempted suicide himself. During the day of 18 August, the young chief of staff wrote a number of suicide notes, including one short note that said "I can no longer work together with the Reichsmarschall [Goering]. Long live the Fuehrer!" He also wrote a memorandum to Hitler that was critical of his boss, Goering. He then shot himself in his office on the command train of the Luftwaffe, in what is now Goldap, Poland (at the time part of East Prussia). It was near Hitler's command post, the Wolf's Lair in East Prussia.[19] He was 44 years old.

OTHER SOVIET KILL CLAIMS

Claims of German planes shot down by Second Air Army over the Voronezh Front, 5–18 July 1943[20] compared to reported losses by German VIII Air Corps.

Type	Number Claimed	German Losses	Ratio of Claims to Losses
Ar-66	–	1	–
Do-215	7	–	–
Fiat	5	–	–

Type	Number Claimed	German Losses	Ratio of Claims to Losses
Fw-189	3	1	3.00
Fw-190	73	11	6.64
He-111	47	15	3.13
Hs-123	5	–	–
Hs-126	36	2	18.00
Hs-129	–	3	–
Ju-87	223	17	13.12
Ju-88	77	10	7.70
Me-109	341	37	9.22
Me-110	5	–	–
Not Stated	–	14	–
Total	822	111	7.41

German planes claimed by unit, 5–18 July 1943[21]

Unit	Claims
I Assault Corps	121
I Bomber Corps	16
IV Fighter Corps	175
V Fighter Corps	451
291st Assault Division	48
Total	811

PERSONAL KILL CLAIMS

While individual Soviet airmen claims of kills cannot be systematically checked, as detailed German logs do not exist, they can be compared to the reported daily losses of the VIII Air Corps. This is illustrative and, not surprisingly, demonstrates that the pattern of overclaiming kills also applies to a pilot's personal totals.

4 July
A list of personal victory claims is provided in the Second Air Army records for the V Fighter Corps for 4 July. They also provide the location of the engagement, and all locations are in the Voronezh Front or Fourth Panzer Army area. See Table 10.2.

The VIII Air Corps reports losing 2 Ju-88s and one Me-109 on 4 July.

Kozhevnikov is possibly Hero of the Soviet Union Anatolii Leonidovich Kozhevnikov of the 438th Fighter Regiment, who scored 27 victories in his career. Karmin is possibly Aleksandr Leontyevich Karmin of the 27th Fighter Regiment, who scored 19 victories and 14 shared kills in his career. Mikhalev may be Vasilii Pavlovich Mikhalev of the 508th Fighter Regiment who scored 26 victories and 14 shared kills in his career. Stroikov may be Nikolai Vasilyevich Stroikov of the 508th Fighter Regiment who scored 14 victories and 21 shared kills in his career. Orlovskii, Oleinikov, Dernik and Stepanobyim have not been identified.

5 July
The following claims are made for the 8th Guards Fighter Division:

Sr. Lt. Belikov	4 kills
Sr. Lt. Danin	4 kills
Sr. Lt. Sementsov	3 kills
Lt. Nikanorov	3 kills

The following claims are made for the 205th Fighter Division:

Sr. Lt. Gulayev	4 kills
Jr. Lt. Shpak	4 kills
Capt. Nasonov	3 kills

These 25 claimed kills (out of 76 claimed by the V Fighter Corps) exceed the actual 19 losses suffered by the VIII Air Corps on this day.

Hero of the Soviet Union Oleg Stepanovich Belikov of the 19th Fighter Regiment scored 15 kills and 14 fractional kills in his career. Sementsov is probably Hero of the Soviet Union Mikhail Ivanovich Sementsov of the 40th Fighter Regiment who scored 19 kills and 12 shared kills in his career. Nikanorov is probably Hero of the Soviet Union Pyotr Mikhailovich Nikanorov of the 166th Fighter Regiment who scored 17 kills and 5 shared kills in his career. Gulayev is probably two-time Hero of the Soviet Union Nikolai Dmitriyevich Gulayev of the 27th Fighter Regiment who scored 55 kills and 5 shared kills in his career. Danin and Nasonov have not been identified. Shpak is Jr. Lt. I. N Shpak who was shot down on 9 July.[22]

Ace Claims
A summation of the claimed kills made by Soviet aces that could be compared to the actual German losses is provided in Table 10.3.

THE LAST AIR OFFENSIVE

It would appear that 55% of these claims made by Soviet aces are not correct, or are misidentified as to plane type. As all claims made were of Me-109 or Fw-190s fighters, gull-wing Ju-87s, or twin engine Ju-88s or He-111s, it does not appear that misidentification is the major cause of these incorrect claims. It is not known if this is a representative sample of the accuracy of Soviet ace claims.

Table 10.2: V Fighter Corps Claims for the 4th of July 1943

Pilot	Claim	Location
Sr. Lt. Kozhevnikov	2 Ju-88	Olkhovka-Aleksandrovka
Sr. Lt. Karmin	1 Ju-87	30 km SW of Belgorod
Jr. Lt. Orlovskii	2 Me-109	Streletskoye
Jr. Lt. Mikhalev & Stroikov	2 Me-109	Shelkovo, Klemenkovo
Jr. Lt. Oleinikov	1 Me-109	Streletskoye, Dmitriyevka
Jr. Lt. Dernik	1 Me-109	Tomarovka
Jr. Lt. Stepanobyim	1 Me-109	own side of lines

Table 10.3: Claimed Kills by Soviet Aces Compared to Actual German Losses

Soviet Ace	Kill Claims Checked	Not a Possible Kill
Ivan Kozhedub	4	2
Nikolai Gulayev	12	10[23]
Kirill Yevstigneyev	5	2
shared kills	2	2
Arsenii Vorozheikin	4	0
shared kills	1	1
Vatalii Popkov	3	2
Sergei Luganskii	5	3
Ivan Syitov	1	1
Nikolai Krasnov	2	1
Fyodor Arkhipenko	2	0
shared kills	3	2
Sergei Glinkin	2	0
Vasilii Merkushev	2	0

ACES AT KURSK

Soviet Ace	Kill Claims Checked	Not a Possible Kill
Nikolai Dunayev	4	1
Ivan Gnezdilov	2	0
Ilya Andrianov	2	1
Oleg Smirnov	1	0
Aleksandr Vyibornov	2	0
Ivan Ulitin	2	0
Anatolii Shamanskii	2	1*
Anatolii Kozhevnikov	9	3
	72	32

* Duplicate claim

A similar type of check of German ace claims is not possible because so many more Soviet planes of different types were shot down each day. Rarely is there a day where a German claim can be disproved, unless one can compare a specific time and location. The claims that were checked are shown below, but little can be determined from this tally.

German Ace	Claims Checked	Not a Possible Kill
Erich Hartmann	20	0
Gunther Rall	13	0
Johannes Wiese	30	2
Kurt Braendle	14	2
Joachim Kirschner	22	0
Total	99	4

Overall, in light of Soviet claims from 4 to 18 July reported in excess of German losses by more than eight times, it is not surprising that many individual claims cannot be confirmed. This does bring into question the validity of all Soviet ace totals. On the other hand, the fact that German claims for 4 to 18 July were almost equal to Soviet losses during that time does provide some level of confidence in the accuracy of German claims. Still, one notes that the Luftwaffe claimed 220 planes shot down by air and 40 by antiaircraft on 5 July, when the Soviets reported losing 189, so one should not place too much reliance on the accuracy of these claims.

Yet based upon this limited sample, it does appear that the German ace claims are usually valid while the Soviet claims are clearly inflated, and possibly inflated by several times.

GERMAN AIR EFFECTIVENESS VERSUS THE TANKS OF THE FIRST TANK ARMY

The First Tank Army initially consisted of three tank and mechanized corps and had three tank brigades and one tank regiment added to it during the battle. They primarily faced the German XLVIII Panzer Corps, although its XXXI Tank Corps faced off against the Leibstandarte SS Panzer Grenadier Division for several days. They reported the total losses of tanks, by cause for 4-18 July. That report is below:

Table I: Krsk, Soviet 1st Tank Army Strength and Loss by Unit, 4–18 July 1943[24]

Unit/Tank Type	Participated	Lost	Artillery	Air	Burned	Breakdown
3rd Mechanized Corps						
T-34	195	145	20	0	108	17
T-70	35	16	3	0	10	3
6th Tank Corps						
T-34	155	146	13	5	106	22
T-70	32	30	5	2	19	4
31st Tank Corps						
T-34	175	146	32	3	102	9
T-70	42	32	7	0	10	15
180th Tank Brigade						
T-34	43	37	2	0	33	2
T-70	23	18	0	0	16	2
T-60	6	3	0	0	1	2
86th Tank Brigade[25]						
T-34	41	27	0	0	27	0
T-70	3	1	0	0	1	0
T-60	9	3	0	0	3	0
23rd Heavy Tank Regiment						
KV-1 and KV-2	11	8	1	1	5	1
192nd Tank Brigade						
Grant	31	25	1	0	21	3
Stuart	24	11	0	0	9	2
Total	825	648	84	11	471	82

As can be seen from this report, of 648 tanks lost from 4 to 18 July 1943, only 11, or less than 2% of their losses, were lost due to air. We suspect this figure is low, and there are other scattered reports that indicate a higher level of losses due to air, but it does not appear from this report and many other reports on the battle that German air was a primary killer of Soviet tanks.

ACES AT KURSK

Notes

1. Interview with Maj.Gen. (ret.) Dieter Brand on 20 April 1999.
2. Col. Raymond F. Toliver and Trevor J. Constable, *The Blond Knight of Germany* (Ballantine Books, New York, 1970), page 60.
3. Jill Amadio, *Guenther Rall: A Memoir: Luftwaffe Ace & NATO General* (Tangmere Productions, Santa Ana, CA, 2002), page 198.
4. Cajus Bekker, page 255.
5. See Bergstrom, *Kursk*, page 131.
6. Hooton, *War over the Steppes*, page 177. For the record he reports that Second Air Army lost 372 aircraft while the Seventeenth Air Army lost 244.
7. Fond: Second Air Army, Opis: 4196, Delo: 39, page 9.
8. This relationship was suggested to me by Dr. Richard Harrison in 1994.
9. A briefing based upon this data was presented to Col. Fyodor Sverdlov in October 1994, who was a staff officer for the Eleventh Guards Army at Kursk and later a professor at the Frunze Military Academy. After presenting the chart showing Soviet claims to German losses, Sverdlov stated that "the enemy always suffers 30% more losses than you."
10. Their strength are given as:

22 June 1941	1,339 bombers
10 July 1941	688 bombers
22 October 1941	439 aircraft (92 TB-3s, 9 Pe-2s, 28 fighters)
22 December 1941	226 serviceable aircraft (182 DBs, 84 TB-3s, some TB-7s and some ER-2s)
5 March 1942	341 bombers
May 1942	329 bombers (114 heavy)
November 1942	479 bombers (63 heavy)
1 July 1943	740 bombers

    See Hooton, *War over the Steppes*, pages 103, 105, 106, 158, 165
11. The ADD committed 450 bombers, including all their Pe-8s, to *Operation Kutuzov*, their offensive to the north of Kursk against Orel. See Hooton, *War over the Steppes*, page 177. He reports for 5-18 July 1943 that the Second and Seventeenth Air Armies flew 16,170 sorties, including 4,712 at night. He reports that elements of the ADD (operating in the south?) flew 1,521 sorties. On page 178 he reports that for the defensive phase, 5-11 July 1943 in the north and 5 – 18 July 1943 in the south, 90% of the ADD sorties were against German defenses and troop concentrations and only 217 sorties were against rail and airfield targets.
12. For example, Hooton, *War over the Steppes*, page 52, states that: "what analysis later demonstrated—only five per cent of fighter pilots became aces (five or more victories), but they account for 40 per cent of all victories." His source is not footnoted. Also see Mike Spick, *The Ace Factor* (Naval Institute Press, Annapolis, MD, 1988) and Robert L. Shaw, *Fighter Combat* (Naval Institute Press, Annapolis, MD, 1985).
13. Khazanov, page 73.
14. Hardesty and Grinberg, Appendix 3. The sorties for July 5-12 1943 include ADD and the aviation of the PVO.
15. For the defensive phase, which covered 7 or 8 days, the Soviet air force averaged 4,023 or 3,520 sorties a day. For the counteroffensive phase, which has data for 12 July to 18 August (37 or 38 days) it was more like 2,086 sorties a day.
16. Polak, page 10. German strength in July 1943 on the Eastern Front was around 2,500 planes. It had declined to 1,732 by the end of the year and was never above 2,000 thereafter. Meanwhile, Soviet air strengths kept increasing. See Ellis, page 233 and Hooton, pages 186-187.
17. The air battles around Yassy, Romania in late April and into early June 1944 were significant in size, with the Germans exceeding a thousand sorties in a day. See Hardesty and Grinberg, pages 286-295.
18. There is a claim in many accounts that Adolf Hitler called Jeschonnek on the afternoon of 17 August or the morning of 18 August to again criticize the Luftwaffe, telling him "You know what to do" or "You

know what is left for you to do now." This story apparently comes from Field Marshal Erhard Milch, the Air Inspector General, who testified that Jeschonnek had a story stormy session with Hitler. This entire story is disputed and dismissed by Prof. Richard Suchenwirth, *Command and Leadership in the German Air Force* (USAF Historical Division, Aerospace Studies Institute, Air University, July 1969), page 288. Suchenwirth states "It is untrue, as Milch has claimed, that Jeschonnek had had a heated discussion with Hitler on the afternoon preceding his suicide, during which Hitler had told him that the failures were his responsibility and that he "ought to know now what was expect of him." This account is denied by those who were best informed about the situation."

19. Suchenwirth, pages 284-290. Many accounts state that Jeschonnek committed suicide at Hitler's command post, the Wolf's Lair in East Prussia, on 18 or 19 January 1943. His gravestone gives his date of death as 18 January 1943 (see https://ww2gravestone.com/people/jeschonnek-hans/). The date of his death was officially posted as 19 January 1943 by Hermann Goering to disconnect it from the Peenemunde bombing so as to hide the manner and reason for his death. They also published that he died from a hemorrhage of the stomach.
20. Fond: 303, Opis: 4196, Delo: 39, page 9.
21. Fond: 302, Opis: 4196, Delo: 39, page 12.
22. Khazanov, page 56.
23. See Tables II.20 and II.21 in Appendix II. If the loss claims are based on the VIII Air Corps reports there are only two claims that are possible. If they are based upon the quartermaster report then up to seven claims are possible. The quartermaster report may include planes damaged in accidents, with mechanical problems, and planes that returned from combat but were later written off as too damaged.
24. The data were found in reports of the First Tank Army (Fond: 299, Opis: 3070, Delo: 226). Obvious math errors in the original document have been corrected (the total lost column did not always agree with the totals by cause). The total participated column evidently reflected the starting strength of the unit plus replacement vehicles. "Burned'" in Soviet wartime documents usually indicated a total loss, however it appears that in this case "burned" denoted vehicles totally lost due to direct fire antitank weapons. "Breakdown" apparently included both mechanical breakdown and repairable combat damage.
25. Note that the brigade report (Fond: 3304, Opis: 1, Delo: 24) contradicts the army report. The brigade reported that a total of 28 T-34s were lost (9 to aircraft and 19 to "artillery") and one T-60 was destroyed by a mine. However, this report was made on 11 July, during the battle, and may not have been as precise as the later report recorded by 1st Tank Army. Furthermore, it is not as clear in the brigade report that "artillery" referred only to indirect fire HE and not simply lo both direct and indirect fire guns.

Appendix I

GERMAN AND SOVIET TERMINOLOGY

Conventions

Unit Numbers   The convention followed here is that platoons, companies, regiments and divisions are identified by Arabic numerals, battalions and corps are identified by Roman numerals, while armies are spelled out. However, all battalions numbered above 10 are identified by Arabic numerals.

Heights, hills, points   Many locales on the battlefield are named for the height in meters identifying them on a map. These places are referred to as "heights," although in some cases, as "hills," especially if the author knew that this height was a clearly defined hill. They are used interchangeably. Some heights are only marked on the maps by a point referencing the additional height above the surrounding terrain (i.e. +1.8 meters). These are referred to as "points."

German Unit Names   The units in a German panzer division usually were prefaced by "panzer," for example the 3rd Panzer Reconnaissance Battalion. In all cases, this "panzer" is removed except where the unit is actually an armored unit or refers to their armored infantry (panzer grenadiers), even though they are usually truck-mounted. The same applies for panzer artillery regiments and other units of a German armored division.

Soviet Unit Names   The Soviets often referred to units as "independent" or "separate." This was not consistently applied in their own reports and therefore it is not used here. It does not create any problems, as there were no two units in the battle with the same designation except for one being "separate." Also the extended honorific names of the Soviet units are not used in most cases (i.e. 42nd Prilukskaya, Order of Lenin, Red Star, Order of Bogdan Khmelnitskii Guards Rifle Division). For those Soviet units that are referred to as antitank artillery brigades, regiments or battalions, we usually do not include the word artillery.

We do capitalize the first letter of the word "front" when it is used as a formation name (Voronezh Front, Steppe Front) as opposed to when it is used to describe the front or the front line.

GERMAN AND SOVIET TERMINOLOGY

German Terminology I have tried to minimize the use of German military terms in this book, even though many may be well known. The ones regularly used in this book are as follows, and are not italicized.

Abteilung Literally this means a "detachment." It is usually used for a unit larger than a company and up to a battalion in size. It is a term mostly used for artillery units, reconnaissance units and assault gun units (which were part of the artillery arm). It was translated throughout this book as battalion, as for most purposes that is what it is. The Soviet equivalent, the "divizion", is also translated as battalion.

The term is also used to designate provisional or temporary armies, like Army Abteilung Kempf. This is translated as Provisional Army Kempf as opposed to the meaningless (at least in English) Army Detachment Kempf.

Arko This is a German abbreviation for artillery commander. These were regimental-type headquarters set up to command corps and army artillery assets.

Das Reich This means the empire, realm, rule, or nation, as in Third Reich. It was the name given to the "Das Reich" SS Division.

Flak This is a German abbreviation for "Flieger Abwehr Kanone," literally aircraft defense gun or antiaircraft. It is used to refer to antiaircraft units, their fire and the shell bursts from such fire.

Fusilier This is a term from the seventeenth century that refers to a soldier armed with a fusil, a light flintlock musket. They were originally artillery guards. Although the fusil ceased being used after the Napoleonic Wars, the term has continued to this day as an honorific for certain units. In this book, the term Fusilier is only used to refer to one of the two armored infantry (panzer grenadier) regiments of the Gross Deutschland Division (the other being the Grenadier Regiment).

Grenadier This is a seventeenth century term that refers to grenade-throwing infantryman. They were usually stronger men who received extra pay. By the Napoleonic Wars, these units had mutated into elite troops. The term continues to this day as an honorific for certain units. During the Second World War, many German infantry regiments were renamed "grenadier" regiments, but without any other changes being made to the unit. For this book, they are called what they are, which is infantry regiments.

In this book, the term grenadier is only used to refer to one of the two armored infantry (panzer grenadier) regiments of the Gross Deutschland Division (the other being the Fusilier Regiment).

Gross Deutschland This means Greater Germany. It was a regular German Army division (not SS!) recruited from throughout Germany as a whole rather then from traditional regional recruiting areas. This was the reason for this name. The division received preferential treatment in personnel and equipment and was generally considered an elite unit in the German Army. The actual German spelling is Großdeutschland or Grossdeutschland. We chose to "Americanize" the spelling.

KampfGruppe   This literally means "battle group," and is the same as the US combat team or task force. It was a temporary organization created from different units. In practice, a seriously depleted division could also be referred to as a kampfgruppe.

K-Bridge   This is a deployable bridge used by the German engineers. There were also B-Bridges, H-Bridges and J-Bridges. They were transported in a platoon-size bridging column that was often named for the type of bridge they carried.

Bridge Set K was the standard box girder pontoon-and-trestle bridging equipment for panzer divisions. Bridge Set B was the standard pontoon-and-trestle bridging equipment for most German divisions. Bridge Set J was designed to carry the new heavy tanks and assault guns.

Landsers   A German slang term for a common soldier, similar to "GI."

Lehr   This means "training" or "demonstration." It was applied to certain units that were responsible for developing tactical doctrine for their particular arm. They were often used as regular combat units.

Leibstandarte   This literally means "life standard" (standard as in a flag or banner) or more correctly "body guard." It was the SS unit originally created as the personal bodyguard for Adolf Hitler.

LSSAH   Common abbreviation used for the Leibstandarte SS Adolf Hitler Division.

Nazi   This is the German abbreviation for the National Socialist German Workers Party (Nationalsozialistische Deutsche Arbeiterpartei or NSDAP). This was a very small political party (originally called the German Workers Party) that was formed in 1919 by a toolmaker named Anton Drexler and which Adolf Hitler joined that same year. In 1933, Adolf Hitler, at the head of this party, became Chancellor of Germany. The Nazis were a fascist (dictatorial) and intensely nationalistic political party as well an ideology. Not all Germans were Nazis, although party membership numbered in the millions.

Nebelwerfer   This literally means "smoke (or fog) thrower." It was the five- or six-tubed rocket launcher that fired either high explosive or smoke rockets. Neither very accurate nor long-ranged, it could quickly lay down a considerable volume of fire or smoke. It was similar to the Soviet Katyusha.

OKH   This is a German abbreviation for the Oberkommando des Heeres (Senior Commander of the Army or German Army High Command). It was the headquarters of the

GERMAN AND SOVIET TERMINOLOGY

German Army and included the Army General Staff. At the time of the Battle of Kursk, its commander was Adolf Hitler and his chief of staff was General Kurt Zeitzler.

OKW This is a German abbreviation for the Oberkommando der Wehmacht (Senior Commander of the Armed Forces or High Command of the Armed Forces). It was the headquarters and staff for all German armed forces. For most of its existence, its commander was Adolf Hitler, his chief of staff was General Wilhelm Keitel, its chief operations officer was General Alfred Jodl. Most of its officers were from the Army General Staff.

Panzer This means tank or armored. The word was originally used for body armor, but has come to mean a German tank in both English and German. A panzer division is an armored division. A panzer is a tank.

Panzer Jaeger This literally means "tank hunter." For all practical purposes it means antitank and consists of towed 37mm, 50mm and 75mm guns as well as the self-propelled antitank units using 75mm armed Marders.

Panzer Grenadier This means armored grenadiers or armored infantry. It is a title for the infantry in a panzer division or a panzer grenadier division. It does not usually mean mechanized infantry, as most of the infantry in German armored units were truck transported and fought on foot. Normally only one battalion in a division was actually mounted in halftracks (armored transports).

Panzer Grenadier Division This means an armored infantry division. Many of these divisions in the German Army were motorized infantry divisions with limited armor assets. The German Army by the middle of 1943 had also created five large panzer grenadier divisions, all of which were committed or held in reserve for the Belgorod Offensive. These large armored divisions included more infantry, more armor and more support troops than either an armored division or a regular panzer grenadier division. They were Gross Deutschland, Leibstandarte SS Adolf Hitler, Das Reich SS, Totenkopf SS and Viking SS Panzer Grenadier Divisions (which was shy on armor compared to the other divisions).

SS This is a German abbreviation for their security section (schutzstaffel). They were a branch of the Nazi party that started as bodyguards for party members and when the party came to power, also provided their concentration camp guards. They were also formed into a military wing to provide a small separate, politically motivated and politically reliable armed force. As such, they had their own training centers, recruitment, rank system, etc. They received preferential treatment in personnel.

Stuka This is a German abbreviation for "sturzkampf," literally diving or falling combat. It came to refer to the most famous of these aircraft, the Junkers Ju-87 dive bomber, their units and also to their dive bombing attacks.

Sturmgeschuetz   This literally means "assault gun." It was a fixed gun mounted on an armored Panzer III chassis. Although part of the artillery branch, it was a "tank-like" vehicle and often used as such.

Totenkopf   This literally means "Death's Head." It refers to the Totenkopf SS Division. It was originally formed from units assigned to guard concentration camps.

Viking   This means Viking (spelled "Wiking" in German), a Nordic wanderer and warrior from the Middle Ages. It refers to the Viking SS Division, which was made up of mainly Germans, some Dutch and Belgians, but was supposed to rely heavily upon Scandinavian (Danish, Norwegian, Swedish and Finnish) volunteers.

Werfer   This means "launcher" and is sometimes used as shorthand for nebelwerfer.

Soviet Terminology

As the Soviet terminology is less well known to many American readers, less of it was used in the text. Still, a few terms and conventions do appear in the book.

Balka   This is a Russian word that translates as gully or ravine.

Bolshevik   This means the "majority faction" of the Russian Communist party, even though for most of their history this was not true (the other branch being Mensheviks). This was the faction of the party that was more radical, aggressive and was led by Lenin. It is this faction which seized power and established the USSR.

Kolkhoz   This was a Soviet abbreviation for a collective farm, nominally run by the farmers with some land allotted for personal use.

Mechanized   As a convention, Soviet armored infantry formations are referred to as mechanized instead of armored infantry, so as to easily distinguish them from the German panzer grenadier (armored infantry) units. As with German panzer grenadiers, they were usually equipped with truck transport as opposed to armored transport. This matches Russian terminology.

MTS   This is the Soviet abbreviation for the Machine and Tractor Stations that supplied most of the agricultural machinery used by the kolkhozes.

NKVD   This was the People's Commissariat of Internal Affairs. This was the name of the Soviet secret police from 1934 to 1946, replacing the previous name OGPU and later known as the KGB. They served a wide range of functions, including internal and external security and espionage. As they controlled the Ministry of the Interior, they also included border security and NKVD combat units.

GERMAN AND SOVIET TERMINOLOGY

Rifle As a convention, Soviet infantry units are referred to as Rifle instead of infantry, so as to easily distinguish them from the German infantry units. This matches Russian terminology and German usage.

RKKA The Workers' and Peasants' Red Army. This was the abbreviation for the full name of the Soviet Army. It was renamed the Soviet Army after the Second World War.

Soviet This means the Soviet Union. It is used in preference to Russia or Russian, since the Soviet Union was a multinational state that had non-Russians in senior positions of leadership (including the head of the state, Joseph Stalin).

Sovkhoz This was a Soviet abbreviation for a Soviet collective farm. It was usually larger than a kolkhoz and was state-financed and under direct state control and management.

STAVKA This was the staff of the Supreme High Command for the Soviet Armed Forces. It was the supreme Soviet headquarters, headed by Josef Stalin and with Generals Zhukov and others as members. It reported to the State Defense Committee, also headed by Stalin. It was the equivalent of the German OKW.

Tank As a convention, Soviet armored units are referred to as tank instead of armored, so as to easily distinguish them from the German panzer (armored) units. This matches Russian terminology and German usage.

USSR Union of Soviet Socialist Republics, or the Soviet Union. This was the communist state established by the Bolsheviks in 1922 that encompassed most of the areas of the old Russian Empire (it did not include Finland or Poland). It was a larger nation in territory and population than modern Russia.

Abbreviations

The following abbreviations are used in this book.

AA	Antiaircraft
Art	Artillery
AT	Antitank
ATR	Antitank Rifle
Bde	Brigade
Bn	Battalion
Bty	Battery (an artillery company)
Co	Company
Col.	Colonel
Col.	Column (a type of bridging platoon)
Con	Construction

D	Division
Eng	Engineer
GD	Gross Deutschland
Gds	Guards
GRD	Guards Rifle Division
Hq	Headquarters
Hvy	Heavy
ID	Infantry Division
KIA	Killed in Action
Lt.	Lieutenant
Lt. Col.	Lieutenant Colonel
MC	Mechanized Corps
MG	Major General
MIA	Missing in Action
Mtn	Mountain
Mtr	Mortar
MTS	Machine and Tractor Station
Pn	Platoon
PoW	Prisoner of War
Pz	Panzer
PzD	Panzer Division
PzGr	Panzer Grenadier
PzGrD	Panzer Grenadier Division
RD	Rifle Division
Rgt	Regiment
Sgt	Sergeant
SP	Self-Propelled
T	Tank
TC	Tank Corps
WIA	Wounded in Action

Transliteration conventions

For German, Americanized spellings were used. Umlauts were not used, and instead the umlaut "a" was replaced with "ae," the umlaut "o" was replaced with "oe," while the umlaut "u" was replaced with "ue."

For Russian, there are several different competing transliteration systems that have fallen in and out of favor over the decades, most individually generated. The Library of Congress system seems to have recently gained popularity. It makes extensive use of the apostrophe to represent soft sounds and uses an "i" for certain variations of Russian letters. This leads to words like "Dal'niaia." The average English language speaking person simply does not know how one is supposed to pronounce an apostrophe. I consider this transliteration system to be an overly scholarly interpretation that loses track of the purpose of a transliteration system, which is to serve people who are not familiar with the language! As the majority of readers have neither the time, inclination nor need to learn the basics of the Russian language, I have used a transliteration scheme that makes use of "y" to represent the soft sound in front of the verbs. This turns "Dal'niaia" into "Dalnyaya" and "Iakovlevo" into the more pronounceable "Yakovlevo." This appears to be a more practical solution for the lay reader.

Specifically, those Russian letters that are transliterated with more than one English letter include the "ж" which becomes "zh," the "х" becomes "kh," "ц" becomes "ts," "ч" becomes "ch," "ш" becomes "sh," "щ" becomes "shch," "ы" becomes "yi," "ю" becomes "yu," "я" becomes "ya." Both "и" and "й" (ikratkoye) are transliterated "i." I did not transliterate "e" to "ye" except when it follows a vowel, otherwise we would have produced spellings like "Vyesyelyii" as opposed to "Veselyii." The hard sound "ъ" is ignored. The soft sound "ь" is represented by a "y" when it precedes a "hard" vowel, otherwise it is ignored. The "ё" (umlaut) is transliterated the same as the "e."

In a few cases, we do not do a direct transliteration as described above where the word or place is commonly known in English. This includes Russia, Moscow and Byelorussia.

Nationalities

There are a number of nationalities referred to in this book. They are briefly defined below.

Caucasian There were a large number of nationalities in the area of the Caucasus Mountains, including Georgians, Armenians, Azerbajainis, Chechens, Ossetians, and others.

Cossacks These are mostly (but not exclusively) a European people who speak Russian. They are descended from horsemen with a tradition of military service and their own independent clan traditions.

Georgians This is a European people in the Caucasus Mountains who speak Georgian, an Indo-European language.

Germans This is a central European people who speak a Germanic dialect and are members of the nation of Germany.

Jewish This is a people scattered across Europe who practice the Jewish religion. They were considered a separate nationality by both the German and Soviet governments.

Kazakhs This is a Central Asian people who speak a Turkish language.

Mongols This is an East Asian people who speak Mongolian. It is also a term applied loosely to the Oriental and Turkish peoples who were commanded by Genghis Khan and his successors in the Middle Ages.

Russians   This is an Eastern European people who speak Russian. In some cases, the word is used to refer to the Soviet Army or Soviet soldiers, as the Russians made up the largest national group in the Soviet Union.

Slavs   This is a term that covers the people of the central and eastern European language group that includes Polish, Czech, Croatian, Serbian, Russian, Ukrainian, etc.

Tatars   This is a loosely applied term that refers to a variety of Mongol or Turkish people, now primarily applied to various Turkish people.

Turkestan   This is a central Asian area, populated by a people (Turkmens) who speak a Turkish language.

Ukrainians   This is an eastern European people who speak the Slavic language of Ukraine. It is closely related to Russia and mutually intelligible. The original "Rus" state was formed around the Ukrainian city of Kiev. It was the second largest national group in the former Soviet Union.

Uzbeks   This is a central Asian people who speak a Turkish language.

Comparative Ranks

The German and Soviet ranks systems were very similar and easily comparable, and are also similar to that of the US Army in the Second World War and now. The confusion to some readers is caused by the US use of the rank of Brigadier General whereas the lowest general officer rank in the German and Soviet Army was Major General. The modern German Army uses a ranking convention for general officers similar to the US See Tables I.1 and I.2.

In this book SS officers are usually referred to by their German Army rank equivalent. This expedient was adopted so as not to introduce a lot of German terms to the text, or to use strange sounding English translations of the ranks such as "Assault Banner Leader."

Table I.1: Comparative German Ranks

US Army	German Army	SS Rank	
(Cadet)	Ensign		
2nd Lieutenant	Jr. Lieutenant	Untersturmfuehrer	(Junior Assault Leader)
1st Lieutenant	Sr. Lieutenant	Obersturmfuehrer	(Senior Assault Leader)
Captain	Captain	Hauptsturmfuehrer	(Captain Assault Leader)
Major	Major	Sturmbannfuehrer	(Assault Banner Leader)
Lt. Colonel	Lt. Colonel	Obersturmbannfuehrer	(Senior Assault Banner Leader)
Colonel	Colonel	Standartenfuehrer	(Standard Leader)

GERMAN AND SOVIET TERMINOLOGY

US Army	German Army	SS Rank	
(no equivalent)		Oberfuehrer	(Senior Leader)
Brigadier General	Major General	Brigadefuehrer	(Brigade Leader)
Major General	Lt. General	Gruppenfuehrer	(Group Leader)
Lt. General	General of the . . .	Obergruppenfuchrer	(Senior Group Leader)
General	Colonel General	Oberstgruppenfuehrer	(Col. Group Leader)
General of the Army	Field Marshal	Reichsfuehrer SS	(SS Reich Leader)

Note: In this book, the author uses the German ranks, not their translated US comparative rank.

Table I.2 Comparative Soviet Ranks

US Army	Soviet Army
(Cadet)	Ensign
2nd Lieutenant	Jr. Lieutenant
1st Lieutenant	Sr. Lieutenant
Captain	Captain
Major	Major
Lt. Colonel	Lt. Colonel
Colonel	Colonel
Brigadier General	Major General
Major General	Lt. General
Lt. General	Colonel General
General	General of the Army
General of the Army	Marshal of . . .
(no equivalent)	Marshal of the Soviet Union

Appendix II

AIR CAMPAIGN STATISTICS

In the process of collecting data on the air campaign, a lot of miscellaneous charts and tables were assembled. These are presented here as a supplement to the text of the book.

Air Force Organizations

German Air Force
The German Air Force was organized into air fleets (or air forces), of which there were a total of eight during the war, and four on the Eastern Front at its peak. Each fleet was usually commanded by a Colonel General or Field Marshal. They reported to the Supreme Commander of the German Air Force, which was Reich Marshal Hermann Goering. The chief of staff was General Jeschonnek. Each air fleet had a number of air corps or other commands under its control. An air corps was usually commanded by a Lt. General or General. The air corps on the Eastern Front tended to be an area command with units attached to it as the situation required. Beneath the air corps could be air divisions. In the case of the VIII Air Corps, it did not have any, although the Sixth Air Fleet in the north had a mixture of air corps and air divisions, all of which reported directly to it. The divisions were usually commanded by a Major General, Lt. General or General. The basic combat unit of the German Air Force was the Geschwader. This was the equivalent of a US wing or a UK group, consisting of 100 to 120 aircraft and usually commanded by a Major, Lt. Colonel, Colonel or Major General who usually flew operations with their command. The Geschwader or Wing was usually broken into three Gruppe and a staff squadron, with many units having a fourth Group for operational training, but these were often used for operations, usually separate from the main body of the unit. The Gruppe is the equivalent of a US group or a UK wing, consisting of 30 to 40 aircraft, and usually commanded by a Captain, Major or Lt. Colonel. It was not that unusual for German fighter groups to have more than 40 aircraft. The Gruppe was usually broken into three Staffel and a staff section of 3 to 4 aircraft. The Staffel was the equivalent of a US or UK squadron, consisting of 9 to 12 aircraft and usually commanded by a Senior (First) Lieutenant or Captain. The squadron was further broken down into sections of three or four aircraft called a Kette, or a Schwarm, if fighters. These were equivalent to a US or UK flight. They were commanded by Lieutenants or NCOs. Unlike the US and UK, the Germans made extensive use of NCOs as pilots.

AIR CAMPAIGN STATISTICS

A fighter squadron consisted of 20 to 25 pilots and around 150 ground crew. A group of 40 to 50 fighters had around 500 ground personnel.

Soviet Air Force

The Soviet air force was organized in a structure similar to an army. Attached to each Front was an air army of variable size. Within each air army were a number of corps, divisions and regiments, based upon the needs of the operation. Corps were divided into two or three divisions, divisions were divided into two or three regiments and regiments were divided into three squadrons. An air regiment had about 30 planes.

Prior to the war, the air forces were divided organizationally into the Aviation of the Central Command (later the bomber air force), the Aviation of the Military Districts, air armies (mainly mixed air divisions), and the military aviation (corps and squadrons). In June 1941 there were 79 air divisions and 5 brigades; moreover, the aviation had increased by 80% compared to the year 1939. The majority of the aircraft were of the old models, but by 22 June 1941, new and modern fighters MiG-3, Yak-1, LAGG-3, the low-flying attack aircraft Il-2, and the bomber Pe-2 were being deployed. Overall there were 2,739 aircraft. On the first day of the war, 1200 airplanes were lost on the ground and in the air (the Byelorussian Military District alone lost 738 airplanes). The aviation was, basically, spread among the combined armies. The long-range bomber air force was put together in February 1942, in subordination to STAVKA (Major General A. Golovanov).

Starting in May 1942 the air armies of variable personnel were forming, and in fall of 1942 the air corps of the Supreme High Command Reserve was formed for airlifts to important locations. In December 1944, the Long-range Air Corps was restructured into the Eighteenth Air Army (four air corps), in subordination to the leadership of the Military Air Force. By mid-summer 1944, Soviet aviation solidly won the supremacy in the air. Toward the end of 1944, there were a total of 16 air armies. By January 1945, these had 15,500 airplanes, the majority of the new types made in USSR, and some were received from the USA and UK.[1]

VIII Air Corps Order of Battle

No surviving order of battle for the VIII Air Corps could be located. There are three primary sources for determining their order of battle. One is the VIII Air Corps liaison officer report in the Second Army's files for 5 July, which lists the number of sorties by the unit conducting them and their plane type.[2] Next is the march plan for the VIII Air Corps that was located in the III Panzer Corps files.[3] The other, and least reliable, is Seidemann's (VIII Air Corps commander) post-war interview, which provides an order of battle and his estimate of the unit strengths.[4]

These were then cross-checked to the Luftwaffe quartermaster report of German planes lost and the claims of kills for 5 July.[5] More accurate strength estimates were provided by the "Flugzeugbestand und Bewegungsmeldungen, 3.42–12.44."[6] There are additional secondary sources that have been examined, including Klink. These sources have been combined to create the following order of battle table.[7]

Table II.1: VIII Air Corps Fighters

Unit Name	Number and Type of Planes, 1 July[8]
3rd Fighter Wing[9]	
II Group	2 Me-109 G-2
	31 Me-109 G-4
III Group	32 Me-109 G-4[10]
52nd Fighter Wing[11]	1 Me-109 G-4
	3 Me-109 G-6
I Group	34 Me-109 G-6
III Group	36 Me-109 G-4
	6 Me-109 G-6

Table II.2: VIII Air Corps Ground Attack

Unit Name	Number and Type of Planes, 1 July
1st Ground Attack Wing[12]	None
I Group	52 Fw-190 A-5
II Group (5th, 6th & 7th Sqdns)	5 Fw-190 A-5 (staff)
	2 Fw-190 F-3 (staff)
	3 Fw-190 A-5/U3 (5th Squadron)
	10 Fw-190 F-3 (5th Squadron)
	7 Fw-190 A-5/U3 (6th Squadron)
	6 Fw-190 F-3 (6th Squadron)
	16 Hs-123 B-1 (7th Squadron)
4th Squadron	17 Hs-129 B-2
8th Squadron	16 Hs-129 B-2
4th Sqdn/2nd Ground Attack Wing[13]	17 Hs-129 B-2
8th Sqdn/2nd Ground Attack Wing ?	10 Hs-129 B-1/2
Antitank Squadron/51st Fighter Wing[14]	15 Hs-129 B-1/2

Table II.3: VIII Air Corps Stukas

Unit Name	Number and Type of Planes, 1 July
2nd Stuka Wing[15]	2 Ju-87 D-3
	1 Ju-87 D-5
I Group	36 Ju-87 D-3
	1 Ju-87 D-5

AIR CAMPAIGN STATISTICS

Unit Name	Number and Type of Planes, 1 July
II Group	6 Ju-87 D-1
	28 Ju-87 D-3
	2 Ju-87 D-5
III Group	1 Ju-87 D-1
	33 Ju-87 D-3
	1 Ju-87 D-5
10th Squadron (Panzer)	0 ?
77th Stuka Wing[16]	1 Ju-87 D-1
	2 Ju-87 D-3
I Group	5 Ju-87 D-1
	35 Ju-87 D-3
II Group	41 Ju-87 D-5
III Group ?	3 Ju-87 D-1
	33 Ju-87 D-3

Table II.4: VIII Air Corps Bombers

Unit Name	Number and Type of Planes, 1 July
3rd Bombardment Wing[17]	1 Ju-88 A-4
I Group	34 Ju-88 A-4
II Group	33 Ju-88 A-4
	4 Ju-88 C-6
III Group ?	1 Do-217 K-1
27th Bombardment Wing[18]	1 He-111 H-11
	1 He-111 H-16
I Group	21 He-111 H-6
II Group	1 He-111 H-11
	33 He-111 H-16
III Group	1 He-111 H-11
	33 He-111 H-16
14th Squadron	10 He-111 H-16
55th Bombardment Wing[19]	4 He-111 H-16
II Group	8 He-111 H-6
	2 He-111 H-14
	37 He-111 H-16
III Group	2 He-111 H-6
	6 He-111 H-11

299

Unit Name	Number and Type of Planes, 1 July
	26 He-111 H-11/R1
	12 He-111 H-16
14th Squadron ?	0 ?
I Group/100th Bombardment Wing[20]	4 He-111 H-6
	12 He-111 H-11
	1 He-111 H-14
	21 He-111 H-16

Table II.5: VIII Air Corps Other Air Units

Unit Name	Number and Type of Planes, 1 July
6th Close-range Reconnaissance Group[21]	0 ?
3.(H)/32 ?	8 Fw-189 ?
5.(H)/32	9 Hs-126 B-1
7.(H)/32	3 Fw-189 A-2
	4 Fw-189 A-2 trop.
	2 Fw-189 A-3
2.(H)/33	8 Me-110 G-3
3rd Long-range Reconnaissance Group[22]	0 ?
2.(F)/11	10 Ju-88 D-1
2.(F)/22	10 Ju-88 D-1
	2 Ju-88 D-5
2.(F)/100	11 Ju-88 D-1
	2 Ju-88 D-5
Harassment Bomber Group[23]	60[24]
VIII Air Corps Transport Squadron[25]	13 Ju-52
Royal Hungarian Air Division[26]	
Fighter Group	30 Me-109
Dive Bomber Group	30 Ju-87
Ground Attack Squadron	12
Close-range Reconnaissance Squadron	9
Long-range Reconnaissance Squadron	9
Total Aircraft	1,093

AIR CAMPAIGN STATISTICS

Table II.6: Served in Army Group South Area

And sent missions into Belgorod-Kharkov area	
2nd Close-range Reconnaissance Group[27]	3 Me-109 G-4
1/2 NAG	9 Me-109 G-4
	2 Me-109 G-6
	2 Me-109 G-6 trop.
No record of missions sent to Belgorod-Kharkov area	
10th Squadron/5th Night Fighter Wing[28]	14 aircraft (?)
Night Fighter Flight, Fourth Air Fleet[29]	4 aircraft (?)
4.(F)/122 ?	8 Ju-88 D-1
	2 Ju-88 D-5
	2 He-111 H-6
4.(F)/Night ?	7 Do-17P
	4 Do-217 K-1
Wekusta 76 (weather squadron)	7 Ju-88 D-1

Assigned to the VIII Air Corps was a Hungarian air contingent. A second, more detailed, order of battle is presented in Table II.7.[30]

Table II.7: Hungarian Air Contingent Order of Battle

Unit	Airfield	Commander	Aircraft Type[31]	Number
I Long-range Reconnaissance Group	Major Gyula Timar			
1/1 Reconnaissance Squadron	Kharkov-Osnova	Captain Adorjan Mersich	Ju-88 D-1/2	
3/1 Tactical Reconnaissance Squadron	Kharkov-Grobly	Captain Imre Telbisz	Fw-189 A	12[32]
4/1 Bomber Squadron	Kharkov-Southeast	Captain Tihamer Ghyczy	Ju-88 A-4 & Ju-88 C-6	
V Fighter Group	Kharkov-South	Major Aladar Heppes*		Me-109
5/1 Fighter Squadron	Kharkov-Voychenko	Captain Gyorgy Ujszaszy	Me-109 F-4/G-2	
5/2 Fighter Squadron	Kharkov-Voychenko	Captain Gyula Horvath	Me-109 F-4/G-2	

* Lt. Colonel Aladar Heppes was credited during the war with eight claimed kills and four unconfirmed kills.[33]

The Hungarian 2/2 Dive-bomber Squadron, commanded by Captain Jeno Korosy, was probably not at Kursk.[34] In August it is claimed that it had 11 Ju-87 D-3s and 1 Ju-87 D-5.[35] The total number of Hungarian Aircraft as of 1 July 1943 is given as: 30 bombers, 30 fighters, 12 ground attack and 18 reconnaissance. Most likely the 12 ground attack planes were not there, nor were all 30 bombers, so there were probably around 63 or less Hungarian manned aircraft at Kursk.[36]

Table II.8: VIII Air Corps Commanders[37]

Unit Name	5 July Location	Commander
Fourth Air Fleet	Dnepropetrovsk	Gen. Otto Dessloch
VIII Air Corps	Mikoyanovka	Gen. Hans Seidemann
II/3rd Fighter Wing	Rogan	Maj. Werner-Kurt Braendle
III/3rd Fighter Wing	Bessonovka	Maj. Wolfgang Ewald* (acting) Captain Walter Dahl[38]
52nd Fighter Wing	Bessonovka	LtCol. Dieter Hrabak
I Group	Bessonovka	Capt. Helmut Bennemann** (acting) Captain Johannes Wiese
III Group	Ugrim	Maj. Hubertus von Bonin*** Capt. Guenther Rall (6 July)
1st Ground Attack Wing	Varvarovka	Maj. Alfred Druschel
I Group	Bessonovka	Maj. Georg Doerffel
II Group	Bessonovka	Capt. Frank Neubert
Antitank Commander	Captain Bruno Meyer[39]	
4th Squadron	Varvarovka	Sr. Lt. George Dornemann (?)[40]
8th Squadron	Varvarovka	Lt. Orth (?)
4th Sqdn/2nd Ground Attack Wing****	Varvarovka	Capt. Matuschek (?)
8th Sqdn/2nd Ground Attack Wing****	Varvarovka	Sr. Lt. Oswald (?)
Antitank Squadron/51st Fighter Wing		Sr. Lt. Hans Jentsch[41]
2nd Stuka Wing	Krestovoi	LtCol. Dr. Ernst Kupfer
I Group	Kharkov-North	Capt. Wilhelm Hobein
II Group	Kharkov-North	Maj. Hans-Karl Stepp

AIR CAMPAIGN STATISTICS

Unit Name	5 July Location	Commander
III Group	Kharkov-North	Capt. Walter Krauss
		Capt. Hans-Ulrich Rudel, 19 July*****
10th Squadron (Panzer)	Kharkov-North	Sr. Lt. Helmut Schuebe[42]
77th Stuka Wing	Tolokonnoye	Maj. Helmut Bruck
I Group	Tolokonnoye	Maj. Werner Roell
II Group	Tolokonnoye	Capt. Helmut Leicht
III Group	(?)	Capt. Franz Kieslich
3rd Bomber Wing	Poltava	LtCol. Lt. Lehwess-Litzmann
I Group	Poltava	Maj. Joachim Joedicke
II Group	Poltava	Major Juergen de Lalande[43]
III Group	Poltava	Maj. Horst Bengsch
27th Bomber Wing Hq	Dnepropetrovsk	Col. Hans-Henning Frhr. von Beust
I Group	Dnepropetrovsk	Capt. Joachim Petzold (?)
II Group	Dnepropetrovsk	Major Karl-August Petersen[44]
III Group	Kharkov-Voichenko	Capt. Karl Mayer (?)
14th Squadron	(?)	
55th Bomber Wing	Rogan	LtCol. Dr. Ernst Kuehl
II Group	Rogan(?) & Stalino	Maj. Heinz Hoefer
III Group	Rogan & Stalino	Maj. Wilhelm Antrup
14th Squadron	Poltava	Sr. Lt. Mathias Bermadinger
I/100th Bomber Wing	Poltava	Captain Hans-George Baetcher[45]
6th Close-range Recon. Group	Veterinar	Capt. Heribert Rinke ?
10th Flak Division		MG Franz Engel

* Command ended on 14 July due to being shot down and captured.
** Bennemann was injured on 10 May 1943 and in convalescence.
*** Command change from Bonin to Rall occurred on 6 July when Bonin was promoted to take command of the 54th Fighter Wing.
**** The main body of the 2nd Ground Attack Wing was in Italy; only the Hs-129 squadrons were in Russia.
***** Command change to Rudel occurred on 19 July as Krauss was killed the night of 16/17 July.

There are other slightly different similar listings available.[46] Due to the paucity of German records, it is difficult to resolve with confidence all the differences in the listings, although some of these differences may be resolved with additional research, especially in the personnel files.

The Other German Aces

The Luftwaffe produced over 5,000 aces during the course of the war. German kill claims are based upon a mix of records, as most of the Luftwaffe records did not survive the war. The standards for German claims were as rigorous as any air force, and as such these claims are probably not grossly over-inflated. The astoundingly high number of claims by German aces, especially when compared to any other air force, war, or theater, is fundamentally due to three factors. First, the war on the Eastern Front operated continuously for four years at a high level of intensity. There is no other campaign with a similar intensity and duration. Second, the Soviet air force was not particularly adept but was used actively, aggressively, and fought with courage. As such, they often took unusually high losses and the Germans were able to maintain favorable kill ratios. Third, the Germans kept their aces in combat throughout the war.

There were two fighter wings involved in the southern part of the Battle of Kursk, the 3rd and 52nd Fighter Wings:

The 3rd Fighter Wing
Although less famous than the 52nd Fighter Wing, as witnessed by its kill claims on 5 July, it was not any less effective than the 52nd Fighter Wing. See Table IV.10 for the pilots identified as having been at the fighting in the south around Belgorod during the month of July.

The 52nd Fighter Wing
Based on airplanes downed, the German 52nd Fighter Wing was the single most accomplished air formation in the history of warfare. At the time of Kursk, its pilots included the three men who would become the highest scoring aces in the history of air warfare, Erich Hartmann, Gerhard Barkhorn and Guenther Rall. Among the ten highest scoring German aces of the war, five of them flew for the 52nd Fighter Wing.

The head of the 52nd Fighter Wing was Dietrich Hrabak (125 kills to his credit during the war). The I Group was headed by the absent Captain Helmut Bennemann (93 kills to his credit during the war),[47] the II Group was headed by Captain Helmut Kuehle (16 kills to his credit during the war) and included Barkhorn (301 kills to his credit for the war). The II Group was not present at Kursk. The III Group was led by Major Hubertus von Bonin (77 kills to his credit during the war) and on 6 July by Guenther Rall (275 kills to his credit for the war), and included Hartmann (352 kills), Walter Krupinski (197 kills), Friedrich Obseler (120 kills) and Edmund Rossmann (93 kills).

Its pilots who participated in the Battle of Kursk, along with their total wartime victories, are listed in Table II.11.

AIR CAMPAIGN STATISTICS

Table II.9: Claimed German Kills by Unit, 5 July 1943

	Total Claimed Kills, 5 July
Staff II/3 JG	5
4/3 JG	24
5/3 JG	26
6/3 JG	14
Staff III/3 JG	2
7/3 JG	15
8/3 JG	11
9/3 JG	11
Staff/52 JG	3
Staff I/52 JG	19
1/52 JG	13
2/52 JG	8
3/52 JG	5
Staff III/52 JG	4
7/52 JG	17
8/52 JG	14
9/52 JG	9
I/100 KG	1
2/2 StG	1
3/1 SG	1

Table II.10: Claimed Kills by 3rd Fighter Wing

	Total Victories	Scoring Ranking[48]	Victories on 5 July	Unit
Sr. Lt. Joachim Kirschner	188	20th	8	5/3 JG
Maj. Werner-Kurt Braendle	180	21st	5	II/3 JG
Sgt. (Uffz.) Gerhard Thyben	157	31st	–	6/3 JG
Capt. Wilhelm Lemke	131	54th	3	9/3 JG
Sr. Lt. Emil Bitsch	108	86th	6	8/3 JG

ACES AT KURSK

	Total Victories	Scoring Ranking[48]	Victories on 5 July	Unit
Sr. Lt. Werner Lucas	106	89th	4	4/3 JG
M. Sgt. Hans Schleef	99	106th	3	7 & 4/3 JG
T. Sgt. Hans Gruenberg	82	–	6	5/3 JG
Maj. Wolfgang Ewald	78	–	2	III/3 JG Captured 14 July
M. Sgt. Alfred Surau	46	–	4	9/3 JG
Lt. Hans Frese	44	–	4	4/3 JG
Lt. Juergen Hoeschelmann	44	–	1	7/3 JG
Lt. Ernst-Heinz Lohr	37	–	2	6/3 JG
Sgt. Emil Zibler	36	–	–	9/3 JG Missing 5 July
Capt. Karl-Heinz Langer	30		1	7/3 JG
Lt. Raimond Koch	26	–	2	8/3 JG
Lt. Hartwig Dohse	24	–	4	5/3 JG
Lt. Winfried Schmidt	19	–	2	6/3 JG
Sgt. Rudolf Traphan	13		2	5/3 JG
Others (multiple kills on 5 July)				
Sgt. (Uffz.) Franz Birnstill	7		3	7/3 JG
Sgt. (Uffz.) Arnold Bringham			2	5/3 JG
Lt. Wolfgang Chichorius			3	4/3 JG Killed 7 July
Sgt. Eyrich			3	6/3 JG
Sgt (Uffz.) Geyer			3	7/3 JG
Lt. Hans Reiser			3	4/3 JG Killed 10 July
Airman 1st Class Hans Schilling			2	6/3 JG Injured 5 July, Killed 11 July
Lt. Hermann Schuster			4	4/3 JG
Sr. Lt. Paul-August Stolte	5		3	6/3 JG

AIR CAMPAIGN STATISTICS

Table II.11: Claimed Kills by 52nd Fighter Wing

	Total Victories	Scoring Ranking	Victories on 5 July	Unit
Lt. Erich Hartmann	352	1st	4	7/52 JG
Captain Guenther Rall	275	3rd	–	III/52 JG
Sr. Lt. Walter Krupinski	197	16th	2	7/52 JG Injured 5 July
Lt. Franz Schall	137	42nd	–	3/52 JG
Walter Wolfrum	137	42nd	–	
Capt. Johannes Wiese	133	50th	12	I/52 JG
LtCol. Dietrich Hrabak	125	62nd	3	Staff/52 JG
Lt. Friedrich Obseler**	120	69th	–	8/52 JG
Lt. Berthold Korts	113	80th	4	8/52 JG
M. Sgt. Franz Woidich	110	83rd	2	3/52 JG
Sr. Lt. Paul-Heinrich Dahne	99	106th	4	2/52 JG
M. Sgt. Edmund "Paule" Rossmann	93	–	3	Staff III & 7/52 JG Captured 9 July
Lt. Johann-Hermann Meier	78	–	6	1/52 JG
Hubertus von Bonin	77*	–	–	III/52 JG
Capt. Josef Haiboeck	77	–	3	1/52 JG
Lt. Johannes Bunzek	75	–	2	7/52 JG
Sgt (Uffz.) Karl Heinz Meltzer	74	–	4	8/52 JG
M. Sgt. Karl "Fox" Munz	60	–	2	Staff I/52 JG
M. Sgt. Walter Jahnke	58	–	4	Staff I/52 JG
Sgt. Hermann Wolf	57	–	2	9/52 JG
Sgt. Karl-Friedrich Schumacher	56	–	–	III/52 JG Wounded 5 July
Sgt. Wilhelm Hauswirth	54	–	1	8/52 JG Killed 5 July
M. Sgt. Guenther Toll	49	–	4	Staff III & 7/52 JG
Lt. Karl-Heinz Pluecker	42	–	1	I/52 JG
Sgt. (Uffz.) Werner Hohenberg	32	–	4	8/52 JG Injured 9 July

	Total Victories	Scoring Ranking	Victories on 5 July	Unit
Lt. Herbert Fraenzel	18	–	2	1/52 JG
Sgt. Manfred Lotzmann	15	–	–	8/52 JG Killed 5 July
Others (multiple kills on 5 July)				
Sgt. Heinz Kurten			2	9/52 JG
Lt. Ernst Lohberg			4	7/52 JG Injured 7 July Missing 9 July

* Includes four kills in Spanish Civil War.
** Lt. Obseler took command of the 8th squadron on 6 July 1943 according to Rall, *My Logbook*, but claimed no kills in the month of July.

Other German Aces

Kurt-Werner Braendle   Kurt Braendle was born on 12 January 1912 in Ludwigsburg in Wuerttemberg. Due to his passion for flying he was also a civilian glider and airplane pilot and a flight instructor. He joined the Luftwaffe in 1935. Assigned to the 53rd Fighter Wing he claimed 14 victories on the Western Front. He was injured in an accident during the French Campaign. He was involved with the Russian Campaign at the start but was transferred in October to the west and in December to the Mediterranean Theater. Now a captain, in May of 1942 he took command of the II Group of the 3rd Fighter Wing and went back to the Eastern Front. He was awarded the Knight's Cross on 1 July 1942 after 49 kills and a very successful summer July and August, he was awarded Oak Leaves on 27 August 1942 for 100 victories.

Already one of the highest scoring aces on the Eastern Front, he claimed his 150th victory in July 1943. In August 1943, he was transferred back to the Western Front and killed in action west of Amsterdam on 3 November 1943 by fighters of the Royal Canadian Air Force.

Before the Battle of Kursk he was credited with 144 or 146 victories. On 5 July he claimed four Il-2s and 1 Yak-1, he claimed 2 Il-2s on 6 July, and Il-2 and two La-5s on 7 July, two La-5s on 14 July, and a "Yak-4" and a Boston on 17 July. The two claims for the 17th can be questioned as no Yak-4s were deployed in the Second or Seventeenth Air Armies and no Bostons or other two engined bombers were reported lost by these two air armies on the 17th.[49] He was credited during the war with 170 or 172 kills or 180 kills.[50]

Hubertus von Bonin   Huberus von Bonin was born in Potsdam 3 August 1911. He first fought in Spain as part of the German Condor Legion where he claimed four Spanish

AIR CAMPAIGN STATISTICS

Republican fighters. He claimed his first victory of the Second World War in May 1940. In the fall of 1941, he took command of the III Group, 52nd Fighter Wing. On 17 November 1942, he was awarded the Knight's Cross for 51 victories. On 6 July 1943 he was promoted to the command of 54th Fighter Wing, transferring from the south of Kursk to the north of Kursk. Bonin was killed in action on 15 December 1943, shot down by Soviet P-39 Airacobras. He was credited with 77 kills.

Wolfgang Ewald   Wolfgang Ewald was born 26 March 1911 in Hamburg. He initially served in the German Army, but transferred to the Luftwaffe in 1935. He participated in the Spanish Civil War, Polish Campaign, French Campaign and in the Battle of Britain. After serving in staff assignments, he was returned to combat in April 1942. Major Ewald was awarded a Knight's Cross in December 1942. At Kursk, he was the commander of the III Group, 3rd Fighter Wing. His plane was hit by Soviet antiaircraft near Belgorod on 14 July 1943 and he was forced to parachute over enemy lines. Taken prisoner, he was held until December 1949. He later served in the West German Air Force, retiring as a Lt. Colonel. He passed away 24 February 1995.

He is credited with 78 aerial victories: one in the Spanish Civil War, one during the Battle of Britain, and 76 on the Eastern Front.

Dietrich Hrabak   Dietrich Hrabak was born in 1914 near Leipzig. He entered the German Navy in 1934, becoming friends with Johannes Steinhoff at that time. He was transferred to the Luftwaffe in November 1935 and was noted for crashing a number of aircraft during training. He took command of the Vienna Fighter Group and was shot down 1 September 1939 on his first mission over Poland. He scored his first kill on 13 May 1940 near Sedan. He flew in the Battle of Britain and had 18 kills to his credit when he was transferred east in spring 1941.

He was assigned to the 54th Fighter Wing and was involved in the invasion of Greece and in the war in the northern half of Russia. He transferred south to command the 52nd Fighter Wing in October 1942. His old friend Steinhoff was the II Group commander there already. Hrabak flew for the entire length of the war, from 1939 to 1945, scoring 125 victories, with 18 of them on the Western Front. Most of these were scored before the end of 1943. He flew over 800 combat sorties, and was shot down seven times but never wounded.

After the war, he worked as a sales manager for a machinery company and then joined the German Air Force in 1955. He retired as a Major General on 1 October 1976.

Joachim Kirschner   Joachim Kirschner was born 7 June 1920 at Niederloessnitz, Saxony. He joined the Luftwaffe in 1939 and claimed his first victory in August 1941. He was awarded the Knight's Cross on 23 December 1942. At this point, he had over 50 claimed kills.

At Kursk, he was with the 5th squadron of the 3rd Fighter Wing. He was the second highest scoring German pilot on 5 July, after Wiese. He is credited with 8 or 9 kills that day. He is credited with 21 or 22 kills from 5 July thought 12 July 1943.[51] Like Braendle, he also claimed his 150th victory in July.

He was awarded Oak Leaves on 2 August 1943 after being credited with 170 victories. In fall of 1943 he was made commander of the IV Group of the 27th Fighter Wing and transferred from the Eastern Front. On 17 December 1943 he was shot down in Croatia by pilots from the U.S. Air Force 57th Fighter Group. Kirschner safely bailed out but landed in a Yugoslavian partisan controlled area. He was captured and killed by firing squad.

He is credited with 188 career kills.

Other Soviet Aces at the Battle of Kursk[52]

Because of the nature of the air campaign from 1942 to 1945, like the Germans, many of the top Soviet aces were located in the south. Some of the other major scorers who were at the Battle of Kursk include:

Arsenii Vorozheikin Arsenii Vasilyevich Vorozheikin was born 28 October 1912 in the Nizhnii Novgorod (Gorkii) area. He entered the Red Army in 1931, serving with cavalry units for three years before going to flight school and getting his wings in 1937. He gained his first combat experience fighting the Japanese in Mongolia in 1939, where he scored six kills. He then participated in the war against Finland in 1940, but was not credited with any kills there. He attended the Air Force Academy in 1942 and after graduation was assigned to the very depleted 728th Fighter Regiment in September of 1942 on the Kalinin Front. At this stage the unit was down to six planes and 10 pilots and still using the woefully slow I-16s.[53] The regiment converted to Yak-7bs in March 1943 and in July Vorozheikin was promoted to Captain and a squadron leader. This regiment was then shifted down to the Fifth Air Army, and on 9 July transferred over to the Second Air Army.

Vorozheikin drew his first blood against the Luftwaffe on 14 July while leading a fighter sweep of six Yak-7s. Between Bogoroditskoye-Belinikhino-Shakhovo they got into a fight with 40 Ju-87s and 6 Me-109s. He claimed two Ju-87s on his own and a combined kill with one other member of his squadron. His squadron claimed nine kills in this fight.[54] On this day, the IV Fighter Corps was patrolling this area while the Germans made extensive use of Stukas, including in front of the III Panzer Corps attack zone. Still, the losses appear to be overstated, as the Germans only lost three Ju-87s this day.

Vorozheikin continued to score until he was pulled from combat in October 1944 due to a conflict with his regiment commander. At this point he was deputy regiment commander and a major. He then took up training of front line units and saw little combat, although he did claim an Ar-234 jet in April 1945. He scored 52 victories during the war (including the six from Manchuria) and 13 shared victories. He flew 300 sorties and had 90 encounters. He was twice awarded the Hero of the Soviet Union. He was the Soviet Union's sixth highest scoring ace.

He continued service after the war, graduating from the General Staff Academy in 1952 and retiring in 1957 at the rank of Major General.

AIR CAMPAIGN STATISTICS

During the Battle of Kursk, Vorozheikin was credited with four solo kills and one shared kill. This included on 14 July a Ju-87 at Prokhorovka, a Ju-87 at Shakhovo, an Me-109 at Shakhovo, and a shared kill of an Hs-126 also at Shakhovo. On 16 July he claimed an Me-109 at Shakhovo.[55] This matches the reports of kills provided by the 728th Fighter Regiment that are included in Appendix II. The Germans do not report an Hs-126 as lost on the 14th, although one is reported as lost on the 15th.

Nikolai Skomorokhov Nikolai Mikhailovich Skomorokhov was born in the Saratov area in May 1920. He joined the military in December 1940 and was awarded his wings in 1942. He joined the 164th Fighter Regiment on 29 November 1942, flying LaGG-3s.

He was still a developing pilot at the start of the battle, credited with only three kills and one shared kill before July. He is credited with no kills during the Battle of Kursk but claimed two kills and a shared kill on 24 July 1943 in operations outside of the Kursk battle area. He began scoring steadily and was promoted to Captain in the second half of 1943 and continued scoring, especially in 1945. He was never wounded. He was twice awarded the Hero of the Soviet Union.

He continued service after the war, graduating from the Frunze Academy in 1949 and the General Staff Academy in 1958. Skomorokhov rose to Marshal of Aviation in 1981 but was later killed in an automobile accident near Moscow.

Vladimir Bobrov Vladimir Ivanovich Bobrov was an older pilot, having fought in the Spanish Civil War where he gained 13 kills along with four shared kills. He was a squadron leader at the start of the invasion, scoring his first victory against the Luftwaffe on 22 June 1941. He took command of the 27th Fighter Regiment on 4 April 1943 (renamed in September 1943 the 129th Guards Fighter Regiment), which developed into one of the top Soviet units. This unit on 6 July attacked 12 Me-109s and 27 Ju-87s with 10 Yak-1s lead by Bobrov. They claimed ten German planes destroyed for no losses.[56] The German VIII Air Corps lost only seven planes this day.

Bobrov continued as the regiment's commander, ending the war as a Lt. Colonel. Bobrov was the 11th highest scoring Soviet ace, but was never awarded the Hero of the Soviet Union. Every other ace listed below was awarded the Hero of the Soviet Union at least once, so this exception was highly unusual. He apparently was in disfavor due to "character problems." He had 43 personal victories to his credit, 24 shared victories and 112 engagements. In May 1944 he had been expelled from membership of the Communist Party "for misbehavior in everyday life and violation of party ethics." In March 1945 he was reinstated.

He continued service after the war, being promoted to Colonel in 1948. For "violations in the service" he was later demoted to Major and was again promoted back to Colonel in 1958. He became a lecturer at Kharkov State University. He passed away in 1970 at the age of 54. He was posthumously awarded the title of Hero of the Soviet Union on 20 March 1991, nine months before the Soviet Union ceased to exist.

Vatalii Popkov Vatalii Ivanovich Popkov was born in Moscow 1 May 1922 and entered service 15 September 1940. He was awarded his wings the following year and was posted to a flying school. In April 1942 he was assigned to the 5th Guards Fighter Regiment operating around Rzhev flying LaGG-3s. His first kill was in May 1942 and he scored his fifth victory on 5 August. The regiment was then assigned La-5s and redeployed to Stalingrad. He scored seven victories in the Stalingrad area, but these were nullified in a disciplinary action by Zhukov against the fighter arm.

Popov scored three kills at Kursk on 6 July, with three Me-109s claimed to east of Maslova Pristin, Ternovaya and east of Bezlyudovka.[57] These three kills cannot be confirmed by German records.[58] He claimed other kills in July but they were outside the battle area.[59] On 3 August, he was shot down, forced to bail out and sustained serious burns. Upon his recovery he took command of the first squadron of the regiment and began to score regularly. During this time, he claimed to have shot down German ace Wilhelm Batz near Izyum in August 1943. Batz was briefly captured and Popkov met him during his interrogation.[60] Popkov was wounded in 17 April 1945 when he rammed a Ju-88 over Berlin, but was back in action the following day.

After the war he was placed in command of the 739th Fighter Regiment and then served as deputy commander for the 324th Fighter Regiment in Korea, where he was credited with three kills against the United States. He graduated from the Air Force Academy and in 1964 from the General Staff Academy. He was promoted to Lt. General and in 1980 became a lecturer at the Soviet Air Force Academy.

He scored a total of 41 kills and one shared kill. This does not include the three kills in Korea nor the 7 kills disallowed by General Zhukov. He flew over 300 sorties and had 117 encounters. He was awarded Hero of the Soviet Union twice. During his career, he claimed to have flown 53 different types of aircraft.

Sergei Luganskii Sergei Danilovich Luganskii was born in Vernyii (Alma-Ata or Almatyi in what is now Kazakhstan) on 1 October 1918 and joined the army in 1938. He completed pilot training two years later and served in the war with Finland. He was promoted to squadron leader of the 162nd Fighter Regiment in October 1941. At Stalingrad he was credited with destroying an Me-109 with his Yak-1 on 14 September 1942 by ramming. He was then credited in Soviet sources with shooting down the Italian ace Gibelli with some 50 victories.[61] This is a questionable claim as the top-scoring Italian ace of the war had only 26 kills and no ace named Gibelli has been identified. Luganskii then conducted a second ram in the Kirovograd area in 1943 that claimed a German bomber. He was promoted to Captain and made a squadron leader in the 270th Fighter Regiment. He participated in the Kursk fighting, claiming up to 16 kills between 5 July and 23 August 1943.[62]

In May 1944 he took over command of the regiment. In early 1945, he was sent to the Air Force Academy. He was eventually promoted to Major General and retired in 1964. He died on 16 January 1977. He is credited with 37 kills and 6 shared victories, flew 417 sorties, and engaged in 200 encounters. He was awarded the Hero of the Soviet Union twice and was the Soviet Union's 16th highest scoring ace.

Vasili Zaitsev Vasili Aleksandrovich Zaitsev was born 10 January 1911 in the Moscow region and enlisted in the Soviet air force in 1932. He completed his pilot training a year later and

AIR CAMPAIGN STATISTICS

was a squadron commander in the 129th Fighter Regiment when the war began. Based on the Baltic coast and armed with MiG-3s, he claimed his first kill on 5 July 1941. He was promoted to captain in 1941. Involved in the defense of Moscow, his regiment was re-designated the 5th Guards Fighter Regiment in December and re-equipped with LaGG-3s. He operated near Rzhev in the summer of 1942, was awarded Hero of the Soviet Union in May 1942 for 12 kills in 115 sorties as of January 1942. He was also promoted to major and took over the regiment in September 1942. Re-armed with La-5s in November 1942, the regiment was shifted down to Stalingrad and then on to Kursk. By then he had been promoted to Lt. Colonel.

In August 1943 he was awarded Hero of the Soviet Union a second time, this time credited with 22 kills in 299 sorties. His 5th Guards Fighter Regiment would become the most successful fighter regiment in the Soviet air force, with 739 victories claimed for the war. He was reputed to be one of the great Soviet fighter leaders. He was promoted to full colonel in 1944 and took command of a fighter division. He ended the war with 34 claimed kills, 19 shared kills in 427 sorties and 163 engagements.

Seriously injured late in the war with damage to his spine, he was in hospitals for the next two years. He retired in 1946 and only in February 1947 was he able to walk again. Unable to fly again, he headed an aero club. In 1957 he was appointed director of a tire repair plant but retired in 1959. He passed away in 1961, just 50 years old.

Kozhedub was awarded Hero of the Soviet Union three times. Six of the other seven pilots whose biographies we have listed were awarded the Hero of the Soviet Union twice. The exception is Bobrov, who was never awarded a Hero of the Soviet Union while he was alive.

FIVE SOVIET FIGHTER REGIMENTS

For the Kursk Data Base project we collected the daily operational reports for the Second, Fifth and Seventeenth Air Armies, among other records. These were complete enough in detail that they sufficed for that work. We later went back and collected the records for five of the fighter regiments involved in the fighting. A brief summary of their actions is provided below. Between the three air armies, there were at least 40 fighter regiments. In this sampling of these regiments, three from the Second Air Army, one from the Seventeenth Air Army and one from the Fifth Air Army. Of the three fighter regiments of the Second Air, one was from the IV Fighter Corps, one from the V Fighter Corps and one from 291st Assault Division.

The Fifth Guards Fighter Regiment at Kursk
The Soviet 5th Guards Fighter Regiment was part of III Mixed Corps of the Seventeenth Air Army during the battle. It was commanded by the ace Major Vasilii Zaitsev (1911-1961), twice Hero of the Soviet Union who was credited with 34 kills

during the war. The unit's deputy commander was ace Lt. Vitalii Popkov (1922-2010), also twice Hero of the Soviet Union who was credited with 41 kills during the war. The Chief of Staff was Major Kalashnikov.

The 5th Guards Fighter Regiment was the highest scoring Soviet air regiment of the war with 739 victories claimed. They report that on 28 June they had 23 La-5s. Material losses in July 1943 are recorded as six La-5s shot down in aerial combat, five La-5s shot down by antiaircraft, two La-5s did not return from combat missions, four pilots were killed, one pilot did not return from combat mission, one La-5 was destroyed during the bombing of its airfield and one U-2 crashed.

Pilots in the regiment who they report kills for:

Date	Pilot	Plane	Time	Notes
7 July	Lt. Shumilin	Me-109G	0710-0817	
7 July	Jr. Lt. Belyakov	Me-109	0855-0945	
7 July	Jr. Lt. Glinkin	Fw-190	0855-0945	
7 July	Lt. Bayevskii	Me-109	1440-1610	
7 July	Lt. Yaremenko	Ju-88	1730-1835	
7 July	Jr. Lt. Glinkin	He-111	1730-1835	
7 July	Captain Dmitriyev	Ju-52	1730-1835	
7 July	Major Pindyur	Me-109	2000-2110	
7 July	Lt. Stokolov	Me-109	2000-2110	
7 July	Jr. Lt. Bugreyev	Me-109	2000-2110	
7 July	Jr. Lt. Kalsin	Me-109	2000-2110	
7 July	Jr. Lt. Sverlov	Me-109	2000-2100	***

Their reported losses were:

Date	Pilot	Plane	Time	Notes
7 July	Lt. Shumilin		1730-1835	*
7 July	Jr. Lt. Belyakov		1730-1835	**
7 July	Jr. Lt. Sidorets		1730-1835	Did not return
7 July	Jr. Lt. Sverlov	Me-109	2000-2100	***

* Lt. Shumilin after an air battle made a forced landing on wheels in the area of Mikhailovka. The pilot was seriously wounded
** Hit by fire from antiaircraft artillery and an Fw-190, pilot crossed the front line and made a landing. Pilot was wounded in the legs. Plane was burned on the ground by German artillery and mortar fire.
*** but he himself was caught in fire by two Me-109s, as a result, the La-5 burned and the pilot died.

AIR CAMPAIGN STATISTICS

Note that this may not be a complete listing of claims and losses for the period for which we have records (4-18 July 1943). For 7 July, they claimed eight Me-109s and four other planes at a loss of four planes, two pilots lost and two pilots wounded. On 7 July, the German VIII Air Corps lost 4 or 5 Me-109s (see Tables II.20 and II.21). This was but one fighter regiment of the 26 fighter regiments in the Second and Seventeenth Air Armies on 7 July 1943.

For subsequent days they report:

Date	Pilot	Plane	Time	Notes
9 July	Lt. Shtokolov	Me-109	0715-0845	*
13 July	Jr. Lt. Lavrenko	Fw-189	0620-0715	**
16 July	Jr. Lt. Popkov	Fw-190	0455-0620	***
16 July	Lt. Syitov & Eremenko	He-111	0455-0620	
16 July	Lt. Shtokolov	He-111	0455-0620	
16 July	Lt. Bayevskii	He-111	0455-0620	
16 July	Lt. Syitov	Me-109	0455-0620	
16 July	Jr. Lt. Yermolayev	Me-109	0455-0620	
16 July	Jr. Lt. Glinkin	Fw-189	0940-1010	Not a kill****
17 July	Lt. Syitov	2 Ju-87	0630-0810	Not in Kursk area
17 July	Lt. Syitov & Lt. Nikitin	Fw-189	0630-0810	*****
17 July	Lt. Popkov & Lt. Pchelkin	Me-109	1110-1230	
17 July	Lt. Bugreyev	Me-109	1404-1615	
18 July	Jr. Lt. Pchelkin	He-111	0454-0620	
18 July	Major Pendyur	Me-109	0454-0620	
18 July	Lt. Col. Zaitsev	Me-109	1828-2005	
18 July	Captain Dmitriyev	Me-109	1828-2005	

* Knocked down one Me-109, which went off with a course of 270 degrees.
** In the area of Dolgenkaya at a height of 300 meters Jr. Lt. Lavrenko attacked an Fw-189, who knew how to turn down and was lost against the background of the forest.
*** Above the target at an altitude of 2,500 meters, Popkov entered an air battle with three Fw-190s. He shot down one Fw-190 which fell in the Yurkovo area.
**** Attacked an Fw-189. The German aircraft was able to find a cloud.
***** They attacked an Fw-189 and knocked him down. The plane went in a southerly direction.

In the first two cases, we suspect a kill was not achieved. What really stands out on this list is the claim of three He-111s shot down on the 16th. Neither the VIII Corps air liaison officer nor the Luftwaffe quartermaster reports any He-111s lost. It appears the VIII Corps lost only 3 planes that day, although the 5th Guards Fighter Regiment is claiming seven. It is possible that they could have engaged planes from the German IV Air Corps as they were operating outside of the area of the Battle of Kursk. On 16 July, the VIII Air Corps only reported 30 bombing sorties as the corps bombers units were now committed to action in the south with the IV Air Corps.

Their reported losses were:

Date	Pilot	Plane	Time	Notes
16 July	Major Kulik		0455-0620	*
17 July	Lt. Yeremenko		1330-1510	**
17 July	Lt. Nikitin		1955-2055	Did not return
18 July	Lt. Glinkin		0454-0620	Did not return

* Major Kulik was shot down in a dogfight, the pilot jumped with a parachute and landed at Lozovaya, receiving burns on his face and hands.
** When approaching Kravtsov, 2 Fw-190s attacked La-5 Yeremenko (a hydraulic system was punctured) the flyer landed on the border of Puchenach airfield, the pilot was unharmed

This is a total of 29 planes shot down (including 16 Me-109s) for a lost of eight (four killed or missing, three wounded). The Fifth Guards Fighter Regiment reports for the month that they shot down 53 planes (33 Me-109s) and destroyed on the ground 11. All indications are that actual German losses were much lower than that.

The 27th Fighter Regiment at Kursk
The 27th Fighter Regiment was part of the V Fighter Corps of the Second Air Army. It was commanded by Vladimir Bobrov, who became the 11th highest scoring ace of the Soviet air force, although he was never awarded Hero of the Soviet Union. It also included two times Hero of the Soviet Union Nikolai Gulayev, who became the fourth highest scoring ace of the Soviet air force and may have been the highest scoring ace if he had not been wounded in June 1944. On 1 July the regiment consisted of 55 officers, 96 sergeants and 18 privates. They were armed with 50 rifles.

The regiment started the battle with 25 Yak-1s. On 4 July twenty of the Yaks were based at Svinopogorelovka, two at Luchki, two at Sukho-Solotino and one at Arkhangelskoye. On 5 July they flew 24 planes on 62 sorties for a total flight time of 51 hours and 29 minutes. They lost four Yaks, which did not return to their aerodromes. They claimed 25 enemy planes shot down (including 10 Me-109s), which is clearly optimistic.

On 6 July, they flew only 12 planes for 35 sorties for 28 hours and 36 minutes of flight time. They claimed 12 more kills. Their own losses were one Yak-1, which failed to return. He was reported at 1210 to be Jr. Lt. Drepin. Also on the 6th it was reported between 1410 and 1530 that Jr. Lt. Lusto made a forced landing six kilometers north of

AIR CAMPAIGN STATISTICS

Belenikhino. At the end of the day, they reported 11 planes based at Svinopogorelovka, one at Pravorot and one at Arkhangelskoye. They started reporting their claimed kills by name on 6 July. They are listed below.

Date	Pilot	Plane	Time	Notes
6 July	Captain Chepinota	Ju-87	1210	Fell 3 km south of Yakovlevo
		Hs-126	1210	Fell in area of Yakovlevo
6 July	Jr. Lt. Tinkin	Fw-190	1210	Fell in area of Ternovka
6 July	Jr. Lt. Kotrusov & Jr. Lt. Karpov	Hs-126	1210	Fell east of Byikovka
6 July	Sr. Lt. Gulayev	Fw-190	1210	Fell west of Verkhopenye
6 July	Captain Chepinota	Ju-88	1410-1530	Fell 3 km south of Mukhanin
6 July	Captain Chepinota	Ju-87	1410-1530	Fell 2 km south of Olkhovka
6 July	Sr. Lt. Karmin	Ju-87	1410-1530	Area of Zadelnoye
6 July		Me-109	1802-1905	Fell in area of Verkhopenye

As convincing as this series of reports looks with nine claimed kills, they probably exaggerated German losses. According to German records, they lost a total 7 to 11 planes on 6 July. The VIII Air Corps was facing up to 26 different Soviet fighter regiments and considerable Soviet antiaircraft.

For 7 July they only flew 10 planes on 41 sorties for 41 hours and 45 minutes of flight time. At 1320 they reported that Jr. Lt. Kotrusov did not return. At the end of the day, they reported 10 planes based at Svinopogorelovka and one at Arkhangelskoye. Their claims were:

Date	Pilot	Plane	Time	Notes
7 July	Sr. Lt. Gulayev	Ju-87	1245-1350	area of Belenikhino and Verkhopenye
7 July	Jr. Lt. Shpak	Ju-87	1245-1350	Fell in the area of Belenikhino
7 July		Hs-126	1320	Fell at the southern outskirts of Belenkhino
7 July		Fw-189	1705-1805	Fell northwest of Gostishchevo.

For 8 July they again flew 10 planes on combat missions and four on non-combat missions for 28 sorties for 28 hours and 2 minutes of flight time. They now had 15 planes at Svinopogorelovka and one at Arkhangelskoye. The number of planes flown each day is recorded below. The number of planes ready to fly declined after the

first day and the regiment flew 3 or 4 sorties a day for the next two days to maintain presence. Their activity declines after 7 July.

Date	Planes Flown	Sorties	Flight Time	Notes
4 July	15	34	20 hours, 26 minutes	Claimed 1 Ju-87
5 July	24	62	51 hours, 29 minutes	
6 July	12	35	28 hours, 36 minutes	3 sorties a day
7 July	10	41	41 hours, 45 minutes	4 sorties a day
8 July	14	28	28 hours, 2 minutes	
9 July	14	27	18 hours, 29 minutes	
10 July	6	9	4 hours, 30 minutes	
11 July	3	8	4 hours, 30 minutes	
12 July	7	13	8 hours, 45 minutes	
13 July	7	7	2 hours, 55 minutes	
14 July	12	12	6 hours	
15 July	0	0		
16 July	0	0		
17 July	10	10	4 hours, 30 minutes	

Their claimed kills for these days include:

Date	Pilot	Plane	Time	Notes
8 July	Sr. Lt. Gulayev	Me-109	1250-1415	Fell 1-2 km south Belenikhino.
9 July	Jr. Lt. Shapkin	Me-109	0955	Fell in the area of Prokhorovka
12 July	Captain Chepinota	2 Ju-87s	0953-1103	
12 July	Sr. Lt. Gulayev	2 Ju-87s	0953-1103	Fell in the area of Prokhorovka
		Fw-190	0953-1103	Fell in the area of Prokhorovka
12 July	Sr. Lt. Karmin	Ju-87	1128-1230	Fell in the area of Rozhdestvenka
12 July	Jr. Lt. Ivanov	Ju-87	1128-1230	Fell in the area of Kochetovka

For 9 July, the regiment took a heavy hit with one Yak-1 not returning from his combat mission and two others shot down in air battles. Their pilots were killed (including Jr. Lt. Shpak). The regiment only claimed one kill that day. This battle is described in some detail in the records:

> In the area of Prokhorovka at an altitude of 1000 meters, 12 Ju-87s were met escorted by 4 Me-109s. Six Yak-1s went to attack the enemy bombers, while 4 Yak-1s tied up the enemy fighters. At the time of the

attack on the enemy bombers in the area of air combat, a group of 20-25 Me-109 fighters appeared.

As a result of the attack of enemy fighters, our planes were broken up into separate planes and fought in isolation from each other. During the battle, Jr. Lieutenant Shapkin shot down one Me-109 (enemy aircraft fell in the Prokhorovka area).

Our fighters went out of battle by climbing and departing into the clouds.

In the air battle one Yak-1 was shot down (pilot – junior lieutenant Shpak). Two Yak-1s did not return from combat missions; one Yak-1, shot down in an air battle, made an emergency landing in the Ostrenkii area and, by the end of the day, flew the fighter to Svinopogorelovka airfield.

On the 10th, six Yak-1s were moved from the Svinopogorelovka airfield to Arkhangelskoye. There was otherwise little action with only six planes flying three combat sorties (3 hours and 30 minutes) and six non-combat sorties (1 hour). On the 11th only three planes flew eight sorties, only two of them combat. The regiment became more active on the 12th with seven planes flying 13 sorties, and the regiment claiming a rather amazing seven kills (6 Ju-87s, 1 Fw-190) with no losses. Seven Yak-1s flew back to the Svinopogorelovka airfield. They now report seven Yak-1s at Svinopogorelovka, 3 Yak-1s at Arkhangelskoye, and 1 Yak-1 was put into repair in the 40th Regimental Aircraft Workshop. The 27th Fighter Regiment was much less active from the 13th through the 16th and they moved to the rear to Staryii Oskol on 14 July. On 17 July they transferred 13 Yak-1s to the 737th Fighter Regiment, which was part of the 291st Assault Division. They were going to be replaced with lend-lease US manufactured P-39 Airacobras. This ended the 27th Fighter Regiments involvement in this stage of the Battle of Kursk.

They state that during the air battles from 5 to 18 July, the regiment lost 11 aircraft and claimed to have killed 55.

The 240th Fighter Regiment
The 240th Fighter Regiment was part 302nd Fighter Division, IV Fighter Corps of the Second Air Army. The commander of the 302nd Fighter Division was Colonel Litvinov and his chief of staff was Colonel Gareyev.

The 240th Fighter Regiment was the training ground for two the top Soviet aces of the war, Ivan Kozhedub the highest scoring allied ace of the war with 62 claimed kills, and Kirill Yevstigneyev, the fifth highest scoring allied ace of the war with 53 claimed kills. They both had similar backgrounds, having worked training pilots before being assigned to the front. Both Kozhedub and Yevstigneyev were assigned to the 240th Fighter Regiment in March 1943. Yevstigneyev claimed his first kill on 28 March 1943 while Kozhedub did not claim his first kill until 6 July 1943.

The 240th Fighter Regiment from 5 to 18 July was located at Cheryanka. The regiment was commanded by Major Sergei Podorozhnyii. On 1 July the regiment consisted of 64 officers, 103 sergeants and 8 privates. They were armed with 50 rifles. They were flying La-5s.

We do not have daily reports from the regiment. In the period 5 - 18 July they flew 449 sorties for 420 hours and 20 minutes: 200 were covering sorties, 158 were escort, 15 were for exploration, 2 were patrol, 57 were (non-combat?) flights, and 17 were returning planes.

From 4 to 18 July they claimed to have shot down 36 aircraft in 24 air battles, including 13 Me-109s. Their own losses were eight planes and five pilots. They had 17 aircraft repaired and 45 aircraft with minor repairs. On 20 July the regiment had 24 serviceable La-5s and 8 non-serviceable La-5s.

Their losses were:
Jr. Lt. Gomolko was shot down by their own Il-2s when returning from a combat mission in the area of Priznannoye.
Jr. Lt. Voronov was shot down by antiaircraft artillery
Jr. Lt. Mukhin was hit by antiaircraft artillery (the pilot survived)
Lt. Filippov shot down in an air battle in the area of Kochetovka (pilot survived)
Jr. Lt. Kolesnikov hit by anti-aircraft artillery (pilot lives)
Three planes did not return from combat missions: Lt. Aladin, Jr. Lt. Shabanov, and Jr. Lt. Pronin.

"Best People in the Regiment" – according to the regiment records:
Flight Commander: Jr. Lt Yevstigneyev
Deputy command of squadron: Jr. Lt. Grishin
Flight Commander: Jr. Lt. Amelin
Pilot: Jr. Lt. Tretyak
Pilot: Jr. Lt. Rezitskii
Pilot: Jr. Lt. Kozhedub
Pilot: Jr. Lt. Bryizgalov

The 270th Fighter Regiment
The 270th Fighter Regiment was part of the I Assault Corps of the Second Air Army. The I Assault Corps consisted of one fighter division of three regiments armed with Yak-1bs and two assault divisions with a total of six regiments of Il-2s.

It included the top ace, Sergei Danilovich Luganskii, who claimed 37 kills and 6 shared kills during the war, making him the 16th highest scoring Soviet ace of the war. The regiment commander was Major Vasilii Afanasyevich Merkushev who claimed 29 killed during the war. The Deputy Regiment Commander for Political Affairs, or the commissar, was Major Kuzmichev. The chief of staff was Major Ustinov. Also

AIR CAMPAIGN STATISTICS

in the unit at Kursk was Nikolai Panteleyvich Dunayev who claimed 24 kills and 9 shared kills during the war, Ivan Mikheyevich Korniyenko who claimed 24 kills during the war and Nikolai Konstantinovich Shutt who claimed 22 kills during the war.

From 26 June to 12 August 1943, the regiment was based at the aerodrome Solonets-Polyana. On 1 July the regiment consisted of 59 officers, 95 sergeants and 12 privates, of which 34 were pilots. They were armed with only 39 rifles. They reported on 4 July that they were connected by telephone with the 203rd Fighter Division.

Their missions starting 5 July were primarily escort missions for the two divisions of Il-2s in the corps. This did not go that well on the first day. The regiment in the early morning covered the Il-2 attack aircraft who were involved in the attack on the German airfields of Pomerki and Sokolniki. On that mission, between 0427 and 0500, the regiment got into a fight at 1500 meters with two Fw190s. The regiment claimed one Fw-190 shot down. At 0428, while conducting air combat, two Il-2s collided, with one of the pilots descending by parachute.

They also escorted Il-2s which were operating to destroy enemy aircraft in the area of Tomarovka. At 0630 they report that when returning from a combat mission, Major Gnedich led two damaged Il-2s of which one landed ("sat") in the Burluk area and the other landed ("sat") five kilometers south of Valuiki. The regiment ended up reporting three air combats this day with one Fw-190 claimed to have been shot down and two Yak-1s that did not return.

On 6 July the regiment escorted Il-2s, which attacked the men and German tanks in the area of Shebekino and Tomorovka. At 1315 they report that eight Yaks in the area of Butovo-Byikovka at a height of 800 meters were in air combat with 20 Me-109s and 10 Fw-190s. They claimed two kills. At 1750 six Yak-1s in the area Shopino met a single Me-109 which was immediately shot down by Captain Dunayev. At 1805 in the area of Dragunskaya again at a height of 800 meters six Yak-1 got into a fight with six Fw-190s. They claimed one Fw-190.

The weather was reported by the regiment this day was being cloudy to 5 to 6 points, with a cloud height of 800-1500 meters and visibility of 6 to 7 kilometers. They had four air battles this day claiming two Fw-190s and 2 Me-109s. The regiment's own losses were three Yak-1s which did not return from their mission and 1 Yak-1 which was damaged by antiaircraft artillery and made an emergency landing on the fuselage in the area of Barsuk.

On the night of July 6-7, a German bomber dropped FAB-50 bombs at the Solonets-Polyana airfield. The bombs fell on the airfield but there was no damage to the materiel and personnel.

For 7 July they escorted Il-2 to the areas of Dubrova, Solonets and Byikovka. They had five aerial combats with five claimed kills and no losses. At 0540 six Yak-1s at a height of 100 meters in the area of Nizhnyaya Aleksandrovka attacked one Fw-190 and shot it down. At 0825 six Yak-1s in the area of Streletskoye and Bukovo at a height of 800 meters met eight Ju-87s and engaged, resulting in one Stuka shot down. At 0836 in the area of Bukovo they shot down an He-126. At 1840 six Yak-1s in the area of Yakovlevo at a height of 1800 meters engaged two Fw-190s shooting down one. At 1845 the same six Yak-1s engaged 18 Ju-87s and shot down one, which fell in the area of Yakovlevo. Most of the locales for the 6th and 7th were in the area of operations of the German XLVIII Panzer Corps.

For 8 July they mostly covered ground troops in the area of Aleksandrovskii, Belenikhino and Krasnaya Polyana and escorted Il-2s to attack tanks and personnel in the area of Yakovlevo and Teterivino. They ended up with 5 air battles this day, claiming eight planes shot down (including five Fw-190s) while losing one plane in the area of Prokhorovka. The Germans reported losing only one Fw-190 this day in both their liaison officer report and their quartermaster report.

Each air battle is reported on, starting with 0520 in the area of Belenikhino at a height of 700-900 meters where they met 2 Fw-190s who tried to attack the Il-2s. One Fw-190 was shot down and fell to the west of Prokhorovka. And then at 0610 at a height of 2000 meters eight Yak-1s fought an air battle with 20 Fw-190s in the area of Aleksandrovskii and Belnikhino. They claimed four Fw-190s shot down. At 1900 at a height of 800 meters five Yak-1s engaged with four Me-109s and six Fw-190s in the area of Teterivino. They claimed one Me-109 and second one at 1200 meters, and then a Ju-87. This was also the mission where one Yak-1 did not return to the aerodrome.

For communications with the division, they are finally reporting both telephone and radio with the note that during the day communications (with the radio?) worked intermittently. As the regiment continued to operate with low losses, their level of activity on subsequent days remained constant.

For 9 July their primary missions were to escort Il-2s in the area of Belenikhino, Kochetovka, Luchki and Gryaznoye. These missions only resulted in one air battle. At 0830 at a height of 1500 meters 14 Yak-1s in the area Ternovka, in groups of 4-6 aircraft, were involved in air battles with separate groups of Me-109s, Fw-190s and the fictitious He-113s. They claimed four German airplanes shot down. There were no Soviet losses. Again communication with the division was conducted by telephone, which worked intermittently, and by radio, which worked well.

For 10 July their missions were to escort Il-2s in the area of Preznoye, Malyiye Mayachki and Belenikhino. They had three groups of air battles. At 0650 at a height of 1800 meters in the area of Byikovka and Vislyi 11 Yak-1s met a group of 50 Ju-88s, Ju-87 and Me-109s. The air battle resulted in four German planes shot down, including 3 Ju-88s, while their own losses were nothing. On 10 July the Luftwaffe air liaison officer reports only 3 planes lost by the VIII Air Corps while the quartermaster reports indicate that only a Ju-87 and an Me-109 were lost this day. It does not appear that the Germans lost any Ju-88 on 10 July. The regiment does note that telephone and radio communications was excellent.

AIR CAMPAIGN STATISTICS

For 11 July their primary missions were escort Il-2s to attack men and tanks in the area of Luchki, Greznoye and Yakovlevo. They also did ten reconnaissance sorties. They claim only one action but appear to report two. At 1535 at a height of 1,000 meters in the area of Shakhovo, on the way back, the Yak-1 met 3 Ju-88s, resulting in squadron commander Sr. Lt. Shutt's plane being damaged. The plane landed in Bobrov. At 1845 at 1,500 meters in the area of Malyie Mayachki four Yak-1 met 4 Me-109s and 2 Fw-190s who tried to attack the (escorted) Il-2s. An air battle ensued "which was not successful."

For 12 July, their primary mission was again to escort Il-2s in the area of Luchki, Pokrovka, Sukho-Solotino and Yakovlevo. There were no recorded air battles (as defined by them), but while repelling attacks of two Me-109s on the Il-2s, one Me-109 was shot down. At 1925 in the area of Mukhanvoka at a height of 600 meters two Yak-1s attacked two Me-109s, resulting in one Me-109 shot down. One Yak-1 did not return from their mission.

For 13 July their primary mission remained to escort Il-2s, this time to the areas of Melekhovo, Shlyakhovo, Verkhnii Olshanets, Yakovlevo, Mayiye Mayaki. A number of these areas were where the III Panzer Corps was attacking. There were no air battles, no claims and no losses.

The following day their primary mission remained escorting Il-2s to "the area of their fighting." There was one group air battle. At 1237 two Yak-1s at 1800 meters in the area of Kazachye engaged four Me-109s. One Me-109 was claimed. There were no Soviet casualties. The same for the 15th, with again one group air battle. At 1950 four Yak-1s at a height of 300 meters engaged ten Fw-190s, claiming one, again with no losses. Added to the regiment this day were two Yak-7Bs from the 183rd Fighter Regiment. That regiment reported to the IV Fighter Corps. The 16th was more escort missions of Il-2s and two group air battles. At 0655 at a height of 800 meters in the area of Leski and Ivanovka, 3 Yak-1s engaged 9 Hs-123s, the German biplane dive bomber, covered by two Me-109s, downing one He-123. At 1225 at a height of 700 meters in the area of Maloye Yablonovo 1 Yak-1 engaged with two Me-109s with one Me-109 shot down. There were again no Soviet losses. The 17th and 18th were more of the same. At 0650 on the 17th in the area of Berzovka and Zavikovka and Rakovo at a height of 500 meters two Yak-1s engaged two Me-109s and two Fw-190s with one Me-109 and Fw-190 claimed. At 0930 on the 18th in the area of Pokrovka at a height of 1,000 meters two Yak-1s engaged two Me-109s with both claimed as shot down. There were no Soviet losses either of those two days.

What is interesting in these records is the large number of Fw-190s encountered and engaged. Most of the other fighter regiments are primarily engaged with Me-109s. This regiment claims to have shot down 13 Fw-190s and 13 Me-109s from 5 to 18 July. The Me-109 was the primary German fighter at this time in the VIII Air Corps. The Fw-190s was as capable a fighter, but was being used for ground support. According to the VIII Air Corps records, the Germans lost 11 Fw-190s from 5 to 18 July, but lost 36 Me-109s in that same period.

Their operations over the course of the battle consisted of:

Day	Planes	Sorties	Duration
5 July		79	80 hours, 59 minutes
6 July		62	56 hours, 43 minutes
7 July		46	36 hours, 19 minutes
8 July	14 Yak-1s	64	66 hours, 39 minutes
9 July	15 Yak-1s	47	42 hours, 8 minutes
10 July	13 Yak-1s	23	24 hours, 22 minutes
11 July		38	30 hours, 21 minutes
12 July		42	29 hours, 57 minutes
13 July	13 Yak-1s	45	34 hours, 43 minutes
14 July	12 Yak-1s	45	36 hours, 31 minutes
15 July	16 Yak-1s	40	29 hours, 04 minutes
16 July	13 Yak-1s	39	34 hours, 30 minutes
17 July	14 Yak-1s	40	44 hours, 15 minutes
18 July	13 Yak-1s	23	20 hours, 37 minutes

Their claims were:

Date	Pilot	Plane	Time	Notes
5 July	Captain Luganskii	Fw-190	0427-0500	
6 July	Sergeant Kireyev	Fw-190	1315	Area of Butovo-Byikovka
6 July	Captain Dunayev	Me-109	1315	Area of Butovo-Byikovka
6 July	Captain Dunayev	Me-109	1750	Area of Shopino
6 July	Lt. Andrianov	Fw-190	1805	Area of Dragunskaya
7 July	Lt. Odinokov	Fw-190	0540	Area of Nizhnyaya Aleksandrovka
7 July	Lt. Frantsuzov	Ju-87	0825	Area of Streletskoye
7 July	Captain Luganskii	He-126	0836	Area of Butovo
7 July	Major Merkushev	Fw-190	1840	Area of Yakolevka
7 July	Captain Luganskii	Ju-87	1845	Fell in the area of Yakovlevka
8 July	Captain Dunayev	Fw-190	0520	Fell west of Prokhorovka
8 July	Captain Matiyenko	Fw-190	0610	Fell in the area of Gryaznoye
8 July	Sr. Lt. Korniyenko	2 Fw-190s	0610	Fell in the area of Luchki,-Yakovlevka
8 July	Lt. Andrianov	Fw-190	0610	Fell in the area of Yakovlevka
8 July	Jr. Lt. Serbin	Me-109	1900	Fell in the area of Malyie Mayachki

AIR CAMPAIGN STATISTICS

Date	Pilot	Plane	Time	Notes
8 July	Jr. Lt. Minshutin	Me-109	1900	Fell in the area of Prokhorovka
8 July	Lt. Odinokov	Ju-87	1900	Fell in the area of Bolshiye Mayachki
9 July	Major Merkushev	He-113	0830	Fell in the area of Ternovka
9 July	Captain Dunayev	Me-109	0830	Fell in the area of Ternovka
9 July	Sr. Lt. Korniyenko	Me-109	0830	Fell in the area of Luchki
9 July	Jr. Lt. Frantsuzov	Fw-190	0830	Fell in the area north of Pokrovka
10 July	Sr. Lt. Shutt	Ju-88	0650	Fell in the area of Byikovka
10 July	Sr. Lt Shutt	Ju-88	0650	Fell in the area of Tenovka
10 July	Jr. Lt. Gurkov	Me-109	0650	Fell in the area of Vislyi
10 July	Captain Luganskii	Ju-88	0650	Fell in the area of Ternovka
12 July	Sr. Lt. Sechin	Me-109	1925	Area of Mukhanovka
14 July	Captain Luganskii	Me-109	1237	Fell in the area Novo-Oskochnoye
15 July	Sr. Lt. Savitskii	Fw-190	1950	Fell in area south of Belenikhino
16 July	Sr. Lt. Sechin	Hs-123	0655	Fell in the Leski-Ivanovka area
16 July	Jr. Lt. Kireyev	Me-109	1225	Fell in Maloye Yablonovo
17 July	Sr. Lt. Shutt	Me-109	0650	Fell in area of Belenikhino, Zavidovka and Rakova
17 July	Sr. Lt. Korniyenko	Fw-190	0650	Fell in area of Belenikhino, Zavidovka and Rakova
18 July	Lt. Odinovka	Me-109	0930	Fell in the area of Pokrovka
18 July	Jr. Lt. Kireyev	Me-109	0930	Fell in the area of Pokrovka

The 728th Fighter Regiment

The 728th Fighter Regiment started July with the 256th Fighter Division which reported to the Fifth Air Army. The regiment commander was Major Vasilyaka. The Deputy Regiment Commander for Political Affairs, or the commissar, was Lt. Colonel Klyuyev. The commander of the 256th Fighter Division was Hero of the Soviet Union Guards Colonel Gerasimov, his chief of staff was Colonel Kuznetsov, and the Chief of Operational Intelligence was Lt. Colonel Boreiko. The commander of the V Fighter Corps, to which they would soon be assigned, was Guards Major General Golunov. The regiment, a veteran of the Kuban air battles, also included the ace Arsenii Vorozheikin, who would become the 6th highest scoring Soviet ace of the war with 52 claimed kills and 13 shared kills.

The "combat strength" of the regiment (no date given) was 65 officers, 84 sergeants and 19 privates, of which 32 were pilots and 125 were technical staff. The unit was armed with 39 rifles and had 30 Yak-7Bs. The regiment claimed for the battle to have shot down 40 German aircraft at a cost of 10 planes and seven pilots.

Up through 9 July the unit was part of the Fifth Air Army. On 9 July the 256th Fighter Division was transferred to the Second Air Army.

Disposition (their location):
5-9 July: Khorolskoye
9-10 July: Staryii Oskol
10-19 July: (train) station Solntsevo

On 10 July, operating out of Solntsevo, they patrolled in the areas of Kurasovka, Kruglik, Sukho-Solotino and Kochetovka, which resulted in three air battles and three claimed kills. One Yak-7 did not return, allegedly shot down in aerial combat. It was 1st squadron commander Captain Kozhina. Communication was maintained with division headquarter by U-2 aircraft as was also the case for the 11th through the 18th.

On 11 July the regiment covered the areas of Orlovka, Kochetovka, Kadinovka and Verkhopenye. At 1230 eight Yak-7Bs attacked a group of bombers, up to 45 Ju-88s, Ju-87s and He-111s under the cover of 13-15 fighters. At 1430-1635 in the area of Kochetovka, because of the clouds, an Me-109 shot down the Yak-7B of Jr. Lt. Samoilova. Two Yak-7B shot down the Me-109. The cloud cover was 4 to 10 points and a height of 400-1700 meters. Visibility was 6 to 15 kilometers. For the day, the regiment shot down four aircraft and lost one in combat and two that did not return. One pilot killed.

After the heavy losses of the previous day, only ten sorties were flown on the 12th briefly patrolling the areas of Fedayevka, Sovkhoz Stalinino, Kruglik and Fivpya (only 4 hours and 40 minutes of flying time). The following day was more active, with them patrolling the areas of Alksandrovskii, Vasilevka, Belenikhino and Maloye Yablonovo.

On the 14th the regiment again engaged in combat patrolling the areas of Bogoroditskoye, Belenikhino, Shakhovo and Pravorot. There were three group air battles and the regiment ended up claiming 17 aircraft in the area of Prokhorovka, including 7 Ju-87s and 7 Me-109s. These are rather optimistic claims as on this day the German VIII Air Corps lost three or four Ju-87s and two or three Me-109s, and there were certainly other engagements with other air regiments (for example: the 270th Fighter Regiment). No description of these actions is provided in the regiment records we have. Their own losses were three Yak-7Bs that failed to return.

The regiment did not fly on the 15th. They stated that they remained in constant combat readiness for orders from the division. They were still only communicating with the 256th Fighter Division by U-2.

AIR CAMPAIGN STATISTICS

They were again heavily engaged on the 16th with them claiming three group air battles, shooting down 13 airplanes, including 7 Me-109s and 5 Ju-87s. Just for a reality check, the German VIII Air Corps lost from zero up to 2 Me-109s this day and reports losing no Ju-87s in either the air liaison reports or the quartermaster reports. It appears that most, if not all, of the claimed kills for this day are false. The regiments own losses were three Yak-7Bs that failed to return.

For the 17th and 18th, operations were limited. On the 17th they patrolled in the area of Vladimirovka, Kruglik, Hovenkoye and Melovoye. On the 18th they patrolled at a height of 1,000-2,000 meters in the area of Kruglik, Melvoye and Verkhopenye. By 1600 they had relocated to the aerodrome at Dolgte Dudyi. These were no actions and no losses for either of those two days.

Their operations over the course of the battle consisted of:

Day	Planes	Sorties	Duration
10 July	20 Yak-7s	36	26 hours, 07 minutes
11 July	19 Yak-7s	30	31 hours, 16 minutes
12 July	10 Yak-7Bs	10	4 hours, 40 minutes
13 July	22 Yak-7Bs	24	24 hours
14 July	23 Yak-7Bs	24	25 hours, 30 minutes
15 July		0	
16 July	14 Yak-7Bs	26	21 hours, 25 minutes
17 July	10 Yak-7Bs	20	17 hours
18 July	12 Yak-7Bs	23	13 hours, 37 minutes

Their reported claims were:

Date	Pilot	Plane	Time	Notes
11 July	Lt. Timchenko & Lt. Redyugera	Me-109	1430-1635	The pilot jumped with a parachute
14 July	Jr. Lt. Pakhomov	2 Ju-87s		
14 July	Jr. Lt. Pomanov	1 Ju-87		
14 July	Jr. Lt. Timosh	1 Ju-87 & 1 Fw-190		
14 July	Jr. Lt. Milashenko	1 Ju-87 & 1 Fw-190		
14 July	Captain Vorozheikin	2 Ju-87s		
14 July	Captain Vorozheikin	1 Me-109		
14 July	Lt. Kozlovskii	1 Me-109		

ACES AT KURSK

Date	Pilot	Plane	Time	Notes
14 July	Lt. Shiryayev	1 Me-109		
14 July	Sr. Lt. Kirnilov	2 Me-109s		In the area of Shakhovo
14 July	Jr. Lt. Vyibornov	1 Me-109		In the area of Shakhovo
14 July	Captain Vorozheikin & Jr. Lt. Milashenko	1 Hs-126		
14 July	Lt. Annin	1 Me-109		In the area of Shakhovo
16 July	Captain Vorozheikin	1 Me-109		
16 July	Lt. Sachkov	1 Me-109		
16 July	Jr. Lt. Vyibornov	1 Me-109		
16 July	Jr. Lt. Morye	1 Me-109		
16 July	Major Petrushin	2 Ju-87s		Fell in the area of Shakhovo
16 July	Jr. Lt. Shiryayev	1 Ju-87		Fell in the area of Shakhovo
16 July	Lt. Kozlovskii	1 Ju-87		Fell in the area of Shakhovo
16 July	Jr. Lt. Pakhomov	1 Ju-87		Fell in the area of Shakhovo
16 July	by the group	1 He-123		Fell in the area of Dalnii Dolzhik
16 July	Jr. Lt. Milashenko	1 Me-109		Fell in the area of Pravorot
16 July	Jr. Lt. Karnaukhov	1 Me-109		Fell in the area of Pravorot
16 July	Lt Khudyakov	1 Me-109		Fell in the area of Pravorot

Table II.12: Top Soviet Aces at the Battle of Kursk (south)

Name	Fighter Regiment	Rank	Kills	Shared Kills	Sorties	Combats	Remarks
Ivan Nikitovich Kozhedub	240th	1st	62		330	120	4 kills at Kursk
Nikolai Dmitriyevich Gulayev	27th	4th	55	5	248	69	12 kills (2 shared) at Kursk
Kirill Alekseyevich Yevstigneyev	240th	5th	53	3	283	109	7 kills (2 shared) at Kursk
Arsenii Vasilyevich Vorozheikin	728th	6th	52	13	300	90	4 + 1 shared kill at Kursk
Nikolai Mikhailovich Skomorokhov	164th	10th	46	8	605	143	No kills recorded until 24 July 1943

AIR CAMPAIGN STATISTICS

Name	Fighter Regiment	Rank	Kills	Shared Kills	Sorties	Combats	Remarks
Vladimir Ivanovich Bobrov	27th	11th	43	24	112		Rgt CO
Vatalii Ivanovich Popkov	5th Gds	13th	41	1	300+	117	3 kills at Kursk
Sergei Danilovich Luganskii	270th	16th	37	6	417	200	5 kills at Kursk

Table II.13: Other Soviet Aces with Known Kill Claims at Kursk (south)

Name	Fighter Regiment	Rank	Kills	Shared Kills	Sorties	Combats	Remarks
Vasilii Aleksandrovich Zaitsev	5th Gds	24th	34	19	427	163	Rgt CO
Ivan Nikitovich Syitov	5th Gds	29th	34	–	–	–	1 kill at Kursk #1
Nikolai Fyodorovich Krasnov	116th	33rd	32	10	300		Rgt CO, 2 kills at Kursk #2
Fyodor Fyodorovich Arkhipenko	508th	40th	30	14	467	102	5 kills (3 shared) at Kursk #3
Sergei Grigoryevich Glinkin	5th Gds	45th	30		200+		2 kills at Kursk #4
Vasilii Afanasyevich Merkushev	270th	49th	29 or 24	–	418		Rgt CO, 2 kills at Kursk #5
Anatolii Leonidovich Kozhevnikov	438th	67th	27	–	300	69	9 kills at Kursk #6
Aleksandr Vasilyevich Lobanov	41st Gds	71st	26	14	811	83	2 kills 7/07/43
Nikolai Panteleyevich Dunayev	270th	93rd	24	9	500		4 kills at Kursk #7
Ivan Fyodorovich Gnezdilov	516th	100th	24		376	120	1 or 4 kills at Kursk #8
Ilya Filippovich Andrianov	516th		23				2 kills at Kursk #9

	Fighter Regiment	Rank	Kills	Shared Kills	Sorties	Combats	Remarks
Aleksandr Yefimovich Maksimov	247th		22		444	68	2 kills at Kursk #10
Oleg Nikolayevich Smirnov	31st		20	7	404	120	1 kill at Kursk #11
Nikolai Ivanovich Leonov	183rd		20				2 kills at Kursk #12
Aleksandr Ivanovich Vyibornov	728th		20		190	42	2 or 3 kills at Kursk #13
Mikhail Ivanovich Sementsov	41st Gds		19	12	363	83	6 kills at Kursk
Pavel Aleksandrovich Bryizgalov	240th		19		243[63]	61	no kills at Kursk
Ivan Semyonovich Ulitin	116th		17		202	64	2 kills at Kursk #14
Anatolii Fyodorovich Shamanskii	247th		16	1	253	61	2 kills at Kursk #15
Oleg Stepanovich Belikov	88th		15	14	635	114	4 kills at Kursk #16
Nikolai Ivanovich Gorbunov	31st		15		196	40	1 kill at Kursk #17
Aleksandr Konstantinovich Gorovets	88th		11	6	74	11	9 kills at Kursk #18

All the above pilots were awarded the Hero of the Soviet Union. Zaitsev was awarded the medal twice!

Details of claimed kills

#1 According to the Red Falcons website shared a kill of an Fw-189 on 9 July east of Gremyachii, shared a kill of an He-111 on 16 July at the station Studenok. That same day he claimed an Me-109 south of Okr. Zavodskoi. On 17 July he claimed a Ju-87 east of Peropolye and two Ju-87s southeast of Belikaya Kamyishevakha. The claims for 16 and 17 July appear to have been out of the area of the Battle of Kursk and may have been out of the area of responsibility of the German VIII Air Corps. The records we have for the 728th Fighter Regiment only start reporting on 10 July. The 5th Guards Fighter Regiment reports confirm the claims for 16 July but for 17 July credit him with a shared killed of an Fw-189 and 2 Ju-87s. No Fw-189 was lost on 9 July, although the Germans lost one on the 16th.

AIR CAMPAIGN STATISTICS

#2 On 7 July claimed a Me-109 at Yastrebovka-Myasoyedovo and an Ju-87 at Krutoi Log. Claimed two Me-109s on 17 July, but they are out of the area of the Battle of Kursk. The Germans record no Ju-87s are being lost on the 7th.

#3 Arkhipenko's claims vard depending on source. We believe he shot down one Ju-87 on 8 July over Sukho-Solotino and one Ju-87 over Verkhopenye on 9 July. He has shared kills on 7 July of 6/12ths of a Ju-87 and 2/12ths of a Me-109 over Belenikino-Verkhopenye and on 8 July 2/6ths of an He-111 over Pokrovka. The Germans report no Ju-87s lost on the 7th but did lose 4 Me-109s that day. They do report two Ju-87s lost on the 8th (one due to air combat) but no He-111s lost on the 8th. For 9 July, they report 2 Ju-87s lost.

See website: http://airaces.narod.ru/all1/arhipenk.htm and also see Seidl, pages 34-35.

#4 According to Seidl, page 73, a He-111 on 5 July in the vicinity of Kamennaya Yaruga and a Ju-87 on the 23rd. According the Red Falcons website on 4 July he shared a kill of a Fw-189 at Sovetskaya-Lozovenka, on 7 July a He-111 at Kamennaya Yaruga and on 18 July two Ju-88s at Golaya Dolina-Kurulka and 1 Me-109 at Sinichino. The claims on 18 July were of the area of the Battle of Kursk. According to the 5th Guards Fighter Regiment records, Glinkin was credited on 7 July with an Fw-190 and an He-111. On 16 July he attacked an Fw-189 but the records report that the German aircraft was able to find a cloud. On 18 July he is reported to have not returned from a mission at 0454-0620. He obviously survived that ordeal as he continued to claim victories through April 1945.

The Germans lost four He-111s on the 5th and one on the 7th. They also lost Fw-190s on the 7th and a Fw-189 on the 16th but not one on the 4th.

#5 Claimed an Fw-190 on 7 July at Yakovlevo and claimed a He-113 on 9 July at Ternovka. The German quartermaster reports note the loss of 3 Fw-190s on the 7th. The He-113 does not exist but there were other German fighters lost on the 9th.

#6 The claimed kills are 1 Ju-88 on 4 July, 2 Ju-88s and 1 Me-109 on 5 July, 1 He-111, 1 Me-109 and 1 Ju-88 on 6 July and 1 Ju-88 and 1 Me-109 on 7 July.[64] The Second Air Army claims that Kozhevnikov shot down two Ju-88s on the 4th. The Germans did lose two Ju-88s on the 4th, but only one Ju-88 on the 5th and no He-111s or Me-109s on the 6th.

According to the Red Falcons website, he is credited with 2 Ju-88s on 4 July, one at Olkhovatka-Aleksandrovka and the other south of Khutor Alekandrovskii. On 6 July he claims a third Ju-88 at Dmitriyevka and on 8 July claims an Me-109 at Prokhorovka. All of these four claims are possible, although the Me-109 is only reported in the quartermaster records while none of the three Ju-88s that are claimed are reported in the quartermaster record even though they are reported in the VIII Corps air liaison officer reports.

#7 According to Dunayev, he shot down an Me-110 north of Belgorod on the 6th, and a total of 9 planes and 3 shared victories and was seriously wounded on the 17th. According to Seidl's book, he scored near Belgorod on the 6th, over Tomarovka on the 8th, and near Belgorod on the 11th. While leading four Yak-7Bs on the 13th, Dunayev claimed a bomber and a fighter during a large melee with 26 Ju-88s and 17 Me-109s. Seidl states that during the fighting at Belgorod, he was credited with six kills.

According to the Red Falcons' website, he claimed two Me-109s on the 6th, one at Butovo-Byikovka and the other at Shopino. He claimed an Fw-190s on the 8th to the west of Prokhorovka, and an Me-109 on the 9th at Ternovka. He also claimed an Hs-123 on the 23rd at Andreyevskiye.

According to the 270th Fighter Regiment records on 6 July he shot down two Me-109s, one at Butovo-Byikovka and the other at Shopino. On 8 July he shot down an Fw-190 that fell west of Prokhorovka. On 9 July he shot down an Me-109 that fell in the area of Ternovka. These records seem to indicate that the Red Falcons' website is more accurate about Soviet kill claims than many of the formally published sources.

#8 Including two Me-109s on 11 July 1943, near Prokhorovka. Four Me-109s were lost by the VIII Air Corps this day. According to the Red Falcons' website, he only claimed one plane at Kursk, a Me-109 on the 11th southeast of Pokhorovka. This claim is also possible.

#9 On 6 July, six Yak-1s were engaged in escorting nine Il-2s. At 1700 hours at 2,000 meters they were attacked by eight Fw-190s. Andrianov claimed one near Dragunskoye. On 8 July, he claimed another Fw-190 in the Ryazanovka area in a dogfight between eight Yak-1s and 12 Me-109s and six Fw-190s. According to the Red Falcons' website, he claimed an Fw-190 on 6 July at Dragunskoye and an Fw-190 on 8 July at Yakovlevo. The Germans lost no Fw-190s on the 6th, but lost one on the 8th.

#10 As captain and squadron leader, Maksimov on 5 July led six of his squadron on an escort of Il-2s. Near Tomarovka engaged 30 bombers and 12 escorting fighters. Maksimov scored two kills but was wounded, but returned to base.

#11 One Me-109 between Solomino and Bezlyudovka on 11 July. The VIII Air Corps reports that four Me-109s were lost on the 11th. According to the Red Falcons' website, he claimed one Me-109s east of Nizhnii Olshanets on 5 July. This is also a possible claim.

#12 Near Prokhorovka on 10 July claimed two Fw190s while leading 12 Yak-1s and Yak-7Bs in an attack on 15 Fw-190s escorting four Me-109s fighter-bombers. Claim cannot be checked as German VIII Air Corps provides no detailed loss reports for this day (they did report losing three planes this day).

#13 Claimed a Ju-87 on 13 July and two kills on the 14th. The VIII Air Corps does not report the loss of a Ju-87s on the 13th. According to the Red Falcons' website, for 14 July he claimed 1 Ju-87 at Prokhorovka and 1 Me-109 at Ivanovo. On 16 July he claimed one Me-109 at Shakhovo. The 728th Fighter Regiment records report him shooting down an Me-109 on 14 July in the area of Shakhovo. They report him shooting down another Me-109 on 16 July.

#14 According to one source, on 3 July Ulitin's flight of La-5s was attacked by 20 Me-109s. His flight claimed five, of which two were his claims. The Soviets suffered no losses. The

AIR CAMPAIGN STATISTICS

VIII Air Corps suffered no losses this day. According to the Red Falcons' website, on 5 July he claimed an Me-109 west of station Dolbino and on 7 July an Me-109 west of Staraya Tavolzhanka. These two claims are possible.

#15 Shamanskii on 8 July claimed an Fw-190 in the area of Teterevino when six Yak-1s involved in escort became engaged with four German fighters. On 16 July he "forced down" an Me-109 while escorting Il-2s. The Germans lost one Fw-190 on the 8th, but this is the second claim for an Fw-190 on the 8th (see Andrianov). The Germans lost two Me-109s on the 16th. There is no entry for Anatoli Shamanskii in the Red Falcons' data base although he is listed in both Seidl, pages 192-193 and Polak, page 281.

#16 On 4 July Belikov claimed four kills near Belgorod while flying escort for Il-2s. Claim is noted in Second Air Army records. The Germans lost only three planes on this day.

#17 Shot down a German ace (number 17 on aircraft) on 17 July 1943 at Krasnyii Liman (north of Slavyansk). This is outside the battle area covered in this book.

#18 It is claimed that on 6 July Gorovets scored the Soviet record for the greatest number of victories in a sortie. He was returning from a mission to the Vladimirovka and Olkhovatka area when he got separated from the rest of his flight after encountering intense flak. At 1940 he sighted a formation of around 20 German planes. Coming from behind, it is claimed that he shot down nine before he was bounced by four Fw-190s and shot down in flames. He was buried in Zorinskiye Dvoryi.

The Germans report losing only seven planes this day, of which five were reported to be lost to anti-aircraft. No German fighters were lost this day. One is tempted to dismiss this story in its entirety.

Table II.14: Other Soviet Pilots Who Were at Kursk (south)

	Fighter Regiment	Rank	Kills	Shared Kills	Sorties	Combats	Remarks
Grigorii Denisovich Onufriyenko	–	49th	29	–	405		In office of 295th Fighter Division
Aleksandr Alekseyevich Dyachkov	297th	66th	27	1	217	54	#1
Pavel Ilyich Peskov	5th Gds	75th	26	–	326		Have not confirmed he was present
Ivan Pavlovich Laveikin	5th Gds	93rd	24	15	498	106	

ACES AT KURSK

	Fighter Regiment	Rank	Kills	Shared Kills	Sorties	Combats	Remarks
Ivan Mikheyevich Korniyenko	270th	100th	24	–	–		
Nikolai Konstantinovich Shutt	270th		22	–	444	120	
Igor Aleksandrovich Shardakov	5th Gds		21		483	–	
Boris Vasilyevich Zhigulenkov	240th		20	–	200	50	
Valentin Andreyevich Karlov	27th		19	7	246	71	
Mikhail Vasilyevich Lusto	27th		19	1	251	49	
Georgii Arturovich Bayevskii	5th Gds		19	–	232	52	#2
Vasilii Filippovich Mukhin	240th		19	–	340	–	
Nikolai Ivanovich Olkhovskii	193rd		19	–	128	–	
Nikolai Semyonovich Artamonov	193rd		18	8	165	42	
Mikhail Vasilyevich Bekashonok	27th		18	4	170	50	
Ivan Frolovich Shamenkov	427th		18	–	200	–	
Aleksei Mikhailovich Milovanov	193rd		17	5	215	30	
Vasilii Ivanovich Mishustin	88th Gds		17	8	388	68	
Pyotr Mikhailovich Nikanorov	88th Gds		17	5	167	44	
Nikolai Ivanovich Glotov	27th		17	1	203	33[65]	
Stepan Andreyevich Karnach	247th		16	4	346	84	
Nikita Nikiforovich Kononenko	297th		15	9	169	52	
Sergei Ivanovich Lazarev	728th		15	3	131	48	
Anton Dmitriyevich Yakimenko	427th		13	35	241	29	
Pavel Fomich Mushtayev	31st		8	–	–	–	Rgt CO[66]

All these pilots were awarded Hero of the Soviet Union.

AIR CAMPAIGN STATISTICS

Notes

#1 Dyachkov, along with two other drunk pilots, were convicted on 4 June 1944 of murdering a food warehouse manager. All three were convicted to 10 years and demoted. He served his sentence with his unit, continuing to conduct combat missions. He died in a plane crash on 31 March 1945. He only received the Hero of the Soviet Union and other honors posthumously in 1946 (source: Russian Wikipedia article on Dyachkov and Heroes of the Soviet Union website: http://www.warheroes.ru/hero/hero.asp?Hero_id=15642).

#2 attended the same school and knew German ace Wilhelm Batz before the war when his father, a diplomat, was stationed in Berlin.

Table II.15: VIII Air Corps Base Locations and Transfers[67]

Unit Name	30 June Location	Base Transferred to for Operations	Transferred to After Battle
Fourth Air Fleet	Dnepropetrovsk		
VIII Air Corps	Kharkov	Mikoyanovka, 3/4 July	
II/3rd Fighter Wing	Varvarovka	Rogan, 5 July	
III/3rd Fighter Wing	Feldflugplatz 'Uhu'	Bessonovka	'Uhu', 15 July
52nd Fighter Wing	(?)	Bessonovka, 4/5 July	
I Group	Gostagayevskaya	Bessonovka, 4 July	Kuteinikovo, 17 July
III Group	Tamin	Ugrim, 3 July	Orel, 14 July***
1st Ground Attack Wing	Barvenkovo	Varvarovka, 2 July	Orel
I Group	Barvenkovo	Bessonovka, 3/4 July*	Orel
II Group	Anapa	Bessonovka, 3/4 July*	Rudka
4th Squadron	Deblin-Irena	Varvarovka, 4 July	Orel-West, 15 July
8th Squadron	Zaporozhye	Varvarovka, 4 July	Orel-West, 15 July
4th Sqdn/2nd Ground Attack Wing	Varvarovka		Orel-West, 15 July
8th Sqdn/2nd Ground Attack Wing	Varvarovka		Orel-West, 15 July
Antitank Sq./51st Fighter Wing	Orel-West, 15 July		
2nd Stuka Wing	Kharkov-Sortirovka	Krestovoi, 4/5 July**	Orel

335

Unit Name	30 June Location	Base Transferred to for Operations	Transferred to After Battle
I Group	Kharkov-'Hfb' (East?)	Kharkov-North, 2 July	Orel, 12 July
II Group	Kharkov-'Hfb' (East?)	Kharkov-North, 4 July	Tatsinskaya, 20 July
III Group	Kharkov-'Hfb' (East?)	Kharkov-North, 3 July	Tatsinskaya, 20 July
	Kharkov-Sortirovka	Kharkov-North, 4 July	
10th Squadron (Panzer)	Kharkov-East	Kharkov-North (?)	Orel
77th Stuka Wing	Kharkov-Voichenko	Tolokonnoye, 2/3 July	Orel bulge, 16 July(?)
I Group	Kharkov-Voichenko	Tolokonnoye, 3/4 July	Orel bulge, 16 July(?)
II Group	Kharkov-Voichenko	Tolokonnoye, 3/4 July	Orel bulge, 16 July(?)
III Group	(?)	(?)	Orel bulge, 16 July(?)
3rd Bomber Wing	Poltava		
I Group	Poltava		
II Group	Poltava		
III Group	Poltava		
27th Bomber Wing	Dnepropetrovsk	(?)	
I Group	Dnepropetrovsk	(?)	
II Group	Dnepropetrovsk	(?)	
III Group	Kharkov-Voichenko		
14th Squadron	(?)	(?)	
55th Bomber Wing	Rogan		
II Group	Kharkov & Stalino		
III Group	Kharkov & Stalino		Stalino, 18 July
14th Squadron	Poltava		
I/100th Bomber Wing	Stalino	Poltava, 4 July	Stalino, 17 July
6th Close-range Recon. Group	Alekseyevka	Veterinar, 3/4 July	

* All or part of the unit moved from Varvarovka to Bessonovka on the night of 3/4 July.
** According to the march plan, the St.G. 2 was transferred from Kharkov North to Krestovoi. It is unknown whether just the headquarters went there, or all three groups went with it.
*** Transferred to Orel on 14 July and then Ivanovka on 20 July.

AIR CAMPAIGN STATISTICS

During the Kursk Data Base project we never assembled a detailed order of battle for the Second Air Army, nor was it required for that project. A detailed order of battle for the Second Air Army is presented by Christer Bergstrom, Pawel Burchard and Dmitriy B. Khazanov.[68] A compilation of these three efforts is provided below, crosschecked and updated to the Second Air Army records.[69]

Table II.16: Second Air Army Order of Battle

Second Air Army: Lt. General Stepan Krasovskii, Headquarters; Spartak[70]

Parent Formation	Commanders	Locations	Aircraft Types	Notes
I Assault Corps	Lt. Gen. Vasili G. Ryazanov	Berovkii		Transferred 18 July[71]
203rd Fighter Division	MG Konstantine G. Baranchuk	Ostanovka		
247th Fighter Regiment	Lt. Col. Yakov Kutikhin[72]		Yak-1b	
270th Fighter Regiment	Maj. Vasili Merkushev		Yak-1b	
516th Fighter Regiment			Yak-1b	
266th Assault Division	Col. Fyodor G. Rodyakin	Dubki, Valuyki, Urazovo		
66th Assault Regiment	Maj. V. Lavrinenko		Il-2	
673rd Assault Regiment	Lt. Col. Aleksandr P. Matikov		Il-2	
735th Assault Regiment	Maj. Semyon Bolodin		Il-2	
292nd Assault Division	MG Filipp A. Agaltsov	Kulma, Novyii Oskol		
667th Assault Regiment	Maj. Grigori P. Shuteyev		Il-2	
800th Assault Regiment	Maj. Anatoli I. Mitrofanov		Il-2	
820th Assault Regiment	Maj. I. N. Afanasyev		Il-2	
I Bomber Corps	Col. Ivan S. Polbin	Illovskoye		Transferred 20 July[73]
1st Guards Bomber Division	Col. Fyodor I. Dobyish	Ilyinka		
80th Guards Bomber Rgt			Pe-2	
81st Guards Bomber Rgt.	Lt. Col. Vladimir Gavrilov		Pe-2	
82nd Guards Bomber Rgt			Pe-2	
293rd Bomber Division	Col. Gurii V. Gribakin	Trostanka, Ostrogozhsk		

ACES AT KURSK

Parent Formation	Commanders	Locations	Aircraft Types	Notes
23rd Guards Bomber Rgt ?				
780th Bomber Regiment				
804th Bomber Regiment	Maj. A. M. Semyonov			
854th Bomber Regiment	Maj. A. A. Novikov			
IV Fighter Corps	MG Ivan D. Podgornyii	Vasilev Dol		Transferred 18 July[74]
294th Fighter Division	Col. Vladimir V. Sukhoryabov	Pestunovo		
6th Fighter Regiment				
183rd Fighter Regiment	Maj. Andrei Oboznenko		Yak-1b	
427th Fighter Regiment	Maj. Anton D. Yakimenko		Yak-1b	
302nd Fighter Division	Col. Boris I. Litvinov	Shirokii Gul		
193rd Fighter Regiment	G. M. Pyatakov		La-5	
240th Fighter Regiment	Maj. Sergei Podorozhnyii		La-5	
297th Fighter Regiment			La-5	
V Fighter Corps	MG Dmitrii P. Galunov	B. Psinka		
8th Guards Fighter Division	MG Dmitrii P. Galunov*	Trubezh, Oboyan, Ivniya		
40th Guards Fighter Rgt.	Maj. Moisei S. Tokarev		La-5	CO killed 12 July.[75]
41st Guards Fighter Rgt.	Maj. Pavel Chupikov		La-5	
88th Guards Fighter Rgt.	Maj. Stefan S. Rymsha		La-5	
92nd Fighter Regiment				
205th Fighter Division	Col. Yuri A. Nemtsevich	Sukho-Solotino, Kochetovka		
27th Fighter Regiment	Maj. Vladimir I. Bobrov		Yak-1b	
438th Fighter Regiment	Lt. Col. Yakov Utkin		Yak-1b	
508th Fighter Regiment	Lt. Col. Sergei Zaichenko		Yak-7b	
291st Assault Division	Col. Andrei N. Vitruk	Shumakovo		
243rd Assault Regiment ?	Maj. Aleksandr Nakonechnikov		Il-2	

AIR CAMPAIGN STATISTICS

Parent Formation	Commanders	Locations	Aircraft Types	Notes
245th Assault Regiment ?			Il-2	
313rd Assault Regiment ?	Maj. I. D. Borodin		Il-2	
617th Assault Regiment	Maj. Dmitrii L. Lomovtsev		Il-2	
737th Fighter Regiment	Col. Nikolay I. Varchuk		mixed**	
954th Assault Regiment ?			Il-2	
208th Night Bomber Division	Col. Leonid N. Yuzeyev***	Kalinovka		
646th Night Bomber Rgt	Lt. Col. Aleksandr Letuchii[76]			
715th Night Bomber Rgt.	Lt. Col. I. I. Zamyatin			
887th Night Bomber Rgt ?				
60th Independent KAE****?			Il-2	
50th Air Reconnaissance Regiment	Lt. Col. I. Ya. Mironov		Pe-2	
454th Bomber Regiment	Maj. I. A. Tatulov		A-20B	
272nd Independent Army Squadron				

* Under MG D. P Galunov through 6 July 1943, then under command of Col. I. P. Laryushkin.
** The Second Air Army records report the 291st Assault Division conducting operations with Yak-1bs, Yak-7bs and La-5s.
*** Commander is also listed as Col. F. P. Kotlar with Yuzeyev taking over on 10 July.[77]
**** Unit designation is not known.

Table II.17: Soviet Reinforcements during the Battle

The following units may have been added to the Second Air Army's order of battle during the battle:

Parent Formation	Commanders	Locations	Aircraft Types	Notes
256th Fighter Division	Col. N. S. Gerasimov			Attached 9 July[78]
32nd Fighter Regiment	A. S. Patrunin		Yak-9[79]	
91st Fighter Regiment			Yak-1	
728th Fighter Regiment			Yak-7b	

Parent Formation	Commanders	Locations	Aircraft Types	Notes
X Fighter Corps	MG M. M. Golovnia			Attached 23 July[80]
201st Fighter Division	Col. V. A. Sryvkin			
13th Fighter Regiment	Maj. A. K. Lyshkov		La-5 FN	
236th Fighter Regiment	Capt. S. N. Petrukhov		Yak-1	
437th Fighter Regiment	Maj. M. S. Khvostikov		La-5 FN	
235th Fighter Division	MG I. A. Lakeyev			
3rd Guards Fighter Rgt.	Col. D. S. Shpak		La-5	
181st Fighter Regiment			La-5	
239th Fighter Regiment				
V Assault Corps				Attached in July[81]
202nd Bomber Division	Col. S. I. Netshiporenko			Attached 23 July[82]
39th Bomber Regiment	Col. A. Fedorov		Pe-2	
92nd Bomber Regiment	Lt. Col. A. G. Fedorov?		Pe-2	
797th Bomber Regiment			Pe-2	

Table II.18: Second Air Army Strength

Bergstrom, *Kursk,* page 128, reports the following strengths for the Second Air Army:

	Serviceable	Not Serviceable	Total Strength
Fighters	389	85	474
Assault	276	23	299
Bombers	172	18	190
Night Bombers	34	15	49
Reconnaissance	10	8	18
Totals	**881**	**149**	**1030**

The same figures for serviceable aircraft are used for the Second Air Army's created "Correlation of Air Forces."[83] These figures do not agree with the on-hand figures for 1 July 1943 drawn from the Second Air Army records.[84] Those figures show 572 fighters, 306 assault, 117 bombers, 57 night bombers, and 21 reconnaissance (total of 1073). The largest number of planes flown in a day through 6 July shows 348 fighters, 162 assault, 70 bombers, 31 night bombers and 13 reconnaissance (total of 624). The largest number

AIR CAMPAIGN STATISTICS

flown in a day may be the most meaningful figure. See sidebar "Second Air Army Forces (1-6 July 1943)."

A detailed Seventeenth Air Army order of battle is provided in the sidebar "Seventeenth Air Army Forces (5 July 1943)."[85] A detailed Fifth Air Army order of battle is provided in Chapter Five, in the sidebar "Fifth Air Army Order of Battle, 1 July 1943." There are tables published that show the Seventeenth Air Army with 538 planes ready for action at the beginning of July, as opposed to the 735 we show.[86] The figure of 538 appears to be too low and is probably only a partial listing of Seventeenth Air Army's strength. This report probably came from Soviet-era sources.

Table II.19: Fifth Air Army Sortie Count, 4–16 July 1943

	Total	Pe-2	Il-2	Il-2T	Yak-7	Yak-9	U-2	P-39	Total Flying Time
4 July–Combat Sorties									
Training Sorties	108	15	57	18	–	8	10	–	
Planes Flown	36	2	22	3	–	8	1	–	4h/5m
5 July–Combat Sorties	2	–	–	–	–	–	–	2	
Training Sorties	67	–	33	14	5	15	–	–	
Planes Flown	38	–	14	2	5	15	–	2	33h/6 m
6 July–Combat Sorties	12	–	–	–	5	7	–	–	
Training Sorties	81	11	39	6	11	14	–	–	
Planes Flown	51	7	23	1	8	12	–	–	55h/41m
7 July–Combat Sorties	135	–	–	–	30	105	–	–	
Training Sorties	59	12	44	2	–	–	1 UT-2	–	
Planes Flown	106	12	40	1	13	39	1	–	246h/49m
8 July–Combat Sorties	33	–	–	–	4	27	–	2	
Training Sorties	142	67*	67	–	–	–	4 UT-2	4	
Planes Flown	131	32	61	–	4	27	1	6	165h/40m
9 July–Combat Sorties									
Training Sorties	108	48	60	–	–	–	–	–	
Planes Flown	55	14	41	–	–	–	–	–	66h/30m
10 July–Combat Sorties									
Training Sorties	71	15**	54	2	–	–	–	–	
Planes Flown	48	9**	38	1	–	–	–	–	60h/41m

341

ACES AT KURSK

	Total	Pe-2	Il-2	Il-2T	Yak-7	Yak-9	U-2	P-39	Total Flying Time
11 July–Combat Sorties	2	–	–	–	2 La-5s	–	–	–	
Training Sorties	111	85***	15	–	–	–	11	–	
Planes Flown	61	45***	12	–	2 La-5s	–	2	–	63h/50m
12 July–Combat Sorties									
Training Sorties	100	28	33	22	–	–	17 UT-2	–	
Planes Flown	38	9	26	1	–	–	2 UT-2	–	44h/18m
13 July–Combat Sorties	18	–	–	–	8 La-5	–	–	10	
Training Sorties	126	27	45	40	–	–	14 UT-2	–	
Planes Flown	69	10	34	4	8 La-5	–	3 UT-2	10	86h/26m
14 July–Combat Sorties	7	–	–	–	5 La-5	–	–	2	
Training Sorties	116	30	15	70	–	–	1 UT-2	–	
Planes Flown	37	16	11	2	5 La-5	–	1 UT-2	2	41h/11m
15 July–Combat Sorties									
Training Sorties	20	11	9	–	–	–	–	–	
Planes Flown	16	11	5	–	–	–	–	–	25h/10m
16 July–Combat Sorties	2	–	–	–	–	–	–	2	
Training Sorties									
Planes Flown	2	–	–	–	–	–	–	2	1h/33m

* Eight sorties were for photography training
** One Pe-2 trainer flew seven sorties
*** One Pe-2 trainer flew 28 sorties

Table II.20: Comparison of German Loss Reports

	VIII Air Corps Losses	Quartermaster reports:						
		100%	80–95%	60–75%	40–55%	20–35%	not stated or 0–15%	Total
July 4	3	1	–	1	2	1	1	6
July 5	19	25	3	3	8	13	8	60
July 6	7	6	2	–	6	3	5	22
July 7	10	11	–	2	1	10	4	28
July 8	5	8	1	–	1	4	10	24

AIR CAMPAIGN STATISTICS

	VIII Air Corps Losses	Quartermaster reports:						
		100%	80–95%	60–75%	40–55%	20–35%	not stated or 0–15%	Total
July 9	11	17	–	4	1	4	4	30
July 10	3	2	1	2	2	–	3	10
July 11	14	12	1	–	1	3	2	19
July 12	11	6	–	4	3	1	3	17
July 13	5	5	1	1	–	3	3	13
July 14	9	8	–	3	–	4	6	21
July 15	5	2	1	–	–	1	1	5
July 16	3	1	–	2	2	1	–	6
July 17	5	0	–	1	–	1	–	2
July 18	1	0	–	–	1	–	–	1
	111	104	10	23	28	49	50	264

Other German Loss Claims

The German Luftwaffe quartermaster records contain detailed records of German planes damaged and destroyed. They list the plane, the pilot, the squadron, the location and the degree of damage. A plane listed as 100% damaged is destroyed. A plane listed as 60% or greater is certainly seriously damaged and possibly not repairable. Table II.20, a comparison of those percent ratings to the VIII Air Corps loss reports, is illuminating.

The differences from day to day reflect no consistent pattern. It does appear that the VIII Air Corps sometimes underreported Stuka losses. The quartermaster records have been reviewed by unit and location to ensure that only those units involved in the fighting around Belgorod and Kharkov are included. As such, this listing includes some losses in reconnaissance units that are probably not included in the VIII Air Corps list. By the same token, after the 14th, the VIII Air Corps may be reporting losses from units that were out of the area in consideration and which have been culled from the quartermaster reports.

While there are niggling differences between these two lists, they are mostly complementary and provide further confirmation of the nature and accuracy of the German loss reports. Still, there is no reason to believe that either list is exhaustive, complete, or always accurate. For example, Guenther Rall's crash-landing on the 9th and his collision on 12 July are not picked up in the quartermaster reports and the reports list the wrong squadron for Walter Krupinski.

Added to that, the quartermaster report probably lists planes that were damaged or lost to accidents, while the VIII Air Corps report may not list these planes. There are always some non-combat losses in air operations.

As the Soviet Second and Seventeenth Air Army loss reports are daily submissions by those units, for loss comparisons the VIII Air Corps daily loss reports were used for the sake of consistency.

Table II.21: German Losses by Type, VIII Air Corps Reports

	Total	Ar-66	Fw-189	Fw-190	He-111	Hs-126	Hs-129	Ju-87	Ju-88	Me-109
July 4	3	–	–	–	–	–	–	–	2	1
July 5	19	–	–	1	4	1	–	–	1	12
July 6	7	–	–	–	–	–	–	6	1	–
July 7	10	–	–	4	1	–	–	–	1	4
July 8	5	–	–	1	–	–	2	2	–	–
July 9	11	–	–	–	1	–	1	2	–	7
July 10	3	Only total number lost is provided for this day							
July 11	14	–	–	2	3	–	–	4	1	4
July 12	11	Only total number lost is provided for this day							
July 13	5	1	–	1	2	–	–	–	1	–
July 14	9	–	–	1	2	–	–	3	–	3
July 15	5	–	–	1	2	1	–	–	1	–
July 16	3	–	1	–	–	–	–	–	–	2
July 17	5	–	–	–	–	–	–	–	2	3
July 18	1	–	–	–	–	–	–	–	–	1
Total	111	1	1	11	15	2	3	17	10	37

Table II.22: German Losses by Type, Quartermaster Report

	Total	Ju-52	Fw-189	Fw-190	He-111	Hs-126	Hs-129	Ju-87	Ju-88	Me-109	Me-110
July 4	1	–	–	–	–	–	–	–	–	1	–
July 5	25	–	–	2	5	1	1	3	1	13	–
July 6	6	–	–	1	–	–	–	4	–	1	–
July 7	11	–	–	3	3	–	–	–	–	5	–
July 8	8	–	–	1	–	–	–	6	–	1	–
July 9	17	–	–	1	1	–	1	5	1	7	1
July 10	2	–	–	–	–	–	–	1	–	1	–
July 11	12	–	–	2	2	–	–	5	2	1	–
July 12	6	1	1	1	–	–	2	–	–	1	–
July 13	5	–	–	2	2	–	–	1	–	–	–
July 14	8	–	–	–	1	–	1	4	–	2	–
July 15	2	–	–	1	1	–	–	–	–	–	–
July 16	1	–	–	–	–	–	1	–	–	–	–
July 17	0	–	–	–	–	–	–	–	–	–	–
July 18	0	–	–	–	–	–	–	–	–	–	–
Total	104	1	1	14	15	1	6	29	4	33	1

AIR CAMPAIGN STATISTICS

Christer Bergstrom, *Kursk*, pages 129-131 has compiled a detailed list of German losses on 5 July 1943 from his independent research. This listing is summarized below. His listing does provide the names of the killed, wounded and missing aircrew.

Table II.23: German Losses on 5 July 1943

Unit	Plane Type	Damage	Men Lost	Casualty Type	Location	Cause
2.(F)/11	Ju-88 D-1	100%	4	Missing[87]	PQ 71/817	Unknown
NAGr 6	Me-110 G-3	20%	0	–	PQ 61573	Fighter
1./NAGr 2	Me-109 B-4	50%	0	–	Kharkov North Airfield	Technical
5.(H)/32	Hs-126	100%	1	KIA	PQ 67791	Fighter
			1	?		
4./KG 3	Ju-88 A-14	10%	1	KIA	PQ 6179	AA
			1	?		
4./KG 3	Ju-88 A-4	30%	0	–	Poltava Airfield	Landing Accident
5./KG 3	Ju-88 A-4	100%	0	–	PQ 6119	Engine Damage
2./KG 27	He-111 H	20%	1	wounded	Krasnaya-Dorvov	Fighter
2./KG 27	He-111 H-6	?	0	–	Yakovnevo	Fighter
3./KG 27	He-111 H-6	20%	0	–	Krasnaya-Dorvov	Fighter[88]
5./KG 27	He-111 H	–	1	wounded	Belgorod	Fighter
III./KG 27	He-111 H-16	100%	4	KIA	Belgorod	AA
			1	?		
III./KG 27	He-111 H-16	100%	3	wounded	Kharkov-Voychenko	Airfield Landing[89]
6./KG 55	He-111 H-16	20%	0	–	PQ 6156	Fighter[90]
6./KG 55	He-111 H-16	100%	1	KIA	Kharkov	Fighter[91]
			3	wounded		
6./KG 55	He-111 H-16	100%	1	missing	PQ 6132	Fighter
			2	wounded		
1./KG 100	He-111 H-6	45%	1	KIA	Dimitriyevka	Fighters & AA
1./KG 100	He-111 H-16	100%	4	missing	East of Sumy	Fighters & AA
			1	wounded		
3./KG 100	He-111 H-16	45%	1	?	Varvarovka	Fighters & AA
II./JG 3	Me-109 G-4	40%	0	–	Kharkov	Friendly AA[92]

ACES AT KURSK

Unit	Plane Type	Damage	Men Lost	Casualty Type	Location	Cause
4./JG 3	Me-109 G-4	40%	1	wounded	Kharkov-Rogan Airfield	Fighter[93]
5./JG 3	Me-109 G-4	100%	1	wounded	Volchansk	Air Combat
6./JG 3	Me-109 G-4	–	1	wounded	Belgorod	Air Combat
6./JG 3	Me-109 G-4	15%	1	wounded	Belgorod	Air Combat
Stab III./JG 3	Me-109 G-4	100%	1	KIA	PQ 6111	Fighter[94]
7./JG 3	Me-109 G-4	100%	1	?	PQ 5126	Air Combat[95]
7./JG 3	Me-109 G-4	20%	0	–	PQ 6138	Engine Failure
8./JG 3	Me-109 G-4	100%	1	PoW	PQ 613	Ground fire[96]
8./JG 3	Me-109 G-4	30%	0	–	PQ 6138	Technical failure
9./JG 3	Me-109 G-4	20%	1	–	Airfield Orlovka	Technical failure
9./JG 3	Me-109 G-4	100%	1	missing	PQ 61182	Air Combat[97]
I./JG 52	Me-109 G-6	80%	0	–	Airfield Bessonovka	Overturned during landing
1./JG 52	Me-109 G-6	100%	1[98]	KIA	Tomarovka	Pe-2[99]
2./JG 52	Me-109 G-6	100%	1	missing	Belgorod	10 Il-2s[100]
2./JG 52	Me-109 G-6	40%	0	–	?	AA
3./JG 52	Me-109 G-6	100%	1	KIA	Belgorod	Air Combat
6./JG 52	Me-109 G-6	80%	1[101]	wounded	Airfield Ugrim	Overturned during landing
III./JG 52	Me-109 G-4	100%	1[102]	wounded	Northeast of Belgorod	Air Combat
8./JG 52	Me-109 G-4	100%	1[103]	KIA	Ugrim	Air Combat
8./JG 52	Me-109 G-4	100%	1	KIA	Ugrim	Unknown
8./JG 52	Me-109 G-4	100%	1[104]	KIA	Belgorod	AA
9./JG 52	Me-109 G-4	60%	0	–	Zaporozhye-East Airfield	Crashed during landing
9./JG 52	Me-109 G-4	100%	1	missing	Ugrim	Air Combat
1./St.G 2	Ju-87 D-3	70%	2	wounded	PQ 6116	AA
4./St.G 2	Ju-87 D-3	35%	0	–	Kharkov-North Airfield	AA
6./St.G 2	Ju-87 D-3	35%	0	–	PQ 61531	AA
III./St.G 2	Ju-87 D-3	100%	0	–	PQ 6119	AA

AIR CAMPAIGN STATISTICS

Unit	Plane Type	Damage	Men Lost	Casualty Type	Location	Cause
III./St.G 2	Ju-87 D-3	100%	0	–	PQ 67192	AA
9./St.G 2	Ju-87 D 3	100%	2	KIA	PQ 6116	AA
1./Sch.G 1	Fw-190 A-5	35%	0	–	PQ 153	Technical failure[105]
Stab/Sch.G 1	Fw-190 A-5	100%	1	missing	Belgorod	Air Combat
1./Sch.G 1	Fw-190 F-3	15%	0	–	Varvarovka Airfield	Crashed on airfield
2./Sch.G 1	Fw-190 A-5	90%	1	wounded	PQ 6158	Overturned during landing
2./Sch.G 1	Fw-190 A-5	100%	0	–	PQ 6133	Ground fire
5./Sch.G 1	Fw-190 A-5	65%	0	–	Varvarovka	Crashed during landing
5./Sch.G 1	Fw-190 F-3	40%	0	–	Varvarovka	AA
6./Sch.G 1	Fw-190 F-3	15%	0	–	Varvarovka	AA
7./Sch.G 1	Hs-123 B-1	15%	0	–	Varvarovka	AA[106]
7./Sch.G 1	Hs-123 B-1	40%	1	wounded	Varvarovka Airfield	Landing accident

This is a total of 26 planes 100% destroyed and 29 men killed or missing (16 KIA, 13 missing, 21 wounded and one captured). There were also 6 planes 60 to 90% damaged, five of them from crashes on landing and one to AA.[107] Of the planes 60 to 100% destroyed, 4 were lost to fighters, 10 to air combat (including one to a Pe-2 and one to ten Il-2s), 1 to Fighters & antiaircraft, 5 to antiaircraft, 2 to ground fire, 1 to landing, 1 to engine damage, and 2 are unknown. The VIII Air Corps reports 19 planes lost this day. This is 24 planes lost directly to enemy action compared to the 19 reported in the VIII Air Corps report.

Table II.24: Losses by Unit According to Quartermaster Reports, Belgorod-Kharkov area operations

Unit	Plane Type	100%	80-95%	60-75%	40-55%	20-35%	5-15%	Not Stated	Crew: Killed	Missing	Injured	Captured
2(F)/11	Ju-88 D-1	–	–	–	–	1	–	–	1	–	–	–
2(F)/22	Ju-88 D-1	2	–	–	–	–	–	–	–	8	–	–
2(F)/100	Ju-88 D-1	1	–	–	–	–	–	–	–	4	–	–
1/2 NAG	Me-109 G-4/6	–	1	2	3	–	–	–	–	–	–	–

ACES AT KURSK

Unit	Plane Type	100%	80-95%	60-75%	40-55%	20-35%	5-15%	Not Stated	Crew: Killed	Missing	Injured	Captured
	Fi-156	–	–	–	–	1	–	–	–	–	–	–
6 NAG	Me-110 G-3	1	–	–	–	1	–	–	–	–	3	–
	(?)	–	–	–	–	–	–	2	–	–	2	–
	Fw-189 A-5	1	–	1	–	–	–	–	–	3	3	–
5(H)/32	Hs-126	1	–	–	2	–	–	–	1	–	1	–
San. Fl.Ber.	Ju-52 3mg10e	1	–	–	–	–	–	–	–	–	4	–
I/KG 100	He-111 H-6/11/16	2	–	–	3	–	–	–	1	9	1	–
3 KG	Ju-88	1	–	–	–	1	1	–	–	–	–	–
27 KG	He-111*	8	–	1	2	5	2	7	21	14	17	–
55 KG	He-111**	5	–	–	1	2	1	3	10	6	9	–
2 St.G.	Ju-87 D-1/3/5	12	1	3	1	5	–	–	12	2	6	–
77 St.G.	Ju-87 D-3	17	1	–	2	7	10	–	18	6	1	–
1 SG	Fw-190 A-5	5	3	5	3	5	3	1	1	1	5	–
	Fw-190 F-3	9	1	1	3	3	5	1	1	4	4	–
	Fw-190	–	–	–	–	–	–	1	–	–	1	–
7th Sq.	Hs-123 B-1	–	–	–	2	–	1	–	–	–	2	–
4th and 8th Sq.	Hs-129 B-2	4	–	2	2	–	1	–	1	2	–	–
2 SG	Hs-129 B-2	–	–	1	–	–	–	–	–	–	–	–
Pz.Jg. St./51 JG	Hs-129 B-2	1	–	1	–	1	–	–	–	–	–	–
3 JG	Me-109 G-4/6	12	2	5	3	10	7	1	4	2	6	2
52 JG	Me-109 G-4/6	21	2	2	2	4	3	–	8	4	5	2
		104	10	23	28	49	34	16	79	65	70	4

* H, H-2, H-6 and H-16s
** H, H-11 and H-16s

Note: 1(H)/21: reports no losses; 16 NAG: reports no losses; 2(H)/33: reports no losses

AIR CAMPAIGN STATISTICS

Table II.25: German Losses by Cause, VIII Air Corps Report, 4–18 July 1943

	Total	Ar-66	Fw-189	Fw-190	He-111	Hs-126	Hs-129	Ju-87	Ju-88	Me-109	Not stated
Anti-aircraft	10	–	–	–	2	–	–	8	–	–	–
Fighters	1	–	–	–	–	–	–	1	–	–	–
Bomb Explosion	1	–	–	–	–	–	–	1	–	–	–
Missing	6	–	–	1	1	–	–	–	–	4	–
Belly Landing	1	–	–	–	–	–	–	–	1	–	–
Forced landing	11	–	1	2	3	1	–	–	–	4	–
Motor failure	1	–	–	–	–	–	–	–	1	–	–
Crash after takeoff	1	–	–	–	–	–	–	–	1	–	–
SS Corps Flak	1	–	–	–	–	–	–	–	–	1	–
Not stated	78	1	–	8	9	1	3	7	7	28	14
Total	111	1	1	11	15	2	3	17	10	37	14

Table II.26: German Damage by Cause, Quartermaster Report, 4–18 July 1943

	Fw-189	Fw-190	He-111	Ju-52 or Fi-156 or Hs-123	Hs-126	Hs-129	Ju-87	Ju-88	Me-109	Me-110	Not stated
Fighter	1		13	1 Ju-52			16		4	1	1
Air battle with La-5									1		
Air battle with 8 La-5s									1		
Battle with fighter									2		
Belly landing due to fighter fire			1								
Crashed due to fighter fire					1						
Forced landing due to fighter fire			1								
Shot up by a Yak-1 while taking off									1		
Total damaged from fighters	1		15	1	1		16		9	1	1

	Fw-189	Fw-190	He-111	Ju-52 or Fi-156 or Hs-123	Hs-126	Hs-129	Ju-87	Ju-88	Me-109	Me-110	Not stated
Air battle									16		1
Air battle with Pe-2									1		
Battle with 10 Il-2s									1		
Belly landing after aerial combat									1		
Crashed after air battle		1									
Emergency landing after air battle									1		
Emergency landing behind enemy lines after air battle with Il-2									1		
Hit in the "LKW"									1		
Total damaged from air battles		1							22		1

	Fw-189	Fw-190	He-111	Ju-52 or Fi-156 or Hs-123	Hs-126	Hs-129	Ju-87	Ju-88	Me-109	Me-110	Not stated
Flak		12	13	1 Hs-123		9	23	1	4	1	
Crashed due to flak		4							2		
Crashed due to flak fire and burned on impact						1					
Crashed due to own flak									1		
Emergency landing as a result of a flak hit in the radiator									1		
Forced landing due to flak				1 Hs-123	1						
Hit by flak on the far side of the front line									1		
Landing gear damaged due to flak			1								
Damage by own flak									2		
Total damaged from Anti-aircraft		16	14	2	1	10	23	1	11	1	

AIR CAMPAIGN STATISTICS

	Fw-189	Fw-190	He-111	Ju-52 or Fi-156 or Hs-123	Hs-126	Hs-129	Ju-87	Ju-88	Me-109	Me-110	Not stated
Crashed due to weapons hit		1									
Crash landing due to enemy fire									1		
Flak and fighter			5								
Weapons hit			1								
Total damaged from hostile fire		1	6						1		
Total damaged from combat	1	18	35	3	2	10	39	1	43	2	2

	Fw-189	Fw-190	He-111	Ju-52 or Fi-156 or Hs-123	Hs-126	Hs-129	Ju-87	Ju-88	Me-109	Me-110	Not stated
Accident									1		
Belly landing due to bad weather		1									
Belly landing due to running out of fuel		1									
Crash landed because of operating error		1									
Crash landing		4			1		2		4		
Collision in the air with a Ju-87							4				
Collision in the air with a He-111		1									
Collision upon landing									1		
Emergency landing due to collision with crashing enemy aircraft							1				
Flipped over upon landing		2							1		
Flipped over upon landing trying to avoid another rolling aircraft								1			

	Fw-189	Fw-190	He-111	Ju-52 or Fi-156 or Hs-123	Hs-126	Hs-129	Ju-87	Ju-88	Me-109	Me-110	Not stated
Operating Error			1	1				1	5		
Struck an obstacle									1		
Total damaged from accident		10	1	1	1		7	2	13		

	Fw-189	Fw-190	He-111	Ju-52 or Fi-156 or Hs-123	Hs-126	Hs-129	Ju-87	Ju-88	Me-109	Me-110	Not stated
Mechanical											
Belly landing due to burst barrel		1									
Belly landing due to engine damage		1									
Belly landing due to technical problem									1		
Bomb release			1	1			1		1		
Crash due to engine damage		1									
Crash due to technical problems		1									
Crash landing due to technical problems		1									
Engine damage		1						1	1		
Engine fire							1		1		
Engine trouble		2							4		
Erdabweh		4				1			1		
Forced landing due to engine trouble									1		
Landing gear damage		1					2				
Landing gear damage upon landing				1 Hs-123							
Technical problems						2					

AIR CAMPAIGN STATISTICS

	Fw-189	Fw-190	He-111	Ju-52 or Fi-156 or Hs-123	Hs-126	Hs-129	Ju-87	Ju-88	Me-109	Me-110	Not stated
Tire damage upon landing		1									
Tire damage		1									
Total damaged from mechanical		16	1	1			3	4	1	10	

	Fw-189	Fw-190	He-111	Ju-52 or Fi-156 or Hs-123	Hs-126	Hs-129	Ju-87	Ju-88	Me-109	Me-110	Not stated
Other											
Belly landing		1							1		
Crash landing due to fuel shortage			1								
Crashed									1		
Crashed after take-off		1									
Crashed due to explosion							1				
Crash due to explosion of another plane in flight and impact fire							1				
Damaged upon landing							1				
Damaged while taxiing		1							2		
Emergency landing and burned on ground							1				
Emergency landing behind the front line									1		
Exploded in the air							1				
Explosion in the air							3				
Explosion upon landing			1								
Forced landing									1		
Geramt.									2		
Unknown	1	2	3				1	3	6		
Total other losses	1	5	5				9	3	14		

Summation

	Total	Fw-189	Fw-190	He-111	Ju-52 or Fi-156 or Hs-123	Hs-126	Hs-129	Ju-87	Ju-88	Me-109	Me-110	Not stated
Damaged from fighters	45	1		15	1	1		16		9	1	1
Damaged from air battles	24		1							22		1
Damaged from antiaircraft	79		16	14	2	1	10	23	1	11	1	
Damaged from hostile fire	8		1	6						1		
Damaged from accident	35		10	1	1	1		7	2	13		
Damaged from Mechanical	36		16	1	1		3	4	1	10		
Total other Losses	37	1	5	5				9	3	14		
Total	264	2	49	42	5	3	13	59	7	80	2	2

Table II.27: Second Air Army Losses by Type, 4–18 July 1943

	Total	U-2	R-5	Il-2	Pe-2	A-20	La-5	Yak-1	Yak-7	Yak-9	Fighters
July 4	4							1	3		
July 5	114			43	18	1		10	3		39
July 6	51	1		22			12	6	10		
July 7	45			13			18	7	7		
July 8	47	1		16			16	10	4		
July 9	37			15	2		14	6			
July 10	25			12			6	3	2	2	
July 11	19			2			9	7	1		
July 12	28			12	3		2	3	6	2	
July 13	27	1		8	5	1	1	3	1	7	
July 14	24			7	4		5	6		2	
July 15	11			8				2		1	
July 16	29			6	11			5	4	3	
July 17	17	1		13				2	1		
July 18	7		1	3	3						
Total	485	4	1	180	46	2	83	71	42	17	39

AIR CAMPAIGN STATISTICS

Table II.28: Second Air Army Losses by Cause, 4–18 July 1943

	Total	U-2	R-5	Il-2	Pe-2	A-20	La-5	Yak-1	Yak-7	Yak-9	Fighters
Shot down in air combat	34			1	4		3	2	3	9	12
Shot down by fighters	15			7	3		4	1			
Failed to return	333	4	1	110	19	2	73	57	35	8	24
Anti-aircraft	35			20	9		3		1		2
Friendly anti-aircraft	3			2			1				
Ramming	1						1				
Accident	1			1							
Crashed	3				3						
upon returning	1							1			
pilot killed	1						1				
landing, damaged	3						3				
into each other	2				2						
while landing	1							1			
Not stated	2			2							
Forced landings	45			37	1		6				1
damage	2			2							
AA damage	3			3							
Total	485	4	1	180	46	2	83	71	42	17	39

Addenda:
1) Of the planes listed as not returning in the reports of 9–11 July, in fact three Il-2 and 1 Yak-1 returned to their units. During this period, another Yak-1 was found to have made a forced landing.

Table II.29: Seventeenth Air Army Losses by Type
(for only those missions that were judged to be in the Belgorod area or that attacked the VIII Air Corps, 4–18 July 1943)

	Total	U-2	R-5	Il-2	Pe-2	TB-3	La-5	Yak-1
July 4								
July 5	75			66			7	2
July 6	28		1	21		1	3	2
July 7	42	1		28		3	6	4
July 8	14			13				1
July 9	9			8			1	
July 10	–							

	Total	U-2	R-5	Il-2	Pe-2	TB-3	La-5	Yak-1
July 11	–							
July 12	3			3				
July 13	1			1				
July 14	6			3				3
July 15	–							
July 16	4			2			2	
July 17	–							
July 18	–							
Total	182	1	1	145		4	19	12

Table II.30: Losses not included as related to the Kursk operations

July 6	2 Yak-1s from I Mixed Corps
July 15	1 Yak-1 from III Mixed Corps,
	1 Pe-2 from 39th Reconnaissance Rgt
July 16	2 Pe-2s from reconnaissance missions
July 17	7 Il-2s and 1 Yak-1 from III Mixed Corps
	2 Il-2s and 1 La-5 from IX Mixed Corps
	1 TB-3 from 244th Bomber Division
July 18	5 Yak-1s from I Mixed Corps
	4 Il-2s, 1 Yak-1, 1 La-5 from III Mixed Corps
	5 Il-2s, 1 La-5 from IX Mixed Corps
	4 TB-3s from 244th Bomber Division

Table II.31: Seventeenth Air Army Losses by Cause
(for only those missions that were judged to be in the Belgorod area or that attacked the VIII Air Corps)

	Total	U-2	R-5	Il-2	Pe-2	TB-3	La-5	Yak-1	Yak-7
Shot down in air combat	16			12		2		2	
Failed to return	149	1	1	123		1	16	7	
Anti-aircraft	7			2			2	3	
German attack on airfield	1						1		
Crashed	1					1			
Probably made a forced landing	6			6					

AIR CAMPAIGN STATISTICS

Table II.32: Other Soviet Loss Reports

The Second Air Army reports the following losses for 5–18 July 1943:

	Total	Shot down in Air Combat	Shot down by Antiaircraft	Failed to Return	Forced Landing
Fighters	288	26	8	138	116
Assault Aircraft	246	11	20	137	78
Bombers	47	4	3	18	22
Night Bombers	6			6	
Total	587	41	31	299	216

Of those making forced landings:

	Able to Fly to Their Airfields	Evacuated Back to their Units	Remained on the Field
Fighters	20	60	36
Assault Aircraft	19	30	29
Bombers	3	13	6
Total	42	103	71

Table II.33: Total Irreplaceable Losses

Fighters	172
Assault Aircraft	168
Bombers	25
Night Bombers	6
Total	371

Table II.34: Losses for the Month of July 1943

Unit	Type	Combat	Non-Combat	In repair
I Assault Corps	Assault	71	4	2
	Fighter	28	2	1
I Bomber Corps	Bomber	36	5	–
IV Fighter Corps	Fighter	61	3	1
V Fighter Corps	Fighter	117	9	2
208th Night Bomber Div.	Night Bomber	3	4	–
291st Assault Div.	Assault	91	6	57

Unit	Type	Combat	Non-Combat	In repair
	Fighter	19	1	12
454th Bomber Rgt	Reconnaissance	4	–	–
Total		430	34	75

Data from the Soviet General Staff Study on the Battle of Kursk
On the Second and Seventeenth Air Armies

The Soviet General Staff study on the Battle of Kursk, dated March-April 1944, had this oddly named table for the operations of the Second and Seventeenth Air Armies.[108]

Aircraft Sorties Over Soviet Territory by Enemy Aircraft (5-18 July)

Date	Our Aviation							Enemy	
	Second Air Army		Seventeenth Air Army		LRA	Total			
	Day	Night	Day	Night		Day	Night	Day	Night
5 July	1,274	48	446	123	–	1,720	171	1,947	11
6 July	820	72	458	197	85	1,278	354	873	26
7 July	847	83	689	192	163	1,536	438	829	15
8 July	957	96	228	174	275	1,185	545	692	25
9 July	658	60	187	183	161	845	404	1,577	28
10 July	455	69	71	149	231	526	449	1,105	17
11 July	539	57	56	183	45	595	285	528	21
12 July	759	109	134	164	–	893	273	530	8
13 July	659	156	118	151	112	777	419	271	35
14 July	865	200	168	114	144	1,033	458	1,195	43
15 July	328	151	35	146	193	363	490	261	–
16 July	723	219	203	143	112	926	474	403	7
17 July	484	135	–	–	–	484	135	140	22
18 July	436	199	–	–	–	436	199	55	17
Totals	9,804	1,654	2,793	1,919	1,521	12,597	5,094	10,406	275

The Soviet General Staff study data on sortie counts is similar to the data we have assembled. The data we have for the Second and Seventeenth Air Armies operations are taken directly from the daily air army reports as drawn from the archives. The Soviet General Staff study may have used these same reports, or used higher level reports or other assembled reports for their study. But there are minor differences between ours and their reports, so most likely they used other higher level or assembled reports for their study. For example, we have the Second Air Army flying 1,296 daytime sorties on 5 July. The Soviet General Staff study has them flying 1,274. There are also minor differences over the next two days, but the two sets of counts are the same for 8 and 9 July and then vary slightly for most of the subsequent days (except for the 15th and 16th, where they again match). After the 5th, the largest difference is on the 12th, where our reports record 10 more daytime sorties. These are very minor differences. The Second Air Army nighttime sorties match in all cases between the counts we assembled from the air army daily reports and what the Soviet General Staff study reports.

The Seventeenth Air Army is a little more complex as some of their missions were flown into the battle area while other of their missions were flown completely out of the battle area defended by the Voronezh Front. For the Kursk database project, I ended up reviewing each reported mission as to where it operated and made a judgment as to whether this mission was in the area of the Belgorod offensive or not. It does not appear that the Soviet General Staff study did that. For the 5th through the 16th, their estimate more closely matches with the total number of sorties flown by the Seventeenth Air Army than it does with my lower count of the number of sorties flown in the battle area. On eight of those 12 days in question, their totals match the total we drew from the Seventeenth Air Army daily reports. The day they most differ was on 7 July when they reported 50 more sorties than we counted. We did re-check the original report and our total is 639.[109] Suspect their number of 689 is a typo. As the Soviet General Staff study may have been drawn from a later aggregate report, there are multiple opportunities for typos.[110]

On the other hand, in the table we assembled of Seventeenth Air Army daytime sorties we had a lower count for "only those that were in the Belgorod Area or attacked the VIII Air Corps" (see table in Chapter Four). It is consistently lower from the 5th through the 16th, which the worse variance being on the 7th, where we count 588 as valid sorties in the battle area, whereas the Soviet General Staff study reports 689. On the 17th we count none in the area and on the 18th we count 12 sorties.

Still there are a couple of observations we can make from this comparison. First, is that the Soviet General Staff study reports of Soviet sorties flown is fairly accurate in that it matches with records we have from the Second and Seventeenth Air Armies. This is important to note as we rely on the Soviet General Staff study for the count of sorties for the Sixteenth Air Army.

Second, is that they focus on the dates for the battle of 5 to 18 July. The Germans were attacking from the 5th through 15 July, there were then two days of rest, and the Soviets started attacking on 18 July. The Germans then conducted a controlled withdrawal starting the 19th ending on 24 July. The period of 5 to 18 July was also the period covered by the Kursk database.

There are two other tables in the Soviet General Staff study on Kursk that relate to the Second and Seventeenth Air Army. They are provided below:[111]

The Air Struggle Along the Enemy's Main Axis

	Air Battles	Enemy Losses			Second Air Army Losses			
		Fighter	Bomber	Total	Fighter	Bomber	Assault	Total
5 July	81	71	83	154	36	15	27	78
6 July	64	40	65	105	23	–	22	45
7 July	74	44	78	122	24	–	13	37
8 July	65	54	52	106	24	1	16	41
9 July	62	49	22	71	16	1	15	32
10-14 July	152	112	93	205	49	14	75	138
15-18 July	43	45	27	72	(the figures in the line above cover from 10-18 July)			
Totals	541	415	420	835	172	31	168	371

Now, these figures have been discussed before. The losses of the German VIII Air Corps was 111 planes, against the 835 claimed here. The losses of the Second Air Army according to the records we reviewed was 481 planes from 5 to 18 July (see Appendix II, Table II.27), against the 371 reported here. This report also does not include Seventeenth Air Army claims or losses. The Seventeenth Air Army's losses were significant (182 planes). So, it does appear that the Soviet General Staff study basically leaves out 292 out of their 663 airplanes losses (44% of their losses), effectively under reporting their air losses by almost half.

This is concerning, for it does appear that Soviet General Staff study is understating the Second Air Army losses, omitting the considerable losses from the Seventeenth Air Army and of course, grossly overclaiming the number of German aircraft shot down. This was in an internal classified report that was supposed to be an analysis of the battle. Hard to properly analyze if your data is not correct.

The final table related to the fighting in the south shows the following:

Date	Fighters	Assault Aircraft	Bombers			Total	% of Fighter Operations	
			Day	Night Total	Night Long-range		Total	Day
5-10.7	4,657	2,119	314	2,361	915	9,451	49	65
11-14.7	2,104	878	316	1,435	301	4,733	44	64
15-18.7	1,277	598	334	1,298	305	3,507	36	58
Totals	8,038	3,595	964	5,094	1,521	17,691	45	64

Again, these figures are similar to what we have. We report 11,657 sorties for the Second Air Army and 6,503 sorties for the Seventeenth Air Army (and 4,384 sorties for "only those that were in the Belgorod Area or Attacked the VIII Air Corps"). We do not have a figure of Long Range Aviation, but note that this apparently included 1,521 night missions. This had to have a fairly limited impact in the immediate battlefield area, as it is suspected that many of these night missions by Long Range Aviation were probably not conducted near the front lines.

AIR CAMPAIGN STATISTICS

The Luftwaffe Records

The Luftwaffe, being the younger service and personally headed by the Deputy Fuehrer of the Reich, Hermann Goering, was a more politically motivated, or "Nazified" organization than the German Army. The Luftwaffe had moved its records out of Berlin as it became threatened by the Soviet advance in 1945. Adolf Hitler, as the Reich was crumbling, gave the order to destroy all records. The Luftwaffe records were sitting in rail cars when the order was received. This was done with great efficiency by the Luftwaffe, unlike the German Army, which mostly ignored the order.[112] As such, almost no Luftwaffe unit records survived the war. Most of what exists are the Ministry of Air Records and some limited surviving personal files (e.g., Rhodan & Milch). These top-level records provide few details on the actual Luftwaffe air operations during the Battle of Kursk.

The Luftwaffe did have air liaison officers attached to the army. In the case of the neighboring Second Army, this unit kept the records of their liaison officers. Thus, we have a daily count of the number of sorties and by mission for the battle.

What we do not have is any German record, other than a few scattered references, of where these missions went each day. As much of the underlying analysis in this book relies on looking at relative combat performance of units, it has been important to make some determination as to the degree of air support given on each day to each German unit. The only alternative source is the Soviet reports of German overflights. While this is very far from an ideal source, in the absence of any other material, this source was relied upon. A complete quoting of the reports from the Soviet records and the subsequent analysis from those is provided later. They are the underlying basis of the air figures used in each of the engagement files.

Table II.35: Summation of Daytime Ground Attack Type Sorties
(Stuka, Assault, Bombing and Ground Attack Sorties)

Date	German	Soviet	Ratio
4	160	0	N/A
5	1,942	486	4.00
6	1,356	442	3.07
7	1,444	400	3.61
8	1,380	404	3.42
9	1,266	291	4.35
10	529*	158	3.35
11	801	152	5.27
12	411	354	1.16
13	402	343	1.17
14	1,131	401	2.82
15	541	126	4.29
16	278	340	.82
17	?	211	N/A
18	0	187	N/A
Total	11,641	4,295	2.71

* Estimated

ACES AT KURSK

Notes

1. These two paragraphs come primarily from a write-up prepared by Col. Fyodor Sverdlov in 2001.
2. Second Army air liaison officer records (T312, R1242, page 001151).
3. NARA RG-242, T314, R197.
4. Seidemann manuscript, *The 'Zitadelle" Offensive, Eastern Front, 1943: Luftwaffe Participation* (manuscript T-26, written in Newstadt, 1 November 1947 by Writer No. 737, General Seidemann).
5. Provided courtesy of Christer Bergstrom.
6. Provided courtesy of Michael Holm through *The Lutwaffe, 1933–1945* website. These records were pulled from the Bundesarchiv in Freiburg (RL 2 III/876).
7. This order of battle was also cross-checked to Klink, page 336 and Hooton, *Eagle in Flames*, page 316. It was not possible to entirely resolve the differences between the various orders of battle.
8. Unless otherwise noted, all plane strengths come from the "Flugzeugbestand und Bewagungsmeldungen" (RL 2 III/876) assembled by Michael Holm.
9. Seidemann claims there were three groups. Hooton, *Eagle in Flames*, page 315, indicates only two groups, the II and III Groups. Film C. 2032/ II indicates the following units making kills in the Belgorod area on the 5th of July are the II and III Group, and the 4th through 9th Squadrons. The quartermaster loss reports also indicate the same. The unit strength reports show the staff of JG3 with no aircraft. Michael Holm shows the staff and the I Group back in Germany at this time.
10. An estimate, as the reporting ends in May 1943. There were 32 Me-109 G-4s on 1 June.
11. The Second Army air liaison records for 5 July 1943 state "II + III/J.G. 52," yet both Seidemann and Klink claim there were three groups. Hooton, *Eagle in Flames*, page 316, claims it had the staff, I, II, and III Groups, and 15th Squadron. The unit status reports indicate that the 15th Squadron had no airplanes at this time. Film C. 2032/II clearly indicates that the I and III Groups and their squadrons were in the Belgorod area and scoring kills on the 5th of July. The quartermaster loss reports indicate the same and that the II Group was in Anapa (on the Black Sea). Michael Holm also indicates that the II Group was in Anapa. Even though this contradicts the Second Army air liaison records, this clearly appears to be the case.
12. Seidemann states it had two groups, while Klink states three. Hooton, *Eagle in Flames*, page 316, states that it had its staff, and I & II Group. The march plan clearly shows the staff, I and II Group and 4th and 8th Squadrons and an antitank command. From the quartermaster loss reports, it is clear the unit had its staff, I, 1, 2, 3, II, 5 and 6/1 SG armed with both Fw-190 A-5s and Fw-190 F-3s. The 7/1 SG was armed with Hs-123 B-1s. The 4 (Pz) and 8 (Pz) were armed with Hs-129 B-2s. This matches the existing airplane status reports, as there is no III Group.
13. The extent of participation of the 2nd Ground Attack Wing is a source of some confusion and is not listed in many sources. The main body of the 2nd Ground Attack Wing was in Italy according to Michael Holm, except for these two squadrons, which were at Varvarovka. The quartermaster loss reports only show an Hs-129 B-2 lost in the Belgorod-Kharkov area on the 17th of July by 4.(Pz.)/2 SG. Hooton, *Eagle in Flames*, page 316, states that the staff and I Group of the Second Assault Wing were there with Hs-129s from the I Group and Fw-190s. Seidemann identifies a 4th Antitank Ground Attack Group, 9th Ground Attack Wing in his manuscript, and estimates it had 60 planes. This unit was not formed until 18 October, but was under command of Bruno Meyer and created from the 4th and 8th Squadrons of the 1st and 2nd Assault Wings and the Tank Hunting Squadron from the 51st Fighter Wing. Klink, page 336, states that there were two antitank squadrons in addition to the three groups of the 1st Ground Attack Wing and shows two or three groups of the 2nd Ground Attack Wing with the Sixth Air Fleet. It is clear that the 4.(Pz.)/2 SG was there. It is uncertain if 8.(Pz.)/2 SG was there.
14. Hooton, *Eagle in Flames*, page 316, states that there was a tank hunting squadron with Hs-129s from the 51st Fighter Wing. This is confirmed by the quartermaster loss records.
15. Staff and three groups identified in march plan. Seidemann also notes "plus 1 Antitank Squadron." This is Rudel's experimental antitank squadron armed with 37mm guns. Two experimental units had been working with Ju-87 G-1s at the time. They were 1. and 2./Versuchkommando fur Panzerbekampfung. The 1st Squadron became 10.(Pz)/StG 1 on 17 June 1943. The 2nd Squadron on 17 June 1943 became the 10.(Pz.) of the 2nd Stuka Wing. The airplane status report shows eight Ju-87 G-1s (and 1 D-1 and 2 D-3s) with the 1st Squadron on 1 July, but none with the 2nd Squadron. Instead the 2nd Squadron

AIR CAMPAIGN STATISTICS

had 8 Ju-87 D-1s, and 11 Ju-87 D-3s as of 1 July, but they are all transferred out during the month. On 1 August it shows 8 Ju-87 G-1s transferred in.

16. The march plan notes only the staff and I and II Groups. Seidemann, page 194, states that it had three groups. Klink, page 336, states two. Hooton, page 316, states it had its staff, and Groups I, II & III. Whether the III Group is there is not known for certain.

17. This formation is not listed in Klink, page 336. Instead it lists one group from Bombardment Wing 51. Hooton, *Eagle in Flames*, page 316, lists it with the Sixth Air Fleet and lists III Group/51st Bombardment Wing with the VIII Air Corps (with Ju-88s). The Second Army air liaison officer records for 5 July lists "KG 3" as does Seidemann, page 194. Seidemann only shows it with a strength of 70. Writer #762 in post-war study T-26, The "Zitadelle" Offensive, Eastern Front, 1943: Luftwaffe Participation in the Areas of the German OREL Armies, page 165, states that the I, II and III Groups of the 3rd Bombardment Wing, armed with Ju-88s, were up north with the Sixth Air Fleet. This account sometimes records units as being there that were later transferred. Michael Holms shows the staff and Groups I, II and III based in Poltava at this time. He shows the III Group of the 51st Bombardment Wing in Bryansk at this time. It had 21 Ju-88s as of 1 July 1943.

It is hard to claim that the unit was not with the VIII Air Corps on 5 July when it is clearly listed as such in the Second Army air liaison records. The unit was reported to have three Ju-88s damaged on 5 July in the Belgorod area.

With the III Group having only one plane, it may have not been involved with the offensive.

18. Hooton, *Eagle in Flames*, page 316, states it had only I & III Groups and the 14th Squadron. This appears to be incorrect as the 1, 2, 3, II, 4, 5, 6, III, 7 and 14/27 KG are all reported in the loss reports in the Belgorod-Kharkov area between 4 and 15 July.

19. Seidemann, page 194, states that it had three groups. Klink, page 336, states two. Hooton, *Eagle in Flames*, page 316, states it had the staff and Groups I, II & III.

The III Group of the 55th Bomber Wing was there, as its records survive. Even then, it appears that only its He-111 H-11Rs participated in the Kursk Offensive. They were operating out of Rogan and flew a maximum of 88 sorties in a single day. The unit's He-111 H-16s did not participate in the offensive, as they were based in Stalino. They flew a maximum of 11 sorties in a day.

The III/55th Bombardment Wing started with 46 planes. Looking at the groups of missions flown, it appears that the group operating out of Rogan had at least 40 and as many as 46 He-111 H-11s. The group operating out of Stalino had at least 7 He-111 H-16s.

The quartermaster reports records losses in the Belgorod-Kharkov area for the 5th through the 13th of July from the 5, 6, 7, 8, 9/55 KG. Michael Holm shows the I Group in Germany and a 14th Squadron in Poltava. There are no airplane status reports for the 14th Squadron until January 1944.

20. This group is not listed in Seidemann, page 194, but is identified by name in the Second Army air liaison record for 5 July 1943 (T312, R1242, page 001151). Klink, page 336, and Hooton, *Eagle in Flames*, page 316, also list this unit. Hooton states it was armed with He-111s. A pilot from this unit claims a kill on 5 July (Film C. 2032/II) and the Luftwaffe quartermaster report shows losses (He-111s) in the Belgorod area for the 1st, 2nd and 3rd Squadrons for the 5th through the 7th of July.

21. Seidemann, page 194, identified the unit by type and estimated it had 40 aircraft. The unit is identified by name in the march plan. Hooton, *Eagle in Flames*, page 316, lists the following reconnaissance units:

1 NAG:	3.(H)/31, 2.(H)/31	Fw-189
6 NAG:	3.(H)/32, 5.(H)/32	Fw-189, Hs-126, Me-110
	7.(H)/32, 2.(H)/33	
9 NAG:	1.(H)/21, 7.(H)/32	Fw-189
14 NAG:	5.(H)/11, 5.(H)/41	Fw-189, Me-110

The duplicate listing of 7.(H)/32 is not explained. Michael Holm reports that 5.(H)/32 & 2.(H)/33 served under 6th NAG while 7.(H)/32 was under 9th NAG.

The close-range reconnaissance units are clearly identified from the quartermaster damage reports as having sent flights into the area are the 1/2 NAG (Me-109), 2 NAG (Me-109), 6 NAG (Fw-189 and Me-110), and 5.(H)/32 (Hs-126).

The 3.(H)/32 has no status reports after July 1942, when it transferred its 8 Hs-126s out of the unit. It is assumed to have upgraded to Fw-189s. This unit may not have been here, or may even have been disbanded at this time.

22. This unit is identified as a long-range reconnaissance squadron in Seidemann's manuscript with an estimated strength of 10. It is not identified by Klink. It is identified by name by Hooton, *Eagle in Flames*, page 316, and is listed as consisting of the "4.(F)/11" armed with Ju-88s, the "4.(F)/Nacht" armed with Do-17s, He-111s, and Do-217s and the "Wekusta 76" armed with Ju-88s. This last unit, being a weather squadron, was probably not exclusively used in the Belgorod-Kharkov area.

    The reconnaissance units are clearly identified from the quartermaster damage reports as having sent flights into the area are the 2(F)/11, 2(F)/100, and 2 (F)/22. They were all flying Ju-88 D-1s.

23. This unit is identified in Seidemann's manuscript. Klink states that there were two harassing squadrons. Hooton, *Eagle in Flames*, states there were six squadrons (number one through six) and credits them with having Ar-66s, Do-17s, Fw-58s, Fw-189s, Go-145s, He-46s, Hs-126s, W-34s.

24. This is Seidemann's estimate, page 194, and it seems reasonable if all six squadrons were deployed in the Kharkov-Belgorod area.

25. This unit is identified in Seidemann's manuscript with an estimated 12 Ju-52s. There were definitely Ju-52s conducting medical evacuation in the Belgorod-Kharkov area.

26. Details of the division are provided by Seidemann. The air liaison officer records identified this unit on 5 July (which only sent up 12 sorties that day), and clearly identified that there were Hungarian Me-109s on the 5th and Hungarians Ju-88s on the 17th.

    Hooton, *Eagle in Flames*, page 316, identifies the units as the 2nd Hungarian Air Brigade, consisting of:

5/1 Fighter Group	Me-109
102/1 Bomber Squadron	Ju-88
102/2 Dive Bomber Squadron	Ju-87
1st Reconnaissance Squadron	Ju-88
3/1 Tactical Reconnaissance Squadron	Fw-189
4/1 Bomber Squadron	

    Also see Table II.7 below for a more descriptive order of battle. There may have only been around 63 aircraft with this unit at Kursk.

27. The close-range reconnaissance units clearly identified from the quartermaster damage reports as having sent flights into the area are the 1/2 NAG (Me-109), 2 NAG (Me-109), 6 NAG (Fw-189 and Me-110), and 5.(H)/32 (Hs-126).

28. Hooton, *Eagle in Flames*, page 316. This unit is not listed in Seidemann's account. Hooton does not provide a source for his order of battle. Michael Holm does state that the 10th and 12th Squadrons were divided into several detachments and operated under the Sixth Air Fleet in Smolensk-Bryansk area and the Fourth Air Fleet in the Poltava-Stalino area. This potentially places them in the area of the Kursk battlefield. There is no evidence of any night fighter missions being flown in the Belgorod area.

    As of 1 July, the III Group (consisting of a staff and three squadrons) of the 5th Night Fighter Wing had 42 aircraft: 1 Me-110 E-2, 8 Me-110 F-4s, 1 Me-110 G-4, 9 Do-217 Js, 5 Do-217 Ns, 1 Ju-88 C-4 and 17 Ju-88 C-6s.

29. Hooton, *Eagle in Flames*, page 316. This unit is not listed in Seidemann's account. It might be a flight from the 12th Squadron of the 5th Night Fighter Wing.

30. From Bergstrom, *Kursk*, page 125 and the Pawel Burchard order of battle at http://www.yogysoft.de/pawel/_kursk/odbs/Lfl4_odb.htm. They differ in a number of details. Order of battle also reviewed the accounts of the Hungarian air force provided in Gyula Sarhidai, Gyorgy Punka and Viktor Kozlik, *Hungarian Eagles: The Hungarian Air Forces 1920-1945* (Hikoki Publications, Aldershot, UK, 1996).

31. Aircraft types are from the Pawel Burchard order of battle. The Bergstrom listing is similar.

32. The Pawel Burchard order of battle gives a strength of 12 and the date of 18 May 1943. Sarhidai, page 31, sates that they received 12 Fw-189s in March 1943 and flew their first missions on 22 May 1943.

33. Sarhidai, page 42.

34. This unit is not listed in the Bergstrom order of battle. It was probably not at Kursk. The note in Pawel Burchard's order of battle states that: "Anf. Juni 1943 in Ausb. auf dem Fl.Platz Kiew Post Wolinski Mitte Aug. Einsatz im Verband II./St.G. 77" indicating that is was in Kiev in June 1943 and did move to Kharkov area until August. Sarhidai, page 31, states that the squadron was sent out to the front in July 1943 and took part the battles in the region Kharkov from August.

AIR CAMPAIGN STATISTICS

35. According to Pawel Burchard order of battle.
36. The strength figures are from Bergstrom, *Kursk*, page 125. The figures do not seem to match well with his order of battle. If 12 Fw-189s are with the 3/1 Tactical Reconnaissance Squadron, then it follows that there are only 6 Ju-88s with the 1/1 Reconnaissance Squadron (which is reasonable). This would leave 30 bombers and 12 ground attack planes to be assigned to the 4/1 Bomber Squadron, which would seem to be incorrect. The 4/1 Bomber Squadron probably did not have more than 15 bombers.
37. All commander designations drawn from Michael Holm, *The Luftwaffe, 1933–45* (www ww2 dk), unless otherwise noted.
38. From Pawel Burchard order of battle, www.yogysoft.de
39. Bergstrom, *Kursk*, page 124 has his base location at Zaporozhye, Burchard has his base location as Warwarowka as of 5 July and on the night of 13 July he moves to Orel-West. Burchard has the AT command/1st SchG at Saporoschje to 8 July 1943 and then at Warwarowka from 8 July 1943.
40. Bergstrom, *Kursk*, page 124 provides his first name. The Pawal Burchard order of battle also states the same.
41. Bergstrom, *Kursk*, page 124. The Pawel Burchard order of battle also lists him.
42. Bergstrom, *Kursk*, page 124. The Pawel Burchard order of battle also lists him.
43. Bergstrom, *Kursk*, page 124.
44. Bergstrom, *Kursk*, page 124. The Pawel Burchard order of battle also lists him.
45. Bergstrom, *Kursk*, page 124. The Pawel Burchard order of battle also lists him.
46. There is a similar listing provided in Bergstrom, *Kursk*, page 124 that list the units, airfield, commander, aircraft type and number of aircraft available (as of 1 July 1943). The differences between these two listings are:

    1. The location of II/3rd JG is listed as Kharkov-Rogan and Ugrim
    2. Bergstrom lists II/52nd JG at Kharkov-Rogan and under command of Gerhard Barkhorn. This unit was clearly not at Kursk and remained in the south.
    3. The location of the staff/I SchG is listed at Bessonovka
    4. The location of the five antitank squadrons is listed at Zaporozhye with them moving to Varvarovka on 8 July, while we have four them at Varvarovka.
    5. The commander for 8th/1st SchG is listed as Captain Rudolf Heinz Ruffner
    6. The commander of the 4th/2nd SchG. 1 is listed as Major Matuschek.
    7. The location of the I/2nd StG is listed at Kharkov-East
    8. The commander for I/2nd StG is listed as Captain Bruno Dilley
    9. The commander for I/77th StG is listed as Captain Karl Henze
    10. The location for III/77th StG is listed as Kharkov-West
    11. The commander for III/77th StG is listed as Major Georg Jacob
    12. The location of the I/3rd KG is listed as Stalino and Poltava.
    13. We list III/3rd KG (3rd Bomber Wing). Bergstrom does not.
    14. The rank of commander of 27th KG is given as Lt. Colonel (vice Colonel).
    15. The location of the staff/55th KG is listed as Kharkov-Rogan and Stalino.
    16. Bergstrom provides commanders for II/3rd KG, II/27th KG, I/110th KG, 10th/2 StG, and AT Sqn/51st JG. They have been added to this list.
    17. He lists eight reconnaissance and transportation units that are not listed in our order of battle. They are: 1) 1./NAGr 6 – 1.(H)/21, 2) 2./NAGr 16, 3) 1./NAGr 2 – 4.(H)/10, 4) 5.(H)/32, 5) 2.(H)/33, 6) Transportstaffel Fl.K.VIII, 7) Flugbereitschaft FL.K.VIII, 8) San.Flugbereitschaft 3.

There is also a listing on page 125 of the units in the Fourth Air Fleet in the Army Group South area that are "available for operations the Belgorod combat zone on 5 July 1943."

There is also a website by Pawel Burchard that presents a detailed order of battle for the VIII Air Corps for July. It also lists units, aircraft, commanders, and plane types. It is similar to Bergstrom's listing. It does list II/52nd JG under Gerhard Barkhorn as being at Kharkov-Rogan as at 4 August 1943. It also lists the same five reconnaissance groups that Bergstrom lists and provides a similar order of battle for the Hungarian air units. Significant differences include:

1. The location of II/3rd JG is listed as Rogan from 5-15 July 1943 (which agrees with our listing).
2. The location for III/52nd JG is listed as Ugrim from 3-13 July, then Orel from 14-19 July.
3. The location for HQ/1st SchG is listed as Besonowka.
4. The location for I/1st SchG is listed as Besonowka/Warwarowka and then as Orel from 14 July 1943.

ACES AT KURSK

5. The location for II/1st SchG is listed as Besonowka/Warwarowka and then Barwenkowo from 20 July 1943.
6. The location for I/2nd StG is listed as Kharkov-East and the command is Captain Bruno Dilley. This is the same as in Bergstrom's list.
7. The location for II/2nd StG is listed as Krestowoj
8. The location for III/2nd StG is listed as Krestowoj.
9. The commander for I/77th StG is listed as Captain Karl Henze. This is the same as in Bergstrom's list.
10. The location for III/77th StG is listed as Kharkov-West. This is the same as in Bergstrom's list.
11. The commander of III/77th StG is listed as Major Georg Jakob. This is the same as in Bergstrom's list.
12. The III Bomber Wing is not listed (!)
13. The location for I/27th KG is listed as Melitopol (to 4 July 1943), Charkow-Woltschenko (to 17 July 1943) and Charkow-Rogan (to 5 August 1943).
14. The location for II/27th KG is listed as Melitopol (to 3 July 1943), Charkow-Woltschenko (to 17 July 1943), Seschtschinskaja (to 20 July 1943) and Schatalowka (to 9 August 1943).
15. The location for III/27th KG is listed as Melitopol (to 3 July 1943) and Charkow-Woltschenko (to 8 August 1943).
16. The location for 14th/27th KG is listed as Poltawa to 8 August 1943.
17. The rank of commander of 27th KG is listed as Lt. Colonel (vice Colonel).
18. The location of HQ/55th KG is listed at Charkow-Rogan and Stalino (to 3 august 1943)
19. His order of battle lists a 7. Staffel, 8. Staffel, 9. Staffel and Eis-Staffel III./K.G. 55 while we do not. He does not list the 14th Squadron.
20. The location for I/100th KG is listed as Poltava 4 – 17 July and Stalino 17 July – 3 August 1943.
21. The location for 4.(Pz.)/Sch./G 1, 8/(Pzx)/Sch.G. 1 4.(Pz.)/Sch.G. 2, 8.(Pz.)/Sch.G. 2 and Pz.Jagd. Staffel/J.G. 51 is given as Saporoschje to 8 July 1943 and then Warwarowka on 8 July 1943 for the first two units, Mikojanowka for the third unit and Charkow for the fifth unit listed.
22. The commander of the 8.(Pz.)/Sch.G. 1 is listed as Captain Rudolf-Heinz Ruffner. This is the same as in Bergstrom's list.
23. The rank of the commander of the 4.(Pz.)/Sch.G. 1 is given as Major (the same as in Bergstrom's list) and Major Matuschek is listed as killed 19 July 1943.
47. He was convalescing from a wound received on 10 May 1943 and was not present.
48. The scoring ranking varies slightly depending on which list is used. For example, the Aces of WW2 website (https://acesofww2.com/germany/) listing varies from the Wikipedia "List of World War II Flying Aces" (https://en.wikipedia.org/wiki/List_of_World_War_II_flying_aces) starting with the 5th entry, where Wikipedia lists Walter Nowotny and the other list does not. This also occurs on the 19th entry and the 27th entry (in this case Wikipedia does not list Heinz Schmidt). The Wikipedia list also does not mention Karl-Friedrich Schumacher, III/52 JG (56 victories). Neither list mentions Emil Zibler, 9/3 JG (36 victories). Neither list seems definitive. The Wikipedia listing was used for this ranking.
49. The Yak-4 was claimed in Ost 61281, northeast of Belgorod, 20 kilometers southeast of Prokhorovka. The Boston was claimed in Ost 61164, Yakovlevo. This was the Second Air Army's area of operations. On the 17th, the 454th Bomber Regiment is reported by the Second Air Army to have flown seven sorties by seven Bostons. They report no losses for them.
50. Victory listing is from the Wikipedia article on Kurt Braendle, which provides the details two slightly differing lists, one by Prien, Stemmer, Rodeikie and Bock which credit him with 172 kills and the other by Matthews and Foreman which credit him with 170 kills. Several other accounts claim 180 kills.
51. His claimed kills are listed as:

Date	Time	Plane	Remarks
5 July	0331	Il-2	Ost 60234 Bolshaya Babka
5 July	0340	Il-2	Ost 61844 NE of Kharkov or 25 km NE of Kharkov
5 July	0341	Yak-1	Ost 61841 NE of Kharkov or 25 km NE of Kharkov
5 July	0344	Il-2	Ost 60142 NE of Kharkov or 25 km ENE of Kharkov
5 July	0408	La-5	Ost 60193 NE of Kharkov or 15 km SE of Kharkov
5 July	1806	Il-2	Ost 61353 W of Belgorod or 15 km ENE of Belgorod

AIR CAMPAIGN STATISTICS

5 July	1817	Il-2	Ost 61472 SW of Belgorod or 5 km S of Belgorod
5 July	1824	Il-2	Ost 61623 SE of Belgorod or 20 km SE of Belgorod
5 July	1832	Il-2	Ost 61651 SE of Belgorod or 15 km NW of Volkansk
6 July	1731	Yak-1	Ost 61241 N of Belgorod or 10 km S of Prokhorovka
6 July	1743	Il-2	Ost 61484 SE of Belgorod or 15 km ESE of Belgorod
6 July	1750	La-5	OSt 61634 W of Schtschekekino or 20 km north of Volkansk
7 July	0344	Il-2	Ost 61623 SE of Belgorod or 20 km SE of Belgorod
7 July	0350	Il-2	Ost 61484 E of Borisovka or 15 km ESE of Belgorod
7 July	0402	Il-2	Ost 61623 vicinity of Toplinka train station or 20 km SE of Belgorod
7 July	1226	Yak-1	Ost 61162 SE of Verkhopenye or 15 km SW of Prokhorovka
7 July	1946	La-5	Ost 61864 Stary Shaltov or 15 km SE of Belyi Kolodes
8 July	0409	La-5	Ost 70153, Shrednii-Burluk or 15 km NW of Valuiiki
10 July	1712	Yak-1	Ost 62883 NE of Prokhorovka or 20 km NE of Prokhorovka
10 July	1716	Yak-1	Ost 62882 Prokhorovka or 20 km NE of Prokhorovka
11 July	0940	Yak-1	Ost 61212 E of Verkhopenye or SW of Prokhorovka
12 July	1658	Yak-1	Ost 62794 Bogoroditskoye or 15 km NW of Prokhorovka

The first location given is from Prien, et al. The second location given is from Matthews and Foreman. They sometimes disagree. The first kill on this list in only in the Prien listing.

Of those, none can be ruled out as kills by comparison to the Soviet records of losses.

52. Relied almost exclusively on Seidl, *Stalin's Eagles*, for the biographies. Claims are cross-checked to the Second Army air liaison officer reports from the VIII Air Corps.
53. Seidl, page 218.
54. Seidl, page 218. Although he does not footnote his sources, this is clearly drawn from a Soviet account.
55. Source is the kill list at: http://airaces.narod.ru/mongol/vorojeyk.htm
56. Seidl, page 49. Note that Seidl has the 27th Fighter Regiment flying P-39s. They flew Yak-1s according to the unit records and according to Evgeniy Mariinskiy *Red Star Airacobra: Memoirs of a Soviet Fighter Ace 1941-45* (Helion & Company Ltd, Solihull, England, 2006), pages vii & viii.
57. Kills from the Red Falcons website: http://airaces.narod.ru/all1/popkov.htm.
58. The air liaison officer records no Me-109s lost on the 6th while the quartermaster reports only one lost. See Tables II.20 and II.21.
59. According to Red Falcons website, and Fw-190 at Yurkovo on 16 July and an Me-109 and Fw-190 at Petropolye on 20 July. That claimed kill on 16 July is also noted in the 5th Guards Fighter Regiment along with a shard killed of an Me-109 on the 17th of July.
60. Seidl, page 175.
61. Seidl, page 138.
62. According to Seidl, page 138, he is credited with 14 kills at Kursk between 5 July and 6 August 1943. On the Red Falcons website, Luganskii is credited on 5 July with an Fw-190 at the aerodrome at Sokolniki. On 7 July he claimed an Hs-126 at Novo-Aleksandrovka and a Ju-87 at Yakovlevo. On 10 July he claimed a Ju-88 at Ternovka. On 14 July he claimed at Me-109 at Novo-Oskochnoye. This last claim may have been out of the battle area. The 270th Fighter Regiment records also report all five of these claims in the same locales expect for the Hs-126, which they record as being brought down at Butovo. Of these five claims, neither of the claims on 7 July are possible according the liaison or quartermaster reports and the claim of a Ju-88 on the 10th looks improbably. See Tables II.20 and II.21.

The Red Falcons listing includes eight more planes from 23 July to 7 August 1943 and three planes for 17-23 August for a total of 16 planes since the beginning of July.
63. Seidl, page 53 records 243 sorties while page 311 records 248.
64. Source of list was letter from Christer Bergstrom to this author, dated 19 May 2002.
65. This pilot was not listed in *Stalin's Eagles*. Data comes from http://airaces.narod.ru/all0/glotov_n.htm.
66. According to Polak, page 230 he had 8 victories in 1941. He is not listed in Seidl. There are detailed biographies of him on the Red Falcons website, which also state he is credited with 8 claimed kills.
67. Base locations drawn from march plan for VIII Air Corps dated 30 June, and from Micheal Holm, *The Luftwaffe, 1933– 45* website. The base locations on 30 June and the place to and dates the units were transferred out of the Belgorod are not confirmed.
68. Bergstrom, *Kursk*, page 127, the Pawel Burchard order of battle, and Khazanov, page 128.

69. As the Russian names and locations were drawn from transliterated Swedish and German text, it may not precisely match the transliteration used in the rest of this book. The Second Air Army records that we have include their daily operational reports (Fond: 2nd Air Army, Opis: 4196, Delo: 29, vol. 2) and other supporting status reports (Fond: 2nd Air Army, Opis: 4196, Delo: 39; Fond: 302, Opis: 4196, Delo: 39; Fond: 2nd Air Army, Opis: 4213, Delo: 16). We did not pull up corps, division or regiment reports.

We do have a status report for 1 July that lists out the personnel strengths and ground based equipment for each unit (Fond: 2nd Air Army, Opis: 4201, Delo: 15, pages 313-359). It confirms the order of battle for all but seven of the aviation regiments. The 1 July record lists the four regiments of the 208th Night Bomber Division as the 331st Independent, 620th, 646th and 715th. Two are different from the order of battle. For the 291st Assault Division it only lists four regiments instead of six: 61st, 617th, 241st Assault Regiment and the 737th Fighter Regiment. Furthermore the 61st and 241st Assault Regiments are not listed in the order of battle. The 203rd Fighter Division is not listed under the I Assault Corps. They list three regiments for the 294th Fighter Division (IV Fighter Corps) instead of two. The third regiment is the 6th Fighter Regiment. For the 8th Guards Fighter Division, they list the 92nd Fighter Regiment instead of the 620th Fighter Regiment. The 23rd Guards Bomber Regiment is not listed in the 1 July report.

This 1 July report also lists a 1st Independent Transport Squadron at Arkhangelskoye with 1 Yak-6, 2 R-5s, 2 R-7s, 3 U-2 and 1 S-2; it lists the 372nd Independent Aviation "Connection" with 1 Yak-6 and 8 U-2s; and it lists an element from the Seventeenth Air Army of 4 officers, 4 sergeants, and 2 U-2s. These units are not listed in the order of battle nor do they appear the Second Air Army daily reports.

It is possible that the differences between the 1 July list (which is from the unit records) and these published orders of battle are because of units being shifted in and out of the Second Air Army in the first couple of days of July.

We have the same listing for 20 July 1943. It still lists the 6th Fighter Regiment with the 294th Fighter Division and the 92nd Fighter Regiment instead of the 620th Fighter Regiment with the 8th Guards Fighter Division, so we have added them to the order of battle. The 203rd Fighter Division is still not listed with the I Assault Corps. The 291st Assault Division is still listed as consisting of only four regiments (61st, 241st, 617th Assault Regiments and 737th Fighter Regiment). The 208th Night Bomber Division is listed as consisting of only three regiments (620th, 646th and 715th). The 23rd Guards Bomber Regiment is not listed in either the 1 or the 20 July report.

Question marks were left next to the units that we were not able to confirm were present from the Second Air Army records in our possession.

70. All Second Air Army reports we have are filed from Zavodnyi. We have not been able to locate Zadovnyi or Spartak on a map.
71. The Fifth Air Army's Operational Report #383, 0800, 19 July 1943 states that "According to the STAVKA directive of July 18, the following units were operationally subordinated to the Fifth Air Army: 1st Assault Corps (266th Assault Division, HQ at Dubki; 292nd Assault Division, HQ at Kulma; 203rd Assault Division, HQ at Ostanovka) and the IV Fighter Corps (Corps HQ at Vasilev Dol; 294th Fighter Division, HQ at Bolshaya Khopan; 302nd Fighter Division, HQ at Shirokii Gul). The VIII Mixed Corps and the X Fighter Corps were subordinated to other units." See Fond: 5th Air Army, Opis: 4999, Delo: 66. The corps was transferred around 20 July 1943 to the Fifth Air Army according to the Pawel Burchard order of battle.
72. Bergstrom, *Kursk*, page 127 has him listed as Lt. Col. Yakov Kutikhin. Pawel Burchard has him listed at Lt. Col. A. N. Kutikhin.
73. The corps was transferred around 20 July 1943 to the Fifth Air Army according to the Pawel Burchard order of battle.
74. The corps was transferred around 20 July 1943 to the Fifth Air Army according to the Pawel Burchard order of battle.
75. This is according to the Pawel Burchard order of battle.
76. According to the Pawel Burchard order of battle the commander's name is I. A. Letutshij.
77. This is according to the Pawel Burchard order of battle.
78. Operational Report #367, 2000, 9 July 1943 states that "256th FD (32nd FRgt, 91st FRgt and 728th FRgt) was shifted to the Staryii Oskol airfield as part of the Second Air Army." (Fond: 5th Air Army, Opis: 4999, Delo: 66). Pawel Burchard shows the corps receiving the 256th Fighter Division from the Fifth Air Army on the 9th.

AIR CAMPAIGN STATISTICS

79. According to Bergstrom, *Kursk*, page 75, the 32nd Fighter Regiment and the 91st Fighter Regiment both had some of the 43 new Yak-9s. Fifth Air Army records report for 1 July 1943 that the 256th Fighter Division had 33 Yak-9s ready for action and 19 not ready, and had 28 Yak-7bs ready for action and 12 not ready.
80. Pawel Burchard shows the corps being attached around 23 July. The corps is listed in the Second Air Army's "Aircraft Park" records for July with 154 fighters on 1 July 1943, and it is shown to have received another 80 fighters from other units during the month.
    The Fifth Air Army records report for 1 July 1943 that the 201st Fighter Division had ready for action 22 Yak-1s and 23 La-5s, while the 235th Fighter Division had 50 La-5s ready for action.
81. The corps is listed in the Second Air Army's "Aircraft Park" records for July with 139 assault aircraft on 1 July 1943.
82. Pawel Burchard shows the corps being attached around 23 July.
83. See Fond: 2nd Air Army, Opis: 4196, Delo: 39, page 1 (back).
84. See Fond: 2nd Air Army, Opis: 4196, Delo: 39. These records also show totals for the X Mixed Fighter Corps (154 Fighters) and V Assault Corps (139 Assault) for a total of 1,426 planes (although the totals given only add up to 1,366). We do have Xerox copies of the original documents.
85. Bergstrom provides an order of battle for the Seventeenth Air Army on page 128 as does Pawel Burchard and Khazanov, page 128.
    The only additional information provided is the unit commanders (the names are transliterated differently than most names in this book). He shows: I Mixed Corps commander is MG Vladimir I. Shevchenko, III Mixed Corps commander is MG Vladimir I. Aladinski and the IX Mixed Corps commander is MG Oleg V. Tolstikov. The commanders of the divisions are: 288th Fighter Division is Col. Boris A. Smirnov, 5th Guards Assault Division is Lt. Col. Leonid V. Kolomeytsev, 207th Fighter Division is Col. Aleksandr P. Osadchiy, 290th Assault Division is Col. Pavel I. Mironenko, 295th Fighter Division is Col. Nikifor F. Balanov (given as Col. A. A. Silvestrov in the Burchard list), 305th Assault Division is Lt. Col. Nikolay G. Mikhyevichev, 306th Assault Division is Col. Aleksandr Miklashevskiy (given as Col. A. F. Isupov in the Khazanov list), 244th Bomber Division is MG Vasiliy I. Klevtsov, and the 262nd Night Bomber Division is Col. Gennadiy I. Belitskiy.
    Some regiment commanders are listed including the 866th Fighter Regiment (Maj. Pyotr Ivanov, given as Maj. S. Kuzin in the Burchard list), 5th Gds Fighter Regiment (Maj. Vasiliy A. Zaytsev), 814th Fighter Regiment (Maj. Mikhail V. Kuznetsov), 867th Fighter Regiment (Maj. Semyon Indyk), 299th Assault Regiment (Maj. Stepan K. Ananin), 775th Assault Regiment (Maj. Nikolay I. Zubanev), 31st Fighter Regiment (Maj. P. F. Mushtaev), 164th Fighter Regiment (Maj. Aleksey Melentyov), 449th Bomber Regiment (Maj. M. I. Malov, or I. I. Malov in Burchard list), 861st Bomber Regiment (Lt. Col. N. A. Nikiforov), 370th Night Bomber Regiment (Lt. Col. Vasilyevskiy), 97th Guards Night Bomber Regiment (Maj. A. B. Styazhkov) and 39th Reconnaissance Regiment (Lt. Col. Aleksey Fyodorov).
    The Bergstrom and Burchard orders of battle list the 737th Fighter Regiment with both the Second and Seventeenth Air Army.
86. See Bergstrom, *Kursk*, page 128 and also Dmitriy B. Khazanov, *Air War Over Kursk: Turning Point in the East* (SAM Publications, Bedford, UK, 2010), page 14. They list the number of planes serviceable (538) and not serviceable (73). These figures are low compared to other figures, including the order of battle provided on sidebar "Seventeenth Air Army Forces (5 July 1943)" in Chapter Two, which shows 735 planes (See Fond: 17th Air Army, Opis: 6518, Delo: 28). Also see the section on "Soviet Preparations" in Chapter Two, the "Seventeenth Air Army Order of Battle, 6 July 1943" and the "Seventeenth Air Army Order of Battle, 7 July 1943" in Chapter Four.
    The specific figures by plane type are: Fighters 163 serviceable (43 unserviceable), Assault 239 (27), Bombers 76 (2), Night Bombers 60 (1), and Reconnaissance 0 (0). In contrast, on 5 July the Seventeenth Air Army flew 216 fighters and 5 reconnaissance planes. See: Operational Report #185, 2300, July 5, 1943, Fond: 370, Opis: 6518, Delo: 174.
87. Khazanov, page 53, has a passage for 5 July 1943 that states; "Soviet forces held their ground firmly, however, and many senior German officers were still sure of the final outcome, which is confirmed by the interrogation of the Ju 88D flight crew from 2(F)/11, shot down by Sergeant Omelchenko from the 183rd IAP at an altitude of 7,000m outside Alekseevka. Captured German *Leutnant* H. Schultz stated that his crew had been ordered to monitor the retreat of Soviet units from the area north and east of Belgorod towards Korocha, Novyii Oskol, and Oboyan. However, they did not see any retreat."
    Bergstrom, *Kursk*, page 129, does list the missing pilot of the Ju-88 D-1 as Lt. Hans Schultz.

88. Says "Shot down by fighter." Not sure how you are shot down and sustain only 20% damage.
89. Says "Exploded during landing" with 100% damage.
90. Also say "shot down by fighter" but only sustained 20% damage. By definition 20% damage means "Medium damage that can be repaired through small repair works at the unit" (see Bergstrom, *Kursk*, page 131).
91. Says "Forced-landed after getting hit by fighter. Damage 100%."
92. Says "shot down by friendly Flak. Damage 40%."
93. Says "Hit by fire from Yak-1 during take-off. Damage 40%"
94. Says "Air combat with fighter. Pilot bailed out but parachute failed to open completely. Damage 100%"
95. Says "Forced-landed following air combat. 100%."
96. Says "Shot down by ground fire. Pilot later died of wounds. Damage 100%." PoW means pilot was captured and became a prisoner of war.
97. Says "Belly-landed in hostile territory following air combat. Damage 100%." The pilot was Fw. Emil Zibler, an ace with 36 kills. According to Bergstrom, *Kursk*, page 31, advancing German troops found his bell-landed Me-109 the next day, but without a trace of the pilot. The Luftwaffe Fighter Pilots website (http://www.luftwaffe.be/missing-in-action-jg-3/) gives the location of PQ 61182 as being 10 kilometers north of Belgorod.
98. Ofw. Basilio Maddalena, pilot of the Italian Air Force.
99. Says "Shot down in air combat with Pe-2…Damage 100%."
100. Says "Air combat with 10 Il-2s. Damage 100%"
101. Sr. Lt. Walter Krupinski. Described as "Overturned during landing following battle damage in air combat with fighters. Damage 80%." 80% damage is defined as "Write-off category. Certain parts could be used as spare parts for other aircraft." (see Bergstrom, *Kursk*, page 131).
102. Sgt. Karl-Friedrich Schumacher, later credited with 56 kills before he died in Romania on 31 May 1944.
103. Sgt. Manfred Lotzmann, credited with 15 kills according to Khazanov, page 54.
104. Sgt. Wilhelm Hauswirth, credited with 54 kills. Described as "Shot down by Flak over hostile territory. Damage 100%."
105. Says "Crash landed due to technical failure. Damage 35%."
106. Says "Force-landed after getting hit by Flak fire. Damage 15%"
107. Three were from "overturned on landing", two were from "crashed during landing", and one was from "hit by flak" but returned to base. The figure 60-80% damaged is defined as "Write-off category. Certain parts could be used as spare parts for other aircraft" (see Bergstrom, *Kursk*, page 131).
108. Glantz and Orenstein (2013), page 252.
109. Specifically reported as 639 missions: 428 fighter sorties, 156 assault aircraft sorties, 41 bombers sorties and 14 reconnaissance sorties. The reports for each of the air divisions and corps match these totals, except for the 244th Bomber Division report which claims that 38 TB-3s flew 45 sorties, of which 34 bombers carried out 34 (?) and four reconnaissance planes carried out four. See Operational Report #187, 2300, 7 July 1943, HQ, 19th Air Army, Rovenki (Fond 370, Opis: 6518, Delo: 174, pages 10-12).
110. For example, it could be during the creation of the aggregate report, in the transition of the aggregate report to the study, in the preparation for printing of the original report, in the translation of the study into English or in the preparation of the printing of the translated report.
111. Glantz and Orenstein (2013), pages 253 and 255.
112. Conversations with Trevor N. Dupuy, 1993.

Appendix III

THE STRUCTURE OF THE GERMAN GROUND OFFENSIVE

The German offensive in the south initially consisted of 16 divisions organized into five corps. The primary offensive force was two large armored corps, the XVIII Panzer Corps and SS Panzer Corps whose operated next to each other and were both pushing north. The XVIII Panzer Corps primarily consisted, from west to east, of the 3rd Panzer Division, the Gross Deutschland Panzer Grenadier Division, and the 11th Panzer Division. The SS Panzer Corps consisted of the Leibstandarte SS Adolf Hitler Grenadier Division, the Das Reich SS Panzer Grenadier Division and the Totenkopf SS Panzer Grenadier Division. These corps had around 600 tanks each. They received the lion's share of German close air support.[1]

To the left (west) of the two attacking panzer corps was the LII Corps, consisted of three infantry divisions. From left to right (west to east) they were the 57th Infantry Division, 255th Infantry Division, and the 332nd Infantry Division. The 332nd Infantry Division was attached as often as not to the XVIII Panzer Corps and operated to protect and cover its left (western) flank. The other two divisions primarily sat opposite the Soviet Fortieth Army, involved in very little offensive action.

Initially, advancing in the area between the two panzer corps was the 167th Infantry Division. After several days it started transferring to the right (eastern) flank of the SS Panzer Corps.

To the south of three corps, which were all under command of the Fourth Panzer Army, were the three corps under command of Provisional Army Kempf. They were deployed north to south along the Donets River and were facing east. The most northern corps was the III Panzer Corps, initially deployed from north to south with the 168th Infantry Division, 6th Panzer Division, 19th Panzer Division and 7th Panzer Division. They had around 400 tanks and less infantry and other support compared to the other two panzer corps. They were originally supposed to push to the northeast so as to protect the Fourth Panzer Army's flank, but they ended up effectively first pushing east across the Donets River and then later pushing north.

To the south of them was Corps Raus. It consisted initially of two infantry divisions, the 106th and 320th. It was later joined by the 198th. They were to push east across the Donets River and to cover the flank of the III Panzer Corps. They ended up taking heavy casualties on the first day of the offensive (5 July 1943) and ended up doing a more limited advance across the river.

To the south of them was the XXXXII Corps of two infantry divisions, which was not involved in the offensive.

Deployed opposite the German LII Corps was the Soviet Fortieth Army of seven divisions. Deployed opposite the two German panzer corps advancing north was the Soviet Sixth Guards Army of seven divisions, the First Tank Army of three tank and mechanized corps, two independent tank corps (V Guards and II Guards) and later the reinforcing II Tank Corps, X Tank Corps, Fifth Guards Tank Army of three tank and mechanized corps, and the Fifth Guards Army of seven divisions. Deployed opposite the III Panzer Corps and Corp Raus was the Seventh Guards Army of seven divisions. In the second echelons and in reserve with the Sixty-Ninth Army of five divisions and the XXXV Guards Rifle Corps of three divisions. These forces ended up being committed against elements of the Fourth Panzer Army and Provisional Army Kempf. A day-by-day account of the movement and engagements for each German and Soviet division is provided in my book *Kursk: The Battle of Prokhorovka*.

The German air support was primarily provided to the two panzer corps advancing to the north. The Soviet Seventeenth Air Army primarily provided air support to the forces opposing the III Panzer Corps and Corps Raus. In fact, for much of the operation, the Soviets maintained air superiority over these units.

Provided below is the deployment for 4 July and 18 July 1943. Also provided is the armor strength for 4 July, 11 July and 18 July 1943.

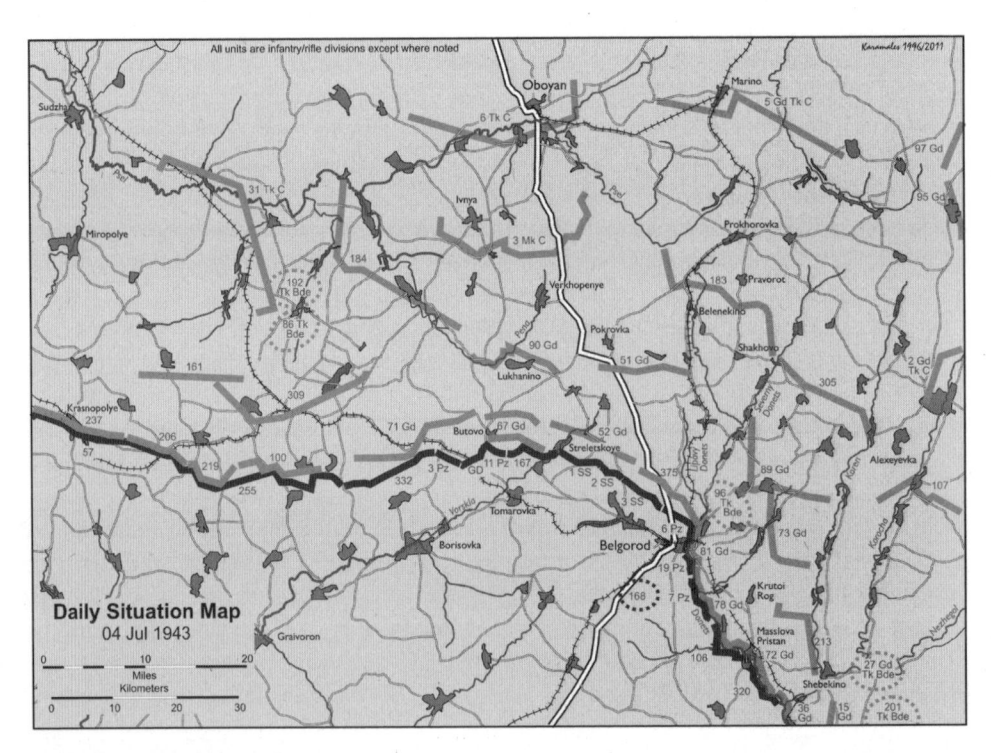

Daily Situation Map, 4 July 1943.

THE STRUCTURE OF THE GERMAN GROUND OFFENSIVE

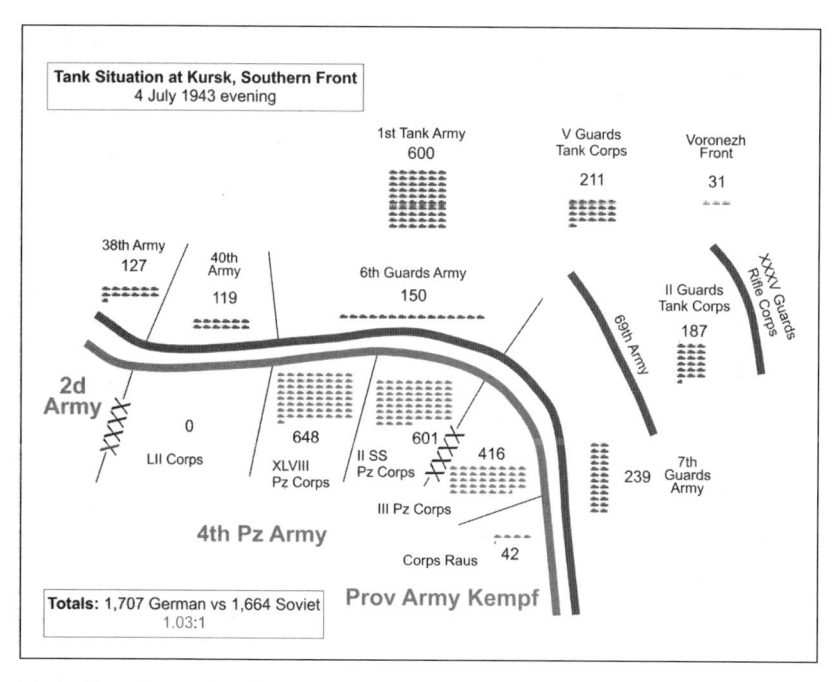

Tank Situation at Kursk, Southern Front, 4 July 1943, evening.

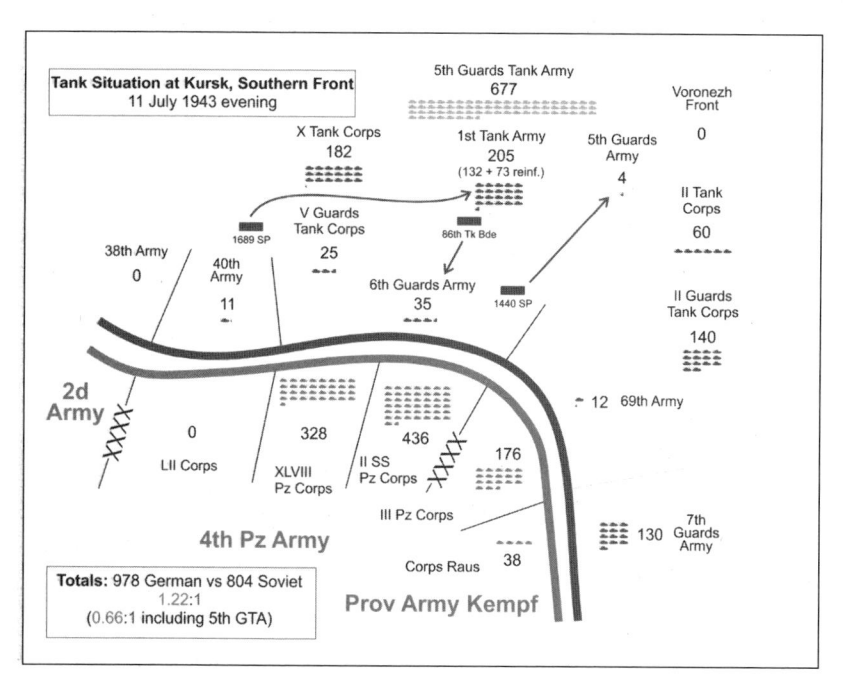

Tank Situation at Kursk, Southern Front, 11 July 1943, evening.

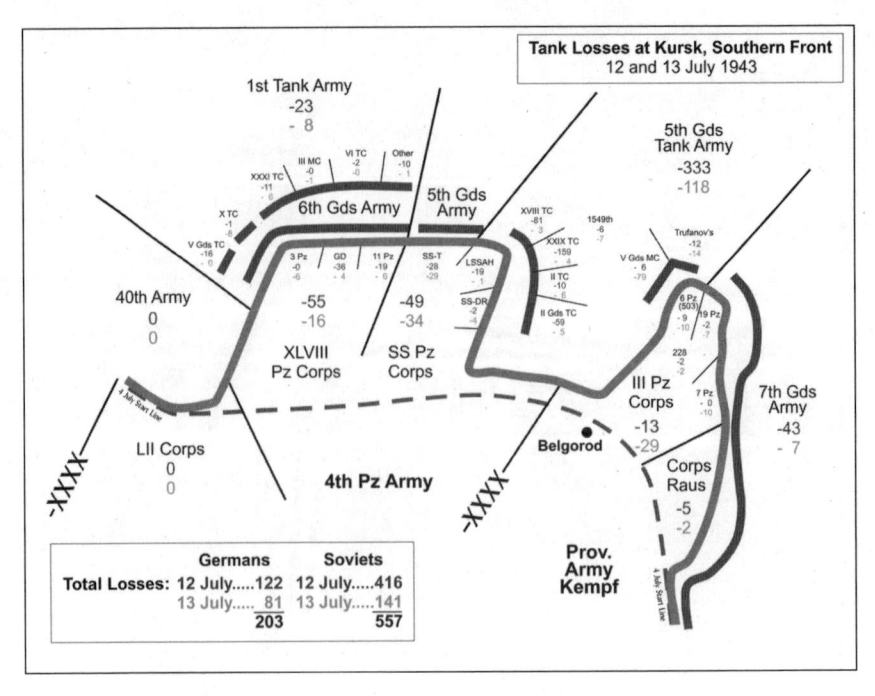

Tank Losses at Kursk, Southern Front, 12 and 13 July 1943.

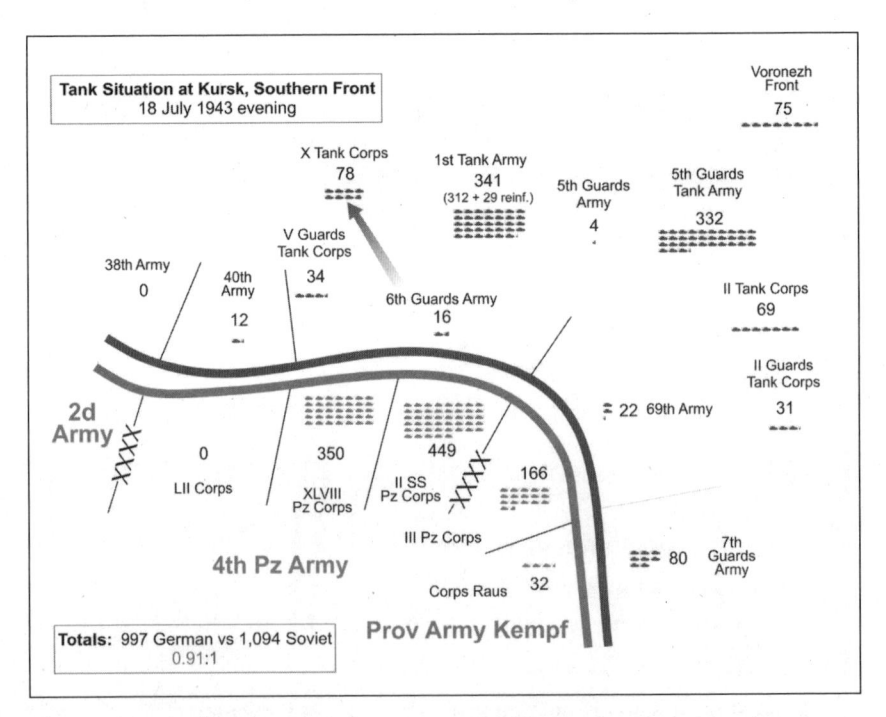

Tank Situation at Kursk, Southern Front, 18 July 1943, evening.

THE STRUCTURE OF THE GERMAN GROUND OFFENSIVE

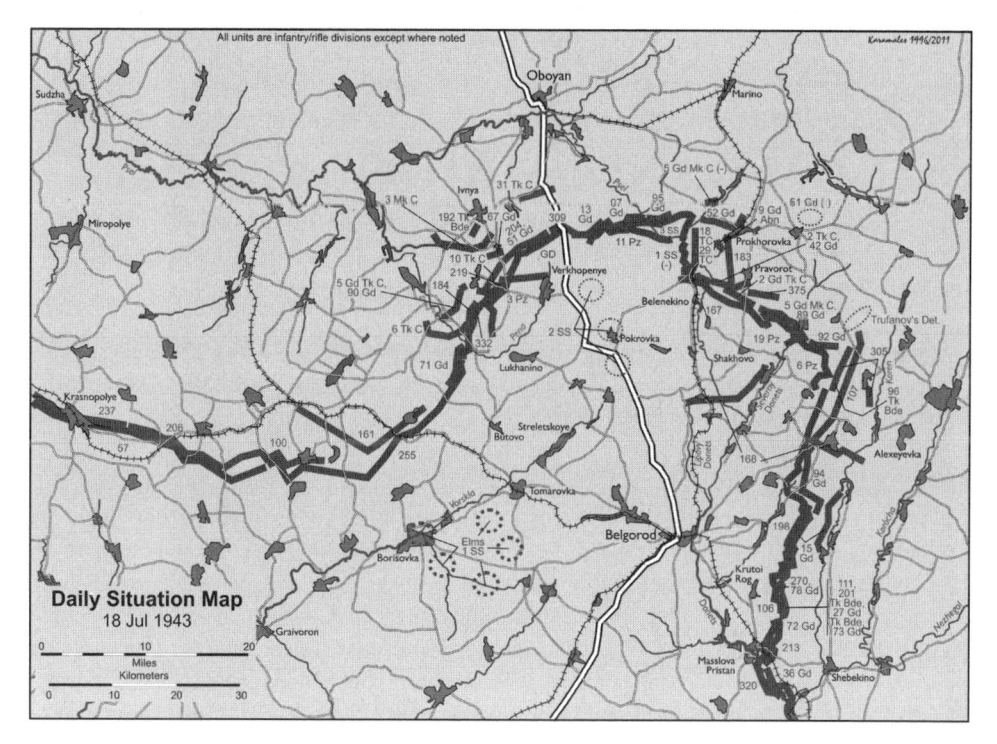

Daily Situation Map, 18 July 1943.

Appendix IV

COMMANDER BIOGRAPHIES

The German Commanders

General Otto Dessloch (Fourth Air Fleet)
Otto Dessloch was born 11 June 1889 in Bamberg in Unterfranken. He was a Bavarian officer in the First World War and served as a pilot, earning the Iron Cross 1st and 2nd Class and wound badges. In 1916 he crashed in Switzerland, was interned there and was exchanged, returning back to service in 1917 and eventually commanded a fighter squadron. He is credited with one kill during the war.

He joined the Luftwaffe in 1933, before it officially existed, and received refresher flight training. He was promoted to Lt. Colonel in October 1934, made Colonel in April 1936 and was promoted to Major General on 1 January 1939. Dessloch commanded the 32nd Air Division, then the 6th Air Division in 1939 and then took command of the II Flak Corps. Promoted to Lt. General on 19 July 1940, he continued to command the II Flak Corps under the Fourth Air Fleet during Barbarossa. He was promoted to General of Anti-aircraft Artillery on 1 January 1942. In early 1942 he commanded the Tactical Battle Command North in addition to the II Flak Corps. He then took over command of I Flak Corps, remaining with the Fourth Air Fleet. From 25 November 1942 to 6 February 1943 he was commander of the Luftwaffe Command Caucasus. This was renamed Luftwaffe Command Kuban, which he continued to command until sometime in March 1943. As these were general commands that included aircraft and anti-aircraft units, this returned Dessloch back to commanding flying forces, instead of just anti-aircraft.

He took over temporary command of the Fourth Air Fleet on 13 June 1943. He was promoted to Colonel General on 1 March 1944 and continued as temporary commander of the Fourth Air Fleet until 1 June 1944. In August 1944, he took over command of the 3rd Air Fleet in the west and later reclaimed command of the Fourth Air Fleet, Air Command Four, and finally the Sixth Air Fleet.

He was awarded the Knight's Cross on 24 June 1940 and Oak Leaves on 10 May 1944. He passed away 13 May 1977 in Munich.

Colonel General Hans Jeschonnek
Hans Jeschonnek was born 9 April 1899 in Hohensalzan in the Prussian province of Posen, now part of Poland. His father was an assistant secondary school master. He became an officer candidate on 10 August 1914, became a lieutenant and was wounded in 1915. He started flying in 1917 and served with Fighter Squadron 40 in 1918. He earned the Iron Cross First and Second Class during the war and was credited with two kills.

COMMANDER BIOGRAPHIES

He stayed in the German Army, serving with cavalry regiments among other assignments. He graduated from the General Staff College in 1928 and was the class valedictorian. He transferred to the air force in 1933 and became an adjutant to Erhard Milch. He eventually ended up leading training commands from July 1936 to September 1937 and was promoted to Lt. Colonel in 1937. He was then moved to the General Staff of the Luftwaffe on 1 October 1937, where he would remain for the rest of his career. He was promoted to Colonel on 1 November 1938 and became the Chief of Staff of the Luftwaffe on 1 February 1939. He was promoted to Major General in August 1939, was awarded the Knight's Cross in October 1939, promoted to General of the Air Corps in July 1940 (skipping the rank of Lt. General), and then to Colonel General in March 1942. He was slated to take command of the Fourth Air Fleet, even though he had never held a combat command, and had held no command since he was a Lt. Colonel. After this transfer did not occur, trapped in the job of Chief of Staff of the Luftwaffe, he committed suicide on 18 August 1943 in East Prussia (now Goldap Poland).

His younger brother Gert served in the navy and later the West German Navy. His son Friedrich eventually became a Brigadier General in the post-war German Army and an author.

Major General Hans Seidemann (VIII Air Corps)
Hans Seidemann was born 18 January 1902 in Garlin, Brandenburg, in Eastern Germany. He was part of the Prussian Cadet Corps in the First World War but was too young to serve in the war. He joined one of the "Free Corps" units in the east in 1919, joined the German Army in 1920, and was promoted to Lieutenant 1 December 1922. He began flying in 1924 and trained in the late 1920s at the secret German training facility at Lipetsk, in the Soviet Union. Seidemann developed into a famous pilot, participating in the third and fourth FAI International Tourist Plane Contest Challenge in 1932 and 1934. He won the London to Isle of Man air race in 1937. He was chief of staff of the Condor Legion in Spain from January 1938 until May 1939.

By the start of the war, he had risen to Lt. Colonel and was the chief of staff to Lt. General Richthofen's VIII Air Corps during the Polish Campaign, French Campaign, and the Battle of Britain. For part of July 1940, Seidemann directed operations just before the Battle of Britain when Richthofen was absent. He was promoted to Colonel on 1 October 1940 and transferred that same month to serve as chief of staff of Kesselring's Second Air Fleet. He remained with them until August 1942 in their operations in the west and the east. He was awarded the Knight's Cross on 20 March 1942 and was promoted to Major General on 24 August 1942. He then replaced General Otto Waldau as commander of Air Command (Fliegerfuehrer) Afrika in August 1942, supporting Rommel's operations at Alam Halfa and El Alamein and his retreat to Tunisia. In early February, his command was renamed the Tunis Air Corps and he commanded some 300 aircraft until mid-April.

After the fall of Tunis, he returned to the Eastern Front where he replaced General Martin Fiebig as VIII Air Corps commander, taking command 19 May 1943. Promoted to Lt. General 1 January 1944, he continued commanding the VIII Air Corps until the end of the war. He was awarded Oak Leaves on 18 November 1944 and was promoted to General of the Air on 1 March 1945. At the time of the surrender, the VIII Air Corps had been renamed the Eighth Air Fleet, and he was the one who gave the order to Hartmann and Graf to fly to surrender to the British while the rest of their squadron surrendered to the Soviets. Hartmann's disobeyal of this order resulted in him being turned over to the Soviet Union by the US and his subsequent imprisonment for 10 years in Soviet prisons.

Seidemann surrendered to the West and prepared a post-war account of the air battles of Kursk. He ended his post-war career as sales manager for a firm in Duesseldorf. The month he was to retire, he passed away from a heart attack 21 December 1967 in Braunschweig (Brunswick), Lower Saxony, West Germany.

The Soviet Commanders

Lt. General Stepan Krasovskii (Second Air Army)[1]
Stepan Akimovich Krasovskii was born on 7 August 1897 in the village of Glukhi, Mogilev oblast, Byelorussia, into a family of peasants. He graduated from the four-year village school, and the five-year agricultural school, and then worked on his father's farm. From 1916 he was called into the Tsarist army, but did not participate in combat. In April 1917 he became a private in the Red Guards, and in May 1918, the Red Army. He was in combat on the eastern and Tsaritsyn fronts and in the Caucasus until 1924.

In 1918, he became "almost from his own will" a motor-mechanic in an air detachment located not far from his regiment and worked there in war conditions for two years. In 1920, as an educated man and already a member of the Bolshevik party, he was appointed commissar of this detachment, where he served in this capacity for 6 years! Certainly, he learned to fly and flew in combat missions. In 1926, he was sent to study at the one-year school for pilots, which he finished successfully, and then commanded an air detachment for seven years.

By 1934–1935, he was commander of an air brigade composed of four detachments. In 1936 Krasovskii finished a one-year operational program at the military aviation academy; he commanded for another year the air brigade; and from 1937, commanded an air corps in the Leningrad military district. He was married to a Latvian woman from Vindava, and in the purges of 1937 he could have been put into prison for that, but was passed by (Latvia was an independent country at that time). Krasovskii's air corps had three brigades of new TB-3 bombers.

During the Soviet-Finnish War in the winter of 1939–1940, Krasovskii commanded an air brigade and was simultaneously the commander of the air force operating to the north of the Fourteenth Army. He was promoted to Major General on 6 April 1940. In the summer of 1940, Major General Krasovskii was appointed as aide to the air force commander of the Northern Caucasus Military District. For part of 1941, he was in charge of aviation for the Bryansk Front. In May 1942, the aviation units of the Bryansk Front were formed into the Second Air Army. Major General Krasovskii became its commander. On 4 July 1942 Krasovskii was replaced at the Second Air Army by Colonel Konstanin Smirnov.[2] This was probably related to the problems the Soviets were having holding back the advance of the German army during Operation Brunswick (often referred to as Case Blue). Krasovskii was returned to duty during the time of the counterattack near Stalingrad. In November 1942,

COMMANDER BIOGRAPHIES

Krasovskii was charged with the mission to form the Seventeenth Air Army, partly from his own Second Air Army. He was promoted to Lt. General on 20 December 1942. He fulfilled this mission successfully, handed over the Seventeenth Air Army to Lieutenant General of Aviation Vladimir Sudets in March 1943, and returned to his Second Air Army. One of Krasovskii's contributions in those times was his use of ground support aircraft as fighters (!).

On the eve of the Kursk battle, the aviators of the Second Air Army, already in the Voronezh Front, carried out about 3,000 combat flights over the approaching enemy troops in March 1943 alone. Prior to the beginning of the Kursk battle, Krasovskii concentrated his forces on destroying the enemy's airplanes on their airfields. "Destroying the enemy's planes in the air is more difficult than on land," he remarked.

Stepan Krasovskii remained as the commander of the Second Air Army until practically the end of the war. This army was part of the Bryansk Front, Southwestern Front (Battle of Stalingrad), Voronezh Front (Battle of Kursk) and then the First Ukrainian Front, in this order. In total, during all the war years, it carried out more that 300,000 combat flights and its pilots led 6,000 air battles. Highly decorated, 280 of its aviators were awarded the "Hero of the Soviet Union" title, including Krasovskii, who received the title on 29 May 1945 for exhibiting courage and heroism. Twenty of its pilots received the title twice and Aleksandr Pokryishkin received it three times. From 6 June 1940, Krasovskii was Major General of Aviation; from December 1942, Lieutenant General of Aviation; from February 1944, Colonel General of Aviation; and from May 1959, Marshal of Aviation.

The commander of the Second Ukrainian Front, Marshal Konev, wrote in Krasovskii's evaluation after the successful Lvov-Sandomir offensive:

> His uncontrollable energy inspires the pilots to pursue feats. He often gets out to the airfields and in the headquarters of the infantry and trooper corps to organize collaborative actions. He was able to concentrate the blow of more than 1500 planes on the large enemy groupings approaching Lvov. Up to 100 German tanks were destroyed.

Krasovskii inflicted massive air strikes on the Vistula River and the Sandomir operation base. During the "time of muddy roads" in 1944, Krasovskii was the first to suggest using the highway Breslau-Berlin, in need of only a few repairs, for the take off and landing of the low-flying attack aircraft and fighters. The first one to test this "airfield" successfully was the division commander, Colonel Pokryishkin. During the Berlin operation, the Second Air Army was based on 82 airfields, but Krasovskii managed it skillfully, focusing and refocusing his air corps and divisions, precisely coordinating with the situation on land, and clearing the way for the ground troops.

After the war, Krasovskii commanded the air forces of several military districts. For a long period of time, from 1956 to 1970 he was the director of the Gagarin Military Aviation Academy for officers. From 1970 he was in the Ministry of Defense group of general inspectors. Despite his declining years, Krasovskii often times instructed and helped new military aviation formations. He died on 21 April 1983 at the age of 85 of pneumonia, and was buried in Novodevichye Cemetery in Moscow.

ACES AT KURSK

Konev wrote about Krasovskii in his memoir "The year 45":

> [He was an] old soldier, experienced combat commander, with excellent knowledge not just of the aviation but also of the strategy of ground troops and their use in aviation. He successfully led large scale operations…

Lt. General Vladimir Sudets (Seventeenth Air Army)[3]

Vladimir Aleksandrovich Sudets was born on 23 October 1904 in Ukraine, in the city of Nizhnedneprovsk, into the family of a locksmith. His grandfather was a foundryman. He was Ukrainian by nationality. Sudets worked as a locksmith himself after finishing the primary school. In 1925, he voluntarily entered the Soviet Army, after which he graduated from the two-year military-technical school of the air force in Leningrad in 1927 and flight school in 1929. From 1929 to 1933, he served as a pilot, flight commander, commander, and a commissar of an independent aviation unit.

From there he went to Mongolia where from 1935 to 1937 he trained Mongolian pilots and commanded the first national air force units. He wanted to get into the Frunze Military Academy, but was not admitted, having the following written in his report:

> Rejected. While in Mongolia, he befriended regiment commander Vainer, who was a "people's enemy".

He was also out of luck in his personal life. Before he went to Mongolia, he got married "fast" to a young woman (it was "fashionable" to marry pilots in those days). But the marriage did not work out; he divorced, and was left with a one-year-old son. While he was enrolled at the Academy, he remarried and divorced for the second time. But the third marriage, to the doctor of his bomber corps, whom he spent all the war years with, turned out successful. For his service in Mongolia, he was awarded the Order of the Red Banner and the Mongolian Republic's Order of the Red Banner twice. His pre-war evaluations were somewhat unusual:

> He loves to fly. He flies devotedly—a master of his work. However, he is short-tempered and irritable when disturbed from the airplanes. He commands the bomber corps confidently. He makes decisions competently, fast and without errors. Take note of his family relationships.

He served as flight commander, squadron commander and, from 1939 to 1940, during the Soviet-Finnish war, he was an air brigade commander. On the eve of the Soviet-Finnish war, Sudets managed to complete the accelerated eight-month course of the Air Force Academy. From November 1940 he was commander of a long-range bomber force corps and a Colonel.

From the beginning of the war Sudets commanded this bomber corps on the southwestern sector. From August 1941 he was air force commander of the Fifty-first Army in the Crimea, and from October in the Volga Military District. Following this, from September

COMMANDER BIOGRAPHIES

1942 he commanded a bomber air corps. From March 1943 until the end of the war he was commander of the Seventeenth Air Army.

While in charge of the Seventeenth Air Army, Sudets participated in the Battle of Stalingrad as part of the Southwestern Front, which delivered the main blow during the counterattack. He supported skillfully the armored corps that was breaking forth, provided the encirclement of the Hungarian and Italian armies on the neighboring Voronezh Front during the Ostrogozhsk-Rossoshansk operations, supported the attack in Donbass, and participated in air operations for gaining air supremacy in the South during the spring of 1943. No matter how diverse the missions were, he always acted firmly, bravely, without special regard for "the authority," always taking the responsibility on himself.

During the Battle of Kursk, while operating on the neighboring (from the left) Southwestern Front, Sudets managed not only to deliver massive bombings on the approaching tank convoys of the enemy, but also to cover its neighbors with his fighter divisions. According to the biographer, Col. Fyodor Sverdlov, he was not sure that this was always in agreement with the Army General R. Ya. Malinovskii, who commanded the Southwestern Front.

During the war years, the army carried out more than 200,000 flights, and 229 of its pilots received the title of Hero of the Soviet Union, including Colonel General of Aviation Sudets on 28 April 1945, who was "right on target" more than once for bringing into the air battle a division or even a regiment. The Seventeenth Air Army contributed to the foundation and development of the Air Force in Bulgaria and Yugoslavia.

After the war, Sudets was appointed Chief of Staff and Deputy Commander of the Air Force. In 1950 he graduated from the Military Academy of the General Staff and returned to his prior position. In 1955 he became Marshal of Aviation. From 1962 to 1966 he served as air defense commander and Deputy Minister of Defense. As the years went by, Sudets' health worsened. By the end of 1966, at his request he became an inspector for the Ministry of Defense. In this request he wrote, "Due to frequent heart attacks, I am no longer able to work the way I must and wish to, and so I no longer wish to work the way am able to." Sudets remained loyal until the end to his independence, will power, strong character and his military duty.

Sudets passed away in Moscow on 6 May 1981 and was buried in Novodevichye cemetery. For his military service, Sudets was awarded the "Hero's Golden Star"; the titles "National Hero of Yugoslavia" and "Hero of Mongolia"; he was awarded the Order of Lenin four times; the Order of the October Revolution; the Order of the Red Banner five times; the Orders of Suvorov and Kutuzov of the 1st Class; the Order of Kutuzov of the 2nd Class; the Order of the Red Star; the Order for Service to The Homeland in the Armed Forces of the 3rd Class; medals and many foreign orders.

Lt. General Sergei Goryunov (Fifth Air Army)[4]

Sergei Kondratyevich Goryunov was born on 7 November 1899 in the village of Ushakovka, Republic of Mordoviya, into a peasant's family. He was Russian. Goryunov received a pretty good education for those times—he graduated from the 7-year college-seminary in Kasan. He worked for two years as a village school teacher, but he joined the Red Army in 1918. As he was well educated, Goryunov was sent right away to take courses for officers, which he finished in 1919, and then courses for work in the headquarters, which he finished in 1920. Those courses, taught for the most part by former combat experienced tsarist officers who switched to the Red Army, gave him a not-so-bad tactical education. He served as platoon and company commander and as instructor in Mongolia until 1923. However, service in the infantry did not satisfy him and so he eagerly went into aviation, which, although small at the time, was a promising field.

Starting his career over at 24, he entered as an enlisted cadet the Borisoglebsk Pilot School, which later graduated many famous pilots (V. Chkalov, M. Gromov, V. Kokkinaki and others). After a year of aviation training, he was admitted into the Advanced Aviation School, which he finished in 1927. Being an excellent pilot, he remained to be an instructor there, in the position of unit and, later, squadron commander. In 1930, Goryunov was admitted into the Military Aviation Academy, which he finished successfully in 1934. He served as commander of a squadron for bombers for two years, and in 1937 he was assigned to command an air brigade for bombers. He was Kombrig (Commander of the Brigade) starting in February 1938. In 1939 he finished the special courses in aviation at the General Staff Academy. His many years of education, great flying experience, good operational mind, and high cultural level enabled Goryunov's appointment to command the air force of the Kalinin Military District.

In the winter of 1939–1940, during the Soviet-Finnish war, he commanded the air force of the Seventh Army, acting on delivering the main blow. The aviation of the army completed its tasks successfully, enabling the ground troops to advance 200km and take Vyiborg. On 4 May 1940, Goryunov became division commander, and on 4 June 1941, while working in the headquarters of the Soviet Army's air force, he became Major General of Aviation. He knew the staff work, but did not love it, and from January 1941 he commanded the air force of the Kharkov military district. With the beginning of the war he commanded the air force of the Eighteenth Army, which was formed from this district.

From November 1941 to May 1942 Goryunov commanded the air forces of the North Caucasus Military District. On 3 June 1942, he became commander of the Fifth Air Army, just formed from the air force of the North Caucasus Military District. He was promoted to Lieutenant General of Aviation on 28 May 1943 and exactly a year later to Colonel General of Aviation. The Fifth Air Army participated in the battle for the Caucasus and supported the troops of the North Caucasus Front, the Black Sea fleet, and landing-parties in many difficult operations. In the spring of 1943, the Fifth Air Army participated in the air battles in the Kuban area.

The Fifth Air Army participated in the Battle of Kursk as part of the Steppe Front. In the course of the defensive battle, the army supported the neighboring Voronezh Front. The Fifth Air Army distinguished itself in the Belgorod-Kharkov operation, the battle for the Dnepr, and a series of offensive operations in Ukraine. Throughout all these, Goryunov's principle of action was the same: a massive blow by the [air] army on the main direction of the ground forces. The Fifth Air Army was successful in Hungary, Austria and Czechoslovakia. During all the war years, this army performed about 180,000 combat airplane sorties. The army saw 138 of its pilots and navigators, including Goryunov himself on 28 April 1945, awarded the title of Hero of the Soviet Union, and four of them were awarded this title twice.

COMMANDER BIOGRAPHIES

After the war, until May 1946, Goryunov continued commanding this army, then for three years he led the Seventeenth Air Army (following Sudets) in the southern group of the troops in Austria. For a year he commanded the Fifty-seventh Air Army in Lvov (the Trans-Carpathian Military District). Being true to himself, Goryunov finished in 1950–1951 an advanced course of studies at the General Staff Academy, and then again until November 1956 he commanded the Sixty-ninth Air Army in the Kiev Military District. In total, Goryunov commanded air armies all through the war, from 1941 until 1956, nonstop for 15 years.

Suddenly, following a routine inspection of the troops, an order by Marshal G. Zhukov, Minister (Deputy) of Defense of the USSR, dated 12 November 1956, came out: "For repeated flight incidents during combat and aviation training in the Sixty-ninth Air Army, the commander of the army, Colonel General Goryunov to be removed and pensioned off."[5]

Goryunov took this harsh and perhaps unfair blow, and grew thin and old. He continued to live in Kiev, where he died on 10 October 1967. He was buried there with honors.

For his military service, Goryunov was awarded the Hero of the Soviet Union, twice the Order of Lenin, five times the Order of the Red Banner, the Order of Suvorov and Kutuzov of the 1st Class, the Order of Suvorov of the 2nd Class, medals, and foreign orders. The Order of the Red Revolution, established on 31 October 1967, and immediately awarded to all military leaders of the Second World War, was not conferred on Goryunov even posthumously. How exactly he was at fault—today no one will ever find out.

Table IV.1: Chiefs of Staff and Commissars[6]

Unit	Chief of Staff	Military Council Members
2nd Air Army	MG F. I. Kachev	MG S. N. Romazanov
5th Air Army	MG N. G. Seleznyov	MG V. I. Alexeyev
17th Air Army	MG N. M Korsakov	MG V. N. Tolmachev

Notes

1. This bio comes primarily from a write-up prepared by Col. Fyodor Sverdlov in 2001.
2. Hooton, page 123. A number of other sources indicate that Krasovskii was in command of the Second Air Army from May to October 1942 with Smirnov taking over from October 1942 to March 1943. Hooton, page 136 has him returning to favor and returning to duty in November 1942 when he took over the Seventeenth Air Army. Also see website: http://www.soldat.ru/force/sssr/rkka/vvs/06_komva.html which shows Krasovskii in charge until 4 July 1942 and Smirnov taking over until Krasovskii returns in late March of 1943.
3. This section on Sudets was prepared by Col. Fyodor Sverdlov in 2001 for this book and presented as is with some minor editing
4. This bio comes primarily from a write-up prepared by Col. Fyodor Sverdlov in 2001.
5. Col. Fyodor Sverdlov included a harsh criticism of Zhukov's management style. To quote Col. Sverdlov about this dismissal:

"Where, in what army, in what country, are there no flight incidents during aviation training? Is the fault of the air army commander really that big in this? No! This is simply leadership by Zhukov. Think about the man [Goryunov], about the 15 years of impeccable leadership in air armies—including the war years, about the man, who in the crucial moments of combat, personally led regiments into air strikes, the man who finally became a very experienced and educated military aviation leader and had by law three more years left to serve—this is Zhukov's leadership style."

Without knowing the specifics of the incident, it is hard to determine if there was a strong basis for his dismissal or any other factors behind it.

6. *The Battle of Kursk* (Progress Press Publishers, USSR, 1974), pages 334–40. Spelling of names is in accordance with their transliteration.

BIBLIOGRAPHY

The following bibliography refers only to those books that were actually referenced or reviewed for writing this book. It does not attempt to list all the books on the subject.

Secondary Sources
Accoce, Pierre, and Pierre Quet, *A Man Called Lucy* (Berkley Medallion Books, New York, 1968).
Aganov, S. Kh., ed., *Inzhenernyie Voiska Sovetskoi Armii 1918–1945* (Voyenizdat, Moscow, 1985).
Agte, Patrick, *Jochen Peiper, Kommandeur Panzerregiment Leibstandarte* (Kurt-Vohwinckel-Verlag, 82335 Berg am Stamberger See, I. Auglage, 1998).
Agte, Patrick, *Michael Wittmann and the Tiger Commanders of the Leibstandarte* (Stackpole Press, Mechanicsburg, PA, 2006).
Amadio, Jill, *Guenther Rall: A Memoir: Luftwaffe Ace & NATO General* (Tangmere Productions, Santa Ana, CA, 2002).
Ananyev, I. M., *Tankovyie Armii v Nastuplenii* [Tanks Armies in the Offensive] (Voyenizdat, 1988).
Axell, Albert, *Stalin's War: Through the Eyes of his Commanders* (Arms and Armour, London, 1997).
Barbier, M. K., *Kursk: The Greatest Tank Battle 1943* (Amber Books Ltd., London, 2002).
Barnett, Correlli, *Hitler's Generals* (Grove Weidenfeld, New York, 1989).
Bauer, Eddy, *Illustrated World War II Encyclopedia* (H. S. Stuttman, Inc, Westport, CT, 1978).
Bekker, Cajus, *The Luftwaffe War Diaries* (Ballantine Books, New York, 1966).
Belyayeva, L. G., ed., *Marshal Zhukov: Kakim my ego Pomnim* (Izdatelstvo Politicheskoi Literaturi, Moscow, 1988).
Bergstrom, Christer, *Kursk: The Air Battle: July 1943* (Ian Allen Publishing, Hersham, UK, 2007).
Bergstrom, Christer, *Black Cross, Red Star: Air War over the Eastern Front: Volume 5: The Great Air Battles Kuban and Kursk, April-July 1943* (Vaktel Books, Eskilstuna, Sweden, 2020).
Bingham, James, *Infantry Tank Mk II Matilda, Armour in Profile No. 15* (Great Bookham, UK, 1967).
Boog, Horst, Gerhard Krebs, Detlef Vogel, Derry CookRadmore (translator), *Germany and the Second World War: Volume VII: The Strategic Air War in Europe and the War in the West and East Asia, 1943–1944/5* (Oxford University Press, Oxford, 2006).
Bradley, Dermot, Karl-Friedrich Hildebrand, Markus Roverkamp, *Die Generale des Heeres 1921–1945* (Biblio Verlag, Osnabruck, 1993).
Brief Tactical-Technical Guide, National Commission for the Defense of the USSR (Moscow, 1943).
Bullock, Alan, *Hitler and Stalin, Parallel Lives* (Vintage Books, New York, 1993).
Butler, Rupert, *SS-Leibstandarte: The History of the First SS Division 1933–45* (MBI Publishing Company, St. Paul, MN, 2001).
Caidin, Martin, *The Tigers are Burning* (Hawthorn Books, Inc., New York, copyright 1974, pre-publication copy).
Carell, Paul, *The Scorched Earth: The Russian-German War 1943–44* (Schiffer Military/Aviation History, Atglen, PA, 1994).

Carius, Otto, *Tigers in the Mud: The Combat Career of German Panzer Commander Otto Carius* (Stackpole Books, Mechanicsburg, PA, 2003).

Chamberlain, Peter, and Chris Ellis, *British and American Tanks of World War II* (Arco Publishing Company, New York, 1969).

Chamberlain, Peter, and Hilary Doyle, technical editor Thomas L. Jentz, *Encyclopedia of German Tanks of World War Two* (Revised Edition, London, 1993).

Chaney, Otto Preston, *Zhukov* (Revised edition, University of Oklahoma Press, Norman and London, 1996).

Clark, Alan, *Barbarossa: The Russian-German Conflict, 1941–45* (Quill, New York, 1985, originally published 1965).

Clodfelter, Micheal, *Warfare and Armed Conflicts* (McFarland & Company, Inc., Jefferson, NC & London, 1992).

Comnena, Anna, *The Alexiad of Anna Comnena*, translated from Greek by E. R. A. Sewter (Penguin Books, London, 1969).

Conquest, Robert, *The Great Terror, A Reassessment* (Oxford University Press, Oxford, 1990).

Cross, Robin, *Citadel: The Battle of Kursk* (Michael O'Mara Books Limited, London, 1993).

Deutsch, Harold C., and Dennis E. Showalter, eds., *What If? Strategic Alternatives of WWII* (The Emperor's Press, Chicago, 1997).

Drogovoz, I. *Zheleznyii Kulak RKKA: Tankovyie i Mekhanizirovannyiye Korpusa Krasnoi Armii 1932–41 gg.* (Izdatelskii dom, Moscow, 1999).

Dupuy, Trevor N., *Attrition: Forecasting Battle Casualties and Equipment Losses in Modern War* (HERO Books, Fairfax, VA, 1990).

Dupuy, R. Earnest, and Trevor N. Dupuy, *The Harper Encyclopedia of Military History* (Harper Collins Publishers, New York, 1993).

Dupuy, T. N., *A Genius for War, The German Army and General Staff, 1807–1945* (HERO Books, Fairfax, VA, 1984).

Dupuy, T. N., and Paul Martell, *Great Battles of the Eastern Front: The Soviet-German War, 1941–1945* (Bobbs-Merrill Company, Indianapolis, IN, 1982).

Dupuy, Trevor N., ed., *International Military and Defense Encyclopedia* (Brassy's [US], Inc., Washington, New York, 1993).

Dupuy, Trevor N., David L. Bongard, Richard C. Anderson, Jr., *Hitler's Last Gamble, The Battle of the Bulge, December 1944–January 1945* (Harper Collins Publishers, New York, 1994).

Dupuy, Trevor N., Curt Johnson, David L. Bongard, *The Harper Encyclopedia of Military Biographies* (Harper Collins Publishers, New York, 1992).

Dupuy, Trevor N., Curt Johnson, Grace P. Hayes, *Dictionary of Military Terms, A Guide to the Language of Warfare and Military Institutions* (H. W. Wilson Company, New York, 1986).

Dyer, D. P., *Infantry Tank Mark III "Valentine," Bellona Military Prints No. 34 & 38* (Great Bookham, UK, 1972 & 1974).

Ellis, John, *World War II: The Encyclopedia of Facts and Figures* (The Military Book Club, USA, 1995).

Erickson, John, *The Road to Berlin* (Phoenix Giants, London, 1996, 1983).

Ferguson, Niall, *The Pity of War, Explaining World War I* (Basic Books, New York, 1999).

Forczyk, Robert, *Kursk 1943: The Northern Front* (Osprey Publishing, Oxford, 2014).

Forty, George, *Tank Aces from Blitzkrieg to the Gulf War* (Sutton Publishing, Stroud, UK, 1997).

Frieser, Karl-Heinz, *Germany and the Second World War: Volume VIII: The Eastern Front 1943–1944: The War in the East and on the Neighbouring Fronts* (Oxford University Press, Oxford, 2017).

Funk & Wagnalls Standard Reference Encyclopedia (Standard Reference Works Publishing Company, Inc., New York, 1962).

BIBLIOGRAPHY

Galland, Adolf, *The First and the Last, The Rise and Fall of the German Fighter Forces 1938–1945* (Bantam Books, New York, 1982).
Garlinski, Josef, *Swiss Corridor* (J. M. Dent & Sons, Ltd., London, 1981).
Glantz, David M., *From the Don to the Dnepr, Soviet Offensive Operations December 1942–August 1943* (Frank Cass, London, 1991).
Glantz, David M., *Stumbling Colossus: The Red Army on the Eve of World War* (University of Kansas Press, Lawrence, KS, 1998).
Glantz, David M., and Jonathan M. House, *The Battle of Kursk* (University of Kansas Press, Lawrence, KS, 1999).
Glantz, David M., and Jonathan House, *When Titans Clash, How the Red Army Stopped Hitler* (University Press of Kansas, Lawrence, KS, 1995).
Glantz, David M., and Harold S. Orenstein, Kursk 1943: *The Soviet General Staff Study* (self published, 1997). Originally published as *Sbornik Materialov po Izucheniyu Opyita Voinyi, No 11, Mart–Aprel 1944 g.* (Collection of Materials for the Study of War Experience, No. 11, March–April 1944) (Military Publishing House of the Peoples' Commissariat of Defense, Moscow, 1944). Full title: *Upravleniye po Ispolzovaniyu Opyita Voinyi Generalnogo Shtaba Krasnoi Armii, Sbornik Materialov po Izucheniyu Opyita Voinyi, No 11, Mart–Aprel 1944 g* (*Directorate for the Use of War Experience of the Red Army General Staff, Collection of Materials for the Study of War Experience, No 11, March–April 1944*).
Goode's School Atlas (Rand McNally & Company, New York, 1943).
Gorlitz, Walter, *History of the German General Staff, 1657–1945* (Praeger, New York, 1957).
Gorlitz, Walter, *Strategie der Defensive: Model* (Limes Verlag, Wiesbaden & Munchen, 1982).
Gorlov, Sergei Alekseyevich, *Sovershenno Sekretno: Alyans Moskva-Berlin, 1920–1933 gg.* (OLMA-PRESS, Moscow, 2001).
Great Patriotic War: 1941–1945 Encyclopedia (Sovetskaya Entsiklopediya, Moscow, 1985).
Halder, Franz, *The Halder War Diary* (Presidio Press, Novato, CA, 1988). Edited by Charles Burdick and HansAdolf Jacobsen.
Handbook on U.S.S.R. Military Forces (War Department Technical Manual TM 30-430, War Department, November 1945).
Hardesty, Von and Ilya Grinberg, *Red Phoenix Rising: The Soviet Air Force in World War II* (University Press of Kansas, Lawrence, Kansas, 2012).
Harrison, Richard W., *The Russian Way of War, Operational Art, 1904–1940* (University Press of Kansas, Lawrence, KS, 2001).
Harrison, Richard W., *Architect of Soviet Victory in World War II: The Life and Theories of G. S. Isserson* (McFarland & Company, Jefferson, NC, 2010).
Hart, Sir Basil Liddell, editor-in-chief, *History of the Second World War* (Marshall Cavendish USA Ltd., New York, 1973; 1966).
Hart, S., and R. Hart, *German Tanks of World War II* (Brown Books, Dallas, 1998). Hinsley, F. H., et al., *British Intelligence in the Second World War* (three volumes, HMSO, London, 1979–1988).
Hooton, E. R., *Eagle in Flames, The Fall of the Luftwaffe* (Arms & Armour Press, London, 1997).
Hooton, E. R., *War over the Steppes: The Air Campaigns on the Eastern Front 1941-45* (Osprey Publishing, Oxford, 2016).
Irving, David, *Hitler's War* (Viking Press, New York, 1977).
Ismagilov, R., et al., *Tanki Mira* (Tanks of the World) (Rusich, Smolensk, 2001).
Istoriya Velikoi Otechestvennoi Voinyi Sovetskogo Soyuza, 1941–45 (*The History of the Great Patriotic War of the Soviet Union, 1941–45*) (Voennoye Izdatelstvo, Moscow, 1960–65), Volume 3.
Istoria Vtoroi Mirovoi Voinyi, 1939–1945 (*The History of the Second World War, 1939–1945*) (Moscow, 1973–80, Volume 7).
Jentz, Thomas L., *Germany's Panther Tank* (Schiffer Military/Aviation History, Atglen, PA, 1995).

Jentz, Thomas L., *Panzertruppen: The Complete Guide to the Creation & Combat Employment of Germany's Tank Force, 1933–42* (Schiffer Military History, Atglen, PA, 1996).

Jentz, Thomas L., *Panzertruppen II: The Complete Guide to the Creation & Combat Employment of Germany's Tank Force, 1943–45* (Schiffer Military History, Atglen, PA, 1996).

Jukes, Geoffrey, *Kursk: The Clash of Armor* (Ballentine Books, New York, 1969).

Jung, Hans-Joachim, *The History of PanzerRegiment GrossDeutschland* (J.J. Fedorowicz, Winnipeg, Canada, 2000).

Just, Gunther, *Stuka Pilot Hans-Ulrich Rudel* (Schiffer Military History, Atglen, PA, 1986).

Kennedy, Paul, *The Rise and Fall of the Great Powers, Economic Change and Military Conflict from 1500 to 2000* (Random House, New York, 1987).

Khazanov, Dmitriy B., *Air War Over Kursk: Turning Point in the East* (SAM Publications, Bedford, UK, 2010).

Kinder, Hermann, and Werner Hilgemann, translated by Menze, Ernest A., *The Anchor Atlas of World History* (Anchor Books, New York, 1974).

Klink, Ernst von, *Das Gesetz Des Handelns, Die Operation "Zitadelle" 1943* (Deutsche Verlags-Anstalt, Stuttgart, 1966).

Kohn, George C., *Dictionary of Wars* (Facts on File Publications, New York, 1986). Kolomiyets, Maksim, *Panteryi na Kurskoi Duge* (Panther's at the Kursk Bulge) (Izdatelstvo Strategiya KM, Moscow, 2002).

Kolganov, K. S., ed., *Razvitiye Taktiki Sovetskoi Armii v Godi Velikoi Otechestvennoi Voĭni (1941–1945 gg.)* (Voyenizdat, Moscow, 1958).

Kolomiyets, M., and I. Moshchanskii, *Tanki Lend-Liza* (The Tanks of Lend-Lease) (Eksprint, Moscow, 2000).

Kolomiyets, M., and M. Svirin, *Kurskaya Duga* (Kursk Bulge) (Eksprint, Moscow, 1998).

Koltunov, G. A., and B. G. Solovyev, *Kurskaya Bitva* (The Battle of Kursk) (Voyennoye Izdatelstvo, Moscow, 1970).

Koltunov, G. A., and B. G. Solovyev, *Ognennaya Duga* (Voyenizdat, Moscow, 1973).

Koltunov, G. A., and B. G. Solovyev, *Kurskaya Bitva* (The Battle of Kursk) (Voyennoye Izdatelstvo, Moscow, 1983).

Kratkii Taktiko-Tekhnicheskii Spravochnik (A Short Tactical-Technical Handbook) (Moscow, 1943).

Kries, John F., *Air Warfare and Air Base Air Defense* (Office of Air Force History, United States Air Force, Washington, DC, 1988).

Krivosheyev, G. F., ed., *Grif Sekretnosti Snyat: Poteri Vooruzhennyikh sil SSSR v Voinakh, Boyevyikh Deistviyakh i Voyennyikh Konfliktakh. Statisticheskoye Issledovaniye* (The Mark of Secrecy has been Removed: Losses of the USSR Armed Forces in Wars, Combat Actions and Military Conflicts. A Statistical Study) (Voyennoye Izdatelstvo, Moscow, 1993).

Krivosheyev, G. F., ed., *Belikaya Otechestvennaya bez Grifa Sekretnosti: Kniga Potep* (The Great Patriotic War without the Mark of Secrecy: Book of Losses) (Veche, Moscow, 2010).

KTO byil Kto v Velikoi Otechestvennoi Voine 1941–1945 (Who Was Who in the Great Patriotic War 1941–1945) (Izdatelstvo "Respublika", Moscow, 1995).

Kurowski, Franz, *Infantry Aces* (Ballentine Books, New York, 2002).

Kurowski, Franz, *Panzer Aces* (Ballentine Books, New York, 2002) and (J. J. Fedorowicz Publishing, Winnipeg, Canada, 1992).

Kurowski, Franz, *Panzer Aces 2* (J. J. Fedorowicz Publishing, Inc., Winnipeg, Canada, 2000).

Langer, William L., *An Encyclopedia of World History* (Houghton Mifflin Company, Boston, 1952).

Larionov, V., N. Yeronin, B. Solovyov, V. Timokhovich, *World War II: Decisive Battles of the Soviet Army* (Progress Publishers, Moscow, 1984).

Lawrence, Christopher A., *Kursk: The Battle of Prokhorovka* (Aberdeen Books, Sheridan, CO, 2015).

BIBLIOGRAPHY

Lincoln, W. Bruce, *Red Victory, A History of the Russian Civil War* (Simon & Schuster, New York, 1989).
Longford, Elizabeth, *Wellington: The Years of the Sword* (World Books, Suffolk, 1971).
Lopukhovskii, Lev, *Prokhorovka: Bez Grifa Secretnosti* (Eksmo, Yauza, Moscow, 2005). Losik, O. A., *Stroitelstvo i Boyevoye Primeneniye Sovetskikh Tankovyikh Voisk v Godyi Velikoi Oteschestvonnoi Voinyi* (Formation and Combat Use of Soviet Tank Troops During the Years of the Great Patriotic War) (Moscow, 1979).
Lucas, James, *Hitler's Enforcers, Leaders of the German War Machine 1933–1945* (Arms and Armour Press, London, 1996).
Lucas, James, *War on the Eastern Front, The German Soldier in Russia, 1941–1945* (Military Book Club, USA, 1991).
Madej, W. Victor, ed., *The Russo-German War: June 1941–June 1943* (Game Publishing Company, Allentown, PA, 1983).
Madej, W. Victor, ed., *The Russo-German War: July 1943– May 1945* (Valor Publishing Company, Allentown, Pennsylvania, 1986).
Madej, W. Victor, *Russo-German War: Summer-Autumn 1943* (Valor Publishing Company, Allentown, PA, 1987).
Mann, Chris, *SS-Totenkopf: The History of the 'Death's Head' Division 1940–45* (MBI Publishing Company, St. Paul, MN, 2001).
Mattson, Gregory L., *SS-Das Reich: The History of the Second SS Division 1941–45* (MBI Publishing Company, St. Paul, MN, 2002).
Mawdsley, Evan, *The Russian Civil War* (Allen & Unwin, Boston, 1987).
McEvedy, Colin, and Richard Jones, *Atlas of World Population History* (Penguin Books, Ltd, Middlesex, England, 1978).
McGuirl, Thomas (text research), Remy Spezzano (photo research), et al., *God, Honor, Fatherland: A Photo History of Panzergrenadier Division Grossdeutschland on the Eastern Front 1942–1944* (RZM Imports, Inc., Southbury, CT, 1997).
Medicus, Thomas, *In den Augen meines Grossvaters* (In the Eyes of my Grandfather) (Munich, Deutsche VerlagsAnstalt, 2004).
Mikoyan, A. I., *Tak Byilo* (Moscow, Vagrius Publishers, 1990).
Muller, Richard, *The German Air War in Russia* (The Nautical & Aviation Publishing Company of America, Baltimore, MD, 1992).
Murray, Williamson and Allan R. Millett, *A War to be Won: Fighting the Second World War* (2000).
Murzayev, N., *Pekhota Ognennoi Dugi: Strelkovyie Soyedineniya i Chasti v Kurskoi Bitve* (Tsentralno-Chernozemnoye Knizhnoye Izdalelstvo, Voronezh, 1987).
The Military Balance, 1997/98 (The International Institute for Strategic Studies, Oxford University Press, London, 1997).
Naimark, Norman M., *The Russians in Germany: A History of the Soviet Zone of Occupation* (The Belknap Press of Harvard University Press, Cambridge, MA, 1997).
Nechayev, Gen.Lt. E. A., ed., *Meditsinskoye Obespecheniye Sovetskoi Armii v Operatsiyakh Velikoi Otechestvennoi Voinyi, 1941–1945 gg.* (The Soviet Army's Medical Service in Operations of the Great Patriotic War, 1941–1945) (Volume I, Voyennoye Izdatelstvo, Moscow, 1991).
Newton, Steven H., *Kursk: The German View* (Da Capo Press, Cambridge, MA, 2002).
Nevshemal, Martin, *Objective Ponyri: Defeat of the XXXXI. Panzerkorps at Ponyri Train Station* (Leaping Horseman Books, Sydney, Australia, 2015).
Nipe, George M. Jr., *Decision in the Ukraine, Summer 1943, II SS and III Panzerkorps* (J. J. Fedorowicz Publishing, Inc. Winnipeg, Canada, 1996).
Parotkin, Ivan, *The Battle of Kursk* (Progress Press Publishers, USSR, 1974).
Paul, Wolfgang, *Brennpunkte: Die Geschichte der 6. Panzerdivision (1. leichte) 1937–1945 (Krefeld, Hontges, 1977) Perechen Obyedinenii i Soyedinenii Sovetskikh Voorruzhennyikh sil, vkhodivshikh v*

sostav deistvuyushchei armii v period Velikoi Otechestvennoi voinyi 1941–1945 (Institut Voyennoi Istorii, Moscow, 1992).

Pavlov, Ivan Vladimirovich, and Mikhail Vladimirovich Pavlov, *Sovetskiye Tanki i Samokhodno-Artilleriiskiye Ustanovki (1939–1945 gg.)* (Arsenal-Press, Moscow, 1996).

Polak, Tomas with Christopher Shores, *Stalin's Falcons: The Aces of the Red Star* (Grub Street, London, 1999).

Quarrie, Bruce, *Hitler's Samurai, The Waffen-SS in Action* (Arco Publishing, Inc., New York, 1983).

Ready, J. Lee, *World War Two: Nation by Nation* (Arms and Armour Press, London, 1995).

Restayn, J., and N. Moller, *Operation "Citadel": A Text and Photo Album, Volume 2: The North* (J. J. Fedorowicz Publishing, Inc., Winnipeg, Canada, 2006).

Reynolds, Michael, *The Devil's Adjutant: Jochen Peiper, Panzer Leader* (Sarpedon, New York, 1995).

Ryabkov, Andrei, *Boyevoi Put divizii i brigad strelkovyikh i vozdushno-desantnyikh voisk Krasnoi Armii v Velikoi Otechestvennoi Voine* (Spravochnik, Sankt-Peterburg, 2008).

Salisbury, Harrison E., *The 900 Days: The Siege of Leningrad* (De Capo Press, New York, 1985).

Samokhodnyie Ustanovki Krasnoi Armii (The Red Army's Self-Propelled Guns) (Moscow, 1945).

Sarhidai, Gyula, Gyorgy Punka and Viktor Kozlik, *Hungarian Eagles: The Hungarian Air Forces 1920-1945* (Hikoki Publications, Aldershot, UK, 1996).

Schneider, Wolfgang, *Tigers in Combat, Vol. I* (J.J. Fedorowicz Publishing, Inc., Winnipeg, Canada, 1994).

Schneider, Wolfgang, *Tigers in Combat, Vol. II* (J.J. Fedorowicz Publishing Inc., Winnipeg, Canada, 1998).

Schrank, David, *Thunder At Prokhorovka: A Combat History of Operation Citadel, Kursk, July 1943* (Helion & Company, Solihull, England, 2013).

Seaton, Albert, *The Russo-German War 1941–1945* (Presidio Press, Novato, CA, 1993, 1971).

Seidl, Hans D., *Stalin's Eagles, An Illustrated Study of the Soviet Aces of World War II and Korea* (Schiffer Military History, Atglen, PA, 1998).

Shirer, William L., *The Rise and Fall of the Third Reich, A History of Nazi Germany* (Simon and Schuster, New York, 1960).

Slaughterhouse: The Encyclopedia of the Eastern Front (The Military Book Club, Garden City, NJ, 2002).

Sokolov, B. V., *Tainyi Vtoroi Mirovoi* (Mysteries of the Second World War) (Veche, Moscow, 2000).

Spaeter, Helmuth, *The History of the PanzerKorps GrossDeutschland, Volume 2* (J. J. Fedorowicz Publishing, Winnipeg, Canada, 1995).

Spielberger, Walter J., *Panther & Its Variants* (Schiffer Military/Aviation History, Atglen, PA, 1993).

Strokov, ed., *Istoriya Voyennogo Iskusstva* (Voyenizdat, Moscow, 1966).

Suchenwirth, Prof. Richard, *Command and Leadership in the German Air Force* (USAF Historical Division, Aerospace Studies Institute, Air University, July 1969).

Sverdlov, F. D., *Neizvestnoye o Sovetskikh Polkovodtsakh* (Unknown Facts about Soviet Captains) (Moscow, 1995).

Sverdlov, Fyodor, *Tankmen* (Novosti Press Agency Publishing House, Moscow, 1984).

Tank KV: Kratkoye Rukovodstvo Sluzhbyi (The KV Tank: A User's Manual) (Voyennoye Izdatelstvo, Moscow, 1942).

Tarrant, V. E., *The Red Orchestra, The Soviet Spy Network Inside Nazi Europe* (Cassel, London, 1998).

Tarrant, V. E., *Stalingrad, Anatomy of an Agony* (Leo Cooper, London, 1992).

Taubman, William, *Khrushchev: The Man and His Era* (W.W. Norton & Co., New York, 2003).

Thomas, Franz; Gunter Wegmann *Die Ritterkreuztrager der Infanterie* (Biblio Verlag, Osnabruck, 1998).

Thomsett, Michael C., *The German Opposition to Hitler, The Resistance, the Underground, and Assassination Plots, 1938–1945* (McFarland & Company, Inc., Jefferson, NC, 1997).

BIBLIOGRAPHY

Time Almanac 1999, Borgna Brunner, ed. (Information Please, New York, 1998).
Toliver, Col. Raymond F., and Trevor J. Constable, *The Blond Knight of Germany* (Ballantine Books, New York, 1970).
Toliver, Col. Raymond F., and Trevor J. Constable, *Horrido! Fighter Aces of the Luftwaffe* (Bantam, New York, 1979).
Torchinov, V.A., A.M. Leontiuk, compilers, *Vokrug Stalin: Istoriko-Biograficheskii Spravochnik* (Filologicheskii Fakultet Sankt-Peterburgskogo Gosudarstvennogo Universiteta, St. Petersburg, 2000).
Tsirlin, A. D., et al., *Inzhenernyie Voiska v Boyakh za Sovetskuyu Rodinu* (Voyenizdat, Moscow, 1970).
Urlanis, B., Ts., *Istoriya Voyennyikh Poter* (History of War Losses) (Poligon, Saint Petersburg, 1994).
Volkogonov, Dmitri, *Stalin, Triumph and Tragedy* (Prima Publishing, Rocklin, CA, 1992).
Voyennoye Iskusstvo vo Vtoroi Mirovoi Voine i v Poslevoyennyii Period (Strategiya i Operativnoye Iskusstvo) (Military Art in the Second World War and the Postwar Period (Strategy and Operational Art)) (Moscow, 1988).
Voyennoye Iskusstvo vo Vtoroi Mirovoi Voine (Strategiia i Operatiynoye Iskusstvo) (Military Art in the Second World War (Strategy and Operational Art)) (Moscow, 1973).
Voyenno-Istoricheskii Zhurnal (Military History Journal), 1968, Number 6. "Dokumentyi i Materialyi: Kurskaya Bitva v Tsifrakh."
The War in the East. The Russo-German Conflict, 1941–45 (Simulations Publications, Incorporated, New York, 1977).
Warlimont, Gen. Walter, *Inside Hitler's Headquarters 1939–45* (Pesidio, Novato, CA, 1964).
Weal, Elke C., John A. Weal, and Richard F. Barker, *Combat Aircraft of World War Two* (Macmillan Publishing Co., Inc., New York, 1977).
Werth, Alexander, *Russia at War, 1941–1945* (Carroll & Graf Publishers, Inc., New York, 1964, 1984).
Whiting, Charles, *Jochen Peiper: Battle Commander SS Leibstandarte Adolf Hitler* (Leo Cooper, Barnsley, South Yorkshire, 1999).
Zalesskii, K. A., *Stalin's Empire: A Biographical Encyclopedia Dictionary* (Imperiya Stalina. Biograficheskii entsiklopedicheskii Slovar) (Veche, Moscow, 2000).
Zamulin, Valeriy, *Demolishing the Myth: The Tank Battle at Prokhorovka, Kursk, July 1943: An Operational Narrative* (Helion and Company Ltd, Solihull, UK, 2011).
Zamulin, Valerii Nikolayevich, *Prokhorovka: Neizvestnoye Srazheniye Velikoi Voinyi* (Prokhorovka: the Unknown Battle in the Great War) (Tranzitkniga, Moscow, 2005).
Zamyatin, MG N. M., Cols P. S. Boldyirev, F. D. Vorobyev, LtCols N. F. Artemyev, I. V. Parotkin, *Bitva pod Kurskom* (The Battle of Kursk) (Voyennoye Izdatelstvo Narodnovo Komissariata Oboronyi, Moscow, 1945).
Zetterling, Niklas and Anders Frankson, *Kursk 1943: A Statistical Analysis* (Frank Cass, London, 2000).
Zetterling, Niklas, *Normandy 1944, German Military Organization, Combat Power and Organizational Effectiveness* (J. J. Fedorowicz Publishing, Inc., Winnipeg, Canada, 2000).
Zetterling, Niklas, and Anders Frankson, *The Korsun Pocket: The Encirclement and Breakout of a German Army in the East, 1944* (Casemate, Philadelphia & Newbury, 2008).
Ziemke, Earl F., *Stalingrad to Berlin: The German Defeat in the East* (Center of Military History, the United States Army, Washington, DC, 1987, 1968).
Zolotarev, V. A., G. A. Sevostyanov, eds. *Velikaya Otechestvennaya Voina, 1941–1945, Vol 2*. (Nauka, Moscow, 1998–99).

Published Accounts from Participants

Below, Nicolaus von, *At Hitler's Side: The Memoirs of Hitler's Luftwaffe Adjutant 1937–1945* (Greenhill Books, London, 2001).
Chistyakov, Gen-Col. I. M., et al., *Po Prikazu Rodinyi* (On Orders from the Motherland) (Moscow, 1971).

Chistyakov, Col. Gen. I. M., *Sluzhim Otchizne* (We Serve the Fatherland) (Voyenizdat, Moscow 1975). Second Edition issued in 1985.
Getman, Gen. A. L., *Tanki Idut Na Berlin* (The Tanks are Heading to Berlin) (2nd edition, Moscow, 1982).
Goebbels, Joseph, *Die Tagebucher von Joseph Goebbels* (The Diary of Joseph Goebbels) (K.G. Saur, Munchen, 1993).
Guderian, Heinz, *Panzer Leader* (abridged) (Ballantine Books, New York, 1967)
Guderian, Heinz, *Panzer Leader* (The Noontide Press, Costa Mesa, CA, 1990).
Heiber, Helmut, and David M. Glantz, eds., *Hitler and His Generals: Military Conferences 1942–1945* (Enigma Books, New York, 2003).
Ivanovskii, E. F., *Tankmen Began the Attack* [Ataku Nachinali Tankistyi] (Military Publishing House (Voyennoye Izdatelstvo, Moscow, 1984).
Katukov, Marshal M. E., *Na Ostriye Glavnogo Udara* (To the Spearhead of the Main Blow) (Moscow, Voyenizdat, 1974, and 2nd edition, Moscow, 1976).
Khrushchev, Nikita (translated and edited by Strobe Talbott), *Khrushchev Remembers* (Little, Brown and Company, Boston, 1970).
Khrushchev, Nikita, *Khrushchev Remembers, The Glasnost Tapes* (Little, Brown and Company, Boston, 1990).
Konev, Marshal I. S., *Zapiski Komanduyushchego Frontom, 1943–1944* (A Front Commander's Notes, 1943–1944) (Moscow, 1972).
Krasovskii, Aviation Marshal S. A., *Zhizn v Aviatsii* (A Life in Aviation) (Moscow, 1960).
Krivoshein, S. M., *Ratnaya Byil* (A War Story) (Moscow, 1962).
Manstein, Erich von, *Lost Victories* (Henry Regnery Company, Chicago, 1958).
Mellenthin, MG F. W. von, *Panzer Battles* (Ballentine Books, New York, 1984).
Moskalenko, Marshal K. S., *Na Yugo-Zapadnom Napravlenii, 1943–1945* (On the Southwestern Axis, 1943–1945) (Moscow, 1972).
Rall, Gunther, *My Logbook: Reminiscences 1938-2006* (NeunundzwanzigSechs Verlag, Moosberg, Germany, 2006).
Ribbentrop, Rudolf von, "Erzaehlende Kriegsgeschichte: New geboren—bei Prochorowka" (Tales of War History: Born Again—at Prokhorovka), published in "Der Freiwillige" (The Volunteer), 35th year, issue 7–8, July/August 1989.
Rosen, Richard Freiherr von, *Panzer Ace: The Memoirs of an Iron Cross Panzer Commander from Barbarossa to Normandy* (Greenhill Books. London, 2018).
Rotmistrov, P. A., *Tankovoye Srazheniye pod Prokhorovkoi* (The Tank Battle at Prokhorovka) (Moscow, Voyennoye Izdatelstvo, 1960).
Rotmistrov, P. A., *Stalnaya Gvardiya* (Steel Guards) (Moscow, Voyennoye Izdatelstvo, 1984).
Rudel, Hans Ulrich, *Stuka Pilot* (Bantam Books, New York, 1979, originally published 1958).
Stahlberg, Alexander, *Bounden Duty: The Memoirs of a German Officer 1932–45* (Brassey's [UK], London, 1990).
Vasilevskii, Marshal A. M., *Delo Vsei Zhizni* (The Cause of a Lifetime) (Sixth edition, Moscow, 1989).
Zhadov, Gen. A. S., *Chetyire Goda Voinyi* (Four Years of War) (Moscow 1978).
Zhukov, Marshal G. K., *Vospominaniya i Razmyishleniya* (Memoirs and Reminiscences) (Moscow, Izdatelstvo Novosti, 1971).
Zhukov, Marshal G. K., *Vospominaniya i Razmyishleniya* (Memoirs and Reminiscences) (eleventh edition, Moscow 1992).
Zhukov, G., *Reminiscences and Reflections* (Progress Publishers, Moscow, 1985).
Zhukov, Georgi K., *Marshal Zhukov's Greatest Battles* (Harper and Row, New York, 1969).

BIBLIOGRAPHY

Reprints from Archival Sources
Russkii Arkhiv: Velikaya Otechestvennaya, Vol 15-4(3), Prelyudiya Kurskoi Bitvyi, Documentyi i materialyi 6 Dekabrya 1942 g.–25 Aprelya 1943 g. (Terra, Moscow, 1997). Russkii Arkhiv: Velikaya Otechestvennaya, Vol 15-4(4), Kurskaya Bitva, Dokumentyi i materialyi 27 Marta–23 Avgusta 1943 goda (Terra, Moscow, 1997).
Russkii Arkhiv: Velikaya Otechestvennaya, Vol 16-5(3), Stavka Verkhovnogo Glavnokomandovaniya, Dokumentyi i materialyi 1943 god (Terra, Moscow, 1999).
Russkii Arkhiv: Velikaya Otechestvennaya, Vol 23-12(3), Generalnyii Shtab v Godyi Velikoi Otechestvennoi Voinyi, Dokumentyi i Materialyi 1943 god (Terra, Moscow, 1999).

Limited Publication Sources
(*The Dupuy Institute* and HERO reports are available through the website www.dupuyinstitute.org)

Anderson, Richard C., Jr., "Artillery Effectiveness versus Armor," *The International TNDM Newsletter*, Volume I, Number 6, pages 26–29.
Bauman, Walter J., *Quantification of the Battle of Kursk* (U.S. Army Concepts Analysis Agency, provided in a letter to Chris Lawrence from Walter J. Bauman dated 19 August 1998).
Bergstrom, Christer, Copies of research for *Black Cross, Red Star* series of books on the air war in the east, provided May 2002.
Chrisman, Jeff, Copies of research on panzer commanders.
The Dupuy Institute, *Final Report for Capture Rate Study, Phases I and II* (The Dupuy Institute, McLean, VA, 6 March 2000).
The Dupuy Institute, *Final Report for The Battle of Kursk; Southern Front: A Validation Data Base* (The Dupuy Institute, McLean, VA, 1996).
The Dupuy Institute, *The Kursk Data Base* (The Dupuy Institute, McLean, VA, 1996, revised 2002). Christopher A. Lawrence, Program Manager.
The Dupuy Institute, *A Measure of the Real-world Value of Mixed Mine Systems* (The Dupuy Institute, McLean, VA, 20 June 2001).
The Dupuy Institute, *The Military Consequences of a Complete Landmine Ban* (Vietnam Veterans of America Foundation, Washington, DC, Summer 2001).
The Dupuy Institute, *Military Consequences of Landmine Restrictions* (Vietnam Veterans of America Foundation, Washington, DC, Spring 2000).
The Dupuy Institute, *Photoguide for Belgorod Trip, 18–20 September* (The Dupuy Institute, McLean, VA, 1995).
The Dupuy Institute, *Soviet Barriers and Fortifications on the Southern Front, Battle of Kursk, 4–18 July 1943, A Supplemental Appendix to the Kursk Data Base* (The Dupuy Institute, McLean, VA, 1996).
Gaetzschmann, Kurt, *Pz.Abt.51 Heerestruppe–II./Pz.Rgt. 33 9. Pz.Div. 1943–45* (Self-published, 1984).
Glantz, David M., *Atlas and Survey: Prelude to Kursk, The Soviet Central Front Offensive, February–March 1943* (Self-published, 1998).
Glantz, David M., *Atlas of the Battle of Kursk* (Self-published, 1997).
Glantz, David M., *Atlas of the War on the Eastern Front (1941–1945)* (Self-published, 1996).
Glantz, David M., Letter to Christopher A. Lawrence dated 14 August 1995 regarding Soviet Army order of battle and establishment (TOE) strength during the Kursk Operation.
Historical Evaluation and Research Organization (HERO), *A Study of Breakthrough Operations* (HERO, Dunn Loring, VA, October 1976).
Historical Evaluation and Research Organization (HERO), *German and Soviet Replacement Systems in World War II* (HERO, Dunn Loring, VA, July 1975).

Isserson, G. S., *Osnovyi Oboronitelnoi Operatsii* (Fundamentals of the Defensive Operation), published in 1938 by the RKKA General Staff Academy.
Jung, Lt Col. Jakob, *Consumption of Ammunition by Land Forces Since 1939* (unpublished Bundeswehr study, Bergisch Gladback, FRG, 1986).
Kelley, Greg, with Jason Long, *Romanian Armour in World War II* (Web published, 5/99), (http://orbat.com/site/ sturm vogel/romafv.html).
Sverdlov, Fyodor D., Unpublished research notes on Soviet captures of German Prisoner of War, faxed to *The Dupuy Institute* between 26 June 1998 and 14 August 1998.
Sverdlov, Fyodor D., Battle summary prepared for *The Dupuy Institute* (not published, 1998).
Sverdlov, Fyodor D., Interviews with Soviet soldiers and airmen at Kursk, prepared for *The Dupuy Institute* by him and associates, 1998–2000.
Sverdlov, Fyodor D., Soviet commander biographies prepared for The Dupuy Institute in 2000.
Whiting, Theodore E., Carrel I. Tod, and Anne P. Craft, *The United States Army in World War II, Statistics, Lend-Lease* (Office of the Chief of Military History, Washington, DC, 15 December 1952).

Foreign Military Studies
The US Army historical section in Europe produced a series of reports written by various senior German officers after the war, usually from 1946 to 48. These reports are very useful, but often fairly general. They tend to reflect the views of one individual and are sometimes written with only a minimal amount of research and primary source documentation. They are usually secondary sources and should be used with caution. The major ones used for this study are:

Breith, General der Panzertruppen Hermann, *Breakthrough of a Panzer Corps Through Deeply Echeloned Russian Defense During the Battle of Kharkov in July 1943* (D-258).
Busse, General der Infantrie Theodor, *The "Zitadelle" Offensive* ("Operation Citadel"), Eastern Front, 1943 (T-26).
Guderian, Generalobert a.D Heinz, *Representation of Armored Interests, 1938–1945* (P-041a, Historical Division, Headquarters, United States Army, Europe, 1952).
Moebius, Rolf, German Heavy Armor (D-226).
Poppe, Generalleutnant Friedrich, *Teilnahme der 255. Infantrerie Division an der Kursk Offensive Juli–August 1943 mit anschliessendem ausbrechen aus einem Kessel auf Achtyrka (Unternehmen Zitadelle)* (D-336).
Seidemann, Hans, *The 'Zitadelle" Offensive, Eastern Front, 1943: Luftwaffe Participation* (manuscript T-26, written in Newstadt, 1 November 1947 by Writer No. 737, General Seidemann).
Von Strachwitz, Hyazinth *Ein Beitrag zur Geschichte des deutschen Widerstandes gegen das nationalsozialistische Regime* (A Contribution to the History of German Resistance to the National Socialist Regime) (MS #B-340, Allendorf, February 1947).
Wienskowski, Hellmuth von, *Materialsammlung fur die Darstellung des deutschen Angriffs auf Kursk (operation Zitadelle) im Juli 1943* (Chapter 12, T-9, 11 January 1953).
Wienskowski, Hellmuth von, *Materialsammlung fur die Darstellung der russischen Offensiven gegen die deutschen Heeresgruppen A, sud und Mitte vom Juli bis September 1943* (Chapter 12, T-9, 31 October 1953).
Zeitzler, Generaloberst A. D. Kurt, *Das ringen um die grossen entscheidungen im zweiten weltkriege* (D-406).
Commitment of German Armor 1943–45, MS #C-033, October 1948, author unknown, but an addendum was added by LtG. Oldwig von Natzmer, who was chief of staff of Gross Deutschland Division during Kursk.
German Order of Battle Charts (D-427).

BIBLIOGRAPHY

German Tank-Strengths and Loss Statistics (P-069).

Writer No. 742, *"Zitadelle" [Operation Citadel], Fourth Panzer Army Attack, July, 1943* (T-26, Part B, Chapter II).

Writer No. 750, *The Battle Fought by the Second Panzer Army and the Ninth Army in the Orel Bend Between 5 July and 18 August, 1943* (T-26, Part B, Chapter III).

Writer No. 762, *The "Zitadelle" Offensive, Eastern Front, 1943, Luftwaffe Participation in the Area of the German OREL Armies* (T-26).

Writer No. 856, *The "Zitadelle" Offensive, Eastern Front, 1943, Sector of Provisional Army Kempf* (Part B, Chapter I, T-26).

Articles and Websites

Fesenko, Col. Yu. (Doctor of technical sciences), Maj. S. Zhuravie, "The Battle of Kursk and 'Desert Storm,'" *Voyennyii Vestnik* [Military Herald], 1993, #5.

Frieser, Karl-Heinz, "Schlagen aus der Nachhand—Schlagen aus der Vorhand. Die Schlachten von Char'kov und Kursk 1943," from Foerster, Roland G., *Gezeitenwechsel im Zweiten Weltkrieg?* (Verlag E.S. Mittler & Sohn, Hamburg, 1996).

Frolov, Aleksandr, "Citadel—93, The Americans are Programming the Battle of Kursk," *Sovetskaya Rossiya*, 13 July 1993.

Galitsan, Col. A., and Col. L. Pavlov, "Nekotoryie Osobennosti Operativnogo Iskusstva i Taktiki," *VoyennoIstoricheskii Zhurnal* #7, 1973.

John, Mark (Reuters), "General who foiled coup attempt on Hitler dies," *The Seattle Times*, 6 October 1997.

"General Remer, Ein Leben fur Deutschland," *National Journal*.

Holm, Michael, *The Luftwaffe, 1933–45* (www.ww2.dk)

Khodarenok, Mikhail, *Pervaya Prokhorovka* (The First Prokhorovka), *Nezavisimoye Voyennoye Obozreniye* [Independent Military Review], 16 May 2003.

Khrushchev, Nikita S., *Special Report to the 20th Congress of the Communist Party of the Soviet Union, Closed session, February 24–25, 1956* (The New Leader, 1962).

Koltunov, G. A., "Kursk: The Clash of Armor," article in *The History of the Second World War*, 1966. (Marshall Covendish, USA Ltd., 1974).

Kozlov, Col. L., "Sovershenstvovaniye Protivotankovoi Oboronyi Strelkovyikh Soyedinenii," *Voyenno-Istoricheskii Zhurnal* #3, 1971.

"Kurskaya Bitva v Tsifrakh," *Voyenno-Istoricheskii Zhurnal* #6, 1968.

Lee, Martin A., "The Strange Saga of Hitler's Bodyguard," *The Consortium*, 1997. Lexicon der Wehrmacht (http://www.lexikon-der-wehr marcht.de).

Long, Jason, *Panzerkeil* (http://www.sturmvogel .orbat.com/Panzerkeil.html).

Miller, Michael D., Axis Biographical Research http://www .geocities.com/~orion47/).

Nipe, George M. Jr., *Kursk Reconsidered: Germany's Lost Victory*. (Article at www.theblitz.org).

Parada, George, "Hans-Ulrich Rudel," *Achtung Panzer* website, 1999.

Pechenkin, A. A., "Generals perished not only in battles," *Nezavisimaya Gazeta* (Independent Newspaper), 17 June 2005.

The Red Falcons (or Air Aces) website: *Nasheyi Rodinyi Krasnyie Kokolyi [Our Homeland Red Falcons]*: http://www.airaces.ru/.

Remer, Otto Ernst, "My Role in Berlin on July 20, 1944," *The Journal of Historical Review*, Volume 8, No. 1: pages 41-53.

Ritterkreuztraeger 1939–1945 (http://www.ritterkreuz traeger-1939-45.de).

RKKA in World War II (http://www.armchairgeneral.com/ rkkaww2).

The Russian Battlefield (http://www.battlefield.ru).

Sazonov, Col. I., "Razvitiye Takticheskoi Oboronyi v Velikoi Otechestvennoi Voine," *Voyenno-Istoricheskii Zhurnal* #9, 1968.
Sokolov, B. V., "The Cost of War: Human Losses for the USSR and Germany, 1939–1945," *The Journal of Slavic Military Studies*, Vol. 9, No. 1 (March 1996), pp. 152–193 (Frank Cass, London, 1996).
Stevenson, Richard W. "John Cairncross, Fifth Briton in Soviet Spy Ring, Dies at 82." *New York Times*, 10 October 1995.War Heroes website: *Geroi Stranyi [Country's Heroes]:* http://warheroes.ru/main.asp?l=0.
Weber, Mark, "War Hero Fled to Spain to Avoid 'Thought Crime' Imprisonment: [Otto Ernst] Remer Dies in Exile," *The Journal of Historical Review*, Volume 17, Number 1, January/February 1998.
Wendel, Marcus, Axis History Factbook (www.axishistory. com).
Zamansky, Dan, *How were German air force resources distributed between different fronts in the years 1941 to 1943 and what are the implications of this case study for understanding the political economy of the period?*: http://www.ww2.dk/Dan%20Zamansky%20-%20The%20 Study.pdf.
Zamulin, V. N., and L. N. Lopukhovskii, "Prokhorovskoye Srazheniye. Mifyi i realnost" (Battle of Prokhorovka. Myths and Reality), *Voyenno-Istoricheskii Arkhiv* [Military Historical Archives], No 9(33) *Sentyabr 2002*, (Tserera, Moscow, 2002 & 2003); No 10(34) *Oktyabr 2002*; No 11(35) *Noyabr 2002*; No 12(36) *Dekabr 2002*; No 1(37) *Yanvar 2003*; No 2(38) *Fevral 2003*; and No 3(39) *Mart 2003*.

German Archival Material

The author conducted extensive research of the files for:
  Commanding General of the Army (OKH)
  OKH Quartermaster Reports
  Inspector General of Infantry
  Commanding General of Armaments and Replacements
  Army Group South
  Fourth Panzer Army
  Provisional Army Kempf
  All five participating corps
  All 17 participating divisions
  Second Army (for Luftwaffe data)
  Luftwaffe records (T321, R154)
  Selected Federal German Archives Records

Also reviewed:
  Army Group Don
  Army Group B
  First Panzer Army
  Sixth Army
  Ninth Army
  XVII Corps
  XXIV Panzer Corps
  LVII Panzer Corps
  Tigerfibel, Tiger I (RG 242, D656/27)

BIBLIOGRAPHY

Soviet Archival Material

The author had extensive research conducted of the files for:
   National Commission for the Defense of the USSR
   Second Air Army
   Fifth Air Army
   Seventeenth Air Army
   All seven participating armies
   Thirty-eighth Army
   All 11 participating rifle corps
   All 10 participating tank and mechanized corps
   All 37 participating airborne, rifle and guards rifle divisions
   252nd Rifle Division
   All six participating separate tank brigades
   All 59th, 60th, 148th, 167th & 245th Tank Regiments
   1st Guards Motorcycle Regiment
   5th, 6th, 9th, 26th & 29th Antiaircraft Artillery Divisions
   14th, 27th, 28th, 29th, 30th, 31st & 32nd Antitank Brigades
   27th, 33rd & 36th Gun Artillery Brigade
   12th Mortar Brigade
   29 different artillery, mortar and guards mortar regiments

US Archival Material (from National Archives and Library of Congress)
Headquarters, Third United States Army, Office of the Assistant Chief of Staff, G-2, Interrogation Report No. 30, 15 August 1945. Interview conducted by Edmund L. King, Major, Infantry, Chief of Interrogation Section.

Office of Strategic Services, Research and Analysis Branch, Current Intelligence Series no. 13, "The Kursk-Orel Campaign July 5–August 10," 13 August 1943.

War Department, Office of Assistant Chief of Staff, G-2, "Magic" Summary, Nos. 454, 455, 458, 460, 465, 468, 469, 474, 475, 483, 488, 490, 501, 502, 572 and 624 from 23 June to 10 December 1943.

1:50,000 Soviet 1942 maps that were captured from the Germans

1:50,000 German 1942 maps that were copied from Russian maps

U.S. Turkish Military Attache Report of 23 July 1943 prepared by Brigadier General Richard G. Tindall.

The Interviews

The Battle of Kursk was in 1943. The men in battle, many as young as 17, would now (in 2000) be at least 74 years old. Many of the surviving veterans are older than that. This book was the last chance for many of these veterans to tell their stories. For this book we interviewed 28 German veterans and 84 Soviet veterans. The interviews were originally intended to supplement the accounts, but the depth, interest and details of many of these stories resulted in them becoming a significant part of this book. In most cases the veterans were interviewed in person by a volunteer, usually retired military, who was working for the author. The interviews were not recorded, as this was felt to greatly hinder conversation. Instead, the interviewer took notes and prepared a transcript of the interview later. As such, what is being "quoted" from the veterans in this book are not direct quotes, but are summation, sometimes very detailed, of what the interviewee said. As such, all the interviews are placed in italics. They are not placed in quotation marks, and the words used are not necessary a direct quote from the interviewee. Where it is, we placed the interview in quotes.

The German Interviews
For this book, 28 German veterans of the battle were interviewed. The sole interviewer was Dieter Brand, Major General (Ret.) Bundeswehr. General Brand personally knew four of the people due to their service together in the Bundeswehr (the post-war West German Army). Twenty-six of the interviews were conducted in person, with one conducted by letter and phone and one by letter. All the German interviews were translated by Wulf-Deitrich Brand. The depth and detail of the German interviews was quite good. This is certainly due to the interviewer. A significant number of these veterans had been interviewed before, many had studied the battle since and some had even written books (Jung and Rall). As such, it is possible that some of the German interviews were influenced by post-war accounts.

The Soviet Interviews
For this book, we collected over 80 Soviet interviews. The interviews were conducted by Col. Fyodor Sverdlov, Col. Anatolii Vainer, Major General G. G. Nessonov, or Col. Valerii Akimov. The first two gentlemen were veterans of the Second World War and Col. Akimov is also a combat veteran (Afghanistan). Most of the Soviet interviews were translated by Tatiana S. Lawrence. These were supplemented by two interviews conducted by the author, both in conjunction with his trips to Belgorod.
The Soviet interviews were not conducted with the same depth and detail as the German interviews. As such, they were not used to the same extent as the German interviews.

Sources for the Chapters
Most of this book was developed from the archived records of the Soviet and German Armies. Where unit records were used, we have usually not listed the individual records or footnoted them, due to space considerations. The records used are on file at *The Dupuy Institute* and listed in detail in the *Final Report for The Battle of Kursk: Southern Front: A Validation Data Base* (The Dupuy Institute, McLean, VA, 1996).

For the German side the air chapters were drawn from a mix of existing Luftwaffe records and a wide variety of secondary sources. The Luftwaffe did manage to destroy most of their records before the war ended, leaving a real dearth of unit records. The German Second Army air liaison officer left records, which are used for the sortie counts. These records tend to be interspersed and interchangeably. As such, this usage tends to be heavily footnoted.

For the Soviet side, we have the records of the Second, Fifth and Seventeenth Air Armies. The records are detailed, comprehensive and complete. There are also detailed regimental records and personnel records. We did not systematically access them in the original Kursk Data Base project, but have occasionally accessed them since then. Some of these are also available on-line. The Soviet discussion of air operations is not heavily footnoted as most of what is reported is drawn directly from the various air army files. The use of other sources is footnoted.

BIOGRAPHICAL INFORMATION

Christopher A. Lawrence is a professional historian and military analyst. He is the Executive Director and President of *The Dupuy Institute*, an organization dedicated to scholarly research and objective analysis of historical data related to armed conflict and the resolution of armed conflict. *The Dupuy Institute* provides independent, historically-based analysis of lessons learned from modern military campaigns.

Mr. Lawrence was the program manager for the Ardennes Campaign Simulation Data Base, the Kursk Data Base, the Modern Insurgency Spread Sheets and for a number of other smaller combat data bases. He participated in studies on casualty estimates (including estimates for Bosnia and Iraq) and studies of air campaign modeling, enemy prisoner of war capture rates, medium weight armor, urban warfare, situational awareness, counterinsurgencies and other subjects for the US Army, Department of Defense, the Joint Staff and the US Air Force. He has also directed a number of studies related to the military impact of banning antipersonnel mines for the Joint Staff, the Los Alamos National Laboratories and the Vietnam Veterans of America Foundation.

His published works include papers and monographs for the Congressional Office of Technology Assessment and Vietnam Veterans of America Foundation, in addition to over 40 articles written for limited distribution newsletters and over 60 analytical reports prepared for the Department of Defense. He is the author of *America's Modern Wars: Understanding Iraq, Afghanistan and Vietnam* (Casemate Publishers, Philadelphia & Oxford, 2015), *Kursk: The Battle of Prokhorovka* (Aberdeen Books, Sheridan, CO, 2015), *War by Numbers: Understanding Conventional Combat* (Potomac Books, Lincoln, NE, 2017), *The Battle of Prokhorovka* (Stackpole Books, Mechanicsburg, PA, 2019), *The Battle for Kyiv: The Fight for Ukraine's Capital* (Frontline Books, Yorkshire & Philadelphia, 2023) and, with Jay Karamales, *Hunting Falcon: The Story of WWI German Ace Hans-Joachim Buddecke* (Air World, Yorkshire & Philadelphia, 2024).

Mr. Lawrence lives in northern Virginia near Washington, D.C., with his wife and son.